Managing Web Service Quality:
Measuring Outcomes and Effectiveness

Khaled M. Khan
Qatar University, Qatar

T0325006

Information Science REFERENCE

INFORMATION SCIENCE REFERENCE

Hershey · New York

Director of Editorial Content: Kristin Klinger
Director of Production: Jennifer Neidig
Managing Editor: Jamie Snavely
Assistant Managing Editor: Carole Coulson
Typesetter: Jeff Ash
Cover Design: Lisa Tosheff
Printed at: Yurchak Printing Inc.

Published in the United States of America by
        Information Science Reference (an imprint of IGI Global)
        701 E. Chocolate Avenue, Suite 200
        Hershey PA 17033
        Tel: 717-533-8845
        Fax: 717-533-8661
        E-mail: cust@igi-global.com
        Web site: http://www.igi-global.com

and in the United Kingdom by
        Information Science Reference (an imprint of IGI Global)
        3 Henrietta Street
        Covent Garden
        London WC2E 8LU
        Tel: 44 20 7240 0856
        Fax: 44 20 7379 0609
        Web site: http://www.eurospanbookstore.com

Library of Congress Cataloging-in-Publication Data

Managing web service quality : measuring outcomes and effectiveness / Khaled M. Khan, editor.

       p. cm.

Includes bibliographical references and index.

Summary: "This book is for strategic decision makers as it discusses quality issues related to Web services"--Provided by publisher.

ISBN 978-1-60566-042-4 (hbk.) -- ISBN 978-1-60566-043-1 (ebook)

1. Web services--Management. 2. Management information systems. I. Khan, Khaled M.

TK5105.88813.M35 2009

006.7'6--dc22

                              2008013148

British Cataloguing in Publication Data
A Cataloguing in Publication record for this book is available from the British Library.

All work contributed to this book set is original material. The views expressed in this book are those of the authors, but not necessarily of the publisher.

Table of Contents

Section I
Development and Application

Chapter I

Andrew Simpson, Oxford University Computing Laboratory, UK
David Power, Oxford University Computing Laboratory, UK
Douglas Russell, Oxford University Computing Laboratory, UK
Mark Slaymaker, Oxford University Computing Laboratory, UK
Ghita Kouadri Mostefaoui, Oxford University Computing Laboratory, UK
Graeme Wilson, Oxford University Computing Laboratory, UK
Xiaoqi Ma, Oxford University Computing Laboratory, UK

Chapter II

Abdelghani Benharref, Concordia University, Canada
Mohamed Adel Serhani, United Arab Emirates University, UAE
Mohamed Salem, University of Wollongong, Dubai, UAE
Rachida Dssouli, Concordia University, Canada

Chapter III

Krishna Ratakonda, IBM T. J. Watson Research Center, USA
Deepak S. Turaga, IBM T. J. Watson Research Center, USA

Section II
Description and Composition

Detailed Table of Contents

Section I
Development and Application

Chapter I

> *Andrew Simpson, Oxford University Computing Laboratory, UK*
> *David Power, Oxford University Computing Laboratory, UK*
> *Douglas Russell, Oxford University Computing Laboratory, UK*
> *Mark Slaymaker, Oxford University Computing Laboratory, UK*
> *Ghita Kouadri Mostefaoui, Oxford University Computing Laboratory, UK*
> *Graeme Wilson, Oxford University Computing Laboratory, UK*
> *Xiaoqi Ma, Oxford University Computing Laboratory, UK*

Chapter I focuses upon some experiences in the development, testing, and deployment of systems
built on Web services to support a variety of distributed healthcare applications. The middleware that
underpins these applications has been developed to meet the needs of various applications, with these
applications being drawn from the areas of healthcare delivery, research, and training. The very nature
of the applications that the middleware supports—and their associated data—means that non-functional
properties such as usability, maintainability and dependability are key concerns, and necessarily influence the development processes.

Chapter II

> *Abdelghani Benharref, Concordia University, Canada*
> *Mohamed Adel Serhani, United Arab Emirates University, UAE*
> *Mohamed Salem, University of Wollongong, Dubai, UAE*
> *Rachida Dssouli, Concordia University, Canada*

This chapter proposes an approach to provide a unique central console for management of both functional and non-functional aspects of Web Services. It aims at the development of a framework to provide management features to service providers and clients by supporting management activities all along the lifecycle. The framework allows service providers to consider management activities while developing their Web Services. It allows clients to select appropriate Web Services using different criteria. Clients make also use of the framework to check if the Web Services, they are actually using or planning to use, are behaving correctly in terms of quality requirements.

Chapter III

This chapter presents an overview of research and development efforts across several different technical communities aimed at enabling efficient and standardized end-to-end delivery of multimedia content over a service oriented architecture. It focuses primarily on issues related to quality of service specification, measurement, and enforcement for different multimedia distribution applications in this space.

Chapter IV

This chapter proposes virtualization techniques of Web services. It argues that standard high-availability techniques based on the use of Web servers; business-logic-based caching systems; dynamic binding of Web services by programming the access to SOAP message content from the business logic layer; and other kinds of current open problems can now be handled using a common unique technique.

Section II
Description and Composition

Chapter V

This chapter focuses on the problem of the proper definition of non-functional properties and methods that may be applied in order to estimate their values. First of all, a reader is familiarized with the concept of non-functional properties and different views on the quality of Web services. Then, selected approaches to obtain values of non-functional properties are presented. The focus of attention is a Web services profiling that seems to be one of the most promising methods to perform this task. The framework presented in this chapter was implemented and tested within the EU Adaptive Services Grid project.

Kyriakos Kritikos, Institute of Computer Science, FORTH, Greece
Dimitris Plexousakis, Institute of Computer Science, FORTH, Greece

This chapter provides a detailed definition of QoS for WSs and the importance of QoS in WS management. An analysis of the requirements that are imposed on the WS Description and Discovery processes based on QoS is given along with a review of related work in QoS-based WS description and discovery, highlighting the main deficiencies of recent approaches. Then, a complete semantic approach for QoS-based WS description and discovery is presented and analyzed. The chapter concludes by drawing directions for further research.

Michael C. Jaeger, Berlin University of Technology, Germany
Matthias Werner, Operating Systems Group, TU Chemnitz, Germany

This chapter discusses the current status quo in the area of QoS-aware Web services. The issue is divided into three sub-issues: description, management and monitoring. By this discussion, this chapter puts research about dependability in relation with ongoing QoS-related efforts in the Web services domain. Thus it identifies how these efforts can be combined in to form order a dependable Web services platform.

Frederic Montagut, SAP Labs France, France
Refik Molva, Institut Eurecom, France
Silvan Tecumseh Golega, Hasso-Plattner-Institut, Germany

This chapter presents a new procedure towards automating the composition of transactional Web services. This composition procedure does not take into account functional requirements only but also transactional ones based on the Acceptable Termination States model. The resulting composite Web service is compliant with the consistency requirements expressed by business application designers and its execution can easily be coordinated using the coordination rules provided as an outcome of the approach. An implementation of the theoretical results based on OWL-S and BPEL technologies is further detailed as a proof of concept.

Enrico Pontelli, New Mexico State University, USA
Tran Cao Son, New Mexico State University, USA y
Chitta Baral, Arizona State University, USA

This chapter presents a comprehensive logic programming framework, designed to support intelligent composition of Web services. The underlying model relies on the modeling of Web services as actions, each described by a logic programming theory. This view allows the use of logic-based planning to address the Web service composition problem, taking advantage of the fact that logic-based planning enables the elegant introduction of a number of extensions and generalizations (e.g., dealing with incomplete knowledge and preferences). The theory describing each Web service is encoded as a logic programming module, and different semantics are allowed within different modules, thus better reflecting the practical use of different service description formalisms and ontologies.

Section III
Testability and Security

Chapter X

Daniel Brenner, University of Mannheim, Germany
Barbara Paech, University of Heidelberg, Germany
Matthias Merdes, Heidelberg Mobil International GmbH, Germany
Rainer Malaka, University of Bremen, Germany

This chapter proposes a methodology that can be used to enhance the testability of Web services. In general, however, testing Web services is much more challenging than testing normal software applications—not because they are inherently more complex, but because of the limited control and access that users of Web services have over their development and deployment. In order to effectively test Web services under these conditions special measures and approaches need to be taken to enhance their testability. The chapter argues that right from the early phases of development, the testability of services needs to be taken into account and "designed into" services.

Chapter XI

Ghita Kouadri Mostefaoui, Oxford University Computing Laboratory, UK
Zakaria Maamar, Zayed University, UAE
Nanjangud C. Narendra, IBM India Research Lab, India

This chapter presents the research initiative known as Aspect-oriented Framework for Web Services (AoF4WS). This initiative looks into the role of aspect-oriented programming in enhancing Web services with non-functional properties that are orthogonal to the primary functional requirements of Web services, without the need for extensive reprogramming. This enhancement helps to promote a clear separation between the functional and non-functional aspects of Web services, thereby resulting in easier adaptability and maintainability. The AoF4WS initiative is therefore demonstrated using two projects, namely security concerns of Web services, and self-healing Web services.

Chapter XII

Ty Mey Eap, Simon Fraser University, Canada
Marek Hatala, Simon Fraser University, Canada
Dragan Gašević, Athabasca University, Canada
Nima Kaviani, University of British Columbia, Canada
Ratko Spasojevic, TELUS Security Solutions, Canada

This chapter proposes an open security framework that is based on the concept of personal identity management. Semantic Web research is seeking to develop expert Web services that are a composition of specialized Web services of multi-organizations. It is argued in the chapter that when all the alternatives are exhausted, the industry will come to the conclusion that only the concept of personal identity management is the only approach to provide true user-centric identity management and give users control over the management of their identities.

Chapter XIII

Vishal Dwivedi, Infosys Technologies Limited, India
Srinivas Padmanabhuni, Infosys Technologies Limited, India

This chapter primarily focuses on two aspects. First, the security requirements for Web services and the currently available stack of security mechanisms and frameworks for achieving security at various levels of Web-service implementation; Second, how these could be utilized to built security SLAs which could be enforced on Web services. Later this chapter suggests a conceptual model to represent these SLA clauses and present an approach to enact them.

Section IV
Maintainability and Management

Chapter XIV

Fatih Oguz, Valdosta State University, USA

This chapter describes a research study with an objective to explore and describe decision factors related to technology adoption. The study utilized theories of Diffusion of Innovations and Communities of Practice as frameworks and a case study of Web services (WS) technology in the Digital Library (DL) environment to develop an understanding of the decision-making process.

      Bijoy Majumdar, Infosys Technologies Limited, India
      Krishnendu Kunti, Infosys Technologies Limited, India
      Mohit Chawla, Infosys Technologies Limited, India
      Terance Bernard Dias, Infosys Technologies Limited, India
      Lipika Sahoo, Infosys Technologies Limited, India

This chapter details out the challenges faced in service evolution management and the key activities involved, and their role in SOA quality. Change is the only constant, and this concept holds good for services too. Service maintenance is the most tedious and longest phase of service lifecycle. The more complex the service, the more difficult it is to maintain it. Service maintenance and service evolution mandate a series of best practices and selective models to apply for better execution and administration.

      Pauline Ratnasingam, University of Central Missouri, USA

This chapter aims to examine the extent of Web services usage and quality applying the balanced scorecard methodology in a small business firm as an exploratory case study. This chapter contributes to guidelines and lessons learned that will inform, educate and promote small businesses on the importance of maintaining the quality of Web services.

Foreword

Let me first open this foreword with a note on what this book is not all about. It is not a book about what Web services are, the detailed programming implementation of Web services, or the architecture of Web services; rather, this is a book about Web services quality. Quality properties influence the Web services products. With the increasing complexity of information systems and their integration with Web services, there is a need for a minimum level of quality assurances. This book is a reflection of quality issues of Web services as an important topic. It attempts to address the often-neglected quality aspects of Web services. I have seen many books on Web services, but this book is different in the sense that it focuses largely on quality issues of Web services. The quality properties addressed in this book are testability, dependability, maintainability, usability, security, quality of service (QoS) of multimedia delivery, and measurement and management of QoS. Barely focusing on the technical programming issues of Web services and ignoring the quality issues of the technology can lead to the adaptation process of Web services failure.

This book is an effort to further the response of the researchers and practitioners to the needs for quality achievement, and it reflects the increasing interest in quality Web services. Systems quality is not just about good quality; these are integral attributes and properties of Web services throughout the lifecycle of the system. Many excellent books have been written on Web services, but there is a relative lack of literature on Web services that focuses solely on the quality issues of this technology. My former student Khaled Khan's book definitely represents a little contribution to fill this gap. I have known him since 1989 and he has a passion for the quality of software systems. As a result, in 2005, he edited a book on software maintenance and evolution. In this book on Web services quality, Khaled does a good job of bringing the quality issue of Web services to focus. The collection of selected chapters sheds some light on various quality issues related to Web services. He has managed to achieve a good balance between the technical details of quality aspects and of managerial aspects of the issue; the right blend of these makes reading of the book more enjoyable.

The book includes several chapters with advanced research output. However, the Preface written by Khaled provides a couple of introductory paragraphs of Web services basics as well as sets the scene of the book. Some case studies presented in the book illustrate how the Web services can be effectively used to achieve quality requirements of enterprises. Some real-life examples discussed in various chapters pull together the theory and issues discussed elsewhere in the book. The chapters are presented in an easy-to-understand way. The issue of quality in Web services certainly gives a compelling reason to read this book, and to apply or develop further the underlying concepts discussed in the book. The chosen topics are timeless, and the relevancy of the presented issues remains for a long time. Undoubtedly, this text will become an important reference for many Web services researchers, developers, as well as users.

Professor Torbjørn Skramstad
Norwegian University of Science and Technology
February 2008

Torbjørn Skramstad is a professor of computer science at the Norwegian University of Science and Technology, NTNU, and chief research scientist in DNV Research and Innovation. He has more than 35 years of experience from the software engineering and software development field as a software engineer, consultant, project manager, and professional technical expert. He has also been quality manager in one of Norway's largest software companies. His main areas of experience and expertise include software development methodologies, software quality assurance, software metrics, software project risk analysis, project management, and independent software verification/validation. Dr. Skramstad covers theoretical aspects combined with an extensive practical experience. His current interests are in the area of assessment of dependability critical software and systems.

Preface

Web services are increasingly becoming an important area of business processing and research for distributed systems. Around 15 years ago, starting with the first move in the form of simple object access protocol (SOAP), Web services have steadily become a reality. In the past 15 years or so, several technological developments have brought the issues of integrating enterprise information systems to each other as they need software functionalities which they themselves do not have: first, the creation of distributed systems which are running over global networks and support distributed functionalities; second, abetted by Internet technologies, the characteristics and strategies of the modern business model have significantly changed; and third, the business competitiveness and complexities have also changed dramatically (Khan & Zhang, 2005). Web services support loosely coupled integrations between various services running on a broad range of technology platforms. As pointed out by Manes (2003), the main difference between the Web services and their previous technologies is that earlier technologies supported only one way of communication which required the installation of the same technology platform and same communication protocols. Web services technology allows easy integration between two applications, but it does not mean that a flawless service is guaranteed.

The basic idea behind Web services is that a specific functionality of software running on one machine of an enterprise is accessible to another machine running at another enterprise using specific protocols over the Internet. Providing seamless access to systems functionality without downloading the software is the main concept behind Web services. Web services represent independent software products that interact with other systems to deliver a software service or functionality. The independence and interactions are essential for the robust integration with other systems.

In a nutshell, three standard technologies are used in Web services: SOAP, universal description, discovery, and integration (UDDI), and Web services description language (WSDL). These three technologies facilitate service level collaboration among software services. SOAP is a lightweight protocol that enables communication across all languages, that is, a piece of code written in one language (e.g., Java) communicates to another piece of code written in a different language (e.g., C++). This flexibility provides the power of interoperability between software systems. UDDI is a registry in where different services advertise their availability to other application services. The services could be easily discovered by other application systems just before they are integrated. WSDL is used to specify the format of the services and their contracts. The service contract describes what will be offered, what procedures will be used, and the use of service (Manes, 2003). The description of a Web service written in WSDL is entered in the UDDI registry. The description includes the name of the service, arguments required to use the service, a briefing of the functionality a Web service offers, and so forth.

In the past, enterprises knew their precise business functions clearly. However, it is not the case in the modern business environment which is highly dynamic. Today, enterprises try to explore new opportunities almost every day, and engage in varieties of functionalities with different enterprises, and are heavily dependent on distributed technologies. Most of the enterprises base themselves on Internet to increase the functional capabilities of their information systems. In order to keep its business competitive with others, an enterprise has to support a variety of functionalities. It is not feasible for the enterprises to enable their information systems to support all possible functionalities that their businesses need. To provide multiple functionalities, most enterprises are realizing that they need loosely coupled easy-to-integrate technologies on which their application systems will base on. There has been a growing interest in deploying such easy-to-compose software services over the Web to support a variety of systems functionalities to the enterprise requirements.

Through Web services, the Internet is becoming an open global computing platform that facilitates business transactions between independent and heterogeneous systems within and across organizational boundaries. Web services have the ability to be composed with other independent services dynamically in order to achieve high level functionality. These allow business processes to be available over the Internet as well as different applications to communicate with each other using standard Internet. Different types of services ranging from entertainment, finance, healthcare, to high-tech real-time computations are being currently offered by various service providers.

Let us look at Amazon.com, Google, or even Yahoo; most of the functionalities we see in these sites are integrated into the portal of other enterprises' Web sites, such as weather, travel, maps, Web searches, and so forth (Lefebvre & Cimetiere, 2001). For instance, Amazon.com offers Web services for its product search, cart system, and wish lists. eBay uses Web services such as item search, bidding, and auction creation. FedEx uses Web services that are connected to its package shipping and tracking systems. Each enterprise gets much wider exposure to their business environments using Web services. These services are aimed for direct integration with each other within and across enterprises to form Internet-based systems and perform cross-application transactions (Han, Kowalczyk, & Khan, 2006). The relevant services need to be dynamically discovered and composed with little human intervention to form a collaborative application system. Building applications by dynamically integrating services from different locations certainly supports rapid development. This can be achieved by investing much less than required for procuring an information system.

In Web services, we see a great need and potential to develop a new framework for open, dynamic integration of business services with predicable quality outcomes. With the widespread proliferation of Web services, delivering quality has become a critical challenge for the service providers. Service quality determines the ultimate success of the Web services; it is, therefore obvious that an important selling point of different competing services is the assurance of a certain level of quality.

THE CHALLENGES

Despite the positive predictions, and grand success stories, some major technical challenges exist. Web services have not yet become the universally accepted silver bullet for Web-based business integration. The challenges are how to ensure the overall quality of Web services. In Web services the system needs to satisfy the functional requirements of the target application systems in carrying out a transaction or forming a specific virtual organization under a set agreement. The formation of such a collaborative application system and its continued viability is to be based on the compatibility of the functional as well as quality properties and requirements of individual services and their integrations. It is not enough that only the functional requirements are met. It is equally important to ensure that associated quality properties are also satisfied along with the functional requirements. Let us illustrate this phenomenon with a scenario.

Assume a number of travel related enterprises such as tour operators, hotels, and car rental companies are willing to collaborate their businesses by integrating their computerized information systems to deliver sustained services to their customers in a seamless and improved way. These enterprises deal with a whole range of functions related to their businesses, such as making flight booking, hotel reservation, renting cars, organizing shuttling services from and to airports, and so forth. For example, a tour operator may book hotels and car rental in addition to making flight reservation. In that case, the information systems running at the tour operation need to dynamically integrate to a third party software owned by a different enterprise to book the hotels. The system of tour operator may or may not satisfy the quality requirements of the hotel booking system or vice versa. These quality requirements raise several concerns ranging from security to usability, such as:

- How do we dynamically and automatically verify, check, and ensure before an integration that the quality requirements of two different services are compatible to each other for a viable composition?
- What happens if the hotel reservation Web service modifies its connection parameters or it becomes unavailable after it has been advertised or after serving for a while?
- How can the reliability of the car rental Web service be measured and communicated?
- How do these Web services know about the changing security requirements and privileges of each other?
- What kinds of mechanisms are required for maintaining a seamless collaboration among these Web services?
- How does an application system achieve a predictable response time before using third-party services?
- How do the software engineers test Web services that are provided by different vendors running on remote machines?
- How does the provider of a service test a Web service under all its operating environments with all types of unknown applications systems that it would eventually collaborate?

These are the obvious challenges that need to be addressed. Current service-oriented technologies do not provide the solutions to such obvious requirements. The available technology solutions aiming to simplify integration of different software services through a standard interoperability are not adequately addressing the quality concerns such as security, testability, composability, dependability, maintainability, manageability, deployability, interoperability, and so on. While the concepts of Web services appear to be very attracting to enterprises, satisfying the quality requirements during the service integration and service delivery is still an open challenge. Effectively tackling this challenge represents the next major trend in Web services research, and as a result, it requires new perspectives, new concepts, and new techniques to deal with the quality issues of Web services.

SEARCHING FOR A SOLUTION

To address the challenges, the approach that we take in this book is to present a broad perspective on Web services quality. The focus in this book is, therefore, on the technical as well as managerial issues related to quality of Web services. This book provides insights into various quality attributes such as testability, security, dependability, maintainability, usability, composability, and so forth. We understand that the quality issues such as requirements and assurances for two different Web services cannot be the same, but there are underlying similarities in addressing the issue for most enterprise systems.

The main objective of this book is to focus on advances in Web services quality. This will increase awareness of the importance of quality in a Web services context. It seeks to promote the advances in quality issues related to Web services by exchanging views and ideas within the information technology community. The book emphasizes how important it is to achieve and manage quality for Web services as well as using Web services. We believe that this book will bring much-needed focus to some important aspects of Web services quality, and foster more interest in this pressing topic.

This book features research work as well as experience reports on a wide range of topics related to quality aspects of Web services. It does not intend to initiate an academic debate on the need for Web services; instead, it focuses on how Web services could provide quality achievements in an organization, and how quality Web services could be developed.

REFERENCES

Han, J., Kowalczyk, R., & Khan, K. (2006, December 6-8). *Security-oriented negotiation for service composition and evolution.* Paper presented at the IEEE Conference on Asia Pacific Software Engineering Conference (APSEC '06), Banglore.

Khan, K., & Zhang, Y. (2005). *Managing corporate information systems evolution and maintenance. Hershey*, PA: IGI Global, Inc.

Lefebvre, A., & Cimetiere, J. (2001). *Foreword by Mougin, P. & Barriolade, C. for Web services, business objects and component models* (white paper) (pp. 4-6). Orchestra Networks.

Manes, A. (2003). *Foreword by Hagel, J. & Brown, J. for understanding the power (and limitations) of Web services.* Retrieved June 8, 2008, from http://www.johnseelybrown.com/fwd_manesbook.html

READERSHIP

This book is primarily aimed at information systems researchers as well as practitioners who are interested in nonfunctional aspects of Web services. We assume basic familiarity with the concepts of Web services. To support a variety of readers, most of the chapters are kept relatively self-contained. More specifically, the book will suit:

- Researchers, who like to keep track of the quality issues related to Web services, and who will find the book a rich source of material.
- Practitioners such as systems designers, managers, software architects, and planners responsible for the strategic decision of an enterprise for technology evaluation, or for the software integrators who will find this book in its entirety useful.
- Graduate students who may find enough detail on various research issues in Web services. This book could also serve as reference reading for the senior undergraduate students.

ORGANIZATION OF THE BOOK

The chapters of the book are grouped into four parts corresponding to four broad themes: Section I: Development and Application; Section II: Description and Composition; Section III: Testability and Security; and Section IV: Maintainability and Management.

Chapter I focuses upon some experiences in the development, testing, and deployment of systems built on Web services to support a variety of distributed healthcare applications. The middleware that underpins these applications has been developed to meet the needs of various applications, with these applications being drawn from the areas of healthcare delivery, research, and training. The very nature of the applications that the middleware supports—and their associated data—means that nonfunctional properties such as usability, maintainability, and dependability are key concerns, and necessarily influence the development processes.

Chapter II proposes an approach to provide a unique central console for management of both functional and nonfunctional aspects of Web services. It aims at the development of a framework to provide management features to service providers and clients by supporting management activities all along the lifecycle. The framework allows service providers to consider management activities while developing their Web services. It allows clients to select appropriate Web services using different criteria. Clients also make use of the framework to check if the Web services they are actually using or planning to use are behaving correctly in terms of quality requirements.

Chapter III presents an overview of research and development efforts across several different technical communities aimed at enabling efficient and standardized end-to-end delivery of multimedia content over a service-oriented architecture. It focuses primarily on issues related to quality-of-service specification, measurement, and enforcement for different multimedia distribution applications in this space.

Chapter IV proposes virtualization techniques of Web services. It argues that standard high-availability techniques based on the use of Web servers, business-logic-based caching systems, dynamic binding of Web services by programming the access to SOAP message content from the business logic layer, and other kinds of current open problems can now be handled using a common unique technique.

Chapter V focuses on the problem of the proper definition of nonfunctional properties and methods that may be applied in order to estimate their values. First of all, a reader is familiarized with the concept of nonfunctional properties and different views on the quality of Web services. Then, selected approaches to obtain values of nonfunctional properties are presented. The focus of attention is a Web services profiling that seems to be one of the most promising methods to perform this task. The framework presented in this chapter was implemented and tested within the EU Adaptive Services Grid project.

Chapter VI provides a detailed definition of QoS for Web services (WSs) and the importance of QoS in WS management. An analysis of the requirements that are imposed on the WS description and discovery processes based on QoS is given along with a review of related work in QoS-based WS description and discovery, highlighting the main deficiencies of recent approaches. Then, a complete semantic approach for QoS-based WS description and discovery is presented and analyzed. The chapter concludes by drawing directions for further research

Chapter VII discusses the current status quo in the area of QoS-aware Web services. The issue is divided into three subissues: description, management, and monitoring. By this discussion, this chapter puts research about dependability in relation with ongoing QoS-related efforts in the Web services domain. Thus it identifies how these efforts can be combined in order to form a dependable Web services platform.

Chapter VIII presents a new procedure towards automating the composition of transactional Web services. This composition procedure does not take into account functional requirements only but also transactional ones based on the acceptable termination states model. The resulting composite Web service is compliant with the consistency requirements expressed by business application designers and its execution can easily be coordinated using the coordination rules provided as an outcome of the approach. An implementation of the theoretical results based on OWL-S and BPEL technologies is further detailed as a proof of concept.

Chapter IX presents a comprehensive logic programming framework designed to support intelligent composition of Web services. The underlying model relies on the modeling of Web services as actions, each described by a logic programming theory. This view allows the use of logic-based planning to address the Web service composition problem, taking advantage of the fact that logic-based planning enables the elegant introduction of a number of extensions and generalizations (e.g., dealing with incomplete knowledge and preferences). The theory describing each Web service is encoded as a logic programming module, and different semantics are allowed within different modules, thus better reflecting the practical use of different service description formalisms and ontologies.

Chapter X proposes a methodology that can be used to enhance the testability of Web services. In general, however, testing Web services is much more challenging than testing normal software applications, not because they are inherently more complex, but because of the limited control and access that users of Web services have over their development and deployment. In order to effectively test Web services under these conditions, special measures and approaches need to be taken to enhance their testability. The chapter argues that right from the early phases of development, the testability of services needs to be taken into account and "designed into" services.

Chapter XI presents the research initiative known as aspect-oriented framework for Web services (AoF4WS). This initiative looks into the role of aspect-oriented programming in enhancing Web services with nonfunctional properties that are orthogonal to the primary functional of Web services, without the need for extensive reprogramming. This is an enhancement to a separation between the functional and nonfunctional aspects of Web services, thereby resulting in easier adaptability and maintainability. The AoF4WS initiative is therefore demonstrated using two projects, namely, security concerns of Web services and self-healing Web services.

Chapter XII proposes an open security framework that is based on the concept of personal identity management. Semantic Web research is seeking to develop expert Web services that are a composition of specialized Web services of multiorganizations. It is argued in the chapter that when all the alternatives are exhausted, the industry will come to the conclusion that only the concept of personal identity management is the only approach to provide true user-centric identity management and give users control over the management of their identities.

Chapter XIII primarily focuses on two aspects: first, the security requirements for Web services and the currently available stack of security mechanisms and frameworks for achieving security at various levels of Web-service implementation; and second, how these could be utilized to build security SLAs, which could be enforced on Web services. Later this chapter suggests a conceptual model to represent these SLA clauses and presents an approach to enact them.

Chapter XIV describes a research study with an objective to explore and describe decision factors related to technology adoption. The study utilized the theories of diffusion of innovations and communities of practice as frameworks and a case study of Web services technology in the digital library (DL) environment to develop an understanding of the decision-making process.

Chapter XV details out the challenges faced in service evolution management and the key activities involved, and their role in SOA quality. Change is the only constant, and this concept holds good for services too. Service maintenance is the most tedious and longest phase of service lifecycle. The more complex the service, the more difficult it is to maintain it. Service maintenance and service evolution mandate a series of best practices and selective models to apply for better execution and administration.

Chapter XVI aims to examine the extent of Web services usage and quality, applying the balanced scorecard methodology in a small business firm as an exploratory case study. This chapter contributes to guidelines and lessons learned that will inform, educate, and promote small businesses on the importance of maintaining the quality of Web services.

Khaled M. Khan, PhD
Qatar University
February 2008

Acknowledgment

The editor would like to acknowledge the help of all involved in the collation and review process of the book, without whose support the project could not have been satisfactorily completed. I am immensely grateful to my fellow professionals, well-wishers, and colleagues who were of great help to me in bringing out this book. A very special "thank you" goes to Mehdi Khosrow-Pour of IGI Global, whose enthusiasm and encouragement motivated me to initially accept his invitation for taking on this endeavors. Deep appreciation and gratitude is due to all authors who submitted the manuscripts, revised their chapters multiple times, and resubmitted the camera-ready chapters in time.

I would also like to thank all members of the Editorial Advisory Board for providing their thoughtful advice regarding the organization of the chapters and other helpful editorial suggestions for enhancing its content. In particular, Andrew Simpson of Oxford University and Nanjangud C. Narendra of IBM Research Lab (India) provided very useful suggestions regarding the organization of the chapters. Some of the authors of the chapters included in this book also served as referees for chapters written by other authors. Thanks go to all those who provided constructive and comprehensive reviews. Some of the members of the Editorial Advisory Board set the benchmark of their review. Support from Sikander Mahmood Khan from Campsie Library, Canterbury City Council is highly acknowledged for managing all paper work and correspondence archives. His timely archiving process of documents and management of my mail is deeply appreciated.

I would also like to thank Qutaibah Malluhi, Head, Department of Computer Science and Engineering, Qatar University and Leanne Ryland, then acting Head, School of Computing and Mathematics, University of Western Sydney, Australia for their constant support in terms of generous allocations of photocopier use, printing resources, and most importantly, my time during my stay with these two universities for this 18-month-long project.

Special thanks also go to the publishing team at IGI-Global whose contributions throughout the whole process from inception of the initial idea to final publication have been invaluable. In particular to Rebecca Beistline and Deborah Yahnke who continuously prodded via e-mail for keeping the project on schedule.

And last but not least, my family for their unfailing support and encouragement during the months it took to give birth to this book.

In closing, I again wish to thank all of the authors for their insights and excellent contributions to this book.

Khaled M. Khan, PhD
Qatar University
February, 2008

Section I
Development and Application

Chapter I
The Development, Testing, and Deployment of a Web Services Infrastructure for Distributed Healthcare Delivery, Research, and Training

Andrew Simpson
Oxford University Computing Laboratory, UK

Ghita Kouadri Mostefaoui
Oxford University Computing Laboratory, UK

David Power
Oxford University Computing Laboratory, UK

Graeme Wilson
Oxford University Computing Laboratory, UK

Douglas Russell
Oxford University Computing Laboratory, UK

Xiaoqi Ma
Oxford University Computing Laboratory, UK

Mark Slaymaker
Oxford University Computing Laboratory, UK

ABSTRACT

The ultimate effectiveness in terms of quality achievements should be a key concern of systems built from Web services. To this end, in this chapter we focus upon our experiences in the development, testing, and deployment of systems built on Web services to support a variety of distributed healthcare applications. The middleware that underpins these applications—termed SIF for service-oriented interoperability framework—has been developed to meet the needs of various applications, with these applications being drawn from the areas of healthcare delivery, research, and training. The very nature of the applications that the middleware supports—and their associated data—means that nonfunctional properties such as usability, maintainability, and dependability are key concerns for us, and necessarily influence our development processes.

INTRODUCTION

In this chapter we report upon our experiences in utilising open standards and technologies in the development of service-oriented interoperability framework (SIF), a system that is being developed to support the secure transfer and aggregation of clinical data for use in applications as diverse as the provision of support for patients suffering from long-term conditions, image analysis for cancer research, and radiologist training.

SIF is built on technologies that are portable, interoperable, standards-based, freely available, and, where possible, open source, with a view to developing solutions that require minimum buy-in from end users and are straightforward for application developers to code against. The effective reuse of existing data, stored in legacy systems, can only be facilitated by an approach based on interoperability and open standards and this is a key motivation for adopting the approach that we have.

There are, however, drawbacks associated with taking such an approach. Many aspects of proprietary solutions or toolkit approaches that already exist have had to be developed 'from scratch.'

The principles upon which the middleware is based were developed through experiences in the e-DiaMoND project (Brady, Gavaghan, Simpson, Mulet-Parada, & Highnam, 2003), in which a consortium developed a 'grid' to support various applications pertaining to breast cancer, and were reported by Power, Politou, Slaymaker, and Simpson (2005).

SIF—in various forms—is being used to underpin the efforts of three interdisciplinary projects: Generic Infrastructure for Medical Informatics (GIMI) (Simpson, Power, Slaymaker, & Politou, 2005), NeuroGrid (Geddes, Lloyd, Simpson, Rossor, Fox, Hill et al., 2005), and a prototype demonstrator project for the UK's National Cancer Research Institute (NCRI) Informatics Initiative (Pitt-Francis, Chen, Slaymaker, Simpson, Brady, van Leeuwen et al., 2007; Slaymaker, Simpson, Brady, Gavaghan, Reddington, & Quirke, 2005). Early versions of the technology are underpinning NeuroGrid and the NCRI demonstrator project (with an overview being reported by Simpson, Power, Slaymaker, Russell, and Katzarova [2007]); a more recent version—offering greater levels of functionality—is being used to underpin GIMI. The responsibility for the development and the deployment of the middleware for all of these projects lies with the present authors.

It is, perhaps, worth considering each of the projects in turn.

The main aim of GIMI is to develop a generic, dependable middleware layer capable of:

*   (in the short term) supporting data sharing across disparate sources to facilitate healthcare research, delivery, and training;
*   (in the medium term) facilitating data access via dynamic, fine-grained access control mechanisms; and
*   (in the longer-term) interfacing with technological solutions deployed within the National Health Service (the UK's free-at-point-of-service national healthcare provider).

The key deliverable of a middleware layer is being complemented by three applications, that is, the self-management of long-term conditions, image analysis for cancer care, and training and auditing for radiologists, that utilise it.

NeuroGrid is concerned with tackling problems that are currently holding back widespread data sharing, with the principal aim of the 3-year project being to develop a distributed collaborative research environment to support the work of neuroscientists. The potential benefits of the NeuroGrid platform include the streamlining of data acquisition, the aiding of data analysis, and providing improvements to the power and applicability of studies. In order to validate the technological solutions being developed, the project involves three exemplars that are helping drive the technology development. The Dementia exemplar requires real-time transfer and processing of images with a view to assuring image quality prior to the patient leaving the examination. The Stroke exemplar is establishing and testing mechanisms for interpretation and curation of image data, which are essential to the infrastructure of many multicentre trials in common brain disorders. The Psychosis exemplar is testing the capabilities of NeuroGrid to deal with retrospective data, assimilate material into databases, and facilitate data analysis.

Finally, the National Cancer Research Institute Informatics Initiative has facilitated funding to bring together researchers from various disciplines to demonstrate the utility of a multiscale, multidisciplinary approach to enhancing the information that can be derived from data collected within a clinical trial. The intention is to develop a prototype system to relate MRI images to the consequence macro images and to demonstrate the application of medical image analysis (developed for radiological scale images) to macro slides.

It is through GIMI that the functionality of SIF is being extended to make it a truly usable system with high-speed transfer, and a 'plug-in' approach that allows domain specialists to develop new applications in a straightforward fashion and the technical details of data sources to be abstracted from end users being key aspects in this respect. GIMI, though, is more than SIF; for example, GIMI incorporates novel aspects to authentication and authorisation. While being complementary to SIF, these mechanisms can be used in a stand-alone fashion. It is, therefore, the middleware framework, SIF, that is the focus of this chapter, rather than GIMI, which is a specific instantiation of SIF that includes additional functionality aspects.

The primary contribution of this chapter is to consider the development process involved in SIF—in terms of development, testing, and deployment—with a view to demonstrating the effective use of an emerging technology, in the form of Web services, to support a variety of applications with many essential nonfunctional requirements.

The structure of the remainder of this chapter is as follows.

In Section 2 we discuss the context of the work described in the chapter; we describe the motivation for, and the work carried out in support of, the aforementioned GIMI, NeuroGrid, and NCRI demonstrator projects. In addition, we consider some of the use cases associated with the applications and how they have influenced the design of SIF.

In Section 3 we describe the architecture of our system. The architecture is based on the principles of Power et al. (2005), who describe a secure health grid architecture which is sympathetic to the necessary legal and ethical guidelines.

In Section 4 we consider our choice of, and experiences with, Web services technologies. We make particular reference to the Web service specifications utilised within our framework, with vendor support being particularly relevant in this respect. We also discuss the development process that we have taken in support of the various projects.

In Section 5 we concentrate on a neglected area, that is, the testing of Web services. The complexity of our system—in particular the fact that there are various 'flavours' of SIF supporting the different projects—means that this activity is nontrivial.

In Section 6 we discuss the approach taken to the building and deployment of SIF in support of the projects it underpins. Again, the fact that various versions of SIF support different projects means that this is not as straightforward as it might be; however, an appropriate automated solution has been developed.

Finally, in Section 7 we summarise the contribution of this chapter and indicate potential areas for future work. In this respect, we are actively investigating applications drawn from other domains.

BACKGROUND

The 'e-health' arena has received significant exposure in recent years; there is a UK-based Web site (www.e-health-insider.com) with daily updates; there are dedicated journals (*Telemedicine and e-Health, The e-Health International Journal,* etc.); there are conferences associated with the subject (e.g., www. e-healthconference.com). Despite the inconsistent use and application (and even representation ['e-health' or 'eHealth']) of the term, the most common interpretation of the term is consistent with the definition of Eysenbach (2001):

e-health is an emerging field in the intersection of medical informatics, public health and business, referring to health services and information delivered or enhanced through the Internet and related technologies. In a broader sense, the term characterizes not only a technical development, but also a state-of-mind, a way of thinking, an attitude, and a commitment for networked, global thinking, to improve health care locally, regionally, and worldwide by using information and communication technology.

The subject of e-health is of particular relevance within the United Kingdom, where a National Programme for Information Technology (NPfIT) within the National Health Service (NHS) is being developed at significant cost to the public purse. The system being developed in England—as distinct from systems being developed in Wales, Northern Ireland, and Scotland—is now referred to as Connecting for Health (CfH). CfH promises to deliver various aspects of functionality: the 'spine'—the Care Record Service (CRS)—which is supposed to contain the electronic healthcare records of all patients in the country; electronic prescription of drugs; and 'choose-and-book,' which is the electronic booking of appointments. The UK is, of course, not unique in this sense. Similar 'cradle-to-grave' systems are being—or have been—developed throughout Europe and in Australia, Canada, and the USA (Cornwall, 2002).

Postulated benefits of the system include increased quality of care, increased efficiency, and increased patient autonomy. The system is not without its critics, though, with most criticisms pertaining to security and confidentiality. (The interested reader is referred to Anderson [1996, 1999] for overviews of the relevant issues and Becker [2005] for an excellent—if slightly outdated—survey of criticisms of the issues pertaining to CfH.)

In a slightly different context, the field of 'health grids' (or 'healthgrids'; again, the nomenclature is inconsistent) has emerged. The inconsistency of the term 'grid,' which, depending on context, can mean large-scale data federation or super computing (whether via super computers or cycle scavenging) is unhelpful, but it is possible to make a clean distinction between 'compute grids' and 'data grids,' with the former being concerned with offering the opportunity to provide unparalleled processing power to facilitate, for example, analysis of 3D images or real-time visualisation and the latter offering the opportunity to share information between sites to allow distributed data analysis.

Early 'health grid' projects, such as e-DiaMoND (Brady et al., 2003) and MammoGrid (Amendolia, Brady, McClatchey, Mulet-Parada, Odeh, & Solomonides, 2003) used toolkit-based approaches in their development; Globus Toolkit (GT) version 3 in the case of e-DiaMoND and AliEn in the case of Mammogrid. The emergence of Web services technologies has meant that 'second generation' projects, such as CancerGrid (Calinescu, Harris, Gibbons, Davies, Toujilov, & Nagl, 2007)—which uses Microsoft's .NET technologies—have become 'truly' service-oriented. Other projects have utilised, for example, the more recent GT version 4 and the UK's grid toolkit solution produced by the Open Middleware Infrastructure Institute (OMII).

Our view in developing SIF is that we would like an open framework that meets the needs of the applications with which we are concerned. Rather than developing an infrastructure that attempts—and fails—to meet the needs of a disparate collection of applications, we have focussed initially on a specific domain. Further, interoperability is key; rendering existing data and systems useless due to hardware and software choices runs counter to the open and interoperable philosophy that Web services are purported to support.

Our concern, then, is the facilitation of data sharing with a view to delivering distributed healthcare research, delivery, and training, with data access control residing with data owners and domain specialists having the freedom to develop applications that meet their own needs. To this end, we have been developing a lightweight infrastructure based on Java and Web services to facilitate such data sharing, with the data owner retaining absolute control over who can access what data, when the data can be accessed, and where the data can be accessed from.

It is, perhaps, worth reprising the use cases of Power et al. (2005) to illustrate some of the intended functionality of SIF.

- **Distributed queries of patient data.** A user wishes to query the data held on a subset of the hospitals that form the health grid. Each hospital is allowed to decide its own policy for data access. The user should receive the combined results containing only data that they are permitted to access.
- **Working at a remote site.** A doctor is working at a remote hospital, which is part of the health grid. The doctor should be able to access data from their home hospital, though their request may be subject to a policy that differs from the one used when they are at their home institution.
- **Delegation of access permissions.** A senior health professional would like to grant access to data to a colleague. This access should be temporary, and could be granted to either a named individual or a group of people.
- **External access.** Either a health professional working from home or an individual patient wishing to see their own records should be able to access data in accordance with the local hospital's access control policy. The hospital would use a different policy for such external access than would be used for requests from a remote hospital. This use case differs from the others as the request comes from outside of the current virtual organisation.[1]
- **Modification of data.** Having made a clinical decision about a case, a doctor wishes to modify the data stored in the health grid. A doctor will only be able to modify data if a hospital's policy allows it. Each hospital is responsible for the data it stores and as such it should keep a record of all modifications made. This use case is similar to the delegation of access permissions described above, with the only difference being that the data—rather than the policy—is being changed.

- **Transferring patient records.** In this use case a patient has moved and is now being treated at a new hospital. As the patient is likely to stay at the new hospital for some time, it would make sense to move their data. To be able to move the data it will first need to be read: this may involve a distributed query as data may already be present at other hospitals. The data will then need to be deleted from one hospital and copied to another — as the responsibility for it has transferred. This will involve the modification of data. Finally the access policies at both of the hospitals may need to be changed to reflect the change of ownership of the data.

Initially, we are concerned with sharing research data. In the longer term, interoperation with systems deployed within the NHS seems an achievable goal; research has been characterised as a 'secondary use' for NPfIT. Support for such secondary use of routinely-collected data (at least within the United Kingdom) was recently voiced by the editors of the *Journal of Medical Internet Research* (Powell & Buchan, 2005):

One aspect of electronic care records which has received little attention is the potential benefit to clinical research. Electronic records could facilitate new interfaces between care and research environments, leading to great improvements in the scope and efficiency of research. Benefits range from systematically generating hypotheses for research to undertaking entire studies based only on electronic record data ... Clinicians and patients must have confidence in the consent, confidentiality and security arrangements for the uses of secondary data. Provided that such initiatives establish adequate information governance arrangements, within a clear ethical framework, innovative clinical research should flourish. Major benefits to patient care could ensue given sufficient development of the care-research interface via electronic records.

Of course, for such a joined-up approach to work in practice, it will first be necessary to consider the confidentiality and security of patient records, and, in particular, appropriate anonymisation and pseudonymisation of data. Only then will it be desirable for electronic care records to facilitate new interfaces between healthcare delivery and clinical research environments. This is the goal of the secondary user service (SUS). The 'plug-in' approach we have developed should mean that SUS can simply be treated as another data source for researchers.

SIF

The roots of our work can be found in our experiences within the e-DiaMoND project (Brady et al., 2005). There, a collaborative team developed what might be termed an 'application-level grid' in which the application is the only way to access the underlying 'grid.'

The technologies on which e-DiaMoND was based were GT3, open grid service architecture-data access and integration (OGSA-DAI), Java 1.4.2, IBM DB2 (with information integrator), and IBM content manager (with information integrator for content), all of which ran on top of the IBM AIX operating system.

The e-DiaMoND project was successful in many respects: the world's largest collection of digitised mammograms was collected and each mammogram had associated (anonymised) patient data to enable its use for training and research purposes; a stable four-node grid was established; the system supported high-speed federated querying and file retrieval; and a number of demonstration applications were developed.

However, the project had its limitations from a technical perspective. First, Globus Toolkit 3 contained Linux-only legacy GT2 code; it required very specific releases of Java, for example, 1.4.2, and GWSDL, which was used by GT3 and never became a standard. Second, the proprietary technologies that were used required all nodes to be up and running for federation to work, and, inevitably, would have resulted in a rather expensive solution.

While the e-DiaMoND project delivered a working grid, terms associated with the 'grid vision'—such as heterogeneity and interoperability—were clearly not characteristics of e-DiaMoND. As such, Power et al. (2005) propose a vision for health grids, which is cogniscent of the legal and ethical requirements on such systems within the UK. Other drivers—such as interoperability, the accommodation of legacy systems, and the requirement for low end-user buy-in—have resulted in the development of SIF.

Early versions of the middleware underpin NeuroGrid and the NCRI demonstrator project, and these have been reported by Simpson et al. (2007). In the following, we shall focus our discussion on GIMI.

The philosophy behind the middleware is that issues pertaining to secure transfer and data federation are abstracted from the end user. The middleware is agnostic to the kind of data that are shared; furthermore, it is agnostic to what is done to that data. Via a 'plug-in' mechanism, domain specialists develop applications to federate and manipulate remotely held data; via a GIMI node, data providers make their data available. To use the 'grid' analogy that has been popularised in recent years, the middleware supports various distinct grids, with, within GIMI, there being one for an application that supports patients with long-term conditions, one for an application that allows data sharing for the training of image analysis algorithms, and one that allows a radiologist training tool to access large, geographically disperse collections of mammograms.

Figure 1 illustrates the architecture of a NeuroGrid node. Web-based distributed authoring and versioning (WebDAV) (Whitehead, 1998) folders are used to provide scratch space for operations. Users communicate with the WebDAV server over HTTPS with mutual authentication enabled; this establishes a secure channel over which insecure messages can be passed. WebDAV plays a key role in the SIF architecture. First, there is no standard high-speed and secure way of transferring binary data using

Figure 1. A NeuroGrid node

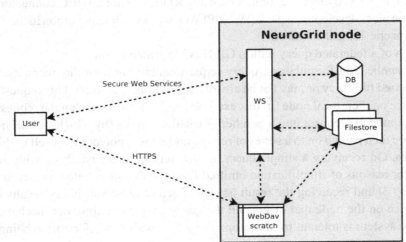

Figure 2. A GIMI federated query

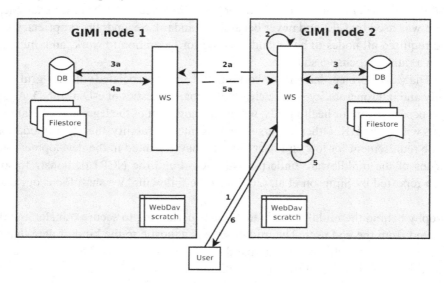

SOAP messages; WebDAV allows us to both get files from and put files to Web servers in a secure way efficiently. Second, WebDAV allows the user to browse, upload, and download files directly to their scratch space using a variety of third party WebDAV clients; this is especially useful when wrapping the Web services with a portal. The WebDAV folders also provide an ideal location for any intermediate results that might be generated by algorithms that do not belong in the file-store but may be of interest to the user. A file-store and a database of metadata provide part of the back-end of the system, with all interactions occurring through Web service calls. We separate image data from patient and metadata (with appropriate references between the two to guarantee referential integrity).

The use of the Apache Derby database management system—which is written entirely in Java, is easy to install, and has a minimal system footprint—was chosen as it enhances the interoperability and portability of the underlying infrastructure. (Although the default database management system of choice is Derby, it is perfectly feasible for us to use any RDBMS with a JDBC connector) We are using Sun's Java Web services development pack (JWSDP) Web service implementation in the Sun customised version of the Apache Tomcat container.

The execution of a federated query within GIMI is illustrated below.

Initially, the application formulates a query request containing both the query itself and a list of servers to be queried (this may or may not be abstracted from the end user). This request is then passed to the Web service on their local node (in this example, node 2). On receiving the request, the Web service then decomposes the request into a number of smaller, simple (by which we mean nonfederated) queries, which are then passed on to a series of remote nodes (and, potentially, itself). This is illustrated as steps 2 and 2a. On receiving a simple query, a Web service will first check with the local access control policy (for reasons of simplification omitted from the diagram) before presenting the query to the database (step 3) and receiving the result (step 4). Each of these subsidiary results is passed back to the Web service on the node that originated the query (step 5). A time-out mechanism is in place meaning that the system is tolerant to unresponsive modes, with this information being passed to the application. These subsidiary results are then joined together—according to a manner specified by the original request—before the aggregate result is passed back to the application.

The current system offers support for multiple SQL databases per node, direct querying via JDBC, homogeneous (SQL UNION) and heterogeneous (JOIN) federation, and support for algorithms via a 'plug-in' interface.

Plug-ins come in three varieties, that is, data, file, and algorithm. By using a standard plug-in interface for each of the three types, it becomes possible to add heterogeneous resources. Importantly, there is no need for the resource being advertised through the plug-in system to directly represent the physical resource. What is advertised as a single data source may come from any number of physical resources, or even another distributed system. In the longer term, we anticipate that a variety of sources—relational databases, XML databases, picture archiving and communication systems (PACS) systems, local file systems, network file systems, and potentially the NHS secondary uses service—will be accessible via plug-ins.

The approach we take ensures that our system can be built and deployed (and redeployed) in a straightforward fashion. Our 'users' are data owners—who wish to share data with collaborators—and application developers, be they portal developers, clinical researchers, medical image analysts, training tool gurus, or (in the longer term) healthcare providers.

The focus of the next three sections is to concentrate on the development processes that allow us to deliver specific application-focused robust service-based infrastructures from a common core. The common code base, the requirements derived from seven very different applications, and the nature of the data involved have combined to mean that a disciplined and structured approach to development, testing, and deployment is essential. Much of the Web services literature is focused upon the development of single-server applications; the focus of this chapter is the development and deployment of a system built out of distributed Web services. Ensuring the effectiveness and usefulness of our software is a key driver. Maintainability, compositionality, reuse, and interoperability are not simply 'buzz words' to us; they are essential qualities if our software is to be useful to our target end user audience.

IMPLEMENTATION

The design of the previous section has its roots in a key driver: in building our systems, we would like to use technologies that are portable, interoperable, standards-based, freely available, and (where possible) open source with a view to providing middleware that requires minimum buy-in from end users and is straightforward for application developers to code against. In this section we consider the technology choice that we have made and consider the development process undertaken.

Technology Choice

When initially embarking upon this path, there were a number of options available to us: Web services resource framework (WSRF), Globus Toolkit 4, the open middleware infrastructure institute (OMII) stack, and WS-I+. Each had its advantages and disadvantages: WSRF was more likely to become a standard to industry backing, but was openly criticised by some in the academic community (e.g., Parastatidis, Webber, Watson, & Rischbeck, 2005); GT4 would no longer have the dependency on legacy C code that GT3 suffered from, but as it was to be WSRF-based it would have to adapt to any future standard;

and the OMII stack had the support of the UK e-science community, but early releases needed specific versions of Linux and were computation-focused. WS-I+, however, had more positives than negatives in that by being based on the Web services interoperability (WS-I) standard—plus a choice of limited additional WS-* standards (+)—interoperability was likely to be maximised.

Further decisions still had to be made though; the choice of Web service libraries still had to be made, for example. IBM WebSphere, Microsoft .NET, and BEA WebLogic (amongst others) were ruled out due to the fact that they were not portable, freely available, or open source. Axis was portable, freely available, and open source, but was ruled out on the grounds that it had limited support for WS-security. We chose to utilise the JWSDP as—although it was not open source—it was portable and freely available. Furthermore, it provided good support for WS-security.

The current system utilises: Linux for the server operating system (although the system has also been deployed to Windows and Macintosh platforms); Java 2 Standard Edition 5.0; Apache Tomcat 5.0 and Java Web Services Development Pack 2.0; Apache 2.2 using OpenSSL; the Apache Derby database management system; the Ant build tool; and the Eclipse development platform. The prime motivation for using Java-based technologies is the provision of platform-independence; using Web services allows maximum interoperability with client implementations in a variety of languages. We are also using the Apache Web server, which is available for most platforms. The technologies we have chosen to create the GIMI infrastructure were chosen to ensure that it would be as portable and interoperable as possible. We have attempted to choose solutions with excellent cross-platform support and which are at least freely available, if not open source.

The decision to implement our own framework has meant that some functionality that would have 'come for free' from a standard grid toolkit has had to be developed ourselves. Examples of such aspects include certificate authority management, proxy certificates and delegation, service registries, file storage and retrieval, and remote code execution.

However, our goal was to build a secure lightweight service-oriented system using standards-based cross-platform tools. We have managed to do this in a way that has maximised portability without sacrificing speed or security. Rather than making our lives more difficult, not using a grid toolkit has enabled us to develop a system with precisely the features that we need. Further, despite the rejection of a toolkit-based approach and the embracing of Web services, the infrastructure does meet the criteria of the 'grid checklist' of Foster (2002): 'a Grid is a system that: coordinates resources that are not subject to centralized control ... using standard, open, general-purpose protocols and interfaces ... to deliver nontrivial qualities of service.'

Code Structure

Each of the three projects follows a (broadly) similar structure. Application developers build their applications on top of the middleware with a view to accessing remotely held data; data providers make their data available—and configure policies—via the middleware. Domain experts are responsible for application development, data owners are responsible for making their data available, and middleware development and deployment is the responsibility of the authors. In this fashion, systems built on interdisciplinary expertise are possible, with dependencies being minimised. A simplified view of this state of affairs is given in Figure 3. (In reality, the federation and local Web services are located in the same container.)

Figure 3. Division of responsibility

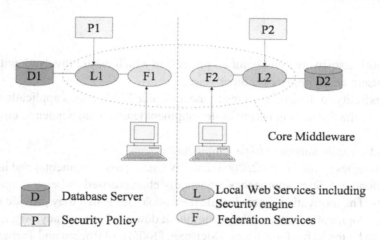

As the code base is itself modular (and flexible), we have deployed not one system but four: a mammography grid; a long-term conditions grid; NeuroGrid; and the aforementioned pilot system for the National Cancer Research Institute. The functionality offered by the four systems differs dramatically. For example, the access control mechanism in place for NeuroGrid is relatively simple, while the NCRI demonstrator project does not require access to compute facilities. As such, a modular approach to development has been taken.

Certain aspects of functionality—with the secure transfer of data being an obvious example—are consistent across all projects; as such, they might be thought of as being associated with core functionality. The imaging and pathology demonstrator requires heterogeneous federation, that is, federation across data sets with different data schemas, while NeuroGrid does not. GIMI offers fine-grained access control and high-speed data transfer, and even within GIMI there are differences between the applications: the long-term conditions application is intended to link to systems containing 'real' patient data in the near term; the radiologist training grid is essentially a closed system; and the image analysis for cancer research grid requires developers to be able to code—and test—new algorithms constantly.

Logically, then, we may think of the code structure as being almost tree-like, with each individual system inheriting aspects of functionality from 'lower down' the tree.

- Core
  - ○ NeuroGrid
  - ○ I&P (for imaging and pathology demonstrator)
  - ○ GIMI
    - ➢ Long-term conditions grid
    - ➢ Image analysis for cancer research grid
    - ➢ Radiologist training grid

This state of affairs gives rise to a number of key principles, that is, an iterative development cycle involving relatively short 'bursts', close end-user engagement, constant refactoring (Fowler, 2000), and a reliance on rigorous testing are key for successful delivery.

An Agile Approach

The need to

- develop working software quickly for all projects in which we are involved, with the early enthusing of end users being impossible otherwise;
- have the flexibility to develop systems to meet the needs of various applications; and
- accommodate the fluctuating nature of development teams in an academic environment

led us to adopt an agile approach to development.

Agile methodologies (Ambler, 2002, 2005) usually encompass incremental and iterative approaches to software development. Such approaches are usually characterised as being *lighter* than more traditional approaches. The motivation for such agile methodologies is that they provide sufficient structure to support the development process, without bogging it down in bureaucracy. Arguments against agile methodologies can be found by, for example, McBreen (2003) and Boehm and Turner (2004), with criticisms including the lack of structure and 'up-front' design provided by such approaches.

Those who subscribe to the *agile manifesto* value

- Individuals and interactions over processes and tools;
- Working software over comprehensive documentation;
- Customer collaboration over contract negotiation; and
- Responding to change over following a plan.

The manifesto gives rise to a number of *principles*, which are particularly pertinent in the context of this chapter.

- Welcoming changing requirements, even late in development. Agile processes harness change for the customer's competitive advantage.
- Delivering working software frequently, from a couple of weeks to a couple of months, with a preference to the shorter timescale.
- Building projects around motivated individuals. Give them the environment and support they need, and trust them to get the job done.

The use of emerging technologies to underpin systems with evolving requirements makes an agile approach essential.

TESTING

Recent efforts in the area of testing systems based on Web services can be divided into two categories: the use of ready-to-use tools (of either commercial or open source varieties), such as Apache-JMeter, IBM-TestStudio and Parasoft-SOAPtest, and the development of research prototypes for testing specific aspects of Web services functionalities.

When surveying current contributions on testing Web services, model-based testing emerges as a salient direction, and constitutes a sound basis for the practical testing of systems built on Web services. However, a significant proportion of the proposed techniques reported in the literature tend to target specific aspects of Web services. Frantzen, Tretmans, and de Vries (2006), for example, investigate the use of symbolic transition systems to approach testing coordinated Web services, with related contributions being made by Fu, Bultan, and Su (2004) and Heckel and Mariani (2005).

With respect to the testing of commercial Web services—where access to the source code is limited, if not impossible—monitoring is an essential strategy. In this case, the process is conducted from a user's perspective and relies on the service interface rather than on its implementation (Canfora 2005).

Relatively little literature exists on the topic of the *practical* testing of systems based on Web services, with the most relevant contributions concentrating on testing specific aspects of Web service-based systems, such as XML schema and WSDL (Offutt & Xu, 2006; Xu, Offutt, & Luo, 2005).

Our key requirements of interoperability and accessibility for application developers, together with our focus on iterative development, have led us to give careful consideration to the testing of our software, with the approach being taken inevitably relying on the careful selection of multiple testing tools and techniques.

Test Derivation

When considering the testing of large-scale systems, performance testing, load testing, and stress testing are all essential. Despite the fact that these terms can be rather loosely defined at times, essentially they refer to different—and complementary—activities. Performance testing is mainly dedicated to measuring the response time of the Web service under a certain workload, load testing is dedicated to analysing a Web service when it is invoked simultaneously by many clients, and stress testing is aimed at ensuring that, for example, a Web service recovers gracefully when one of its resources (e.g., database, port, or server) is no longer available. While definitions abound of these categories of testing, practical advice on how to undertake the activities is limited.

While these categories of testing are clearly important parts of any distributed or Web application testing plan, sticking religiously to this classification for deriving tests is unsatisfactory due to the fact that the categories do not cover all aspects of the system; indeed, it may very well be the case that they ignore the critical ones.

In our case, we initiated our study from the use cases associated with the various applications; in cases in which such documents are not available, a verbal description of the (intended) functionalities of the Web services infrastructure and/or its source code could be used instead. As new aspects of functionality are being incorporated continuously, tests are carried out iteratively following the regression testing paradigm.

Service-oriented architectures raise a set of testing challenges and issues. The issues highlighted by Canfora and Di Penta (2006) are devoted to the different kinds of testing that might be carried out by the services' stakeholders, such as developers, service providers, service integrators, and end users. Since a single development team at Oxford is undertaking most of these responsibilities, we have more freedom with respect to the types of tests that can be run on the system. Nevertheless, the 'test the worst things first' principle of Canfora and Di Penta (2006) is a key driver in our test set selection, with this being manifested as 'test the most critical aspects first.'

Based on the nature of the project, a collection of guidelines has been derived. The intention of these guidelines is to drive the testing project with a view to achieving the optimum trade-off between cost, time, and quality.

Top-down approach. A combination of the 'test the worst thing first' principle and our layered architecture has led us to adopt a top-down approach to testing. The API layer (the upper layer) is tested first, since it provides the starting point for middleware developers to extend the framework with new functionalities. The extension/customisation process is more likely to introduce bugs than the client-side artefacts layer (the lower layer), which relies on standard code for SOAP management, XML parsing, and so forth.

Incremental testing. The requirements on the middleware are evolving constantly as new applications are considered. As such, tests also follow an incremental pattern. To ensure that this process works, we utilise two main technologies: a version control system and a continuous build framework. The former relies on Subversion,[2] which is a version control system that offers advanced functionality. We rely on the Subversion plugin, SubEclipse, which is available for the Eclipse IDE. This is of particular benefit since multiple developers are working on the project simultaneously and the latest version of the code base is needed for control by the continuous build. The latter is achieved using CruiseControl,[3] an open source framework that supports continuous build processes, including testing. CruiseControl can be configured to run periodically in order to reduce code integration problems. It affords a Web-based user interface for monitoring the project status, displaying testing results history, and sending notifications regarding the status of the build.

Test automation. While test automation is a laudable aim, it is not possible (or, indeed, desirable) to automate all tests; over time, some tests may have no real prospect of being rerun, and, as such, their presence becomes useless. The question of when automation should be employed is an interesting one (Marick, 1998; Pettichord, 1996). Potential strategies include trading-off the time needed to develop tests against the generated cost. It emerges (implicitly) from the contributions of Pettichord (1996) and Marick (1998) and (explicitly) from our practical experiences that taking the decision to automate a given test is dictated by the constraints of the specific context. Indeed, only the developers and testers can evaluate if a test needs to be added to the automated test suite. In our context, automation of a specific test (or a test suite) is driven by two main factors. The first is the automation of tests that relate to satisfying obligations that are contractual in nature. For example, being able to create a temporary folder on a grid node and then to move a medical image to the newly created folder is a key function that might be present at any time of the development process. These kinds of tests are effectively acceptance tests. This first class of tests is more related to ensuring that the defined scenarios are still achievable. The second is to automate the underlying support code upon which the earlier code relies. This helps in scoping the source of any bug and helps to realise the top-down approach.

The choice of adequate frameworks and tools. Many tools and frameworks for the purpose of testing Web services are available. Some of these tools are dedicated to testing Web services from a developer's perspective, while others allow testing from a consumer's perspective. In the latter case, testers have no access to the code and the used tools mainly perform direct invocations of the Web services under different conditions. The first type—which is of interest to us—allows access to the code and is mainly used by the developers of the Web services in order to reduce bugs for the sake of delivering a software release. Our preference is to utilise freely available, open source Java-based tools where possible. This choice has the additional benefit that often such tools are continuously evaluated by the research and development communities.

Test Implementation

We now consider the different types of tests that have been undertaken.

Functional Correctness

The aim of functional testing is to verify the achievability of the functional requirements. In order to devise the tests relevant to this class of testing, we rely on the system use cases. In our context, actors are medical staff, including general practitioners, specialist nurses, and consultants, whose tasks pertain to healthcare delivery, and researchers, who are typically more interested in querying medical data sources for the purposes of statistical analysis and research. Verifying the functional correctness of our code consists of testing scenarios on manipulating patient data, transferring medical images, retrieving medical data, and so forth.

Some use cases require the development of a single test application, while others require multiple independent tests. Complex use cases are refined to smaller ones, with tests being devised accordingly. This approach allows the testing of both higher level functionalities and fine-grained functionalities. For example, to test the storing of retrieved data requires connecting to and creating a WebDAV folder and transferring a result set into it. Such a fragmentation of tests equates to testing smaller scenarios of the parent use case. More complicated use cases require the inclusion of the use cases they depend on.

It follows that there is no direct mapping between the number of use cases and the effective tests to implement and run, and this should be borne in mind in any test plan. Additionally, despite the fact that the main use cases are mined from the requirements, some of them emerge as a result of adding helper elements to the system. These helpers are important and sometimes vital to the health of the whole system. For instance, a *healthcheck* Web service has been implemented for the sake of checking periodically the status of deployed nodes. Including such components of the system into the testing process is valuable.

Performance and Load Testing

The performance of a Web service can be evaluated by measuring its response time and throughput. These two parameters are the quality of service indices end users can see and understand, so they are used to compare between multiple Web services providing the same functionality. For performance and load testing, JMeter[4] is a commonly used tool. JMeter provides GUIs for specifying the testing parameters such as the number of concurrent threads, the type of the request, and the number of requests by time interval. The main issue here is that the implementation of SIF Web services is not trivial; the system supports extra functionalities not accessed by JMeter. For example, in order to manage sessions, SIF relies on a 'ticketing' system (Simpson et al., 2007). This creates and publishes a ticket to be used as an identification token during the multiple invocations of the Web service by the same client. Thus, to be able to have more control on the tests to perform we rely instead on GroboUtils,[5] a free Java package, which extends JUnit with multithreaded functionalities. The framework allows the simulation of heavy Web traffic. Multiple unit tests can be run simultaneously for the aim of assessing the limitations of Web services. It provides code patterns to use for building tests and, since the tests are implemented manually, GroboUtils gives developers greater control over the code they write to run tests.

Stress Testing

Stress testing is used to evaluate the behaviour of the system in case of unavailability of one or many of its resources; as such, deriving the set of stress tests relies on identifying these resources. Corresponding stress tests are carried out by turning off one or many of these processes. The following is a list of relevant resources our system relies on:

- Our software provides a distributed infrastructure connecting multiple nodes across the network. Corresponding stress tests include shutting down a node or blocking its communication port during interaction.
- Web servers for running Web services and WebDAV.
- Apache Derby databases.
- Medical files and WebDAV folders to transfer files to.
- Available disk space for storing data.

Concretely, the results of stress testing are used to update the source code in order to force it to fail in a proper manner (e.g., not corrupting data or producing unrecoverable errors).

Unit Testing

Unit testing is used to validate that units of source code are working correctly, and is dedicated to testing small modules rather than verifying the high-level behaviour of the system. It is thus not sufficient by itself but is commonly used as a complement to the other types of testing discussed in the previous sections. In Java, units usually correspond to methods, and we make use of the JUnit framework V4.0[6] to test all the methods present in the API. In addition to being the most established tool for testing Java programs, JUnit is also supported by the Eclipse IDE and generated tests can be run as an Ant task.

Unit tests are released into the code repository along with the code they test and are run periodically to make sure the multiple iterations of code performed by the different developers have not broken any functionality.

BUILDING AND DEPLOYMENT

In earlier sections we have alluded to the fact that the requirements for, and the subsequent middleware that is deployed for, each of the projects supported by SIF vary. This, clearly, has had an impact upon the building and deployment of our systems.

We have had to address the problem of maintaining a growing code-base with clear dependency chains, while at the same time being able to build and deploy any such chain quickly and efficiently. In order to achieve this, we have adopted a project structure for our code-base that is related to the class inheritance model of the code itself.

There are several different parts to our code structure, most of which can be extended to provide additional functionality. Figure 4 illustrates the structure that we have used.

Here, the folders represent 'levels' in our code structure. The SIF level contains all of the code that is generic across all of the projects, and can be thought of as being the 'base' from which everything else is built.

Figure 4. SIF code structure

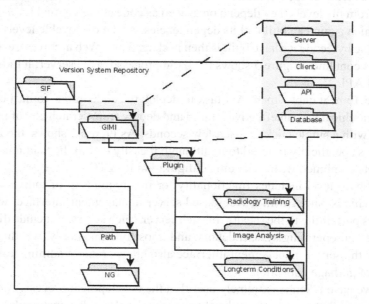

The inset box in the diagram shows the four main parts of our code-base. Each of these can be extended at a 'higher level' to add increased functionality. The plug-in level, for example, adds a large amount of additional functionality on the server side; and because the server largely contains server-side Web service code, this is mirrored by client-side Web service code in the client, which, in turn, must be accessible via the API. In actuality, the plug-in functionality also requires some additional database tables, and these go in the database section. These extensions can, and do, happen at every level of the code-base and are analogous to the principle of inheritance in object orientation. In fact, in most cases, the extensions truly are extended classes.

A further example of extending the code at a higher level is that of the predefined database queries for NeuroGrid. As NeuroGrid has database tables not used anywhere else (and, of course, stored in the database part of NeuroGrid), these predefined queries would be useless to any other project, and, as such, they are at the NeuroGrid level. In contrast, the code to upload any file to the file-store is generic to all levels and is stored at the SIF level.

Each of the code levels is entirely buildable within themselves (although they will, of course, depend on anything below them); this has the consequence that each level can be tested in isolation. The highest level in our code structure are the deployable endpoints of the system; not only can these be built, but they can also be deployed to a suitable Web service container.

As we have chosen to use Java, we use Ant—the Java build system—to build our code. The most interesting part of the build system is the implementation of the Web services on the server-side. The Ant scripts to build each part of each level of the code are contained locally to that code. For example, all of the code to build a GIMI server is contained local to itself. However, because the GIMI server code depends on other parts of the GIMI level, as well as the SIF level, it must also include those parts when it builds them.

The actual order of building is complicated by the usage of Web services and the fact that we use the client-side API in the server to do onward calls. First, the client code must be built (this generates the

Web service stubs which the API implements), then we can build the API. Both of these are capable of building the code from the levels they depend on as well as code at their actual level. Now we can build the server code, which again can build all its dependencies. At the deployable levels such as long-term conditions (LTC), the bytecode we have built is then packaged into Web archives, ready for deployment into a Web services container. Figure 5 shows the build process for the server; it hides the necessity to build the stubs and API.

We then use the Tomcat deployment Ant task to deploy the code into a Tomcat container. Because Ant scripts are hierarchical we can effectively build and deploy from scratch any of the deployable end-points of our code with a single click in just a few seconds. As Figure 5 shows, the LTC level actually has no Web services specifically tailored to it (although it easily could). Instead it uses all the services in its parent projects combined with a custom configuration for LTC.

Part of the SIF base level includes functionality for the monitoring of individual nodes within a deployed system. This is paired with a Web-based server management interface, which is capable of displaying statistics pertaining to the 'health' of each server. Such statistics include disk space, memory usage, architecture and operating system details, and, most fundamentally, whether the node is alive or not. In addition, the server management interface also allows remote administration, including the remote activation of garbage collection.

The approach we have taken is extremely useful in the development process. A developer can easily redeploy a server so that it will reflect the changes the developer has just made to the code, which, obviously, speeds up the development process greatly.

It is standard procedure when using any version control system to branch one's code before releasing it. This is so that if bugs are reported on a release, the developer can easily retrieve the code used in that release, and, furthermore, so that fixed versions of the code can then be released without releasing any development features currently in progress in the 'trunk' branch (the main development branch).

As our code is organised into a large number of projects, creating a new branch of the code can be a very time-consuming task if undertaken manually. We have, therefore, automated this process by

Figure 5. The SIF build process

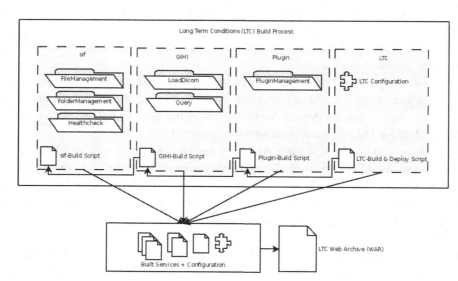

utilising some extensions to Ant, which allow it to interoperate with a subversion repository. A single Ant script iterates through all the projects, branching each one.

Once a branch for release has been created, it then remains to build the code and package it. As described above, the code to build the WAR files for server deployment is held in the deployable projects such as LTC-server; before that can be called, however, the release script checks out the version of the code to build into a release. By specifying a branch, it will check out that code from the version repository and then build it (optionally deploying the WAR files to a Tomcat container). It can also checkout, build, and package the client API code and appropriate documentation for distribution to application developers.

The appropriate use of automation of this kind is vital to maintaining a rapid development cycle and ensuring that releases are of a suitable quality. For example, typically when building a distributed system, one key problem to address is the deployment to each node in the system of the latest release of the code. Using our build system, we can deploy to servers in a scalable fashion, picking up custom configurations for each node in the process.

CONCLUSION

In this chapter we have described the development, testing, and deployment of Web services-based middleware for the support of distributed healthcare research delivery and training applications. The system has been developed by a team of researchers based at Oxford University Computing Laboratory, and has been used to support seven application areas drawn from three collaborative interdisciplinary projects.

In deciding to adopt an approach based on Web services we have faced significant challenges (e.g., we have had to develop our own versions of aspects that would have come for free had we taken a grid toolkit approach, such as certificate authority creation), but we have also realised significant benefits: SIF provides interoperability in a lightweight fashion with exactly the functionality that application developers require.

We have realised various other benefits by taking this approach.

First, the architecture is based on the assumption that data resides with their owners, as does (legal and ethical) responsibility and the rights to determine data access permissions. Second, as SIF is fundamentally technology- and application-agnostic, it gives rise to the potential to support many different systems. Third, SIF assumes that legacy systems have integral value; there are no preconceived schemas, ontologies, or interfaces that render legacy data incompatible, that is, a file is a file is a file. It is the *applications* that determine compatibility: lower level interoperability is achieved via the use of open standards, while higher level—or semantic—interoperability is achieved on an application-by-application, or domain-by-domain basis.

The use of an agile approach, coupled with appropriate tool support, is essential in environments such as ours; but even then, there are hurdles to overcome. One of the major issues that we have faced is that current toolkits for Web services are very much focused on a single server being contacted by multiple clients; as such, they are clearly being intended for systems that are using Web services merely as an alternative to traditional HTML-based solutions. Other challenges include the fact that commercial extensions to 'standards' often result in implementations that are nonstandard, which rather compromises the notion of standards and interoperability being at the heart of Web services.

To date, the applications supported by SIF have been drawn exclusively from the healthcare arena, albeit to support applications spanning delivery, research, and training. In the near future, we intend to evaluate SIF in the context of applications drawn from other domains, with the biological sciences being the immediate (and in some ways obvious) first choice.

ACKNOWLEDGMENT

The authors are grateful to the National Cancer Research Institute, the Technology Strategy Board, and the Medical Research Council for funding various aspects of the research described in this chapter.

REFERENCES

Ambler, S. W. (2002). *Agile modelling: Effective practices for extreme programming and the unified process.* John Wiley & Sons.

Ambler, S. W. (2005). *Managing agile projects.* Lightning Source UK Ltd.

Amendolia, S. R., Brady, J. M., McClatchey, R., Mulet-Parada, M., Odeh, M., & Solomonides, T. (2003). MammoGrid: Large-scale distributed mammogram analysis. In *Proceedings of the 18th Medical Informatics Europe Conference (MIE '03)* (pp. 194-199).

Anderson, R. (1996). Patient confidentiality: At risk from NHS-wide networking. In B. Richards & H. de Glanville (Eds.), *Current perspectives in healthcare computing* (pp. 687-692). BJHC Books.

Anderson, R. (1999). Information technology in medical practice: Safety and privacy lessons from the United Kingdom. *Medical Journal of Australia, 170,* 181-185.

Becker, M. (2005). *CASSANNDRA: Flexible trust management and its application to electronic health records.* Unpublished doctoral thesis, University of Cambridge Computer Laboratory.

Boehm, B., & Turner, R. (2004). *Balancing agility and discipline: A guide for the perplexed.* Addison-Wesley.

Brady, J. M., Gavaghan, D. J., Simpson, A. C., Mulet-Parada, M., & Highnam, R. P. (2003). eDiaMoND: A grid-enabled federated database of annotated mammograms. In F. Berman, G. C. Fox, & A. J. G. Hey (Eds.), *Grid computing: Making the global infrastructure a reality* (pp. 923-943). Wiley.

Calinescu, R., Harris, S., Gibbons, J., Davies, J. W., Toujilov, I., & Nagl, S. (2007). Model-driven architecture for cancer research. In *Proceedings of the 5th IEEE International Conference on Software Engineering and Formal Methods.* IEEE Computer Society Press.

Canfora, G. (2005). User-side testing of Web services. In *Proceedings of the 9th European Conference on Software Maintenance and Reengineering.* IEEE Computer Society Press.

Canfora, G., & Di Penta, M. (2006). Testing services and service-centric systems: challenges and opportunities. *IT Professional, 8*(2), 10-17.

Cornwall, A. (2002). Electronic health records: An international perspective. *Health Issues, 73.*

Erl, T. (2005). *Service-oriented architecture: concepts, technology, and design.* Prentice-Hall.

Eysenbach, G. (2001). What is e-health? *Journal of Medical Internet Research, 3*(2), e20.

Foster, I. (2002). What is the grid? A three point checklist. *GRID Today, 1*(6). Retrieved May 20, 2008, from www.gridtoday.com/02/0722/100136.html

Fowler, M. (2000). *Refactoring: Improving the design of existing code.* Addison-Wesley.

Frantzen, L., Tretmans, J., & de Vries, R. (2006). Towards model-based testing of Web services. In A. Bertolino & A. Polini (Eds.), *Proceedings of the International Workshop on Web Services Modeling and Testing (WS-MaTe 2006)* (pp. 67-82).

Fu, X., Bultan, T., & Su, J. (2004). Analysis of interacting BPEL Web services. In *Proceedings of the 13th International Conference on World Wide Web* (pp. 621-630).

Geddes, J., Lloyd, S., Simpson, A. C., Rossor, M., Fox, N., Hill, D., et al. (2005). NeuroGrid: Using grid technology to advance neuroscience. In *Proceedings of the 18th IEEE Symposium on Computer-Based Medical Systems (CBMS)*. IEEE Computer Society Press.

Heckel, R., & Mariani, L. (2005). Automatic conformance testing of Web services. In *Proceedings of the FASE 2005* (Springer Verlag LNC S3442, pp. 34-48).

Marick, B. (1998). When should a test be automated? In *Proceedings of the International Quality Week, 1998.*

McBreen, P. (2003). *Questioning extreme programming.* Addison-Wesley.

Offutt, J., & Xu, W. (2006). Generating test cases for Web services using data perturbation. *SIGSOFT Software Engineering Notes, 29*(5), 1-10.

Parastatidis, S., Webber, J., Watson, P., & Rischbeck, T. (2005). WS-GAF: A framework for building grid applications using Web services. *Concurrency and Computation: Practice and Experience, 17*(2-4), 391-417.

Pettichord, B. (1996). Success with test automation. In *Proceedings of the Quality Week, 1996.*

Pitt-Francis, J., Chen, D., Slaymaker, M. A., Simpson, A. C., Brady, J. M., van Leeuwen, I., et al. (2006). Multimodal imaging techniques for the extraction of detailed geometrical and physiological information for use in multi-scale models of colorectal cancer and treatment of individual patients. *Computational Mathematical Methods in Medicine, 7*(2/3), 177-188.

Powell, J., & Buchan, I. (2005). Electronic health records should support clinical research. *Journal of Medical Internet Research, 7*(1), e4.

Power, D. J., Politou, E. A., Slaymaker, M. A., & Simpson, A. C. (2005). Towards secure grid-enabled healthcare. *Software: Practice and Experience, 35*(9), 857-871.

Simpson, A. C., Power, D. J., Slaymaker, M. A., & Politou, E. A. (2005). GIMI: Generic infrastructure for medical informatics. In *Proceedings of the 18th IEEE Symposium on Computer-Based Medical Systems (CBMS)*. IEEE Computer Society Press.

Simpson, A. C., Power, D. J., Slaymaker, M. A., Russell, D., & Katzarova, M. (2007). On the development of secure service-oriented architectures to support medical research. *The International Journal of Healthcare Information Systems and Informatics 2*(2), *75-89.*

Slaymaker, M. A., Simpson, A. C., Brady, J. M., Gavaghan, D. J., Reddington, F. & Quirke, P. (2006). A prototype infrastructure for the secure aggregation of imaging and pathology data for colorectal cancer care. In *Proceedings of the 19th IEEE Symposium on Computer-Based Medical Systems (CBMS).* IEEE Computer Society Press.

Whitehead, J. (1998). Collaborative authoring on the Web: Introducing WebDAV. *Bulletin of the American Society for Information Science, 25*(1), 25-29.

Xu, W., Offutt, J., & Luo, J. (2005). Testing Web services by XML perturbation. In *Proceedings of the 16th IEEE International Symposium on Software Reliability Engineering* (pp. 257-266).

ENDNOTES

[1] We take the term *virtual organisation* to mean a dynamic collaboration involving existing autonomous real organisations.

[2] http://subversion/tigris.org

[3] http://cruisecontrol.sourceforge.net

[4] http://jakarta.apache.org/jmeter/

[5] http://groboutils.sourceforge.net

[6] http://www.junit.org

Chapter II
Multi–Tier Framework for Management of Web Services' Quality

Abdelghani Benharref
Concordia University, Canada

Mohamed Adel Serhani
United Arab Emirates University, UAE

Mohamed Salem
University of Wollongong, Dubai, UAE

Rachida Dssouli
Concordia University, Canada

ABSTRACT

Web services are a new breed of applications that endorse large support from main vendors from industry as well as academia. As the Web services paradigm becomes more mature, its management is crucial to its adoption and success. Existing approaches are often limited to the platforms under which management features are provided. In this chapter, we propose an approach to provide a unique central console for management of both functional and nonfunctional aspects of Web services. In fact, we aim at the development of a framework to provide management features to providers and clients by supporting management activities all along the lifecycle. The framework allows/forces providers to consider management activities while developing their Web services. It allows clients to select appropriate Web services using different criteria (e.g., name, quality, etc.). Clients also make use of the framework to check if the Web services they are actually using or planning to use are behaving correctly. We evaluate the Web services management features of our framework using a composite Web service.

INTRODUCTION

Web services standard is a recent paradigm of emerging Web components. It combines a set of technologies, protocols, and languages to allow automatic communication between Web applications through the Internet. A Web service is any application that exposes its functionalities through an interface description and makes it publicly available for use by other programs. Web services can be accessed using different protocols, different component models, and running on different operating systems. They usually use hypertext transfer protocol (HTTP) (W3C, 1999) as a fundamental communication protocol, which carries exchanged messages between Web services and their clients. Web services use extensible markup language (XML)-based (W3C, 2006) messaging as a fundamental means of data communication.

Research on Web services has focused more on interfacing issues, that is, simple object access protocol (SOAP) (W3C, 2004), Web services description language (WSDL) (WSDL, 2001), and universal description, discovery, and integration (UDDI) (OASIS, 2005). Until recently, considerable efforts have been conducted to address the issues of management of Web services in service-oriented architecture (SOA).

Web services management is among the hot issues that are not yet mature. Ongoing research from academia and industry are still emerging. Management of Web services is critical for their success because they are being actually used in a wide range of applications, ranging from entertainment, finance, and healthcare to real-time critical applications. Management issues in Web service can be divided into two dimensions: (1) management of functional aspects, namely fault management, and (2) management of nonfunctional aspects such as quality of service (QoS). Quality of a Web service, referred to as QoWS in this chapter, reflects the quality of a Web service, both in terms of correctness of functional behaviour and level of supported QoS. A Web service supporting QoWS is said to be QoWS-aware.

Nowadays, management of Web services is highly platform-dependent which implies the following limitations: (1) management features are usually available to Web services providers but often not to other partners (e.g., clients, third parties); (2) management solutions are usually restricted to only one management aspect, functional or nonfunctional; and (3) most of management solutions require considerable amount of computer and network resources to be deployed and used.

The first limitation restricts the utilization of management information to providers who are using it to assess the QoWS of their Web services. However, other entities involved in SOA industry might need to use this information as well. Clients can use this information during discovery and selection of Web services so they can figure out those with desirable QoWS. Moreover, many providers are likely to offer Web services providing similar functionalities but with quite different QoWS. In such a competitive market, attraction and loyalty of clients are primarily based on high standards of provided QoWS.

In SOA, a significant amount of work is taking place to allow both Web services providers and their clients to define and concisely use QoWS during publication, discovery, and invocation of Web services. For example, to select from a set of potential Web services, the one which is mostly available, and has a low response time and/or an acceptable utilization fee is preferable.

This chapter presents our approach for management of Web services. This approach provides a unique central environment for management of both functional and nonfunctional aspects of Web services. In fact, we aim at the development of a framework to provide management features to Web services providers and clients by supporting management activities all along the lifecycle of a Web service, from specification to invocation. The framework allows/forces providers to consider management activities while developing their Web services. In fact, the provider should concisely and precisely describe QoWS factors during design and implementation of the Web service. These factors will/shall be used latter by clients to select appropriate Web services during the discovery and selection operations. Clients also make use of the framework to check if the Web services they are actually using or planning to use are behaving correctly in terms of functional and nonfunctional facets.

The concepts presented all along this chapter will be illustrated in details through a case study. A Web service example will be used to show how different phases of the Web service development lifecycle must be conducted while promoting good practices for advanced management activities. At each phase, information and documents required by the management framework are produced and their impact on management is thoroughly discussed.

This book chapter is organized as follows. The next section provides background information required for nonexpert readers to follow the flow of ideas in following sections. The following section discusses related work in management of Web services and their limitations. A composite Web service used to illustrate our management framework is introduced. The subsequent section details, in a step-by-step tactic, how different management activities proposed by our framework can be conducted at each phase during the development of a Web service. We show then promising experimental results while using the framework to manage the Web service introduced hereafter. We close the chapter by presenting conclusions and insights for ongoing and future work.

BACKGROUND

Web services are a new variant of Web applications. It is a new paradigm which allows different applications to communicate automatically with each other over the Internet. They are self-contained, self-describing, modular applications that can be published, located, and invoked across the Internet (Wahli, 2002). The endeavor of this new paradigm is to allow applications to be delivered over the Internet and to run across all kinds of computers and platforms.

A Web service is any application that can be published, located, and invoked through the Internet. Each Web service has a Web service description language document (WSDL)(W3C, 2001), which consists of an XML (W3C, 2006) document providing all required knowledge to communicate with the Web service, including its location, supported transport protocols, messages formats, list, and signatures of published operations.

A Web service can perform any kind of transactions that may range from getting a city's temperature to a more complicated transaction, like for instance, searching and/or building the best travel packages from specific travel agencies. The main objective of Web services is to allow, at a high level of abstraction, applications to be accessible over the Internet. They can be of great use, for instance, for 3G networks operators to expose their core network functionalities to third parties (3GPP, 2003) and for digital imaging where they can provide an important benefit to the digital photography industry. The common picture exchange environment (CPXe) (CPXe, 2005), a Web service business framework, will make transfer and printing of digital images as suitable as the use of films.

SOA defines three roles (i.e., provider, requester, and registry) and three operations (i.e., publish, find, and bind). The relationship between the roles and the operations are illustrated in Figure 1. Additional information on the Web services architecture can be found by Kreger (2001).

The starting point in Web services activities is the development, deployment, and publication of the Web service by its provider. When a requestor (client) needs a specific Web service, the client probes the registry for a list of potential Web services. The returned list contains matching records; each record contains required information to connect to the corresponding Web service. Based on a set of criteria (i.e., location, availability, etc.), the requestor selects a suitable Web service and binds to it.

Web services can be developed either from scratch or by composition. Composition of Web services is the process of aggregating a set of Web services to create a more complete Web service with a wider range of functionalities. This composition has a considerable potential of reducing development time and effort for new applications by reusing already available Web services.

Currently, there are standards or languages that help in building composite Web services, such as: Web services flow language (WSFL) (Leymann, 2001), DAML-S (Ankolekar, Burstein, Hobbs, Lassila, Martin, McDermott et al., 2002), Web services conversation language (WSCL) (Banerji, Bartolini, Beringer, Chopella, Govindarajan, Karp et al., 2002), Web services choreography interface (WSC) (Arkin, Askary, Fordin, Jekeli, Kawaguchi, Orchard et al., 2002), and business process execution language (BPEL) (Andrews, Curbera, Dholakia, Goland, Klein, Leymann et al., 2003). These languages make the Web services composition process easier by providing concepts to represent partners and orchestrate their interactions. BPEL, which represents the merging of IBM's WSFL and Microsoft's XLANG, is gaining a lot of interest and is positioned to become the primer standard for Web service composition.

RELATED WORK

Most works on Web services focus on their development and deployment. Management of Web services (W3C, 2002), and in particular fault and performance management, are not yet a well-studied area. However, some interesting works have to be cited.

Existing approaches for management of Web services include approaches from network management and those that have been developed specifically for Web services. The approaches that have been used

Figure 1. Service oriented architecture

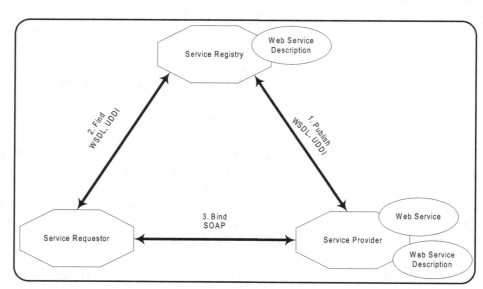

for network management for a long time seem to be a candidate for the management of Web services. However, their main drawbacks are due to the major differences between Web services and network components, and the need for the participation of a component in its management. In fact, most network components (devices) run standardized protocols that have specific and known attributes to be managed. Manufacturers of components running proprietary/no-standard protocols and/or applications often provide their customers with specific management agents/applications or well-defined sets of APIs.

In network oriented approaches, simple network management protocol (SNMP) (Case, Fedor, Schoffstall, & Davin, 1990) is based on TCP/IP and the client/server communication mode. In this approach, an agent associated with a management information base (MIB) (Perkins & McGinnis, 1997), communicates with a management station by processing *get* (report the value of an attribute) and *set* (modify the value of an attribute) messages and generating *trap* messages (unsolicited notification). Thus, SNMP management system requires a SNMP agent, a MIB, and a management station (manager).

The common management information protocol (CMIP) (ISO/IEC, 1998) fulfills in the OSI reference model protocol stack (ISO/IEC, 1989), a role similar to that of SNMP in TCP/IP. CMIP has many advantages compared to SNMP, including the number of available commands and the possibility to operate over TCP/IP. However, complexity and long development time, especially CMIP over TCP/IP (CMOT) (Warrier, Besaw, LaBarre, & Handspicker, 1990), have kept its adoption pervasively.

A considerable amount of work in the Web services community is dedicated to the determination of the requirements and the definition of specific approaches for Web services management. These approaches can be divided into two main groups: approaches based on active testing and approaches requiring the Web service (architecture) to support management interfaces. The World Wide Web (W3) Consortium presents a set of requirements that Web services management architectures should satisfy to provide management features (W3, 2004). This includes the definition of standard metrics, management operations, and methodologies for accessing management capabilities. The complying architectures must provide a manageable, accountable, and organized environment for Web services operations. It must support at least resource accounting, usage auditing and tracking, performance monitoring, availability, configuration, control, security auditing and administration, and service level agreements. Another approach in which the Web service provides specific interfaces for management is presented by Farrell and Kreger (2002). The developer is supposed to supply commands and APIs for management operations that are invoked by the management system.

Casati, Shan, Dayal, and Shan (2003) classify the management of Web services into three levels: infrastructure-level, application-level, and business-level. The infrastructure-level deals with the Web service platform while the application-level focuses on the Web services themselves. The business-level takes into consideration the conversations between a Web service and its client

Management approaches presented by W3 (2004), Farrell and Kreger (2002), and Casati et al. (2003) assume that the Web service will provide management operations that one can invoke. Developers of Web services have then to develop and deploy these operations in addition to the core business operations the Web service is offering.

A couple of management tools to be integrated into Web services environment are already available. Hewlett Packard's Web service management engine (HP, 2007) is a collection of software components that enables some management features, including the definition and the enforcement of service level agreement (SLA). Parasoft (2006) provides a set of tools (e.g., SOAPTest, .TEST, WebKing) to assist during the lifecycle of a Web service. These tools have to be installed and configured, thus requiring extra resources and introducing new cost for Web services providers.

There has been a considerable amount of work on testing Web services in the last couple of years. The work can be divided into two main groups: works targeting functional aspects of Web services and works tackling nonfunctional. The first group is concerned with the correctness of interactions between Web services and their clients while the second group is concerned with QoS management of Web services.

Functional Management

The majority of work on functional management is based on active testing where appropriate test cases have to be carefully generated, executed, and their results analyzed. This unavoidable phase of active testing has, however, practical limitations. First of all, exhaustive testing is impractical for quite large Web services. In fact, test cases can not cover all possible execution scenarios that a Web service will have to handle while serving clients' requests. The size of test cases is bounded by the cost a Web service's provider is willing to spend on testing activities. Usually, active testing stops whenever developers are confident that the Web service is good enough to be put into the market.

Many recent results were published lately describing test cases generation methods for Web services; they are mainly based on static analysis of WSDL documents. Xiaoying, Wenli, Wei-Tek, and Yinong (2005) present a method for test data generation and test operation generation based on three types of dependencies: input, output, and input/output. Jiang, Xin, Shan, Zhang, Xie, and Yang (2005) propose a method for test data generation in which a set of tests is randomly generated based on the WSDL document. ChangSup, Sungwon, In-Young, Jongmoon, and Young-Il (2006) combined both EFSM models and WSDL documents to generate test cases.

QoS Management

QoWS management includes definition of QoS attributes, QoS publication, discovery, validation, and monitoring. Existing approaches for QoS management can be classified into two groups: one based on extending related technologies including WSDL and UDDI to support QoS and the other mandating independent entities to perform some or all of QoS management tasks.

In the first category, W3C (2003) extends SOAP header to include QoS information. WSDL is also extended to describe QoS parameters, their associated values, computation units (e.g., millisecond, request/second), and so forth. UDDIe, a UDDI extension, consists of extending the current UDDI data structure with QoS information (ShaikhAli, Rana, Al-Ali, & Walker, 2003). The aim of these extensions is to allow QoS-based publication and discovery of Web services.

In the second group, solutions are presented for one or more of the following QoS management operations:

- **QoS attributes:** The first step in QoS management is the definition of evaluation's criteria and attributes. A set of attributes have been defined, studied, and used in software engineering for a long time (Fenton & Pfleeger, 1997; Gray & MacDonell, 1997; Salamon & Wallace, 1994).
- **QoS publication and discovery** (Kalepu, Krishnaswamy, & Loke, 2004; Ran, 2003; Serhani, Dssouli, Hafid, & Sahraoui, 2005): This operation allows providers to include QoS information in WSDL. This information is then used by requestors when selecting the appropriate Web service in terms of functional and QoS requirements.

- **QoS verification** (Kalepu et al., 2004; Serhani et al., 2005; Tsai, Paul, Cao, Yu, & Saimi, 2003): This operation allows the provider to certify that the QoS claimed by the Web Service is accurate.

- **QoS negotiation** (Serhani et al., 2005): If the available published QoS requirements do not satisfy a client's needs, negotiation operations and strategies can be followed to reach an agreement on different QoS attributes.

- **QoS monitoring** (Benharref, Glitho, & Dssouli, 2005; Benharref, Dssouli, Glitho, & Serhani, 2006; Ho, Loucks, & Singh, 1998; Schmietendorf, Dumke, & Reitz, 2004; Yuming, Chen-Khong, & Chi-Chung, 2000): Performs monitoring of Web services during interactions with clients to assess if the QoS attributes agreed upon in previous points are delivered.

Discussion

All the solutions presented above fit in one or more of the following categories:

1. Platform-dependent
2. Assume that a Web service will participate in its management by providing specific interfaces (e.g., W3C architecture)
3. Are based on active testers

The usage of platform-dependent management approaches is restricted to the targeted platform. When management features are embedded to the hosting platform, they are only available to the provider and cannot be used by clients or third party certification entities. A client might need management information for two tasks: (1) during discovery and selection to select the appropriate Web service, and (2) during invocation to assess the quality of the interactions. The client must rely on management information made available by the Web service provider and has no mean of verifying it. Moreover, information used in assessing the behavior is taken from one location, that is, at the provider's side. There are many situations, in composite Web service for example, where this information should be gathered from different sources and locations.

The Web services architecture becomes more complex if it has to support management features in addition to its basic functions. The performance of the Web service and its hosting platform is also degraded due to these additional features. Moreover, developers of Web services have to also implement the needed interfaces and APIs to support management. Since these features will be used somehow sporadically, the return on investment of their development and deployment might be relatively low.

Once a Web service is interacting with clients, active testing cannot be used to monitor, in real time, the correctness of interactions. Moreover, application of generated test cases consumes resources and may disturb the Web service.

Since management of Web services is somehow at its earlier stages, related work usually concentrates more on provision of management features without evaluating the overhead they generate. In order to select the appropriate management approach, a potential user must be able to evaluate it in terms of usefulness and associated cost.

Furthermore, most of the existing work on management of Web services does not tackle management issues at the earlier phase of their development. However, management features need to be addressed as early as possible in the development process, especially during the design and implementation phases.

For example, design for manageability will describe manageability scope and functions. Moreover, it will expose a Web service as a manageable entity providing some of the following capabilities (Farrell & Kreger, 2002): operations, events, interfaces, status, configuration, and metrics that can be used for managing and controlling Web services.

To solve some of the limitations of related work cited above, this chapter presents a novel framework for management of Web services. This framework considers QoWS management issues from earlier phases of the development lifecycle of a Web service. These issues are specified during specification and design, verified and certified before deployment, published with the WSDL document, used during discovery and selection, and passively monitored during invocation of the Web service.

To illustrate the applicability of our approach for management of Web services, we will be using a case study all along the chapter's sections to demonstrate how each management task, at each development phase, can be achieved. Introduction to this case study and its utilization context are given in the next section.

CASE STUDY

For the end of year meetings, a general manager has to meet with managers from different departments (e.g., Sales, R&D, etc.). Managers are located in different locations and, because of their busy timetables, they cannot meet in a single location. A practical alternative is to conduct these meetings in a series of teleconferences. Only mangers are concerned and only those of them who are in their offices can join a conference. This is implied by security issues since confidential information will be exchanged during meetings and communication between different locations is secured (e.g., VPN). At the end of each meeting, meetings' reports must be printed and distributed among all participants.

The manager decides to use available conferencing Web services. Such Web services should allow creation of conferences, and the addition and removal of participants to conferences depending on their profiles and physical locations. At the end of each meeting, the Web service should be able to submit produced reports for printing and deliveries.

The general manager is highly concerned with the environment in which meetings will be carried out using Web services. A thorough QoWS-based discovery and selection operation had lead to the utilization of "conferencing Web service" (CWS), a QoWS-aware composite Web service, which performs all of the required tasks. The manager decides to make use of the monitoring feature of the management framework to assess the QoWS of the CWS.

To perform all these tasks, the CWS is a composition of the following basic Web services (Figure 2):

- **Presence:** This Web service contains information on managers' profiles (e.g., name, address, location, status, position, and availability).
- **Sensors:** This Web service detects the physical location of managers.
- **Call Control:** This Web service creates and manages multiparty conferences (e.g., initiates conferences, adds/removes participants, and ends conferences).
- **Printing:** At some points during conferences or later on, managers may want to print documents (e.g., meeting reports, etc.). The printing Web service will print these documents and keeps them for shipping.

Figure 2. Composite/basic Web services

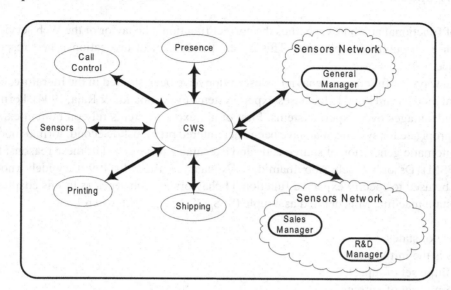

- **Shipping:** Documents printed during and after the conference should be distributed among participants at different locations. The CWS informs the shipping Web service of the location of the documents to be shipped and their final destinations.

WEB SERVICES MANAGEMENT FRAMEWORK

For a better exploitation of Web services, a Web services lifecycle is supposed to integrate features such as QoWS factors' precise definition, QoWS specification, QoWS-based discovery and selection, and QoWS monitoring. This implies that these features need to be addressed in earlier phases through Web services development process, especially during the design phase, then ultimately in the implementation phase, and possibly during selection and invocation of the Web service. QoWS management information, for example, is first specified then published to be later on discovered by clients using QoWS-aware discovery. Our approach is to investigate possibilities to augment the development process of Web services with the above important features.

In the subsequent sections, we will describe how management of QoWS should be supported during development, publication and deployment, discovery, selection, and invocation.

During Development of the Web Service: Behavior's Specification

The first step in a QoWS-aware development and utilization of Web services is the selection and concise definition of factors that will characterize the quality of a Web service. As cited above, these factors are divided into functional and nonfunctional aspects.

Functional Aspects

Definition of functional attributes specifies the correct functional behavior of the Web service for each invocation of each published operation. This covers the content of invocations, their responses, and their sequence.

Two main ways for functional behavior's description have been studied in the literature, concentrating on formal models and knowledge bases/expert systems (Vijayananda & Raja, 1994). Formal models have many advantages over expert systems. First of all, expert systems rely on human expertise and are more appropriate for systems that have been encountered previously. Second, formal models can be useful for automatic generation of source code and executable test cases. For these reasons, finite state machines (FSM) (Dssouli, Saleh, Aboulhamid, En-Nouaary, & Bourhfir, 1999), a widely known formal model, will be used to specify expected functional behaviors of Web services in this chapter.

A finite state machine M is defined as a tuple $(S, S_0, X, Y, D_S, \delta, \lambda)$, where

- S is a set of states,
- $S0 \in S$ is the initial state,
- X is a finite set of inputs,
- Y is a finite set of outputs,
- $D \subseteq S \times X$ is the specification domain,
- $\delta: D^S \rightarrow S$ is the transfer function, and
- $\lambda: D^S \rightarrow Y$ is the output function.

The machine starts at S_0. Whenever an input is received, λ computes the corresponding output and δ determines the corresponding next state(s).

An FSM can be represented by an XML document as illustrated in Figure 3, which gives a partial overview of the FSM machine of the CWS. The root of the document (*fsm*) has an attribute (*name*) and a set of children which represents states. The name is a textual description of the Web service. Each child has a name, the attribute (*initial*), and a set of *transitions*. The name is a textual description of the state while the attribute "initial," if set to YES, indicates that this is the initial state of the machine. A transition has four attributes: *ID*, *input*, *output*, and *next*. The first attribute is a textual description of the transition, the second attribute identifies the event that triggers this transition if the machine is in the associated state, the third attribute is the output generated when firing that transition, and the last attribute specifies the state that the machine will reach after firing the transition.

Nonfunctional Aspects: QoS

QoS consists of a set of factors or attributes such as response time, reliability, availability, accessibility, and so forth. Information on QoS attributes can be specified in many different ways. It can be described in a separate document, embedded within the description of functional behavior, or as an extension to WSDL document. However, to allow QoWS-aware discovery and selection of Web services, QoWS attributes should be available within the WSDL document. The client indicates preferences in terms of QoWS when probing the registry. The registry returns then a list of available Web services providing required operations with requested QoWS.

Figure 3. XML representation of an FSM machine

```
<fsm name="Conferencing Web Service ">
 <state name="Init" initial="YES">
        <transition ID="t1"         input="Config_Valid" output="True" next="Ready"/>
        <transition ID="t2"         input="Config_Invalid" output="False" next="Init"/>
 </state>
 <state name="Ready" initial="NO">
<transition ID="t3"          input="CreateConf_Valid" output="True" next="ConfCreated"/>
 </state>
 <state name="ConfCreated" initial="NO">
        <transition ID="t4"          input="AddUser"output="True" next="ConfCreated"/>
 </state>
...
</fsm>
```

The first step in extending SOA with QoS is the definition of QoS attributes. In this chapter, we will focus on the following attributes:

- **Processing Time (PT):** This is a measure of the time a Web service takes between the time it gets a request and the moment it sends back the corresponding response. PT is computed at the Web service's provider side.
- **Maximum Processing Time (MxPT):** This is the maximum time the Web service should take to respond to a request.
- **Minimum Processing Time (MnPT):** This is the minimum time the Web service should take before responding to a request. Unlike PT, which is a dynamically computed attribute, MnPT and MxPT are statically defined and $MnPT \leq PT \leq MxPT$.
- **Response Time (RT):** It consists of the time needed between issuing a request and getting its response. It is measured at the client's side to include the propagation time of requests and responses.
- **Maximum Response Time (MxRT):** This is the maximum accepted time, for the client, between issuing a request and getting its response.
- **Minimum Response Time (MnRT):** This is the minimum time, for the client, between issuing a request and getting its response. This attribute in unlikely to be used since the client is usually more interested in MxRT. For the client, $RT \leq MxRT$ must always be satisfied.
- **Availability:** This is a probability measure that indicates how much the Web service is available for use by clients. It can also consist of the percentage of time that the Web service is operating.
- **Service Charge (SC):** It defines the cost a client will be charged for the Web services utilization. SC can be estimated by operation, type of requests, period of utilization, session, or by volume of processed data.
- **Reputation:** This is a measure of Web services' credibility. It depends basically on previous end users' experiences while using the Web service. Different users may have different opinions on the same Web service. The reputation value can be given by the average ranking given to the Web service by several users.

MnPT, MxPT, availability, and SC are related to profiles of users of the Web service. This profiling is based on the type of subscriptions of clients and/or the QoWS they are willing to pay for. For example, a gold-subscribed user must be served quicker (MnRT = 0) than a bronze-subscribed user (MnRT > 1ms).

Figure 4 illustrates embedded QoS attributes in the definition of the operation tag within the WSDL document of the CWS.

Before Deployment and Publication: QoWS Verification and Certification

Once a Web service is developed, it must be tested to verify whether it is correct with regards to the behavior's specification document produced during preceding development phases. The management framework has features that a Web service's developer can use to verify and certify the Web service's behavior. This certification information is then published with the WSDL description of the Web service so potential clients will use it.

Verification and certification procedures enable providers to evaluate QoWS of their Web services prior to the publication. Our approach consists of a two-phase verification and certification technique, which is conducted by a verifier Web service and a certifier Web service (Figure 7). The first phase consists of verifying the WSDL document, including the QoWS parameters description. The second phase consists of applying a measurement technique to compute the QoWS metrics stated in the Web service interface and compares their values to those claimed in the WSDL document. This is used to verify the conformity of a Web service to its description from a QoWS point-of-view (QoWS testing). Therefore, a set of QoWS test cases are defined and used as input to QoWS verification. The configuration and generation of these test cases is described in detail by Serhani et al. (2005). Once the Web service passes the verification tests, the certifier issues a conformance certificate to certify that QoWS

Figure 4. QoWS in WSDL document

```
<?xml version="1.0" encoding="UTF-8"?>
<wsdl:portType name="ConferenceService">
 <wsdl:operation name="addUser" parameterOrder="userAddresse callID">
  <wsdl:input message="intf:addUserRequest" name="addUserRequest"/>
  <wsdl:output message="intf:addUserResponse" name="addUserResponse"/>
            <Profile name="GOLD">
                 MnPT = NULL
                 MxPT = 10ms
                 SC= "$10"
            </Profile>
            <Profile name="SILVER">
                 MnPT = 10ms
                 MxPT = 30ms
                 SC= "$5"
            </Profile>
 </wsdl:operation>
</wsdl:portType>
```

claims are valid. This certificate will be considered as a key differentiator between Web services offering similar functionalities. The verifier and certifier perform the following tasks:

- It asks for information about the provider and its Web service (e.g., servers' resources capacity, connections used, Network information, etc.).
- It checks the WSDL files of the target Web services (e.g., location, interface, and implementation description)
- It makes sure that all published operations are available.
- It verifies the QoWS described in WSDL. The QoWS verifier can initiate, if necessary, additional tests to validate other information provided in the WSDL document. This information concerns QoWS attributes classification (e.g., definition, computation logic, and upper and lower bounds).
- It stores the verification report in a specific-purpose database.

During Discovery and Selection: QoWS-based Discovery and Selection

In standard SOA, the find operation is based on the name of the Web service. A client is likely to get a list of Web services following a basic find operation issued to a UDDI registry. Alternatively, an intelligent find operation must consider, in addition to the name, QoWS information verified and certified in the previous phase, so the returned list of Web services is somehow short and concise.

Our framework defines how an intelligent discovery operation should look like and how it can be used. Discovering a Web service will be based on its functionalities as well as its QoWS. We automated the processes of publication and discovery of Web services based on QoWS using a supporting application (Figure 5), which allows the following tasks:

- **Publication:** In order to publish their Web services using our application, providers should supply the Web service name, description, and the location of its WSDL document. This document is then parsed to validate its content and to display the list of QoWS information. The validation process verifies the correctness of published operations in addition to the QoWS information. The provider can add/remove/modify QoWS attributes before publication. At this stage, the WSDL document is validated and the provider publishes the QoWS-enabled WSDL document.
- **Discovery:** The application allows the user to query the registry while specifying the Web service name and the set of required QoWS attributes and their related values. The list of Web services descriptions that fulfill the client's requirements is displayed via the application interface. The frame contains corresponding Web services and their associated QoWS information.

During Invocation: QoWS Monitoring

During interactions between a Web service and its client, it might be necessary to assess if the Web service is behaving as initially specified and claimed in previous subsections. This assessment will require a continuous online monitoring of interactions between the Web service and its client.

Online monitoring of Web services requires passive observers (Benharref et al., 2005, 2006). A passive observer receives a copy of all exchanged messages between a Web service and its client and checks their validity. Passive observation of systems modeled as FSM is usually performed in two steps (Lee, Netravali, Sabnani, Sugla, & John, 1997):

Figure 5. UDDIe client's application for QoWS-driver publication and discovery

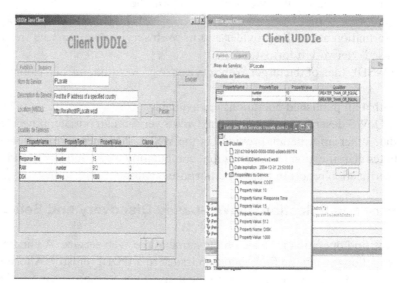

QoWS Validation before publication Q   oWS-based discovery of Web Services

1. **Passive Homing (or state recognition):** In this step, the observer is brought to a state equivalent to the one that the Web service might be in. If no such state is found, a fault is immediately reported. The set of messages leading to this state is known as the homing sequence. This first step is required if observation starts while the Web service and its client already exchanged some messages. These messages will not be available to the observer but the latter can figure out a homing sequence to determine the appropriate state.

2. **Fault Detection:** Starting from the state identified in the previous step, the observer checks the observed behavior against the system's specification. If an observed event is not expected then a fault is immediately reported.

The observation in distributed architectures requires the selection of a number of observers and their best locations (where to get copies of exchanged messages). The number and location of the points of observation affect significantly the detection capabilities of the observation architectures. For example, if the observed Web service is a composite Web service, it might be more interesting (in terms of misbehavior detection) to consider a network of observers, that is, an observer for each Web service rather than a unique observer for the composite Web service. In such architectures, cooperation of all observers can generate pertinent information for Web services management. The consideration of a global observer (for the composite Web service) and local observers (for composing Web services) presents a framework where this cooperation can be orchestrated for the benefit of better misbehavior detection.

Our Web services management framework offers two monitoring architectures as depicted in Figure 6, which shows a mono-observer architecture (Benharref et al., 2005) and multiobserver architecture (Benharref et al., 2006).

Figure 6. Monitoring architectures

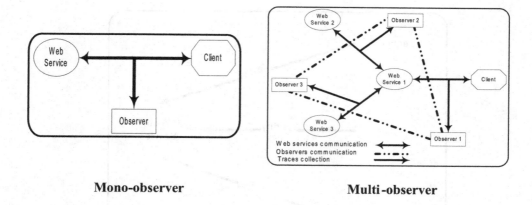

Mono-observer   **Multi-observer**

Three types of interactions are illustrated in Figure 6. Web services communication refers to the SOAP-based communication between Web services and their clients. Traces collection consists of forwarding messages exchanged between the observed Web service and its client to local observers. Observers communication conveys information between observers. This information is divided into three categories:

3. **Configuration information:** During configuration of different observers, local observers must indicate to the global observer which Web service they are observing and where they are located. The global observer needs this information to identify observers and associates the traces it will receive to appropriate observers/Web services.
4. **Traces from local observers to the global observer:** Whenever a local observer gets a trace, it sends it to the global observer.
5. **Notifications of faults:** If the global observer detects a fault, it informs other local observers. In the case where a local observer detects a fault, it informs the global observer. The latter informs remaining local observers that misbehavior has been observed elsewhere and they should be aware of some specific traffic/actions.

Traces collection mechanisms studied by Benharref et al. (2005) show that mobile agents present the least overhead. Whenever an entity wants to use monitoring architectures, it invokes a Web service observer (WSO) that generates a set of mobile observers and sends them to locations specified during invocation.

Except specification of expected behaviors of Web services which has to be done by the provider, other management operations presented in previous sections are performed by invoking the verifier, the certifier, and the observer, three Web services provided by the management framework. These components and their associated operations are illustrated in Figure 7.

Different steps discussed above have been applied to a set of Web services to illustrate their applicability. The next section shows an example of application to the CWS introduced earlier in this chapter.

Figure 7. Management framework components and operations

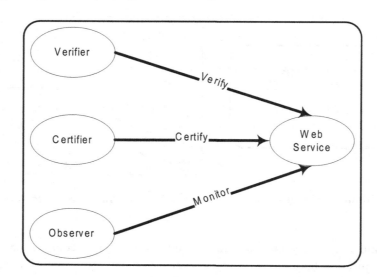

EXPERIMENTATION AND RESULTS

As indicated earlier, CWS is a composite Web service for management of teleconferences, printing, and shipping of teleconferences reports. Experimenting with the framework using this Web service required implementation and deployment of a dozen of Web services.

Implementation Issues

All Web services, including the WSO, are implemented in BEA WebLogic (BEA, 2004). Mobile observers get traces using SOAP handlers, which are available within the BEA platform. A SOAP handler, a specific-purpose Java class, intercepts a request/response to/from a Web service before it gets to the core Web service or the client respectively, and can also perform operations on it. In our case, the SOAP handler sends each intercepted request or response in a user datagram protocol (UDP) datagram to the concerned mobile observer all along with the date at which this event occurred to allow the observer to assess QoS attributes such as response time. The mobile observer checks this trace and forwards it to the global observer.

To be able to detect lost UDP datagrams, a sequence number field is used. When a mobile observer detects a lost datagram (wrong/not expected sequence number), it suspends the misbehavior detection and reperforms the homing procedure. It restarts the detection once this procedure is achieved correctly. Since the behavior/operation of SOAP handlers within all observed Web services is similar, a unique (generic) SOAP handler is developed and then distributed to all providers participating in the observation.

The overhead of the management framework can be quantitatively evaluated with regards to required computer resources and generated network overhead. Both analytical analysis and experimentations showed that most of the overhead is related to the online monitoring. In fact, the verification and certification operations are straightforward and usually conducted off-line, that is, before the Web service is made available to clients. Moreover, all required resources are located at the verifier and certifier Web services providers. For these reasons, overhead analysis presented in upcoming subsections will concentrate on online monitoring, especially traces collection.

Monitoring

In addition to the observation of the CWS, the manager wants to make sure that all the steps are performed according to the agreed on contract and QoWS. Fortunately, all the providers accept to participate, to some extent, in the monitoring. The provider of the CWS will host all mobile observers using the Jade platform (Jade, 2007). This provider will also supply WSDL documents and FSM models of each of the basic Web services. Basic Web services providers will configure SOAP handlers for traces collection and forward.

The observation procedure of CWS is performed following the steps detailed below and illustrated in Figure 8. To keep the figure simple, just one Web service handler and one Web service client[1] are depicted in the figure.

1. The manager invokes the WSO, providing different locations of mobile observers.
2. The WSO generates a mobile agent and sends it to one of the destinations submitted during invocation in Step 1.
3. Once the mobile agent gets into its destination, it clones itself as many times as required to observe all Web services.
4. The mobile agent observing the CWS becomes the global observer; other mobile observers are local.

Figure 8. Multiobserver deployment

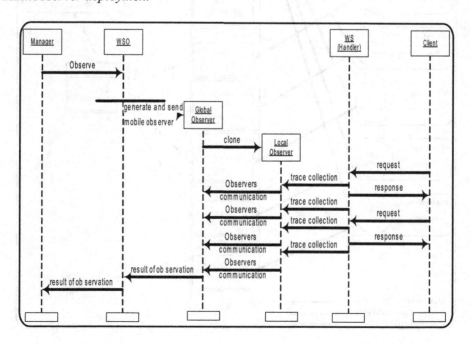

5. SOAP handlers forward traces to appropriate mobile observers.
6. Local observers analyze these traces and forward them to the global observer.
7. Whenever misbehavior is detected (by global or local observers), correlation then fault location is initiated by the global observer to find the faulty Web service.
8. The global observer reports to the WSO.
9. The WSO reports to the manager.

Each local observer is listening to a UDP port to receive events from SOAP handlers. The global observer is listening to two different UDP ports: one to receive events (request or response) from local observers and another port to receive information on detected misbehaviors by local observers. The SOAP handler sends each event between a client and its Web service to the attached local observer. The latter forwards this event to the global observer and checks the validity of this event. If misbehavior is detected, the local observer notifies the global observer. Figure 9 shows the overall configuration of interacting client, Web services, mobile observers, and communication between these entities.

Figure 9. Multiobserver configuration for monitoring of CWS

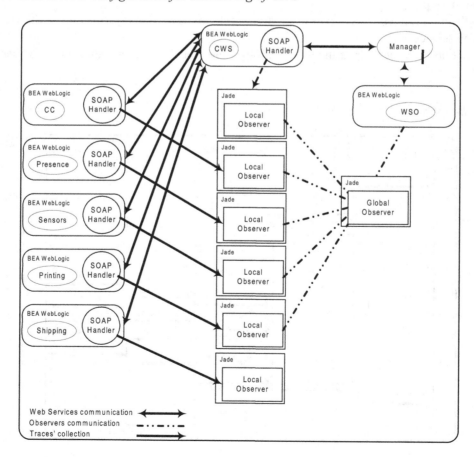

Processing CPU and Memory Utilization

Computer resources (CPU and memory) used by traces collection entities are somehow insignificant with regards to the minimal standard configuration of actual personal desktops/laptops. Except for the mobile agent approach, CPU and memory utilization are so low that they are even difficult to precisely evaluate.

For mobile observers, CPU and memory utilization on a laptop equipped with an AMD Athlon 64/3000+ processor and 512MB RAM, CPU and memory utilization are as follows:

- **Hosting a mobile platform:** If the mobile agent administration interface is located on the laptop, the CPU utilization varies between 2% and 4%. For memory, it uses around 30 Megabytes.
- **Joining a mobile platform[2]:** If the mobile agent platform is running on a remote computer, joining it requires 12 MBytes memory at the laptop and around 2 MBytes on the host running the administration interface. For CPU, there is almost no impact at both sides.
- **Receiving a mobile observer:** When a mobile observer is received, it requires around 27 MBytes of memory. For CPU, there is a high utilization during 1 to 2 seconds while initializing and displaying the graphical interface of the mobile observer, then the CPU utilization goes back to previous level
- **Processing traces:** Even in the worst case where traces are received with a very small delay, the CPU used by the mobile observer for analyzing them is around 2%. However, there is no additional memory utilization.

Network Load

The network load introduced by the observation is classified into load due to the deployment of mobile agents and load due to the traces collection process.

Deployment Load

Since all observers are located at the composite Web service provider's side, only one mobile agent is generated by the WSO. The size of the traffic to move a mobile agent is around 600 Kilobytes (600 KB).

Traces Collection Load

Generally, for each interaction between a Web service and its client, 2 UDP datagrams are generated: a first datagram from the SOAP handler to the local observer, and a second datagram from this local observer to the global observer. Whenever a local observer detects misbehavior, a third datagram is sent (fault notification). The average size of a datagram is 150 bytes. So, each response/request pair introduces 4 datagrams if everything goes fine, 5 datagrams if one of the events is faulty, or 6 datagrams if both are faulty. We suppose that faults will not occur very often, and then few fault notifications will be generated. This assumption is realistic since all Web services are supposed to undergo acceptable testing process before their deployment. The traces collection load then is reduced to the forward of events, that is, 4 datagrams for a request/response pair. This represents a load of 600 bytes.

Results and Analysis

To illustrate the detection capabilities of our architecture, we injected faults to some Web services and/or in the network and monitored the behavior of observers (Table 1). The observers have been able to detect most of the injected faults.

A fault that cannot be detected occurs when the last event in a communication between a Web service and its client is lost (see Figures 10 and 11). As discussed earlier, traces are sent as UDP packets. To be able to detect lost packets and recover the observation, a sequence number attribute is used. An observer detects a lost packet if the sequence number of the following packet is different than expected. When a lost packet carries the last event in a communication, observers will not be able to detect this incident since no future packets will arrive. Table 1 shows brief descriptions of some of the executed scenarios and the reactions of observers (both local and global) to the fault.

CONCLUSION

Web services are a new generation of Web applications. This new paradigm of communication puts more emphasize on business-to-business interactions rather than the business-to-consumer transactions model that the Internet was largely providing. Management of Web services is of prime importance for all entities involved in service oriented architecture. In an environment where the interacting components are not known a priori, can be on different operating systems and platforms, and coded in different programming languages, the management of Web services is very challenging compared to the management of traditional distributed systems.

In this chapter, we have developed a framework to provide management features to Web services providers and clients by supporting management activities all along the lifecycle of a Web service, from development to invocation. The framework encourages providers to consider management activities while developing their Web services by specifying QoWS attributes. It allows clients to select appropri-

Table 1. Some of the executed scenarios

Target Web Service	Fault description	Comments
CWS	Submit a printDocument request before creating a conference	Fault detected by local and global observer
Call Control	Add a user before creating a conference	Fault detected by local and global observer
Presence	Try to add a user to the conference that is not recognized by the Presence service	Fault detected by local and global observer
Shipping	Request shipping of a document that has not been submitted for printing	Fault detected by local and global observer
Shipping	A trace collection event (shipDocument response) from a handler to the local observer is lost (Figure 10)	Neither the local observer nor the global observer will detect the fault.
Shipping	A trace collection event (shipDocument response) or a fault notification from a local observer to the global observer is lost (Figure 11)	The global observer will not be able to detect the fault or process the notification (correlation)

Figure 10. Trace lost before getting to local observer

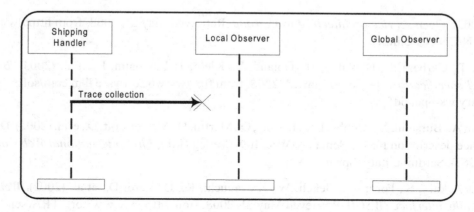

Figure 11. Trace or fault notification lost before getting to global observer

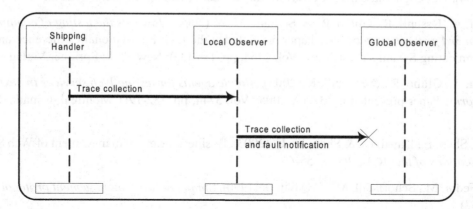

ate Web services using QoWS information published previously by providers. Clients also make use of the framework to check if the Web services they are actually using or planning to use are behaving correctly in terms of functional and nonfunctional facets. A prototype of the framework has been developed and used in management of a set of Web services. In this chapter, a conferencing Web service has been used to evaluate the effectiveness and the overhead of the framework.

As a future work, we intend to enhance the framework by providing support to other management operations, such as fault isolation and repair. Work is in progress to implement the remaining components of the framework and to evaluate the overall features of the framework on a large scale Web services environment.

REFERENCES

3GPP. (2003). *Open service architecture workgroup.* Retrieved May 21, 2008, from http://www.3gpp.org/TB/CN/CN5/CN5.htm

Andrews, T., Curbera, F., Dholakia, H., Goland, Y., Klein, J., Leymann, F., et al. (2003). *BPEL4WS version 1.1 specification.* Retrieved May 21, 2008, from ftp://www6.software.ibm.com/software/developer/library/ws-bpel.pdf

Ankolekar, A., Burstein, M., Hobbs, J. R., Lassila, O., Martin, D., McDermott, D., et al. (2002). DAML-S: Web service description for the Semantic Web. In S. Verlag (Ed.), *First International Web Conference* (pp. 348-363). Sardinia, Italy: Springer Verlag.

Arkin, A., Askary, S., Fordin, S., Jekeli, W., Kawaguchi, K., Orchard, D., et al. (2002). *Web service choreography interface (WSCI).* Retrieved May 21, 2008, from http://www.w3.org/TR/wsci/

Banerji, A., Bartolini, C., Beringer, D., Chopella, V., Govindarajan, K., Karp, A., et al. (2002). *WSCL: The Web services conversation language.* Retrieved May 21, 2008, from http://www.w3.org/TR/wscl10/

BEA. (2004). *WebLogic plateform.* Retrieved May 21, 2008, from http://www.bea.com

Benharref, A., Dssouli, R., Glitho, R., & Serhani, M. A. (2006). *Towards the testing of composed Web services in 3rd generation networks.* Paper presented at the IFIP International Conference on Testing of Communicating Systems (TestCom) (Vol. 3964, pp. 118-133). New York: Springer Verlag.

Benharref, A., Glitho, R., & Dssouli, R. (2005). *Mobile agents for testing Web services in next generation networks.* Paper presented at MATA 2005 (Vol. 3744, pp. 182-191). Montreal, Canada: Springer Verlag.

Casati, F., Shan, E., Dayal, U., & Shan, M.-C. (2003). Business-oriented management of Web Services. *Communications of the ACM, 46*(10), 55-60.

Case, J., Fedor, M., Schoffstall, M., & Davin, J. (1990). S*imple network management protocol (SNMP)* (RFC 1157).

ChangSup, K., Sungwon, K., In-Young, K., Jongmoon, B., & Young-Il, C. (2006). *Generating test cases for Web services using extended finite state machine.* Paper presented at the IFIP International Conference on Testing of Communicating Systems (TestCom) (pp. 103-117). New York: Springer Verlag.

CPXe. (2005). *I3A standards - initiatives - CPXe.* Retrieved May 21, 2008, from http://www.i3a.org/i_cpxe.html

Dssouli, R., Saleh, K., Aboulhamid, E., En-Nouaary, A., & Bourhfir, C. (1999). Test development for communication protocols: Towards automation. *Computer Networks, 31*(17), 1835-1872.

Farrell, J. A., & Kreger, H. (2002). Web services management approaches. *IBM Systems Journal, 41*(2), 212-227.

Fenton, N. E., & Pfleeger, S. L. (1997). *Software metrics: A rigorous and practical approach* (2nd ed.). Boston: PWS Pub.

Gray, A. R., & MacDonell, S. G. (1997). Comparison of techniques for developing predictive models of software metrics. *Information and Software Technology, 39*(6), 425-437.

Ho, S., Loucks, W. M., & Singh, A. (1998). Monitoring the performance of a Web service. In *IEEE Canadian Conference on Electrical and Computer Engineering* (Vol. 1, pp. 109-112). Waterloo, Ontario, Canada: IEEE Press.

HP. (2007). *Open view.* Retrieved May 21, 2008, from http://www.managementsoftware.hp.com

ISO/IEC. (1989). *7498, information processing systems -- open systems interconnection – basic reference model.* Author.

ISO/IEC. (1998). *9596, information technology -- open systems interconnection -- common management information protocol.* Author.

Jade. (2007). *Java agent development framework.* Retrieved May 21, 2008, from http://jade.tilab.com

Jiang, Y., Xin, G.-M., Shan, J.-H., Zhang, L., Xie, B., & Yang, F.-Q. (2005). A method of automated test data generation for Web services. *Chinese Journal of Computers, 28*(4), 568-577.

Kalepu, S., Krishnaswamy, S., & Loke, S. W. (2004). Verity: A QoS metric for selecting Web services and providers. In *Fourth International Conference on Web Information Systems Engineering Workshops* (pp. 131-139). Rome, Italy: IEEE Computer Society.

Kreger, H. (2001). *Web services conceptual architectures (WSCA 1.0)* (white paper). IBM Software Group.

Lee, D., Netravali, A. N., Sabnani, K. K., Sugla, B., & John, A. (1997). *Passive testing and applications to network management.* Paper presented at the International Conference on Network Protocols (pp. 113-122). Atlanta: IEEE Computer Society.

Leymann, F. (2001). *Web service flow language (WSFL) 1.0.* Retrieved May 21, 2008, from http://www-4.ibm.com/software/solutions/Webservices/pdf/WSFL.pdf

OASIS. (2005). *Universal description, discovery, and integration.* Retrieved May 21, 2008, from http://www.uddi.org/

Parasoft. (2006). *SOATest.* Retrieved May 21, 2008, from http://www.parasoft.com/jsp/products/home.jsp?product=SOAP

Perkins, D., & McGinnis, E. (1997). *Understanding SNMP MIBs.* Upper Saddle River, N.J.: Prentice Hall PTR.

Ran, S. (2003). A Framework for Discovering Web Services with Desired Quality of Services Attributes. In *International Conference on Web Services* (pp. 208-213). Las Vegas, Nevada: CSREA Press.

Salamon, W. J., & Wallace, D. R. (1994). *Quality characteristics and metrics for reusable software.* National Institute of Standards and Technology.

Schmietendorf, A., Dumke, R., & Reitz, D. (2004). SLA management - Challenges in the context of Web-service-based infrastructures. In *IEEE International Conference on Web Services (ICWS)* (pp. 606-613). San Diego, CA: IEEE Computer Society.

Serhani, M. A., Dssouli, R., Hafid, A., & Sahraoui, H. (2005). A QoS broker based architecture for efficient Web services selection. In *International Conference on Web Services (ICWS)* (Vol. 2005, pp. 113-120). Orlando, FL: IEEE Computer Society.

ShaikhAli, A., Rana, O. F., Al-Ali, R., & Walker, D. W. (2003). UDDIe: An extended registry for Web services. In (pp. 85-89). Orlando, FL, USA: IEEE Computer Society.

Tsai, W. T., Paul, R., Cao, Z., Yu, L., & Saimi, A. (2003). Verification of Web services using an enhanced UDDI server. In *Eighth IEEE International Workshop on Object-Oriented Real-Time Dependable Systems* (pp. 131-138). Guadalajara, Mexico: IEEE.

Vijayananda, K., & Raja, P. (1994). *Models of communication protocols for fault diagnosis.* Swiss Federal Institute of Technology.

W3. (2004). *Web services endpoint management architecture requirements.* Retrieved May 22, 2008, from http://dev.w3.org/cvsWeb/2002/ws/arch/management/ws-arch-management-requirements.html?rev=1.7

W3C. (1999). *HTTP.* Retrieved May 22, 2008, from http://www.w3.org/Protocols/

W3C. (2001). *Web services description language.* Retrieved May 22, 2008, from http://www.w3c.org/TR/wsdl

W3C. (2002). *Web services management concern* (white paper). W3C Consortium.

W3C. (2003, November). *QoS for Web services: Requirements and possible approaches.* Author.

W3C. (2004). *Simple object access protocol.* Retrieved May 22, 2008, from http://www.w3c.org/TR/soap

W3C. (2006). *eXtensible markup language.* Retrieved May 22, 2008, from http://www.w3c.org/XML

Wahli, U. (2002). *Self-study guide: WebSphere studio application developer and Web* services (1st ed.). Retrieved May 22, 2008, from http://www.books24x7.com/marc.asp?isbn=0738424196

Warrier, U., Besaw, L., LaBarre, L., & Handspicker, B. (1990). *The common management information services and protocols for the Internet (CMOT and CMIP)* (RFC 1189).

WSDL. (2001). *Web services description language.* Retrieved May 22, 2008, from http://www.w3c.org/TR/wsdl

Xiaoying, B., Wenli, D., Wei-Tek, T., & Yinong, C. (2005). WSDL-based automatic test case generation for Web services testing. In *International Workshop on Service-Oriented System Engineering* (pp. 207-212). Beijing, China: IEEE Computer Society.

Yuming, J., Chen-Khong, T., & Chi-Chung, K. (2000). Challenges and approaches in providing QoS monitoring. *International Journal of Network Management, 10*(6), 323-334.

ENDNOTES

[1]   When a composite Web Service invokes a basic Web Service, it is said to be a client of that Web Service.

[2]   A node can host a mobile observer if it is running a mobile agent platform administration interface or is joining a remote platform.

Chapter III
Quality Models for Multimedia Delivery in a Services Oriented Architecture

Krishna Ratakonda
IBM T. J. Watson Research Center, USA

Deepak S. Turaga
IBM T. J. Watson Research Center, USA

ABSTRACT

In this chapter we present an overview of research and development efforts across several different technical communities aimed at enabling efficient and standardized end-to-end delivery of multimedia content over a service-oriented architecture (SOA). We focus primarily on issues related to quality of service (QoS) specification, measurement, and enforcement for different multimedia distribution applications in this space.

INTRODUCTION

In this chapter we present an overview of research and development efforts across several different technical communities aimed at enabling efficient and standardized end-to-end delivery of multimedia content over a service oriented architecture (SOA). We focus primarily on issues related to quality of service (QoS) specification, measurement, and enforcement for different multimedia distribution applications in this space. In order to do this, we first describe state-of-the-art in multimedia delivery architectures, and standardization efforts in coding, networking, and multimedia quality modeling. We then consider the implications of building SOA-based realizations of such multimedia applications, and identify the appropriate integrated service policies, mechanisms, architecture, and metrics that may be used to successfully design and deploy them. We not only describe the current state-of-the-art in this space, but also identify emerging trends, describe problems, discuss solutions, and most importantly, provide insights into the feasibility and applicability of these solutions to specific problem areas.

With the current availability of digital content, and underlying infrastructure improvements in network bandwidth and user devices, there is a rapidly expanding set of applications that require delivering multimedia to remote users. This includes traditional applications such as videoconferencing and video on demand, as well as several new applications enabled by enterprises, and the peer-to-peer (P2P) and gaming environments. Multimedia delivery requires orchestration across several different aspects, such as content generation, underlying infrastructure, end-user device capability, user preferences, service provider capabilities, and so forth. There is need for a standardized set of mechanisms that allow these distributed and heterogeneous components to successfully interact with each other to build an end-to-end multimedia delivery system.

A service-oriented architecture provides several mechanisms for describing precisely the capabilities of distributed components, providing directory services to locate appropriate service providers, and providing interface descriptors that allow connecting such components to compose workflows. It also provides policy mechanisms to support service level agreements (SLA), and specifies requirements on the desired QoS. Hence, there has been significant interest in using SOA-based architectures to deliver multimedia for several of these applications.

This is significantly different from the way several multimedia applications are currently constructed, as it requires traditional multimedia researchers to acknowledge the presence of a distributed infrastructure where the delivery mechanism is not under the control of any single provider. For example, a typical situation will have different providers providing content, infrastructure hosting, and end-user services. The situation is further complicated by the fact that a content provider would like to work with multiple end-user services providers. A key challenge that needs to be addressed in this space involves the development of appropriate models of *end-to-end QoS* for multimedia delivery. Such models are critical prerequisites for the successful deployment of any multimedia delivery application within the SOA framework. For instance, models for QoS are essential for users and service providers to be able to formulate the right SLAs and being able to enforce them. This also requires changing several of the established paradigms in prioritizing and delivering multimedia services over a tightly controlled network infrastructure. Capability negotiation, dynamic load balancing, security, privacy, and robustness of the heterogeneous environment are all very important considerations.

Traditional research in this field has often been from two distinct perspectives: the SOA side and the multimedia side. Researchers in SOA often use very simplistic QoS models for multimedia, and often ignore critical metrics relevant to the quality of the multimedia experience (e.g., user preferences, content characteristics, encoding, artifacts, etc.). On the other hand, multimedia researchers have built sophisticated models to measure multimedia quality and perform network bandwidth optimization; however, they have lacked a good mechanism to specify or enforce delivery policies that typically cover a broad spectrum of systems components. In this chapter, we bring together the established and emerging developments across both these fields, and connect these to QoS specification, measurement, and enforcement for different multimedia applications.

This chapter is organized as follows. We start, in Section 0, with an overview of multimedia delivery architectures currently used, in terms of the media formats, network protocols, and delivery mechanisms. In Section 0, we present the potential impact of the infrastructure issues (i.e., varying delivery architectures, network protocols, content access, etc.) on multimedia quality, and show examples of the resulting multimedia quality variations. We then describe metrics developed within the multimedia community to capture the end-to-end quality in Section 0, and present the standardization efforts in this space. In Section 0, we describe the special requirements that SOA-based realizations of multimedia delivery place on the infrastructure, delivery mechanisms, and the underlying standards and algorithms. We then describe how these media requirements can be translated into SLAs and additionally into service policies, and how such media-specific SLAs can be monitored and enforced to provide QoS guarantees. We present emerging trends in multimedia delivery and SOA, and describe applications in business and enterprise settings, as well as application for user communication and content sharing in Section 0, and finally conclude in Section 0.

OVERVIEW OF MEDIA DELIVERY SOLUTIONS

There are several different end-to-end solutions currently in use for delivery of networked multimedia content. Some of the popular solutions are proprietary, such as those based on Microsoft Windows Media, Apple QuickTime, or Real Networks software. The key disadvantage of these proprietary solutions is the limited control and flexibility they provide solution developers in terms of using different content and service providers to construct their desired applications. Additionally, they also limit interoperability and reuse of solutions and components across different service offerings. In contrast, there are several significant industry efforts to develop open standards-based end-to-end solutions. Such end-to-end solutions consist of specifications for different types of standardized delivery models, underlying physical network infrastructure, and several transport and multimedia compression standards, and descriptions of how these may all be put together. In this section we describe different delivery models and standards for end-to-end networked multimedia solutions.

Delivery Models and Network Infrastructure

Multimedia delivery/distribution services may be classified into three categories (Xiang, Zhang, Zhu, Zhang, & Zhang, 2004):

- Centralized
- Content Distribution Network (CDN)-based
- Peer-to-Peer (P2P)

Centralized approaches use one multimedia server (or central server cluster) to support multiple clients. Although this architecture is widely deployed in many distribution services, its performance is limited, as it is susceptible to bottlenecks at the server or in the network. Server clustering or mirroring (Xiang, Zhang, Zhu, & Zhong, 2001) techniques have been proposed to enhance its service availability, however, this architecture is still not as scalable or flexible as the either the CDN or the P2P architectures.

CDN-based multimedia distribution services, for example, Akamai, deploy a number of servers at the edge of the network, to efficiently redirect user requests, for reduced request latency and balanced load across servers. However, the capacity of the edge servers is designed more in line with handling nonmedia Web traffic, and they are often overwhelmed by streaming media services. This limits the use

Figure 1. Different delivery models: Centralized (left), CDN (center), and P2P (right)

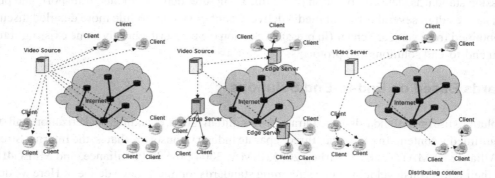

of a CDN-based architecture for a large scale multimedia distribution service over the Internet. Several issues, such as server placement, content distribution, request routing, policies for management and enforcement, and server scheduling in order deal with dynamic and "flash" variations of demand in an efficient manner, are active areas of research (Cohen, Katzir, & Raz, 2002; Kangasharju, Roberts, & Ross, 2002; Turaga, Chen, & Caviedes, 2002; Zhang, Wang, Du, & Su, 2000).

Recently, there has been much interest in P2P computing and communication as well distribution services (Yiu, Jin, & Chan, 2007). Examples of P2P systems include BitTorrent, Napster, Gnutella, Freenet, CenterSpan, and so forth. In a P2P-based distribution service, individual clients host content in their local store and distribute this to other clients. Hence, resource (bandwidth) contributions from individual peers allow sharing of data by a large community at very low cost, as there is no need for dedicated servers[1] and any network maintenance cost is minimal. However, providing streaming service over P2P networks is still a challenging task because of their inherent instability and unreliability. The most challenging issues in P2P networks are dynamic content location and routing, and distributed streaming with QoS provisioning. These challenges arise because peers have dynamic uptimes with arbitrary arrival and departure times, and determine their resource contributions dynamically and selfishly. Additionally, peers are often constrained in terms of the resources that they can contribute to the system, and this varies dynamically. There has been a significant effort to tackle these issues by building hierarchical service routing frameworks with overlays on top of the physical P2P network. Additional efforts have focused on game theoretic solutions that model research exchanges among peers as a dynamic game with rational decision makers, and identify necessary and sufficient conditions for stability, equilibrium, and so forth. There are several additional directions for research in this space, and more details can be obtained from Yiu et al. (2007) Tran, Hua, and Do (2002, 2004), Xu, Hefeeda, Hambrusch, and Bhargava, (2002), Padmanabhan, Wang, Chou, and Sripanidkulchai (2002), Eger and Killat (2006), and van der Schaar and Chou (2007).

The selection of an appropriate delivery model brings with it several corresponding advantages and disadvantages, and solution developers need to be aware of these tradeoffs in order to be able to construct the optimal solution designed for their client requirements. Besides these delivery models, there are also several underlying network infrastructure and application layer issues that can affect the quality of the delivered multimedia. These include the use of unicast, multicast, broadcast or simulcast, use of reliable transport control protocol (TCP) vs. unreliable user datagram protocol (UDP) transport, nature of the physical network medium, that is, wired vs. wireless, and application layer issues such as media compression standards. The combination of the infrastructure, delivery model, transport, and physical medium can result in several different media delivery configurations. While more detailed discussions can be obtained from van der Schaar (in press), in Section 0 we describe briefly some existing standards based on end-to-end solutions and protocols.

Standards Based on End-to-End Solutions

These solutions use open standards-based strategies for initialization, encoding, packetization, and streaming of multimedia content. In particular, three separate industry consortia, that is, the Internet Streaming Media Alliance (ISMA) (Fuchs & Färber, 2005; ISMA, 2004), the 3GPP alliance, and MPEG4IP have focused their efforts on developing open streaming standards for multimedia delivery. Here we describe the ISMA initiative and the underlying media formats and transport protocols it supports.

ISMA is a nonprofit corporation founded to provide a forum for creating end-to-end specifications that define an interoperable implementation for streaming rich media (e.g., video, audio, and associated data) over IP networks. *ISMA specifications* are implementation agreements that allow ISMA members, as well as the market at large, to develop streaming products and solutions with the expectation that cross-platform, multivendor interoperability with other products in the delivery chain is possible. The stated goal of ISMA is to use existing standards and contribute to those still in development to complete its specifications.

ISMA Specification 2.0 was released in 2005. The basic architecture of the ISMA specification includes a media server/s, an IP network, and a media client, with intermediate systems in the transmission chain such as storage, transcoders, and caches/proxies. The functional areas addressed in the specification are:

- Audio-Video Coding Format
    ○ Audio format: MPEG-4 Advanced Audio Codec (AAC) and High Efficiency-AAC (HE-AAC), including 5.1 surround support;
    ○ Video format: MPEG-4, Advanced Video Codec (AVC), also known as ITU-T H.264;
    ○ Media storage: MPEG-4 and AVC File Format
- Transport Protocols
    ○ Media transport: Real-time Transfer Protocol (RTP), Real Time Control Protocol (RTCP);
    ○ Media control and announcement: Real Time Streaming Protocol (RTSP), Session Description Protocol (SDP).

The architecture, including several different profiles of the specification is shown in Figure 2.

The different profiles correspond to different application requirements in terms of video quality and bit-rate, ranging from medium quality 1.2 Mbps all the way to high quality 15 Mbps. The audio and video formats are based on the ISO MPEG-4 (MPEG-4, 1998; Koenen, 2002; Ebrahimi & Pereira, 2002; van der Schaar, Turaga, & Stockhammer, 2005) standard. MPEG-4 includes algorithms for audio-visual coding in multimedia applications, digital television, and interactive graphics applications. MPEG-4 was specifically designed to go significantly beyond the pure compression efficiency paradigm (van der Schaar et al., 2005) under which MPEG-2 (1994) and ITU-H.263 (ITU-T, 1996) were developed, and it includes several functionalities to cover content-based interactivity and universal access. Specifically,

Figure 2. ISMA 2.0 architecture

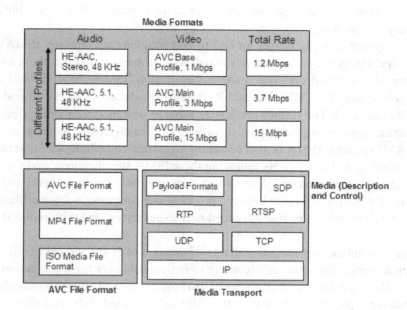

MPEG-4 was the first major attempt to standardize object-based coding, efficient compression across a wide range of target bit-rates and receiver devices, and several novel algorithms for scalability and error resilience. The current AVC standard (MPEG-4 Part 10) (Wiegand, Sullivan, Bjontegaard, & Luthra, 2003) provides great flexibility in the selection of encoder configurations and parameters for extremely efficient video compression. The popularity of MPEG-4 audio and video has led to it being supported even by all major proprietary players in the multimedia arena, including Microsoft Windows Media, Real Networks (plug-in from Envivio), and Apple QuickTime (version 6 and beyond).

The transport protocol suite recommended by ISMA is based on RTP (Kikuchi, Nomura, Fukunaga, Matsui, & Kimata, 2000; Schulzrinne, 1996; van der Meer, Mackie, Swaminathan, Singer, & Gentric, 2003). RTP can be used for media-on-demand, as well as interactive services such as Internet telephony and IP television (IPTV). RTP consists of a thin data transport protocol along with a control protocol called RTCP. The data protocol includes support for timing reconstruction, loss detection, security, and content identification, while RTCP provides support for real-time conferencing of groups of any size within a local area network (LAN). This includes support for source identification and support for gateways like audio and video bridges, as well as multicast-to-unicast translators. RTCP also provides support for the synchronization of different media streams. While UDP/IP is the initial target networking environment for RTP, efforts have been made to make it transport-independent so that it could be used over other transports such as TCP, connection-less network protocol (CLNP), IPX, and so forth. RTP does not address the issue of resource reservation or quality of service control; instead, it relies on resource reservation protocols such as reservation protocol (RSVP) for this purpose.

In conjunction with RTP for streaming, the ISMA specification uses RTSP for media control and SDP for describing streaming media initialization parameters. RTSP allows a client to remotely control a streaming media server, issuing VCR-like commands such as "play" and "pause," and allowing time-based access to files on a server. SDP is intended for describing multimedia sessions for the purposes of session announcement, session invitation, and other forms of multimedia session initiation, such as for describing multicast sessions.

Finally, when required building blocks for end-to-end solutions are missing, ISMA also produces its own technical specifications, collaboratively across its members, and makes these available for the market. An example is the ISMA encryption and authentication (ISMA, 2004). ISMACryp is a specification for encrypting content in MP4 files and RTP transport and provides end-to-end protection for storage and during transport. The framework is extensible to new media encodings, can be upgraded to new cryptographic transforms, and applies to various key management, security, and digital rights management (DRM) systems. ISMA is also currently investigating techniques for second generation DRM, closed captioning, and so forth. By following these ISMA specifications, and the available open standards on which these are based, any developer/system integrator can build multimedia delivery solutions that allow seamless interworking between products and components from different multimedia vendors and service providers, to enable advanced user experiences, and with reduced cost and time to market.

We would like to conclude this section with a brief mention of 3GPP and MPEG4IP. 3GPP specifications are targeted specifically towards streaming of multimedia over third generation (3G) wireless networks. The MPEG4IP project was recently created to provide an open-source standards-based system for encoding, streaming, playing, and broadcasting MPEG-4 encoded audio and video.

IMPACT OF DELIVERY MODELS AND NETWORK INFRASTRUCTURE ON VIDEO QUALITY

Different network infrastructure and delivery configurations influence key attributes that determine multimedia quality. In this section we first describe these network dependent attributes and contributory factors that affect them under different network and infrastructure configurations. We then describe the interaction of these with the application layer attributes and the combined impact on multimedia quality.

Network Dependent Attributes that Impact Multimedia Quality

These attributes include content availability, timing issues including delay and jitter, issues with packet losses and bit errors and packet delivery order, and finally, issues with bandwidth variations. These network dependent attributes interact with application layer attributes such as content characteristics, compression and packetization strategy used, error resilience and error concealment mechanisms, and constraints on power, complexity, and resource availability at encoder and decoder to finally determine the multimedia quality. Additional factors that may also affect user perceived video quality include user preferences and end-user devices and so forth.

Content Availability

Content availability is determined primarily by the selected delivery model and the popularity of the desired content. Complexity, bandwidth, or resource constraints, and failures at the centralized server, edge server, or from source peers are primary causes for content being disrupted or not being available when desired. This problem is often worsened by the presence of flash demand. There are several algorithms for automatic and dynamic content discovery and request routing (Kabir, Manning, & Shoja, 2002; Stoica, Morris, Karger, Kaashoek, & Balakrishnan, 2001; Zhang, 2001; Sripanidkulchai, 2001) being developed for the different delivery models to maximize content availability.

Delay, Data Loss, and Bandwidth Variations

While these different attributes may lead to different kinds of impairments in the video quality, they are often caused by similar underlying factors. These factors range from the selected delivery model, transport protocols, network infrastructure, congestion and packet loss[2], all the way to complexity and resource constraints at source and destination. These factors may also include effects of firewalls, load balancing in the network, timing drifts in the system, wireless interference and fading, or other factors such as mobility (of receivers or senders) and so forth.

Delay can result in dropped (too late to display) audio and video packets, causing perceptually annoying temporal artifacts (e.g., motion jerkiness, missing sounds/words) and even loss of synchronization between different media types. Similarly, packet and data losses lead to missing content at the decoder that can create spatial, temporal, or joint spatio-temporal artifacts, with error propagation due to motion compensated predictive coding. This leads to artifacts such as blurring, ringing, blockiness, color imperfections, and temporal motion jerkiness, some of which are shown in Section 0. Variations in streaming bandwidth manifest themselves as either delays or packet and data losses, thereby creating a similar set of artifacts.

There have been efforts to quantify the perceptual impact of delay, packet loss, and bandwidth variations on multimedia quality (Calyam & Lee, 2005; Claypool & Tanner, 1999) and on building management and buffering techniques (Jeffay & Stone, 1995; Zhang, 2001) to overcome this impact. There is also work on building error resilience (Kumar, Xu, Mandal, & Panchanathan, 2006; Takishima, Wada, & Murakami, 1995; Turaga, 2006; van der Schaar, 2007; Wang & Zhu, 1998; Zhang, Yang, & Zhu, 2005; Zhu & Kerofsky, 1999) and robustness through source coding, channel coding, and joint source-channel coding. At the same time, efforts on building decoder only robustness solutions, using error concealment (Valente, Dufour, Groliere, & Snook, 2001; Yan & Ng, 2003; Zeng & Liu, 1999) methods, have also been pursued. Optimization strategies to minimize the impact on video quality when content is being received from multiple sources are being investigated (Padmanabhan et al., 2001; van der Schaar, 2007; Wang, Riebman, & Lin, 2005).

Jitter

Unlike delay, the primary cause of jitter is congestion in the network that leads to additional queuing or buffering delays at routers across several hops, leading to irregular interarrival times between consecutive packets. While most jitter may be smoothed out by buffered and delayed playback (Zhang, 2001) at the receiver, this may not be possible for real-time applications. In such cases it has been found that jitter affects the temporal properties of multimedia and the resultant perceptual quality almost as severely as packet losses and errors (Chang, Carney, Klein, Messerschmitt, & Zakhor, 1998; Claypool & Tanner, 1999).

Complexity and Resource Constraints

Resource constraints at the encoder can result in poor compression or packetization, while resource constraints in the decoder can result in discard of data, improper error handling, and concealment. Resource constraints in the network can result in congestion, leading to delays, packet drops, and bandwidth variations. Trading off rate-distortion performance against resilience, delay, and complexity constraints is an emerging area of research interest (van der Schaar, 2007).

Examples of Video Artifacts

We conclude this section with examples of different video impairments and artifacts that are created by the above described attributes. We first show spatial artifacts, including blockiness, blurring, and high frequency artifacts such as ringing, for different video sequences in Figure 3, Figure 4, and Figure 5. These sequences are standard common intermediate format (CIF), that is, resolution 352×288 at 30 frames per second, and are taken from the set to evaluate compression algorithms.

While blockiness and ringing are caused by the introduction of additional high-frequencies (blocks edges in the case of blockiness) or corruption of the existing high frequency components, blurring is caused by the removal of these high frequency components. Each one corresponds to different visual impacts, depending on severity and content characteristics such as texture, motion, and so forth in the scene. We also show some examples of temporal artifacts in Figure 6 for the football sequence, a high motion action scene at CIF resolution and 7.5 frames per second.

In the figure we show examples of jerkiness and reference frame mismatch. Jerkiness is caused by the loss of information for Frame 3, causing the decoder to replace it with the previous frame (error concealment by frame replication), thereby leading to a break in the continuous motion. Furthermore, due to this substitution there is a reference frame mismatch for Frame 4 (which was predicted from the actual Frame 3, but is compensated from the concealed Frame 3, that is, Frame 2) leading to several visible motion artifacts. These artifacts affect the end-to-end quality depending on the nature of the application, characteristics of the content, and preferences of the user. In the next section we describe some standard metrics that account for some of these issues to objectively capture the multimedia quality.

Figure 3. Blockiness in foreman sequence - original (left) and blocky frame (right)

Figure 4. Blurring in mobile sequence - original (left) and blurred frame (right)

Figure 5. Ringing and high frequency noise in mobile sequence - original (left) and noisy frame (right)

ESTIMATING END-TO-END MULTIMEDIA QUALITY

There are several metrics that have been developed to estimate multimedia quality, specifically for networked multimedia applications. In this section we describe some of these metrics based on the discussion by Clark (2006).

Types of Multimedia Quality Metrics

Quality metrics may be subjective or objective. Subjective metrics are computed by averaging opinion scores from human evaluators under a set of precisely defined viewing and listening conditions, while objective metrics are computed automatically from the content. While subjective metrics present the most accurate assessment of multimedia quality, they are extremely expensive to compute. Recent advances have led to the development of several objective metrics that can approximate subjective metrics effectively. Additionally, quality metrics may be categorized into full reference, reduced (partial) reference, and no (zero) reference. While full reference metrics require comparison of the received multimedia

Figure 6. Motion jerkiness and temporal error propagation in football sequence

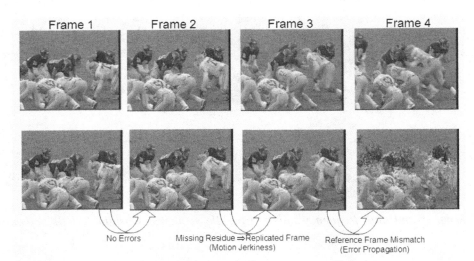

content against the original content, reduced reference metrics require only comparison of features derived from original and received content, and no reference metrics are computed after analysis of only the received content. An example of estimating these metrics, as explored by Voran and Wolf (2000), is shown in Figure 3.

Full reference metrics are often impractical in real deployment scenarios, as they require availability of source content at receiver, and the computation is often intensive, as it requires processing every pixel after spatio-temporal alignment of the original and received content. However, the resulting estimated quality is accurate, and often correlates well with subjective perceptual measurements. A widely used simple full reference metric is peak signal to noise ratio (PSNR), which measures the mean squared error between the original and received content, normalized by the maximum value that the original signal can take. PSNR is expressed in decibels (dB), with 35 dB and higher corresponding to acceptable video quality, and 20 dB or lower corresponding to unacceptable video quality. Several other full reference metrics for video include moving pictures quality metric (MPQM) (van den Lambrecht, 1996), video quality metric (VQM) (Wolf & Pinson, 2000), and continuous video quality evaluation (CVQE) (Masry & Hemami, 2004) for low bit rate video. VQM has been incorporated into the ITU-T J.144 (ITU-T, 2004) standard. Reduced reference metrics (Le Callet, Viard-Gaudin, Pechard, & Caillault, 2006; Wolf & Pinson, 2004) approximate full reference metrics by estimating quality from features extracted from the multimedia content.

No reference metrics (Fu-Zheng, Xin-Dai, Yi-Lin, & Shuai, 2003; Le Callet et al., 2006; Turaga et al., 2002) are often computed by analyzing the decoded multimedia as well as the compressed bitstream (to extract some information about the coding parameters). Commercial solutions such for no reference quality metrics include VQmon and Psytechnics Video IP metric. Similar efforts have also led to the development of several metrics for audio and speech quality (Barbedo & Lopez, 2004; Cai, Tu, Zhao, & Mao, 2007; Hendriks, Heusdens, & Jensen, 2007; Hu, He, & Zhou, 2006; Rix, Beerends, Hollier, & Hekstra, 2001; Rohani & Zepernick, 2005).

Figure 7. Full reference (top), partial reference (middle), and no reference (bottom) quality estimation

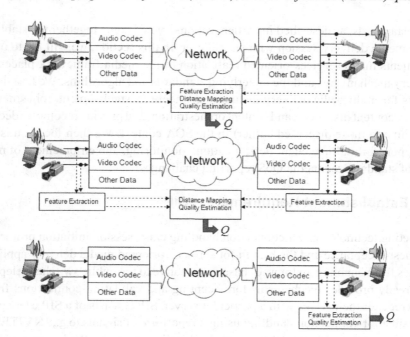

Standards-Based Multimedia Quality Metrics

The Video Quality Experts Group (VQEG) has actively focused on developing several objective video quality metrics. There is ongoing standardization activity in parallel within several committees (Clark & Pendleton, 2006) that has led to the following metrics being defined:

- **Video Service Transmission Quality (VSTQ):** A video encoding format independent measure of the ability of the network to transport video. This is derived in terms of the attributes such as delay, packet loss, jitter, and so forth.
- **Video Service Picture Quality (VSPQ):** A video encoding dependent estimate of the viewing quality of the video. This combines network attributes with multimedia characteristics, compression, and so forth.
- **Video Service Audio Quality (VSAQ):** An estimate of the quality of the audio stream.
- **Video Service Multimedia Quality (VSMQ):** An overall metric that includes video quality, audio quality, and audio-video synchronization
- **Video Service Control Quality (VSCQ):** A metric that estimates the response times for control requests (such as rewind, seekm etc.) that also affect the quality of experience.

More details on their computation is discussed by Clark and Pendleton(2006). These standardized metrics may be used by solution developers to measure the end-to-end quality of networked multimedia for a diverse set of applications over different network configurations.

SOA AND MEDUA DELIVERY STANDARDS

There are many standards, as described in earlier sections, which come together to establish, maintain, and terminate a media delivery session with an end user. In this section, we will try to understand the special requirements that a services-oriented realization of the media framework places on the infrastructure, delivery mechanisms, and the underlying standards and algorithms. We first describe different requirements for multimedia delivery including connection establishment, robustness, midstream quality variations, content discovery, and content orchestration, and provide recommended standardized solutions (from among those discussed earlier) in the SOA context. We then focus on issues involved in providing support for multiple client tiers, creation, monitoring, and enforcement of media-specific SLAs, and use of standardized media QoS reporting challenges

Connection Establishment Requirements: SIP

Although competing technologies for connection handling exist, session initiation protocol (SIP) probably has the widest acceptance and the best fit for services-oriented media delivery applications. SIP's motivation comes from enabling an Internet-based alternative to the public switched telephone network (PSTN). SIP already provides mechanisms for accepting and validating connections from users and enables them to register themselves with a particular server. SIP consists of a SIP user agent (SIP-UA), which is responsible for connection handling using a repertoire of signals (e.g., INVITE, REGISTER, BYE, CANCEL, and ACK). Media delivery applications leverage the SIP-UA to manage their connections to other SIP clients. Note that proxies, end users, SIP servers, and registrars all use the same SIP-UA protocol. Recent literature (e.g., Liu, Chou, Li, & Li, 2004) details industry efforts in building Web services interfaces to access SIP functionality in an implementation agnostic setting. Although enabling SIP service access through a Web service interface seems like the right approach, it is very important to explore the need for additional features that need to be addressed to make this approach practical in a services oriented setting.

The advantage of this approach is that SIP can now become one part of a distributed business application that uses other Web services to enable features such as billing, customer authentication, resource management, load balancing, and so forth. These services can be orchestrated as part of a business process that involve SIP invocation as one of the services. An example of using SIP in conjunction with other Web services is shown in Figure 8.

The disadvantage of this approach is that calls to SIP-UA are typically stateful and refer to events initiated by other calls in the past; the paper uses a message queue and an event table to manage state. This may present problems in scaling the application to a multiserver environment and in turn its ability to serve a large number of clients. Other examples of systems using Web services wrappers around SIP functionality include those discussed by Wu, Fox, Bulut, Uyar, and Huang (2006) and Uyar and Fox (2005a, 2005b).

Robustness to Delivery Models and Network Infrastructure: TCP vs. UDP

Once a connection is established, using a protocol like SIP, media delivery is performed using RTP (over both TCP and UDP). Network congestion leads to packet delays or lost packets that lead to translate to pauses in the media playback, glitches, blockiness and decoding errors, as described in Section 0. In

Figure 8. Illustration: Wrapping SIP using Web services to interact with other Web-services

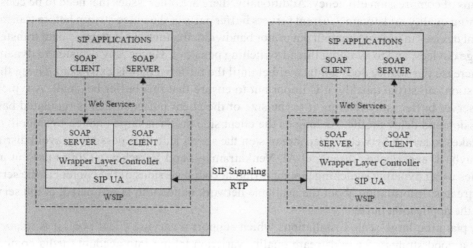

terms of network bandwidth consumption, UDP shows a better utilization profile than TCP. However, media compressed with existing standards do not typically show graceful degradation in the presence of lost packets. As mentioned earlier, there is a vast amount of literature on error recovery in the presence of packet loss using unreliable transport mechanisms. However, none of the proposed techniques provide a robust solution that has been accepted by a significant community of users. Thus, we believe that the preferred mode of transmission should use TCP as the underlying transport mechanism, especially for noninteractive content.

It may be unavoidable to use UDP when the number of users is large or due to the nature of the video broadcast. One such situation is live event multicast over cellular networks; the real time nature of the broadcast and the limited amount of bandwidth available on the network would pre-empt the use of TCP. In such cases, it is important that the media should be encoded in such a way as to quickly recover from errors in the case of lost packets. This involves trading off the compression efficiency with redundancy for error resilience. Thus, attempting to provide a robust media delivery service to end users requires careful orchestration and planning in terms of both the compression standards used to encode the content and the network transport.

Midstream Quality Variation Requirements

In many media delivery settings, it is necessary to either reduce or increase the bit-rate at which video is being transmitted to client devices in the middle of a media delivery transaction. This is necessary to cope with both network bandwidth variations and the changing size of the client pool. Infrastructure resources are typically never sized to accommodate the worst-case bandwidth, and media transactions typically have a long duration, necessitating midstream quality variation under heavy usage. Most client devices and current compression standards (MPEG-4) support changes in bit rate and other media compression settings (such as display resolution, number of audio channels etc) on the fly.

Support for switching the quality of the video stream requires using either spatio-temporal-SNR scalable (Li, 2001; Radha, van der Schaar, & Chen, 2001; Woods, 2006) compression solutions, or by explicitly inserting refresh/switch points during compression. However, both these solutions come with a cost in terms of compression efficiency. Additionally, there are other issues that need to be considered when switching quality midstream. Current servers buffer parts of the video stream before transmitting it to the client devices in order to smooth out minor bandwidth fluctuations, optimize data transfer from media storage devices, and to avoiding thread switching penalties. Hence, any decision to dynamically reduce or increase the quality does not take effect until the buffered data is exhausted. Given that network congestion can strike quickly, it is important to ensure that this buffer be small. A typical way to size the server buffer is by relating it to the size of the client buffer, which is regulated based on the compression and delay profile. As long as the client side buffer is large enough to smooth out the duration it takes to switch between video streams on the server side, it is possible to avoid disruptions in media playback experience. Turaga, el Al, Venkatramani, and Verscheure (2005) present adaptation strategies using dynamic switching among different coded versions of the content at the server for live video streams. Information about the available network bandwidth is estimated, at the server, by monitoring the application buffer.

Thus, in planning large-scale installations which support a varying client pool, it is important to put in place a good strategy for midstream quality variation taking into account media compression settings, client, and server buffer management strategies.

Location-Aware Streaming Requirements

In a distributed environment, it is quite possible that many service providers may be able to provide the same media content. Given the typically large bandwidth required to serve media files, it may be convenient to ensure that the location of the service provider is close to the end user. This becomes an important constraint to consider when other parameters such as cost of the service, the quality of the media served, and so forth are on par. Establishing the connection with the right server which has the ability to service the client (in terms of load level) and also is geographically best situated is essential in terms of ensuring a consistent QoS throughout the delivery process. Typical SIP connections are point-to-point and do not address the fact that the target can be one of a collection of servers rather than an individual server into account. A simple approach to enable this would require the invocation of a Web service API that can be used to select the closest server that satisfies all the client requirements prior to instantiating a connection using SIP or other chosen point-to-point connection creation protocols. This may be built on top of several algorithms in literature for location aware streaming (Ge, Ji, & Shenoy, 2002; Pai, Aron, Banga, Svendsen, Druschel, Zaenepoel, et al., 1998).

Content Discovery Requirements

Closely associated with the previous topic of finding the closest server that satisfies the client's preferences is the ability to discover content. In Section 0, we referred to several research efforts in designing intelligent approaches for content discovery. However, these efforts focus primarily on locating the *source* of the content a client is interested in, and do not consider the harder issue of locating *content* itself that users may be interested in. In most media delivery settings, end users would like to explore a database of available content before making a selection. From a QoS perspective, ensuring that standard metadata exists to describe the nature of the content (its compression settings, video/audio resolution, geographic location, etc.) is critical in ensuring that end users not only find the content that interests them, but also at a delivery quality that is satisfactory. Currently no such industry-wide standards exist. MPEG-7 (Martinez, 2002) is an existing standard for describing multimedia content metadata for universal access. However, MPEG-7 does not fully support the kind of metadata needed for content distribution support, and needs several extensions especially for content discovery in the context of a specific application/domain. This has led to limited acceptance of MPEG-7 in the industry. Thus, a more targeted content description mechanism which leverages parts of MEPG-7 may be appropriate in the context of a services oriented architecture; however, any such description has to be an industry standard to succeed.

Content Choreography Requirements

Content choreography refers to delivering composite media content to the end users composed of content aggregated from multiple providers in a seamless fashion (Roczniak, Janmohamed, Roch, El Saddik, & Lévy, 2006). Most commercial Internet sites already use content choreography to some degree in showing advertisements before the start of the main video content. Although such advertisements are currently stored locally, the natural next step is for this content to be managed by "ad servers," as already happens in the case of typical banner ads that appear on most Internet sites. An example of content choreography across Web-services, end-user devices, and applications in the context of media conferencing (using standard and commercial solutions) is shown in Figure 9.

Adding advertisements, and potentially nonadvertisement content (e.g., in the context of a news broadcast) from multiple sources poses issues in ensuring the content has compatible compression settings and does not pose delivery problems; for example, the failure in an ad server should not result in a disruption in the delivery of the content from the main server. Adequate mechanisms that "time out" the content access from a server may be used for this purpose. Another approach is to cache the content

Figure 9. Illustration of content choreography for media conferencing services

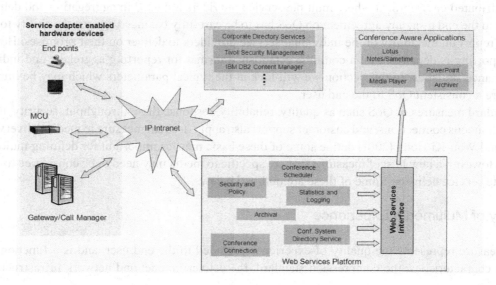

from the distributed servers at the local site prior to doing dynamic composition. The choice of the right approach is dependent on the nature of the application at hand.

Support for Multiple Client Tiers

An important feature in building a large scale media delivery system is the need to support a gradation in the quality of service provided to different clients depending on the service level agreement in place. This is especially important in the SOA context as multiple service providers can come together dynamically to provide a composite service to the end user. In supporting this model, individual service providers may offer different levels of service to support other service providers who package this into a set of composite services that they provide to the end user. As a practical example, a media delivery service provider in China may be providing functionally similar services to local service providers as well as other service providers in USA. However, the service level agreements that are negotiated with these two sets of "clients" may be radically different. A simple approach to dealing with tiered services is to keep separate sets of servers and other infrastructure to support each tier. However, this approach is both inflexible and not scalable. A better approach is being able to service all clients using the same servers but use policies on the server to govern how each client should be treated. In this context, Rata-konda, Turaga, and Lai (2006) consider a server cluster consisting of servers with different capacities and capabilities serving multimedia streams to clients with different priorities and QoS requirements. This includes the design of algorithms that dynamically determine which server a new client request is directed to, as well as the particular QoS, in terms of the video representation that is served to the client. At the same time, existing client connections may be modified to accommodate the new client request. In such a scenario, it becomes clear that supporting midstream quality variation to quickly react to changes in the client pool both in terms of size of the client pool, as well as its constitution in terms of types of clients, is an important consideration.

Creation and Monitoring of Media-Specific SLAs

In a distributed environment where multiple service providers are used in aggregating and delivering content to the end user, any agreement on QoS has to be carefully balanced against the ability to monitor and report on the ability of the individual service providers to deliver on their promises. However, such reporting is dependent on a common established format for reporting aggregate and individual performance statistics. In this section we will look at the typical parameters which may be important to ensure a consistent QoS to the end user.

Standard measures of QoS such as quality, reliability, response time, throughput, security, number of simultaneous connections, and customer support also apply in equal measure to media delivery. Park, Baek, and Won-Ki Hong (2001) define some of these basic metrics important for defining multimedia SLAs. However, a new host of measures that are specific to media may need to be considered to ensure adequate service delivery. Some of these are outlined below.

Quality of Multimedia Experience

This measure represents the quality of experience provided to the end user, and is a function of the content characteristics, the compression standard, the delivery model and network infrastructure, as well as the end-user device and preferences. Such a composite measure may be computed using metrics defined in Section 0.

Consistency of Throughput

This measure defines the consistency in achieving a certain throughput to a client. In the case of live media streaming, achieving a consistent throughput is important, as any sustained disruption in throughput manifests as an interruption in the media playback. Thus, it is not sufficient to guarantee average throughput. It is important to also guarantee average throughput over each time slice; the size of the time slice will depend on the buffers present at the server and client devices. In the case of prerecorded media, the consistency requirement can be relaxed by ensuring that the size of the buffer at the client device is large.

Robustness

Robust media delivery requires the ability to manage one or more hardware or software failures in a manner that is transparent to the end user. However, this requires careful planning, as the switch in the server would also mean (typically) a loss in any contextual information maintained at the server for the specific client. This is probably best managed at the client side rather than at the server side.

Fidelity

Since the same media object is typically available at multiple fidelities and high fidelity equates to higher client bandwidth, defining the right measure to track the fidelity experienced by the client is complicated. For example, when there is network congestion, delivering a lower fidelity may be more acceptable than an interruption in service.

Utilization

Any broad utility computation has to take into account the number of clients served, the priorities of these clients (in the case of tiered services), the fidelity of the videos served to these clients, and the consistency in end-user experience. Ratakonda et al. (2006) give an example of such a utility function.

EMERGING AND EXISTING MOTIVATION APPLICATIONS

There are several current and emerging applications driving the need for large scale multimedia distribution and networking-based services. The first set of applications lie in the Enterprise Multimedia Communications space. In recent times, digital media have been acknowledged as standard data type and is expected that digital media will become the medium for business-business, business-employee, and business-customer communications (Turaga, Ratakonda, & van der Schaar, 2001; Dorai & Kienzle, 2004). Enterprises are beginning to explore the use of digital media in improving the effectiveness and efficiency of their business processes. The digital media lifecycle in an enterprise environment includes activities ranging from creation and management, going all the way to distribution and transaction

(Figure 6). It is clear that multimedia streaming will be used by corporations, especially for corporate communications, in-service training (e-learning), product launches, performance reporting, and delivery of real-time financial information for e-commerce. In this context it is critical to realize a SOA-based multimedia delivery architecture to allow for flexible content discovery, creation, management, streaming, billing, and consumption. The second set of enabling applications lie in the voice over IP (VoIP) space. Among the main advantages that VoIP has over PSTN include the ability to provide easy integration with other services available over the Internet, including video, message or data exchange, audio conferencing, and location independence. From Wikipedia, nearly a third of North American companies, besides individual users, were already using VoIP services. This is only expected to grow rapidly, for both individual users as well as companies.

The third set of applications lie in the IPTV space. IPTV has rapidly gained popularity, especially in Europe, with over 40 million current subscribers. There is ample room for growth in the rest of the world with the need for several integrated services-based solutions for IPTV-converged services for interactivity, video on demand, and triple play (voice, video, Internet). The fourth set of applications lies in the surveillance space. The demand for surveillance has not only been from large public (i.e., airports, traffic management) and private corporations, but also from several individual users who want to monitor several different aspects of their personal space. The fifth set of applications lies in the space of networked gaming, where different sets of games are using integrated media-based services as part of the virtual environments. One of the largest set of applications lies in the P2P space, with several existing protocols such as BitTorrent, Coolstreaming, and so forth that are beginning to explore the use of streaming media over P2P networks. These are growing very rapidly, with a recent estimate suggesting that more than a fifth of the traffic over the Internet corresponds to P2P traffic. Finally, with the popularity of personalized multimedia creation, management, and sharing services available from sites like YouTube, there are several different emerging applications in the personal media space. Future research into SOA-based multimedia streaming will both drive and be driven by the successful deployment of some of these applications and the identification of other novel applications. Finally, we

Figure 10. Digital media lifecycle in enterprise environments

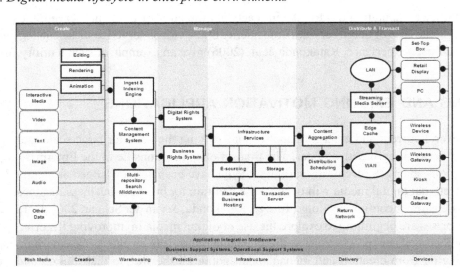

want to mention that real solutions for multimedia streaming and distribution need to be combined with provisioning and management of mixed-media information and high-level semantic analysis to satisfy business scenario requirements.

CONCLUSION

It is clear that emerging trends in both SOA and media delivery are leading to an increased interest in delivering media over SOA; however, there are a number of factors that one needs to consider while designing a system that uses elements of both technologies. In this chapter, we presented the trends that currently affect the multimedia landscape as the use of SOA becomes more widespread. We reviewed both standards-based and proprietary media delivery architectures, standards, and protocols that are currently in use. The interplay between infrastructure and media delivery architectures was covered and its impact on media quality was identified. Key metrics for measuring media quality, which play a crucial role in defining enforceable service level agreements, and the organizations involved in the standardization effort were covered. We also showed how the emergence of SOA affects the infrastructure, architecture, and the key players involved.

REFERENCES

3GPP. Retrieved May 23, 2008, from http://www.3gpp.org/

Akamai. Retrieved May 23, 2008, from http://www.akamai.com/

Apple QuickTime. Retrieved May 23, 2008, from http://www.apple.com/quicktime/

Barbedo, J. G. A., & Lopez, A. (2004). A new strategy for objective estimation of the quality of audio signals. *IEEE Latin America Transactions (Revista IEEE America Latina), 2*(3).

BitTorrent. Retrieved May 23, 2008, from www.bittorrent.com

Cai, L., Tu, R., Zhao, J., & Mao, Y. (2007). Speech quality evaluation: A new application of digital watermarking. *IEEE Transactions on Instrumentation and Measurement, 56*(1), 45-55.

Calyam, P., & Lee, C.-G. (2005). *Characterizing voice and video traffic behavior over the Internet.* Paper presented at the 20th International Symposium on Computer and Information Sciences (ISCIS 2005), Istanbul, Turkey.

CenterSpan. Retrieved May 23, 2008, from http://www.centerspan.com/

Chang, Y.-C., Carney, T., Klein, S. A., Messerschmitt, D., & Zakhor, A. (1998). Effects of temporal jitter on video quality: Assessment using psychophysical methods. In *Proceedings of the SPIE: Human Vision and Image Processing.*

Clark, A. (2006). *Clarifying video quality metrics*. Retrieved May 23, 2008, from http://www.tmcnet.com/news/2006/04/11/1561303.htm

Clark, A., & Pendleton, A. (2006). *RTCP XR - IP video metrics report blocks.* Retrieved May 23, 2008, from http://www.telchemy.com/reference/draft-clark-avt-rtcpxr-video-01.pdf

Claypool, M., & Tanner, J. (1999). The effects of jitter on the perceptual quality of video. In *Proceedings of the ACM Multimedia*, Orlando.

Cohen, R., Katzir, L., & Raz, D. (2002). Scheduling algorithms for a cache pre-filling content distribution network. In *Proceedings of the IEEE InfoCom'02.*

Dorai, C., & Kienzle, M. (2004). Challenges of business media. *IEEE Multimedia, 11*(4).

Ebrahimi, T., & Pereira, F. (2002). *The MPEG-4 book.* Prentice Hall.

Eger, K., & Killat, U. (2006). *Bandwidth trading in unstructured P2P content distribution networks.* Paper presented at the Sixth IEEE International Conference on Peer-to-Peer Computing (P2P'06) (pp. 39-48).

Freenet. Retrieved May 23, 2008, http://freenet.sourceforge.net/

Fuchs, H., & Färber, N. (2005). ISMA interoperability and conformance. *IEEE Multimedia, 12*(2), 96-102.

Fu-Zheng, Y., Xin-Dai, W., Yi-Lin, C., & Shuai, W. (2003). *A no-reference video quality assessment method based on digital watermark.* Paper presented at the 14th IEEE Proceedings on Personal, Indoor and Mobile Radio Communications, 2003. PIMRC 2003, 3(7), 2707 - 2710.

Ge, Z., Ji, P., & Shenoy, P. (2002). *A demand adaptive and locality aware (DALA) streaming media server cluster architecture.* Paper presented at the ACM Conference on Networking and Operating System Support for Audio and Video (NOSSDAV'02), Miami.

Gnutella. Retrieved May 23, 2008, from http://www.gnutella.wego.com/

Hendriks, R. C., Heusdens, R., & Jensen, J. (2007). An MMSE estimator for speech enhancement under a combined stochastic–deterministic speech model. *IEEE Transactions on Audio, Speech and Language Processing, 15*(2), 406-415.

Hu, X., He, G., & Zhou, X. (2006). *PEAQ-based psychoacoustic model for perceptual audio coder.* Paper presented at the 8th International Conference on Advanced Communication Technology, 2006, ICACT 2006, Phoenix Park, Korea.

ISMA. (2004). Retrieved May 23, 2008, from http://www.isma.tv/

ITU-T Recommendation H.263. (1996). *Video coding for low bit rate communication.* Author.

ITU-T Recommendation J.144-2004. (2004). *Objective perceptual video quality measurement techniques for digital cable television in the presence of a full reference.* Author.

Jeffay, K., & Stone, D. (1995). An empirical study of delay jitter management policies. *Proceedings of ACM Multimedia Systems, 2*(6), 267-79.

Kabir, M., Manning, E., & Shoja, G. (2002). Request-routing trends and techniques in content distribution network. In *Proceedings of the International Conference on Computer and Information Technology*, Dhaka, Bangladesh.

Kangasharju, J., Roberts, J., & Ross, K.W. (2002). Object replication strategies in content distribution networks. *Computers and Communications, 24*(4), 367-383.

Kant, K., Tewari, V., & Iyer, R. (2001). *Peer to peer computing: The hype, the hard problems, and quest for solutions.* Paper presented at the IEEE International Conference on Network Protocols 2001.

Kikuchi, Y., Nomura, T., Fukunaga, S., Matsui, Y., & Kimata, H. (2000). *RTP payload format for MPEG-4 audio/visual streams* (RFC 3016).

Koenen, R. (2002). *MPEG-4 overview* (MPEG Output document, N4668). Jeju, Korea.

Kumar, S., Xu, L., Mandal, M. K., & Panchanathan, S. (2006). Error resiliency schemes in H.264/AVC standard. *Elsevier Journal of Visual Communication and Image Representation (Special issue on Emerging H.264/AVC Video Coding Standard), 17*(2).

Le Callet, P., Viard-Gaudin, C., Pechard, S., & Caillault, É. (2006). No reference and reduced reference video quality metrics for end to end QoS monitoring. *IEICE Transactions on Communications, 2006 E89-B*(2), 289-296.

Li, W. (2001). Overview of fine granularity scalability in MPEG-4 video standard. *IEEE Transactions on Circuits and Systems for Video Technology, 11*(3), 301-317.

Liu, F., Chou, W., Li, L., & Li, J. (2004). WSIP - Web service SIP endpoint for converged multimedia/multimodal communication over IP. In *Proceedings of the IEEE International Conference on Web Services (ICWS'04)*, San Diego.

Martinez, J. (2002). MPEG-7: Overview of MPEG-7 description tools, part 2. *IEEE Multimedia, 9*(3), 83-93.

Masry, M., & Hemami, S. (2004). A metric for continuous quality evaluation of compressed video with severe distortion. *Signal Processing: Image Communication, 19*(2).

Microsoft Windows Media. Retrieved May 23, 2008, from http://www.microsoft.com/windows/windowsmedia/default.mspx

MPEG-2: ISO/IEC International Standard 13 818-2. (1994). *Generic coding of moving pictures and associated audio information: Visual.* Author.

MPEG 4: ISO/IEC International Standard, 14 496-2. (1998). *Information technology—coding of audio-visual objects: Visual.* Author.

MPEG4IP. Retrieved May 23, 2008, from http://mpeg4ip.sourceforge.net/

Napster. Retrieved May 23, 2008, from http://www.napster.com/

Padmanabhan, V. N, Wang, H. J., Chou, P. A., & Sripanidkulchai, K. (2002). *Distributing streaming media content using cooperative networking.* Paper presented at the ACM Conference on Networking and Operating System Support for Audio and Video (NOSSDAV) 2002, Miami.

Pai, V., Aron, M., Banga, G., Svendsen, M., Druschel, P., Zaenepoel, W., et al. (1998). *Locality-aware request distribution in cluster-based network services.* Paper presented at the 8th International Conference on Architectural Support for Programming Languages and Operating Systems (ASPLOS-VIII), San Jose, CA.

Park J-T., Baek, J-W., & Won-Ki Hong, J. (2001, May). Management of service level agreements for multimedia Internet service using a utility model. *IEEE Communication Magazine.*

Psytechnics video. Retrieved May 23, 2008, from IP metric http://www.psytechnics.com

Radha, H., van der Schaar, M., & Chen, Y. (2001). The MPEG-4 fine-grained scalable video coding method for multimedia streaming over IP. *IEEE Transactions on Multimedia, 3*(1).

Ratakonda, K., Turaga D. S., & Lai, J. (2006). *QoS support for streaming media using a multimedia server cluster.* Paper presented at the IEEE Globecom 2006.

Real Networks. Retrieved May 23, 2008, from http://www.realnetworks.com/products/media_delivery.html

Rix, A. W., Beerends, J. G., Hollier, M. P., & Hekstra, A. P. (2001). Perceptual evaluation of speech quality (PESQ): A new method for speech quality assessment of telephone networks and codecs. In *Proceedings of the IEEE Acoustics, Speech, and Signal Processing, Conference (ICASSP '01),* Salt Lake City, Utah.

Roczniak, A., Janmohamed, S., Roch, C., El Saddik, A., & Lévy, P. (2006, May 17-19). SOA-based collaborative multimedia authoring. In *Proceedings of the 2nd Montréal Conference on e-Technologies (MCeTECH'06),* Montréal, Canada.

Rohani, B., & Zepernick, H.-J. (2005). An efficient method for perceptual evaluation of speech quality in UMTS. In *Proceedings of Systems Communications, 2005.*

Rosenberg, J., & Schulzrinne, H. (2002). *SIP: Session initiation protocol* (RFC 3261). IETF Network Working Group.

RTSP. Retrieved May 23, 2008, from http://www.ietf.org/rfc/rfc2326.txt

Schulzrinne, H. (1996). *RTP profile for audio and video conferences with minimal control* (Standards Document RFC 1890).

SDP. Retrieved May 23, 2008, from http://www.ietf.org/rfc/rfc2327.txt

Sripanidkulchai, K. (2001). *The popularity of Gnutella queries and its implications on scalability.* O'Reilly's. Retrieved May 23, 2008, from www.openp2p.com

Stoica, I., Morris, R., Karger, D., Kaashoek, M., & Balakrishnan, H. (2001). *Chord: A scalable peer-to-peer lookup service for Internet applications.* Paper presented at the ACM Special Interest Group on Communications Conference (SIGCOMM 2001), San Diego.

Takishima, Y., Wada, M., & Murakami, H. (1995). Reversible variable length codes. *IEEE Transactions on Communications, 43,* 158-162.

Tran, D., Hua, K., & Do, T. (2002). Scalable media streaming in large P2P networks. In *Proceedings of the ACM Multimedia Conference (SIGMM 2002),* Juan Les Pins, France (pp. 247-256).

Tran, D., Hua, K., & Do, T. (2004). A peer-to-peer architecture for media streaming. *IEEE Journal on Selected Areas in Communications, Special Issue on Recent Advances in Service Overlay Networks, 22*, 121-133.

Turaga, D. S., Chen, Y., & Caviedes, J. (2002). *PSNR estimation for compressed pictures.* Paper presented at the IEEE International Conference on Image Processing (ICIP), Rochester, NY.

Turaga, D. S., el Al, A. A., Venkatramani, C., & Verscheure, O. (2005, July). *Adaptive live streaming over enterprise networks.* Paper presented at the ICME.

Turaga, D. S., Ratakonda, K., & van der Schaar, M. (2001). *Enterprise multimedia streaming: Issues, background and new developments.* Paper presented at the IEEE International Conference on Multimedia and Exposition, Amsterdam, Holland.

Turaga, D. S., & van der Schaar, M. (2007). Cross-layer packetization and retransmission strategies for delay-sensitive wireless multimedia transmission. *IEEE Transactions on Multimedia, 9*(1), 185-97.

Uyar, A., & Fox, G. (2005a, May). Investigating the performance of audio/video service architecture I: Single broker. In *Proceedings of the 2005 International Symposium on Collaborative Systems.*

Uyar, A., & Fox, G. (2005b, May). Investigating the performance of audio/video service architecture II: Broker network. In *Proceedings of the 2005 International Symposium on Collaborative Systems.*

Valente, S., Dufour, C., Groliere, F., & Snook, D. (2001). An efficient error concealment implementation for MPEG-4 video streams. *IEEE Transactions on Consumer Electronics, 47*(3), 568-578.

van den Lambrecht, C. J. (1996). *Color moving pictures quality metric.* Unpublished doctoral thesis, EPFL.

van der Meer, J., Mackie, D., Swaminathan, V., Singer, D., & Gentric, P. (2003). *RTP payload format for transport of MPEG-4 elementary streams* (RFC 3640).

van der Schaar, M., & Chou, P. (2007). *Multimedia over IP and wireless networks: Compression, networking, and systems.* Elsevier Press.

van der Schaar, M., Turaga, D. S., & Sood, R. (in press). Stochastic optimization for content sharing in P2P systems. *IEEE Transactions on Multimedia.*

van der Schaar, M., Turaga, D. S., & Stockhammer, T. (2005). *MPEG-4 beyond video compression: Object coding, scalability and error resilience.* Digital Library of Computer Science and Engineering, Morgan Claypool.

Video Quality Experts Group (VQEG). Retrieved May 23, 2008, from http://www.its.bldrdoc.gov/vqeg/

Voran, S., & Wolf, S. (2000). *Objective estimation of video and speech quality to support network QoS efforts.* Paper presented at the 2nd Internet2/DoE Quality of Service Workshop, Houston.

VQEG 2000. *Final report from the video quality experts group on the validation of objective models of video quality assessment.*

VQmon. Retrieved May 23, 2008, from http://www.telchemy.com/vqmonsavm.html

Wang, Y., & Zhu, Q.-F. (1998). Error control and concealment for video communication: A review. *Proceedings of the IEEE, 8*(5), 974-997.

Wang, Y., Riebman, A. R., & Lin, S. (2005). Multiple description coding for video delivery. *Proceedings of the IEEE, 93*(1), 57-70.

Wiegand, T., Sullivan, G. J., Bjontegaard, G., & Luthra, A. (2003). Overview of the H.264/AVC video coding standard. *IEEE Transactions on Circuits and Systems for Video Technology, 13*(7), 560-76.

Wikipedia. Retrieved May 23, 2008, from http://en.wikipedia.org/wiki/Voice_over_IP

Winkler, S. (2005). *Digital video quality.* Wiley Interscience.

Wolf, S., & Pinson, M. (1999). Spatial-temporal distortion metrics for in-service quality monitoring of any digital video system. In *Proceedings of the SPRI Multimedia Systems.*

Woods, J. (2006). *Multidimensional signal, image, and video processing and coding.* Elsevier.

Wu, W., Fox, G., Bulut, H., Uyar, A., & Huang T. (2006, May). Service oriented architecture for VoIP conferencing: Research articles. *International Journal of Communication Systems Archive, 19*(4).

Xiang, Z., Zhang, Q., Zhu, W., Zhang, Z., & Zhang, Y.-Q. (2004). Peer-to-peer based multimedia distribution service. *IEEE Transactions on Circuits and Systems for Video Technology, 6*(2), 343-55.

Xiang, Z., Zhang, Q., Zhu, W., & Zhong, Y. (2001). *Cost-based replacement policy for multimedia proxy across wireless Internet.* Paper presented at the IEEE GlobeCom'01, San Antonio.

Xu, D., Hefeeda, M., Hambrusch, S., & Bhargava, B. (2002). On peer-to-peer media streaming. In *Proceedings of the IEEE International Conference on Distributed Computing Systems (ICDCS 2002),* Wien, Austria.

Yan, B., & Ng, K. W. (2003). A novel selective motion vector matching algorithm for error concealment in MPEG-4 video transmission over error-prone channels. *IEEE Transactions on Consumer Electronics, 49*(4), 1416-1423.

Yiu, W.-P. K., Jin, X., & Chan, S.-H. G. (2007). Challenges and approaches in large-scale P2P media streaming. *IEEE Multimedia, 14*(2), 50-59.

Zeng, W., & Liu, B. (1999). Geometric structured based error concealment with novel applications in block based low-bit-rate coding. *IEEE Transactions on Circuits and Systems for Video Technology, 9*(4), 648 -665.

Zhang, Z.-L., Wang, Y., Du, D. H. C., & Su, D. (2000). Video staging: A proxy-server- based approach to end-to-end video delivery over wide-area networks. *IEEE/ACM Transactions on Networking, 8,* 429-442.

Zhang, Q., Xiong, Y., & Zhu, W. (2001). *Testing scheme QoS probing tool—uProbe* (Microsoft internal report). Microsoft.

Zhang, F. P., Yang, O. W., & Cheng, B. (2001). *Performance evaluation of jitter management algorithms.* Paper presented at the Canadian Conference on Electrical and Computer Engineering, 2001, Toronto, Canada.

Zhang, Q., Yang, F., & Zhu, W. (2005). Cross-layer QoS support for multimedia delivery over wireless Internet. *EURASIP Journal on Applied Signal Processing 2005, 2*, 207-219.

Zhu, Q. F., & Kerofsky, L. (1999). Joint source coding, transport processing, and error concealment for H.323-based packet video. In *Proceedings of the SPIE Visual Communications and Image Processing* (Vol. 3653, pp. 52-62).

Chapter IV
Virtual Web Services:
Extension Architecture to Alleviate Open Problems in Web Services Technology

Julio Fernández Vilas
University of Vigo, Spain

Jose J. Pazos Arias
University of Vigo, Spain

Ana Fernández Vilas
University of Vigo, Spain

ABSTRACT

Several open issues in Web services architecture are being solved by using different kinds of solutions. Standard high-availability techniques based on the use of Web servers, business-logic-based caching systems, dynamic binding of Web services by programming the access to a SOAP message content from the business logic layer, and other kinds of current open problems can now be handled using a common unique technique. What we propose is to apply virtualization techniques to Web services.

INTRODUCTION

When referring to current Web service architecture, a very important aspect to take care of is the one related to the separation of roles and the meaning of each role inside the architecture. Although the distinction between client, provider, and directory is clear, a great part of the Web services technology is based on a Web service offered by a provider (Booth, Haas, McCabe, Newcomer, Champion, Ferris et al., 2004). That is, according to the roles of the current proposed architecture, the provider is intimately related to the Web service it actually offers. In fact, both Web service and provider are used as only one role inside the architecture, called service provider. Several open problems of the current architecture can be solved by redefining this way of conceiving the roles inside the architecture.

Within the current architecture, the relation between client and provider has been established based on the use of two concepts:

- *Binding.* It is a process performed at development-time, consisting of adapting client software to the definition or description of a Web service.
- *Invocation.* It takes place on runtime, and it can be defined as the process by which a running client application calls a Web service.

The revised version of the W3C architecture redefines and merges these two concepts as "interaction." According to an "interaction" between client and provider, the binding is performed in a static way, so the way invocations must be performed is predefined. According to this:

- Dynamic binding cannot be performed, or, at least, not in an automatic way. There are different options based on the use of metadata ("Web services invocation framework," 2007) that enable the use of dynamic binding, but it is always mandatory to use metadata to access application data.
- Once a client application is bound to a concrete Web service, the execution of the application will be bound to the service provider selected, initially, at development-time. It will be necessary to bind a new Web service if we decide to use a new service provider. And this means that it will be necessary to develop new code to adapt the client application to the new interface of the new Web service. Although it is possible to change the location of the server providing the Web service without needing to make any modification to client application code, this will be only useful for those providers that have developed and published a Web service in the same way, that is, with the same parameters (its names and types), the same namespaces, and so forth.
- If a client application wants to use more than one provider in order to invoke the same equivalent service (offered by different service providers), the developer must bind the client application to each one of the Web services.

These and other less relevant problems have their origin in the fact that the role of "service provider" is not distinguished from the role of "Web service provider." When we talk about service-oriented architectures (SOA) (Barry, 2003; Vinosky, 2002), we usually use the terms "clients" and "providers," and we always relate these term with the use of services. We think it is necessary to slightly change the terminology, and use the terms "client application" when we refer to a SOA client, and "Web service provider" when we refer to a SOA provider.

In addition, we propose the creation of two new roles (as seen in Figure 1): the service provider (differentiated from the Web service provider), and the client entity (differentiated from the client application). The appearance of these two new roles will led us to a mandatory role separation. That is, Web services architecture is now composed of five roles: client entity, client application, directory, Web service provider, and service provider.

Figure 1. New roles

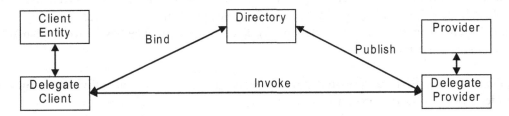

STATE OF THE ART

In the following subsections we will analyze the state of the art in several open issues in the Web services technology.

High Availability (HA)

When using production systems, the availability of a system is one of the most important issues to care about. HA is not considered as a part of the Web services architecture, but infrastructure providing companies (e.g., application servers, Web servers, load balancers, etc.) propose to increase the availability of a Web service by means of enhancing the availability of its underlying infrastructure.

There are two alternative ways to enhance the availability of a system:

- **Fault-tolerant systems**. All the hardware components in a fault-tolerant system are redundant (memory, processor, etc.), so, in case of a component fault, the whole system will continue running.
- **Cluster systems**. A cluster system is made of several computers (servers) that communicate using a high speed local area network (LAN). If a server fails, the whole cluster will continue running.

It is also possible to find mixed hardware configurations where fault-tolerant systems are used to build a fault-tolerant cluster, like Sysplex® (Nick, Chung, & Bowen, 1996), and cluster systems are made up of nodes build with redundant components.

As a result of hardware availability enhancement, providers protect their systems in order to offer the highest possible availability. But client's point of view is really different. If a provider stops accepting and responding invocations due to a problem in any hardware or software component (or even in the network), what clients notice is a system outage, that is, 0% availability, since the clients do not have any other way of invoking the service.

This situation can really happen, and it is due to the fact that the providers protect the implementation, while clients invoke an interface. Actually, all issues related with production systems of Web services (i.e., availability, scalability, etc.) have had no special attention inside current Web services architecture. The solution to all of them is always focused oi the implementation, not the interface.

Due to these lacks, client applications cannot have an assured minimum availability, since they are bound to a concrete provider, who may not comply with the conditions of a contract with that client. If clients could select automatically a provider when detecting an error condition, the availability of the service (independently of the provider used) would increase. This increment would be obtained independently of the availability of the implementation.

When enhancing the availability of a Web service, as we have mentioned above, protecting the implementation is not enough. The interface, what clients really use, should be equally protected. How? Just untying interface and implementation so the point where request from clients are received and the point where they are solved are really different and independent.

In order to reach this independence we propose the use of **indirect invocation**, so the interface can be published at an intermediate layer (responsible of dialoguing with clients), and the implementation is performed at a different layer, far from clients and invoked from the intermediate layer. This way, the intermediate layer can have some decision capabilities in order to, by publishing one only interface, invoke different implementations that reside in different points or nodes.

Quality of Service (QoS)

The term quality of service (QoS) refers to a set of techniques and technologies used with the aim of offering predictable results. For example, QoS techniques are used to assure a minimum bandwidth, a limited error rate, or a percentage of network availability. QoS is actually a concept that can be applied to any entity that provides a service, and from this point of view, a Web service can be analyzed from a QoS optic.

Variables like performance, response time, or availability can be used to measure the QoS of a Web service. But clients are also interested in other type of variables, that is, variables related to the provider of the service, and not just the Web service. That is, clients may be interested in things like provider cost or reliability. Once again, it is very important to separate the roles of service provider and Web service provider. Actually, we are talking about the need of differentiating "service metrics" (provider related) from "Web service metrics" (Web service related).

From clients' point of view, it is very important to know the value of a Web service's availability, for instance. But it is even more important to know the value of the availability of a service depending on the cost of that service. This assertion can be applied to any number of variables.

Independently of the number of variables that a client wants to handle, it is necessary for the client to handle them separately, differentiating the ones that define the behaviour of a Web service from those that define the behaviour of a Web service provider. The interface of a Web service has several associated metrics, but the implementation of that service has another different set of metrics.

There are several works published related to the QoS issue (e.g., Conti, Kumar, Das, & Shirazi, 2002; Menasce, 2002), but all of them only care about defining metrics, and they do not offer an architecture for implementing QoS. In addition, they do not offer the possibility to differentiate Web service metrics from provider metrics.

Weller (2002) analyzes a theoretical mechanism for qualifying Web services. According to this study, a new component is added to the standard architecture components, that is, the qualification repository, where clients store qualifications about providers, and other clients request qualifications about providers in order to perform an invocation. The repository computes and stores all qualifications about providers.

Our purpose of indirect invocation based on the use of expressions allows the use of any kind of variables in order to qualify a Web service and/or a service provider, and to obtain a unique value that can be used to select the most appropriate Web service at a given moment, according to a concrete QoS.

Multiprovider

As Web services technology grow, more provider companies will use it. That is, client entities will have an opportunity to enhance client applications, since they can use an increasing number of providers that will offer the same or equivalent service. But, for instance, they will differentiate in their availability, cost, or performance.

This ability to use more providers will become an additional new work when developing client applications, since each provider will use its own namespaces, schemas, parameters, and so forth. So, it will be mandatory to write ad-hoc code to integrate each one of the used providers into client applications, and developers will need to carry out more expensive and cost-consuming development processes.

Our purpose based on the virtualization of Web services, permits, in a natural way, to use multiple providers for only one Web service. As we will see below, Web services are published in a virtual way, while implementation of Web services can be performed by multiple different providers.

Error Management

The common lifecycle of a client application using Web services includes, at least, the following processes:

- To look for a Web service and a provider.
- To locate the description of the Web service (Web service definition language [WSDL] document).
- To perform a binding process, in order to build proxies, which will be the ones used to perform the invocations. This process will normally produce a set of modules that hold the definitions of: (i) the class of input data, (ii), the class of output data, and (iii) the invocable methods with its input and output parameters according to previous defined classes.

When a client application invokes a Web service, it is responsible of checking and handling any error condition that can occur. The following checklist should be implemented inside client applications:

- Invoke service.
- Check error.
- If invocation is not successful, determine if invocation can be retried.
- Retry the invocation a finite number of times.
- If invocation cannot be performed, send an error.

Let us consider having a client application bound to a Web service, and we want to stop using our current provider in order to use a new one (due to its low availability, for instance). We will have to modify our client application in order to delete all the references to the old provider and add new references (i.e., URL, types, namespaces, etc.) to the new provider.

In addition, it is usual (and it will become more usual in the future) to have more than one provider for the same service, in such a way that if one provider fails, client applications can invoke another provider.

With the aim of increasing the availability of client application, developers can decide to add more providers (and bind them) to that client application. This way, client application can retry invocation with a provider in case of an error of another one. But, according with what we have said above, a new checklist should be used:

- Invoke service.
- Check error.
- If invocation is not successful, determine if invocation can be retried.
- Retry the invocation a finite number of times.
- Select a new provider from the list of candidates and try again.
- If invocation cannot be performed, send an error.

As we can see, development and maintenance processes get more complex as we add more flexibility and availability to client applications. By using our purpose, we will be able to build Web services whose implementation is based on the selection and usage of several different and equivalent providers. This way, we will have a chance to enhance the availability of client applications without the need of complex development processes.

Caching

It is easy to understand how to implement a caching system when we talk about Web pages (HTML pages, images, etc., that is, static information). However, where (and how) can we apply caching techniques to Web services entirely based on the use of dynamic information (i.e., SOAP messages in response to different SOAP requests)? Our purpose enables the use of caching inside Web services technology, but it is important to take into account the fact that caching techniques can be applied to Web services only under specific circumstances:

- The number of invocation requests is large enough. If so, there will be a significant increase in performance when using a caching system.
- There is at least a method (a WSDL port, let us call it a "cacheable method") whose response to a request can be repeated along time without any variation in SOAP responses. If not, it may not be adequate for implementing caching mechanisms.
- The results received by clients invoking a cacheable method when the response is cached must not differ from those received by clients when the response is not cached.

Different applications in real life can be eligible to be implemented using cacheable Web services. Some examples of cacheable Web services are:

- A Web service that provides weather forecast, where changes in responses are not expected to occur in a short time.

- A Web service to obtain stock market share prices. Although this is a typical real time application (clients obtain real prices on each invocation), consider how the service runs when there are no changes to price, or when the stock market is close.
- A Web service to obtain the status of an item in relation to a stock management service (e.g., available quantity, type, model, etc.).

ARCHITECTURE DEFINITION

Our proposed architecture for the use of virtual Web services (VWS) determines the existence of, at least, five components (Figure 2): a client (client entity), a delegate client (client application), a service provider, a delegate provider (Web service provider), and a VWS engine. The client is the one who needs a service and, by the use of a delegate client, performs an invocation. The service provider is the one that publishes and offers a service through a delegate service provider. In our VWS architecture, invocations are not performed directly from the delegate client (typically a client application) to the delegate service provider (typically a Web service), but rather the delegate client performs an invocation to a VWS engine, who acts as an intermediary, and the engine performs an invocation to the delegate provider.

The VWS engine is not a virtual server. It is a standard server, and it should be implemented in the same way as a server used to process standard Web service invocations. The term "VWS engine" refers to a server that is capable of understanding virtual Web service definitions. That is, it can receive, process, and respond to standard Web service invocations, and, in order to process a request, the engine uses VWS definitions to select and invoke the most suitable Web service.

IMPLEMENTATION AND DEFINITION LANGUAGES

Any application that is able to use a standard Web service can be bound to a virtual Web service. Our virtualization technology provides a definition language (an XML-based language). This language (VWS definition language [VWSDL]) is used to write VWS documents. Clients do not use VWS documents, since these documents are just a definition of an implementation of a virtual Web service, and this definition is only useful to VWS engines. Our proposed language has been defined as a stand-alone language, that is, not as a WSDL extension, since its intended use is completely different. Even though the main objective of both languages is the same (describe a Web service), the way in which services are described are completely different.

Figure 2. Virtualization-based architecture

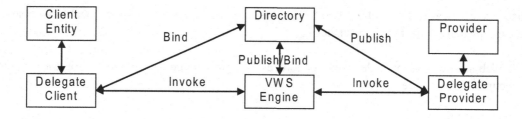

VWS documents are used to describe virtual Web services, and they must contain, at least, a list of methods provided by the service (using the method elements, as shown in Figure 3). In addition, for each method published inside a service, we must specify the input and output parameters, and their corresponding data types.

As shown in Figure 3, each `method` element has its own `name` and `type` attributes. The `type` attribute is used to specify the type of implementation that is being defined. For instance, the `equivalent` value states that, in order to execute a virtual method, a set of "equivalent" services are available to accomplish the execution. The content of a `method` element is also used to specify a list of Web services and methods that will be invoked in order to complete the execution of a method. All those Web services and their methods represent in fact the implementation of a virtual method, and they are specified (inside the `method` element) using so many `invoke` elements as needed.

In SOAP language, parameters are nominal, that is, input parameters sent to methods use the name of the elements (XML elements). The same happens with return parameters. Let us suppose that we build a virtual method that receives a parameter called "P1" and returns a parameter called "RP." This represents a little restriction in the way we write the method and invoke elements, since the name of the parameters used in the virtual method must match the ones used in real methods. If a match can be found, the invoke elements can be used without a problem. When such a match cannot be found, a `map` element should be used to solve this situation. The `map` element can contain a set of `in` and `out` elements that are used to specify the correspondence between virtual parameters and real parameters. Inside each subelement (`in` or `out`), we must write an origin parameter name and a destination one, so the engine knows how to map the parameters before and after each invocation.

It is possible to find equivalent services that use similar parameters with different data types; a price is a typical example that can be handled using integer types or float types. In situations like this, a conversion process must be performed. This conversion is expressed via the `type` attribute. It is also

Figure 3. Sample method declaration

```
<method name="getPrice" type="equivalent" cos="COS#1">
    <select name="COS#1" expression="0.7*adjust(availability)+0.3*reverseAdjust(cost)" />
    <select name="COS#2" expression="0.5*adjust(availability)+0.5*adjust(security)" />
  <input>
    <parm name="ticker" type="xsd:string"/>
  </input>
  <output>
    <parm name="name" type="xsd:string"/>
    <parm name="value" type="xsd:float"/>
    <parm name="date" type="xsd:date"/>
  </output>
  <invoke id="2" method="sendItToMe" location="http://a.com/s1.wsdl">
    <map>
        <in origin="/ticker" target="t"/>
        <out origin="/name/shortName" target="/name"/>
        <out origin="/price" target="/value" type="relaxed"/>
    </map>
  </invoke>
    <...>
</method>
```

possible to map a simple type to an element contained inside a complex one using XPath expressions, that is, assigning a simple value extracted from a DOM node.

The use of the map element brings much new functionality to the virtualization technique, since parameter mapping between virtual and real services lessens the coupling level between client applications and service implementations. Some benefits we obtain include deploying new versions of implementation Web services with the same interface, and new interface versions using the same implementation Web services.

Expressions

In order to explain the expression system, let us consider the existence of three variables that can be used to define a Web service and/or a provider: availability, cost, and security.

When a client application needs to invoke a service, the client must decide which would be the most appropriate provider. Normally, a client would choose the one that has the lowest cost, the highest availability, and the highest security level. In our example, the client should choose service B according to the cost, service A according to the availability, service C according to the security level. To solve situations like this, what our VWS architecture proposes is to build an expression that combines all the variables and gives a unique value, pondering each one of the variables using factors. This way, a sample expression combining all three variables could be written as Expression (1).

$$0.6*A + 0.3*C + 0.1*S \tag{1}$$

where A represents the availability, C is the cost, and S is the security level. To be able to write expressions in which we can mix different types of variables, having each one its own unit (milliseconds, dollars, etc.), we must apply a conversion factor in order to represent all the variables within the same scale. In addition, we should keep in mind the fact that some variables maximize the value of the whole expression by means of their maximum values (availability, for instance), while other variables do the same with their minimum values (cost, for instance).

In order to unify scales, ranges, and units for all variables used in an expression, the function adjust can be used. In addition, for variables whose minimum values represent a maximum scoring, the function `reverseAdjust` is available. Expression (1) can be rewritten as Expression (2) using these new functions.

$$0.6 * \text{adjust}(A) + 0.3 * \text{reverseAdjust}(C) + 0.1 * \text{adjust}(S) \tag{2}$$

When an invocation request is received at the VWS engine, the engine must calculate the scaling factors to unify the scale of the variables that will be used in the expression. An example is shown in Figure 3 (select elements).

Complex Expressions

Two additional methods will allow writing complex expressions: complex variables and time-variables. A complex variable is a new variable that is created using a combination of simple ones. In Expression

(3), a variable defined as G is used to hold a value that represents a global score for a provider, using A, C, and S.

$$G = 0.6 * adjust(A) + 0.3*reverseAdjust(C) + 0.1 * adjust(S) \qquad (3)$$

$$adjust ((W*G_{i-1} + G_i) / (W + 1)) \qquad (4)$$

On the other hand, time-variables allow writing expressions that involve present and past values of a variable. For example, Expression (4) can be used to obtain a global qualification for a provider, where time is taken into account by using two global-score values (i.e., G_{i-1} for the previous computed value of G and G_i for the present value of G), and a weighting factor (W) that is used as a stabilization mechanism.

External Variables

Our virtualization architecture does not impose any kind of constraint when writing expressions or using variables, and so we can use external variables managed by an external entity. For example, we could write an Expression (5) that includes an external status variable (T) indicating the status of the Web service. If a Web service is "out-of-service," we can set T to zero, and the VWS engine will stop selecting it.

$$T *(0.4*reverseAdjust(C) + 0.6*adjust(A)) \qquad (5)$$

Extension Mechanisms

Our virtualization architecture proposes the use of two additional mechanisms in order to help clients in having some decision capabilities over the evaluation process. The main objective of these mechanisms is to give the clients the ability to drive the evaluation process performed at the VWS engine.

The first mechanism is based on the use of classes of service (CoS). A CoS is defined (according to our purpose) by writing a concrete expression inside a method element (using a `select` element). More than one CoS can be defined by writing so many `select` elements as needed, identifying each of them with a name. Each `select` element represents in fact a given class of service. Once several classes of service have been defined inside a VWS document, clients can specify what CoS to use in each invocation by using SOAP extensions.

If a client does not specify what CoS to use, the VWS engine should use a default CoS in order to perform an invocation.

Figure 4. Sample restriction

```
<retriction select="(availability &gt; 95) and (cost &lt; 20)" cos="COS#2" />
```

The second extension mechanism allows the client applications to prune the list of eligible Web services. Clients can send, attached to the SOAP requests, a set of conditions that implementation Web services must fulfill (Figure 4). This way, when the VWS engine has to perform an evaluation, it will consider only those services that fulfill the client's conditions.

The base for the implementation of our extension mechanisms is the use of SOAP header elements. Like other standards, we propose to add specific extension information to the header of SOAP response messages. The information contained in a SOAP header must obey a schema in order to use our cache purpose, that is, a virtual Web services extension language (VWSEL) (Fernández, Pazos, & Fernández, 2005), created as an extension of our VWSDL (Fernández, Pazos, & Fernández, 2004). VWSEL is used in our virtualization-based architecture to offer clients a chance to send processing information to VWS engines, such as classes of service, lists of providers, preferences about caching, and so forth.

Client applications must understand VWSEL in order to use VWS extensions. It is important to note that clients who do not understand VWSEL can still work without a problem, since a SOAP message (aside from including VWSEL data) is still a standard SOAP message that can be processed by client applications, engines, and providers.

It is responsibility of every Web service to decide what information will be included inside the VWSEL section of SOAP messages. Web services should use VWSEL documents to send only caching information to clients.

QUALIFICATION AND EVALUATION

Variables are used inside our solution to achieve the automation of two processes:

*   A **qualification process:** The VWS engine computes and stores statistical information in a database after selecting and invoking a Web service. The same or another engine will use that statistical data in a later moment.
*   An **evaluation process:** By means of this process, a VWS engine reads statistical information stored in the database, with the aim of selecting and invoking the most suitable Web service to accomplish the execution of a virtual service method.

We have already seen how to build expressions in which we can put together all we know about the way a given Web service works. The objective of expressions is to achieve quick and automated qualification and evaluation processes. Theoretically, every time a Web service is invoked, the VWS engine should update the statistical data related to that service.

Nevertheless, by means of a good performance, it could be good practice not to store all the gathered statistical data. As an alternative, we can decide to store the data associated to only a part of the invocations performed. This could be a recommendable way of working, but the percentage of data stored must be big enough, so they can be representative of the total number of invocations.

The process of updating the statistical database must be performed in an automated way, and this automation requires that the variables used in the process can be immediately computed after a service invocation. That is, the engine cannot update a variable that represents the time spent by a provider in serving orders. Actually, variables that cannot be computed from a service invocation are usually provider-related variables, and not service-related ones. Provider-related variables should be considered as external variables, that is, user-managed variables.

Let us suppose that we have developed a client application that uses a Web service to provide a book selling service over the Internet. Let us consider two sample variables: delivering time and package quality. Neither one can be computed when invoking the service since they are provider-related variables.

Provider-related variables, as it happens with service-related ones, can be either quantitative or qualitative, so the same conversion process used in service-related variables can be applied to provider-related ones. In the previous example, delivering time is a quantitative variable, while package quality is a qualitative variable.

The evaluation process of a provider-related variable can be performed the same as the service-related variables evaluation. Actually, both types of variables can be mixed in the same expressions, because one type of variables and the other should be correctly adjusted when performing an evaluation.

However, the qualification of a provider cannot be performed in an automatic way, because the values of variables (provider-related) can be unknown during the lifecycle of an invocation. When using expressions that include provider-related variables, the VWS must have access to data that represent the behavior of the providers in previous invocations. That is, a process external to the engine must update the statistics database. This way, when the VWS engine computes an expression, it can do it without caring about the type of variables used (service- or provider-related), since all the data will be available. From the point of view of the engine, there is no difference between one type of variables and the other.

Rating Subsystem

Our virtualization architecture proposes the use of an optional "rating server" as an extra component that should be in charge of managing statistical data. That is, the rating subsystem is in charge of the qualification and the evaluation processes in the previous section. The VWS engine and the rating server could be the same machine. However, in a big production system, an independent rating subsystem could be used.

The rating system defined inside our QoS architecture is not concerned with the quality of the server nor the client, but with the quality of the services and the providers. Our purpose does not care about the way the rating server is implemented.

When the VWS engine receives an invocation request, it must send a query to the rating server in order to select the most suitable Web service provider. Querying the rating server is a process that can be performed on each invocation or periodically, depending on the VWS engine criteria. Something similar occurs when the engine needs to update statistical data on the rating server. Additionally, in order to optimize the number of accesses to the rating server, the VWS engine could store the statistical data of all the invocations and update the server only at predefined intervals using summarized information. In production environments, it can be interesting to build rating systems that do not use real data obtained from the results of the execution of services, but only sampled data, because of performance reasons.

The rating server location is a major issue. A corporate server can be used, so it will be used as a "provider repository." Alternatively, a public rating server managed by a third-party company can also be used. In this case, the reliability of the rating system will depend on the trust placed in the provider of the rating server.

APPLICATIONS: HIGH AVAILIBLITY

Cluster Implementation

A VWS document that describes a virtual Web service whose invocations can be solved by a set of providers corresponds to what we call a "cluster of Web services." By using VWS documents, clusters can be built by using engines and providers. Our virtualization model establishes the existence of two types of nodes inside a cluster. The first type is the principal node. This node will be in charge of receiving service invocation requests. We must place the VWS documents inside the principal node. The second type is the nonprincipal node or provider node, and it is in charge of executing requests received from principal nodes.

Using the method and invoke elements of the VWS documents we can establish a relation between real and virtual services. This way, we can create a cluster architecture where the cluster's principal node (a VWS engine) will be the one in charge of receiving client requests and distributing the workload across cluster nodes (Web service providers).

According to this structure, if a provider (a cluster node) fails, the VWS engine will redistribute pending invocation requests, and the operative nodes in the cluster should take charge of unassigned workload. This way, the whole cluster continuity can be guaranteed. However, there are still some problems to solve. How can we accomplish such a load balancing system? How can we deal with a planned or unplanned node outage? How can we select the most suitable provider in each moment? The next sections will provide answers to these questions.

Building a Web Services-Based Cluster

Let us suppose that we have a Web service (WS1), with a method (M1). If we want WS1 to be a highly available Web service, we must deploy it to a cluster. The deployment process requires the Web service to be deployed to each one of the nonprincipal nodes in the cluster. This way, more than one instance of the Web service can be used, and these instances can be executed at different nodes. All of them are said to be equivalent.

To get our VWS engine up and running we must create a VWS document to define a virtual Web service (VWS1) that would contain, at least, a virtual method (VM1) (it is important to note that clients do not use the VWS documents to perform the binding; they use a standard WSDL document derived from the VWS document). Inside the VWS document, we must specify how the virtual method execution should be accomplished. We need to include, at least, three XML elements inside the VWS document: a service element describing the service; a method element that describes the method we want to publish (including its input and output elements); and one or more invoke elements. These invoke elements are the ones in charge of describing how and where the method implementation must be made.

When a method execution request for the VM1 method arrives to the VWS engine, the engine must select the most suitable provider in order to complete the request. Once a provider has been selected, a real service (implementation service) will be invoked, sending it input parameters as needed. After service execution, the engine will receive the return parameters from the real service and it will send them back to the client application. For the whole cluster to run accurately, the VWS engine has to decide which provider node would be the most suitable to perform an execution. The engine should use some selection criteria in order to maximize cluster performance.

Node Selection

After the VWS engine receives a request, the engine must select a cluster node that can accomplish the invocation request. To do it, the engine will examine the content of the method element included in a VWS document describing the virtual service. Among the providers detailed in the invoke elements (included in the method element), the VWS engine will choose the best prior to each real service invocation. This concept, the best, is a concept that can change along time.

Our virtualization model proposes the use of expressions to select the most appropriate provider prior to each invocation. Each method element inside a VWS document should include an expression. This expression must reflect which the priorities are when a provider has to be selected. Let us consider Expression (6)

$$0.7*A+0.3*R \tag{6}$$

where A is the availability and R is the response-time, and they represent historical data about a given Web service. Prior to a Web service invocation, the VWS engine must compute the values associated with all services specified in the invoke elements inside a method element, then compare all result values, and, finally, invoke the service with the highest score.

In order to unify scales, ranges, and units for all variables used in an expression, the function `adjust` can be used. In addition, for variables whose minimum values represent a maximum scoring, the function `reverseAdjust` is available. So, Expression (6) could be perfectly adjusted and rewritten like Expression (7):

$$0.7*adjust(A)+0.3*reverseAdjust(R) \tag{7}$$

Cluster Maintenance

To succeed in having a 100% available system, methods that allow performing maintenance on the cluster must be available. When we need to perform any kind of maintenance, we meet with the need for stopping part of the system. If we want to stop a node without interrupting activity, we should use an "upDown" variable and add it to all expressions used inside the cluster. This way, we can rewrite Expression (7) as Expression (8):

$$upDown * (0.7*adjust(A)+0.3*reverseAdjust(R)) \tag{8}$$

If we want to remove a node from the cluster, we must set the value of the upDown variable to zero, and the node will stop receiving new execution requests. That is, the node enters a draining state, and when there are no pending requests, the node can be removed from the cluster.

Node Error Detection

During normal cluster operation, errors can appear that can cause two different effects: increments in response time, and fatal errors like a node outage. The VWS engine is the element in charge of dealing with those kinds of errors.

If the response time of a given node is increased more than usual, the normal operation of the engine should make that node stop being used. This can be accomplished by adding a variable called R (response time) to all expressions. For example, using Expression (7) providers with the lowest response time will always get a high qualification value, while providers with a high response time would stop being selected for an invocation. If a node outage is detected, then the VWS engine should stop invoking services on that node. To deal with this situation the VWS engine must use the upDown variable, like in Expression (8).

When does the provider be used again? A simple procedure for dealing with this situation would consist on using a polling technique (PING or repetitive TCP-open). A most appropriate method consists on having a mechanism that allows the provider to send a notification to the engine, in order to notify the new state. VWS engines must provide a Web service, including a specific method (let us name it "upDownPort" method). Using upDownPort, providers can notify its actual state. Moreover, the upDownPort can also be used to stop a cluster node (by modifying the upDown variable value).

Scalability

Scalability problems are usually solved using two different types of solutions: vertical scalability, achieved by improving hardware configuration of the cluster nodes, and horizontal scalability, where new nodes can be added to the cluster. If we decide to use vertical scalability, we will find no problems when implementing virtualization, since Web services are completely independent on the hardware infrastructure. If we decide to use horizontal scalability as a way to extend the whole cluster capacity, we must search for alternative cluster structures, when building virtual services.

Our virtualization model sees the cluster as a tree, in which the root node is the VWS engine, and the provider nodes are leafs in that tree. The first way in we can extend a cluster consists on adding leafs to the tree (Figure 5).

The virtualization model also proposes another type of scalability, that is, hierarchical scalability. With VWS, we can publish virtual Web services and use them as if they were "traditional" (standard) Web services. A virtual service implementation can be done using another virtual service, and so we can build cluster structures that contain intermediate nodes. According to this, the root node of the cluster would be a VWS engine, leaf nodes would be provider nodes, and intermediate nodes should be implemented as a mixture of both a root node and a leaf node. Intermediate nodes should behave as a root node in order to send requests to leaf nodes under it, and as a leaf node that receives requests from a root node. In Figure 5, an expansion of "Node 2" has caused the creation of an intermediate node and the addition of two new nodes.

Figure 5. Hierarquical scalability

APPLICATIONS: QOS

When developing software that uses Web services, things like the uncertainty associated to the Internet (e.g., unpredictable workload, uncertain and highly oscillating number of users, etc.), must be taken into account. In addition, the quality of the providers used (i.e., its availability, reliability, response time, etc.), will have a great impact on client's applications.

All the providers are different, and clients always want to use the best one. This concept, the best, is a concept that changes along time, due to network outages, server outages, high response times, and so forth. In order to use the best Web service from the best provider, we need to use systems that gather statistical information about providers and their services. That statistical information should be updated with time, so client applications always invoke the best service and provider according to that statistical data. As we have seen, our virtualization architecture proposes the use of three elements that enable the selection of the most suitable service and provider:

- A qualifying method for each one of the services and providers.
- A way to obtain historical qualifications of previous invocations.
- An element in charge of computing the qualifications and performing an evaluation using the information gathered previously.

A correct operation of the assign-and-compute-qualifications system depends directly on choosing the appropriate variables, like availability, reliability, cost, or performance.

The election of the right units for the variables is a mandatory step before using a qualification system. Although there are variables like response time that can be easily measured, there are other variables like "provider security level," which are expressed using qualitative values (e.g., low level, high level, etc.). A simple way of managing the qualitative variables consists of assigning value ranges (using techniques similar to those used in fuzzy logic). This way we can map qualitative values to numeric values.

Let us suppose that we build a virtual service, and its implementation is made using three standard Web services (A, B, and C) that are equivalent (i.e., same functionality). We have decided to use the following variables to select the most appropriate service for each invocation: cost, availability, and security level. Cost is a variable whose value is established by the provider (provider-related variable), while availability and security level refer to a Web service (service-related variable).

Applying virtualization techniques to QoS problems is very easy. It only requires writing expressions that represent the QoS metrics that we want to take into account equally to the expression system we have showed for HA issues. Typically, in clusters of Web services, we will use Web service-related variables, while in QoS problems we will use a mix of Web service provider-related variables and service provider-related variables.

APPLICATIONS: CACHING

It is possible to define at least two different caching structures in Web services architecture. The first one is a two level caching architecture (2LCA), which involves the existence of two entities: server and client. This caching architecture is not new, and caching is applied here using a typical caching implementation, like the one used by Web browsers that access Web servers directly. Three-level caching architecture (3LCA) is also possible. This kind of architecture is likely to occur in an environment where intermediate elements are an active part of the whole architecture. In a 3LCA, a third component appears, the intermediate element, which can also be an active actor in the caching system.

Our purpose is a very good solution to improve the performance of Web service-based applications, especially in stressed environments (with high volume of invocations). In addition, our purpose, far from the traditional HTTP cache system, gives a high degree of freedom to Web service developers, since our purpose, based on the use of extra information that is sent with SOAP messages (VWSEL), allows Web service programmers to control the way that messages are cached by client entities. That is, our purpose allows developers to control a cache system in a different way on each invocation, depending on the execution logic of the Web service.

There are some works on improving Web services performance by using caching; some of them are based on several different programming mechanisms. Goodman (2002) presents a solution based on the use of a cache object. This object is a Java object that must be managed from the Web service logic. This solution does not avoid network traffic, since invocation must be received at application code, in order to access the abovementioned cache object.

Other kinds of solutions are based on the use of HTTP headers to manage the expiration of the HTTP responses. In "Perform Output Caching with Web Services in Visual C#.NET" (2003), the use of programming attributes (similar to compilation directives) is proposed. The use of the `WebMethod` attribute, together with the `CacheDuration` property, allows a simple way to control the TTL of the response. Again, this solution is based on the use of HTTP, enforcing a dependency between a Web service (and its business logic) and a transport layer (HTTP). In addition, it is a static mechanism, that is, programmers cannot control the duration of a response depending on the logic of the Web service.

RELATED WORK

Virtualization is being successfully applied to many other environments, such as storage virtualization, network virtualization, and hardware virtualization. What we propose here is to virtualice software, creating new virtual components (e.g., VWS) with which we can achieve a degree of decoupling and independence between clients and providers greater than the one we could achieve with standard Web services.

The architecture we propose is innovative as a global solution for a range of problems that have only been addressed individually so far. Problems related to SLA management, quality of service, or high availability are the subject of study by public and private entities, but the solutions proposed are specific for each one of these issues: architectures and languages to support SLA management (Dan, Ludwig, & Pacifici, 2003; Ludwig, Keller, Dan, King, & Franck, 2003; Sahai, Machiraju, Sayal, Jin, & Casati, 2002), metrics for QoS (Barry, 2003), and software and hardware architecture intended to improve the availability of the implementation of Web services, but not their interface, which is what clients perceive as a Web service. We have also discussed about these issues our 2004 work.

At the same time, the use of intermediate elements (the engines in our proposal) is a technique that is being implemented in some software platforms, but always with a specific use and using proprietary languages and/or systems. For example, WS-DBC (Brose, 2003) uses an intermediate element as a security system, while WS-Gateway (Venkatapathy & Holdsworth, 2002) isolates the private networks of clients and/or providers, also supporting certain protocol changes (e.g., from SOAP to HTTP/POST).

The work we have performed on caching systems has a close relation with the theories exposed by Cao and Irani (1997) and Cao and Liu (1997) and other works. Moreover, the same as the theories exposed by Chankhunthod, Danzig, Neerdaels, Schwartz, and Worrell (1996) and Worrell (1994), our caching purpose will add even greater benefits when applied to a hierarchic architecture, like the one we proposed in 2004, based on the use of VWS engines in charge of routing SOAP messages.

CONCLUSION AND FUTURE WORK

There exist several ways to apply the proposed architecture to the current Web services technology. Those forms represent different implementations and lead to obtaining different functionalities depending on the localization of the VWS engine. Basically, we can distinguish three alternatives, depending on whether the engine is located: (1) in the private network of the client, (2) in the private network of the service provider, and (3) in the Internet, being accessible to both client and service provider.

In case (1) above (point 1 in Figure 6), the use of an engine offers the following functionalities:

- It makes the software of the client independent of that of the delegate provider, because the engine allows both of them to change their interfaces without affecting the other, as long as the engine can map the different structures of the SOAP messages exchanged in the invocations.
- Provider independence. Virtual Web services allow the adding, modifying, and removing of providers without affecting the client, that is, without any need for the client to modify its applications.
- Proxy. The use of the engine allows client applications to invoke Internet Web services even when they have cannot connect to anything beyond its private network.
- Automated error management. Because the methods of the virtual services are built from a list of Web service providers that is functionally equivalent, the engine can control the errors that take place and, when a provider fails, try to use another one. This occurs unnoticed for client applications.
- Cache. As we have seen, it is possible to cache client requests, noticeably improving response times. Take as an example the case of a Web service that offers share prices on the closing of financial markets, or a weather forecast Web service.

An engine placed inside the provider's private network (point 2 in Figure 6) fundamentally allows the building of Web services cluster systems, where the VWS engine acts as a controller node for the cluster, in charge of receiving requests and routing them to a certain node that is selected depending on the workload of each node (point 3 in Figure 6). Other possible functionalities are:

- Firewall. The VWS engine allows providers residing in a private network to be invoked from outside that network, keeping a high security level inside of it.
- When used as a cluster controller, it allows for the introduction of modifications in a node of the cluster while keeping the others unchanged, making it possible to perform software testing with a minimal impact in the construction of a new Web service in case of an error.

Figure 6. Sample architecture implementation

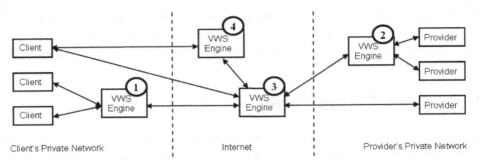

Last, in case (3) (Internet engine), its main use is that of a broker, that is, the engine acts like an intermediate component in the network that puts clients and service providers in contact (point 3 in Figure 6), moreover offering the following main functionalities:

- Decoupling between delegate client and delegate provider, due to the fact that the definition of virtual services makes it possible to modify the interface of the delegate providers (Web services) without changing the client software.
- Use of multiple providers.
- Error control and management.

What we propose is to use a common language for the description of virtual Web services, which at the same time provides a standard way to construct the interfaces that intermediate elements must offer through standard WSDL documents. We also propose an extension of the standard architecture in order to support VWS in such a way that it be compatible with current architecture.

VWS can help developing Web services with rich features like high availability, performance optimization, QoS, error management, and so forth.

The overall performance of the proposed architecture (whichever its use) will greatly depend on the variables and expressions used for the description of virtual Web services. It has to be noted that the VWS engine introduces a new overhead inside the execution architecture, since requests must be received and rerouted to the appropriate provider. However, this overhead is not significant when compared to the benefits obtained with our architecture.

Using VWS developers can build atomic Web services that can be published and subsequently consumed by resource-constrained devices like mobile phones or PDA; that is, virtual Web services can be used as a personalization mechanism regarding client requirements in order to simplify its use in such device types.

VWS technology is the base for other works that extend the use of our model. Regarding these other features of our model:

- We can use the VWS documents to build composite Web services. This work is in progress, and we are defining a set of different types of invocations. Our goal is to develop a Web services programming language (WSPL, as an extension of VWSDL) that supports basic programming structures (e.g., if-then-else, do-while, etc.). Its objective is to provide a simple composition method.
- We plan to integrate WSLA with our Web service descriptions. This way, a VWS engine can be used to analyze each invocation of a Web service and evaluate SLOs after each invocation.

Our proposal is not disruptive in its implementation, because it can coexist with the current architecture with no problems at all. Ideally, in fact, both architectures should coexist, because the standard one shall be used for easy problems in controlled environments, like the invocation of Web services in a corporate network.

REFERENCES

Barry, D. (2003). *Web services and service-oriented srchitectures: The savvy manage's guide.* Morgan Kauffman.

Booth, D., Haas, H., McCabe, F., Newcomer, E., Champion, M., Ferris, C., et al. (2004). *Web services architecture.*

Brose, G. (2003). Securing Web services with SOAP security proxies. In *Proceedings of the International Conference on Web Services* (pp. 231-234).

Cao, P., & Irani, S. (1997). Cost-aware WWW proxy caching algorithms. In *Proceedings of the 1997 Usenix Symposium on Internet Technologies and Systems (USITS-97).*

Cao, P., & Liu, C. (1997). Maintaining strong cache consistency in the World-Wide Web. In *Proceedings of the 7th International Conference on Distributed Computing Systems.*

Chankhunthod, A., Danzig, P., Neerdaels, C., Schwartz, M., & Worrell, K. (1996). A hierarchical Internet object cache. In *Proceedings of the 1996 USENIX* (pp. 153-163).

Conti, M., Kumar, M., Das, S. K., & Shirazi, B. (2002). Quality of service issues in Internet Web services. *IEEE Transactions on Computers , 6*(51), 593-594.

Dan, A., Ludwig, H., & Pacifici, G. (2003). *IBM.* Retrieved May 25, 2008, from http://www-106.ibm.com/developerworks/library/ws-slafram

Fernández, J., Pazos, J., & Fernández, A. (2004a). An architecture for building Web services with quality-of-service features. In *Proceedings of the 5th WAIM.*

Fernández, J., Pazos, J. J., & Fernández, A. (2004b). High availability wit clusters of Web services. In *Proceedings of the 6th APWeb* (pp. 644-653).

Fernández, J., Pazos, J., & Fernández, A. (2005). Optimizing Web services performance using caching. In *Proceedings of the 2005 NWeSP* (pp. 6-16).

Goodman, B. D. (2002). Accelerate your Web services with caching. *developerWorks Journal.*

Ludwig, H., Keller, A., Dan, A., King, R. P., & Franck, R. (2003). *Web Service Level Agreements (WSLA) Project.* Retrieved May 25, 2008, from http://www.research.ibm.com/wsla

Menasce, D. A. (2002). QoS Issues in Web services. *IEEE Internet Computing, 6*(6), 72-75.

Nick, J., Chung, J. Y., & Bowen, N. S. (1996). Overview of IBM system/390 parallel sysplex. In *Proceedings of 10th International Parallel Processing Symposium (IPPS)* (pp. 488-495). IEEE Computer Society.

Perform output caching with Web services in visual C#.NET. (2003). Microsoft Support.

Sahai, A., Machiraju, V., Sayal, M., Jin, L. J., & Casati, F. (2002). *Automated SLA monitoring for Web services.* Paper presented at the 13th IFIP/IEEE International Wokshop on Distributed Systems (DSOM*)* (pp. 28-41).

Venkatapathy, S., & Holdsworth, C. (2002). *An introduction to Web services gateway.* Retrieved May 25, 2008, from http://www-106.ibm.com/developerworks/Webservices/library/ws-gateway/

Vinosky, C. (2002). Web services interaction models. Current practice. *IEEE Internet Computing, 3*(6), 89-91.

Web services invocation framework. (2007). Retrieved May 25, 2008, from http://ws.apache.org/wsif

Weller, S. (2002). *Web services qualification.* Retrieved May 25, 2008, from http://www-106.ibm.com/developerworks/library/ws-qual

Worrell, K. (1994). *Invalidation in large scale network object caches.* Unpublished master's thesis, University of Colorado.

Section II
Description and Composition

Chapter V
Profiling of Web Services to Measure and Verify their Non–Functional Properties

Witold Abramowicz
Poznań University of Economics, Poland

Monika Kaczmarek
Poznań University of Economics, Poland

Dominik Zyskowski
Poznań University of Economics, Poland

ABSTRACT

The following chapter focuses on the problem of the proper definition of non-functional properties and methods that may be applied in order to estimate their values. First of all, a reader is familiarized with the concept of non-functional properties and different views on the quality of Web services. Then, selected approaches to obtain values of non-functional properties are presented. The focus of attention is Web services profiling that seems to be one of the most promising methods to perform this task. The framework presented in this chapter was implemented and tested within the EU Adaptive Services Grid project.

INTRODUCTION

The paradigm of service-oriented architecture (SOA) is currently one of the most popular approaches followed by modellers and IT developers in order to build IT systems. The potential of SOA is being strengthened by the growing popularity of Web services technology. Web services allow for encapsulation of business functionalities provided using IT infrastructure and easy integration with other systems via standard communication protocols. Globalization, along with a tendency to outsource some activities, boosts the exploitation of Web services in enterprise applications.

One of the essential elements needed to ensure the success of Web services (as well as Semantic Web services) technology is a proper Web service description to be used not only in order to invoke a Web service, but also to discover it and perform composition. The common agreement is that a Web service should be represented by its surrogate, describing its functional, non-functional, and behavioural characteristics. The functional features focus on what a Web service does, the non-functional ones on how it does it, and the behavioural ones inform us which parties are involved in the process of service provisioning. Whereas, there seems to exist a common agreement on how the description of the functional and behavioural properties of a service should look like and its role in Web services' interactions; there is still an ongoing discussion about the scope and the methods that should be used to express the non-functional side of a Web service.

Within the last few years, a number of different approaches to define non-functional properties and quality of service (QoS) models for Web services have been proposed. Each of them defines a different set and understanding of non-functional properties as well as QoS features. Yet, as shown in this chapter, these initiatives are still not mature enough as they focus mostly on the technical aspects of a Web service and, in most cases, disregard the business ones. Another problem that appears, once the model of non-functional properties is defined, relates to the methods that can be utilized in order to obtain values of defined properties. Various techniques to carry out this task were proposed. They differ in terms of reliability, trustworthiness, as well as the issue of continuous provisioning of up-to-date values of parameters.

The following chapter focuses on the problem of definition of non-functional properties and methods to estimate their values. The special focus is assigned to the Web services profiling, being, in our opinion, one of the most promising methods to perform this task. The chapter is organized as follows. First, we present our understanding of non-functional properties and quality of service. In the following section, the methods to compute values of non-functional properties are discussed. The following section outlines current methods to compute values of non-functional properties. Then, the concepts of service profiling, service profile, and its elements are presented. Moreover, in this section we also describe the technical details of service profiling system implemented within the Adaptive Services Grid project. Finally, the summary follows.

NON-FUNCTIONAL PROPERTIES OF WEB SERVICES

To fully exploit the advantages of Web services technology, as indicated in the introduction section, their proper description is required. The common agreement is that a Web service should be represented by its surrogate, providing information on its functional (what a Web service does), non-functional (how it does it), and behavioural characteristics (which parties are involved in the process of service provisioning). However, before the initiatives in the area of Web services description are presented, differences between a service and a Web service, being crucial for our further discussion, need to be mentioned.

A service is usually defined as a provision of value in some domain (Preist, 2004) or seen as a business activity that often results in intangible outcomes or benefits (Baida, Gordijn, Omelayenko, & Akkermans, 2004). Let us consider an example of a person who wants to buy a book on knowledge representation published by Springer. The service this person is looking for is the provisioning of books with the specified constraints. A provision is in fact independent on how the supplier and provider interact (Lara & Olmedilla, 2005), that is, it does not really matter at this point whether the requester goes to a bookshop or uses the Amazon.com portal to buy the book of interest.

A Web service in turn may be defined as a computational entity accessible over the Internet (using particular standards and protocols) (Preist, 2004). The focus is assigned here to the way that the requester and provider interact with each other (Lara & Olmedilla, 2005). In the considered example with a book, a bookshop (e.g., Amazon.com) may provide a component accessible via Web service standards (i.e., a Web service) to request the book. Therefore, a Web service is a technical implementation, an interface to a real-world service defined as a certain activity undertaken on behalf of a certain entity. Final users are in fact more interested in the real service they get, rather than in the interface itself. Hence, Web services may be considered as two inseparable parts: a technical interface (described using Web service description language (WSDL) and a real (business) functionality (described by other means) the interface provides access to.

The above perception of a service and Web services entails a question what kind of a Web services description is required for the needs of interactions with and between Web services. A Web service is an interface used to request the actual provisioning of a real-world service fulfilling the requester needs. Therefore, for example, in order to discover a Web service and use it to request a required service, the technical description of a Web service (the interface) is of course crucial but not sufficient. What is also indispensable is the description of a real world service and non-functional properties of both a service and a Web service. The way consumers interact with traditional services and their requirements regarding their description are a result of social and economic interactions that have been taking place for many years. If Web service providers do not consider this fact, they will fail. Therefore, a Web service description should adhere to the well-established requirements of the consumers and cover not only functional, but also non-functional properties (NFP) of a service (Abramowicz, Kaczmarek, & Zyskowski, 2006), (Abramowicz, Kaczmarek, Kowalkiewicz, & Zyskowski, 2005).

Reviewing the Web service description initiatives at least two things should to be taken into account, namely the scope of such a description and formalism used to express it. There are many initiatives in the area of service description. The earliest ones, like WSDL (W3C, 2007), focused mainly on purely technical details needed in order to invoke a Web service (such as its interface, ports, bindings, etc.) and were expressed using XML notation. Then the other initiatives, like UDDI registry (UDDI, 2004), adding few non-functional properties to the Web service description followed. Finally, the semantic initiatives like OWL-S (W3C, 2004), WSMO (Roman et al., 2006), or SAWSDL (Farrel & Lausen, 2006) expressed using the logic-based language, such as, for example, Web services modeling language (WSML) or resource description framework (RDF) and trying to also capture information on the real-world service standing behind the Web service interface were undertaken.

Having a look at those initiatives, one thing may be quite easily noticed. There seems to exist a common agreement on how the description of the functional properties of a service should look like and its role in Web services interactions. However, there is still an ongoing discussion on the scope and methods that should be used to express the non-functional side of a service.

Functional properties represent the capability of a Web service. These properties are mainly related to the input and output parameters as well as constraints/a state of the world before and after service execution. Therefore, in most cases either the functionality is expressed as only information on inputs and outputs (like in WSDL where input and output parameters required by a service are defined) or as the semantically annotated quadruple IOPE (inputs, outputs, preconditions, and effects) in OWL-S or pre- and post-conditions defined within WSMO. The functional properties are used mainly for the needs of discovery and composition of Web services. The mechanisms operating on all of the above mentioned formalisms are already implemented and work more or less efficiently in various projects (Abramowicz, Haniewicz, Kaczmarek, & Zyskowski, 2006a; Kuster, Koenig-Ries, Stern, & Klein, 2007; Liu, Peng, & Chen, 2006).

In turn, the non-functional properties play a crucial role in almost all service interactions (to mention only selection, discovery, and filtering). Non-functional properties of a service may be defined as anything that exhibits a constraint over the functionality (O'Sullivan, Edmond, & Hofstede, 2002). In fact, non-functional parameters are distinctive criteria for the success of businesses offering their services using Web services technology. They allow differentiating between Web services offering the same (or quite similar) functionality, as, in most cases, service substitutes differ when it comes to the values of specific non-functional properties. Their role became even more important, as nowadays Web services are not only used internally, but also support collaboration between various organizations. In consequence, final users (especially business users) desire to know in advance the real quality and non-functional properties of external services they are to use.

The non-functional parameters may be represented as qualitative and quantitative measures of a Web service (or a service). The nonquantitative ones include security or transactions, whereas quantitative ones include such attributes as cost or time. NFP should of course include business constraints and interservice dependencies, if possible. However, different types of services require different properties describing them and which properties are necessary depends on the domain, intended use, and users' requirements. If services are to be used to automate B2B and B2C models, they have to be described in a proper manner and meet specific business requirements. The table below presents a few exemplary non-functional parameters.

The non-functional model for Web services is still under development. Each of the already mentioned service description initiatives or standards like WSDL, UDDI, OWL-S, WSMO, or SAWSDL treats non-functional properties in different ways. No non-functional properties can be expressed using WSDL. A list of non-functional parameters provided by UDDIs includes only some attributes such as, for example,: provider name, service name, and category. In turn, OWL-S and WSMO take into account a wider range of NFP (than, for example, UDDIs), including not only information on service providers,

Table 1. A few exemplary non-functional parameters

Parameter name	Definition
execution price	an amount of money that needs to be paid to the service provider for service execution
latency time	a round-trip time between sending a request and receiving a response
average (maximum) response time	an average (maximum) time needed for the packet of control data to get to the provider's server (where the service is executed) and then return to the requester
robustness	ability of a service to act properly if some of the input parameters are missing or incorrect
availability	probability whether a service is capable of processing the client's request or not at a certain time
charging method	by execution unit, subscription, or by data chunk size and so forth.
payment method	information on method of payment (wire transfer, etc.)

Table 2. Overview of the support of the selected Web services description approaches to NFP

Web services description	Approach to NFP
WSDL	Nonfunctional properties are neglected
UDDI	Defines a set of non-functional properties of a service provider (included in BusinessEntity) such as: address, phone number, e-mail address, and some meta data about a service as, for example, service category
OWL-S	Includes the following non-functional properties: service name, text description, quality rating, and service category; all are stored in the ServiceProfile class. The list may be extended using the ServiceParameter from the ServiceProfile class.
WSMO	It recommends a set of NFP for each element of a Web service description (e.g., contributor, creator, date, and so forth) provided by the Dublin Core Metadata Initiative. WSMO does not provide a model for the non-functional properties of a service (Toma, 2006), but there is an on-going work in this direction.
O'Sullivan's approach	(O'Sullivan et al. (2002) describe a set of the most relevant non-functional properties for Web services and their modelling. Exemplary concepts considered are as follows: service provider, locative model, temporal model, service availability, obligations, price, payment, discounts, trust, security, and so forth.

but also some performance-related information, such as execution time and so forth. The short overview of non-functional aspects supported by the selected Web services description approaches is presented in the following table.

The lack of a real support (i.e, languages, methodologies, tools) for non-functional properties may result from the following issues (Eenoo, Hylooz, & Khan, 2005; Rosa, Cunha, Freire, & Justo, 2002; Toma, 2006):

- Non-functional properties are usually too abstract and most of the time they are stated informally;
- In some cases there is no clear distinction between the functional and non-functional aspects of a service;
- Non-functional properties are often considered to be represented only after the functional and behavioural have been described;
- Non-functional properties very often conflict and compete with each other (e.g., availability and performance);
- Complexity of modelling non-functional properties (difficult to formalize).

DUALITY IN WEB SERVICES QUALITY

Quality of a Web service may be defined as an extent to which a Web service provisioning process as well as delivered results meet expectations of a user. It is a subset of non-functional properties of a Web service. When considering the quality concept of Web services their dual character (the relation to the real world services) should be taken into account. Therefore, in defining quality of service one needs to consider two aspects: the quality of a Web service implementation (the interface), and the quality of a real service (available through a Web service interface). That is why a QoS concept for Web services should be divided into two separate groups, namely, quality of execution (QoE) and quality of result

(QoR) as proposed by Abramowicz, Filipowska, Kaczmarek, Kaczmarek, Kowalkiewicz, Rutkowski et al. (2006). Let us consider a simple route planning service which is a part of the Adaptive Services Grid project's demonstration scenario (Noll, 2004).

QoR of this service may be defined as:

- A service provider's statement on the overall quality of the result provided by the service (low/ high, etc.). It should be understood as follows. To what extent should a user trust the provided route description? Is it adequate and reliable? Does it show exactly what a user wanted? Will a user following the obtained route reach the desired destination point? Other parameters may be also considered (e.g., the route description, the resolution and colours of the image, and accuracy). These characteristics have a crucial impact on the satisfaction of a user and are a part of the QoR concept.

- Users' feedback (assessment) understood as their satisfaction from the returned result (not from the interface through which they communicate with a service) expressed in a defined scale. However, it would be very difficult, if not impossible, to collect such information from users. They would rather provide an overall evaluation of both a service implementation and real service effects.

The QoR concept is domain specific. In fact, it is very difficult, if not impossible, to define a measure that would hold for all possible services. It is not the case with QoE, which is independent of the domain and rather easy to compute. The quality of execution relates to the underlying technology (i.e., technical and network-related aspects). The following properties may be a part of the QoE model:

- **Response latency:** Time needed for the control data to get to the service and back to the client.
- **Maximal throughput:** How many requests a provider is able to process in a given time period.
- **Execution duration:** Time needed to fulfil a user request (time between sending a request and receiving an answer).
- **Execution price:** Amount of money a user needs to pay in order to use an interface to the service.
- **Service robustness:** The ability of a service to act properly if some of the input parameters are missing or incorrect (e.g., the wrong coordinates or incorrect data types, etc.).

Table 3. RoutePlanning service example (Noll, 2004)

Service name	Route Planning Service
Description	Creates a route description for the customer's coordinates and the given attraction. The route description consists of a coloured high-resolution picture and a textual description.
Nonfunctional Properties	
Service Name	Map24RoutePlanningService
Provider Name	Map24.de
Information Quality	High
Functional Properties	
Preconditions	Location ls, Location lg
Positive Effects	RouteDescription rd, hasRoute (rd, r)

Table 4. Comparison of QoR and QoE

Quality of Result	Quality of Execution
Quality of a real service	Quality of an interface (WS implementation)
Domain specific	Domain independent
Very hard to measure and monitor	Rather easy to measure and monitor
In most cases has no impact on QoE	May have an impact on QoR

The following table summarizes our short discussion on the differences between the QoR and QoE concepts.

Another aspect that needs to be mentioned is the difference between an execution price and a service price. A service price is the amount of money a user has to pay for a real service; for example, when using a route planning it is a price of the attraction ticket (e.g., ticket to the cinema) (it influences QoR). In this case, an execution price is the amount of money we have to pay for using the interface to book tickets, not a price of the ticket itself (it influences QoE). When buying a book at Amazon.com, the execution price is 0 (using the Amazon Web page to search and order is free), but the service price is the price of the book and the delivery costs. In case of information services (such services where output returned by a service is equal to the effect we wanted to obtain) it is rather unclear whether the price we have to pay for the information is a service price or execution price, and the classification may depend on many factors.

Most of the current initiatives aiming at providing definitions and descriptions of quality dimension address only some generic parameters (mostly network related), such as execution price and duration, availability and reliability, and so forth (Liu, Ngu, & Zeng, 2004; Menasce, 2002; Zeng, Benatallah, Dumas, Kalagnanam, & Sheng, 2003), and do not differentiate between the QoR and QoE concepts. More parameters, considering also QoR, are presented by O'Sullivan et al. (2002), but they are not widely used in practice. Moreover, QoR properties are not considered in most of the methods trying to compute the values of non-functional properties. Therefore, in the remaining part of this chapter, whenever a reference to QoS is made, it refers to those quality parameters of a service that are computable (therefore, in most cases they exclude QoR parameters). Whenever a clear differentiation needs to be made between quality of result and quality of execution, respective terms are used.

METHODS AND APPROACHES TO DERIVE VALUES OF NON-FUNCTIONAL PROPERTIES

The simplest way to derive values of NFP is to rely on service providers advertising this information. However, taking directly the values advertised by a service provider is not advisable. It requires users to trust the accuracy of the values declared by service providers. However, service providers do have an interest in overestimating NFP of their services, so a solution allowing measurement of (programmatically) the values of NFP for verification purposes is needed. Moreover, values of non functional parameters are often assumed to be constant in time and space (service location), but they may change, depending on the details of the service request, execution environment, and so forth. For example, the response time of a Web service may be less than 5 minutes during the working days, but during the weekends, it may be less than 1 minute as the interest in the particular service decreases.

To avoid the problems of accuracy of non-functional properties' values given by service providers, some other methods to derive (or verify) their values are needed (Abramowicz et al., 2005). Ran (2003) proposes a QoS model using a QoS certifier to verify published QoS criteria. The approach requires all Web services providers to advertise their services with the QoS certifier. However, this approach does not take into account the dynamism of the environment and the fact that the values of a Web service change in time. The approach does not provide, for example, methods to update the QoS values automatically and it lacks the details regarding the verification process.

Sheth, Cordoso, Miller, and Kochut (2002) propose a QoS middleware infrastructure that requires a built-in tool to monitor metrics of NFP automatically. Such an approach requires the willingness of service providers to give up some of their autonomy. It may also require service providers to cover execution costs. Moreover, if the polling interval is set to too long, the QoS will not be up-to-date. If the polling interval is set to too of a short time, it might incur a high performance overhead. A similar approach emphasizing a service reputation, is proposed by Maximilien and Singh (2002a, 2002b).

Another approach obtains information on values of QoS parameters from the users themselves. When collecting quality information from the users feedback, each user is required to evaluate QoS (and at the same time QoR) of the consumed service. The main advantage of this approach is that QoS values can be computed based on the real user experience (up-to-date runtime execution data). The main disadvantage is the fact that a user judgment is not objective; users use different definitions of quality, have different past experiences, and so forth.

In other approaches called "*a'posteriori approach*" (Casati, Castellanos, Dayal, & Shan, 2004) QoS values are solely collected through an active monitoring. The monitoring can be performed by a user, service broker or platform, dedicated QoS registry (Kuropka & Weske, 2006; Liu et al., 2004), or an already mentioned QoS certifier (Ran, 2003). The data are collected from the actual consumption of a service and therefore are accurate and objective. One avoids the necessity to install rather expensive middleware in order to constantly check large numbers of service providers. However, there is a high overhead since QoS must be constantly checked for a large number of Web services. On the other hand, the approach that relies on a third party to rate or endorse a particular service provider is expensive and static in nature.

When the service related data collection is envisioned through, for example, workflow monitoring or user feedback, another important issue is how to compute the values of quality-related parameters from the collected data. There are a few initiatives to solve the problem. One of them (Maximilien & Singh, 2004) suggests performing an analysis of past executions of atomic and composite services by using data mining and workflow log mining techniques. Moreover, some statistical methods can be applied as well (Liu et al., 2004).

Workflow management systems are a very important infrastructure for complex applications. They usually register the start and completion of activities as well as other events that occur during execution. This information is stored as workflow log files (Aalst, Zhang, Shanahas, & et al., 2003) that further are processed using workflow and process mining techniques. The goal of workflow mining is to find a workflow model on a basis of a workflow log (Aalst et al., 2003). In turn, process mining is a method of distilling a structured process description from a set of real executions (Aalst et al., 2003). Many methods to perform these tasks were developed (e.g., probabilistic workflow mining, or Petri nets [Aalst et al., 2003]) and may be successfully applied also to the Web services area.

In the next section, the Web services profiling, being an alternative method to derive the values of non-functional properties of a Web service, is presented.

WEB SERVICE PROFILING, SERVICE PROFILE, AND ITS ELEMENTS

Service profiling is a process of computation of values of non-functional properties. The main goal of service profiling is to create service profiles of atomic and composite services. A service profile may be defined as an up-to-date description of a selected subset of non-functional properties of a service. It not only characterizes a service but also allows for services comparison based on aggregated values of non-functional parameters and, in consequence, selection of a service most suited to the requirements of a user.

In order to compute the values of non-functional properties, service profiling needs first to collect information on services executions, aggregate it, and then derive required information. The raw data may come from multiple data sources. Every source has its own specific purpose and provides different information. The following possible sources of information that further feed the profiling system with appropriate data may be distinguished: service registries, monitoring data, data coming from service level agreements (SLA) storing information on contracted QoS values, feedback from service consumers about obtained service quality, and so forth.

The aim of the Web services profiling is to perform fair and open NFP computation. Therefore, as the service execution history data are the most objective and reliable source of information on the service, they are in fact the primary source of information. The Web services profiling does not perform only the core workflow mining. It analyses log files in order to obtain data needed for the profiling process, but, in addition, it takes advantage of the raw data collected from service properties defined in SLA, published by service providers, and obtained from users' feedback. For instance, it compares contracted values from SLA against these from execution. In consequence, it is possible to check to what extent the agreement between a provider and a consumer is fulfilled. Moreover, appropriate algorithms may discover which values of particular parameters are, for example, likely to be guaranteed by providers.

Service profiling is, in our opinion, a trustworthy method of service quality measurement. It does not rely on providers' declarations about quality of their services. Statistical procedures used to compute values, data coming from execution logs, and so forth, assure high reliability of results of service profiling. The information declared initially by a service provider might be verified by what is stated in SLA, being approved by its provider and then by the results of the analysis of execution data. This kind of verification increases the reliability of our mechanism and we do not need a third party to verify the correctness of the values of profile parameters as procedures are transparent and parameters precisely defined. In addition, a service profiling mechanism is generic (a number of parameters it operates on may be easy modified) and independent of the service description provided by a service provider.

Service Profile

As already stated, a service profile may be defined as an up-to-date description of a subset of non-functional properties of a service. It allows for services comparison based on non-functional parameters and selection of the service most suited to the requirements of a user.

In order to create an adequate service description one needs to consider that the collected or derived data, taken into account by a service profiling mechanism, may differ in terms of its stability in time. Regarding the type of information on services, we can distinguish three main categories:

- **Static Information:** Values of service properties that do not change over time, such as name of the service, and are provided by a service provider.
- **Semistatic Information:** Values of service properties that may change over time, such as quality of service and price. This information changes periodically, but not very often.
- **Dynamic Information:** Values of service properties that may be (and usually are) different in every execution of the service. It relates mainly to the network related quality of service.

From the profiling point of view, the most interesting parameters are the dynamic and semistatic ones. In addition, parameters that are estimated and finally included in a service profile may be simple reflections of service behaviour or adequately aggregated to show an overall quality of a service. Therefore, we consider two groups of non-functional properties:

- **Simple Properties:** Values of service properties that can be monitored on an individual level. This is mostly information presented in service level agreements. Such properties may include, for example, latency time, execution cos,t and so on.
- **Derived Properties:** Where additional manipulation is needed (performed by a service profiling system). Such properties may include reliability, availability, or, in our case, a synthetic indicator.

Our belief is that a service profile should be easily interchanged between building blocks of SOA systems. In order to allow for simple messaging and processing of profiles, we decided to represent them

Figure 1. Service profile structure - class diagram

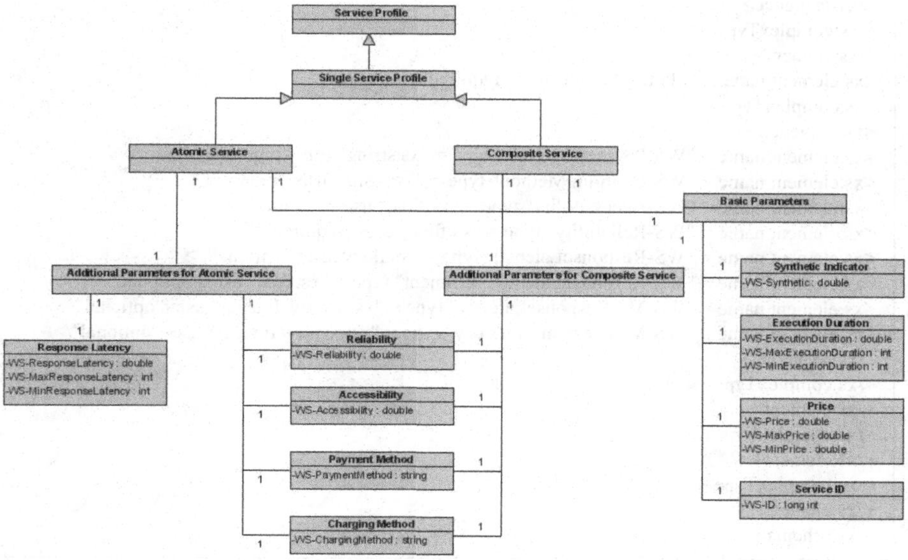

as XML documents. The greatest advantage of this solution is that XML schema is easily verifiable and interpretable by machines. A standardized form of a service profile makes it easy to be adapted in industrial applications.

Because of flexibility of service profiling, the set of parameters included in a profile may vary due to different quality parameters considered in different IT systems. The exemplary structure of a profile (as seen in Figure 1) was derived based on the requirements defined in the already mentioned ASG project.

The excerpt of a service profile schema is presented in the Listing 1. Please note that for some parameters, average, minimal, and maximal values are determined. These values may be helpful when a

Listing 1. Excerpt of exemplary service profile schema

```xml
<?xml version="1.0" encoding="UTF-8"?>
<xs:schema xmlns:xs="http://www.w3.org/2001/XMLSchema">
<xs:element name="ProfileData">
<xs:complexType>
<xs:element name="ServiceProfile" use="required">
<xs:complexType>
<xs:element name="BasicData" use="required">
<xs:complexType>
<xs:sequence>
<xs:element name = "WS-ID" type = "xs:string" use="required"/>
<xs:element name = "WS-Price" type = "xs:float" use="required"/>
<xs:element name = "WS-MinPrice" type = "xs:float" use="required"/>
<xs:element name = "WS-MaxPrice" type = "xs:float" use="required"/>
<xs:element name = "WS-ExecutionDuration" type = "xs:float" use="required"/>
<xs:element name = "WS-ExecutionDurationFulfilment" type = "xs:float" use="required"/>
<xs:element name = "WS-MinExecutionDuration" type = "xs:positiveInteger" use="required"/>
<xs:element name = "WS-MaxExecutionDuration" type = "xs:positiveInteger" use="required"/>
<xs:element name = "WS-Synthetic" type = "xs:float" use="required"/>
<xs:element name = "WS-SlaFulfilmentIndicator" type = "xs:float" use="required"/>
</xs:sequence>
</xs:complexType>
</xs:element>
<xs:element name="AdditionalData" use="required">
<xs:complexType>
<xs:sequence>
<xs:element name = "WS-PaymentMethod" type = "xs:string" use="required"/>
<xs:element name = "WS-ChargingMethod" type = "xs:string" use="required"/>
<xs:element name = "WS-Accessibility" type = "xs:float" use="required"/>
<xs:element name = "WS-Reliability" type = "xs:float" use="required"/>
<xs:element name = "WS-ResponseLatency" type = "xs:float" use="optional"/>
<xs:element name = "WS-ResponseLatencyFulfilment" type = "xs:float" use="optional"/>
<xs:element name = "WS-MinResponseLatency" type = "xs:positiveInteger" use="optional"/>
<xs:element name = "WS-MaxResponseLatency" type = "xs:positiveInteger" use="optional"/>
</xs:sequence>
</xs:complexType>
</xs:element>
</xs:complexType>
</xs:element>
</xs:complexType>
</xs:element>
</xs:schema>
```

Figure 2. Types of Web services events. Based on Aalst et al. (2003)

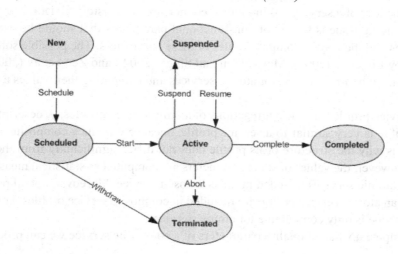

user precisely expresses the user's needs on quality parameters. Therefore, a user may specify that the user is looking for a service where parameters meet accurately expressed criteria.

Additionally, a service profiling system may offer provider profiles that show how, in general, services of a given provider behave. They may be useful to represent the overall quality of services provided by a concrete provider. These profiles are more quality-oriented, whereas service profiles are more performance-oriented. In this case, quality orientation means that time-related QoS parameters are less important than the fact whether a given service was accessible or produced expected results.

Service Profile Computation

The most popular information sources for service profiling are execution logs. These log files usually have a strictly defined structure (Aalst et al., 2003), so the automated processing of them is feasible and algorithms are rather straightforward. For example, the execution duration may be easily counted as a difference between end time and start time of a service execution (these values are stored in the log file). Of course, to compute the values of other parameters other methods may be required. For instance, in order to compute the value of a reliability parameter, a profiling system needs to keep track of service execution states. In our approach, we consider the finite state machine of Web service transitions as shown in the Figure 2.

Therefore, it is possible to determine the number of started services that were completed. Thus, the assessment of reliability parameter is not a problem. A similar approach is used for accessibility parameter computation. For more details please refer Kowalkiewicz, Ludwig, Kaczmarek, and Zyskowski (2005). In the Table 5 we present an exemplary set of non-functional properties and outline methods of their computation.

When creating a service profile the time horizon is taken into account. A user may need a particular instance of a service only once in a given point of time or may need to use the service a few times in a given time period. Therefore, the horizon of the prognosis should be considered. In the first case, short-time information about a service is important, and in the second case, more attention should be paid to the long-term behaviour of a service, taking into account also more historical data.

Another challenging issue is the set of non-functional parameters that should be used to describe composite services and the way to compute values of these parameters. The possible solutions may be found presented by Liu et al. (2004), Maximilien and Singh (2004), and Zeng et al. (2003). They suggest using a similar set of attributes, as for atomic services and computing their values using statistical methods.

Composite service profiles are the aggregations of atomic service profiles. A description of a composite service profile is very similar to a service profile, because it treats a composite service like an atomic one. That is why the structure of its profile does not differ significantly from the profile of an atomic service. However, the values of some parameters are computed as statistical measures based on characteristics of atomic services included in the composed service. Moreover, not all parameters that are computed for an atomic service profile are included in composite service profiles. For example, the response latency value is only computable for atomic services.

In order to compute a value of quality parameters of a composite service we can proceed twofold:

- The execution log mining may be performed in order to compute values of parameters using methods similar to these for atomic services;
- A composite service execution plan may be used to compute *hypothetical value* of quality parameter. Such plans are usually described using business process execution language for Web services (BPEL4WS) language. First, the average values for each atomic service included in the composition are computed, then the plan is analysed, the critical path is identified, and the hypothetical value is computed. For instance, the execution duration of the composite service is computed as a sum of execution durations of services being on the critical path. Other calculations include analysis of workflow patterns, determination of how many times services were executed (in case of loops), and so forth. Details about such computation are given by Kowalkiewicz et al. (2005).

It can be very interesting to rank services according their quality. In order to do that, a method that would allow one to compare objects (in our case, services) with regard to different properties that describe these objects was defined. Our decision was to take advantage of the multiple criteria analysis (MCA) that ideally fitted to our needs. We used the MCA method to rank services based on their quality attributes. This ranking was created by computing a synthetic indicator reflecting the overall service quality. Then, it was possible to compare the values of synthetic indicators of several services and make

Table 5. Some parameters of service profile and their computation methods

Parameter name	Computation method
Execution duration	Difference between end and start time of service execution
Accessibility	Number of successful invocations divided by all the invocations in a given time period
Reliability	Number of successful executions divided by all of the executions in a given time period
Price	Average price in a given period of time
Synthetic indicator	Statistical aggregation of all considered parameters denoting an overall quality of a service

a choice between them. The detailed description of MCA and the procedure to compute the value of a synthetic indicator is described by Abramowicz, Haniewicz, Kaczmarek, and Zyskowski (2006b).

Dynamic Service Profiling in the Adaptive Services Grid Project

Taking into account the issues discussed in the previous section, the architecture of the service profiling system should consist of at least a few components. It should include the repository that will store the data gathered by the system and should have component(s) responsible for communication with the data sources. Moreover, it should provide interfaces that allow all interested parties to ask queries. Finally, it should have the profiling mechanism, responsible for analysing the data and deriving/computing the values of parameters, to be included in a service profile.

As an example of the architecture of service profiling system, the dynamic service profiling component of the Adaptive Services Grid project, may be presented. The main goal of the ASG project (Kuropka & Weske, 2006) was to develop a proof-of-concept prototype of a platform for adaptive services discovery, creation, composition, enactment, as well as negotiations and service profiling. In order to support the above-mentioned interactions, the ASG platform and mechanisms require the ability to differentiate and compare different services and service substitutes (services having the same functionality). There are some requirements that need to be met in order to make the service differentiation feasible. First, the non-functional parameters must be taken into account, as every customer perceives the service not only from the side of what functionality it gives, but is also interested in non-functional properties of the service. The next issue is to deliver a QoS model that everybody would accept. Such a standardized QoS model is the first step to the agreement on monitoring mechanisms, common SLAs, and other elements that should be a part of every mature marketplace. The last challenge is to create adequate description of a service that will give a user hints about the distinctive features of service substitutes. Thanks to the monitoring, it should be possible to analyse the information coming from service executions, SLA violations, and so forth. Based on the execution data and users' preferences, it is reasonable to create

Figure 3. Service delivery process in the ASG. ©Krause, 2005 (used with permission)

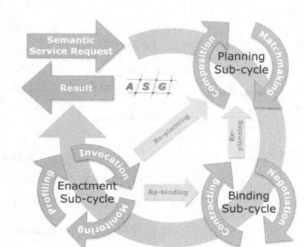

a service profile which reflects QoS values of a given service in a considered time horizon. Moreover, the user should be capable of ranking these profiles and choosing the most suitable Web service. Such a mechanism is implemented in the Adaptive Services Grid platform (Kuropka & Weske, 2006) using a dynamic service profiling (DSP) mechanism. The ASG service delivery process is presented in the figure below.

The architecture of a dynamic service profiling (see Figure 4) system, being a part of the entire ASG platform, consists of a few components (Abramowicz, Kaczmarek, Kowalkiewicz, & Zyskowski, 2006):

- Data collector, which is responsible for collecting data (by either a push or a pull method) from different sources, processing them, and saving properly aggregated to the DSP repository.
- Service profiler, which is responsible for deriving QoS attributes to answer requests. The Service profiler creates an up-to-date profile of a service (or a provider), whenever it receives a query. Two types of queries may be distinguished: a request for a profile of composed service, taking time horizon into consideration; and a request for profiles and a ranking of a set of atomic services, taking time horizon into consideration. When creating profiles, the service profiler uses the following data about services: data from the provider's declaration (service registry), and values of service attributes form the past execution (DSP repository). In order to create a profile, the appropriate values of characteristics, depending on the prognosis horizon, are computed. Then, based on the computed values a synthetic indicator for a service is created. As an interaction with a user is not implemented, default user preferences are used. After computing the indicators for all of the services returned for the given query, services can be compared and the best of them can be identified.
- DSP repository, which is the internal persistent data storage fed by the data collector and responsible for storing all data relevant to service profiles. Only the data collector can change information in the DSP repository. Other subsystems have read-only access to the repository.
- Event Manager, which handles workflow events. The event manager is the subcomponent responsible for processing workflow events and receiving execution logs. If any crucial information is included in such an event, it is passed to the data collector for further analysis.

Figure 4. Architecture of DSP system

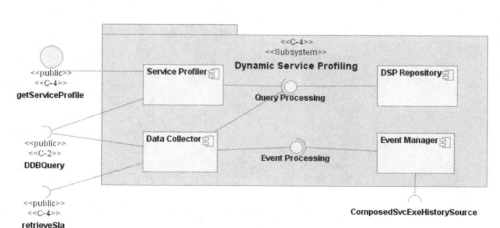

As verified in the prototype implementation within the ASG project, such an architecture fulfils goals and requirements of a service profiling system.

SUMMARY

This chapter familiarizes users with the idea of Web services profiling. As a background, the current initiatives in the field of Web services description, especially non-functional properties and methods to derive the values of these properties, were presented. Moreover, the readers were introduced to different approaches to the quality-of-service concept. The focus of the chapter was placed on Web service profiling successfully implemented within the ASG system. A service profile, in its final state, aggregates all measured values of quality parameters to give a user the holistic view on a service quality. Taking into account information from profiles, it is possible to select the most suitable service, with regard to the user-specific quality expectations.

REFERENCES

Aalst, W. v. D., et al. (2003). Workflow mining: A survey of issues and approaches. *Data Knowledge Egineering, 47*(2), 237-267.

Abramowicz, W., Filipowska, A., Kaczmarek, M., Kaczmarek, T., Kowalkiewicz, M., Rutkowski, W., et al. (2006). *Service interdependencies: Insights into use cases for service compositions.* Paper presented at the IFIP 2006.

Abramowicz, W., Haniewicz, K., Kaczmarek, M., & Zyskowski, D. (2006a). *Automatic Web services interactions - requirements, challenges and limits from the F-WebS system perspective.* Paper presented at the International Conference on Next Generation Web Services Practices, Seoul, Korea.

Abramowicz, W., Haniewicz, K., Kaczmarek, M., & Zyskowski, D. (2006b). *Filtering of Semantic Web services with F-WebS system.* Paper presented at the The Semantic Web: ASWC 2006 Workshop.

Abramowicz, W., Kaczmarek, M., Kowalkiewicz, M., & Zyskowski, D. (2005). *A survey of QoS computation for Web services profiling.* Paper presented at the 18th International Conference on Computer Applications in Industry and Engineering (ISCA), Honolulu.

Abramowicz, W., Kaczmarek, M., Kowalkiewicz, M., & Zyskowski, D. (2006). *Architecture for service profiling.* Paper presented at the Modelling, Design and Analysis for Service-Oriented Architecture Workshop in conjunction with the 2006 IEEE International Conferences on Services Computing (SCC 2006) and Web Services (ICWS 2006), Chicago.

Abramowicz, W., Kaczmarek, M., & Zyskowski, D. (2006). *Duality in Web services reliability.* Paper presented at the International Conference on Internet and Web Applications and Services (ICIW'06). Guadeloupe, French Caribbean.

Baida, Z., Gordijn, J., Omelayenko, B., & Akkermans, H. (2004). *A shared service terminology for online service provisioning.* Paper presented at the Sixth International Conference on Electronic Commerce (ICEC04), Delft, The Netherlands.

Casati, F., Castellanos, M., Dayal, U., & Shan, M. C. (2004, November 2004). *Probabilistic, context-sensitive and goal-oriented service selection.* Paper presented at the ICSOC'04, New York.

Eenoo, C. V., Hylooz, O., & Khan, K. M. (2005). *Addressing non-functional properties in software architecture using ADL.* Paper presented at the 6th Australian Workshop on Software and Systems Architectures - AWSA'05, Brisbane, Australia.

Farrel, J., & Lausen, H. (2006). *Semantic Annotations for WSDL.* DERI Innsbruck.

Kowalkiewicz, M., Ludwig, A., Kaczmarek, M., & Zyskowski, D. (2005). *Documented mechanisms for dynamic service prpofiling and agreement life-cycle management* (ASG internal deliverable, FP6-IST-004617).

Krause, H. (2005). *Next generation service delivery: Adaptive services grid, European project, 2007.*

Kuropka, D., & Weske, M. (2006, January). *Die adaptive services grid platform: Motivation, potential, funktionsweise und anwendungsszenarien.* Paper presented at the EMISA Forum.

Kuster, U., Koenig-Ries, B., Stern, M., & Klein, M. (2007, May 8-12). *DIANE: An integrated approach to automated service discovery, matchmaking and composition.* Paper presented at the WWW 2007, Banff, Alberta, Canada.

Lara, R., & Olmedilla, D. (2005, June). *Discovery and contracting of Semantic Web services.* Paper presented at the Position Paper for the Workshop on Frameworks for Semantics in Web Services, Innsbruck, Austria.

Liu, Y., Ngu, A. H. H., & Zeng, L. (2004, May). *QoS computation and policing in dynamic Web service selection.* Paper presented at the 13th International Conference on World Wide Web (WWW), New York.

Liu, C., Peng, Y., & Chen, J. (2006). *Web services description ontology-based service discovery model.* Paper presented at the International Conference on Web Intelligence (WI 2006).

Maximilien, E. M., & Singh, M. P. (2002a). Reputation and endorsement for Web services. *ACM SIGecom Exchanges, 3*(1), 24-31.

Maximilien, E. M., & Singh, M. P. (2002b). *Conceptual model of Web services reputation.* SIGMOD Record.

Maximilien, E. M., & Singh, M. P. (2004, November, 2004). *Towards autonomic Web services trust and selection.* Paper presented at the ICSOC'04, New York.

Menasce, D. A. (2002). QoS issues in Web services. *IEEE Internet Computing, 6*(6), 72-75.

Noll, J. (2004). *ASG based scenarios in telecommunications, telematics and enhanced enterprise IT.* Retrieved May 26, 2008, from http://asg-platform.org

O'Sullivan, J., Edmond, D., & Hofstede, A. T. (2002). What's in a service? Towards an accurate description of non-functional properties of Web services. *Distributed and Parallel Databases,* (12), 117-133.

Preist, C. (2004, November). *A conceptual architecture for Semantic Web services.* Paper presented at the International Semantic Web Conference 2004 (ISWC 2004).

Ran, S. (2003). A model for Web services discovery with QoS. *ACM SIGecom Exchanges, 4*(1), 1-10.

Roman, D., et al. (2006). *WWW: WSMO, WSML and WSMX in a nutshell.* Paper presented at the First Asian Semantic Web Conference (ASWC 2006).

Rosa, N. S., Cunha, P. R., Freire, L., & Justo, G. R. (2002, March 29, 2005). *Process NFL: A language for describing non-functional properties.* Paper presented at the 35th Annual Hawaii International Conference (HICSS), Hawaii.

Sheth, A., Cordoso, J., Miller, J., & Kochut, K. (2002, July). *QoS for service-oriented middleware.* Paper presented at the 6rh World Multiconference on Systemics Cybernetics and Informatics (SCI02).

Toma, I. (2006). *Non-functional properties in Web services.* DERI.

UDDI. (2004). *UDDI Version 3.0.2.* UDDI Spec Technical Committee.

W3C. (2004). *Owl-s: Semantic markup for Web services.* Retrieved May 26, 2008, from http://www.w3.org/Submission/OWL-S/

W3C. (2007). *WSDL 2.0.* Retrieved May 26, 2008, from http://www.w3.org/TR/wsdl20

Zeng, L., Benatallah, B., Dumas, M., Kalagnanam, J., & Sheng, Q. Z. (2003, May). *Quality driven Web services composition.* Paper presented at the 12th International Conference on World Wide Web (WWW), Budapest, Hungary.

Chapter VI
Enhancing the Web Service Description and Discovery Processes with QoS

Kyriakos Kritikos
Institute of Computer Science, FORTH, Greece

Dimitris Plexousakis
Institute of Computer Science, FORTH, Greece

ABSTRACT

As the Web service (WS) paradigm gains popularity for its promise to transform the way business is conducted, the number of deployed WSs grows with a fast rate. While sophisticated semantic discovery mechanisms have been devised to overcome the UDDI's syntactic discovery solution in order to increase recall and precision, the amount of functionally equivalent WSs returned is still large. One solution to this problem is the description of the nonfunctional aspects of WSs, including quality of service (QoS). QoS encompasses the performance of WSs and can be used as a discriminating factor for refining WS advertisement results. However, most efforts presented so far are purely syntactic in nature and do not capture all aspects of QoS-based WS description, leading to imprecise syntactic discovery mechanisms. In this chapter, a definition of QoS for WSs is provided and its important role in WS management is emphasized. An analysis of the requirements that are imposed on the WS description and discovery processes based on QoS is given along with a review of related work in QoS-based WS description and discovery, highlighting the main deficiencies of recent approaches. Then, a complete semantic approach for QoS-based WS description and discovery is presented and analyzed. The chapter concludes by drawing directions for further research.

INTRODUCTION

Web services (WSs) are modular, self-describing, loosely-coupled, platform, and programming language-agnostic software applications that can be advertised, located, and used across the Internet using a set of standards such as SOAP, Web service description language (WSDL) (Christensen, Curbera, Meredith, & Weerawarana, 2001), and UDDI. They encapsulate application functionality and information resources, and are made available through standard programmatic interfaces. Service-oriented architectures (SOAs) (Papazoglou, 2003) promise to enable the creation of business applications from independently developed and deployed services. A key advantage of SOAs is that they enable services to be dynamically selected and integrated at runtime, thus enabling system flexibility and adaptability, which are vital autonomic attributes for modern business needs.

The dynamic selection of services in SOA is actually the outcome of the WS discovery process. This process takes as input the description of the requested WS and the descriptions of the advertised WSs that are published in WS registries or repositories. It is separated into two subprocesses: matchmaking and selection. The matchmaking subprocess matches each WS advertisement with the WS request. The resulting matches are ordered in decreasing order based on user-given criteria by the WS selection subprocess. As a result, WS requesters are assisted in selecting the best candidate WS according to their criteria. The dynamic integration of WSs is the task of the WS composition process that in turn depends on the WS discovery process. However, this process is out of the scope of this chapter and will not be further analyzed.

Unfortunately, current techniques for WS discovery only partially address the SOA vision. These techniques rely on static descriptions of service interfaces and other general nonfunctional service attributes for publishing and finding WSs. This situation creates two problems. First, syntactic discovery efforts return results with low precision and recall. Second, no means are provided in order to select among multiple services that appear to deliver the same functionality.

The first problem is addressed by combining *Semantic Web* and WS technologies. Ontologies are used, which provide meaning to concepts and relationships between them and thus lead to semantic WS descriptions and discovery algorithms. These enhanced discovery algorithms equipped with Semantic Web technologies provide more precise and recallable results. One recent result of the joint Semantic Web and WS efforts is OWL-S (Sycara et. al., 2003), which is a W3C member submission.

The second problem can be addressed by taking into account a big subset of all possible nonfunctional properties of WSs, collectively referred to as quality of service (QoS). QoS does not only encompass network characteristics like bandwidth, latency, or jitter but it is used in a broader end-to-end sense. It encompasses any characteristic of the service host, the service implementation, the intervening network, and the client system that may affect the quality of the service delivered. Therefore it has a substantial impact on users' expectations from a service and can be used as a discriminating factor among functionally equivalent WS advertisements. Thus WS descriptions must be enhanced with QoS descriptions. Additionally, WS discovery algorithms should perform QoS-based filtering (matchmaking) and ranking (selection) on WS advertisements in order to produce fewer ranked results.

Unfortunately, all research efforts in QoS-based WS description provide a syntactic, poor, and nonextensible QoS model. This has the effect that concepts like "availability" are matched even if they are differently defined. As a result, QoS-based WS offers and demands are not properly aligned and the QoS-based WS discovery processes return results with low precision and recall. However, even if some form of semantics is used, users tend to have different conceptualizations of the same entities.

So the above problem still remains. In addition, current QoS-based WS discovery algorithms are either ineffective and inaccurate or they do not provide advanced categorization of results. Moreover, they do not produce useful results when the QoS-based WS demands are over-constrained.

The above situation clearly states the need for a complete semantic framework for QoS-based WS description and discovery. This framework is covered by the semantic approach analyzed in this chapter. This approach proposes a semantically rich and extensible QoS model for WS description. In addition, a semantic matching algorithm for the most important aspect of QoS for WSs, the QoS metric, is proposed and analyzed. With the above two proposals, QoS-based WS offers and demands are properly defined and aligned. Finally, a constraint-satisfaction-based approach for QoS-based WS discovery is proposed that is accurate and precise, provides advanced categorization of results, and returns useful results even if QoS-based WS demands are over-constrained.

This chapter is organized as follows: Section "The Role of QoS for Web Services" provides a comprehensive analysis of the conceptualization of QoS for WSs and the main domain-independent QoS attributes. In addition, the role that QoS can play in the management of WSs will be elaborated. In the next section, "Requirements and Related Work for QoS-Based Web Service Description and Discovery", the requirements for successful QoS-based WS description and discovery are analyzed. Based on this analysis, a review of related work highlights the main deficiencies of the presented approaches. These deficiencies give rise to the need for a complete semantic approach for QoS-based description and discovery of WSs. This need is realized by the approach presented and analyzed in section "Proposed Approach." The last section, "Discussion," draws conclusions and identifies open research questions.

THE ROLE OF QOS FOR WEB SERVICES

This section comprises of three subsections. Subsection "QoS Definition" defines the QoS concept in the WS context. Subsection "QoS Attributes Exposure" unveils the domain-independent QoS attributes/metrics that should be incorporated into a QoS-based WS description. Finally, subsection "Benefits of QoS Usage for Web Services" explains the benefits of using QoS for WSs and Web processes (WP).

QoS Definition

The international quality standard ISO 9000 (Liebesman, 1994) describes quality as "the totality of features and characteristics of a product or service that bear on its ability to satisfy stated or implied needs" (Ran, 2003, p. 7). According to Deora, Shao, Gray, and Fiddian (2003), what defines quality is vague, and different views exist in different studies and from different perspectives. The following three views are, however, most common:

- **Quality as Functionality.** This view considers quality in terms of the amount of functionality that a service can offer to its users.
- **Quality as Conformance.** This view sees quality as being synonymous with meeting specifications. For example, if service provider (SP) 1 specified in its service agreement that it would provide 1 Mb/s bandwidth for its news service and SP1 did provide users with 1 Mb/s bandwidth (or more) at all times in its operation, then SP1 is usually considered as offering good quality of service.

- **Quality as Reputation.** This view links quality to users' perception of a service in general. It is worth noting that this perception is typically built over the time of the service's existence.

These different views of quality require QoS to be monitored and measured differently. Quality as functionality characterizes the design of a service and can only be measured by comparing the service against other services offering similar functionalities. Quality as conformance, on the other hand, can be monitored for each service individually, and usually requires the user's experience of the use of the service in order to measure the "promise" against the "delivery." Finally, reputation can be regarded as a reference to a service's consistency over time in offering both functionality and conformance qualities, and can therefore be measured through the other two types of quality over time.

While it is possible to establish all three types of quality for a service in an service-oriented computing (SOC) environment, it is perhaps most interesting and relevant to understand how quality as conformance may be monitored and measured. The reasons for this are the following. First, we regard that the first type of quality can be evaluated by a functional WS discovery engine as a static QoS attribute. Second, the reputation of a service is just an indicator of the overall QoS of the service over time that depends on user expectations and other immeasurable factors (e.g., advertisement, financial and political interests, etc.). So reputation is just another measurable QoS property.

Thus, by the above definition and view, we consider QoS of a WS as *a set of nonfunctional characteristics/attributes that may impact the quality of the service offered by the WS*. If a WS is advertised to have certain values (or range of values) in these QoS attributes, then we say that the WS *conforms* to the provisioning of a certain *QoS level*.

QoS Attributes

As specified in the previous definition, QoS is a set of nonfunctional attributes. However, the big question is what are these attributes and do they affect only the WS implementation? To our opinion, QoS does not only encompass network characteristics like bandwidth, latency, or jitter but it is used in a broader end-to-end sense. It encompasses any characteristic of the service host, the service implementation, the intervening network, and the client system that may affect the quality of the service delivered. In this subsection, after reviewing QoS research for several domains generally applicable to WSs based on the nature of WSs, we select those QoS attributes that are common in these domains and that are directly applicable to WSs. These are the so called cross-domain QoS attributes.

Quality of service has been at the focus of research in several domains. The term "quality of service" has been used for expressing nonfunctional requirements for different areas, such as network research community (Cruz, 1995; Georgiadis, Guérin, Peris, & Sivarajan, 1996; Salamatian & Fdida, 2001) and in real time issues (Clark, Shenker, & Zhang, 1992). There is some research effort in defining QoS in distributed systems. The focus is primarily on how to express the QoS for a system, and how these requirements are propagated to the resource manager to fulfil the QoS requirements (Tian, Gramm, Nabulsi, Ritter, Schiller, & Voigt, 2003). Sivashanmugam, Sheth, Miller, Verma, Aggarwal, and Rajasekaran (2003) present a layered model for representing QoS for telecommunication applications. This model presents service quality function, QoS schema mapping, and price-QoS trade-off. Frølund and Koistinen (1998) present a QoS specification language. They advocate its use for designing distributed object system, in conjunction with the functional design. Sabata, Chatterjee, Davis, Sydir, and Lawrence (1997) categorize the QoS from different viewpoints, that is, application, system, and resource. It specifies QoS in terms of metrics and policy.

All the above research efforts categorize and define QoS from their own perspectives with some overlap between them. However, some QoS attributes have been found to be common in most of the above research efforts and are directly applicable to WSs. These are general, cross-domain QoS attributes, that is, they are independent of the domain the WS adheres to. Of course, there will also be some domain-dependent QoS attributes that will depend on the domain(s) of knowledge a WS applies to. For example, QoS attributes regarding information quality will be important for a data warehouse WS (Lee, Strong, Kahn, & Wang, 2002). Another more specific example is the following: A service such as a car rental service will involve attributes belonging to multiple domains, such as the travel and retail domains. Attributes such as price belong to both domains, but an attribute such as "flexibility of reservation changes" has a specific meaning in the travel domain. However, determining the attributes that apply to a particular domain is nontrivial and needs to be decided by the community of users and providers as they converse towards ways to distinguish and evaluate different offerings. For this reason, we are not going to enumerate and explain the meaning of any possible QoS domain-dependent attribute that characterizes any possible domain.

There are many aspects of QoS important to WSs that are organized into QoS attributes. Each attribute needs to have a set of quantifiable parameters or metrics. As further research is needed in this area, we are not going to reveal any QoS metric. Here, each QoS attribute is briefly described. To facilitate the description, the attributes are grouped into different types. This categorization is based on the research works of Anbazhagan and Nagarajan (2002), Frølund and Koistinen (1998), Lee, Jeon, Lee, Jeong, and Park (2003), Ran (2003), Sumra and Arulazi (2003), and Tian et al. (2003).

Runtime Related QoS

- **Scalability:** The capability of increasing the computing capacity of a service provider's computer system and the system's ability to process more operations or transactions in a given period. It is related to performance.
- **Capacity:** Limit of concurrent requests which should be provided with guaranteed performance.
- **Performance:** A measure of the speed in completing a service request. It is measured by
  - **Response time:** The guaranteed max (or average or min) time required to complete a service request (related to capacity).
  - **Latency:** Time taken between when the service request arrives and the time when the request is being serviced.
  - **Throughput:** The number of completed service requests over a time period. Throughput is related to latency/capacity.
  - **Execution time:** The time taken by a WS to process its sequence of activities.
  - **Transaction time:** The time that passes while the WS is completing one complete transaction.
- **Reliability:** The ability of a service to perform its required functions under stated conditions for a specified period of time. Reliability is also related to the assured and ordered delivery of messages being transmitted and received by service requestors and providers. It can be measured by:
  - **Mean time between failure (MTBF)**
  - **Mean time to failure (MTF)**
  - **Mean time To transition (MTTT)**

- ○ **Availability:** It is the probability the system is up and related to reliability. It can be measured as:

$$A = \frac{\langle upTime \rangle}{\langle totalTime \rangle} = \frac{\langle upTime \rangle}{\left(\langle upTime \rangle + \langle downTime \rangle \right)}$$

Where

<upTime> is the total time the system has been up during the measurement period.
<downTime> is the total time the system has been down during the measurement period.
<totalTime> is the total measurement time, it is the sum of *<upTime>* and *<downTime>*.

- ○ **Continuous availability:** It assesses the probability with which a client can access a service an infinite number of times during a particular time period.
- ○ **Failure masking:** It is used to describe what kind of failures a server may expose to its clients. A client must be able to detect and handle any kind of exposed failure. The types of failure than can be exposed are the following: *failure, omission, response, value, state, timing, late,* and *early.* The above types of failures are based on the categorization from Frølund and Koistinen (1998).
- ○ **Operation semantics:** They describe how requests are handled in the case of failure. We can specify that issued requests are executed *exactlyOnce, atLeastOnce,* and *atMostOnce.*
- ○ **Server failure:** Tt describes the way in which a service can fail. That is, whether it will *halt* indefinitely, restart in a well defined *initialState,* or restart *rolledBack* to a previous checkpoint.
- ○ **Data policy:** When a service fails and then restarts, the client needs to know if data returned by the service are still valid.
- **Robustness/ Flexibility:** It is the degree to which a service can function correctly in the presence of invalid, incomplete, or conflicting inputs.
- **Exception handling:** Since it is not possible for the service designer to specify all the possible outcomes and alternatives (especially with various special cases and unanticipated possibilities), exceptions can be expected. Exception handling is how the service handles these exceptions.
- **Accuracy:** Defines the error rate produced by the service.

Transaction Support Related QoS

- *Integrity*: A two-phase commit capability is the mechanism to guarantee the ACID properties for distributed transactions running over tightly coupled systems as if they were a single transaction. It is more difficult in the WSs environment, as the transactions may involve more than one business partner with the possibility of transactions spanning over long time (hours or days); they are also called long running transactions (LRT). The transaction integrity is still described by ACID properties, although it is a much harder to achieve in this case. It may require different mechanisms.

Configuration Management and Cost Related QoS

- **Regulatory:** It is a measure of how well the service is aligned with regulations.
- **Supported Standard:** A measure of whether the service complies with standards (e.g., industry specific standards). This can affect the portability of the service and interoperability of the service with others.
- **Stability/change cycle:** A measure of the frequency of change related to the service in terms of its interface and/or implementation.
- **Guaranteed messaging requirements:** For example, ensuring the order and persistence of the messages.
- **Cost:** It is a measure of the cost involved in requesting the service.
- **Completeness:** A measure of the difference between the specified set of features and the implemented set of features.
- **Reputation:** The reputation $q_{rep}(s)$ of a service s is a measure of its trustworthiness. It mainly depends on end user's experiences on using the service s. Different end users may have different opinions on the same service. The value of the reputation is defined as the average ranking given to the service by end users, that is,

$$q_{rep}(s) = \frac{\sum_{i=1}^{n} R_i}{n},$$

where R_i is the end user's ranking on a service's reputation and n is the number of times the service has been graded. Usually, end users are given a range to rank WSs. For example, in Amazon.com, the range is [0, 5]. Alternatively, a ranking of an end user to a service can be a vector of values of some QoS attributes. From this vector, a QoS value can be obtained which is then averaged over all user rankings to get the overall reputation of the service.

Security Related QoS

The WS provider may apply different approaches and levels of providing security policy depending on the needs of the WS requestor. Security for WSs means providing *authentication, authorization, confidentiality, traceability/auditability, data encryption*, and *no-repudiation*. Each of these attributes can be supported by the adoption of specific security protocols.

Network Related QoS

Today, WS technologies researchers assume that existing communication infrastructures provide reliable communication. Furthermore, researchers in middleware, WSs, and applications take for granted the resources provided by the underlying networks. On the other hand, research activities in certain communication architectures and protocols are performed with less attention to requirements of actual applications. Therefore, most applications cannot actively consume the QoS that may be supported in the communication networks, and on the other hand, common network technologies do not support application-dependent requirements.

To achieve desired QoS for WSs, the QoS mechanisms operating at the WS application level must operate together with the QoS mechanisms operating in the transport network (e.g., RSVP, DiffServ, MPLS, etc.), which are rather independent of the application. In particular, application level QoS parameters should be mapped appropriately to corresponding network level QoS parameters (Lee et al., 2003; Tian et al., 2003). The communication and cooperation between different layers allow an efficient utilization of the underlying network resources as well as a better support of application-dependent requirements. It must be highlighted that the aforementioned mapping of parameters is not the concern of this report. More information on how to achieve this mapping is provided by Lee et al. (2003) and Tian et al. (2003).

Basic network level QoS parameters include network delay, delay variation, and packet loss, and they are described as follows:

- **Network delay:** It is the average length of time a packet traverses in a network.
- **Delay variation:** It is the variation in the interpacket arrival time (leading to gaps, known as jitter, between packets) as introduced by the variable transmission delay over the network.
- **Packet loss:** The Internet does not guarantee delivery of packets. Packets will be dropped under peak loads and during periods of congestion.

In addition, network management mechanisms may also be involved in controlling and managing QoS for WSs.

Benefits of QoS Usage for Web Services

According to Cardoso, Sheth, Miller, Arnold, and Kochut (2004), Web processes constitute the computing model that enables a standard method of building WS applications and processes to connect and exchange information over the Web. For organizations, the ability to characterize WPs based on QoS has four distinct advantages. First, it allows organizations to translate their vision into their business processes more efficiently, since WPs can be designed according to QoS metrics. For e-commerce processes it is important to know the QoS an application will exhibit before making the service available to customers. Second, it enables the selection and execution of WPs based on their QoS to better fulfil customer expectations and requirements. Third, it makes possible the monitoring of WPs based on QoS to assure compliance both with initial QoS requirements and targeted objectives. QoS monitoring allows adaptation strategies to be triggered when undesired metrics are identified or when threshold values are reached. Fourth, it allows for the evaluation of alternative strategies when adaptation becomes necessary. It is essential that the services rendered follow customer specifications to meet their expectations and ensure satisfaction. *Customer expectations and satisfaction can be translated into the quality of service rendered.* Organizations have realized that quality of service management is an important factor in their operations.

As WPs are composed of WSs, all the above advantages of QoS management of WPs also apply to WSs. So WSs can be designed and implemented according to QoS metrics (properties). They can also be discovered and selected based on their QoS capabilities. In addition, they can be monitored in order to reassure the promised QoS levels to the customers. Moreover, monitoring of QoS for WSs can trigger adaptation strategies when undesired metrics are identified, threshold values are reached, and network or software or hardware errors happen. Now, we will closely examine the advantages of QoS description (management) in other nonbasic activities/functions of the service oriented architecture.

After the process of WS selection, the requester chooses the best WS from an ordered WS advertisement list. However, even if WS clients find the appropriate WS, they are not confident that the WS's described QoS levels will actually be delivered during WS execution. For this reason, the WS client and provider enter a multistep negotiation phase, where they try to agree on a trusted third-party entity monitoring QoS levels delivered, on the penalties that will be imposed when one of the two main parties does not keep up with its promises, and on the validity period of the promises. The result of this negotiation phase is a contract or a service level agreement (SLA) document that will give confidence and trust to the entities providing and consuming the service and will lead and guide the process of WS execution. If agreement is not met, the negotiation is stopped and the WS client contacts the next WS from the returned list of the WS selection phase.

When composing a WS, component services are associated to the individual tasks of the composite WS and are invoked during each execution of the WS. However, the number of services providing a given functionality may be large and constantly changing and some of these services will not always be available due to network problems, software evolution and repair, and hardware problems. One solution to this problem is given at design time by QoS-based WS discovery. Another solution is the runtime selection of component services, during the execution of a composite WS, based on quality criteria (i.e., constraints and preferences) and following a local (Benatallah, Sheng, Ngu, & Dumas, 2002) or a global (Zeng, Benatallah, Dumas, Kalagnanam, & Sheng, 2003) selection strategy. In the latter case, service selection is formulated as an optimization problem and linear programming is used to compute optimal execution plans for composite services.

REQUIREMENTS AND RELATED WORK FOR QOS-BASED WEB SERVICE DESCRIPTION AND DISCOVERY

Requirements for QoS-Based Web Service Description and Discovery

Requirements for QoS-Based Web Service Description

After reviewing related work in QoS-based WS description, we have come up with the following requirements (Kritikos & Plexousakis, 2007) that must be satisfied by a QoS-based WS description model:

- **Extensible and formal semantic QoS model:** In the presence of multiple WSs with overlapping or identical functionality, WS requesters need objective QoS criteria to distinguish WSs. However, it is not practical to come up with a standard QoS model that can be used for all WSs in all domains. This is because QoS is a broad concept that encompasses a number of nonfunctional properties such as privacy, reputation, and usability. Moreover, when evaluating WS QoS, domain specific criteria must be taken into consideration. For example, in the domain of phone service provisioning, the penalty rate for early termination of a contract and compensation for nonservice offered in the service level agreement is an important QoS criteria in that domain. Therefore, an extensible QoS model must be proposed that includes both the generic and domain specific criteria. In addition, new domain specific criteria should be added and used to evaluate QoS without changing the underlying computation (i.e., matchmaking and ranking) model. Last but not least, the semantics of QoS concepts must be described in order to have terms/concepts with specific meaning for both

WS requesters and providers. In this way, QoS attributes like "application availability," which may have different meanings if not formally defined, will have a specific meaning in QoS description. The solution to the above problems is the use of ontologies. Ontologies provide a formal, syntactic, and semantic description model of concepts, properties, and relationships between concepts that is human-understandable and machine-interpretable, providing the means for interoperability. Moreover, they are extensible. In addition, SW techniques can be used for reasoning about concepts or for mapping between ontologies. These techniques can lead to syntactic and semantic matching of ontological concepts and enforcement of class and property constraints (e.g., type checking, cardinality constraints, etc.). Therefore, by providing semantic description of concepts and by supporting reasoning mechanisms, ontologies cater for better WS discovery with high precision and recall. Last but not least, ontologies can help specialized brokers in performing complex reasoning tasks like WS discovery or mediation.

- **Standards compliance:** It is important for the QoS-based WS description model to comply with already widely-accepted standards. In this way, it will be easily adopted by the research community. In addition, it will use all freely-available tools related to these standards for its development.

- **Syntactical separation of QoS-based and functional parts of service specification:** QoS specifications should be syntactically separated from other parts of service specifications, such as interface definitions. This separation allows us to specify different QoS properties for different implementations of the same interface. Moreover, while functional constraints rarely change during runtime, QoS constraints can change during runtime. So the separation of service offerings from WSDL descriptions permits service offerings to be deactivated, reactivated, created, or deleted dynamically without any modification of the underlying WSDL file. Last, an offer could be referenced from multiple WSDL files and thus be reused for different services.

- **Support refinement of QoS specifications and their constructs:** QoS specifications should not only be reused but also refined. This means that we can create a new WS QoS offering by referencing an older one and by adding constraints like refinement of an older QoS restriction or creation of a new one. In addition, templates of QoS offerings can be created and appropriately extended for every domain.

- **Allow both provider and requester QoS specification:** It should be possible to specify both the QoS properties that clients require and the QoS properties that services provide. Moreover, these two aspects should be specified separately so that a client-server relationship has two QoS specifications: a specification that captures the client's requirements and a specification that captures service provisioning. Finally, QoS demands and offers should be specified in a symmetric way, that is, allowing the same level of expressiveness.

- **Allow fine-grained QoS specification:** It should be possible to specify QoS properties/metrics at a fine-grained level. As an example, performance characteristics are commonly specified for individual operations. A QoS model must allow QoS specifications for interfaces, operations, attributes, operation parameters, and operation results. Generally speaking, any service object can have QoS attributes/metrics (e.g., elements defined in WSFL [Leymann, 2001]).

- **Extensible and formal QoS metrics model:** Each QoS attribute is measured with the help of a QoS metric. Each attribute/metric has the following aspects:
  - The value set for the metric (and its allowed value range).
  - The domains that this attribute belongs to. For instance, is it a cross-domain attribute or an attribute specific for a domain?

     °   The weight of the metric relative to its domain and user preferences. This weight can also help in calculating the rank of a QoS offering.

     °   The characteristic of the function from metric values to overall QoS values. For instance, some attributes such as price are monotonic, at least in typical business scenarios.

     °   The temporal characteristic of the metric value. Metrics may have decaying values where the decay function can vary from exponential to a step function.

     °   There must be a description (mathematical or otherwise formal) of how a QoS metric's value of a complex WS can be derived from the corresponding QoS metrics' values of the individual WSs that constitute the complex one. For example, the execution time T_C of a complex WS C, which is defined as a sequence of two WSs A and B, can be computed as the sum $T_A +$ TB of the execution times of the two individual WSs. This description is essential for the automated estimation of the values of QoS metrics for a complex WS that is composed of other WSs and individual operations. So this description is needed for automating the QoS analysis process, a prerequisite for a successful QoS-based WS discovery. In addition, it helps in automating the WS composition process and delaying individual WS selection as late as possible (i.e., at runtime).

     °   Tosic, Esfandiari, Pagurek and Patel (2002) argue for the need for several ontologies that would be used in the formal representation of QoS and other constraints. These ontologies include: ontology of measurement units, ontology of currency units, ontology of measured properties and, ontology of measurement methods. So these ontologies must also be developed.

- **Great expressiveness and correct constraint definition:** A QoS offer or demand (i.e., specification) must be comprised of QoS constraints. Each QoS constraint consists of a name, an operator, and a value (Frølund & Koistinen, 1998). The name is typically the name of a QoS metric, although it can also be the name of a metric *aspect*. The permissible operators and values depend on the QoS metric type. A metric type specifies a domain of values. These values can be used in constraints for that dimension. The domain may be ordered. For example, a numeric domain comes with a built-in ordering ("<") that corresponds to the usual ordering on numbers. Set and enumeration domains do not come with a built-in ordering; for those types of domains we have to describe a user-defined ordering of the domain elements. The domain ordering determines which operators can be used in constraints for that domain. For example, we can not use inequality operators ("<", ">", "<=", "=>") in conjunction with an unordered domain.

Aspects are complex statistical characterizations of QoS constraints, such as *percentile, mean, variance*, and *frequency*. They are used for characterization of measured values over some time period. For example, the percentile aspect could be used to define an upper or lower value for a percentage of the measurements or occurrences that have been observed. Aspects can be proved to be very useful in cases where we want to guarantee that the measurements or occurrences of a QoS metric present some special characteristics and we do not want to produce a new complex metric from the basic QoS metric for each of these characteristics. However, they must be used carefully, especially in cases where many aspects are created for one metric.

QoS constraints are usually connected by the "and" logical operator, although they can also be connected by other logical operators, into expressions. A QoS offer or demand should contain one complete expression or just one constraint.

QoS constraints should be joined into constraint groups (CG) or constraint group templates (parameterized CGs) in order to be reused by many QoS specifications (Tosic, Pagurek, & Patel, 2003). Other reusability constructs can also be created even for expressions.

- **Allow classes of service specification:** Class of service (Tosic, Ma, Pagurek, & Esfandiari, 2003) means the discrete variation of the complete service and QoS provided by one WS. Classes of service can differ in usage privileges, service priorities, response time guarantees, and so forth. The concept of classes of service also supports different capabilities, rights, and needs of potential customers of the WS, including power and type of the devices they execute on. Furthermore, different classes of service may imply different utilization of the underlying hardware and software resources and, consequently, have different prices. Additionally, different classes of service can be used for different payment models. The issues of QoS and balancing of limited underlying resources are particularly motivating for having multiple classes of service for Web services. If the underlying resources were unlimited, all consumers would always get the highest possible QoS. Unfortunately, this is not the case, so it is suitable to provide different QoS to different classes of consumers. Providers of Web services want to achieve maximal monetary gain with optimal utilization of resources. Providing different classes of service and their balancing helps in achieving this goal because of the flexibility to accommodate several classes of consumers. On the other hand, consumers of such Web services can better select the service and QoS they need and are willing to pay for, while minimizing their price/performance ratio.

Requirements for QoS-Based Web Service Discovery

Requirements for QoS-Based Web Service Matchmaking

The QoS-based WS matchmaking process starts when the functional WS matchmaking process ends. To put it in another way, the WS matchmaking process is a composed process consisting of two sequential processes: functional and QoS-based. The functional process filters WS advertisements based on the functional restrictions of the requester. The QoS-based process further filters the results of the functional process based on the QoS restrictions of the requester. So the first requirement is that the output of the functional WS matchmaking process should be the input of the QoS-based WS matchmaking process.

QoS offers and demands that are matched during the QoS-based WS matchmaking process should be specified by the same language. The requirements for this language were expressed in section 3.1.1. In addition, both advertisers and requesters should be encouraged to be honest with their descriptions. Otherwise, they will pay the price of either not being matched or being matched inappropriately. The matching should not be based on keyword search only. Instead, semantic and structural information about each attribute in the service request and advertisement must be taken into consideration. More specifically, there should be *semantic matching* of different QoS metric descriptions.

Irrespective of whether it matches functional or QoS-based descriptions, there are some properties that should hold in every matchmaking system and are the following:

- **Open-world descriptions:** This property states that the absence of a characteristic in the description of an advertisement or request should be dealt as something that either will be refined later or is irrelevant for the user (Noia, Sciascio, Donini, & Mongiello, 2003). In other words, if a characteristic is missing from a WS advertisement, then the matchmaking engine should try to obtain it from the service provider instead of regarding as absent. Otherwise, if a characteristic is missing from a WS request, then the matchmaking engine will consider it irrelevant and will not use it in the matchmaking algorithm.

- **Nonsymmetric evaluation:** This property states that the evaluation may be different depending on whether the matchmaking engine matches a request with an advertisement or the opposite (Noia et al., 2003).

- **User preference consideration:** When the user is not actually exact with the description of what the user wants or when the results of the user's query are huge, the user query must be refined based on user preferences and generic usage patterns (Balke & Wagner, 2003). User preferences depend on the intensions a user has in a specific domain. For example, when the user is in New York, the user usually eats at an Italian restaurant. Generic usage patterns can also be considered that state what are the most common user preferences in a specific domain. For example, if someone wants to organize a business dinner, then a French restaurant must be booked.

- **Symmetry of information exchange and selection:** The process of finding the right service for a given service consumer is not necessarily a one-way process of having the consumer state requirements and select a winner from the matching services. Service providers may wish to receive information from the consumer before deciding to make a particular service available to that consumer. The input to the matchmaking process therefore needs to take account of the demands of both service consumers and providers, relating these demands to information provided by both parties, resulting in a symmetric exchange by service consumers and providers of both information and demands (Facciorusso, Field, Hauser, Hoffner, Humbel, Pawlitzek et al., 2003).

- **Dynamic Service Configuration:** Matchmaking should allow a provider to describe its offer as a skeleton or a generating function that can be used to offer different service configurations (Facciorusso et al., 2003). This can be done in the form of a reference to an external system or alternatively by supplying a script that the matchmaking engine (MME) can evaluate locally. Thus, the MME can generate the specific service offer dynamically at the time of searching. Input to the process that provides the specific value can contain information from the potential consumer; each service configuration can be tailored to the circumstances of the specific consumer. This is needed for several reasons:

  ○ It facilitates an up-to-date description of the service where service properties such as the cost, availability, or quality of service may be subject to variations. Such variations can, for example, be due to load, maintenance, and so forth.

  ○ It provides a way to specify a range of services without having to enumerate all the options associated with them in the MME as this may overload the MME.

  ○ It provides a way to configure the service and the consumer application according to the needs and properties of both parties. This facilitates personalisation of the service.

  ○ It provides a way to integrate existing applications that reside on back-end systems (legacy problem).

In a perfect world, the QoS-based matchmaking system would return to the requester those QoS offers that perfectly match the requester's request. In practice, this fact is highly unlikely to happen. One of the challenges of matchmaking is to locate those services that the requester would choose/select despite their differences from the request. Furthermore, the matchmaker should be able to characterize the distance between the request and the matches found, so that the requester can make an informed decision about which service to invoke. So QoS offers should be grouped according to their rank (distance from request). Suppose that there is a measure or function that tells us if one solution (comprised by a specific value for every user metric) is better than another one (see next subsection). To the best of our knowledge, at least the following categories of results should be provided by the QoS-based matchmaking system with decreasing order of significance:

- **Super matches:** This category contains those QoS offers that have at least one better solution and all other equivalent to those solutions of the QoS request.
- **Exact matches:** This category contains those QoS offers that have a subset of the solutions expressed by the QoS request.
- **Partial matches:** This category contains those QoS offers that have at least one worse solution than those of the QoS request.
- **Fail matches:** This category contains those QoS offers that have only worse solutions with respect to the solution of the QoS request.

Of course, a MME could provide more fine-grained categories than the proposed ones. However, their ranking must be based on the following properties:

- QoS offers expressing the same set of solutions for the same QoS metrics should be given the same rank.
- If a QoS offer O1 has at least one better and no worse solution than the solutions expressed by the QoS offer O2, then O1 should have a better rank than O2.

Suppose that after the matchmaking process has been executed, there are only partial and fail matches. This is an indication of an over-constrained QoS request. Fail matches are of no use and should be discarded. However, partial matches are promising. The reason is that if one (not-very-important) QoS constraint of the QoS request is relaxed or deleted, then it is possible that some partial QoS offers are promoted to higher categories. This process is called constraint relaxation and must be incorporated in the QoS-based MME when the aforementioned case occurs in order to provide more value-added results to the WS requester. More details about constraint relaxation are discussed by Bistarelli, Montanari, and Rossi (1997).

In this paragraph, we indicate some additional requirements imposed on the QoS-based MME which are not obligatory but help in providing more value-added services to WS requesters. These requirements are the following:

- Support of persistent and volatile queries.
- Support of caching of user queries.
- Management of user profiles and general usage patterns. The data model for user profiles must contain information concerning the user role, identity, age, location, preferences, social situation, and so forth. User preferences describe user intentions in specific domains. The general usage patterns describe common usage intentions in various domains. Information about the user profile must be updated every time a user makes a request and must be erased after a long period of

time where the user has not contacted the registry. On the other hand, general usage patterns are never erased but simply updated every time there is a query in a specific domain of knowledge. Of course, in order to get user information, the user must allow for uncovering of the user's personal information. In addition, the user should be able to manipulate the user's profile any time or even erase it.

- The Web services data model used in the registry must hold information about all the possible aspects of a Web service description. In addition, the registry's query language must enable users to describe in every possible aspect their request.

- Management of general or domain-specific QoS properties for a Web service description. This means that the registry's data model must associate a Web service description with general and arbitrary QoS metadata. The update of these metadata can be executed by the particular service provider. However, there must be allowance of third-party annotations of QoS metadata to the WS description.

Requirements for QoS-Based Web Service Selection

In the selection process, the results (especially the best ones) obtained from the discovery process are further ranked in order to get the best result. The selection process is completely personalized (preference-oriented) as the ranking is based on user preferences regarding the QoS criteria that are more important to them (along with the degree of importance) and different users may have different preferences. User preferences can be given separately to the selection algorithm or they can be obtained from the metric ontology. Alternatively, they can be collected and derived from user context. User preferences should include weights given to metrics and to the QoS constraints. Apart from user preferences, other information about the QoS criteria/metrics must be available, like the type and range set of a metric, the groups or domains the metric belongs to, the monotonicity of the metric, and so forth. This other type of information is collected/derived by the description of QoS metrics in metric ontologies.

When the selection algorithm collects all the appropriate input, it starts processing available QoS offers in order to give to each of them a suitable rank/degree according to user preferences. The degree is usually computed from the following formula:

$$\sum_{\forall metric} weight * degree\_of\_promised\_val$$

where the degree of promised value is determined by the metric's utility function (Martín-Díaz, Cortés, Benavides, Durán, & Toro, 2003). For example, if the metric is positively monotonic, then it can be computed by the next formula:

$$degree\_of\_promised\_val = \frac{promised\_val - min}{max - min}$$

where *promised_val* is the promised value of the metric, and min and max are the minimum and maximum value of the metric with respect to the available QoS offers. If the offer promises a range of values for a metric, then the promised_val can be the worse or the best or the average or a combination of worse and best values (Kritikos & Plexousakis, 2006). Other sophisticated selection algorithms are based on normalizations and grouping of QoS metrics (in domains or functional groups), as the one described by Liu, Ngu, and Zeng (2004). The purposes of normalization are: (1) to allow for a uniform measurement of service qualities independent of units; (2) to provide a uniform index to represent service qualities for each provider; and (3) to allow setting a threshold regarding the qualities. The number of normalizations performed depends on how the quality criteria are grouped (i.e., the nesting degree of the groups).

Related Work

In this section, all the current research approaches for QoS-based WS description and discovery will be described and their deficiencies will be analyzed.

First, QoS metrics/measurement ontologies are going to be presented. The first work is included in the DAML ontology library where there is a representation of the CyC upper ontology. In this ontology, general classes of measurement units and currencies are described. However, descriptions of concrete measurement units and currencies are not found. In addition, this ontology is not modularized.

The simple HTML ontology extensions (SHOE) (Heflin & Hendler, 2000) measurement ontology is much simpler than the CyC ontology. It contains some measurement units (metric system) in four categories: length, time, volume, and weight. No relationships (except the one stating a metric belongs to a category) and no derived measurement units are defined.

Tosic et al. (2002) describe that for the specification of constraints for QoS metrics/attributes, five ontologies must be developed from which the most important (the top one) is the metrics ontology. They describe the structure and involved elements in four out of the five ontologies. However, they did not develop any ontology. In addition, the requirements specified are incomplete as each from the four aspects of QoS description needs further analysis.

Now, we are going to analyze the standard approaches for QoS-based WS description. The WSDL is a WS standard dedicated to the syntactic description of the signature of a WS operation. It does not describe QoS constraints for a WS operation.

The UDDI WS standard is dedicated to the description and discovery of WSs. However, it is based on the *tModel* concept which leads to purely syntactic queries. In addition, there is no QoS description of offers or demands in the UDDI description model.

The OWL-S (Sycara et al., 2003) ontology is a semantic approach for the description of WSs. Unfortunately, it only contains an attribute used for rating a WS and not any other QoS description.

Now, other approaches for QoS-based description are going to be presented. Ran (2003) proposes an extension to UDDI. A new data structure type—called *qualityInformation*—is added to the UDDI model that represents description of QoS information about a particular WS. The *qualityInformation* data structure type also refers to *tModels* as references to QoS taxonomies, which also need to be defined in the extended UDDI registry. The proposed approach has many disadvantages. First of all, there is no actual description of the contents of the new data structure and its referenced *tModels*. Second, it relies on the UDDI technology so it can be used only for syntactic matchmaking of WSs. Last but not least, there is no clarification of how the actual QoS matchmaking takes place.

Maximilien and Singh (2002) present an architecture and model of WS reputation (QoS). They propose that for successful description of QoS, three challenges must be dealt: (1) definition of a QoS conceptual model for WS attributes which is reusable across domains such that weights, threshold to QoS attribute values, and user risk tolerance can be defined; (2) semantics to QoS service attributes must be added in order for new attributes to be dynamically discovered and incorporated to the conceptual model of QoS attributes and for successful and more accurate discovery of WSs; (3) reputations should consider time and history of endorsements and ratings. Based on the above requirements/challenges, a conceptual model of WS reputation is proposed which is used for the calculation of a WS reputation. The suggested conceptual model encloses a QoS attributes model. The main disadvantages of this work are the following. First of all, the reputation of a WS is calculated and not its overall QoS. Another disadvantage is that there is no explicit clarification of how the reputation of a WS is calculated. In addition, concepts like QoS constraints and QoS offers and demands are not modelled. Last but not least, a QoS metrics conceptual model does not contain the classes and properties described by Tosic et al. (2002).

Work described by Tosic et al. (2003) and Tosic, Ma et al. (2003), which is called Web service offerings language (WSOL), introduces the concept of "service offering," which is a formal representation of one class of service for a WS and contains formal definitions of various constraints (e.g., functional constraints, QoS constraints, and access rights), management statements, as well as different reusability constructs. This work comes with two stated shortcomings/open issues. The first one is no separation and integration of constraint dimensions. The second one is the improvement of the specification of relationships between service offerings to support both easier and more flexible specification and dynamic adaptation. In addition to these shortcomings, there are some other problems. First of all, there is no specification of the QoS demand of the consumer. Secondly, the matchmaking process is not defined. Additionally, the metrics ontologies are not yet developed. Finally, we were not able to find the WSOL's complete specification so we cannot come into safe conclusions about its stated supported features.

The approaches of Web service level agreement (SLA) (Keller & Ludwig, 2003) and Web service management language (WSML) (Jin, Machiraju, & Sahai, 2002) try not only to provide a specification of SLAs but also to develop a complete framework for the management of SLAs. Comparing these efforts on the specification of SLAs, WSLA provides a better and more accurate language, providing more features and constructs, and satisfies a lot of the requirements we have set for QoS-based WS description. However, we should note that a SLA is different from a QoS offer or demand. It contains more management and responsibility statements; it is more technical and refers to implementation details that are not relevant to the context of WS discovery. Moreover, both of these approaches are purely syntactic and thus not appropriate for semantic WS matchmaking.

Tian et al. (2003) propose a syntactic QoS model enriched with links to ontological concepts. They allow fine-grained QoS specification. Additionally, they also reference (a) protocols used by a WS for security and transaction support, service management and QoS monitoring, and (b) the trusted third-parties that will participate in these protocols. Last but not least, they allow class of service specification. This research work comes with three main deficiencies. First of all, only simple equality constraints are allowed. Second, metrics ontologies are not developed but are just referenced. Finally, there is no specification of how WS discovery takes place.

Finally, research efforts with respect to QoS-based description and discovery are going to be analyzed. QoS modelling language (QML) (Frølund & Koistinen, 1998) was designed according to some basic principles for the support of QoS specification. It contains the following constructs: (a) *contract type*: specification of a QoS dimension that includes definitions for the metrics of this QoS dimension; (b) *contract*: gives particular values/constraints to the fields of a contract type; and (c) *profile*: one service is associated with many (QoS) profiles. One (QoS) service profile P is matched with one client profile Q if all contracts of P *conform* to all the contract of Q. *Contract conformance* is translated into *constraint conformance.* The language for specifying QoS offers or demands is not rich enough and lacks the semantics needed for better matchmaking.

Zhou, Chia, and Lee (2004) extend the DAML-S Web service description language by including a QoS specification ontology. In addition to the DAML-S extension, a novel QoS matchmaking algorithm is proposed, which is based on the concept of *QoS profile compatibility* which states that two QoS ontology descriptions C_1 and C_2 are compatible if and only if their intersection is satisfiable: *compatible*$(C_1,C_2) \Rightarrow \neg(C_1 \cap C_2 \subseteq \bot)$". Matchmaking is performed by a DL reasoner that computes the subsumption relationship of a request R (and of $\neg R$) with all available QoS advertisements. The deficiencies of this research effort are the following: **(a)** the metrics and units classes described do not contain all the appropriate properties and relationships; and **(b)** the QoS metrics values are restricted to have the set $\mathbb{N}^+$ as their range in order to help the DL reasoner in calculating the T-Box subsumption relationships (however, this leads to imprecision and errors that can reach one half of measurement unit); and **(c)** DL reasoners are not very quick and do not support the most complex mathematical expressions.

Oldham, Verma, Sheth, and Hakimpour (2006) offer a semantic framework for the definition and matching of *WS-agreements*. However, only unary QoS metric constraints can be expressed while QoS metric matching could only be enforced by manual incorporation of rules.

Martín-Díaz, Cortés, Benavides, Durán, and Toro (2003) use a *symmetric* and *syntactic* QoS model expressing mathematical constraints for QoS metrics and user preferences. Before matchmaking, a QoS specification is transformed to a *constraint satisfaction problem* (CSP) (Van Hentenryck & Saraswat, 1996), which is checked for *consistency,* that is, if there is an assignment of values to metrics (a solution) such that all the constraints are satisfied. Matchmaking is performed according to the concept of *conformance*, which is used for checking out if every solution to the CSP of the offer is also a solution to the CSP of the demand. After matchmaking, two main result-sets are produced: matched and not matched offers. Concerning WS selection, the (QoS) score of a WS advertisement is calculated as a weighted sum of the weight of each metric multiplied with its utility assessment value, where the assignment of values to metrics is chosen so that the sum is the minimum. That is, for every WS advertisement a *constraint satisfaction optimization problem* (CSOP) is solved in order to produce its score and then all scores are sorted in decreasing order. Solving CSOPs may lead to nonpolynomial computation of solutions, especially if there are nonlinear expressions at the QoS constraints. This is a characteristic of the *class* of CSP problems.

PROPOSED APPROACH

A QoS offering (or demand) of a WS is a set of constraints on some QoS metrics. These QoS metrics quantify QoS attributes/characteristics. Actually, current modelling efforts of QoS offers or demands only differ in the expressiveness of these constraints. However, when it comes to QoS attributes/metrics modelling, these efforts fail. The first reason is because the QoS attribute/metric definition is a syntactic one. As a result, QoS metrics like "average availability" may have different meanings to the parties that describe them or may be computed differently. Another reason is that the QoS metrics model is not rich enough, not incorporating the definition of measurement units, currency units, and measurement methods. This deficiency results in similar QoS metrics that are produced differently or use different measurement units leading to problems in QoS-based WS discovery and monitoring. The last reason of failure is that the QoS metrics model is not extensible to include newly invented metrics while taking care not to change the underlying computation (matchmaking and selection) model.

Due on the above shortcomings in QoS-based WS description, the most prominent QoS-based discovery algorithms fail to perform accurate semantic QoS metric matchmaking and thus produce results with low recall and precision. Therefore, it is clear that there is a need for semantic QoS-based description and discovery of WSs. This need is addressed by our approach (Kritikos & Plexousakis, 2006). First, we propose an upper ontology for QoS-based WS description, called OWL-Q, which extends OWL-S. This ontology describes in a syntactic and semantic way all possible parts of QoS metrics and constraints. It is an ontological description designed into several facets that can easily be extended and enriched. Based on this upper ontology, we also propose the development of a midlevel ontology that will define all domain independent QoS metrics and will be the basis for the definition of new QoS metrics on other low-level ontologies.

Second, in case where QoS-based advertisements and requests refer to different concepts/metrics of the same or different ontologies, we propose a semantic QoS metric matching algorithm that can infer the similarity of two different metrics.

For semantic QoS-based discovery, we propose to extend one of the most promising syntactic QoS-based discovery algorithms by incorporating the aforementioned algorithm and by improving its deficiencies.

OWL-Q for QoS-Based Web Service Description

Based on the design principles and requirements of QoS-based WS description that were set on the previous section, we have developed an OWL-S extension (the requirement **syntactical separation** is satisfied as our ontology can be developed independently from OWL-S), named OWL-Q, for QoS-based WS description of both requests and offers. We have extended the OWL-S ontological description for two reasons: to comply with Semantic WS description standards (**standards compliance**) and to use the OWL ontology formalism (**extensible and formal semantic QoS model**). OWL is one of the most expressive ontology languages and it is a W3C recommendation. Various reasoning tools for OWL have been developed, enabling the enforcement of various class and property constraints, subsumption reasoning, and type-checking. Using these tools the syntactic and semantic validity of QoS descriptions can be checked and the processes of QoS matchmaking and selection can be properly supported.

Our ontology is carefully separated into several facets. Each facet can be developed and extended independently of the other (**syntactical separation** and **refinement of QoS specifications**). Each facet concentrates on a particular part of our QoS WS description. A document describing a QoS WS advertisement or request should reference all the facets of our ontology.

In the sequel, we analyze all facets of the OWL-Q ontology commenting on six images-snapshots of this ontology. Each image contains classes (circles) and properties (arrows). It does not include cardinality constraints and other type of OWL constraints. The reason for using this formalism is due to space limitations of this chapter and in order to show that our ontology can be easily expressed in another ontology language apart from OWL. In addition, even if two QoS-based WS descriptions are expressed based on our ontology model in two different ontology formalisms, the mapping between their concepts can be easily handled.

Connecting Facet

As can be seen in Figure 1, the connecting facet tries to connect OWL-S with OWL-Q and to provide the high-level concepts that are appropriate for defining QoS advertisements and demands. For the connection of the two ontological descriptions, the *QoSAttribute* class is a subclass of OWL-S *ServiceParameter* and references a *ServiceElement*. Subclasses of the latter class are *ConditionalOutput*, *Parameter*, *Input*, *Precondition*, *Effect*, and *Service*. That is a *QoSAttribute* that can reference any *ServiceElement* of a service's functional description (**fine-grained QoS specification**). Finally, a *QoSAttribute* can be static or dynamic (it changes with time) and is measured by one or more static or dynamic *QoSMetric*s, respectively.

Basic Facet

A *ServiceProfile* is associated with many *QoSOffer*s (**classes of service**) or with only one *QoSRequest* (**both requester and service provider QoS specification**). A *QoSRequest* is separated into a *QoSDemand* class and a *QoSSelection* class. The latter class is the actual incarnation of a list of *<QoSAttribute, selectionFactor>* elements useful for the WS selection process. The *QoSSpec* class represents the actual QoS description of a WS. It describes the security and transaction protocols used, the cost of using the service and the associated currency for the cost, the validity period of the offer, or demand an arbitrary OpenMath (Caprotti, Dewar, & Turi, 2004) expression (*om:OMOBJ*). This expression represents what is or must be guaranteed and contains variables which are associated to QoS metrics.

Metric Facet of OWL-Q

The metric facet describes all the appropriate classes and properties used for a proper formal definition of a QoS metric (**QoS attribute model**). This metric facet is actually an upper ontology representing any abstract QoS metric. A specific QoS metric can be created by refining the *QoSMetric* class. Many

Figure 1. Connecting facet of OWL-Q

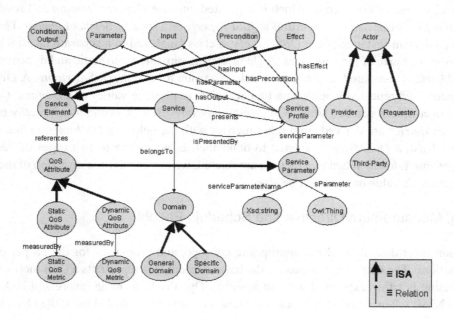

Figure 2. Basic facet of OWL-Q

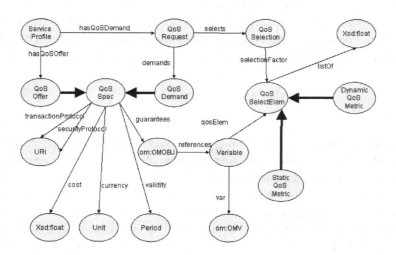

specific QoS metrics (especially the general ones) can be part of a midlevel ontology created for QoS metric reuse. We prefer specialization to instantiation because it allows for a quicker reasoning process. We plan to develop a mid-level ontology defining cross-domain QoS metrics and a low-level ontology for defining QoS metrics for particular domains. The midlevel and low-level ontologies will help WS requesters and providers in describing QoS demands and offers, respectively. The low-level ontology is only used for the (formal) evaluation of our QoS-based WS discovery approach by defining the basic domain-dependent metrics belonging to the domain(s) of a chosen sample application.

The *QoSMetric* is one of the most important classes of OWL-Q representing a QoS metric. The values of a QoS metric are provided by a service provider or a requester or a third-party. A QoS metric belongs to a *Domain* of knowledge, which is separated into one *Generic Domain* and several *Specific Domain*s. It has only one name. It measures a *QoSProperty* on a specific *ServiceElement*. The value type of a *QoSMetric* is an instance of the *QoSValueType* class (analyzed in a separate facet) while the unit of a value is an instance of the *Unit* class. A *QoSMetric* is separated into static and dynamic metrics. A *StaticQoSMetric* is computed only once to produce a value for a *StaticQoSAttribute*. A *DynamicQoS-Metric* is computed repeatedly according to a *Schedule* to produce values of a *DynamicQoSAttribute* that change over time. It can be a simple QoS metric *measuredBy* a *MeasurementDirective* or a complex one. *ComplexMetric*s are derived from other metrics with the help of a *OMFunction* (analyzed later). Last but not least, a *QoSMetric* is related to other metrics according to two types of *Relationship*s: *Independent* and *Related*. When two metrics are related, we can specify the direction of their values or the impact of one's value on the other's value.

Function, Measurement Directive and Schedule Facets

The function facet describes all the appropriate concepts and properties for the proper definition of metric functions. The *OMFunction* class is the basic concept that represents a QoS metric function. A metric function is either expressed with an arbitrary OpenMath formula (expressed in XML via the OpenMath XML schema om:) or with a known OpenMath function (subclass of the *OpenMathSymbol*

Figure 3. Metric facet of OWL-Q

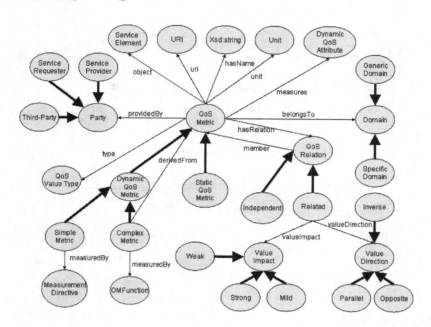

class of the MONET [Caprotti et al., 2004] ontology). A metric function takes as input objects of the *Operand* class, which associate a *QoSMetric* with an OpenMath variable (*om:OMV*) that is used inside the function's formula.

The measurement directive facet describes the concept of measurement directive which is used for the measurement of simple metrics. A *MeasurementDirective* is composed of a *URI* that describes where and how to get a value of a resource's property. A *Schedule* is used to compute the frequency of the computation of a complex metric's value. It has a specific name and is defined either by a starting and ending *Period* of *xsd:dateTime* type or by a time *Interval* that is expressed in specific time units.

Unit Facet

The unit facet formally describes the unit of a QoS metric. A *Unit* has one name, several abbreviations, and synonyms (even in different languages). A *Unit* belongs to a *System of Units* and is associated with the same *QoSProperty* as the one that is measured by the QoS metric of the unit. A *Unit* is separated into *BaseUnit*s, *MultiplesOfUnit*s, and *DerivedUnit*s. The *BaseUnit* class expresses units which are used most of the times in measurements. A *MultipleOfUnit* is associated with a *BaseUnit* and converted to it by a constant (*multiplicationFactor*). It has a name composed of the name of its *BaseUnit* and a prefix. A *DerivedUnit* is proportional to some *Units* and inversely proportional to other *Units*. It also has a *multFactor* that is used to express its mathematical definition in relation to the other (inverse) proportional units. A unit is equivalent to another unit and can be converted to it with the help of the *Equivalence* class. This class correlates the equivalent metrics and defines the OpenMath functions or formulas that are used to convert the values of one unit to the other. A midlevel ontology of units must be developed in order to have a semantic description of specific base units and their alternatives or multiples. This

Figure 4. Function, measurement directive and schedule facets of OWL-Q

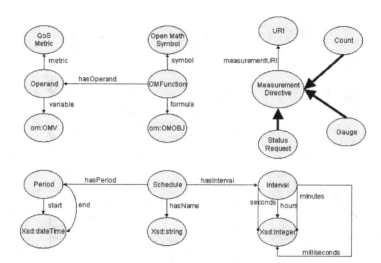

Figure 5. Unit facet of OWL-Q

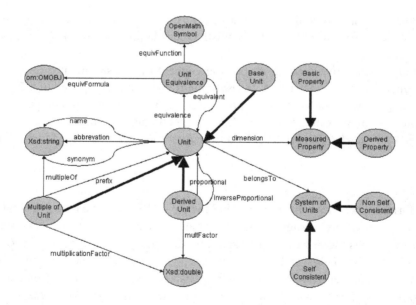

Figure 6. QoS value type facet

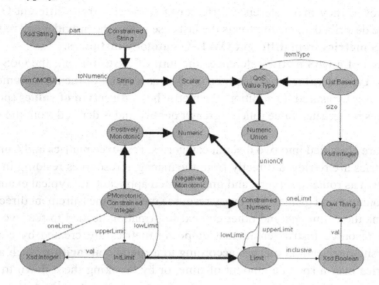

midlevel ontology will be very helpful in converting between values of metrics where these metrics are equivalent but use different units.

QoS Value Type Facet

The *QoSValueType* ontology describes the types of values a QoS metric can take. The *QoSValueType*s can be *Scalar* or *NumericUnion*, or *Listbased* types. *Scalar* value types are simple value types that can be *Numeric* or *String*. *NumericType*s can be *Positively-Monotonic* or *NegativelyMonotonic* in order to show the direction of values of the associated metric. *ConstrainedNumeric* value types represent *Numeric* value types that have (upper, lower, or one) limits (e.g., the Integer set [2,5] or the Integer value {2}). A *String* value type may have a *toNumeric* OpenMath formula that will be used to compute the numeric counterpart of its values. A *ConstrainedString* represents a finite closed *String* list which has specific *String* values as *part*s. The *NumericUnion* class represents value types that are expressed as unions of *Numeric* value types (e.g., [1, 2] U {4} U [9, 11]). The *List-Based* class represents list value types that have a specific size and whose elements are of a specific *QoSValueType*.

Semantic QoS Metric Matching

All current QoS-based WS discovery efforts try to infer if an advertisement constraint involving a particular QoS metric is stricter than a request constraint involving the same QoS metric. However, equivalence of QoS metrics is inferred by the syntactic comparison of their names. As a result, the QoS-based WS matchmaking process fails as it produces results with low precision and recall.

The solution to the above problem is to semantically define and compare two QoS metrics so as to infer that they are the same. For the semantic comparison of two QoS metrics, we have devised a *semantic QoS metric matching algorithm*. This algorithm makes the following assumptions:

- Both the requester and service provider use the OWL-Q semantic language for describing QoS metrics. However, they may reference different QoS metrics from different OWL-Q ontology instances. The described algorithm treats the last case where the provider and requester reference **different QoS metrics** from **different OWL-Q ontology instances**.

- The description of a QoS metric references the **unit** of measurement, the QoS property that is measured, the **type of values** that this metric takes as a result of the measurement, and the **service object** that is measured. In addition, the metric has a **direction of values** (positive, negative) which indicates if a greater value reflects greater quality and is derived from the value type of the metric.

- QoS metrics are classified into two disjoint categories: **resource** metrics and **Composite** metrics. Resource metrics are retrieved directly from the managed resources residing in the service provider's tier, such as routers, servers, and implemented applications. Typical examples of resource metrics are counters and gauges. For every resource metric, a measurement directive is specified, which contains the command and other context information needed to retrieve the metric from the managed resource instrumentation. Composite metrics are created by combining several other (composite or resource) metrics according to a specific **algorithm**, such as averaging one or more metrics over a specific amount of time, or by breaking them down to specific criteria (top 10%, minimum, maximum values of a time series). This is usually done within the service provider's domain but can be outsourced to a third-party measurement service as well. We assume that composite metrics are specified by means of a **function**, that is, a formula describing the input metrics and the arithmetic operations to aggregate them. We further assume that this function is specified in the OpenMath XML language. OpenMath is an emerging standard for representing mathematical objects with their semantics, allowing them to be exchanged between computer programs, stored in databases, or published on the worldwide Web. Translations (called phrase-books) to the internal (math object) representations of popular mathematical engines like **Mathematica** and **Maple** have already been developed for computing the result of OpenMath expressions. In addition, an OWL ontology for the semantic representation of OpenMath objects has been developed in the context of the MONET project (Caprotti et al., 2004). This ontology is used for representing common functions which take only one argument as input and are used for unit transformations or composite metric value computations.

- The requester and service provider use three common ontologies: unit, QoS property, and QoS ValueType. The unit ontology semantically describes the unit used for the measurement prescribed by a QoS metric. The QoS property is an ontology for the semantic description of domain-independent (like throughput, availability and response time) and domain-dependent (e.g., "flexibility of reservation changes" in the travel domain) QoS properties. Finally, the third ontology is used for the semantic description of simple (integer, real, string) and complex QoS types (real number in [0,1], binary integer, list, time series). It is easy to come up and agree with the content of these three ontologies as they usually contain terms/concepts with an easily understood meaning for people/users. Thus they are common and available to every requester and service provider. If this is not the case, then matching algorithms for units, QoS properties, and QoS ValueTypes must be developed and used.

The input to the described algorithm is the following:

- Three ontologies O_1, O_2, O_3. O_1 contain U concepts, each representing a unit. O_2 contains P concepts, each representing a QoS Property. O_3 contains V concepts, each representing a QoS ValueType.
- An ontology instance of a subpart of the MONET ontology describing functions which are subclasses of the *OpenMathSymbol* concept and the OpenMath's XML Schema om: for describing arbitrary OpenMath formulas.
- Two different ontological instances D_1 and D_2 of OWL-Q which include the description of two different QoS metrics M_1 and M_2, respectively. In general, if we have a QoS metric concept M described by an ontology D, then:
  - $M.unit \in U$, where "unit" is a relation associating metrics and unit
  - $M.measures \in P$, where "measures" is a relation associating metrics and QoS Properties
  - $M.type \in V$, where "type" is a relation associating metric and value types

    $$M.object \in ServiceElement = \{Service, Operation,$$
    $$Activity, Flow, Endpoint, Port, Parameter, Input,$$
    $$ConditionalOutput, ...\}$$

    where "object" is a relation associating metrics and service elements
  - If $M.type\ instanceOf\ Number, PositivelyMonotonic \subseteq V$ then $valueDirection(M) = "positive"$ else if $M.type\ instanceOf\ Number, NegativelyMonotonic \subseteq V$ then $valueDirection(M) = "negative"$ else $M.toNumeric\ instanceOf\ om: OMOBJ$. It is stated that if the metric takes numeric values, then it has a positive or negative value direction. Otherwise, a function must be defined that computes the numeric counterpart of every value of the metric.
  - If $M\ subclassOf\ CompositeMetric$, then $M.mearsuredBy\ subclassOf\ OMFunction$ and $M.derivedFrom\ subclassOf\ Metric$. It is stated that if a metric is composite and not resource, then its values are computed by a function and is derived from other metrics.

Main Body of the Algorithm

The algorithm considers three different cases depending on the nature of the compared metrics (i.e., if they are resource metrics or composite):

- If
  $M_1\ subclassOf\ ResourceMetric$ and $M_2\ subclassOf\ ResourceMetric$,
  then
  $$smmatch(M_1, M_2) \equiv (uvmatch(M_1.unit, M_2.unit, M_1.type, M_2.type)$$
  $$\wedge M_1.measures = M_2.measures \wedge M_1.object = M_2.object)$$

Matching of units and types is not going to be analyzed due to space limitation of this chapter. We just note that when the same units are used, the types must be the same. Otherwise, if the units are compatible (one is multiple or equivalent to the other), then the types must be compatible (i.e., if they are constrained, then the transformation of the one type's limits must lead to values equal to the limits of the second). We assume that resource metrics have always numeric values, so there is no meaning to include a comparison of the "toNumeric" math objects. For example, consider two resource metrics: "DownTimeMetric" and "UpTimeMetric". Assume that they both try to measure the "availability" QoS property of a service, they take values from the integers set, and they use the same unit (of time). However, the "DownTimeMetric" has negative value direction while the "UpTimeMetric" has positive value direction. Thus, they are not matched.

- If M_1 *subclassOf ResourceMetric* and M_2 *subclassOf*

$$rcmmatch(M_1, M_2) \equiv (smmatch(M_1, M_2)$$
$$CompositeMetric, \wedge M_2.derivedFrom \cap CompositeMetric = \varnothing$$
$$\wedge M_2.derivedFrom! = M_1)$$

In other words, a resource and a composite metric can be matched if the composite metric is only derived from resource metrics that are different from the compared resource metric and the conditions for resource-to-resource metric match are met. This is the case where we have on one hand a resource metric that is obtained in the form of a high-level reading from systems with advanced instrumentation and on the other hand the same but composite metric that is derived from a resource metric obtained in the form of low-level reading from systems with basic instrumentation. For example, rather than deriving DownTime as a composite metric of time series of a system's status (i.e., resource metric), some systems offer this reading directly. To formally demonstrate the above example, the following hold:

$M_1.unit = $ "sec"$\wedge M_1.measures = Availability$

$\wedge M_1.type = NMonotonicInteger \wedge M_1.object = Service$

$\wedge M_2.unit = $ "sec"$\wedge M_2.measures = Availability$

$\wedge M_2.type = NMonotonicInteger \wedge M_2.object = Service$

$\wedge M_2.derivedFrom = M_3 \wedge M_3.type = Percentage$

It is easy to derive that $!rcmmatch(M_1, M_3)$ and $rcmmatch(M_1, M_2)$.

- If M_1 *subclassOf CompositeMetric* and M_2 *subclassOf CompositeMetric*, then we have the hardest case of all. Let us assume that $M_1.derivedFrom = \{R_1, R_2, \ldots, R_n, C_1, C_2, \ldots, C_m\}$, where R_i *subclassOfResourceMetric* $\forall i \in \{1, \ldots, n\}$ and C_j *subclassOfCompositeMetric* $\forall j \in \{1, \ldots, m\}$. Similarly, we assume that $M_2.derivedFrom = \{R_1', R_2', \ldots, R_{n'}', C_1', C_2', \ldots, C_{m'}'\}$, where R_i *subclassOfresourceMetric* $\forall i \in \{1, \ldots, n'\}$ and C_j' *subclassOfCompositeMetric* $\forall j \in \{1, \ldots, m'\}$. Initially, the algorithm assumes that both of the metrics are resource and executes a resource-to-resource metric match. If this match fails, then we have a failed match. Otherwise, the algorithm continues and tries to match every resource metric R_i of M_1 with every resource metric R_i' of M_2. If there is a match, then it substitutes every occurrence of these matched metrics in the $M_1.measuredBy$ and $M_2.measuredBy$ mathematical expressions with a new variable R_{ij}, where $i \in \{1, \ldots, n\}$ and $j \in \{1, \ldots, n'\}$. Similarly, the algorithm tries to match every composite metric C_j of M_1 with every composite metric C_j' of M_2. If there is a match, then it substitutes every occurrence of these matched metrics in the $M_1.measuredBy$ and $M_2.measuredBy$ mathematical expressions with a new variable C_{ij}, where $i \in \{1, \ldots, m\}$ and $j \in \{1, \ldots, m'\}$. If there are unmatched resource or composite metrics of M_1 and composite or resource metrics of M_2, respectively, then the algorithm tries to match them and assign them a new variable name in the corresponding mathematical expressions of M_1 and M_2. After all of this groundwork, we have a match if the following hold:

$ccmmatch(M_1, M_2) \equiv (smmatch(M_1, M_2)$

$\wedge equivalent(M_1.measuredBy, M_2.measuredBy))$.

In other words, the two composite metrics are matched if the conditions for resource-to-resource metric match are met and they have equivalent functions for computing the derivation of the metrics' values. Two functions (i.e., mathematical expressions) are equivalent if for every instance of their variables, they take the same value. Equivalence of mathematical expressions is generally undecidable but the most powerful mathematical engines like Mathematica and Maple successfully deal with many hard cases.

Example

Let us now examine a complete example of two QoS metrics that try to measure the QoS property of availability. For the first QoS metric "AvailM1," the following hold:

$AvailM1.unit = \varnothing \wedge AvailM1.type = PMonotonicPercentage$

$\wedge AvailM1.measures = Availability \wedge AvailM1.object = Service$

$\wedge AvailM1.derivedFrom = \{DTM1, UTM1\}$

$\wedge AvailM1.computedBy = "1 - DTM1/(UTM1 + DTM1)"$

$\wedge UTM1.unit = "sec" \wedge UTM1.type = PMonotonicInteger$

$\wedge UTM1.object = Service \wedge UTM1.measures = Availability$

$\wedge DTM1.unit = "sec" \wedge DTM1.type = NMonotonicInteger$

$\wedge DTM1.object = Service \wedge DTM1.measures = Availability$

For the second QoS metric "AvailM2," the following hold:

$AvailM2.unit = \varnothing \wedge AvailM2.type = PMonotonicPercentage$

$\wedge AvailM2.measures = Availability \wedge AvailM2.object = Service$

$\wedge AvailM2.derivedFrom = \{DTM2, UTM2\}$

$\wedge AvailM2.measuredBy = "UTM2/(UTM2 + DTM2)"$

$\wedge UTM2.unit = "sec" \wedge UTM2.type = PMonotonicInteger$

$\wedge UTM2.object = Service \wedge UTM2.measures = Availability$

$\wedge UTM2.derivedFrom = "SSM" \wedge DTM2.derivedFrom = "SSM"$

$\wedge DTM2.unit = "sec" \wedge DTM2.type = NMonotonicInteger$

$\wedge DTM2.object = Service \wedge DTM2.measures = Availability$

$\wedge SSM.unit = \varnothing \wedge SSM.type = \{0,1\} \wedge SSM.object = Service$

$\wedge SSM.measures = Availability$

Initially, the algorithm will try to match the two metrics, regarding them both as resource. They match, so it continues. Then, it tries to match resource-to-resource and composite-to-composite ancestral metrics. There a no such pairs, so it then tries to match resource-to-composite metrics. It infers that $rcmmatch(DTM1, DTM2)$ and $rcmmatch(UTM1, UTM2)$. So it replaces DTM1 and DTM2 with DTM, and UTM1 and UTM2 with UTM in the mathematical expressions of both AvailM1 and AvailM2. In other words, it now holds that $AvailM1.measuredBy = "1 - DTM/(UTM + DTM)"$ and $AvailM2.measuredBy = "UTM/(UTM + DTM)"$. Next, the algorithm tries to infer the equivalence of the "measuredBy" expressions of the two metrics. Indeed, it is obvious that $equivalent(AvailM1.measuredBy, AvailM2.measuredBy)$, so the algorithm finally infers that $ccmmatch(AvailM1, AvailM2)$.

QoS-Based Web Service Discovery Algorithm

One of the most prominent QoS-based WS discovery algorithm (Martín-Díaz et al., 2003) expresses each QoS-based WS description as a CSP. Then it separates the QoS-based advertisements into two categories: the ones that satisfy completely the QoS-based request and the others that do not satisfy the request. However, this algorithm presents three major drawbacks: (1) it performs syntactic metric matchmaking producing false negative and false positive results; (2) it does not provide advanced categorization of matches; and (3) it does not deal with cases where all QoS offers do not conform to the (over-constrained) demand.

In the sequel, we present an automated QoS-based WS matchmaking algorithm that exploits OWL-Q and the QoS metric matching algorithm in order to extend the aforementioned algorithm. This algorithm takes as input the QoS offers of all the WS advertisements and the QoS demand of the request in the form of OWL-Q specifications and returns four ordered lists of WS advertisements. It is composed of four parts/processes, which are analyzed in the four following subsections. Finally, the last subsection provides a small example of its application into a set of offers and one demand.

Alignment Process

Before analyzing our discovery algorithm, let us clarify its input. The input consists of I OWL-Q offers $O_i (1 \leq i \leq I, i \in \mathbb{N}^+)$ and one OWL-Q demand D. Every offer O_i guarantees a conjunctive list of goals G_{ij} with $1 \leq j \leq J_i$ and $J_i \in \mathbb{N}^+$. Every goal G_{ij} references K_{ij} metrics M_{ijk}, where $1 \leq k \leq K_{ij}$ and $K_{ij} \in \mathbb{N}^+$. Similarly, the demand D guarantees N conjunctive goals G_n^D, where $1 \leq n \leq N$ and $N \in \mathbb{N}^+$. Each goal G_n^D may have a weight $w_n^D \in [0.0, 1.0) \cup \{2.0\}$ and references L_n metrics M_{nl}^D, where $1 \leq l \leq L_n$ and $L_n \in \mathbb{N}^+$. Goals actually correspond to constraints, so if a demand's constraint has a weight in $[0.0, 1.0)$, then it is considered a *soft* constraint, otherwise it is a *hard* constraint that must be satisfied at any cost. Demand D also references a selection list S of the form (metric, weight).

The alignment process of our discovery algorithm aligns all offers Oi and demand D by finding their common QoS metrics by exploiting the QoS metric matching algorithm. It returns their corresponding CSPs after it has validated that these CSPs are consistent (i.e., they have a solution). If it finds an inconsistent offer CSP, it removes this offer from the discovery algorithm. If the demand's CSP is inconsistent, then the whole discovery algorithm fails. However, the CSPs of the offers are stored. The alignment process relies on the concept of the metric store (MS). The MS stores all unique QoS metrics encountered so far. So when a new QoS spec arrives, we do not need to examine if any of its metrics matches with any metric of all offers or demands but with any metric in the MS. In this way, there is a minimization of all the possible metric-to-metric comparisons. In case of a process failure, the MS's content also stays intact.

The process starts by examining the first QoS offer. It adds all of the offer's unique metrics to the MS and then it transforms it to the corresponding CSP. It solves the CSP and if it is inconsistent, then it adds the offer to a delete list. The process advances in a similar way with the other offers. However, when comparing an offer's metric with the MS, if there is a match, then a list (offer's metric, MS metric) is updated with a corresponding entry. Otherwise, the offer's metric is added to the MS. After all offers are processed, all inconsistent offers are deleted. Then the process works out the QoS demand similarly with the offers with the exception that if its CSP is inconsistent, then the whole discovery algorithm fails.

The transformation of a QoS spec to a CSP is carried out as follows. Initially, the CSP is empty. Then, for every unique metric of the QoS specification, we take two steps. **a)** We check if it was matched or not; If yes, then we get the matching MS metric and its position j in the MS and we add a definition to the CSP: $Xj :: a...b$, where $[a, b]$ is the value range of the matching MS metric. Otherwise, we get the position of the new metric in the MS and we add the definition: $Xj :: a...b$, where $[a, b]$ is the value range of the metric. **b)** For every goal, we check if the metric is contained in its expression. If yes, then if it was new, we update the goal's expression by substituting the name of the metric with the variable Xj; if it was matched, then we update the goal's expression by first substituting the name of the metric with the variable Xj and then applying the scale-to-scale transformation function to Xj in order not to change the meaning of the goal/constraint. After all metrics have been processed, for every goal we add its modified expression as a constraint to the CSP. For example, if the matching MS metric has scale minute and domain [0.0,2.0], the spec's metric has scale second and domain [1,120] and has goal *Metric* >= 100, then we add to the CSP the definition $Xj :: 0.0...2.0$ and the constraint $60 * Xj >= 100$.

Matchmaking Process

This process is based on the concept of conformance (Martin-Diaz et. al., 2003), which is mathematically expressed by the following equivalence:

$$conformance(O_i, D) \Leftrightarrow sat(CSP_i^O \wedge \neg CSP^D) = false \qquad (1)$$

To explain, an offer Oi matches a demand D when there is no solution to the offer's CSP_i^O that is not part of the solution set of the demand's CSP^D. As a CSP is a conjunction of constraints, we can rewrite (1) as

$$conformance(O_i, D) \Leftrightarrow sat(CSP_i^O \wedge \neg CSP^D) = false$$

$$\Leftrightarrow sat(CSP_i^O \wedge \neg(con_1^D \wedge con_2^D \wedge ... \wedge con_m^D)) = false$$

$$\Leftrightarrow sat(CSP_i^O \wedge (\neg con_1^D \vee \neg con_2^D \vee ... \vee \neg con_m^D)) = false$$

$$\Leftrightarrow sat((CSP_i^O \wedge \neg con_1^D) \vee (CSP_i^O \wedge \neg con_2^D) \vee ...(CSP_i^O \wedge \neg con_m^D)) = false$$

$$\Leftrightarrow sat(CSP_i^O \wedge \neg con_1^D) = sat(CSP_i^O \wedge \neg con_2^D) = ... = sat(CSP_i^O \wedge \neg con_m^D) = false$$

So, an offer Oi conforms to the demand D, if and only if all CSP problems—constructed by offer's CSP_i^O, the negation of a demand's constraint $\neg con_j^D$ and the definitions of variables participating in the negated constraint and not defined at the offer's CSP—are unsatisfiable.

This matchmaking process takes as input the CSPs of the offers and the demand and produces four types of results. For each offer's CSP_i^O it checks if it conforms to the demand's CSP^D by constructing N CSP problems (where N is the number of the constraints of the demand) and solving all of them. If all CSPs are unsatisfiable then there are two cases: **a)** if the offer's CSP contains constraints on variables not included at the CSP of the demand, then the offer and its CSP_i^O are put at the *super match* list; **b)** otherwise the offer and its CSP_i^O are put at the *exact match* list. For every CSP (from the N) that a solution is found, a counter is increased, the weight of the demand's constraint is added to a second counter, and the demand's non-negated constraint is put into a list. If at the end of the problem solving the counter equals N, then the offer and its CSP_i^O are put at the *fail match* list. Otherwise, the offer, its CSP_i^O, the value of the two counters, and the demand's violating constraints list are put at the *partial match* list as an entry. The first counter counts the number of satisfiable CSPs (i.e., number of conflicting original constraints of the demand) and the second counter measures the total sum of weights of these conflicting constraints. These constraints of the demand's CSP^D do not allow some solutions of the offer's CSP_i^O to be part of the demand's solution space. If they get relaxed, then the corresponding offer will conform to the demand.

Thus, the matchmaking process produces four types of results: *super*, *exact*, *partial*, and *fail* with decreasing order of significance. Super offers not only conform to the demand but also impose constraints on metrics not referenced by the demand's constraints. Exact offers just conform to the demand by using the same metrics. These two result types represent offers which conform to the demand. Partial offers do not conform to the demand because either they do not use some metrics of the demand or they contain solutions that are not part of the demand's solution space. So, partial results are promising, especially if the first two lists of results are empty. Fail offers contain lower quality solutions with respect to the solutions requested by the demand. If only fail matches are produced, then this is an indication of an over-constrained demand. In this case, the discovery algorithm fails and an appropriate warning is issued to the WS requester.

Constraint Relaxation Process

Assume that the matchmaking process returns only partial and fail type of results. Fail match results are of no use and are not further processed. However, partial results are promising as they represent QoS offers that do not use QoS metrics of the demand or have solutions that are not included in the solution space of the demand's CSP. If the first case holds, then two alternative solutions are possible. The first solution is to find the offer(s) with the smallest set of same undefined variables/metrics and then continue to the next process to order these offers. The user gets back the ordered list and an indicating message that the user's query was relaxed by removing some metrics and their unary constraints. However, this solution is not preferable if these removed variables participate in n-ary constraints ($n \geq 2$) involving not-removed variables as these constraints will also have to be removed.

The second solution of the first case is better and more general. Instead of removing an offer's CSP variables, we ask its service provider to enrich it with definitions of missing metrics and possible constraints on them. Then we restart the discovery algorithm with only these new offers and the original demand.

For the second case, the matchmaking process has provided two metrics for each *partial* offer: number of demand's conflicting original constraints and their total weight. So we order the partial list of offers according first to the total weight and then to the number of the conflicting constraints. In this way, at the top will be offers having the smallest number of hard constraints and the least total weight of weak constraints. So we put these topmost offers along with their conflicting constraints at the exact match list and we move to the last process in order to rank them and return them. However, the user is warned that this ordered list represents exact matches only if the user weakens the corresponding conflicting constraint list from the user's demand.

Selection Process

The goal of the selection process is to rank the best result lists produced by the previous processes. If *super* and/or *exact* matches exist, then they are ranked. Otherwise, there will be only *partial* matches to be ranked. By providing a sorted list of the best possible matches, the WS requester is supported in choosing the best QoS offer according to the requester's preferences, which are expressed by a list associating weights to QoS metrics.

Our selection process (Kritikos & Plexousakis, 2006) extends the one defined by Martín-Díaz et al. (2003) by a) having semantically aligned CSPs of offers; b) the score of each offer is produced by the weighted sum of the score of its worst solution plus the score of its best solution by having two CSOPs solved. More details are discussed by Kritikos and Plexousakis (2006).

Complete Example

To demonstrate our QoS-based WS discovery algorithm, we supply a simple example of its application to a small set of three QoS offers Oi and one demand D. The first offer O_1 references three metrics: a) *Resp1* that measures the QoS property of response time, uses the scale of seconds, and has (0.0, 86400] as value type; b) *Thr1* that measures the QoS property of throughput, uses the scale of requests per second, and has (0, 100000] as value type; c) *Avail1* that measures the QoS property of availability, uses the scale of ratio, and has (0.0, 1.0) as value type; and has the following list of goals: $Resp1 \leq 10.0 \wedge Thr1 \leq 100 \wedge Thr1 \geq 50 \wedge Avail1 \geq 0.9$. The second offer O_2 uses three metrics: **a)** *Resp2* measuring response time, using the scale of minutes, and having (0.0, 1440.0] as value type; **b)** *Thr1*; c) Avail*1*; and has the following list of goals: $Resp2 \leq 0.08 \wedge Thr1 \leq 50 \wedge Thr1 \geq 40 \wedge Avail1 \geq 0.95$. The third offer O_3 uses three metrics: **a)** *Resp2*; **b)** *Thr1*; **c)** *Avail2* measuring availability, using the scale of percentage, and having (0.0, 100.0) as value type; and has the following goals: $Resp2 \leq 0.06 \wedge Thr1 \leq 40 \wedge Thr1 \geq 30 \wedge Avail2 \geq 98.0$. Finally, demand D uses the metrics: a) *Resp1*; b) *Thr1*; c) *Avail2;* and has the following goals: $Resp1 \leq 15 \wedge Thr1 \geq 40 \wedge Avail2 \geq 99.0$. Moreover, the WS requester does not provide weights to the constraints of the requester's demand and associates the following weights to the requester's defined three metrics: $Resp1 \leftarrow 0.3$, $Thr1 \leftarrow 0.3$, $Avail2 \leftarrow 0.4$, while $a = 0.7$ and $b = 0.3$ (Kritikos & Plexousakis, 2006).

We now apply the four processes of our discovery algorithm. The alignment process matches metrics of the offers and the demand, stores first-seen QoS metrics at the MS, and produces four CSPs CSP_i^O and CSP^D. All CSPs have the following three definitions: $X_1 :: (0.0, 86400.0]$, $X_2 :: (0, 100000]$, and $X_3 :: (0.0, 1.0)$. Based on these variable definitions, each CSP has the following constraints: CSP_1^O :

$X_1 \leq 10.0 \wedge X_2 \leq 100 \wedge X_2 \geq 50 \wedge X_3 \geq 0.9, CSP_2^O :$

$X_1 / 60 \leq 0.08 \wedge X_2 \leq 50 \wedge X_2 \geq 40 \wedge X_3 \geq 0.95, CSP_3^O :$

$X_1 / 60 \leq 0.06 \wedge X_2 \leq 40 \wedge X_2 \geq 30 \wedge X_3 \cdot 100 \geq 98.0,$ and CSP^D

$X_1 \leq 15 \wedge X_2 \geq 40 \wedge X_3 \cdot 100 \geq 99.0.$

The matchmaking process checks the satisfiability of 9 CSPs (3 offer CSPs times 3 demand constraints) and produces four lists of results: *Super* = [ ], *Exact* = [ ], *Partial* = [(O_1, CSP_1^O, 1, 2.0, $X_3 \cdot 100 \leq 99.0$), (O_2, CSP_2^O, 1, 2.0, $X_3 \cdot 100 \leq 99.0$), (O_3, CSP_3^O, 2, 4.0, $X_2 \geq 40, X_3 \cdot 100 \leq 99.0$)], *Fail* = [ ]. The constraint relaxation process sorts the partial list based on the third and fourth argument of each entry and produces two lists that are passed to the last process. These lists are: *Exact** = [[(O_1, CSP_1^O), (O_2, CSP_2^O)], $X_3 \cdot 100 \leq 99.0$] and *Partial* = [O_3, CSP_3^O]. Finally, the selection process solves two CSOPs for each of the first two offers, produces one score for each: $Score_1^O \approx 0.37$ and $Score_2^O \approx 0.38$, and returns the following ordered list to the requester: *Matches* = [(O_2, 0.38), (O_1, 0.37)]. However, the WS requester is warned that this list contains offers that do not satisfy the requester's constraint: $X_3 \cdot 100 \leq 99.0$.

As it can be seen from this example, offer O_2 is at the top of the result list as it violates in a significantly lower amount the last constraint of the demand with respect to the amount of violation of O_1. So if O_2 is selected by the WS requester, then the minimum possible constraint relaxation will have been achieved.

DISCUSSION

QoS is a broad concept encompassing many nonfunctional properties of WSs. In this chapter, a definition of QoS for WSs was supplied. Then, the most common and applicable QoS properties were first grouped into QoS categories and then analyzed. Next, the advantages of QoS management in the lifecycle of WSs were broken down with special attention to the WS description and discovery processes.

Most research approaches for QoS-based WS description either lack the semantics or do not provide a rich QoS model which captures every QoS aspect. As a result, the QoS-based WS discovery process fails in producing accurate and recallable results. This conclusion was inferred after a long and deep survey had been conducted. This survey dealt with both the requirements in QoS-based WS description and discovery and the deficiencies of the current research approaches. In this chapter, after the results of the above survey are revealed, a complete semantic framework for QoS-based WS description and discovery is proposed that solves the above deficiencies. For QoS-based WS description, a semantic, formal, rich, and extensible QoS model (as an extension of OWL-S) is proposed that is based on ontologies and captures every aspect of QoS description.

The current QoS-based WS discovery approaches fail because they syntactically compare QoS metrics. For this reason, a semantic QoS metric matching algorithm has been developed. By using this algorithm, the most prominent QoS-based WS matchmaking and selection algorithms were extended in order to provide better results. Besides this extension, some deficiencies of these algorithms were corrected and also their functionality was improved. What remains to be done is the (empirical) evaluation of these extended algorithms in order to show their improvement and correct functionality.

As a future work that will extend the proposed framework, four extensions can be exploited. The first one concerns the development of tools. As for now, very few tools have been developed for the semantic

WS description and none for the QoS specification and querying of WSs. The object of research is more automation for the QoS-based WS description and discovery processes and less user involvement in these processes. Therefore, there is an ongoing need for the implementation of tools. These tools should help the user, whether the user is a WS provider or requester, to describe or query QoS for WSs, to understand and analyze the QoS requirements or performance of the user's application and the impact QoS has on the resources used, and to view the results of the user's query in an appropriate way. In addition, these tools should cooperate with other tools that have been developed and are being used in functional WS description and discovery.

Another extension is the use of advanced techniques for solving over-constrained problems like semiring-based constraint satisfaction (Bistarelli et. al., 1997) as alternatives to the branch-and-bound algorithm used for constraint optimization solving by the majority of CSP engines. In addition, we have identified that the metric of conformance is not perfect as it excludes from the discovery result set offers that provide better solutions than that of the demand. That is why the mathematical definition of conformance is going to be modified appropriately and our QoS-based matchmaking algorithm is going to be altered correspondingly.

OWL-Q should be extended appropriately with the description of the remaining nonfunctional properties, which along with the QoS properties constitute the notion of *class of service*. A special interest is in the subset of these remaining properties called *context* (Broens, Pokraev, Sinderen, Koolwaaij, & Costa, 2004). The result of the incorporation of context is a more accurate and customizable WS discovery process as the tasks of request and input completion, output adaptation, and added-value composition of service-offerings become possible.

The last but very important extension is the realization of QoS-based WS composition. This can be achieved by enforcing global QoS constraints and using for every QoS metric, metric evaluation functions imposed on any possible workflow (WS) composition construct to produce global QoS metric values (Yu & Lin, 2005) through construct reduction. Of course this extension can be implemented only after our semantic QoS-based WS framework is fully implemented.

REFERENCES

Anbazhagan, M., & Nagarajan, A. (2002, January). *Understanding quality of service for Web services.* IBM Developerworks Website.

Balke, W.-T., & Wagner, M. (2003). Cooperative discovery for user-centered Web service provisioning. In L.-J. Zhang (Ed.), *Proceedings of the International Conference on Web Services (ICWS)* (pp. 191-197). LasVegas: CSREA Press.

Benatallah, B., Sheng, Q. Z., Ngu, A. H. H., & Dumas, M. (2002). Declarative composition and peer-to-peer provisioning of dynamic Web services. In *ICDE* (pp. 297-308). San Jose, CA: IEEE Computer Society.

Bistarelli, S., Montanari, U., & Rossi, F. (1997). Semiring-based constraint satisfaction and optimization. *J. ACM, 44*(2), 201-236.

Broens, T. H. F., Pokraev, S., Sinderen, M. J. van, Koolwaaij, J., & Costa, P. D. (2004). *Context-aware, ontology-based, service discovery.* Paper presented at the European Symposium on Ambient Intelligence

(EUSAI), Eindhoven, The *Netherlands* (Vol. 3295, pp. 72-83). Berlin/Heidelberg: Springer. Retrieved June 5, 2008, from http://eprints.eemcs.utwente.nl/7420/

Caprotti, O., Dewar, M., & Turi, D. (2004). Mathematical service matching using description logic and owl. In A. Asperti, G. Bancerek, & A. Trybulec (Eds.), *Mathematical knowledge management (mkm)* (Vol. 3119, pp. 73-87). Bialowieza, Poland: Springer.

Cardoso, J., Sheth, A. P., Miller, J. A., Arnold, J., & Kochut, K. (2004). Quality of service for workflows and Web service processes. *Journal of Web Semantics, 1*(3), 281-308.

Christensen, E., Curbera, F., Meredith, G., & Weerawarana, S. (2001). *Web services description language (wsdl) 1.1* (W3C note). Retrieved June 5, 2008, from http://www.w3.org/TR/wsdl

Clark, D. D., Shenker, S., & Zhang, L. (1992). Supporting real-time applications in an integrated services packet network: Architecture and mechanism. *SIGCOMM Comput. Commun. Rev., 22*(4), 14-26.

Cruz, R. L. (1995). Quality of service guarantees in virtual circuit switched networks. *IEEE Journal on Selected Areas in Communications, 13*(6), 1048-1056.

Deora, V., Shao, J., Gray, W. A., & Fiddian, N. J. (2003). A quality of service management framework based on user expectations. In M. E. Orlowska, S. Weerawarana, M. P. Papazoglou, & J. Yang (Eds.), *ICSOC*(Vol. 2910, pp. 104-114). Trento, Italy: Springer.

Facciorusso, C., Field, S., Hauser, R., Hoffner, Y., Humbel, R., Pawlitzek, R., et al. (2003). A Web services matchmaking engine for Web services. In K. Bauknecht, A. M. Tjoa, & G. Quirchmayr (Eds.), *EC-Web* (Vol. 2738, p. 37-49). Prague, Czech Republic: Springer.

Frølund, S., & Koistinen, J. (1998). Quality of services specification in distributed object systems design. In *Proceedings of the 4th Conference on USENIX Conference on Object-Oriented Technologies and Systems (COOTS '98)* (Vol. 5, No. 4, pp. 179-202).

Georgiadis, L., Guérin, R., Peris, V., & Sivarajan, K. N. (1996). Efficient network QoS provisioning based on per node traffic shaping. *IEEE/ACM Trans. Netw., 4*(4), 482-501.

Heflin, J., & Hendler, J. (2000). Searching the Web with SHOE. Paper presented at the *Artificial Intelligence for Web Search, Papers from the AAAI Workshop. WS-00-01* (pp.   35-40). Menlo Park, CA: AAAI Press.

Jin, L., Machiraju, V., & Sahai, A. (2002, June). *Analysis on service level agreement of Web services* (Tech. Rep. No. HPL-2002-180). USA: Software Technology Laboratories, HP Laboratories.

Keller, A., & Ludwig, H. (2003). The WSLA framework: Specifying and monitoring service level agreements for Web services. *Journal of Network and Systems Management, 11*(1), 57-81.

Kritikos, K., & Plexousakis, D. (2006). Semantic QoS metric matching. In *Proceedings of the European Conference on Web Services, Ecows '06* (pp. 265-274). Washington, D.C.: IEEE Computer Society.

Kritikos, K., & Plexousakis, D. (2007). Requirements for QoS-based Web service description and discovery. *Compsac, 02*, 467-472.

Lee, K., Jeon, J., Lee, W., Jeong, S.-H., & Park, S.-W. (2003, November). *Qos for Web services: Requirements and possible approaches.* World Wide Web Consortium (W3C).

Lee, Y. W., Strong, D. M., Kahn, B. K., & Wang, R. Y. (2002). Aimq: A methodology for information quality assessment. *Information Management, 40*(2), 133-146.

Leymann, F. (2001). *Web services flow language (wsfl 1.0)* (Tech. Rep.). IBM Corporation.

Liebesman, S. (1994, July). ISO 9000: An introduction. *Using ISO 9000 to improve business processes* (Chapter 1). AT&T Corporate Quality Office.

Liu, Y., Ngu, A. H. H., & Zeng, L. (2004). QoS computation and policing in dynamic Web service selection. In S. I. Feldman, M. Uretsky, M. Najork, & C. E. Wills (Eds.), *WWW (alternate track papers & posters)* (pp. 66-73). New York: ACM.

Martín-Díaz, O., Cortés, A. R., Benavides, D., Durán, A., & Toro, M. (2003). A quality-aware approach to Web services procurement. In B. Benatallah & M.-C. Shan (Eds.), *Technologies for e-services (TES)* (Vol. 2819, pp. 42-53). Berlin: Springer.

Maximilien, E. M., & Singh, M. P. (2002). Conceptual model of Web service reputation. *SIGMOD Rec., 31*(4), 36-41.

Noia, T. D., Sciascio, E. D., Donini, F. M., & Mongiello, M. (2003). A system for principled matchmaking in an electronic marketplace. In *Proceedings of the 12th International Conference on World Wide Web, WWW '03* (pp. 321-330). New York: ACM Press.

Oldham, N., Verma, K., Sheth, A., & Hakimpour, F. (2006). Semantic WS-agreement partner selection. In *Proceedings of the 15th International Conference on World Wide Web, WWW '06* (pp. 697-706). New York: ACM Press.

Papazoglou, M. P. (2003). Service-oriented computing: Concepts, characteristics and directions. In *Proceedings of the 4th International Conference on Web Information Systems Engineering, WISE '03* (pp. 3-12). Rome: IEEE Computer Society.

Ran, S. (2003). A model for Web services discovery with QoS. *SIGecom Exch.,* (1), 1-10.

Sabata, B., Chatterjee, S., Davis, M., Sydir, J. J., & Lawrence, T. F. (1997). Taxomomy of QoS specifications. In *Proceedings of the 3rd Workshop on bject-Oriented Real-Time Dependable Systems (WORDS '97)* (pp. 100-107). Washington, D.C.: IEEE Computer Society.

Salamatian, K., & Fdida, S. (2001). Measurement based modeling of quality of service in the Internet: A methodological approach. In *Proceedings of the Thyrrhenian International Workshop on Digital Communications IWDC'01* (pp. 158-174). London: Springer-Verlag.

Sivashanmugam, K., Sheth, A. P., Miller, J. A., Verma, K., Aggarwal, R., & Rajasekaran, P. (2003). Metadata and semantics for Web services and processes. In W. Benn, P. Dadam, S. Kirn, & R. Unland (Eds.), *Datenbanken und informationssysteme: Festschrift zum 60. geburtstag von gunter schlageter* (pp. 245-271). Hagen: FernUniversitÄat in Hagen, Fachbereich Informatik.

Sumra, R., & Arulazi, D. (2003, March). *Quality of service for Web services: Demystification, limitations, and best practices.* Developer.com Website.

Sycara, K., Burstein, M., Hobbs, J., Lassila, O., Mc Dermott, D., McIlraith, S., et al. (2003). *Owl-s 1.0 release.* Retrieved June 5, 2008, from http://www.daml.org/services/owl-s/1.0/

Tian, M., Gramm, A., Nabulsi, M., Ritter, H., Schiller, J., & Voigt, T. (2003, October). *QoS integration in Web services.* Gesellschaft fur Informatik DWS 2003, Doktorandenworkshop Technologien und Anwendungen von XML.

Tosic, V., Esfandiari, B., Pagurek, B., & Patel, K. (2002). *On requirements for ontologies in management of Web services.* Revised Papers presented at the International Workshop on Web Services, E-Business, and the Semantic Web CAISE '02/WES '02 (pp. 237-247). London: Springer-Verlag.

Tosic, V., Ma, W., Pagurek, B., & Esfandiari, B. (2003). *On the dynamic manipulation of classes of service for xml Web services* (Research Rep. No. SCE-03-15). Ottawa, Canada: Department of Systems and Computer Engineering, Carleton University.

Tosic, V., Pagurek, B., & Patel, K. (2003). WSOL: A language for the formal specification of classes of service for Web services. In L.-J. Zhang (Ed.), *Proceedings of the International Conference on Web Services (ICWS)* (pp. 375-381). Las Vegas: CSREA Press.

Van Hentenryck, P., & Saraswat, V. (1996). Strategic directions in constraint programming. *ACM Computing Surveys, 28*(4), 701-726.

Yu, T., & Lin, K.-J. (2005). Service selection algorithms for composing complex services with multiple QoS constraints. In B. Benatallah, F. Casati, & P. Traverso (Eds.), *ICSOC* (Vol. 3826, pp. 130-143). Amsterdam, The Netherlands: Springer.

Zeng, L., Benatallah, B., Dumas, M., Kalagnanam, J., & Sheng, Q. Z. (2003). Quality driven Web services composition. In *Proceedings of the 12th International Conference on World Wide Web, WWW '03* (pp. 411-421). New York: ACM Press.

Zhou, C., Chia, L.-T., & Lee, B.-S. (2004). DAML-QoS ontology for Web services. In *Proceedings of the IEEE International Conference on Web services (ICWS '04)* (pp. 472-479). Washington, D.C.: IEEE Computer Society.

Chapter VII
Web Services Dependability

Michael C. Jaeger
Berlin University of Technology, Germany

Matthias Werner
Operating Systems Group, TU Chemnitz, Germany

ABSTRACT

This chapter presents the definition of relevant terminology and a conceptual model of the basic terms. The chapter starts with the presentation of research in the area of dependability. Based on this, Web service concepts related to the dependability are introduced. The presentation leads into a statement identifying individual quality-of-service (QoS) characteristics for forming dependable Web services. Then, the chapter discusses the current status quo in the area of QoS-aware Web services. This part is divided into three subparts: description, management, and monitoring. This also identifies ongoing efforts as well as efforts that do not show present activity. By this discussion, this chapter puts research about dependability in relation with ongoing QoS-related efforts in the Web services domain. Thus it identifies how these efforts can be combined in order to form a dependable Web services platform.

INTRODUCTION

The Web services as an implementation of the service oriented architecture (SOA) represents a trend in the IT industry for the development of a flexible and unifying software infrastructure. Picking up the Web services idea, software components provide their functionality as a service by using uniform interface description and invocation protocols using XML formats and Internet communication protocols.

One important characteristic in an open, distributed system is that services can appear, disappear, and bound dynamically at run time. The deployment and use of Web services also results in a varying level of quality. The access to Web services can involve the Internet and thus relies, as mentioned above, on its protocols. As the Web pages in the Internet, Web services are provided on a best-effort basis as well. Indeed, Internet protocols are known for their robustness. However, they do not guarantee that a connection can be established and can be held at given characteristics. Thus, for some soft real-time applications such as telephony or brokering stocks, reservation and signalling extensions to the Internet protocols are used, making Web services more reliable. In addition, the basic SOA idea of a loosely coupled provision of services, which also applies to Web services, forms also a problem. The binding of services leaves generally open what time it takes to find a service, to bind a service, and how reliable the service execution will perform. Thus, the use of loose-coupling mechanisms poses a problem regarding a satisfactory overall performance.

These quality of service (QoS) issues with Web services are well known. Thus, several recent developments and approaches have been proposed that extend the Web services with individual attributes, such as security, integrity, reliability, availability, and further characteristics. Today, a large number of proposals and efforts exist that provide research on description formats for QoS-aware Web services (e.g., Tosic, Patel, & Pagurek, 2002; Ludwig, Keller, Dan, King, & Franck, 2003; Ran 2003; Zhou, Chia, & Lee, 2004), a management infrastructure (e.g., Sahai et al., 2002; Wang, Chen, Wang, Fung, & Uczekaj, 2004), and monitoring approaches (e.g., Baresi, Guinea, & Plebani, 2005; Sahai et al., 2002; Tosic, Ma, Pagurek, & Esfandiari, 2004). In the recent years, standards and recommendations from nonprofit organisations have also emerged to form a community-wide consensus for establishing reliable Web services (e.g., WS-reliability) (OASIS, 2004). In summary, the different QoS issues have already been extensively covered in the Web services domain.

An Assessment of Web Services Dependability

The research on dependable computer systems started long before the Web service proposal came to life. For 20 years ago, different efforts have discussed the concept of dependability (Cavano & McCall 1978; IEC 1997; Laprie 1992; Parhami 1988). The motivation of this research is to provide a unifying concept for operational quality issues when using computer systems. The result of this research is a unifying and comprehensive view on the QoS of a system. The importance of a comprehensive work becomes clear, if we consider, for example, the provision of execution or response time guarantees. Time guarantees rely on the correct operation in general.

The research on dependability provides a unifying view on different individual QoS characteristics. Which characteristics are of particular relevance depends on the application case. Thus, a set of relevant characteristics varies depending on the standpoint; often-involved characteristics are the reliability, the availability, maintainability, security, or diagnosability (Parhami, 1988). We think that such a unifying view is also required in the Web service domain. Thus, we present the state of the art of research on dependability in order to create a framework for discussing individual QoS-related efforts in the Web services area. The result is a comprehensive assessment of the state of the art in order to provide an orientation to the research community and industry users to identify the current outcomes, efforts, and also shortcomings in the area of QoS-aware Web services. The work starts with the definition of a common terminology and a conceptual model of basic terms. Then, the current state of the art in the area of QoS-aware Web service developments is presented. In detail, the following parts are proposed:

- Presentation of research in the area of dependability: This involves the discussion of existing definitions of the term dependability. This discussion leads into a statement about which individual QoS characteristics must be considered in order to form dependable Web services.

- Assessment of the current status quo in the area of QoS-aware Web services: This assessment is divided into three main parts, dividing the research about QoS-aware Web services: modelling, integration, and monitoring. This part also identifies ongoing efforts as well as efforts that do not show present activity.
- Analysis of the existing efforts forms the third part: Based on the presentation of the dependability and the assessment in the Web services area, it is determined which of the current efforts are suitable to form a dependable Web services platform. In addition, this analysis also points out which issues are not well covered so far. For example, the diagnosability is a mentioned characteristic in the area of dependable computing. However, to our present knowledge research work in the area of diagnosability of Web services appears to be rare.

The general aim of this work is to put research efforts in the area of dependable systems in relation with ongoing QoS-related efforts in the Web services domain. Thus, a comprehensive overview of both of these fields is provided. One of the anticipated results is to identify how well current individual efforts can be used together in order to form a dependable Web services platform.

DEPENDABILITY

The concept of dependability has changed over the years. As a native of the rather narrow area of fault-tolerance research, it has broadened its semantics and became an "umbrella term." One can observe this development in the publications of Birolini. In 1991, he had warned of the use of the term in a broad sense; however, later in 1997, the author provided exactly such a broad definition. The IEC norm 60050 defines dependability in the following way (IEC 1997, Chapter 191): The collective term used to describe the availability performance and its influencing factors: reliability performance, maintainability performance and maintenance support performance.

Whereas this definition provides a certain generality, it clearly focuses on availability. Several areas that are today counted to issues of dependability are not covered by this definition (e.g., impairments of the security). The scientific community uses today usually a definition of dependability similar to the one presented by Laprie (1995):

Dependability *is defined as that property of a computer system such that reliance can justifiable be placed on the service it delivers. The service delivered by a system is it behaviour as it is perceptible to its user(s); a user is another system (human or physical) which interacts with the former.* (p. 42)

The dependability concept can be decomposed into three aspects: threads on dependability, attributes of dependability, and means to establish or keep dependability. Figure 1 shows these three aspects in relation to the dependability as levels of a tree, which is based on the work of Avizienis, Laprie, and Randell (2001, p. 2). One can find similar structured concepts to measure software quality already by Cavano and McCall (1978). The nodes in this tree each represent a concept while the edges indicate a composition relation, implying that from left to right, a left concept is comprised by the concepts on the right side of the relation. Of special interest are the attributes; they demonstrate the wide range of the dependability concept. The **attributes** of dependability are properties of the system providing a service, and they are:

- The readiness for usage of the system's service leads to availability;
- The continuity of service leads to reliability;
- The nonoccurrence of undesired impacts[1] on the system's environment leads to safety;
- The nonoccurrence of unauthorised disclosure of information leads to confidentiality;
- The nonoccurrence of improper alterations of information or service leads to integrity; and
- The ability to reestablish one or more of the mentioned properties leads to maintainability.

For several properties, measures exist that allow quantification. For example, for the reliability the probability measure exists with the same name that expresses the likelihood that a system provides its service during a given time interval. Regarding the expression, it depends on the definition of the service correctness, that is, which conditions apply for deciding on whether a service is unavailable or failing. This definition is subject of an agreement between service user and service provider. Nondiscrete correctness parameters of a service are frequently named QoS.

The dependability attributes are attributes of the system that a service provides. However, for Web services it is often not clear or at least hard to determine what exactly the providing system is, or what the system borders are, respectively. To outline this fact, one frequently finds that dependability attributes are applied to the service itself, for example, in terms as *service availability* or *service reliability*.

HOW WEB SERVICES COVER DEPENDABILITY

Looking at dependability in the Web services domain, we can see many individual efforts that cover only a part of the entire attributes of dependability. Some extensions only cover the service availability; some other only covers safety issues. Today, we are not aware of any research that introduces a comprehensive framework for providing conceptual and technical extensions to the Web services architecture as introduced by the W3C (Booth, Haas, McCabe, Newcomer, Champion, & Ferris, 2004). When

Figure 1. Dependability tree

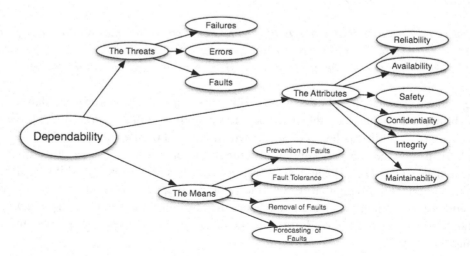

discussing the dependability referring to Web services, we can easily find that some ideas that have lead to the Web services proposal already covers some of the dependability issues introduced above; they come just out-of-the-box when using Web services. Other dependability attributes clearly require extensions to the Web service architecture. Thus, we can distinguish between intrinsic and optional coverage of dependability of Web services.

As an example for an intrinsic support, Web services have been introduced in order to make a distributed computer system less complex and dependencies more explicit. Following these two characteristics makes a Web services application easier to maintain which represents a clear benefit referring to the maintainability of that system. Referring to the previously given structure, focusing on a system's simplicity improves the prevention of faults. On the other side, many external facilities exist that are extensions, add-ons, or optional systems components to a Web service system in order cover other issues of the dependability as introduced in the next section. For example, a reservation mechanism that manages response time guarantees of a service represents such a facility and is a separate extension to existing implementations of Web services.

Dependable SOA

When discussing the SOA, the first question that comes up is what the new improvements about SOA are when considering the component-orientation that evolved several years before. Component-orientation is an architectural pattern proposing to divide a system into individual functional parts. These functional parts should have a well-defined interface and well-defined dependencies regarding the relations of a component to its environment. A component of a system should be replaceable and individually deployable (Szyperski, 1997) as this represents the main objective to design a system in a component-oriented way.

The second main anticipated advantage from component-orientation is to reduce the development complexity when designing and building a system. With defined interfaces and dependencies, the development effort can be split into individual efforts. Thus, the overall complexity is reduced.

The components of a standard personal computer are an example for this approach. A computer system consists of several hardware components. And, no manufacturer designs and builds all the components within an integrated complex development effort. Rather, defined interfaces and dependencies exist for each of the components: sockets for processors, standard interfaces for hard drives and expansion cards, or a bus-system for desktop devices. Based on the standardised interfaces, individual component manufacturers are specialised for the development and production of hard drives, graphic cards, keyboards, and so forth. Moreover, the component orientation eases the replacement of defective or outdated components. If a hard drive becomes too small, it is easily replaced with a larger model. If a keyboard is defective, it is also replaced easily. We can see that the partition of a system into components improves the dependability in the following way:

- **Reduced Development Complexity.** The *reduced development complexity* results in a less error-prone development (Schmidt, 1999). This is an indirect advantage regarding the reliability of the system.
- **Development Reliability.** Defined interfaces and dependencies also improve the testing. The fact that it is explicitly defined how to communicate with a component enables a real-world testing. In such a setup, it is very likely that test and later use of the component will be performed in the same manner. Thus, the efficiency of testing is improved which improves the reliability of the system.

- **Software Maturity.** Another anticipated benefit with component-orientation is also the reuse of existing and evolving software components. For example, Schmidt explains that a common technique to professional software development is to rather take already proven software (components) than a new development (Schmidt 1999). The idea of component-orientation anticipates the reuse of software components and thus improves the reliability.

- **Maintainability.** The ease to remove individual components of a system also supports maintenance activities during a system's runtime. In a component-oriented system, components can be easily removed, and modified or improved components can easily replace previous versions. Also, continuous testing during the runtime of components is improved. For example, in computer systems, the logic board at system start up automatically tests memory components. In this example, different manufacturers have built memory modules and logic board. However, with defined interfaces, both components can interoperate.

In the area of software systems, the component-orientation has been widely adopted because of its clear advantages. Thus, many software systems feature a form of component orientation. Programming APIs and frameworks exist that allow developers to easily implement a component-oriented architecture (e.g., Java Beans [Hamilton, 1997], Enterprise Java Beans [Matena & Stearns, 2000], or the CORBA component model [OMG 1995]).

The SOA picks up the advantages of a component-oriented architecture and extends this approach to build a system that focuses more on the provisioning of services. As a consequence, SOA is not defining a new technology, but it improves the way its functionality is provided. Looking at the Web services implementation, this means the adoption of Internet protocols for the communication between the involved parties and the use of XML for the data. The maturity and robustness of Internet protocols for communication is well known. Thus, these protocols and languages do not only bring the advantage of an easy implementation for different computer platforms, but also they improve the reliability when using Web services.

The Web services architecture also proposes the use of XML. The XML is a widely adopted specification for formatting and encoding documents. It is supported by many applications on many platforms. Many platforms and technologies support the use of XML-based languages. The main reason for using XML and the reason for its success is that it improves the compatibility among the involved parties when exchanging data. By this way, the dependencies to particular platform specific issues are reduced.

- **Proven Technology.** Web services build upon mature and proven Internet protocols. The reuse of these for the communication among the involved parties improves the reliability of the system.

- **Reduced Dependencies.** The use of XML and Internet protocols reduce unnecessary dependencies to particular soft- or hardware platforms. As a consequence, it is easier to replace individual components provided in a Web service environment. Thus, the maintainability is improved.

The previous points have explained the SOA approach and Web services. The essence is that Web services are designed in particular to improve the maintainability and reliability when building and running a distributed software system. We name that intrinsic dependability of Web services which covers the reliability and the maintainability of a system.

WEB SERVICES DEPENDABILITY EXTENSIONS

The previous section has explained what dependability attributes are provided with the design and specification of Web services. It has explained that it is components-orientation and the SOA approach has led to a improvement of reliability and of maintainability when building distributed systems. However, the Web services architecture does not support all other attributes that we have introduced in the previous section (Dependability Section). For example, the confidentiality is not covered at all. In addition, the previous section has explained that using SOA to build a distributed system improved the reliability. However, quantitative reliability measures cannot be applied to these.

Research and industry efforts have proposed several extensions to the Web service architecture in order to improve or to support particular attributes of dependability. We can divide these additions to the Web service architecture into three main categories:

1. **Design and Development.** Additions for designing and building Web services: This leads to the area of modelling languages and methodology.
2. **Integration.** Facilities and conventions that cover the establishment of a service relation: This covers the integration of Web services.
3. **Provision.** Additional software and facilities for controlling and monitoring Web services: This covers the invocation and provision of Web services.

Designing Dependability

As mentioned above, we are not aware of a comprehensive approach for designing dependability issues of a Web services system in general. However, several separate approaches exist that cover individual approaches. Today, we can assume that most software development efforts start with a kind of modelling task, regardless if the development effort leads to an implementation of a model-driven architecture (MDA) (OMG, 2001a) or if it favours the unstructured use of models for the communication among involved parties. Such modelling languages are extensions to the state of the art in software modelling, that is, the unified modelling language (UML) (OMG, 2001b), in most cases. In general, the UML specification supports two main kinds of extensions to customise the use of UML: a), either using the standardised way as an UML profile which refines the given elements of the UML or b), setting attributes to individual elements of a diagram. In the latter case, the expression and the formatting of the attributes must be defined separately.

In the UML world, we can divide the existing approaches into two main categories: approaches that model security aspects and approaches that cover the reliability and its related concepts, such as the availability.

Modelling Security

Referring to the security, there are the three previously introduced aspects, that is, integrity, confidentiality, and the (operating) safety that are supported by two main proposals in the UML area: SecureUML (Lodderstedt, Basin, & Doser, 2002) and UMLsec (Jürjens, 2002). Both approaches extend the UML language by constructs to support security attributes. Lodderstedt et al. have proposed SecureUML. It focuses on the support of confidentiality. The proposal explains how to extend the UML by defining a

UML profile. Besides the new modelling elements, the authors also emphasise that a successful security modelling effort also requires a sound development method. Thus, their motivation was to propose a language that integrates into an MDA-based development environment. The UMLsec proposal (Jürjens, 2002) is a combination of an UML profile and additional consistency tools in order to reason about the correctness of the modelled security attributes. Thus, the focus of the work by Juerjens is not only on the confidentiality but also on other security attributes, such as integrity.

Both approaches have in common that they see the security as mandatory part of the design process when developing systems. Regarding the particular coverage of Web services, Juerjens explains the applicability to an HTTP server and Lodderstedt et al. explain the application of their solution in a component-oriented environment (Basin, Doser, & Lodderstedt, 2003).

Modelling Reliability

Another large area of designing dependability is the area of reliability. As seen for the security, the idea is to assess initial requirements on reliability and to express these requirements within a software model modelling the Web service in its whole or its parts. The extensions are similar to the approaches for the security. The most prominent approach is the UML QoS profile (OMG, 2004), which proposes the modelling of several attributes including reliability, availability, and security. In general, the term QoS refers to attributes that describe a quality when using a system. The concept of QoS subsumes the dependability. Because different authors have proposed the modelling of Web service-based applications using an MDA-based approach (e.g., Skogan, Grønmo, & Solheim, 2004; Grønmo, Skogan, Solheim, & Oldevik, 2004; Bézivin, Hammoudi, Lopes, & Jouault, 2004; Kath, Blazarenas, Born, Eckert, Funabashi, & Hirai, 2004), the UML QoS profile is a natural language for dependency modelling in this area (Grønmo & Jaeger 2005). Additional efforts have proposed a proprietary conceptual model and modelling language for the support of dependability attributes. Examples are the QoS ontology of the Web service QoS framework of Maximilien and Singh (2004), or the QoS model by Ran (2003). Before the UML and its extensions gained the interest of the Web service community, Frølund and Koistinen (1998) proposed a textual modelling language covering several aspects of dependability-named QML.

In summary, the modelling of individual dependability attributes has been covered already. Since the UML is a language for software systems, several authors of the Web service community propose the use of UML for the development of Web service-based systems. However, the community lacks an unifying view that combines the reliability and the security of a system. The UML QoS profile covers the expression of security attributes (the confidentiality, the integrity, and the safety) of the modelled objects. However, the definitions cover the description of either one or two attributes only (e.g., "+safety-level: integer" [OMGm 2004, Section 10.7]) and do not go as far as the UMLsec or SecureUML proposals.

Dependability at Integration

The next part on Web service dependability covers the facilities and languages that cover different attributes of the dependability in order to facilitate agreements for warranting conformance to particular dependability goals. The QoS framework proposal from the ISO calls these mechanisms QoS establishment mechanisms, assuming that individual aspects of dependability can be subsumed under the concept of QoS (ISO/IEC 1997, Section 3.3.3). In essence, these mechanisms cover the establishment between service provider and service consumer. The service provider has particular capabilities that the service provider can offer. And the service consumer has particular requirements on the dependability that the service consumer can express as a precondition for the service invocation.

In the area of Web services, Tosic et al. (2004) has introduced the Web services offerings infrastructure (WSOI). This infrastructure features both, a mechanism to evaluate the conformance of dependability level offers to requirements, and a language that allows both parties to express these offers. This language, named Web services offerings language (WSOL) (Tosic, Patel, & Pagurek, 2002) is tailored for performing the negotiation between the provider and consumer as a part of an integration process on the side of the consumer. The language offers elements to define attributes that allow a numerical expression, such as the response time or an availability percentage. Researchers from IBM have proposed a language with a similar aim called the Web service level agreement (WSLA) (Ludwig et al., 2003) language, which has been recently updated to the Web service agreement language (WS-agreement), (OGF, 2007). Contrary to the WSOL, the WS-agreement also defines the nature of the agreement process that covers several phases. It presumes that particular dependability attributes are defined separately.

Besides the direct communication between service requester and provider there is also the approach to integrate a service broker into the setup of service provider and consumer. The broker maintains a collection of service offers submitted by the provider. Then, a service consumer can query the broker for services meeting the requirements. For this purpose, the universal description discovery and integration (UDDI) (UDDI Spec Technical Committee, 2003) specification is foreseen in a Web service setup. UDDI defines the API and the data model that a broker should implement in order to manage and provide service offerings. Building on the UDDI, extensions and additions exist to manage dependability aspects. Such extensions propose to add new keys to the data model that must be agreed on by all three involved parties. Lee (2003) as well as Ran (2003) have proposed such an extension for the QoS-based selection of Web services. Examples for discussing how to implement the particular extension to a UDDI service are given by Ali Rana, Al-Ali, and Walker (2003) with UDDIe and by Microsoft's (2003) introduction of UDDI. Thus, it is up to the specific application case how to support particular attributes of dependability.

A different approach is to provide dedicated QoS brokers. The already mentioned QoS framework by Maximilien and Singh (2004) involves a separate broker as a component of this setup. Also, Yu and Lin (2005), Serhani, Dssouli, Sahraoui, Benharref, and Badidi (2005) and Wang et al. (2004) propose an architecture featuring a dedicated broker in order to support for particular dependability aspects. In all these cases, a service consumer searching for a particular service is offered a facility to process referring requirements. Compared with the UDDI-based approach, a dedicated broker requires more infrastructures. However, the motivation for establishing a separate broker is to easily support additional functionality. For example, Yu and Lin (2005) propose a broker that automatically maintains statistics on recently measured dependability attributes. Such functionality is not covered so far by the UDDI specification and thus requires a separate system. Same as with the UDDI, the works proposing a dedicated broker do not pose a limitation to particular dependability attributes.

In summary, there are three main ways to support the establishment of agreements for the integration of Web services:

- **Extending Existing Brokers.** The most effortless approach is the extension of existing broker systems, such as the mentioned examples for the UDDI specification. However, this approach only allows the management of dependability descriptions as the UDDI specification does not cover any monitoring or update functionality.

- **Dedicated Brokers.** The provision of dedicated brokers for the management of dependability attributes is a more effort-intense approach, but allows the integration of additional functionality.
- **Direct Negotiation.** As a third approach, researchers propose the direct negotiation between the parties when it comes to the integration of Web services to cover particular dependability attributes.

Besides these three approaches, there is also the possibility to implement dependability facilities into a common platform, both hosting and serving service provider and requester. Then, the service use is not subject to any individual negotiations or queries but overall dependability-ensuring facilities. Wang et al. (2004) have described the architecture of such a Web service-based middleware in order to serve as a service backbone within the Boeing corporation. The WS-reliability, mentioned in the introduction, also proposes an extension to the SOAP in order to improve the protocol with regard to reliability mechanisms like the support for guaranteed deliveries (OASIS, 2004). However, such approaches are special extensions or implementations that require broad adoption by the Web service community. They do not provide the wide acceptance of the basic SOA that makes Web services into an open distributed system and allow the establishment of dynamic application-to-application communication (A2A) at the runtime of the system.

Runtime Dependability

During a Web service invocation, failures can always occur as this is an inherent characteristic of distributed systems. Thus, monitoring of recovery mechanisms must be performed in order to preserve global dependability goals. The recovery mechanism can be of, in essence, two categories. First, a mechanism can perform autonomic, meaning that no particular user interaction is required. Or second, they can require the interaction with the administrator, operator, or user. In both cases, dependability measures must be monitored in order to recognise the failure and initiate referring actions.

Regarding Web services, some autonomic approaches exist that aim to improve the dependability. One among them is from IBM. IBM has introduced the autonomic computing initiative (ACI) (IBM, 2006) that covers models, methods, and technologies in order to equip business IT systems with autonomic mechanisms. The ACI covers many aspects, beginning from the autonomous recovery of bad blocks from a hard drive, an ending up with the load balancing of server applications among clustered computers. The main goal of the ACI is to define a common platform as a standardised interface of autonomic systems in order to improve their manageability and maintainability. In the area of Web services, the ACI proposes autonomic mechanisms for balancing Web service load or automation of software updates or access policy enforcement. In addition to the initiative from IBM, research work also exists that proposes autonomic mechanisms for improving the dependability of Web services by monitoring the state of the Web services and to dynamically replace faulty services with appropriate candidates (Di Marzo Serugendo & Fitzgerald, 2006).

Stepping back to the phase where failures required the interaction of the user or administrator, the basic approach is to provide facilities that monitor attributes of the dependability. Regarding Web services, such monitoring can be either captured by the implementation directly; this is provided, for example, by the SOAP/WSDL implementation named Apache Axis. The software can be configured to send invocation duration and the invocation events to a logging server. Then, such information can be analysed in order to derive statements of the response time, reliability, of availability. Or, as developed by Tosic et al. (2004) for the WSOI, the monitoring features are based on standard handlers of the SOAP implementation.

Menasce (2003) discusses to capture the number of sessions and arrival rate of HTTP requests at the infrastructure level as well as monitoring TCP/IP traffic and the CPU load. In order to capture the HTTP requests, monitoring can take place by some request handling system of the Web service setup, as Web servers can be configured to forward Web service requests. The work of Li, Xu, and Nahrstedt (2001) extends this approach: In their integrated solution, they propose the installation of an additional component. This component serves as a probe that delivers runtime QoS information to external requests.

Besides the platform-based monitoring, the Web services messages can also use a message-oriented architecture or a message-oriented middleware (MOM) respectively. A MOM is placed between the provider and requester. When a requester intends to invoke a service, the request is passed to a MOM, which forwards it to the referring provider. Thus, requester and provider are decoupled. The general advantage is that this reduces the dependencies among the parties and allows for a more flexible message handling as with direct communication (e.g., prioritisation among requesters, load balancing for provided services). Erradi and Maheshwari presented an example of such a MOM for the use with Web services, the wsBus. Besides the research activities, commercial products already exist that facilitate the Web service messaging at large scale in today's enterprises (e.g., IBM's Web Sphere MQ [IBM, 2007] or BEA's Tuxedo [BEA, 2006]). If such a MOM is present in a Web service setup, then appropriate measures can be also taken automatically by logging features of this middleware.

The different approach is to entirely avoid monitoring on the service provider side. Generally, capturing data on the provider side helps the provider to improve the dependability. However, situations exist where users require an independent measure about the provider's dependability. Then, external monitoring has the advantage that the measurements about the dependability of a service are not taken by the provider and thus cannot be manipulated in order pursue dishonest interests. Tsai, Zhang, Chen, Huang, Paul, and Niao (2004) have discussed external testing for assessing the reliability of a Web service. Furthermore, they have presented a method to compute estimation about future reliability values based on the captured values. Although this and the other mentioned approaches are referring to particular attributes of the reliability, these methods are extensible in most cases to all attributes of the dependability.

Future Trend: IPv6

The most nonlocal Web services and practically all services, where client and server are located in different but connected networks, use as transport and network layer protocols of the TCP/IP protocol suite. It is a disadvantage for a number of approaches discussed in the sections above that QoS guarantees are not provided by today's commonly used network layer protocol IP Version 4. Whereas TCP/IP Version 4 is robust against failing of single nodes or communication links (indeed, it was one of that protocol suite's its predecessors' main design goals to survive local failures), it does not cover, for example, timing guarantees. Thus, QoS-related dependability assurance is usually provided at the application layer, based on probabilistic assumptions on the network behaviour.

However, the version 6 of the TCP/IP suite, and especially IP version 6 (IPv6) (Deering & Hinden 1998), support (besides a much larger address space, the main reason for introducing IPv6) QoS control mechanisms, namely the notion of *traffic classes* and *flow labels*.

Traffic classes allow one to distinguish between different types of contents at the network layer and can be seen as a kind of priority notation. Thus, routers can apply different policies to allow *end-to-end* guarantees. Flow labels (Rajahalme, Conta, Carpenter, & Deering, 2004) help to identify related flows. Here, a flow does not necessarily need a to be a 1:1 mapping to a transport connection. Using flow labels allows for establishing *flow states* (Rajahalme, Conta, Carpenter, & Deering, 2004, Section 4) along a connection route, which in turn allow for providing service-specific end-to-end dependability support (and service-specific end-to-end QoS support in general), increasing availability and reliability.[2] In addition, IPv6 supports authentication and encryption. Thus, it supports the two dependability attributes of integrity and confidentiality. Also, IPv6 is expandable. In this way, dependability-supporting properties of new physical and data link layer protocols may be easily integrated and provided to the Web service application.

TCP/IP protocol suite version 6 makes the use of several additional specialised protocols (e.g., IPsec) (Kent & Atkinson, 1998) superfluous and supports many feature that are long-sought by Web service application developers. However, currently it is not clear when and whether at all TCP/IP version 6 will reach a sufficient market penetration to provide a general base for Web service dependability.

SUMMARY AND CONCLUSION

First, the chapter discussed the intrinsic part of the Web service dependability that exists because of its design and specification. Then, several efforts from research and industry were also introduced that have the goal to improve the dependability when developing or using Web services. As the first point, we identified the two main aspects of Web services dependability: the *intrinsic* and *extrinsic* dependability. Furthermore, we proposed to assign the efforts from the extrinsic part of dependability to three categories based on the different stages of the Web services lifecycle: design and development, integration, and usage. In addition, we discussed a future trend resulting from the emerging Internet protocol advances. Figure 2 shows a summary on the two main parts that Web services dependability comprises: its intrinsic dependability and its extrinsic dependability. In addition, Figure 3 shows a taxonomy specifying the methods for the extrinsic part of Web services dependability.

From Figure 3, we can see that the state of the art virtually covers most of the dependability attributes. Only two attributes are missing from the main attributes that we have listed in the Dependability Sec-

Figure 2. Web services dependability overview

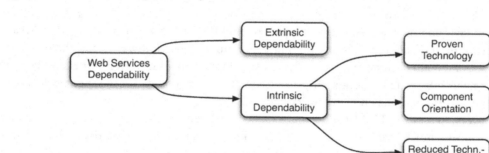

Figure 3. Extrinsic Web services dependability

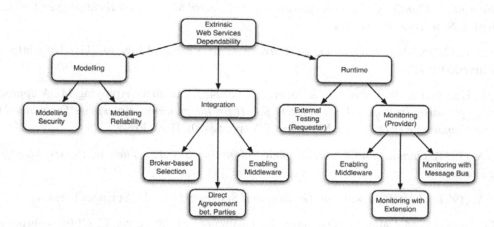

tion. So far, we are not aware of any method of ensuring the *integrity* that is specifically tailored for Web services. Second, the *maintainability* is only supported as an intrinsic characteristic of the Web services design; the component-orientation and the resulting modularity supports maintainability to some extent. An emerging field covering the maintainability is the service governance. However, this concept is currently more related to the organisational aspects of providing a service. Moreover, we need to criticise that many of the approaches that we have mentioned in our work indeed support a particular attribute of the dependability. However, a definition of considered threads is often omitted and thus it remains open what particular threads are specifically covered.

As the next step, we propose to join the efforts and establish a framework and methodology for developing and providing dependable Web services. This work has shown that large areas of Web services dependability have already been covered. The goal of this work is to start establishing an umbrella effort that puts specific approaches referring to the extrinsic Web services dependability in relation to other efforts. The ultimate goal would be a complete set of technologies and a methodology for delivering dependable Web services.

REFERENCES

Ali, A. S., Rana, O. F., Al-Ali, R., & Walker, D. W. (2003, January) UDDIe: An extended registry for Web services. In *Proceedings of the 2003 Symposium on Applications and the Internet Workshops (SAINT'03 Workshops)*, Orlando, FL (p. 85). IEEE Press.

Avizienis, A., Laprie, J.-C., & Randell, B. (2001). Fundamental concepts of dependability. In *Proceedings of the 3rd IEEE Information Survivability Workshop (ISW-2000)*, Boston (pp. 7-12). IEEE Press.

Baresi, L., Guinea, S., & Plebani, P. (2005, September). *WS-policy for service monitoring*. Paper presented at the 6th VLDB Workshop on Technologies for E-Services *(TES'05)* (Vol. LNCS 3811). Springer Press.

Basin, D., Doser, J., & Lodderstedt, T. (2003). Model driven security for process-oriented systems. In *Proceedings of the Eighth ACM Symposium on Access Control Models and Technologies SACMAT '03* (pp. 100-109). New York: ACM Press.

BEA Systems. (2006, May). *Introducing BEA tuxedo ATMI.* Retrieved July 30, 2007, from http://edocs. bea.com/tuxedo/tux91/

Bézivin, J., Hammoudi, S., Lopes, D., & Jouault, F. (2004, September). Applying MDA approach for Web service platform. In *Proceedings of the Eighth IEEE International Enterprise Distributed Object Computing Conference (EDOC'04),* Monterey, CA (pp. 58-70). IEEE Press.

Birolini, A. (1991). *Qualität und Zuverlässigkeit technischer Systeme. Theorie, Praxis, Management.* Springer Press.

Birolini, A. (1997). *Zuverlässigkeit von Geräten und Systemen* (4th ed.). Springer Press.

Booth, D., Haas, H., McCabe, F., Newcomer, E., Champion, M., & Ferris, C. (2004, February). *Web services architecture.* Retrieved October 31, 2007, from http://www.w3c.org/TR/ws-arch/

Cavano, J., & McCall, J. (1978, November). A framework for the measurement of software quality. In *Proceedings of the ACM Software Quality Assurance Workshop* (pp. 133-139). ACM Press.

Deering, S., & Hinden, R. (1998). *Internet protocol, version 6 (IPv6) specification* (RFC No. 2460). The Internet Society.

Di Marzo Serugendo, G., & Fitzgerald, J. (May 2006). *Dependable self-organising software architectures - an approach for self-managing systems* (Tech. Rep. BBKCS-06-05). Birkbeck College, London, UK.

Frølund, S., & Koistinen, J. (1998, December). Quality of service specification in distributed object systems design. *Distributed Systems Engineering Journal, 5*(4).

Grønmo, R., & Jaeger, M. C. (May 2005). Model-driven methodology for building QoS-optimised Web service compositions. In *Proceedings of the 5th IFIP International Conference on Distributed Applications and Interoperable Systems (DAIS'05),* Athens, Greece (pp. 68-82). Springer Press.

Grønmo, R., Skogan, D., Solheim, I., & Oldevik, J. (2004, March). Model-driven Web services development. In *Proceedings of 2004 IEEE International Conference on e-Technology, e-Commerce and e-Service (EEE'04),* Taipei, Taiwan (pp. 42-45). IEEE Press.

Hamilton, G. (1997). JavaBeans™ API specification 1.01. *Sun Microsystems.* Retrieved October 31, 2007, from http://www.es.embnet.org/Doc/Computing/java/beans/beans.101.pdf

IBM Corporation. (2006, June). *An architectural blueprint for autonomic computing* (4th ed.) (IBM Tech. Rep.). Retrieved October 31, 2007, from http://www-03.ibm.com/autonomic/pdfs/ACwpFinal.pdf

IBM Corporation Software Group. (2007, March). Providing a messaging backbone for SOA connectivity. *IBM service oriented architecture solutions white paper.* Retrieved October 31, 2007, from ftp://ftp.software.ibm.com/software/integration/wmq/WS_MQ_Messaging_Backbone_for_SOA.pdf

IEC. (1997). *Dependability and quality of service* (IEC 60050:191) International Electrotechnical Commission.

ISO. (1997). *ISO/ITU-T recommendation X.641 — ISO/IEC 13236: Information technology - quality of service - framework.* Author.

Jürjens, J. (2002, September). *UMLsec: Extending UML for secure systems development.* Paper presented at the Uml 2002 - The Unified Modeling Language: 5th International Conference, Dresden, Germany (Vol. 2460/2002, pp. 1-9). Springer Press.

Kath, O., Blazarenas, A., Born, M., Eckert, K.-P., Funabashi, M., & Hirai, C. (2004, September). Towards executable models: Transforming EDOC behavior models to CORBA and BPEL. In *Proceedings of the 8th International Enterprise Distributed Object Computing Conference (EDOC'04),* Monterey, CA (pp. 267–274). IEEE Press.

Kent, S., & Atkinson, R. (1998). *Security architecture for the Internet protocol* (RFC No. 2401). The Internet Society.

Laprie, J. (1992). *Dependability: Basic concepts and terminology.* Wien, Austria. Springer Press.

Laprie, J. (1995). *Dependable computing: Concepts, limits and challenges.* Paper presented at the 25th International Symposium on Fault-Tolerant Computing, Pasadena (pp. 42-54).

Lee, Y. (2003, October). Matching algorithms for composing business process solutions with Web services. In *Proceedings of the 4th International Conference on E-Commerce and Web Technologies (ECWEB'03),* Prague, Czechoslovakia (pp. 393-402). Springer Press.

Li, B., Xu, D., & Nahrstedt, K. (2001, October). Towards integrated runtime solutions in QoS-aware middleware. In *Proceedings of the ACM Multimedia Middleware Workshop (M3W 2001),* Ottawa, Canada (pp. 11-14). ACM Press.

Lodderstedt, T., Basin, D. A., & Doser, J. (2002, September). SecureUML: A UML-based modeling language for model-driven security. In *Proceedings of the 5th International Conference on the Unified Modeling Language,* Dresden, Germany (Vol. 2460, pp. 426-441). Springer Press.

Ludwig, H., Keller, A., Dan, A., King, R. P., & Franck, R. (2003, January). *Web service level agreement (WSLA) language specification* (IBM Tech. Rep.). Retrieved July 30, 2007, from http://www.research. ibm.com/wsla/WSLASpecV1-20030128.pdf

Matena, V., & Stearns, B. (2000). *Applying Enterprise JavaBeans™: Component-based development for the J2EE™platform.* Addison Wesley.

Maximilien, E. M., & Singh, M. P. (2004, September). A framework and ontology for dynamic Web services selection. *IEEE Internet Computing,* 84-93. IEEE Press.

Menasce, D. A. (January 2003). Automatic QoS control. *IEEE Internet Computing,* 7(1), 92-95.

Microsoft. (2003, February). *Enterprise UDDI services: An introduction to evaluating, planning, deploying, and operating UDDI services.* Retrieved October 31, 2007, from http://www.microsoft. com/windowsserver2003/technologies/idm/uddi/default.mspx

OASIS. (2004, November). OASIS Web services reliable messaging TC. *WS-Reliability 1*(1). Retrieved July 30, 2007, from http://docs.oasis-open.org/wsrm/ws-reliability/v1.1/wsrm-ws_reliability-1.1-spec-os.pdf

OGF. (2007). Web services agreement specification (WS-Agreement) (Open Grid Forum Recommendation Documents [REC]). *OGF Grid Resource Allocation and Agreement Protocol Working Group*. Retrieved October 31st, 2007, from http://www.ogf.org/documents/GFD.107.pdf

OMG. (1995). *The common object request broker: Architecture and specification*. Framingham, MA: Object Management Group, Inc.

OMG. (2001a). *Model driven architecture* (ormsc/2001-07-01). Needham, MA. Object Management Group, Inc.

OMG. (2001b). *Unified modeling language specification version 1.4* (OMG formal document/01-09-67). Needham, MA. Object Management Group, Inc.

OMG. (2004). *UML profile for modelling quality of service and fault tolerance characteristics and mechanisms* (ptc/2004-06-01). Needham, MA. Object Management Group, Inc.

Parhami, B. (1988). From defects to failures: A view of dependable computing. *SIGARCH Comput. Archit. News, 16*(4), 157-168.

Rajahalme, J., Conta, A., Carpenter, B., & Deering, S. (2004). *IPv6 flow label specification* (RFC No. 3697). The Internet Society.

Ran, S. (2003). A model for Web services discovery with QoS. *SIGecom Exch., 4*(1), 1-10.

Sahai, A., Machiraju, V., Sayal, M., & Casati, F. (2002, October). *Automated SLA monitoring for Web services*. Paper presented the Management Technologies for E-Commerce and E-Business Applications: 13th IFIP/IEEE International Workshop on Distributed Systems: Operations and Management, Montreal, Canada (Vol. 2506, pp. 28-41). Springer Press.

Sahai, A., Durante, A., & Machiraju, V. (2002). *Towards automated SLA management for Web services* (Tech. Rep. No. HPL-2001-310). Palo Alto, CA: Software Technology Laboratory, HP Laboratories.

Schmidt, D. C. (1999, January). Why software reuse has failed and how to make it work for you. *C++ Report*.

Serhani, M. A., Dssouli, R., Sahraoui, H., Benharref, A., & Badidi, M. E. (2005, September). QoS integration in value added Web services. In *Proceedings of the Second International Conference on Innovations in Informal Technology (IIT'05)*.

Skogan, D., Grønmo, R., & Solheim, I. (2004, September). Web service composition in UML. In *Proceedings of the 8th IEEE International Enterprise Distributed Object Computing Conf (EDOC'04)*, Monterey, CA (pp. 47-57). IEEE Press.

Szyperski, C. (1997). *Component oriented programming*. Addison-Wesley.

Tosic, V., Ma, W., Pagurek, B., & Esfandiari, B. (2004, April). Web service offerings infrastructure (WSOI): A management infrastructure for XML Web services. In *Proceedings of the IEE/IFIP Network Operations and Management Symposium (NOMS'04),* Seoul, South Korea (p. 817-830). IEEE Press.

Tosic, V., Patel, K., & Pagurek, B. (2002, May). WSOL: Web service offerings language. In *Proceedings of the Workshop on Web Services, e-Business, and the Semantic Web - WES (at CAiSE'02),* Toronto, Canada (Vol. 2512, pp. 57-67). Springer Press.

Tsai, W. T., Zhang, D., Chen, Y., Huang, H., Paul, R. A., & Liao, N. (2004, November). A software reliability model for Web services. In *Proceedings of the IASTED Conference on Software Engineering and Applications,* Cambridge, MA (pp. 144-149). IASTED/ACTA Press.

UDDI Spec Technical Committee. (2003). *UDDI version 3.0.1.* Retrieved June 9, 2008, from http://www.oasis-open.org/committees/uddi-spec/doc/tcspecs.htm

van Schewick, B. (2007). Towards an economic framework for network neutrality regulation. *Journal on Telecommunications and High Technology Law, 5.*

Wang, G., Chen, A., Wang, C., Fung, C., & Uczekaj, S. (2004, September). Integrated quality of service (QoS) management in service-oriented enterprise architectures. In *Proceedings of the 8th International Enterprise Distributed Object Computing Conference (EDOC'04),* Monterey, CA (pp. 21-32). IEEE Press.

Yu, T., & Lin, K.-J. (2005, March). A broker-based framework for QoS-aware Web service composition. In *Proceedings of the 2005 IEEE International Conference on e-Technology, e-Commerce, and e-Services (EEE'05),* Hong Kong, China (pp. 22-29). IEEE Press.

Zhou, C., Chia, L.-T., & Lee, B.-S. (2004, July). DAML-QoS ontology for Web services. In *Proceedings of the IEEE International Conference on Web Services (ICWS'04),* San Diego (pp. 472-479). IEEE Press.

ENDNOTES

[1] Frequently, the undesired impacts are restricted to "catastrophic consequences," (Laprie, 1995).
[2] The cost of using the mentioned measures is the waiving of *application blindness*, which is an issue in the ongoing discussion on network neutrality (van Schewick, 2007).

Chapter VIII
Transactional Composite Applications

Frederic Montagut
SAP Labs France, France

Refik Molva
Institut Eurecom, France

Silvan Tecumseh Golega
Hasso-Plattner-Institut, Germany

ABSTRACT

Composite applications leveraging the functionalities offered by Web services are today the underpinnings of enterprise computing. However, current Web services composition systems make use of only functional requirements in the selection process of component Web services while transactional consistency is a crucial parameter of most business applications. The transactional challenges raised by the composition of Web services are twofold: integrating relaxed atomicity constraints at both design and composition time and coping with the dynamicity introduced by the service-oriented computing paradigm. In this chapter, we present a new procedure towards automating the composition of transactional Web services. This composition procedure does not take into account functional requirements only but also transactional ones based on the acceptable termination states model. The resulting composite Web service is compliant with the consistency requirements expressed by business application designers and its execution can easily be coordinated using the coordination rules provided as an outcome of our approach. An implementation of our theoretical results based on OWL-S and business process execution language (BPEL) technologies is further detailed as a proof of concept.

INTRODUCTION

Web services composition has been gaining momentum over the last years as it leverages the capabilities of simple operations to offer value-added services. These complex services such as airline booking systems result from interactions between Web services that can span over organizational boundaries. Considering the lack of reliability akin to distributed environments, assuring data and transactional consistency of the outcome of cross-organizational workflow-based applications, such as composite applications, is necessary. The requirements that are relevant to assuring consistency within the execution of Web services composite applications are mainly twofold:

- **Relaxed atomicity:** Atomicity of the execution can be relaxed as intermediate results produced by a workflow-based application may be kept despite the failure of a service. The specification process of transactional requirements associated with workflows has to be flexible enough to support coordination scenarios more complex than the coordination rule "all or nothing" specified within the two phase commit protocol (ISO, n.d.).
- **Dynamic assignment of business partners:** Composite applications are dynamic in that the workflow partners or component services offering different characteristics can be assigned to tasks depending on the resources available at runtime. Business partners' characteristics have thus to be combined or composed in a way such that the transactional requirements specified for the workflow are met.

Existing transactional protocols (Elmagarmid, 1992; Greenfield, Fekete, Jang, & Kuo, 2003) are not adapted to meet these two requirements as they do not offer sufficient flexibility to cope, for instance, with the runtime assignment of computational tasks. In addition, existing solutions to combine or compose service providers based on the characteristics they offer appear to be limited when it comes to integrating at the composition phase the consistency requirements defined by workflow designers. These solutions indeed only offer means to validate transactional requirements once the workflow business partners have been selected but no solution to integrate these requirements as part of the composite application building process. The next sections present our approach to overcome these limitations.

Chapter Contributions

In this chapter, we present an adaptive transactional protocol to support the execution of composite applications. The execution of this protocol takes place in two phases. First, business partners are assigned to tasks using an algorithm whereby workflow partners are selected based on functional and transactional requirements. Given an abstract representation of a process wherein business partners are not yet assigned to workflow tasks, this algorithm enables the selection of service providers not only according to functional requirements but also based on transactional ones. In our approach, these transactional requirements are defined at the workflow design stage using the acceptable termination states (ATS) model. The resulting workflow instance is compliant with the defined consistency requirements and its execution can be easily coordinated as our algorithm also provides coordination rules. The workflow execution further proceeds through a coordination protocol that leverages the coordination rules computed as an outcome of the partner assignment procedure.

Chapter Outline

The remainder of the chapter is organized as follows. Section 2 discusses related work and technical background. In section 3, we introduce preliminary definitions and the methodology underpinning our approach. A simple example of composite application is presented in section 4 for the purpose of illustrating our results throughout the chapter. Section 5 introduces a detailed description of the transactional model used to represent the characteristics offered by business partners. In section 6, we provide details on the termination states of a workflow, then section 7 describes how transactional requirements expressed by means of the ATS model are derived from the inherent properties of termination states. Section 8 presents the transaction-aware service assignment procedure and the associated coordination protocol. An implementation of our theoretical results based on Web services technologies including OWL-S (OWL Services Coalition, 2003) and business process execution language (BPEL) (Thatte, 2003) is presented in section 9. Finally, section 10 presents concluding remarks.

TECHNICAL BACKGROUND

Transactional consistency of workflows and database systems has been an active research topic over the last 15 years, yet it is still an open issue in the area of Web services (Curbera, Khalaf, Mukhi, Tai, & Weerawarana, 2003; Gudgin, 2004; Little, 2003) and especially composite Web services. Composite Web services indeed introduce new requirements for transactional systems such as dynamicity, semantic description, and relaxed atomicity. Existing transactional models for advanced applications (Elmagarmid, 1992) are lacking flexibility to integrate these requirements (Alonso, Agrawal, Abbadi, Kamath, Gnthr, & Mohan, 1996); as for instance, they are not designed to support the execution of dynamically generated collaboration of services. In comparison, the transactional framework presented in this chapter allows the specification of transactional requirements supporting relaxed atomicity for an abstract workflow specification and the selection of semantically described services respecting the defined transactional requirements.

Our work is based on the work of Bhiri, Perrin, and Godart (2005), which presents the first approach specifying relaxed atomicity requirements for composite Web services based on the ATS tool and a transactional semantic. Despite a solid contribution, this work appears to be limited if we consider the possible integration into automatic Web services composition systems. It indeed only details transactional rules to validate a given composite service with respect to defined transactional requirements. In this approach, transactional requirements do not play any role in the component service selection process which may result in several attempts for designers to determine a valid composition of services. On the contrary, our solution provides a systematic procedure enabling the automatic design of transactional composite Web services. Besides, our contribution also defines the mathematical foundations to specify valid ATS for workflows using the concept of coordination strategy that is defined later on.

Within the Web services stack, three specifications feature solutions towards assuring the transactional coordination of services: Web services coordination (WS-coordination) (Langworthy, 2005c), Web services atomic transaction (WS-AtomicTransaction) (Langworthy, 2005a), and Web services business activity framework (WS-BusinessActivity) (Langworthy, 2005b). They are often referred to as Web services transaction framework (WSTF). The goal of WS-coordination is to provide a framework that can support various coordination protocols specified in terms of coordination types. When

Figure 1. Principles

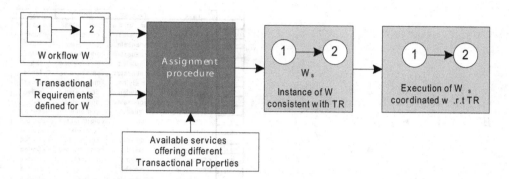

service providers register to transactional coordinators they specify as part of a coordination type the coordination protocol that should be implemented to support a composite application execution. The WS-AtomicTransaction and WS-BusinessActivity specifications are the two main coordination protocols available. Making use of compensation techniques WS-AtomicTransaction requires all participants to be compensatable and to support certain isolation levels; this is in fact an implementation of the two phase-commit protocol. WS-BusinessActivity on the other hand offers a coordination framework suitable for long-running transactions, called business activities. WS-BusinessActivity does not however specify appropriate tools to describe coordination strategies, that is, how the coordination protocol should react in the face of failures so that a composite application can reach consistent termination states. It is, in fact, only mentioned that different strategies are possible in addition to the classical "all or nothing" principle. Besides the Web services transaction framework there are several other initiatives towards establishing transaction management within Web service interactions. The business process execution language for Web services (BPEL4WS) implements the concept of long-running (business) transactions (LRT). It supports coordination of transactions in local BPEL processes. A comparison of BPEL long-running transactions and WS-BusinessActivity and an approach to unify them can be found by Melzer and Sauter (2005). The business transaction protocol (BTP) (Abbott, 2005) specifies roles, interactions, behaviors, and messages to coordinate long-running transactions in the fashion of the WS-BusinessActivity specification.

These various coordination protocols do not however offer adequate support for designers to specify flexible coordination scenarios wherein component services feature different transactional properties such as the ability to compensate the execution of a task or to retry the execution of a failed task. The solution presented in this chapter can be used to augment these standardization efforts in order to provide them with adaptive coordination specifications based on the transactional properties of the component services instantiating a given workflow.

PRELIMINARY DEFINITIONS AND METHODOLOGY

Transactional consistency is a crucial aspect of composite services execution. In order to meet consistency requirements at early stages of the service composition process, we need to consider transactional requirements a concrete parameter determining the choice of the component Web services. In this sec-

Figure 2. Production line process

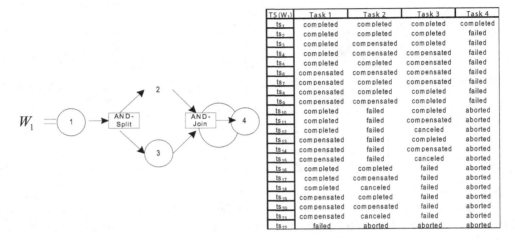

TS (W₁)	Task 1	Task 2	Task 3	Task 4
ts_1	completed	completed	completed	completed
ts_2	completed	completed	completed	failed
ts_3	completed	compensated	completed	failed
ts_4	completed	compensated	compensated	failed
ts_5	completed	completed	compensated	failed
ts_6	compensated	compensated	compensated	failed
ts_7	compensated	completed	compensated	failed
ts_8	compensated	completed	completed	failed
ts_9	compensated	compensated	completed	failed
ts_{10}	completed	failed	completed	aborted
ts_{11}	completed	failed	compensated	aborted
ts_{12}	completed	failed	canceled	aborted
ts_{13}	compensated	failed	completed	aborted
ts_{14}	compensated	failed	compensated	aborted
ts_{15}	compensated	failed	canceled	aborted
ts_{16}	completed	completed	failed	aborted
ts_{17}	completed	compensated	failed	aborted
ts_{18}	completed	canceled	failed	aborted
ts_{19}	compensated	completed	failed	aborted
ts_{20}	compensated	compensated	failed	aborted
ts_{21}	compensated	canceled	failed	aborted
ts_{22}	failed	aborted	aborted	aborted

tion we present a high level definition of the consistency requirements and a methodology taking into account these requirements during the building process of composite applications and later on during the coordination of their execution.

Consistent Composite Web Services

A composite Web service W_s consists of a set of n Web services $W_s = (s_a)_{a \in [1 \ n]}$ whose execution is managed according to a workflow W which defines the execution order of a set of n tasks $W = (t_a)_{a \in [1 \ n]}$ performed by these services (for the sake of simplicity, we consider that one service executes only one task). The assignment of services to tasks is performed by means of composition engines based on functional requirements. Yet, the execution of a composite service may have to meet transactional requirements aiming at the overall assurance of consistency. Our goal is to design a service assignment process that takes into account the transactional requirements associated with W in order to obtain a consistent instance W_s of W as depicted in Figure 1. We consider that each Web service component might fulfill a different set of transactional properties. For instance, a service can have the capability to compensate the effects of a given operation or to reexecute the operation after failure whereas some other service does not have any of these capabilities. It is thus necessary to select the appropriate service to execute a task whose execution may be compensated if required. The assignment procedure based on transactional requirements follows the same strategy as the one based on functional requirements. It is a match-making procedure between the transactional properties offered by services and the transactional requirements associated to each task. Once assigned, the services $(s_a)_{a \in [1 \ n]}$ are coordinated with respect to the transactional requirements during the composite application execution. The coordination protocol is indeed based on rules deduced from the transactional requirements. These rules specify the final states of execution or termination states each service has to reach so that the overall process reaches a consistent termination state. Two phase-commit, the famous coordination protocol (ISO, n.d.), uses, for instance, the simple rule that all tasks performed by different services have to be compensated if one of them fails. The challenges of the transactional approach are therefore twofold.

- Specify a Web service assignment procedure that builds consistent instances of W according to defined transactional requirements, and
- Specify the coordination protocol managing the execution of consistent composite services.

Methodology

In our approach, the services involved in W_s are selected according to their transactional properties by means of a match-making procedure. We therefore need first to specify the semantic associated with the transactional properties defined for services. The match-making procedure is indeed based on this semantic. This semantic is also to be used in order to define a tool allowing workflow designers to specify their transactional requirements for a given workflow. Using these transactional requirements, we are able to assign services to workflow tasks based on rules which are detailed later on. Once the composite service is defined, we can define a protocol in order to coordinate these services according to the transactional requirements specified at the workflow designing phase. The proofs of the theorems underpinning the work presented in this chapter are discussed by Montagut and Molva (2006).

MOTIVATING EXAMPLE

In this section we introduce a simple motivating example that will be used throughout the chapter to illustrate the presented methodology. We consider the simple process W_1 of a manufacturing firm involving four steps as depicted in Figure 2. A first service, order handling service is in charge of receiving orders from clients. These orders are then handled by the production line (Step 2) and in the meantime an invoice is forwarded to a payment platform (Step 3). Once the ordered item has been manufactured and the payment validated, the item is finally delivered to the client (Step 4). Of course in this simple scenario, a transactional approach is required to support the process execution so that it can reach consistent outcomes, as, for instance, the manufacturing firm would like to have the opportunity to stop the production of an item if the payment platform used by a customer is not a reliable one. On the other

Figure 3. Service state diagram

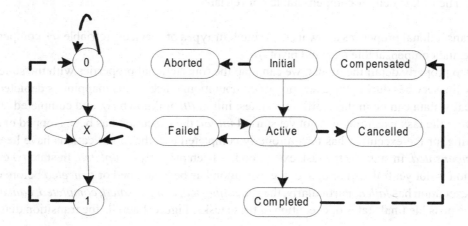

hand, it may no longer be required to care about canceling the production if the payment platform claims it is reliable and not prone to transaction errors. Likewise, customers may expect that their payment platform offer refunding options in case the delivery of the item they ordered is not successful. Those possible outcomes mostly define the transactional requirements for the execution of this simple process and also specify what actions need to be taken to make sure that the final state of the process execution is deemed consistent by the involved parties. This example, although simple, perfectly meets our illustration needs within this chapter as it demonstrates the fact that based on the specified transactional requirements a clever selection of the business process participants has to be performed prior to the process instantiation since, for instance, the selection of both a payment platform that do not offer any refunding options and an unreliable delivery means may result in a disappointed customer. It should be noted that the focus of this example is not the trust relationship between the different entities and we therefore assume the trustworthiness of each of them, yet we are rather interested in the transactional characteristics offered by each participant.

TRANSACTIONAL MODEL

In this section, we define the semantic specifying the transactional properties offered by services before specifying the consistency evaluation tool associated to this semantic. Our semantic model is based on the "transactional Web service description" defined by Bhiri et al. (2005).

Transactional Properties of Services

Bhiri et al. (2005) present a model specifying semantically the transactional properties of Web services. This model is based on the classification of computational tasks made by Mehrotra, Rastogi, Silberschatz, and Korth (1992) and Schuldt, Alonso, and Schek (1999), which considers three different types of transactional properties. An operation, and by extension a Web service executing this task, can be of three types:

- **Compensatable:** The results produced by the task can be rolled back.
- **Retriable:** The task is sure to complete successfully after a finite number of tries.
- **Pivot:** The task is neither compensatable nor retriable.

These transactional properties allow us to define four types of services: retriable *(r)*, compensatable *(c)*, retriable and compensatable *(rc)*, and pivot *(p)*.

In order to properly detail the model, we can map the transactional properties with the state of data modified by the services during the execution of computational tasks. This mapping is depicted in Figure 3. Basically, data can be in three different states: initial *(0)*, unknown *(x)*, and completed *(1)*. In the state *(0)*, either the task execution has not yet started *initial*, the execution has been stopped or *aborted* before starting, or the execution has been properly completed and the modifications have been rolled back or *compensated*. In state *(1)* the task execution has been properly *completed*. In state *(x)* either the task execution is not yet finished or *active*, the execution has been stopped or *canceled* before completion, or the execution has *failed*. Particularly, the states *aborted, compensated, completed, canceled,* and *failed* are the possible final states of execution of these tasks. Figure 4 details the transition diagram for

Figure 4. Transactional properties of services

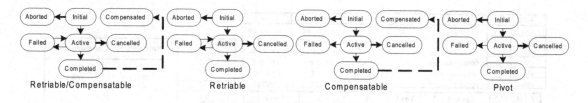

the four types of transactional services. We must distinguish within this model the inherent termination states, that is *failed* and *completed,* which result from the normal course of a task execution and the one resulting from a coordination message received during a coordination protocol instance, that is, *compensated, aborted,* and *canceled,* which force a task execution to either stop or rollback. The transactional properties of the services are only differentiated by the states *failed* and *compensated,* which indeed respectively specify the retriability and compensatability aspects.

Definition 5.1 We have for a given service *s*:

- *Failed* is not a termination state of *s* if *s* is retriable
- *Compensated* is a termination state of *s* if *s* is compensatable

From the state transition diagram, we can also derive some simple rules. The states *failed, completed,* and *canceled* can only be reached if the service is in the state *active.* The state *compensated* can only be reached if the service is in the state *completed.* The state *aborted* can only be reached if the service is in the state *initial.*

Termination States

The crucial point of the transactional model specifying the transactional properties of services is the analysis of their possible termination states. The ultimate goal is indeed to be able to define consistent termination states for a workflow, that is, determining for each service executing a workflow task which termination states it is allowed to reach.

Definition 5.2 We define the operator termination state *ts(x)* which specifies the possible termination states of the element *x*. This element *x* can be

- A service *s* and $ts(s) \in \{aborted, canceled, failed, completed, compensated\}$
- A task *t* and $ts(t) \in \{aborted, canceled, failed, completed, compensated\}$
- A workflow $W = (t_a)_{a \in [1,n]}$ and $ts(W) = (ts(t_1), ts(t_2), ..., ts(t_n))$

- A composite service W_s of *W* composed of *n* services $W_s = (s_a)_{a \in [1,n]}$ and $ts(W_s) = (ts(s_1), ts(s_2), ..., ts(s_n))$

Figure 5. Acceptable termination states of W_1 and available services

ATS$_1$(W$_1$)		Task 1	Task 2	Task 3	Task 4
ats$_1$	ts$_1$	completed	completed	completed	completed
ats$_2$	ts$_6$	compensated	compensated	compensated	failed
ats$_3$	ts$_{14}$	compensated	failed	compensated	aborted
ats$_4$	ts$_{15}$	compensated	failed	canceled	aborted
ats$_5$	ts$_{20}$	compensated	compensated	failed	aborted
ats$_6$	ts$_{21}$	compensated	canceled	failed	aborted

ATS$_2$(W$_1$)		Task 1	Task 2	Task 3	Task 4
ats$_1$	ts$_1$	completed	completed	completed	completed
ats$_2$	ts$_{17}$	completed	compensated	failed	aborted
ats$_3$	ts$_{11}$	completed	failed	compensated	aborted
ats$_4$	ts$_5$	completed	completed	compensated	failed
ats$_5$	ts$_{18}$	completed	canceled	failed	aborted
ats$_6$	ts$_{12}$	completed	failed	canceled	aborted

Available Services		Retriable	Compensatable
Task 1	S$_{11}$	yes	no
	S$_{12}$	no	yes
	S$_{13}$	yes	yes
Task 2	S$_{21}$	yes	no
	S$_{22}$	no	yes
Task 3	S$_{31}$	yes	no
	S$_{32}$	no	yes
Task 4	S$_{41}$	no	no

The operator *TS(x)* represents the finite set of all possible termination states of the element x, $TS(x) = (ts_k(x))_{k \in [1,j]}$. We have especially, $TS(W_S) \subseteq TS(W)$ since the set $TS(W_S)$ represents the actual termination states that can be reached by W_s according to the transactional properties of the services assigned to W. We also define for x workflow or composite service and $a \in [1,n]$:

- $ts(x,t_a)$: the value of $ts(t_a)$ in $ts(x)$
- *tscomp(x)*: the termination state of x such that $\forall a \in [1,n] ts(x,t_a) = completed$

For the remainder of the chapter, $W = (t_a)_{a \in [1,n]}$ represents a workflow of n tasks and $W_S = (s_a)_{a \in [1,n]}$ a composite service of W.

Transactional Consistency Tool

We use the ATS (Rusinkiewicz & Sheth, 1995) model as the consistency evaluation tool for our workflow. ATS defines the termination states a workflow is allowed to reach so that its execution is judged consistent.

Definition 5.3 An *ATS(W)* is a subset of *TS(W)* whose elements are considered consistent by workflow designers for a specific execution of *W*. A consistent termination state of *W* is called an acceptable termination state $ats_k(W)$ thus $ATS(W) = (ats_k(W))_{k \in [1,i]}$. A set *ATS(W)* specifies the transactional requirements defined by designers associated with a specific execution of *W*.

ATS(W) and *TS(W)* can be represented by a table which defines for each termination state the tuple of termination states reached by the workflow task, as depicted in Figure 5. Depending on the application different ATS tables can of course be specified by designers for the same workflow, and for the sake of readability we do not introduce in this chapter an index (as in *ATS$_i$(W)*) in the notation *ATS(W)*. As mentioned in the definition, the specification of the set *ATS(W)* is done at the workflow designing phase. *ATS(W)* is mainly used as a decision table for a coordination protocol so that W_s can reach an acceptable termination state knowing the termination state of at least one task. The role of a coordination protocol indeed consists of sending messages to services in order to reach a consistent termination state given the current state of the workflow execution. The coordination decision, that is, the termination state that has to be reached, made given a state of the workflow execution has to be unique; this is the main characteristic of a coordination protocol. In order to cope with this requirement, *ATS(W)*, which is used as input for the coordination decision-making processs, has therefore to verify some properties that we detail later on.

ANALYSIS OF *TS(W)*

Since $ATS(W) \subseteq TS(W)$, *ATS(W)* inherits the characteristics of *TS(W)* and we logically need to analyze first *TS(W)*. In this section, we first precise some basic properties of *TS(W)* derived from inherent execution rules of a workflow *W* before examining *TS(W)* from a coordination perspective.

Inherent Properties of TS(W)

We state here some basic properties relevant to the elements of *TS(W)* and derived from the transactional model presented above. *TS(W)* is the set of all possible termination states of *W* based on the termination states model we chose for services. Yet, within a composite service execution, it is not possible to reach all the combinations represented by a *n*-tuple $(ts(t_1), ts(t_2),...,ts(t_n))$. The first restriction is introduced by the sequential aspect of a workflow:

- (P_1) A task becomes *activated* if all the tasks executed beforehand according to the execution plan of *W* have reached the state *completed*

(P_1) simply means that to start the execution of a workflow task, it is required to have properly completed all the workflow tasks required to be executed beforehand.

Second, we consider in our model that only one single task can fail at a time and that the states *aborted, compensated,* and *canceled* can only be reached by a task in a given $ts_k(W)$ if one of the services executing a task of *W* has failed. This means that the coordination protocol is allowed to force the abortion, the compensation, or the cancellation only in case of failure of a service. We get (P_2):

- (P_2) if $ts_k(W, t_a) \in \{compensated, aborted, canceled\}$ then $\exists ! l \in [1, n]$ such that $ts_k(W, t_l) = failed$

Classification Within TS(W)

As we explained above, the unicity of the coordination decision during the execution of a coordination protocol is a major requirement. We try here to identify the elements of *TS(W)* that correspond to different coordination decisions given the same state of a workflow execution. The goal is to use this classification to determine *ATS(W)*. Using the properties (P_1) and (P_2), a simple analysis of the state transition model reveals that there are two situations whereby a coordination protocol has different possibilities of coordination given the state of a workflow task. Let two tasks t_a and t_b and assume that the task t_b has failed:

- The task t_a is in the state *completed* and either it remains in this state or it is *compensated*
- The task t_a is in the state *active* and either it is *canceled* or the coordinator lets it reach the state *completed*

From these two statements, we define the *incompatibility from a coordination perspective* and the *flexibility*.

Definition 6.1 Two termination states $ts_k(W)$ and $ts_l(W)$ are said to be incompatible from a coordination perspective if $\exists$ two tasks t_a and t_b such that $ts_k(W, t_a) = completed$, $ts_k(W, t_b) = ts_l(W, t_b) = failed$ and $ts_l(W, t_a) = compensated$. Otherwise, $ts_l(W)$ and $ts_k(W)$ are said to be compatible from a coordination perspective.

The value in $\{compensated, completed\}$ reached by a task t_a in a termination state $ts_k(W)$ whereby $ts_k(W, t_b) = failed$ is called recovery strategy of t_a against t_b in $ts_k(W)$. By extension, we can consider the recovery strategy of a set of tasks against a given task.

If two termination states are compatible, they correspond to the same recovery strategy against a given task. In fact, we have two cases for the compatibility of two termination states $ts_k(W)$ and $ts_l(W)$. Given two tasks t_a, t_b such that $ts_k(W, t_b) = ts_l(W, t_b) = failed$:

- $ts_k(W, t_a) = ts_l(W, t_a)$
- $ts_k(W, t_a) \in \{compensated, completed\}, ts_l(W, t_a) \in \{aborted, canceled\}$

The second case is only possible to reach if t_a is executed in parallel with t_b. Intuitively, the failure of the service assigned to t_b occurs at different instants in $ts_k(W)$ and $ts_l(W)$.

Definition 6.2 A task t_a is flexible against t_b if $\exists ts_k(W)$ such that $ts_k(W, t_b) = failed$ and $ts_k(W, t_a) = canceled$. Such a termination state is said to be flexible to t_a against t_b. The set of termination states of W flexible to t_a against t_b is denoted $FTS(t_a, t_b)$.

From these definitions, we now study the termination states of W according to the compatibility and flexibility criteria in order to identify the termination states that follow a common strategy of coordination.

Definition 6.3 A termination state of W, $ts_k(W)$ is called generator of t_a if $ts_k(W, t_a) = failed$ and $\forall b \in [1, n]$ such that t_b is executed before or in parallel with t_a, $ts_k(W, t_b) \in \{completed, compensated\}$. The set of termination states of W compatible with $ts_k(W)$ generator of t_a is denoted $CTS(ts_k(W), t_a)$.

The set $CTS(ts_k(W), t_a)$ specifies all the termination states of W that follow the same recovery strategy as $ts_k(W)$ against t_a.

Definition 6.4 Let $ts_k(W) \in TS(W)$ be a generator of t_a. Coordinating an instance W_s of W in case of the failure of t_a consists of choosing the recovery strategy of each task of W against t_a and the $z_a < n$ tasks

$$\left(t_{a_i}\right)_{i \in \left[1, z_a\right]}$$

flexible to t_a whose execution is not *canceled* when t_a fails. We call coordination strategy of W_s against t_a the set:

$$CS(W_s, ts_k(W), (t_{a_i})_{i \in [1, z_a]}, t_a) = CTS(ts_k(W), t_a) - \bigcup_{i=1}^{z_a} FTS(t_{a_i}, t_a)$$

If the service s_a assigned to t_a is retriable then $CS(W_s, ts_k(W), (t_{a_i})_{i \in [1, z_a]}, t_a) = \varnothing$

W_s is said to be coordinated according to $CS(W_s, ts_k(W), (t_{a_i})_{i \in [1, z_a]}, t_a)$ if in case of the failure of t_a, W_s reaches a termination state in $CS(W_s, ts_k(W), (t_{a_i})_{i \in [1, z_a]}, t_a)$. Of course, it assumes that the transactional properties of W_s are sufficient to reach $ts_k(W)$.

From these definitions, we can deduce a set of properties:

Theorem 6.5 W_s can only be coordinated according to a unique coordination strategy at a time.

Theorem 6.6 Let $ts_k(W)$ such that $ts_k(W, t_a) = failed$ but not generator of t_a. If $ts_k(W) \in TS(W_S)$ then $\exists \, l \in [1, j]$ such that $ts_l(W) \in TS(W_S)$ is a generator of t_a compatible with $ts_k(W)$. This theorem states that if a composite service is able to reach a given termination state wherein a task t_a fails, it is also able to reach a termination state generator compatible with the latter.

Given a task t_a the idea is to classify the elements of *TS(W)* using the sets of termination states compatible with the generators of t_a. Using this approach, we can identify the different recovery strategies and the coordination strategies associated with the failure of t_a as we decide which tasks can be *canceled*.

Forming *ATS(W)*

Defining *ATS(W)* is deciding at design time the termination states of *W* that are consistent. *ATS(W)* is to be inputted to a coordination protocol in order to provide it with a set of rules which leads to a unique coordination decision in any cases. According to the definitions and properties we introduce above, we can now explicit some rules on *ATS(W)* so that the unicity requirement of coordination decisions is respected.

Definition 7.1 Let $ts_k(W) \in ATS(W)$ such that $ts_k(W, t_a) = failed$. *ATS(W)* is valid if $\exists \, ! \, l \in [1, j]$ such that $ts_l(W)$ generator of t_a compatible with $ts_k(W)$ and

$$CTS(ts_l(W), t_a) - \bigcup_{i=1}^{z_a} FTS(t_{a_i}, t_a) \subset ATS(W)$$

for a set of tasks $(t_{a_i})_{i \in [1, z_a]}$ flexible to t_a.

The unicity of the termination state generator of a given task comes from the incompatibility definition and the unicity of the coordination strategy. A valid *ATS(W)* therefore contains for all $ts_k(W)$ in which a task fails a unique coordination strategy associated to this failure and the termination states contained in this coordination strategy are compatible with $ts_k(W)$. In Figure 5, an example of possible *ATS* is presented for the simple workflow W_1. It just consists of selecting the termination states of the table $TS(W_1)$ that we consider consistent and respect the validity rule for the created $ATS(W_1)$.

DERIVING COMPOSITE SERVICES FROM *ATS*

In this section, we introduce a new type of service assignment procedure, that is, the transaction-aware service assignment procedure which aims at assigning n services to the n tasks t_a in order to create an instance of W *acceptable* with respect to a valid *ATS(W)*. The goal of this procedure is to integrate within the instantiation process of workflows a systematic method ensuring the transactional consistency of the obtained composite service. We first define a validity criteria for the instance W_s of W with respect to *ATS(W)*, and the service assignment algorithm is then detailed. Finally, we specify the coordination strategy associated to the instance created from our assignment scheme.

Acceptability of W$_s$ with Respect to ATS(W)

Definition 8.1 W_s is an acceptable instance of W with respect to $ATS(W)$ if $TS(W_s) \subseteq ATS(W)$.

Now we express the condition $TS(W_s) \subseteq ATS(W)$ in terms of coordination strategies. The termination state generator of t_a present in $ATS(W)$ is noted $ts_{k_a}(W)$. The set of tasks whose execution is not *canceled* when t_a fails is denoted $(t_{a_i})_{i \in [1, z_a]}$.

Theorem 8.2 $TS(W_s) \subseteq ATS(W)$ if $\forall a \in [1, n] CS(W_s, ts_{k_a}(W), (t_{a_i})_{i \in [1, z_a]}, ta) \subset ATS(W)$

An instance W_s of W is therefore an acceptable one if it is coordinated according to a set of n coordination strategies contained in $ATS(W)$. It should be noted that if $failed \notin ATS(W, t_a)$ where $ATS(W, t_a)$ represents the acceptable termination states of the task t_a in $ATS(W)$ then $CS(W_s, ts_{k_a}(W), (t_{a_i})_{i \in [1, z_a]}, ta) = \emptyset$.

Transaction-Aware Assignment Procedure

In this section, we present the procedure that is used to assign services to tasks based on transactional requirements. This algorithm uses $ATS(W)$ as a set of requirements during the service assignment procedure and thus identifies from a pool of available services those whose transactional properties match the transactional requirements associated to workflow tasks defined in $ATS(W)$ in terms of acceptable termination states. The assignment procedure is an iterative process; services are assigned to tasks one after the other. The assignment procedure therefore creates at each step i a partial instance of W noted W_s^i. We can define as well the set $TS(W_s^i)$ which represents the termination states of W that the transactional properties of the i services already assigned allow to reach. Intuitively the acceptable termination states refer to the degree of flexibility offered when choosing the services with respect to the different coordination strategies verified in $ATS(W)$. This degree of flexibility is influenced by two parameters:

- The list of acceptable termination states for each workflow task. This list can be determined using *ATS(W)*. This is a direct requirement which specifies the termination states allowed for each task and therefore introduces requirements on the service's transactional properties to be assigned to a given task; this service can only reach the states defined in *ATS(W)* for the considered task.
- The assignment process is iterative and therefore, as we assign new services to tasks, $TS(W_s^i)$ changes and the transactional properties required to the assignment of further services change as well. For instance, we are sure to no longer reach the termination states $CTS\left(tsk\left(W\right),t_a\right)$ allowing the failure of the task t_a in *ATS(W)* when we assign a service of type (r) to t_a. In this specific case, we no longer care about the states reached by other tasks in $CTS\left(tsk\left(W\right),t_a\right)$ and therefore there is no transactional requirements introduced for the tasks to which services have not already been assigned.

We therefore need to define first the transactional requirements for the assignment of a service after *i* steps in the assignment procedure.

Extraction of Transactional Requirements

From the two requirements above, we define for a task t_a :

- $ATS(W,t_a)$: Set of acceptable termination states of t_a which is derived from *ATS(W)*
- $DIS(t_a,W_s^i)$: This is the set of transactional requirements that the service assigned to t_a must meet based on the previous assignments. This set is determined based on the following reasoning:

(DIS₁): the service must be compensatable if $compensated \in DIS(t_a,W_s^i)$
(DIS₂): the service must be retriable if $failed \notin DIS(t_a,W_s^i)$

Using these two sets, we are able to compute $MIN_P\ (s_a,t_a,W_s^i) = ATS(W,t_a) \cap DIS(t_a,W_s^i)$ which defines the transactional properties a service s_a has at least to comply with in order to be assigned to the task t_a at the *i+1* assignment step. We simply check the retriability and compensatability properties for the set $MIN_P\ (s_a,t_a,W_s^i)$:

- $failed \notin MIN_P\ (s_a,t_a,W_s^i)$ if s_a has to verify the retriability property
- $compensated \in MIN_P\ (s_a,t_a,W_s^i)$ if s_a has to verify the compensatability property

The set $ATS(W,t_a)$ is easily derived from *ATS(W)*. We need now to compute $DIS(t_a,W_s^i)$. We assume that we are at the *i+1* step of an assignment procedure, that is, the current partial instance of *W* is W_s^i. Computing $DIS(t_a,W_s^i)$ means determining whether *(DIS₁)* and *(DIS₂)* are true. From these two statements we can derive three properties:

1. *(DIS₁)* implies that state *compensated* can definitely be reached by t_a
2. *(DIS₂)* implies that t_a can not *fail*
3. *(DIS₂)* implies that t_a can not be *canceled*

The two first properties can be directly derived from *(DIS$_1$)* and *(DIS$_2$)*. The third one is derived from the fact that if a task can not be *canceled* when a task fails, then it has to finish its execution and reach at least the state *completed*. In this case, if a service can not be *canceled* then it can not fail, which is the third property. To verify whether 1, 2, and 3 are true, we introduce the theorems Theorem 8.3, Theorem 8.4, and Theorem 8.5.

Theorem 8.3 The state *compensated* can definitely be reached by t_a if $\exists b \in [1,n] - \{a\}$ verifying **(8.3b)**: s_b not retriable is assigned to t_b and $\exists\, ts_k(W) \in ATS(W)$ generator of t_b such that $ts_k(W, t_a) = compensated$

Theorem 8.4 t_a can not fail if $\exists b \in [1,n] - \{a\}$ verifying **(8.4b)**: (s_b not compensatable is assigned to t_b and $\exists\, ts_k(W) \in ATS(W)$ generator of t_a such that $ts_k(W, t_b) = compensated$) or ($t_b$ is flexible to t_a and s_b not retriable is assigned to t_b and $\forall\, ts_k(W) \in ATS(W)$ such that $ts_k(W, t_a) = failed$, $ts_k(W, t_b) \neq canceled$).

Theorem 8.5 Let t_a and t_b such that t_a is flexible to t_b. t_a is not *canceled* when t_b fails if **(8.5b)**: s_b not retriable is assigned to t_b and $\forall\, ts_k(W) \in ATS(W)$ such that $ts_k(W, t_b) = failed$, $ts_k(W, t_a) \neq canceled$.

Based on the Theorems 8.3, 8.4, and 8.5, in order to compute $DIS(t_a, W_s^i)$, we have to compare t_a with each of the i tasks $t_b \in W - \{t_a\}$ to which a service s_b has been already assigned. This is an iterative procedure and at the initialization phase, since no task has been yet compared to t_a, s_a can be of type (p): $DIS(t_a, W_s^i) = \{failed\}$.

1. if t_b verifies **(8.3b)** then $compensated \in DIS(t_a, W_s^i)$
2. if t_b verifies **(8.4b)** then $failed \notin DIS(t_a, W_s^i)$
3. if t_b is flexible to t_a and verifies **(8.5b)** then $failed \notin DIS(t_a, W_s^i)$

The verification stops if $failed \notin DIS(t_a, W_s^i)$ and $compensated \in DIS(t_a, W_s^i)$. With $MIN_P(s_a, t_a, W_s^i)$ we are able to select the appropriate service to be assigned to a given task according to transactional requirements.

Service Assignment Process

Services are assigned to each workflow task based on an iterative process. Depending on the transactional requirements and the transactional properties of the services available for each task, different scenarios can occur:

i. Services of type *(rc)* are available for the task. It is not necessary to compute transactional requirements as such services match all transactional requirements.

ii. Only one service is available for the task. We need to compute the transactional requirements associated to the task and either the only available service is sufficient or there is no solution.

iii. Services of types *(r)* and *(c)* but none of type *(rc)* are available for the task. We need to compute the transactional requirements associated to the task and we have three cases. First, retriability and compensatability is required in which case there is no solution. Second, retriability (resp.

compensatability) is required and we assign a service of type *(r)* (resp. *(c))* to the task. Third, there is no requirement.

The idea is therefore to assign first services to the tasks verifying *(i)* and *(ii)* since there is no flexibility in the choice of the service. Tasks verifying *(iii)* are finally analyzed. Based on the transactional requirements raised by the remaining tasks, we first assign services to tasks with a nonempty transactional requirement. We then handle the assignment for tasks with an empty transactional requirement. Note that the transactional requirements of all the tasks to which services are not yet assigned are also affected (updated) as a result of the current service assignment. If no task has transactional requirements then we assign the services of type *(r)* to assure the completion of the remaining tasks' execution.

Coordination of W_s

Using the notations introduced so far, we are able to specify the coordination strategy of W_s against each workflow task. We get indeed the following theorem.

Theorem 8.6 Let W_s be an acceptable instance of W with respect to *ATS(W)*. We note $(t_{a_i})_{i \in [1, n_r]}$ the set of tasks to which no retriable services have been assigned.

$$TS(W_S) = \{tscomp(W_S)\} \cup \bigcup_{i=1}^{n_r} \left(CTS(ts_{k_{a_i}}(W), t_{a_i}) - \bigcup_{j=1}^{z_a} FTS(t_{a_{i_j}}, t_{a_i}) \right)$$

Having computed *TS(W)*, we can deduce the coordination rules associated to the execution of W_s.

Figure 6. Transactional architecture

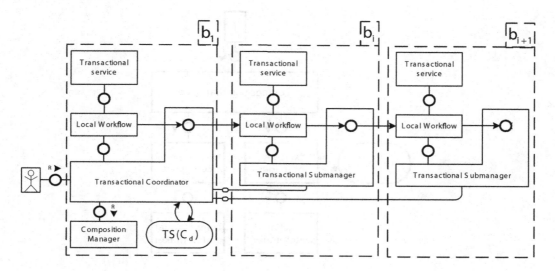

Example

Back to our motivating example, we consider the workflow W_1 of Figure 2. Designers have defined $ATS_2(W_1)$ as the transactional requirements for the considered business application and the set of available services for each task of W_1 is specified in Figure 5. The goal is to assign services to workflow tasks so that the instance of W_1 is valid with respect to $ATS_2(W_1)$ and we apply the assignment procedure presented in section 6.2. We first start to assign the services of type *(rc)* for which it is not necessary to compute any transactional requirements. s_{13} which is available for Task 1 is therefore assigned without any computation. We then consider the tasks for which only one service is available. This is the case for Task 4 for which only one service of type *(p)* is available. We therefore verify whether s_{41} can be assigned to Task 4. We compute $MIN_P(s_a, t_4, W_{1s}^1) = ATS_2(W_1, t_4) \cap DIS(t_4, W_{1s}^1)$.

If $ATS_2(W_1, t_4) = \{completed, failed\}$ and $DIS(t_4, W_{1s}^1) = \{failed\}$ as s_{13} the only service already assigned is of type *(rc)* and the Theorems 8.3, 8.4 and 8.5 are not verified, none the conditions required within these theorems are indeed verified by the service s_{13}. Thus $MIN_P(s_a, t_4, W_{1s}^1) = \{failed\}$ and s_{41} can be assigned to Task 4 as it matches the transactional requirements. Now we compute the transactional requirements of Task 2 for which services of type *(r)* and *(c)* are available and we get $MIN_P(s_a, t_2, W_{1s}^2) = \{failed\}$. As described in the assignment procedure we do not assign any service to this task as it does not introduce at this step of the procedure any transactional requirements to make a decision on the candidate service to choose. We therefore compute the transactional requirements of Task 3 and we get $MIN_P(s_a, t_3, W_{1s}^2) = \{failed, compensated\}$ as Theorem 8.3 is verified with the service s_{41} that is indeed not retriable. The service s_{32} which is of type *(c)* can thus be assigned to Task 3 as it matches the computed transactional requirements. We come back now to Task 2 and compute the transactional requirements once again and we get $MIN_P(s_a, t_2, W_{1s}^3) = \{failed, compensated\}$ as Theorem 8.3 is now verified with the service s_{32} which is indeed not retriable. It should be noted that at this step, the transactional requirements associated to Task 2 have been modified because of the as-

Figure 7. Transactional Web services composition system

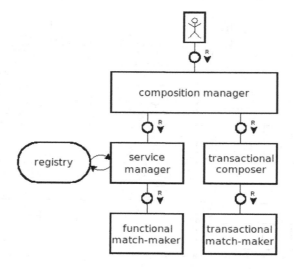

signment of the service s_{32} to Task 3. As the service s_{22} matches the transactional requirements it can be assigned to the task.

COORDINATION OF COMPOSITE APPLICATIONS

In this section an implementation of the work presented in this chapter based on Web services technologies is described. The implementation features the transactional coordination of a cross-organizational composite application that is built based on our transaction-aware assignment procedure. To that respect, the business partners involved in the composite application share their services and communicate through local workflow engines that help them manage the overall collaboration in a distributed manner. These workflow engines are based on the BPEL workflow description language. Of course, the services they share may offer various transactional properties as the ones we detailed so far in the chapter. It is thus required to adapt local workflow engines to integrate into the composite application business logic the transactional model we presented in section 5. The system architecture is depicted in Figure 6. In order to support the execution of cross-organizational composite applications, we implemented in the fashion of the WS-coordination initiative (Langworthy, 2005c) a transactional stack composed of the following components:

- **Transactional Coordinator:** This component is supported by the composite application initiator. On the one hand it implements the transaction-aware business partner assignment procedure as part of the composition manager module and on the other hand it is in charge of assuring the coordinator role of the transactional protocol relying on the set $TS(W_s)$ outcome of the assignment procedure.
- **Transactional Submanager:** This component is deployed on the other partners and is in charge of forwarding coordination messages from the local workflow to the coordinator and conversely.

In the remainder of this section, our implementation is described in terms of the implementation of the transaction-aware partner assignment procedure, the internal communications that take place between the elements deployed on a business partner, and the structure that the BPEL processes deployed on each business partner's workflow engine should be compliant with in order to support the coordination protocol execution.

OWL-S Transactional and Functional Matchmaker

To implement the assignment procedure presented in this chapter we augmented an existing functional OWL-S matchmaker (Tang, Liebetruth, & Jaeger, 2003) with transactional matchmaking capabilities. In order to achieve our goal, the matchmaking procedure has been split into two phases. First, the functional matchmaking based on OWL-S semantic matching is performed in order to identify subsets of the available partners that meet the functional requirements for each workflow vertex. Second, the implementation of the transaction-aware partner assignment procedure is run against the selected sets of partners in order to build an acceptable instance fulfilling defined transactional requirements.

The structure of the matchmaker consists of several components whose dependencies are displayed in Figure 7. The composition manager implements the matchmaking process and provides a Java API

Figure 8. Infrastructure internal communications

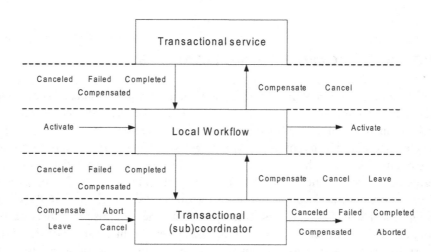

that can be invoked to start the selection process. It gets as input an abstract process description specifying the functional requirements for the candidate partners and a table of acceptable termination states. The registry stores OWL-S profiles of partners that are available. Those OWL-S profiles have been augmented with the transactional properties offered by business partners. This has been done by adding to the nonfunctional information of the OWL-S profiles a new element called *transactionalproperties* that specifies two Boolean attributes that are retriable and compensatable as follows.

```
<tp:transactionalproperties retriable="true" compensatable="true"/>
```

In the first phase of the selection procedure, the business partner manager is invoked with a set of OWL-S profiles that specify the functional requirements for each workflow vertex. The business partner manager gets access to the registry, where all published profiles are available and to the functional matchmaker which is used to match the available profiles against the functional requirements specified in the workflow. For each workflow vertex, the business partner manager returns a set of functionally matching profiles along with their transactional properties. The composition manager then initiates the second phase, passing these sets along with the process description, and the table of acceptable termination states to the transactional composer. The transactional composer starts the transaction-aware business partner assignment procedure using the transactional matchmaker by classifying first those sets into five groups:

- sets including only services of type *(p)*
- sets including only services of type *(r)*
- sets including only services of type *(c)*
- sets including services of types *(r)* and *(c)*
- sets including services of type *(rc)*

Once those sets are formed the iterative transactional composition process takes place as specified above based on the table of acceptable termination states. Depending on the set of available services and the specified acceptable termination states, the algorithm may terminate without finding a solution.

Internal Communications within a Business Partner Infrastructure

In the infrastructure that is deployed on each business partner to implement the transactional protocol presented in this chapter, the transactional coordinator plays the role of interface between the business process and the other business partners when it comes to managing the notification messages exchanged during the execution of the transactional protocol. Some of these messages received by the transactional coordinator should be forwarded to the local business process to take appropriate actions while some others are only relevant to the local transactional (sub)coordinator. The business process may also be require to issue a notification to its local transactional (sub)coordinator when a failure occurs. The messages exchanged between these three layers are derived from the state model depicted in Figure 3. The infrastructure deployed on a given business partner basically consists of three layers:

- **The transactional service layer** representing the business partner's available operations,
- **The local workflow layer** corresponding to the local workflow engine, and
- **The coordination layer** implementing the local (sub)coordinator module.

The message exchanges that can take place on a given business partner between these three layer are depicted in Figure 8. The set of notification messages that is exchanged between the different components of the infrastructure is basically derived from the transactional model depicted in Figure 4. These messages are:

- **Activate:** The activate message is basically issued by the local workflow engine to the local workflow engine of the next business partner involved in the workflow. In fact this message instantiates the process execution on the business partner side.
- **Compensate, Cancel:** The compensate and cancel messages are received at the coordination layer and forwarded to the local workflow layer that forwards them in a second time to the transactional service layer to perform to corresponding functions, that is, compensation or cancellation of an operation.
- **Compensated, Cancelled, Completed:** These messages simply notify that the corresponding events have occurred: compensation, cancellation, or completion of an operation. Issued at the transactional service layer, they are forwarded to the coordination layer in order to be dispatched to the composite application coordinator.
- **Failed:** Issued at the transactional service layer, the failed message is forwarded to the coordination layer in order to be dispatched to the composite application coordinator. If the operation performed at the transactional service layer is retriable, no failed message is forwarded to the local workflow layer as we consider that the retry primitive is inherent to any retriable operation.
- **Abort, Aborted:** The abortion message is received at the coordination layer and acknowledged with an aborted message. Upon receipt of this message, the business simply leaves the composite application execution; no message is forwarded to the other layers since the local workflow has not yet been instantiated.

Figure 9. Transactional BPEL processes (process graphs from ActiveBPEL engine)

Reliable, Retriable

Reliable, Compensatable

- **Leave:** The leave message is received at the coordination layer and the business partner can leave the execution of the composite application execution. The leave message is forwarded to the local workflow layer if the business partner implements an operation that is compensatable. In this case, the business process deployed on the local workflow engine indeed has two possible outcomes, that is, either the results produced by its task are compensated or it can leave the process execution.

Specification of Transactional BPEL Processes

In our implementation, the local workflow engine is implemented using BPEL as the workflow specification language. In order to support the message exchanges identified in section 9.2, the structure of BPEL business processes has to match some templates that we describe in this section. Using the constructs available in the BPEL language, the specification of these transactional BPEL processes is straightforward.

The business process activation is performed using the usual BPEL process instantiation construct <receive> described as follows.

```
<receive createInstance="yes" operation="launch" partnerLink="PLT"
   portType="PT" variable="Data">
 <correlations>
  <correlation initiate="yes" pattern="in" set="CS1"/>
 </correlations>
</receive>
```

The cancel message can be received at any moment during the execution of the process and is thus handled using the <eventHandlers> construct as follows. Of course, the BPEL process has to expose a dedicated operation to receive the cancel message.

```
<eventHandlers>
<onMessage partnerLink="PLT" portType="PT"
   operation="Cancel" variable="workflowid">
 <correlations>
  <correlation set="CS1"/>
 </correlations>
 <terminate/>
 </onMessage>
</eventHandlers>
```

In order to detect the failure of an operation that is not retriable, the <scope> and the <faultHandlers> constructs are used as follows. The failure of the operation is forwarded to the transactional coordination layer inside the <faultHandlers>.

```
<scope name="invokation_try">
<faultHandlers>
 <catchAll>
  <invoke inputVariable="failedid" name="1"
    operation="transacFailed" partnerLink="PLT"
    portType="LocalAdminImpl"/>
 </catchAll>
</faultHandlers>
<invoke inputVariable="DataInc" outputVariable="DataOut"
   name="invoke1" operation="Addition"
   partnerLink="PLT" portType="Add">
</invoke>
</scope>
```

Finally, if the business process implements an operation that is compensatable, the process execution can lead to two possible outcomes depending on whether a compensate or a leave message is received. We use the `<pick>` construct to express this choice as follows.

```
<pick>
 <onMessage partnerLink="PLT" portType="publicPT"
   operation="Leave" variable="workflowid">
 <correlations>
  <correlation set="CS1"/>
 </correlations>
 <empty/>
 </onMessage>
 <onMessage partnerLink="PLT" portType="PT"
   operation="Compensate" variable="workflowid">
 <correlations>
  <correlation set="CS1"/>
 </correlations>
 <invoke inputVariable="serviceid" name="invoke1"
   operation="Compensate"
   partnerLink="PLT" portType="Add"/>
 </onMessage>
</pick>
```

It should be noted that in the listings depicted in this section, we use BPEL correlation sets because the coordination messages are received asynchronously during the process execution and need to be mapped to the appropriate instance of the workflow to be processed by the engine. These BPEL listings can be combined in the design of transactional BPEL processes depending of course on the transactional properties offered by business partners. Two examples of transactional BPEL processes are depicted in Figure 9. For instance, if the task executed by a business partner is not compensatable, the associated BPEL process only ends with the completed notification since it is not required to wait for a leave message. Similarly, a task which is retriable is not surrounded by `<scope>` constructs as there is no fault to catch.

CONCLUSION

We presented an adaptive transactional protocol to support the execution of cross-organizational composite applications. This approach actually meets the requirements that are relevant to assuring consistency of the execution of cross-organizational processes, which are mainly twofold:

- **Relaxed atomicity:** Atomicity of the workflow execution can be relaxed as intermediate results produced by the workflow may be kept intact despite the failure of one partner.
- **Dynamic selection of business partners:** The execution of cross-organizational workflows may require the execution of a composition procedure wherein candidate business partners offering different characteristics are assigned to tasks depending on functional and nonfunctional requirements associated with the workflow specification.

The execution of the protocol we proposed takes place in two phases. First, business partners are assigned to workflow tasks using an algorithm whereby partners are selected based on functional and transactional requirements. Given an abstract representation of a process wherein business partners are not yet assigned to workflow tasks, this algorithm enables the selection of partners not only according to functional requirements but also to transactional ones. The resulting workflow instance is compliant with the defined consistency requirements and its execution can be easily coordinated as our algorithm also provides coordination rules. The workflow execution further proceeds through a hierarchical coordination protocol managed by the workflow initiator and controlled using the coordination rules computed as an outcome of the partner assignment procedure. This transactional protocol thus offers a full support of relaxed atomicity constraints for workflow-based applications and is also self-adaptable to business partners' characteristics.

Besides, a complete transactional framework based on the Web services technologies has been implemented as a proof of concept of our theoretical results. On the one hand, the business partner assignment procedure we designed can be used to augment existing composition systems (Agarwal, Dasgupta, Karnik, Kumar, Kundu, Mittal, et al., 2005) as it can be fully integrated in existing functional matchmaking procedures. On the other hand, our approach defines adaptive coordination rules that can be deployed on recent coordination specifications (Langworthy, 2005c) in order to increase their flexibility.

REFERENCES

Abbott, M. (2005), *Business transaction protocol.*

Agarwal, V., Dasgupta, K., Karnik, N., Kumar, A., Kundu, A., Mittal, S., et al. (2005, May 10-14). A service creation environment based on end to end composition of Web services. In *Proceedings of the WWW Conference*, Chiba, Japan (pp. 128-137).

Alonso, G., Agrawal, D., Abbadi, A. E., Kamath, M., Gnthr, R., & Mohan, C. (1996). Advanced transaction models in workflow contexts. In *Proceedings of the 12th International Conference on Data Engineering*, New Orleans (pp. 574-581).

Bhiri, S., Perrin, O., & Godart, C. (2005, May 10-14). Ensuring required failure atomicity of composite Web services. In *Proceedings of the WWW Conference*, Chiba, Japan (pp. 138-147).

Curbera, F., Khalaf, R., Mukhi, N., Tai, S., & Weerawarana, S. (2003). The next step in Web services, *Communications of the ACM*, *46*(10), 29-34.

Elmagarmid, A. K. (1992). *Database transaction models for advanced applications.* Morgan Kaufmann.

Greenfield, P., Fekete, A., Jang, J., & Kuo, D. (2003, September). Compensation is not enough. In *Proceedings of the 7th International Enterprise Distributed Object Computing Conference (EDOC'03)*, Brisbane, Australia (Vol. 232, pp. 16-19).

Gudgin, M. (2004, June 15-17). Secure, reliable, transacted; Innovation in Web services architecture. In *Proceedings of the ACM International Conference on Management of Data*, Paris (pp. 879-880).

ISO. (n.d.). *Open system interconnection-distributed transaction processing (OSI-TP) model* (ISO IS 100261). Author.

Langworthy, D. (2005a). *WS-atomictransaction.*

Langworthy, D. (2005b). *WS-business activity.*

Langworthy, D. (2005c). *WS-coordination.*

Little, M. (2003), Transactions and Web services, *Communications of the ACM, 46*(10), 49-54.

Mehrotra, S., Rastogi, R., Silberschatz, A., & Korth, H. (1992, June 9-12). A transaction model for multi-database systems. In *Proceedings of the 12th IEEE International Conference on Distributed Computing Systems (ICDCS92)*, Yokohama, Japan (pp. 56-63).

Melzer, I., & Sauter, P. (2005). A comparison of WS-business-activity and BPEL4WS long-running transaction. *Kommunikation in Verteilten Systemen, Informatik aktuell.* Springer.

Montagut, F., & Molva R. (2006, September 18-22). *Augmenting Web services composition with transactional requirements.* Paper presented at the ICWS 2006, IEEE International Conference on Web Services, Chicago (pp. 91-98).

OWL Services Coalition. (2003). *OWL-S: Semantic markup for Web services.*

Rusinkiewicz, M., & Sheth, A. (1995). Specification and execution of transactional workflows. *Modern database systems: The object model, interoperability, and beyond* (pp. 592-620).

Schuldt, H., Alonso, G., & Schek, H. (1999, May 31-June 2). Concurrency control and recovery in transactional process management. In *Proceedings of the Conference on Principles of Database Systems*, Philadelphia (pp. 316-326).

Tang, S., Liebetruth, C., & Jaeger, M. C. (2003). *The OWL-S matcher software.* Retrieved May 29, 2008, from http://flp.cs.tu-berlin.de/

Thatte, S. (2003). *Business process execution language for Web services version 1.1 (BPEL).*

Chapter IX
A Logic Programming Based Framework for Intelligent Web Service Composition

Enrico Pontelli
New Mexico State University, USA

Tran Cao Son
New Mexico State University, USA

Chitta Baral
Arizona State University, USA

ABSTRACT

This chapter presents a comprehensive logic programming framework designed to support intelligent composition of Web services. The underlying model relies on the modeling of Web services as actions, each described by a logic programming theory. This view allows the use of logic-based planning to address the Web service composition problem, taking advantage of the fact that logic-based planning enables the elegant introduction of a number of extensions and generalizations (e.g., dealing with incomplete knowledge and preferences). The theory describing each Web service is encoded as a logic programming module, and different semantics are allowed within different modules, thus better reflecting the practical use of different service description formalisms and ontologies.

INTRODUCTION

One of the main goals of the Semantic Web initiative (Berners-Lee, Hendler, & Lassila, 2001) is to extend the existing Web technology to support the development of intelligent agents, which can *automatically* and *unambiguously* process the information available in millions of Web pages. This led to numerous works on *Web services* and *Web service composition*. The primary goal of Web service composition is to determine an appropriate sequence of Web services to accomplish a user goal. The majority of the existing proposals dealing with Web service composition build on the principle of viewing Web services as *actions*, thus, representing the Web service composition problem as a *planning problem* that can be addressed using existing *planning* techniques. A second popular approach to Web service composition relies on techniques developed in the area of workflow development. The survey by Rao and Su (2004) provides a good overview of various proposals for Web service compositions.

McIlraith and Son (2002) propose to use *GOLOG* (Levesque, Reiter, Lesperance, Lin, & Scherl, 1997), a logic programming based language, for Web service composition. In such a proposal, each Web service is translated to a primitive action. GOLOG provides control-flow constructs, such as **if-then-else**, **while-do**, **sequence** (denoted by ';'), **procedure**, and **test** (denoted by '?'), which can be used to combine the primitive actions into programs. The resulting programs can be provided to a *GOLOG* interpreter for finding the sequence of Web services that need to be executed to achieve the goal of the user. Alternatively, the program can be given to an execution monitoring module, for direct execution. Sufficient conditions for a successful execution of a program are also provided. This direction of work has been adopted by Au, Kuter, and Nau (2005), Kuter, Sirin, Nau, Parsia, and Hendler (2005), and Wu, Parsia, Sirin, Hendler, and Nau (2003), where SHOP2, a hierarchical planning system, is used as the underlying system for automatic Web service composition. The latter work also addressed an important aspect of Web service composition, namely, the problem of incompleteness of information in Web service composition, by adding to the planning algorithm a module for gathering information during the planning process.

Viewing Web service composition as high-level planning is not only natural, but also advantageous for different reasons:

- AI planning has made remarkable progress in the last 10 years, and several robust and scalable planning systems have been developed and are available for use, such as *FF* (Hoffmann & Nebel, 2001), *SHOP* (Nau, Cao, Lotem, & Muñoz-Avila, 1999), SAT-based planners (Kautz & Selman, 1996), and logic programming based planners (Lifschitz, 1999). All these planners can be used as the backbone in the development of systems for Web service composition with an architecture similar to the one described by McIlraith and Son (2002).
- AI planning allows the Semantic Web research community to focus on the development of Web service representation and reasoning languages and tools for translating Web service representation into a planning language.

Indeed, this view of Web service composition has been embraced by many researchers, and a number of tools have been proposed, for example, translators to map Web services encoded using DAML-S or OWL-S to PDDL (PDDL Technical Committee, 1998), a well-known planning language used by many planning systems.

While the use of planning in Web service composition is advantageous, there are a number of issues that need to be addressed before this approach can be widely applied. The first problem, which can be termed as the *service selection problem*, derives from the huge number of available services that can be used to achieve the same goal. The second problem lies in the lack of information in service composition, which imposes additional requirements on the planning system, such as the ability to plan with incomplete knowledge and to handle knowledge producing actions. The third problem centers on the *quality* of the composed service, which can be translated into the problem of planning with preferences, an area of research that has only recently attracted interest from the planning community. The fourth problem derives from the fact that each Web service is often encoded within an ontology or a knowledge base, whose semantics is specified by the service provider, and hence, might be different from service to service. A final problem, that has been recognized very early in the development of the Semantic Web (Berners-Lee & Fischetti, 1999; Berners-Lee et al., 2001), is the need for mechanisms to encode *rules*, for example, rules for the description of Semantic Web services and business rules interchange in e-commerce applications.

Answer set programming (ASP) is a declarative programming framework, originally proposed by Marek and Truszczynski (1999) and Niemelä (1999). To solve a problem in ASP, we translate it into a logic program, whose answer sets correspond one-to-one to solutions of the original problems. ASP has found its way in several real-world applications, for example, diagnosis of components of the space shuttle (Balduccini, Gelfond, & Nogueira, 2006). ASP has been widely adopted in the area of reasoning about actions and planning; it has been applied to solve various forms of planning, such as classical planning, conformant planning, and conditional planning (e.g., Son, Tu, Gelfond, & Morales, 2005; Tu, Son, & Baral, 2006). ASP has been used to incorporate various forms of domain knowledge in planning (Son, Baral, Tran, & McIlraith, 2006a) and to construct plans satisfying multidimensional preferences (Son & Pontelli, 2006). This existing body of knowledge provides the foundations for the development of a logic programming-based framework for Web service composition that addresses all but the problem of dealing with Web services encoded in heterogeneous knowledge bases. This last problem is becoming more and more critical with the development of distinct standards and ontologies for Web service encoding and the wider availability of Web services in the Internet. *This problem will be our main concern in this chapter.*

In this chapter, we propose a logic programming framework for reasoning with distributed heterogeneous knowledge bases that contain rules and facts, that is, we concentrate on the fourth problem faced by the Web service composition problem. Our specific objectives are:

1. The design of a theoretical framework for *reasoning with heterogeneous knowledge bases*, which can be combined with logic programming-based planners for Web service composition. This framework supports:

    a. The interoperation between knowledge bases encoded using different rule markup languages, and

    b. The development and integration of different components that reason about knowledge bases.

2. The development of a prototype of the proposed framework.

The chapter is organized as follows. We start by briefly reviewing the representation of Web services and rules in the Semantic Web, the foundation of logic programming and answer set planning, the use of answer set planning in Web service composition, and discuss the challenges faced by the current architecture for Web service composition. In the successive sections, we describe the main contribution of this chapter, a framework for reasoning with distributed heterogeneous knowledge bases, and its implementation. Finally, we relate our work to other proposals and provide conclusions and indications for future developments.

WEB SERVICES AND LOGIC PROGRAMMING

We begin with a review of the common elements of Web services and the RuleML language, and the basics of logic programming. We then discuss how logic programming can be used in Web service composition and discuss the issues that need to be addressed.

Web Services and RuleML

Many Web service description languages have been proposed (e.g., www.w3c.org). The most recent proposal, WSDL 2.0 (Chinnici, Moreau, Ryman, & Weerawarana, 2007), describes a Web service in terms of

- The kinds of messages that the service will send/ receive (using the **types** element).
- The functionalities of the service (**interface** element).
- The way to access the service (**binding** element).
- The location of the service (**service** element).

In essence, a service can be viewed as a collection of subroutines (or functions), and it is described by a valid WSDL 2.0 document. If a service requesting agent would like to use a service, it needs to place a request with the proper parameters. For example, Figure 1 shows an excerpt from Booth and Liu (2005), used to define the 'checkAvailability' function for a hotel reservation service, which takes three parameters (i.e., checkInDate, checkOutDate, and roomType) and returns either an error message indicating that the date is improper (invalidDataError), or a number indicating the number of available rooms (checkAvailabilityResponse).[1]

Many of the existing Web services are described within some ontology (e.g., an OWL description). More and more are associated with a set of rules (also called a *knowledge base*). Such a knowledge base is often written in one of the variants of the RuleML markup language.

The RuleML initiative[2] is a response to the need of a common XML-based rule markup language, which has precisely defined semantics and enables efficient implementations. In recent years, a significant amount of work has been devoted to develop knowledge representation languages suitable for the task, and a variety of languages for rule markup have been proposed. The initial design (Boley, Grosof, Sintek, Tabe, & Wagner, 2002) included a distinction (in terms of distinct DTDs) between *reaction* rules and *derivation* rules. The first type of rules is used for the encoding of event-condition-action (ECA) rules, while the second is meant for the encoding of implicational and inference rules.

The derivation rules component of the RuleML initiative has originated a family of languages. Figure 2, from Hirtle and Boley (2005), shows the most commonly referred languages; observe that Datalog plays the role of a core language, with simplified versions (e.g., unary and binary Datalog) developed for combining RuleML with OWL (as in SWRL) (Horrocks, Patel-Schneider, Boley, Tabet, Grosof, & Dean, 2004). Various sublanguages have been created to include features like explicit equality (e.g., fologeq), negation as failure (e.g., naffolog), and Hilog layers (e.g., hohornlog). Specific instances of RuleML for handling different aspects of Web services have been proposed (The Policy RuleML Technical Group, 2004).

Kifer, de Bruijn, Boley, and Fensel (2005) argue that any realistic architecture for the Semantic Web must be based on various independent but interoperable languages, one of them being the logic

Figure 1. `CheckAvailability` *function for hotel reservation Web service*

```
. . .
<types>
  <xs:schema
     xmlns:xs="http://www.w3.org/2001/XMLSchema"
     targetNamespace="http://greath.example.com/2004/schemas/resSvc"
        xmlns="http://greath.example.com/2004/schemas/resSvc">
     <xs:element name="checkAvailability" type="tCheckAvailability"/>
      <xs:complexType name="tCheckAvailability">
        <xs:sequence>
          <xs:element  name="checkInDate" type="xs:date"/>
          <xs:element  name="checkOutDate" type="xs:date"/>
          <xs:element  name="roomType" type="xs:string"/>
        </xs:sequence>
     </xs:complexType>
     <xs:element name="checkAvailabilityResponse" type="xs:double"/>
     <xs:element name="invalidDataError" type="xs:string"/>
  </xs:schema>
</types>
<interface  name = "reservationInterface" >
    <fault name = "invalidDataFault" element = "ghns:invalidDataError"/>
    <operation name="opCheckAvailability"
        pattern="http://www.w3.org/ns/wsdl/in-out"
        style="http://www.w3.org/ns/wsdl/style/iri" wsdlx:safe = "true">
        <input messageLabel="In"
              element="ghns:checkAvailability" />
        <output messageLabel="Out"
              element="ghns:checkAvailabilityResponse" />
        <outfault ref="tns:invalidDataFault" messageLabel="Out"/>
    </operation>
```

programming language with negation-as-failure. The use of rule-based languages requires the coexistence of different languages with different semantics and associated reasoning mechanisms, and the need to integrate reasoning across these languages. The need for these languages and their interactions have been extensively discussed (e.g., Kifer et al., 2005; May, Alferes, & Amador, 2005) and it is at the foundation of the most recent work of the Rule Interchange Format working group. It is also important to note that many of the sublanguages of RuleML have been implemented either through translators, for example, GEDCOM (Dean, 2001), which translates to XSB Prolog and JESS, or using independent inference engines, for example,

- j-DREW (Spencer, 2002), a top-down engine for RuleML,
- DR-Device (Bassiliades, Antoniou, & Vlahavas, 2006), an engine supporting defeasible logic and both strong and default negation, and
- CommonRules (Chan & Grosof, 1999), a bottom-up engine for the Datalog sublanguage.

It should be noted that RuleML, WSDL 2.0, and the other markup languages employed when dealing with Web services are simply representation languages. An agent making use of Web services can be developed in any programming language (e.g., JAVA, C++, Perl, etc.). For this reason, previous proposals for Web service composition assume the existence of translators which map Web service descriptions

Figure 2. RuleML language modularization

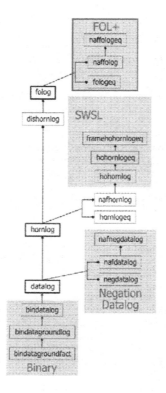

to representations that are more adequate for manipulation and reasoning. For example, McIlraith and Son (2002) map Web service descriptions to situation calculus, while other recent proposals make use of encodings in PDDL; for example, translators of Web service descriptions (in DAML-S) to PDDL (McDermott, Dou, & Qi, 2002).

For the purpose of this chapter, we will assume the existence of translators that map Web service descriptions into a logic programming representation. Many of such tools are already available on the Web (e.g., Rainer, 2005).

Logic Programming

We will consider a logic programming language $\langle \Im, \Pi, \vartheta \rangle$, where $\Im$ is a denumerable collection of function symbols, $\Pi = \Pi_u \cup \Pi_d$ is a denumerable collection of predicate symbols, and ϑ is a collection of variables. Π_u are called user-defined predicates, while Π_d are called built-in predicates. We will assume that $\Pi_u \cap \Pi_d = \varnothing$. We will denote with $ar(\alpha)$ the arity of the symbol $\alpha \in \Pi \cup \Im$. We typically assume that Π_d contains at least the predicates `assert`, `retract`, and `model`.

A *term* is either a variable, an element of $\Im$ of arity 0 (i.e., a constant), or an expression of the form $f(t_1, ..., t_n)$ where $f \in \Im$, $ar(f) = n$ and $t_1, ..., t_n$ are terms. We will say that a term t is ground if it does not contain variables. We will denote with H_P the Herbrand universe for this language, that is, the set of all ground terms.

An *atom* is a formula of the form $p(t_1,...,t_n)$ where $p \in \Pi$, $ar(p)=n$ and $t_1,...,t_n$ are terms. The atom is ground if $t_1,...,t_n$ are ground. A *qualified atom* is a formula of the form $t{:}A$ where t is a ground term (called the *label* of the qualified atom) and A is an atom. In particular, if the predicate p of an atom belongs to Π_d, then the atom can only appear qualified in a rule. A literal is an atom, a qualified atom, or a formula *not A*, where A is an atom/qualified atom. *not A* is also referred to as a negative literal. We will denote with B_p the Herbrand base for this language (i.e., the set of all ground atoms). For an atom (qualified atom, negative literal) l, we denote with $\pi(l)$ the predicate symbol used in l.

A general rule is of the form

$$A \leftarrow B_1,...,B_k \qquad\qquad (1)$$

where A is an atom and $B_1,...,B_k$ are literals. Intuitively, a Rule (1) states that if the literals $B_1,...,B_k$ are true, then we can conclude that A is also true. We view interpretations and models as subsets of B_p. For an atom A, the literal A (resp. *not A*) is true in a model M if $A \in M$ (resp. $A \notin M$).

Depending on the type of programs we wish to represent, different restrictions can be imposed on the rules:

a. **Datalog:** The B_i's in Rule (1) can be only atoms/qualified atoms and the terms used in the literals can be only variables or constants (i.e., of arity 0).
b. **Ground datalog:** The B_i's in Rule (1) can only be atoms/qualified atoms, and the only terms allowed are constants.
c. **Ground binary datalog:** The rules satisfy the conditions of Case (b), and in addition we require all predicates used to construct atoms to have arity at most 2.
d. **Datalog with negation:** The rules have the format as in Case (a) but negative literals (*not A*) are allowed in the body of the rule.

We will refer to a rule as a Ξ-rule (where Ξ is Datalog, ground Datalog, binary Datalog, etc.) to denote a rule that meets the corresponding requirements. A Ξ-program is a collection of Ξ-rules. Given a rule r, we denote with *used(r)* the set of ground terms t such that t is a label of a qualified atom in r. Given a Ξ-program, we denote with

$$used(P) = \{\, t \mid \exists\, r \in P, t \in used(r)\,\}.$$

We also introduce

$$def(P) = \{\, p \mid p \in \Pi, ar(p)=k, \exists r \in P.\ \exists\, t_1,...,t_k, head(r) = p(t_1,...,t_k)\,\}.$$

Intuitively, a Ξ-program encodes a knowledge base, whose semantics is defined by a class of models satisfying certain properties. It should be noted that the semantics of a program might be defined in different ways and depends on the program type. For **Datalog** programs, the least fixpoint semantics can be used (van Emden & Kowalski, 1976). However, for **Datalog with negation** programs, the well-founded (Van Gelder, Ross, & Schlipf, 1991) or the answer set semantics can be used (Gelfond & Lifschitz, 1988).

Planning in Logic Programming and Web Service Composition

A planning problem is specified by a domain, with its properties (called *fluents*) and *actions* with their preconditions and effects, a specification about the initial state of the world, and a formula describing the final state (*goal*). The objective is to determine a sequence of actions that can transform the initial state into a state satisfying the goal.

Logic programming under the answer set semantics was first used in planning by Subrahmanian and Zaniolo (1995) and is now known as *answer set planning* (Lifschitz, 2002). Answer set planning has gained popularity thanks to the development of fast answer set solvers (e.g., *Smodels* [Simons, Niemelä, & Soininen, 2002] and *DLV* [Eiter, Leone, Mateis, Pfeifer, & Scarcello, 1998]). Since our intention is to use logic programming for Web service composition, following the AI planning approach, we will give a brief overview of answer set planning by illustrating its key ideas through an example. As noted earlier, existing tools can be adapted to translate Web service descriptions into the representation discussed in this chapter.

Answer Set Planning

Let us consider the classical AI problem of going to the airport (McCarthy, 1959). In this problem, we have an action, named *drive_home_airport*; in the initial state, we are at home and have a car. We know that driving will bring us to the airport and our goal is to go be at the airport.

In answer set planning, this problem is encoded by a Datalog with negation program that consists of the different groups of rules described below. In each of these rules, T denotes a number between 0 and a predefined constant length, indicating the maximal length of the plan that we wish to compute. The rules

```
action(drive_home_airport)   ←
         fluent(at_home)     ←
       fluent(at_airport)    ←
    fluent(car_available)    ←
```

specify the fluents and the actions of the domain. The rules

```
false    ←   not holds(at_home,T), occ(drive_home_airport), T)
false    ←   not holds(car_available,T), occ(drive_home_airport), T)
```

encode the precondition under which the action drive _ home _ airport can be executed. They state that the action drive _ home _ airport can only occur at the time T if at _ home and car _ available are true at the time T. The rules

```
holds(at_airport,T+1)     ←   occ(drive_home_airport, T)
holds(neg(at_home),T+1)   ←   occ(drive_home_airport, T)
```

say that if the drive _ home _ airport action occurs at the time T, at _ airport and at _ home will be true and false, respectively, at the time T+1. The two rules

```
occ(drive_home_airport,T)       ←  not not_occ(drive_home_airport,T)
not_occ(drive_home_airport,T)   ←  not occ(drive_home_airport,T)
```

are often referred to as *generation rules,* and are used to generate action occurrences. Intuitively, they state that the action either occurs or not. The rules

```
holds(at_airport,T+1)        ←  holds(at_airport, T),
                                 not holds(neg(at_airport), T+1)
holds(neg(at_airport),T+1)   ←  holds(neg(at_airport), T),
                                 not holds(at_airport, T+1)
```

known as *inertial rules*, encode the fact that a fluent normally does not change its value. (We omit the rules for at _ home and car _ available for brevity.)

Finally, the initial state is encoded by a set of facts of the form

```
holds(neg(at_airport),0)   ←
holds(at_home, 0)          ←
```

and the goal is expressed by the rule

```
false   ←   not holds(at_airport,length)
```

Each answer set of the above program corresponds to a plan achieving the goal at _ airport. For example, for length=1, the program yields an answer set corresponding to the plan [drive _ home _ airport]. For more on answer set planning, the interested reader is referred to Lifschitz's (2002) work.

Answer Set Planning and Web Service Composition

Answer set planning can be used for Web service composition, but it requires some modifications and extensions. For example, the functions of the hotel reservation Web service (Figure 1) can be encoded by the following actions:

```
action(checkAvailability(DateIn,DateOut,RoomType))   ←  date(DateIn),
                                                        date(DaeOut),
                                                        type(RoomType)
action(makeReservation(DateIn,DateOut,RoomType))     ←  date(DateIn),
                                                        date(DaeOut),
                                                        type(RoomType)
```

It is reasonable to consider the two following fluents:

*   available: there are some rooms available
*   reserved: the reservation has been successful

Figure 3. Schematic architecture

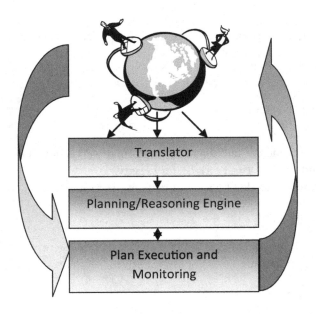

They can be encoded as follows

```
fluent(available)        ←
fluent(reserved)         ←
```

The effect of the action `checkAvailability` is different than the effect of the action `makeReservation`. The execution of `checkAvailability` is *either* `available` *or* `¬available`, while the execution of `makeReservation` is `reserved`. The first action, called *knowledge producing action*, does not change the state of the world (it does not alter the number of available rooms) while the second one does (it reduces the number of available rooms by 1).

Knowledge producing actions are often needed when a reasoner does not have complete information about the state of the world. For example, an agent that uses the above service to place a reservation often does not know whether or not the hotel would have a room. In other words, neither `available` nor `¬available` is true in the initial state. The agent knows about the value of `available` (or `¬available`) after the execution of the action `checkAvailability`. In our previous work (i.e., Son et al., 2005; Tu, Son, & Baral, 2006), we discuss the use of logic programming in reasoning and planning with knowledge producing actions and incomplete information. We also extended answer set planning to incorporate different types of domain knowledge and user preferences (Son, Baral, Tran, & McIlraith, 2006b; Son & Pontelli, 2006).

Current Architecture and Challenges

The techniques developed so far can be used in the implementation of a Web service composition framework similar to other AI-planning Web service composition frameworks (Figure 3). The basic components of this approach are:

- A *translator* which reads Web service descriptions and translates them into an adequate logic programming theory (e.g., a Datalog with negation program).
- A *reasoning/planning engine* which accepts the output of the translator and creates a plan that achieves the goal of the service composition problem.
- An *execution and monitoring* module which is responsible for the execution of the plan.

Architectures analogous to the one depicted in Figure 3 have been successfully implemented, for example, in the development of systems for Web service composition of bioinformatics Web services (e.g., (Pan, Tu, Pontelli, & Son, 2004)). In this application, the results of the translation are Datalog, Datalog with negation, or a similar variant language. The reasoning/planning engine employs the answer set semantics for this program. Furthermore, it is assumed that all necessary information has been incorporated into the encodings of the corresponding services. Although the resulting system is adequate for the mentioned application, the new developments in Semantic Web present two technical challenges to this architecture.

The first problem lies in the fact that knowledge (and hence, Web services) often comes with *reasoning rules,* that were not the focus of earlier Web service description languages, and hence this aspect has not been addressed in previous implementations. The second challenge is the need to consider different semantics embedded in the encoding of a Web service, since the underlying semantics of various RuleML knowledge bases are specified by the knowledge engineers and not by the application developers. In dealing with this problem, we can identify a number of issues that need to be addressed:

1. *Reasoning within one knowledge base:* Being able to reason within a knowledge base implies the ability to interoperate with a computational framework capable of handling the type of knowledge present in the knowledge base (e.g., a Prolog system for hohorn rules, a Datalog system for Datalog rules).
2. *Reasoning across different knowledge bases:* The capability of combining knowledge is essential for intelligent agents (e.g., this is necessary in the context of services composition). This requires
   a. The ability to exchange inference results between different knowledge bases (e.g., the interoperability problem between rules and OWL described by Kifer et al. [2005]);
   b. The ability to combine reasoning results produced by different reasoning engines; and
   c. The ability to properly scope the reasoning w.r.t. a specific knowledge base (e.g., the scoped inference issue described by Kifer et al. [2005]).
3. *Utilizing available knowledge:* This requires the ability to use the results produced by different reasoning processes in the construction/implementation of complex Semantic Web applications.

A Motivating Example

Let us illustrate some of these issues within an example, drawn from the field of bioinformatics. This application domain is particularly interesting with respect to the issue of Web service composition; in recent years a large number of Web services have been developed, and they rely on a large collection of heterogeneous (and often redundant) ontologies and knowledge bases.

The problem at hand is to obtain reliable functional annotation, according to the Gene Ontology (Gene Ontology Consortium, 2007), of the proteins coded by the genes present in the genome of an organism. The input is represented by the NCBI RefSeq id of a genome (i.e., an id of the form *NC_xxxx*).

It has been observed that functional annotations retrieved by AmiGO (the query system to the Gene Ontology Database) are occasionally unreliable (e.g., Andorf, Dobbs, & Honavar, 2007). In particular, it has been observed that some incorrect annotations in the Gene Ontology are characterized by a selection code equal to reviewed computational analysis (RCA). We consider the following services and knowledge bases:

- **NCBI GenBank Genome-to-Protein Search:** This service expects as input the RefSeq of a genome, and produces as results the NCBI ids of the proteins coded by the genes in the considered genome;
- **Protein Class Ontology:** Gene Ontology includes a taxonomy of functional classification of proteins (e.g., its OBO encoding can be found in "Gene Ontology, Edit 1.101, " [2007]). The taxonomy can be directly encoded in Datalog; sample rules extracted are:

```
id(0016301)
name(0016301, 'kinase activity')
namespace(0016301,molecular _ function)
is _ a(0016301,0016772)
...
id(0004672)
name(0004672,'protein kinase activity')
alt _ id(0050222)
xref(reactome(4030))
is _ a(0004672,0016301)
is _ a(0004672,0016773)
...
```

Ontological reasoning allows us, for example, to discover subclasses and superclasses of a given one.

- **Functional Annotation Service:** The input is an id of a protein. If the protein belongs to a class whose functional annotation is not RCA, then the annotation is retrieved from the Gene Ontology annotation database and returned. Otherwise, the annotation is extracted from the UniProt database (and returned in UniProt format). The semantics of this service requires the use of more complex rules (encoded in RuleML using the nafdatalog language). Some of the Datalog with negation rules are:

```
suspect(ProteinClass) ←
    amigo:evidence _ code(ProteinClass,rca)
classification(ProteinClass, FuncAnnotation,go)←
    amigo:is _ a(ProteinClass,FuncAnnotation),
    not suspect(ProteinClass)
classification(ProteinClass,FuncAnnotation,uniprot) ←
    suspect(ProteinClass),
    interpro2go:entity _ xref(ProteinClass,X),
    uniprot:is _ a(X,FuncAnnotation)
```

- **Gene Ontology to InterPro Ontology Mapping:** This mapping, expressed in a ground Prolog facts database is available at the "OBO download matrix" (2007).

Let us assume that the initial state includes the RefSeq NC_003075 (Arabidopsis thaliana chromosome 4) and we are interested only in proteins that are enzyme inhibitors. The genome includes 4,817 coding genes. One of the proteins generated is AT4G00080. The Gene Ontology can be used (through a transitive closure of the is_a relationship) to determine that the protein belongs to the desired class. Accessing the functional annotation, we discover that the protein is annotated as a pectinesterase inhibitor (GO:0046910), but it is RCA. This means that the desired annotation will be extracted from UniProt, and this returns an annotation IPR006501. The mapping between ontologies contains the fact

```
metadata _ db:entity _ xref('GO:0046910','IPR006501')
```

This will eventually produce the same Gene Ontology annotation.

A FRAMEWORK FOR INTEROPERATION AND COMPOSITION

In this section, we describe our framework for interoperation and composition of distributed heterogeneous knowledge bases. We begin with an overview of the approach. We then present the architecture of the component needed to address the challenges faced by the current Web service composition methodology. The precise syntax and semantics of the framework are discussed next.

Overview of the Approach

The objective is to provide a formal logic-based framework that allows the development of the planning/reasoning component of Figure 3. The approach we follow is intuitively depicted in Figure 4. The framework is assembled as a collection of modules, each containing a logic programming theory, potentially requiring a different semantics (e.g., datalog/pure prolog, constraint logic programming, answer set programming, etc.) The modules are the result of a logic programming encoding of the semantics of the Web services description (left side of Figure 4) and of the underlying associated static knowledge (e.g., ontologies – shown on the right in Figure 4). The framework assumes the possibility of dependencies between the different modules, for example, ontologies can be hierarchically defined.

The answer set planner is encoded using a modular view of the action domain. Each service is represented by a logic programming module, which exports the description of the service as an action; in particular, the module exports the description of the action in terms of its executability conditions (predicate `executable`) and its dynamic effects (predicate `causes`). For example, in the case of the functional annotation service mentioned previously, these predicates could be defined as:

```
executable([have _ protein(X), have _ protein _ class(C)])
causes(go _ classification(X,C)) ←
    have _ protein(X),
    have _ protein _ class(Class),
    classification(Class,C,go)
```

```
causes([validated _ annotation,uniprot _ classification(X,C)]) ←
   have _ protein(X),
   have _ protein _ class(Class),
   classification(Class,C,uniprot)
```

The planner will use these predicates to develop plans, for example, using rules like:

```
holds(F,T+1) ←    action(A),
          occ(A,T),
          A:causes(F),
          A:executable(List),
          holds(List,T)
```

where the execution of the action A requires recovering from the corresponding module (which we assume has the same name as the action) the executability conditions (which are tested in the state of the world at time T) and the effects of the action.

Static causal laws will be employed to allow the planner to make use of background knowledge used by the Web services (e.g., ontologies, databases). For example, the protein class ontology, imported as a Prolog module, would allow us to derive rules like:

```
holds(have _ protein _ class(C),T) ←
   holds(have _ protein _ class(C1),T),
   gene _ ontology:is _ a(T1,T)
```

Architecture

The approach adopted in this work relies on the use of a core logic programming framework to address the issues of integration and interoperation. In particular, the spirit of our approach relies on the following beliefs:

- The natural semantics of various languages for Web service description, ontology description, and various levels of the RuleML deduction rules hierarchy can be naturally captured by different flavors of logic programming.
- Modern logic programming systems provide foreign interfaces that allow declarative interfacing to other programming paradigms.

The idea is to combine the *ASP-Prolog* framework of Elkhatib, Pontelli, and Son, (2006)—which allows CIAO Prolog (Bueno, Cabeza, Carro, Hermenegildo, López-García, & Puebla, 1997) programs to access and modify modules containing answer set programming (ASP) code (Niemelä, 1999)—with the notation for modularization of answer set programming of Answar, Baral, and Tari (2005) and Baral, Dzifcak, and Takahashi (2006). The result is a logic programming framework, where modules responding to different logic programming semantics (e.g., Herbrand minimal model, well-founded semantics, and answer set semantics) can coexist and interoperate. The framework provides a natural answer to the problems of use and interoperation of RuleML and other Web service semantic descriptions described earlier. The overall structure is depicted in Figure 4. Most of the emphasis is on the use of answer set programming to handle some of the RuleML sublanguages (e.g., datalog, ur-datalog, nafdatalog, and negdatalog), even though the core framework will naturally support most of the languages (e.g., hornlog and hohornlog).

The problems mentioned in the previous section are addressed by the proposed framework as follows:

- *Issue 1*: CIAO Prolog offers direct access to a collection of modules that support different forms of logic programming reasoning, for example, traditional Prolog, constraint logic programming (over finite domains and reals), fuzzy Prolog, and a declarative ODBC interface. In addition, CIAO Prolog provides a mechanism that allows Prolog programs to invoke Java methods, offering a bidirectional communication and a reflection of Java objects into Prolog. This provides, for example, a natural way to execute Java-based engines (e.g., Jess) and communicate between the core framework and external Java packages. Furthermore, CIAO Prolog includes the PiLLoW library, a standardized Prolog library for Web programming, which provides the framework with capabilities for Web access (e.g., management of URLs) and parsing of HTML and XML documents to Prolog terms. Thus, we envision the core framework as the bridge between distinct execution models for heterogeneous knowledge bases.
- *Issue 2*:
  - *Issue 2(a)*: This issue will be addressed through the introduction of a module system, where different knowledge bases can be encoded (directly or indirectly) as distinct modules. The original import/export of CIAO Prolog can be combined with the languages for answer set modules of Baral et al. (2006) to allow forms of bidirectional communication between the core framework and the modules representing the knowledge bases.
  - *Issue 2(b)*: The core framework will provide the full computational power of Prolog, constraint logic programming, and answer set programming, combined through a sophisticated module and class system. Module interfaces will allow extraction of semantic information from the various knowledge bases (e.g., result of queries, models of knowledge bases) and reason with them.
  - *Issue 2(c)*: The scoped inference is naturally supported by the module system of ASP-Prolog, for example, skeptical and credulous reasoning w.r.t. answer set modules.
- *Issue 3*: This aspect can be handled thanks to the combination, in ASP-Prolog and CIAO Prolog, of Web access capabilities along with the full computational power of Prolog.

We will now introduce the basic structure of our framework for modules and module interoperation.

Module Structure

As mentioned in the introduction to logic programming, we will assume that `assert`, `retract`, `model`,… are elements of $\prod_d$. Given a Ξ-program P, we say that P is pure if neither `assert` nor `retract` appear in the rules of P; otherwise we say that P is impure.

A module is composed of two parts: a module interface and a module body. A module interface has the form

Figure 4. Framework architecture

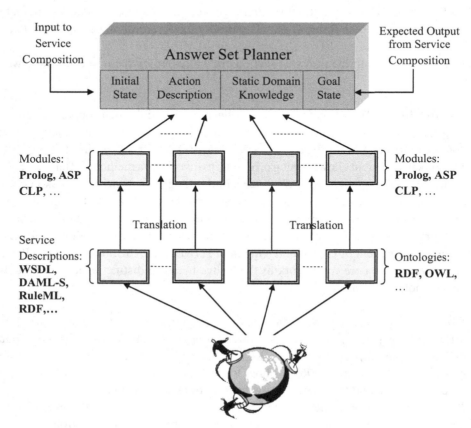

$$\leftarrow \texttt{module} : t$$
$$\leftarrow \texttt{import} : t_1, \ldots, t_k$$
$$\leftarrow \texttt{export} : q_1/k_1, \ldots, q_m/k_m$$

where

- t is a ground term, called the *name* of the module,
- $t_1, \ldots, t_k$ are ground terms, representing names of other modules, and
- $q_1, \ldots, q_m$ are predicates, and are $k_1, \ldots, k_m$ non-negative integers, such that $ar(q_i)=k_i$.

The body of a module is a Ξ-program, for a given Ξ. In that case, we will say that the module is a Ξ-module. Given a module named t, we identify with the *export set of t* (denoted by *exp(t)*) the predicates $q_1, \ldots, q_m$ exported by t. We also identify with *imp(p)* the import set of t, that is, the names of the modules imported by t.

A program $P=\{M_{t_1}, \ldots, M_{t_k}\}$ is a collection of modules named $t_1, \ldots, t_k$. The *graph* of P (denoted by *graph(P)*) is a graph (N,E), where the set of nodes N is $\{t_1, \ldots, t_k\}$ and

$$\left(t_i, t_j\right) \in E \quad \text{iff} \quad t_i \in imp(t_j)$$

A program P is *admissible* if it satisfies the following properties:

- for each t_j we have that $imp(t_j) \subseteq \{t_1, \ldots, t_k\}$; and
- the graph $graph(P)$ is acyclic.

The module structure can be expanded by allowing cyclic dependencies (i.e., two-way communications between modules) as well as OO-style organization of modules (e.g., as described by Baral et al. [2006]). We omit this discussion due to lack of space.

Example: Let us consider the modules associated to the bioinformatics services described earlier. One module, *gene_ontology*, is derived from the Gene Ontology. It will have an overall structure of the form:

```
← module : gene _ ontology
← export : is _ a/2, evidence _ code/2, …

id(0016301)
is _ a(0016301,0016772)
is _ a(0004672,0016301)
is _ a(0004674,0004672)
…
is _ a(X,Y) ← is _ a(X,Z), is _ a(Z,Y)
…
evidence _ code(0016772, rca)
…
```

A second module is obtained from the RuleML semantics of the functional annotation service:

```
← module : validated _ annotation
← import : gene _ ontology, …
← export : executable/1, causes/1, …
suspect(ProteinClass) ←
  gene _ ontology:evidence _ code(ProteinClass,rca)
classification(ProteinClass, FuncAnnotation,go) ←
  gene _ ontology:is _ a(ProteinClass,FuncAnnotation),
  not suspect(ProteinClass)
…
```

The resulting program P will be a set of modules { *planner, gene_ontology, validated_annotation,* …}. □

General Semantics

In order to understand the framework, it is important to clearly define the semantics of the module-based system. We start by considering pure programs, and then we extend the discussion to impure programs.

Pure Programs

In this section, we propose a model-theoretic semantics for programs that do not contain any impure modules. Given a program, a *model naming* function τ is an onto function $\tau: H_p \rightarrow 2^{B_P}$. We will use this function to assign *distinct* names to the models of the different modules. In the rest of this work, we will assume that the function τ is fixed.

Given a program $P = \{M_{t_1}, ..., M_{t_k}\}$, the acyclic nature of *graph(P)* guarantees the ability to construct a topological sort of $\{t_1,...,t_k\}$, say $\eta_1,..., \eta_k$, such that if (η_i,η_j) is an edge of the graph, then $i < j$.

Given the program P and a topological sorting of the modules $\eta_1,..., \eta_k$, we construct the semantics module by module, following the topological sort order. The semantics of each module M_i will be given by a collection of models $\Phi^\tau(M_i)$, where $\Phi^\tau(M_i) \subseteq 2^{B_P}$. Given a Ξ-program T, not containing any qualified atoms and not containing any occurrence of predicates from Π_d, we assume that its semantics $NAT(T)$ is given. For example, if T is a **Datalog with negation** program meeting these conditions, then $NAT(T)$ will be the set of answer sets of T, while if T is a **pure Prolog** program (i.e., definite logic program without extra-logical predicates such as `assert` and `retract`), then $NAT(T)$ contains the least Herbrand model of T.

This suggests a natural way to handle the semantics Φ^τ of a program P. Φ^τ is a mapping of the form $\Phi^\tau: P \rightarrow 2^{B_P}$. Once the topological sort $\eta_1,..., \eta_k$ of the modules is given, we can construct Φ^τ as follows:

- the semantics of M_{η_1} is given, since it does not import any other modules, and
$$\Phi^\tau(M_{\eta_1}) = NAT(M_{\eta_1})$$
- the semantics of M_{η_i} can be constructed by computing the natural semantics of a "reduct" of the module,
$$\Phi^\tau(M_{\eta_i}) = NAT(MR(M_{\eta_i}, \Phi^\tau))$$
as defined next.

Let us consider a module M_{η_i} of P. Then:

- If $t : A$ is a ground qualified atom and $t \in imp(M_{\eta_i})$, then
$M_{\eta_i} \models_{\Phi^\tau} t : A$ iff for each model $M \in \Phi^\tau(M_t)$ we have that $M \models A$.
- If $t : A$ is a ground qualified atom and $t \notin imp(M_{\eta_i})$, then $M_{\eta_i} \models_{\Phi^\tau} t : A$ if there exists $x \in imp(M_{\eta_i})$, $M \in \Phi^\tau(M_x)$ such that $\pi(A) \in exp(x)$, $\tau(t)=M$ and $M \models A$.
- $M_{\eta_i} \models_{\Phi^\tau} t : model(s)$ if $t \in imp(M_{\eta_i})$ and $\tau(s) \in \Phi^\tau(M_t)$.
- If *not* $t : A$ is a ground qualified literal and $t \in imp(M_{\eta_i})$, then
$M_{\eta_i} \models_{\Phi^\tau}$ not $t : A$ if $M_{\eta_i} \not\models_{\Phi^\tau} t : A$.

The *model reduct* of M_i w.r.t. Φ^τ, denoted $MR(M_i, \Phi^\tau)$, is defined as follows:

- Remove from M_i all rules that contain in the body a qualified element l such that $M_i \not\models_{\Phi^\tau} l$.
- Remove from the remaining rules all occurrences of qualified elements.

One can easily see that $MR(M_i, \Phi^\tau)$ is a program without qualified atoms whose semantics is defined by NAT. This allows us to set

$$\Phi^\tau(M_{\eta_i}) = \text{NAT}(MR(M_{\eta_i}, \Phi^\tau))$$

From now on, we will denote with $\Phi^{\tau/P}$ the semantics of a program P.

Example: Let us continue the example we started earlier. The module *gene_ontology* is a Datalog program. Thus, NAT(*gene_ontology*) = { M_0 } where M_0 is its least Herbrand model; some of the elements in M_0 are:

is_a(0016301,0016772), is_a(0004672,0016301),
is_a(0004674,0004672), is_a(0004672,0016772),
is_a(0004674,0016772), is_a(0004674,0016301),...

The module *validated_annotation* is a Datalog with negation program, and its reduct will be performed with respect to the semantics of *gene_ontology* (and the other imported modules). For example, the rule

```
classification(ProteinClass, FuncAnnotation, go) ←
    gene_ontology:is_a(ProteinClass, FuncAnnotation),
    not suspect(ProteinClass)
```

will be grounded and only the instances for which the `is_a` atom is true in M_0 will be kept, for example,

```
classification(0004674, 0016772, go) ← not suspect(0004674)
```

Only the answer sets of the resulting program will be maintained as NAT(*validated_annotation*). □

Impure Programs

We say that a program is impure if it contains impure modules and/or it contains modules that are not based on logic programming. The use of impure programs allows the planner to provide the Web services with knowledge about the state of the world the services will be executed in. It also allows the reasoner to temporarily modify the content of a module (e.g., a module describing an action) to support the planning process. This is particularly important when dealing with very complex plans (Son & Pontelli, 2007) or incomplete knowledge (Tu et al., 2006).

Let $P=\{M_{t_1}, ..., M_{t_k}\}$ be a program; for the sake of simplicity, we assume that $t_1,...,t_k$ is a topological sort of *graph(P)*. We also consider impure programs under the following restrictions:

- The planner is itself a module, encoded using Prolog (pure or impure), and it is represented by the module M_{t_k}.
- The impure predicates `assert` and `retract` are allowed to appear only in Prolog modules.

Because of the nonlogical nature of the impure predicates, we rely on an operational semantics to chaacterize the meaning of programs.

The *state* of a computation is given by a tuple $\langle G, \theta, P\rangle$, where G is a Prolog goal, θ is a substitution, and P is a program. The operational semantics for a goal executed in the module named t_i is defined through a state transition system $\langle G, \theta, P\rangle \rightarrow_i \langle G', \theta', P'\rangle$ where

- If $G = (A \wedge Rest)$ and $\pi(A) \in def(M_{t_i})$, and $h \leftarrow body$ is a variant of a rule in M_{t_i} such that σ is the most general unifier of $A\theta$ and h, then we have that $G'=body \wedge Rest$, $\theta'=\theta\sigma$,[3] and $P'=P$.
- If $G = (t : A \wedge Rest)$, $t_j \in imp(M_{t_i})$, $\pi(A) \in def(M_{t_j})$, t_j is a Prolog module, and $\langle A, \theta, P\rangle \rightarrow_j \langle \square, \theta', P'\rangle$ then we have $G'=Rest$
- If $G = (t : A \wedge Rest)$, $t_j \in imp(M_{t_i})$, $\pi(A) \in def(M_{t_j})$, t_j is an ASP/datalog module, and let σ be a ground substitution fpor $A\theta$ such that $A\theta\sigma$ is true in each model in $\Phi^{v/P}(M_{t_j})$ then we have that $G'=Rest$, $\theta'=\theta\sigma$, and $P'=P$.
- If $G = t : model(t') \wedge Rest$ and $t \in imp(M_{t_i})$, and σ is a ground substitution such that $t'\theta$ is ground and $\tau(t'\theta) \in \Phi^{v/P}(M_t)$, then $G'=Rest$, $\theta'=\theta\sigma$, and $P'=P$.
- If $G = t : A \wedge Rest$ and there exists $t' \in imp(M_{t_i})$, and σ is a substitution such that $(t : A)\theta\sigma$ is ground, $\tau(t\sigma) \in \Phi^{v/P}(M_t)$, and $A\theta\sigma$ is true in $\tau(t\sigma)$, then we have that $G'=Rest$, $\theta'=\theta\sigma$, and $P'=P$.
- If $G = t : assert(Head, Body) \wedge Rest$ and σ is a substitution such that $t\sigma \in imp(M_{t_i})$, then we have that $G'=Rest$, $\theta'=\theta\sigma$, and $P'=(P\backslash\{M_{t\sigma}\})\cup N_{t\sigma}$ where $N_{t\sigma} = M_{t\sigma} \cup \{ (Head \leftarrow Body)\sigma \}$.
- If $G = t : retract(Head, Body) \wedge Rest$ and σ is a ground substitution such that $t\sigma \in imp(M_{t_i})$ and $(Head \leftarrow Body)\sigma \in M_{t\sigma}$, then we have that $G'=Rest$, $\theta'=\theta\sigma$, and $P' = (P\backslash\{M_{t\sigma}\}) \cup N_{t\sigma}$ where $N_{t\sigma} = M_{t\sigma}\backslash\{(Head \leftarrow Body)\sigma\}$.

Given a goal G and a program P with main module M_{t_k}, we say that θ is a solution of G if

$$\langle G, \varepsilon, P\rangle \rightarrow_k^* \langle \square, \theta, P'\rangle$$

where $\rightarrow^*$ denotes an arbitrarily long sequence of transitions.

Example: Let us continue with our example. The ability to perform service composition using logic-based planning provides the added advantage that the plan and the complete trajectory are represented by logic statements, and it is possible to write additional modules to reason about the trajectory. For example:

- Given a list of proteins L we can write a simple query that will provide the functional class to which the majority of the proteins belong to:

```
majority(L, Class) ←
        findall(C,(member(X,L),annotate(X,C)),Funs),
        findall(K-F, ( member(A,Funs),
                    findall(A,member(A,Funs),S),
                    length(S,K)
        ),
              Res),
        keysort(Res,Result),
        last(Result,Class)
annotate(P,F) ←
        assert(planner:initially(have _ protein(P))),
        planner:holds(go _ classification(P,F),length)
```

- Let us assume that the service description includes an estimate of the reliability of the service, provided by the service provider and measuring the ability of the service to quickly respond to a request. This is translated in a fact of the form `low _ load` or `high _ load`. The logic programming module allows the action to successfully return only in case of low load, that is, the definition of the action in the service description module will include

```
executable(...)  :- low _ load.
```

If the resulting plan is sufficiently long, we would like to replace the load information with a pessimistic value, which may reflect the fact that the load figure is not reliable any longer. We could modify the rule used by the planner:

```
holds(F,T+1) ←      action(A), occ(A,T),
        (T > Threshold -> retract(A:low _ load); true),
        A:causes(F), A:executable(List),  holds(List,T)
```

□

FRAMEWORK IMPLEMENTATION

Logical Core Implementation

The implementation of the logical core is based on the combination of two logic programming systems: *CIAO Prolog* (Bueno et al., 1997) and *Smodels* (Niemelä & Simons, 1997). *CIAO Prolog* is a full-fledged Prolog system, with a sophisticated module system, and designed to handle a variety of flavors of logic programming, including constraint logic programming (over reals and finite domains), fuzzy logic programming, and concurrent logic programming. *Smodels* is a logic programming engine which supports computation of the well-founded and answer set semantics for NAF-datalog programs. The proposed system is composed of two parts: a *preprocessor* and the actual CIAO Prolog system.

The input to the preprocessor is composed of

- The main planner module (*Pr*), typically a Prolog module, which extracts information from a planner encoded in ASP;
- A collection of CIAO Prolog modules ($m_1,..., m_n$);
- A collection of ASP modules ($e_1,..., e_m$).

The main task of the preprocessor is to transform the ASP modules to enable their use in the CIAO Prolog system and to manage the interaction with the *Smodels* solver.

The transformation of each ASP module leads to the creation of two entities that will be employed during the actual program execution, that is, an *interface module* and a *model class*. These are described in the following subsections. The preprocessor will also automatically invoke the CIAO Prolog top-level and load all the appropriate modules for execution. The interaction with the user is the same as the standard CIAO Prolog top-level.

Interface Modules

The preprocessor generates one interface module for each ASP module present in the original input program. The interface module is implemented as a standard CIAO Prolog module and it provides the client Prolog modules with the predicates used to access and manage the ASP module. The interface module is created for each ASP module by instantiating a generic module skeleton

The overall structure of the interface module is illustrated in Figure 5. The module has an export list which includes all the predicates used to manipulate ASP modules (e.g., `assert`, `retract`, `model`) as well as all the predicates that are defined within the ASP module.

Each module has an initialization part, which is in charge of setting up the internal data structures and invoke the ASP solver (*Smodels*) for the first time on the ASP module. The result of the computation of the models will be encoded as a collection of *model objects* (see the description of the model classes in the next subsection). The module will maintain a number of internal data structures, including

Figure 5. Structure of an interface module

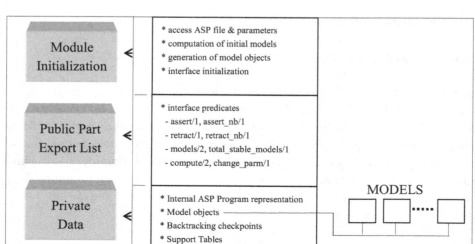

a representation of the ASP code, a representation of the parameters to be used for the computation of the answer sets (e.g., values of constants), a list containing the objects representing the models of the ASP module, a counter of the number of answer sets currently present, and so forth.

The preprocessor creates a graph-module structure which represents the call hierarchy of modules. If a Prolog/ASP module u_p calling another prolog/ASP module u_c then u_p is called the parent module and u_c is one of its children. The tree-module structure is stored in each interface module.

Each interface provides also a `timestamp` predicate, which is used to inform of the time at which the module's semantics have been last computed (recorded as a discrete system time); each interface module will recompute the local semantics whenever the timestamp of one of the imported modules changes. This allows the system to propagate the effect of changes (e.g., `assert/retract`) to all modules that depend on the modified one.

Finally, the preprocessing will add code to handle the different types of goal qualification.

Model Classes

The preprocessor generates a CIAO class definition for each module. The objects obtained from the instantiation of such class will be used to represent the individual models of the module. In particular, for an ASP module we will have one instance for each answer set, while for a Prolog module we will have a single instance, corresponding to the least Herbrand model.

Prolog and ASP modules can obtain reference to these objects (e.g., using the `model` predicate supplied by the interface module) and use them to directly query the content of one model. The definition of the class is obtained through a straightforward parsing of the export declaration of each module, to collect the names of the predicates defined in it; the class will provide a public method for each of the predicates present in the module's export list. The class also defines a public method `add/1` which is used by the interface module to initialize the content of the model.

To facilitate computation, the preprocessor generates an additional module for each ASP module, called `skeptical module`. The module is instantiated to a collection of facts representing the elements that have the same truth value in all answer sets of the corresponding ASP module.

Further Implementation Details

Further details about the implementation of this framework can be found by Pontelli, Son, and Baral (2006). Let us discuss only some significant aspects here.

ASP-State: Every ASP-module has a set of models, atoms, and skeptical model called ASP-states. A stack is used to store the ASP-states which will be used for backtracking. Any change in the ASP-state of an ASP module m, requires that all the ASP ancestor modules of m change their own ASP-states. This can be done with the help of the tree-module structure.

Partial Grounder: In order for the Smodels system to ground the ASP-modules, all qualification of the form $(\alpha: t)$ have to be computed and stored as new facts with a newly created ASP-variable. Therefore, if we have a positive qualification literal $(\alpha: t)$, then the partial grounder will evaluate the predicate t in module α. If α is a Prolog module, then the built-in predicate `findall` is used to compute all possible answers to the goal `?-t`. If α is an ASP-module, then the predicate t is evaluated against the skeptical answers of the ASP-module α. If α is an ASP-model name, then predicate t is computed against the corresponding answer set named α. After that, all ground values of t are added as facts into the ASP-module.

The same rewriting rules are needed for negative qualification literals (*not* α: *t*), domain qualification literals, cardinality qualification literals, and weight qualification literals.

RuleML Specific Issues: RuleML knowledge bases are retrieved and encoded as modules to support the reasoning activities. The translation process relies on the PiLLoW library (which supports HTTP protocol and basic XML manipulation) and the sophisticated XML library provided by CIAO Prolog (which allows XML parsing, URIs management, and even XPath queries). The translation process is performed in two steps. During the first step, the RuleML document is parsed and converted into a Prolog XML representation (as a compound Prolog term). In the second phase, the Prolog XML representation is parsed and translated into logical rules and collected into a module.

The import component of the module is automatically derived by retrieving those atoms used in the program and linking (through URIs) to external components (e.g., used in the `rel` elements). By default, the export list will contain all the `rel` that appear as heads of rules/facts in the knowledge base.

Another specific issue related to RuleML is the inclusion of ECA rules. They can be effectively included in the proposed framework, as discussed by Pontelli, Son, and Baral (2006).

RELATED WORK

The importance of developing languages and frameworks to integrate different aspects of semantic Web reasoning has been highlighted in the literature. Most of the existing focus has been on integrating rule-based reasoning with ontology reasoning. Two relevant contributions in this field are represented by the work of Golbreich (2004) and Laera, Tamma, Bench-Capon, and Semeraro (2004). Golbreich (2004) describes a combination of reasoning about ontologies (encoded in OWL) with rule-based reasoning (with rules encoded in SWRL and processed by the Jess system). Different from our framework, the system is not based on logic programming (relying on Java's Jess platform) and limited to SWRL's rule format.

A wider-breadth approach, and closer to the spirit of ASP-Prolog, is SweetProlog (Laera, Tamma, Bench-Capon, & Semeraro, 2004). SweetProlog offers a platform for integrating rules and OWL ontologies build using logic programming. Rules are encoded using OWLRuleML, which represents an OWL ontology for the RuleML dialect captured by the courteous logic programming scheme (Grosof, 1999). Both rules and OWL ontologies are mapped to Prolog (specifically, the Java-Internet Prolog engine) for interrogation and reasoning. This project has a greater emphasis on integration between a fixed-rule language (the fragment of RuleML captured by OWLRuleML) and OWL ontologies, providing an orthogonal contribution to the integration problem.

A remarkable direction has been explored in the context of the DLV project; `dlvhex` (Eiter, Ianni, Schindlauer, & Tompits, 2006) is an extension of DLV:

- It allows answer set programs to invoke external source of computation, that is, truth value of selected predicates can be achieved through external deduction systems, for example, accessing RDF statements; and
- It allows answer set programs to contain higher-order atoms.

This language has been motivated by similar reasons as those in this chapter, to support semantic Web reasoning (Eiter et al., 2006; Eiter, Lukasiewicz, Schindlauer, & Tompits, 2004), with particular emphasis on integration of ontologies.

Relatively few proposals have appeared in the literature dealing with the high-level integration of different forms of logic programming reasoning, specifically top-down goal-oriented Prolog and bottom-up answer set semantics. ASP-Prolog (Elkhatib et al., 2006), on which the work described in this chapter builds, is a system that provides Prolog programs with the ability to seamlessly access modules processed under answer set semantics. A simplified interface, between the *Smodels* system and XSB Prolog, has been described by Castro, Swift, and Warren (2002).

Lower level interfaces between answer set systems (DLV and *Smodels*) and traditional imperative languages have been developed (Calimeri & Ianni, 2005; Ricca, 2003; Syrjanen, 1998).

CONCLUSION AND FUTURE WORK

In this chapter, we addressed the issue of dealing with heterogeneous Web services in the context of the Web service composition problem. We presented a logic programming framework for intelligent Web service composition and a preliminary prototype of parts of the framework within the ASP-Prolog system. The key idea in our framework is to view Web services as actions and Web service composition as a planning problem. Under this view, Web service documents (e.g., WSDL or RuleML documents) are encoded as logic programs which can be reasoned about and combined using logic programming techniques. The variety of semantics of logic programs supports a natural way to deal with heterogeneous Web service description and ontologies. Furthermore, the use of answer set planning in Web service composition allows us to easily incorporate users' preferences and effectively handle incomplete knowledge.

As future work, we propose to demonstrate the framework on real-world applications, with particular focus on applications on description and manipulation of bioinformatics Web services. The proposed framework is also expected to have a significant role in facilitating the deployment of and reasoning about rule-bases constructed according to the guidelines of the rule interchange format (RIF) initiative (Ginsberg, Hirtle, McCabe, & Patranjan, 2006). Recent developments in RIF have highlighted the importance of being able to merge rule sets, and the requirement of supporting standard ways to characterize rule sets dialects. The proposed framework could easily avail of such standardized identification of dialects to guide the automated translation of RIF rule sets to ASP-Prolog modules.

REFERENCES

Andorf, C., Dobbs, D., & Honavar, V. (2007). Exploring inconsistencies in genome-wide protein function annotations. *BMC Bioinformatics*.

Answar, S., Baral, C., & Tari, L. (2005). *A language for modular ASP: Application to ACC tournament scheduling*. Paper presented at the ASP Workshops.

Au, T. C., Kuter, U., & Nau, D. (2005). *Web service composition with volatile information*. Paper presented at the International Semantic Web Conference (ISWC).

Balduccini, M., Gelfond, M., & Nogueira, M. (2006). Answer set based design of knowledge systems. *Annals of Mathematics and Artificial Intelligence*.

Baral, C., Dzifcak, J., & Takahashi, H. (2006). *Macros, macro calls, and use of ensembles in modular answer set programming.* Paper presented at the International Conference on Logic Programming.

Bassiliades, N., Antoniou, G., & Vlahavas, I. (2006). DR-DEVICE, a defeasible logic reasoner for the Semantic Web. *International Journal on Semantic Web and Information Systems, 2*(1), 1-41.

Berners-Lee, T., & Fischetti, M. (1999). *Weaving the Web: The original design and ultimate destiny of the World Wide Web by its inventor.* Harper.

Berners-Lee, T., Hendler, J., & Lassila, O. (2001). The Semantics Web. *Scientific American, 284*(5), 34-43.

Boley, H., Grosof, B., Sintek, M., Tabe, S., & Wagner, G. (2002). *RuleML design, version 0.8.* Retrieved May 30, 2008, from www.ruleml.org/indesign.html

Booth, D., & Liu, C. K. (2005). *Web service description language primer.*

Bueno, F., Cabeza, D., Carro, M., Hermenegildo, M., López-García, P., & Puebla, G. (1997). *The Ciao Prolog system.* Unpublished manuscript.

Calimeri, F., & Ianni, G. (2005). *External sources of computation for answer set solvers.* Paper presented at the Logic Programming and Non-Monotonic Reasoning.

Castro, L., Swift, T., & Warren, D. (2002). *XASP: Answer set programming with XSB and smodels.* Retrieved May 30, 2008, from xsb.sourceforge.net/manual2/node149.html

Chan, H., & Grosof, B. (1999). *CommonRules.* Retrieved May 30, 2008, from www.alphaworks.ibm.com/tech/commonrules

Chinnici, R., Moreau, J.-J., Ryman, A., & Weerawarana, S. (2007). *Web service description language, version 2.0.*

Dean, M. (2001). *RuleML experiments with GEDCOM.* Retrieved May 30, 2008, from www.daml.org/2001/02/gedcom-ruleml

Eiter, T., Ianni, G., Schindlauer, R., & Tompits, H. (2006). *Effective integration of declarative rules with external evaluations for Semantic-Web reasoning.* Paper presented at the European Semantic Web Conference.

Eiter, T., Leone, N., Mateis, C., Pfeifer, G., & Scarcello, F. (1998). *The KR system dlv: Progress report, comparisons, and benchmarks.* Paper presented at the International Conference on Principles of Knowledge Representation and Reasoning (pp. 406-417).

Eiter, T., Lukasiewicz, T., Schindlauer, R., & Tompits, H. (2004). *Combining ASP with description logics for the Semantic Web.* Paper presented at the Principles of Knowledge Representation and Reasoning,.

Elkhatib, O., Pontelli, E., & Son, T. C. (2006). *A tool for knowledge base integration and querying.* Paper presented at the AAAI Spring Symposium.

Gelfond, M., & Lifschitz, V. (1988). *The stable model semantics for logic programming.* Paper presented at the Logic Programming: Proceedings of the Fifth International Confl and Symp. (pp. 1070-1080).

Gene Ontology Consortium. (2007). *The gene ontology*. Retrieved May 30, 2008, from www.geneontology.org

Gene Ontology, Edit 1.101. (2007). Retrieved May 30, 2008, from http://www.geneontology.org/ontology/gene_ontology_edit.obo

Ginsberg, A., Hirtle, D., McCabe, F., & Patranjan, P.-L. (2006). *RIF use cases and requirements*. W3C.

Golbreich, C. (2004). *Combining rule and ontology reasoners for the Semantic Web*. Paper presented at the RuleML.

Grosof, B. (1999). *A courteous compiler from generalized courteous logic programs to ordinary logic programs*. IBM T.J. Watson Research Center.

Hirtle, D., & Boley, H. (2005). *The modularization of RuleML*. Retrieved May 30, 2008, from www.ruleml.org/modularization

Hoffmann, J., & Nebel, B. (2001). The FF planning system: Fast plan generation through heuristic search. *Journal of Artificial Intelligence Research, 14*, 253-302.

Horrocks, I., Patel-Schneider, P., Boley, H., Tabet, S., Grosof, B., & Dean, M. (2004). *SWRL: A Semantic Web rule language combining OWL and RuleML* (No. SUBM-SWRL-20040521). W3C.

Kautz, H., & Selman, B. (1996). Pushing the envelope: Planning, propositional logic, and stochastic search. In *Proceedings of the 13th National Conference on Artificial Intelligence (AAAI-96)* (pp. 1194-1199).

Kifer, M., de Bruijn, J., Boley, H., & Fensel, D. (2005). *A realistic architecture for the Semantic Web*. Paper presented at the RuleML.

Kuter, U., Sirin, E., Nau, D., Parsia, B., & Hendler, J. (2005). Information gathering during planning for Web service composition. *Journal of Web Semantics (JWS) 3*(2-3), 183-205.

Laera, L., Tamma, V., Bench-Capon, T., & Semeraro, G. (2004). *SweetProlog: A system to integrate ontologies and rules*. Paper presented at the RuleML.

Levesque, H., Reiter, R., Lesperance, Y., Lin, F., & Scherl, R. (1997). GOLOG: A logic programming language for dynamic domains. *Journal of Logic Programming 31*(1-3), 59-84.

Lifschitz, V. (1999). *Answer set planning*. Paper presented at the International Conference on Logic Programming (pp. 23-37).

Lifschitz, V. (2002). Answer set programming and plan generation. *Artificial Intelligence, 138*(1-2), 39-54.

Marek, V., & Truszczynski, M. (1999). Stable models and an alternative logic programming paradigm. *The logic programming paradigm: A 25-year perspective* (pp. 375-398).

May, W., Alferes, J., & Amador, R. (2005). *Active rules in the Semantic Web: Dealing with language heterogeneity*. Paper presented at the RuleML.

McCarthy, J. (1959). Programs with common sense. In *Proceedings of the Teddington Conference on the Mechanization of Thought Processes* (pp. 75-91).

McDermott, D., Dou, D., & Qi, P. (2002). *PDDAML: An automatic translator between PDDL and DAML.*

McIlraith, S., & Son, T. C. (2002). Adapting GOLOG for composition of Semantic Web services. In *Proceedings of the Eighth International Conference on Principles of Knowledge Representation and Reasoning (KR'2002)* (pp. 482-493).

Nau, D., Cao, Y., Lotem, A., & Muñoz-Avila, H. (1999). SHOP: Simple hierarchical ordered planner. In *Proceedings of the 16th International Conference on Artificial Intelligence* (pp. 968-973).

Niemelä, I. (1999). Logic programming with stable model semantics as a constraint programming paradigm. *Annals of Mathematics and Artificial Intelligence, 25*(3,4), 241-273.

Niemelä, I., & Simons, P. (1997). Smodels: An implementation of the stable model and well-founded semantics for normal logic programs. In *Proceedings ICLP & LPNMR* (pp. 420-429).

OBO download matrix. (2007). Retrieved May 30, 2008, from http://www.berkeleybop.org/ontologies/

Pan, Y., Tu, P. H., Pontelli, E., & Son, T. C. (2004). *Construction of an agent-based framework for evolutionary biology: A progress report.* Paper presented at the Declarative Agent Languages and Technologies (DALT).

PDDL Technical Committee. (1998). *Planning domain definition language.* Author.

Pontelli, E., Son, T. C., & Baral, C. (2006). *A framework for composition and inter-operation of rules in the Semantic Web.* Paper presented at the RuleML.

Rainer, W. (2005). *Web service composition using answer set programming.* Paper presented at the Workshop on Planning, Scheduling, and Configuration.

Rao, J., & Su, X. (2004). *A survey of automated Web service composition methods.* Paper presented at the SWSWPC.

Ricca, F. (2003). *The DLV Java wrapper.* Paper presented at the Italian Congress on Computational Logic (CILC).

Simons, P., Niemelä, N., & Soininen, T. (2002). Extending and implementing the stable model semantics. *Artificial Intelligence, 138*(1-2), 181-234.

Son, T. C., Baral, C., Tran, N., & McIlraith, S. (2006a). Domain-dependent knowledge in answer set planning. *ACM Transactions on Computational Logic, 7*(4).

Son, T. C., Baral, C., Tran, N., & McIlraith, S. (2006b). Domain-dependent knowledge in answer set planning. *ACM Transactions on Computer Logic, 7*(4), 613-657.

Son, T. C., & Pontelli, E. (2006). Planning with preferences using logic programming. *Theory and Practice of Logic Programming, 6*, 559-607.

Son, T., & Pontelli, E. (2007). *Planning for biochemical pathways: A case study of answer set planning in large planning problem instances.* Paper presented at the Software Engineering for Answer Set Programming.

Son, T. C., Tu, P. H., Gelfond, M., & Morales, R. (2005). Conformant planning for domains with constraints: A new approach. In *Proceedings of the the Twentieth National Conference on Artificial Intelligence* (pp. 1211-1216).

Spencer, B. (2002). *The design of j-DREW, a deductive reasoning engine for the Semantic Web.* Uni. Pol. Madrid.

Subrahmanian, V. S., & Zaniolo, C. (1995). Relating stable models and AI planning domains. In *Proceedings of the International Conference on Logic Programming* (pp. 233-247).

Syrjanen, T. (1998). *Lparse 1.0: User's manual.* Helsinki University of Technology.

The Policy RuleML Technical Group. (2004). *RuleML-powered policy specification and interchange.* Author.

Tu, P. H., Son, T. C., & Baral, C. (2006). Reasoning and planning with sensing actions, incomplete information, and static causal laws using logic programming. *Theory and Practice of Logic Programming, 7*, 1-74.

van Emden, M., & Kowalski, R. (1976). The semantics of predicate logic as a programming language. *Journal of the ACM., 23*(4), 733-742.

Van Gelder, A., Ross, K., & Schlipf, J. (1991). The well-founded semantics for general logic programs. *Journal of ACM, 38*(3), 620-650.

Wu, D., Parsia, B., Sirin, E., Hendler, J., & Nau, D. (2003). *Automating DAML-S Web services composition using SHOP2.* Paper presented at the The SemanticWeb – ISWC.

ENDNOTES

[1]   For simplicity, we omit the **binding** and **service** elements and the XML namespace definitions.

[2]   www.ruleml.org

[3]   We use the notation $\theta\sigma$ to denote the composition of the two substitutions; we also denote with $A\theta$ to denote the application of the substitution θ to the entity A.

Section III
Testability and Security

Chapter X
Enhancing the Testability of Web Services

Daniel Brenner
University of Mannheim, Germany

Barbara Paech
University of Heidelberg, Germany

Matthias Merdes
Heidelberg Mobil International GmbH, Germany

Rainer Malaka
University of Bremen, Germany

ABSTRACT

For the foreseeable future, testing will remain the mainstay of software quality assurance and measurement in all areas of software development, including Web services and service-oriented systems. In general, however, testing Web services is much more challenging than testing normal software applications, not because they are inherently more complex, but because of the limited control and access that users of Web services have over their development and deployment. Whereas the developers of normal applications, by definition, have full control over their application until release time, and thus, can subject them to all kinds of tests in various combinations (e.g., integration testing, system testing, regression testing, acceptance testing, etc.), users of Web services can often only test them at run-time after they have already been deployed and put into service. Moreover, users of Web services often have to share access to them with other concurrent users. In order to effectively test Web services under these conditions special measures and approaches need to be taken to enhance their testability. Right from the early phases of development, the testability of services needs to be taken into account and "designed into" services. In this chapter we consider these issues and with the aid of a case study we present a methodology that can be used to enhance the testability of Web services.

INTRODUCTION

Service-oriented development is based on the idea of building new software applications using software "services," often built and deployed by third party organizations. It therefore assumes a fundamental separation of concerns between *service developers*, who create and offer services with no knowledge of specific applications to which they may be put, and *service users*, who assemble new applications which use the services available on the Internet or in a company's Intranet.

Since they are themselves software applications, services are typically developed and tested using the same basic practices and techniques used to develop normal software applications, and as a result, they can be expected to exhibit the same levels and variations in quality found in the general population of software applications. However, in service-oriented development, the quality of a service-based application is not just based on the inherent quality of the services it uses, it is also dependent on whether they are used or assembled in the correct way. A system assembled from perfectly correct services may still function incorrectly if it uses the services in a different way to that intended; in other words, if the system's understanding of its contract with a service is different to the service provider's.

This problem exists in all component-based approaches whenever a new application is created from prefabricated parts. However, the situation is more acute in service-based development because service users have much less access to, and control over, their components than in regular component-oriented development approaches using such technologies as EJB, SPRING, or .NET. If the developers are creating all of their own components in-house, they can test larger assemblies of components while the development process is underway (integration testing). And even when some of the components are purchased from a third party, once the first version of the system has been completed they can still often test the full system under controlled conditions in the development/test environment (system testing). Finally, once a traditional component-based system has been delivered to the customer, it can be further tested in the customer's target environment to determine whether it fulfils the customer's needs (acceptance testing) before being made accessible to end users.

In general, none of these traditional testing activities can be carried out in the normal way when developing a service-oriented system, however. First, the final collection of "components" that make up an application is typically not known until deployment-time, making full integration and system testing in the traditional form impossible. Second, many of the "components" may already provide services to other users, and cannot be shut down even temporarily to participate in traditional testing activities in a controlled environment. A new application will often have to share its components with other applications and cannot assume that these will cooperate while it is in testing mode.

Although subtle, these differences have a fundamental impact on the role and goals of testing in the system development process. Because services are in effect independent, multiuser systems in their own right, new applications have to test them at run-time in a way that combines acceptance testing with integration and system testing. In other words, tests of "components" by applications can no longer be regarded as a pure verification exercise, as has traditionally been the case, but must also include an element of "validation" (Boehm, 1984). An application that is connected to a new service at run-time needs to determine whether the service does the "right thing," just as much as it needs to determine whether it does that thing "right."

Building services so that they can be tested in this way requires changes to the way they are traditionally designed and the way that tests are carried out. The purpose of this chapter is to discuss these changes and to present a methodology intended to improve the testability of services. Testability characterizes how easy it is to test a system based on the information provided by it (Voas & Miller, 1995). In the next section we discuss some of the main issues involved in testing services, and describe the basic principles behind the approach. In Section 2 we explain how the basic functionality of services can be modelled in a practical way using UML, and then in Section 0 we explain how services can be extended to enhance their testability. In the following three sections we then consider how to use these enhanced services to design and apply run-time tests. Finally, in Section 0 we round up with some concluding remarks.

To present the ideas in a coherent way, we use a single case study throughout the chapter. This is a so-called "auction house" system whose job is to enable attendees of an auction to interact and participate electronically using standard mobile devices. Unlike fully electronic auction applications like E-bay, the users of this system need to be actually present at a physical auction. The system supports the auctioneer by allowing users to offer and bid for items and conduct payment transactions electronically.

In Figure 1, the auction house service is represented by the big rectangle in the middle. The figure indicates that the auction house uses two other types of services to help it deliver its functionality to auction participants' bank and mail server. The bank, in turn, uses currency converter services to deliver its functionality. It is possible that some of the internal components of the auction house might also be implemented as components, in which case the same principles can be applied to their interfaces as well. However, here we are not concerned with the internal implementation of the auction house service.

SERVICE TESTING

In the following we discuss two important issues in service testing: testing phases and test isolation.

Testing Phases

Web services are essentially software components "designed to support interoperable machine-to-machine interaction over a network" (Austin, Babir, Ferris, & Garg, 2004) (unless explicitly stated otherwise we regard the terms "service" and "Web service" as being synonymous for the purposes of this chapter). As such, they can be developed and tested according to the principle of *contract-driven design* (Meyer, 1992), which holds that the interface between a service and its users should be documented in terms of the rights and obligations of each party. Like parties in a legal contract, the idea is that each party involved in an interaction should know what it may expect and what it must provide in order for an interaction

Figure 1. Overview of the case study

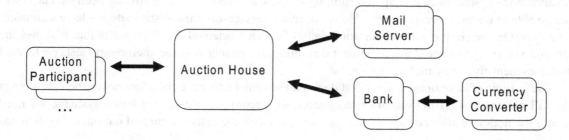

to be completed successfully. The contract therefore defines the criteria by which an interaction can be judged as having succeeded or failed.

With traditional development approaches, two basic forms of testing are used to check that a systems assembled from separate modules does what it is supposed to: "integration testing" and "acceptance testing." Integration testing is a verification technique that focuses on the testing of successively larger groupings of modules, leading up to the system as a whole (for the purpose of this discussion we regard "system testing" as a special case of integration testing). It is performed in the context of the development environment and involves the actual components that will be delivered in the final product, rather than "stubs" or "mocks" for them. According to the terminology of Boehm (1984), integration testing aims to verify that "we are building the system right" according to some well defined description of what the system should do. Acceptance testing, in contrast, is a validation technique which revolves around the testing of a deployed instance of the system in the target execution environment before it is put into service. In Boehm's terminology acceptance testing aims to validate that "we are building the right system" based on the expectations of the customer or users.

In service-oriented development, when systems are assembled from third party services, many of the assumptions which underpin these traditional testing approaches are no longer valid. Integration testing is no longer applicable in its traditional form because the precise composition of a system is not known at development-time when integration testing is traditionally performed. The notion of testing "the system" as an integrated whole at development-time no longer applies in the traditional sense therefore. Testing at development-time is still important, but its role is to test the implementation of a service's provided interface with representative implementations of its required interfaces. A "representative implementation" of a required service can either be a full working version of the service or a stub/mock which mimics the service for a few chosen test cases. Since these tests are performed at development-time and are exclusively focused on verification against a specification, we simply use the term *development-time testing* for this activity.

In the context of service-oriented development neither the notion of integration testing nor the notion of acceptance testing is fully appropriate in its traditional form. The former is not appropriate because integration testing can no longer be fully performed at development-time as has hitherto been the case. The latter is not appropriate because the testing that is performed at deployment-time should no longer focus just on validation as has traditionally been the case. Instead, the testing activities that are performed at deployment-time also need to include tests to verify the assembly of services against the system's specification. It therefore makes sense to combine the notions of integration and acceptance testing into a single activity known as *deployment-time testing*. Such a deployment-time, service testing activity serves the dual roles of validation and verification of the assembled system in its run-time environment.

For a system whose structure remains constant after initial deployment there is clearly no need to revalidate the system once it is up and running because any tests that have already been executed will not be able to uncover new problems. However, many service-oriented systems do not have a constant structure. On the contrary, an important benefit of service-oriented development is that it allows the structure of a system to be changed while it is running. If a change is made, then clearly tests performed at deployment-time may no longer be valid.

The notions of development-time and deployment-time testing are therefore not sufficient to cover the full spectrum of testing scenarios in dynamically reconfigurable service-based systems. We need to add the notion of *service-time testing* as well. Service-time tests are carried out once a system has entered service and is delivering value to users (i.e., is being used to fulfil its purpose). Deployment-time and service-time testing both take place at "run-time" in the sense that they are applied to a "running" system in its final execution environment.

The relationship and role of these different phases in the life-cycle of a service-oriented system are summarized in Figure 2. At the highest level of abstraction, two different phases exist, that is, the development phase, in which the system is developed and tested using representative servers in the development environment, and the run-time phase, in which an instance of the system is connected to actual servers and is running in its final execution environment. The run-time phase is divided into two subphases: the *deployment phase* and the *service phase*. In the deployment phase, the system is set up in its initial configuration and starts to run in its execution environment, but it is not yet delivering service to users. This is important because it allows testing activities to be performed under controlled conditions with known assumptions. In the service phase the system has been put into service and is delivering value to users. During service-time the assumptions that held during deployment-time may no longer be valid.

Test Isolation

As with other development abstractions, an important distinction in service-oriented development is the distinction between types and instances. Service types are classifiers in the UML sense. In other words, service types are templates that can be instantiated to create service instances with specified properties. WSDL files actually contain a mix of both concepts. The first part defines the abstract type exposed by the Web services, while the second part specifies the location and identity of an individual instance.

A common misconception about Web services is that they are stateless because they are often used as facades or wrappers to databases or legacy content providers and are not responsible for maintaining state themselves. However, Web services can actually be stateful objects whose behaviour is dependent on the history of interactions. In fact, from a programming point of view (e.g., assuming Java), Web services are like classes which expose a set of methods (operations) and can have their own internal attributes. A single Java class can even be deployed as a Web services.

From the perspective of testing, these properties of Web services create two significant complications:

1.   The effects of an operation may not be the same each time it is executed (with the same arguments) due to the state of the service, and

Figure 2. Life-cycle phases of a system

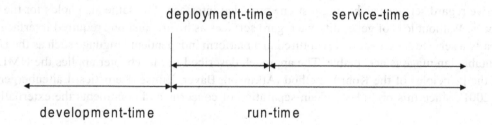

227

2.   The operations exposed by the service may be used by other users while a single user is trying to test it. Thus, the state of the service may not always be known before a service is invoked.

The basic problem is how run-time tests can be performed without having unintended side effects on data or state. In other words, how can the execution of tests and the execution of regular business logic for real users be separated? The testing of a service by one user should not have any effect on the delivery of services to other simultaneous users. To do this it is necessary to intercept each invocation of a service operation and check whether the invocation is part of a test or a regular service request. If the operation is executed from a test, then the test should be *isolated* from the service's response to regular requests.

Web services live in a run-time environment which frees the developer from the burden of developing the functionality which is necessary to interact with the outside world over a network. The Web service is deployed and the functionality offered by the run-time environment is immediately available. This must also include run-time testing functionality built into the run-time environment to support test execution and test isolation. An example for such an environment which the authors have developed is presented by Suliman, Paech, Borner, Atkinson, Brenner, Merdes, et al. (2006).

Several different so-called "test isolation" mechanisms can be identified. One strategy is to prioritize the execution of business logic over the execution of a test. The execution with the lower priority then has to wait. Once the high priority request has been completed, the test is then executed. This strategy can be made more rigorous by ensuring that whenever a regular request is received during the execution of a test, the execution of the test is cancelled and rescheduled.

A second possible test isolation strategy is to just clone the service. A client that wishes to test a service can then work on a copy of the service rather than on the real live version that is servicing user requests. This assumes that it is possible to create a copy of the service easily (and automatically). Through a standardized interface it might even be possible to give the service developer the chance to program the cloning themselves. This would be like a service-driven cloning facility.

FUNCTIONAL INTERFACE SPECIFICATION

The first task to be performed in the development of a service is the creation of a high-level specification. The purpose of this specification is to describe the basic functionality offered by the service (the provided interface) and the basic functionality that it needs from other services (the required interface). It also describes the nonfunctional properties that the service offers and requires. Since a service's specification defines everything that is visible to its clients at run-time, it effectively defines the contract between instances of the service and its run-time clients and servers. In general, a service can support multiple interfaces, but for simplicity we regard these as a single composite interface. Thus, without loss of generality we regard services as having just one provided interface. The same also holds for the required interfaces. Without loss of generality we regard services as having just one required interface.

Ideally a service specification is captured in a platform independent language such as the UML, but any suitable language is acceptable. The approach described in this chapter applies the UML according to the principles of the KobrA method (Atkinson, Bayer, Bunse, Kamsties, Laitenberger, Laqua, et al., 2001), since this provides a clean separation of concerns and documents the externally visible properties of a service in a complete but easy-to-read way. A KobrA service specification involves the creation of three distinct views of a service: the structural view, which describes all structural information that a user of the service needs to be aware of, the functional view, which describes the effects of the operations exported by the service in terms of pre- and post-conditions, and the behavioural view, which describes the allowable sequences of operation invocations in terms of externally visible states and state transitions.

Structural Specification

The structural view describes the information that potential clients of the service need to be aware of when interacting with the service. Primarily, these are the types of the parameters and return values of the service's operations, but it can also include other information such as the service's position in one or more taxonomies, or any important associations that the service maintains.

In KobrA, the structural view of a service is represented as a class diagram. The structural class diagram for the specification of the auction house service is illustrated in Figure 3.

This diagram shows the auction house service, represented as the class with stereotype <<subject>>, together with its required interfaces, represented as the classes with stereotype <<service>>. The AuctionHouse class lists the operations provided by the auction house service.

Functional Specification

The functional view of the service describes the effects of its operations. In general, one operation specification is created for each operation of the service which describes its behaviour in terms of OCL pre- and post-conditions. Figure 4 shows the operation specification of the bid() operation of the AuctionHouse.

Figure 3. Auction house specification class diagram

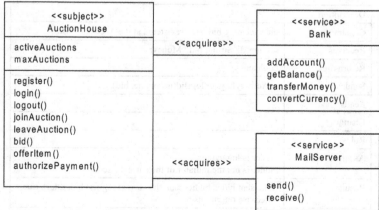

Behavioural Specification

The behavioural view provides a description of any externally visible states that the service exhibits. Figure 5 shows the behavioural model for our auction house example.

The AuctionHouse has two top level states: unconfigured and working. A service enters the unconfigured state when it is first created. In this state it has not been configured and has not been connected to any of its required servers. Only when the configuration operations have been executed, the appropriate dependencies have been set, and the service has been tested the system moves into the working state. This is the state in which the system is servicing user requests. The working state has two substates, that is, idle and active. In the idle state the system is able to respond to a register(), login(), and logout() request, but since there are no active auctions it is unable to respond to requests that relate to active auctions. Only when an offerItem() operation has been invoked and an auction has been started is an AuctionHouse instance is in the active mode so that it can respond to all actions.

Extra-Functional Requirements Definition

A service specification will usually have numerous extra-functional requirements in addition to its functional requirements. In general, these can simply be stated in the requirements document alongside the functional requirements discussed in the preceding sections. Probably one of the most important extra-functional requirements is the reliability or equivalent to the failure rate. One way to state such a requirement is to give the maximum allowed failure rate for each operation, as illustrated in Figure 6 below.

Alternatively, it is possible to define the probability of failure on demand (POFOD) (Sommerville, 2004). For each operation, this value gives the probability that any particular invocation of the operation will fail. If the POFOD and/or the likely failure rate has been defined and the relative execution frequencies have been determined, corresponding POFOD and failure rates can be calculated and specified for the service as a whole.

Figure 4. Specification of the auction house's bid() operation

Name	bid()
Description	
Constraints	the executing bidder is registered at the AuctionHouse
Receives	sessionId : String; bid : Money;
Returns	boolean
Sends	anActivityLogger.logBid(username, bid);
Reads	
Changes	
Rules	
Assumes	bidder is logged in; bidder is not the initiator of the current auction;
Results	if the sent bid is higher than the current highest bid, return true; otherwise return false;

Figure 5. Auction house behavioural model

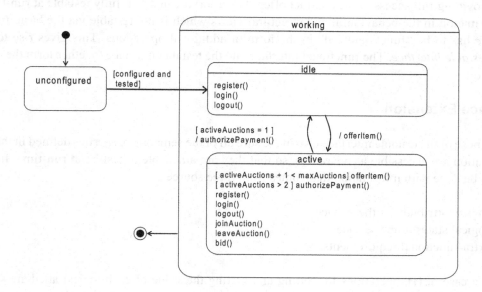

TESTABLE INTERFACE DEFINITION

We refer to the properties of the service that have been defined up to this point as the *functional interface* of the service. This describes the core characteristics of the service as seen by potential users, that is, the contract that it offers. However, not all of the functionality of the service are represented in the operations of the service. Some are defined in the behavioural or structural views and, thus, are not automatically accessible to users at run-time (e.g., states). The next step in the specification process is thus to make sure that *all* behaviour and properties defined in the specification are accessible as operations, not just those operations explicitly identified and specified in the functional view. This is necessary to give users of the service a way of detecting and possibly setting the (logical) states and attributes of a

Figure 6. Reliability requirements

operation	failure rate
AuctionHouse	
register()	0.02
login()	0.03
logout()	0.10
joinAuction()	0.05
leaveAuction()	0.02
bid()	0.002
offerItem()	0.01
authorizePayment()	0.002

service without having direct access to is its internal implementation (and thus breaking it encapsulation). Providing full access to the contract offered by a service makes it fully testable at run-time.

Information in the behavioural and structural views which is not testable via the basic *functional interface* has to be "functionalized" in the form of additional operations. This gives rise to the so-called *testable interface*. The functional interface and the testable interface together form the *extended interface*.

Interface Extension

The purpose of the testable interface is to make sure all of the semantic properties defined in the service specification are accessible as operations so that they are amenable to testing at run-time. In general this can be done with information that comes from three sources:

1. Logical attributes of the service
2. Logical states of the service
3. Extra-functional requirements

In the case of (1), operations for setting and getting the value of each logical attribute should be added. In the case of (2), operations for setting and getting (or confirming) the logical states of services should be added, and in the case of (3), operations for getting the value of each extra-functional quality-of-service (QoS) property should be added. In addition, an operation should be defined for any other semantic information of any kind in the service specification that affects the run-time behaviour of the service and is in principle measurable.

Furthermore, the testable interface could offer operations which support test isolation. These operations indicate whether the service is sensitive to testing (that means tests and business functionality cannot be performed at the same time because of the risks of destroying the service state) or whether it supports the execution of tests in parallel with the business functionality, for example, by offering a specific clone operation.

In this example it would make sense to define the following additional operations in the testable interface of the AuctionHouse:

- **Logical Attributes**
  - setActiveAuctions()
  - getActiveAuctions()
  - getMaxAuctions()
- **Logical State**
  - setIdle()
  - isIdle()
  - setActive()
  - isActive()
  - isWorking()
- **Extra-Functional Requirements**
  - getAllocatedMemory()

- **Test Isolation**
  - cloneAuctionHouse()

These operations are first class citizens of the service interface, and, thus, need to be added to the specification views developed in the previous sections. Each operation needs an operation specification, and should appear in the behavioural and structural views of the service as well. The specification of the extended interface is known as the extended specification of the service. For example, Figure 7 shows the specification of the setActive() operation.

As a result, the extended structural view is shown in Figure 8, and the extended behavioural view is shown in Figure 9.

Figure 7. Operation specification for setActive()

Name	setActive()
Description	sets the service to the "active" state
Results	the service is in the "active" state

Figure 8. Extended structural view

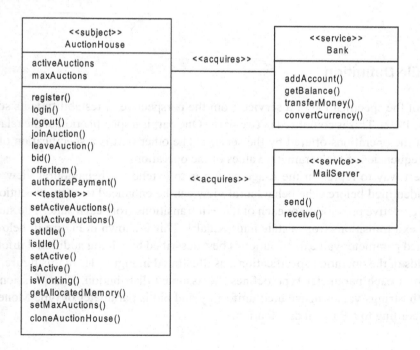

Figure 9. Extended behavioural view

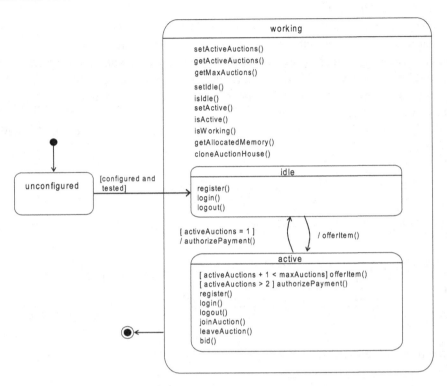

Usage Profile Definition

Another part of the specification of a service from the perspective of testability is its so-called usage profile (Juhlin, 1992). This is composed of two parts. One part is a specification of the relative execution frequencies of the operations offered by the service. The other part is a specification of the expected distribution frequencies of the parameter values of the operations.

The simplest way to represent the usage profile is to extend the behavioural view and operation specification identified before. The behavioural view can be enhanced to show execution frequencies by showing the relative probability of each of the exit transitions from each state. The sum of the probabilities of all exit transitions from a state must equal 1. This is shown in Figure 10 below.

The assumed parameter value distribution is best described by adding additional information to the "receives" fields of the operation specifications, as illustrated in Figure 11. In this figure, the bracketed information after each parameter type defines the assumed distribution. Thus, sessionId is a String parameter with Strings values distributed uniformly and bid is parameter of type Money with values distributed according to a Poisson distribution.

Figure 10. Usage profile – state machine form

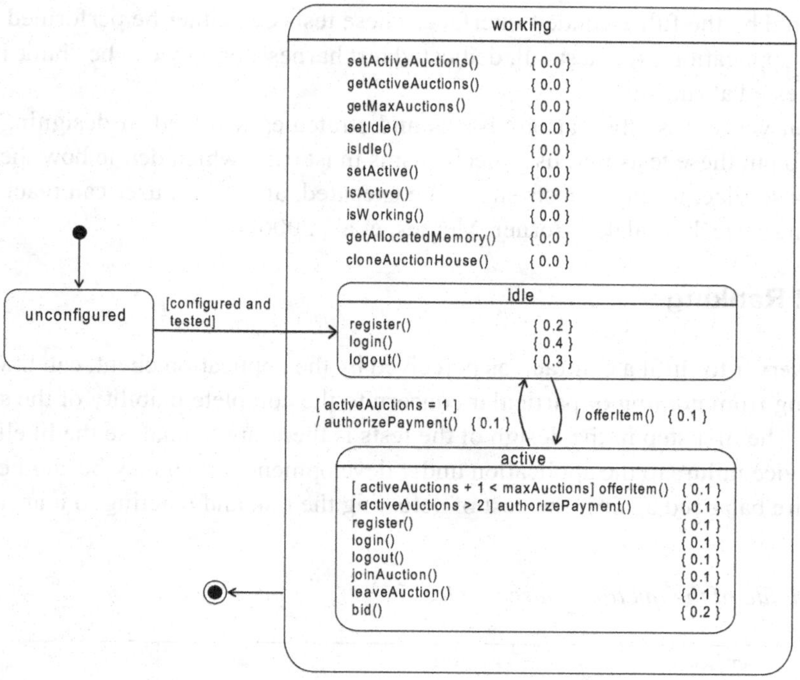

Figure 11. Extended specification of the AuctionHouse's bid() operation

Name	bid()
Description	
Constraints	the executing bidder is registered at the AuctionHouse
Receives	sessionId : String (Uniform); bid : Money (Poisson);
…	…

RUN-TIME TESTING

Once the extended interface of the service has been fully specified it can be turned into an executable system using the normal, widely available tools for implementing services. While under development it should also be tested using the typical defect testing techniques used to test software systems with a well defined interface. Any errors discovered will typically be fixed until a fully functional service is available, which is correct w.r.t. to the usual range and number of test cases. If the service is made available as a Web service, which is usually the case, the implementation process will also result in a WSDL file of the form sketched in Figure 12, which describes the extended interface to the service in a form that can be invoked via SOAP messages.

Developers of new applications can now use this service in their applications. However, in order to have confidence that the service will fulfil their needs, it is advisable for them to test the service using the features offered by the full extended interface. These tests can either be performed during the development of the application using a small, dedicated test harness, or they can be "built-in" to the client application and tested at run-time.

In this section we discuss the various issues and strategies involved in designing such built-in, run-time tests. To put these tests into use, mechanisms must exist which define how these tests can be associated with a service, when the tests should be executed, and how a user can react to a failed test (Atkinson, Brenner, Paech, Malaka, Borner, Merdes, et al., 2006).

Analysis and Ranking

The failure of a server to fulfil a contract, as perceived by the application client, can have various consequences ranging from nothing of particular concern to the complete inability of the service to fulfil its specification. The first step in the design of the tests is therefore to analyse the likelihood and consequences of service failure to the application under development (which may be another service). The identified risks are balanced against the cost of detecting the risk and reacting to it at run-time. Based

Figure 12. WSDL file of the auction house service

```
- <wsdl:definitions targetNamespace="http://auctionhouse.interfaces.application.morabit.org">
  - <wsdl:types>
      <!-- ... -->
  </wsdl:types>
  <!-- ... -->
  - <wsdl:message name="bidResponse">
      <wsdl:part name="bidReturn" type="xsd:boolean"/>
  </wsdl:message>
  - <wsdl:message name="bidRequest">
      <wsdl:part name="in0" type="soapenc:string"/>
      <wsdl:part name="in1" type="tns5:Auction"/>
      <wsdl:part name="in2" type="tns2:Money"/>
  </wsdl:message>
  - <wsdl:portType name="AuctionHouse">
      <!-- ... -->
    - <wsdl:operation name="bid" parameterOrder="in0 in1 in2">
        <wsdl:input message="impl:bidRequest" name="bidRequest"/>
        <wsdl:output message="impl:bidResponse" name="bidResponse"/>
        <wsdl:fault message="impl:CurrencyNotSupportedException" name="CurrencyNotSupportedException"/>
    </wsdl:operation>
  </wsdl:portType>
  - <wsdl:binding name="localhostSoapBinding" type="impl:AuctionHouse">
      <wsdlsoap:binding style="rpc" transport="http://schemas.xmlsoap.org/soap/http"/>
      <!-- ... -->
    - <wsdl:operation name="bid">
        <wsdlsoap:operation soapAction=""/>
      - <wsdl:input name="bidRequest">
          <wsdlsoap:body encodingStyle="http://schemas.xmlsoap.org/soap/encoding/" namespace="http://auctionhouse.interfaces.application.morabit.org" use="..."/>
      </wsdl:input>
      - <wsdl:output name="bidResponse">
          <wsdlsoap:body encodingStyle="http://schemas.xmlsoap.org/soap/encoding/" namespace="http://auctionhouse.interfaces.application.morabit.org" use="..."/>
      </wsdl:output>
      - <wsdl:fault name="CurrencyNotSupportedException">
          <wsdlsoap:fault encodingStyle="http://schemas.xmlsoap.org/soap/encoding/" name="CurrencyNotSupportedException" namespace="http://..." use="..."/>
      </wsdl:fault>
    </wsdl:operation>
  </wsdl:binding>
  - <wsdl:service name="AuctionHouseService">
    - <wsdl:port binding="impl:localhostSoapBinding" name="localhost">
        <wsdlsoap:address location="http://localhost"/>
    </wsdl:port>
  </wsdl:service>
</wsdl:definitions>
```

on a trade-off analysis, tests are designed for the failures with the highest risk-cost ratio. Initially, a risk and cost analysis is performed to analyze the nature of an application's dependency on a service. This is driven by the following questions:

1. What are the types of contract failures that could occur and what is the likelihood of each type occurring?
2. For each failure type, what is the consequence of that failure occurring in terms of the service's ability to provide its own services and in terms of possible effects on the overall system in which an instance of the service might be deployed?
3. What are the estimated costs of detecting this failure in terms of the ability of the application to deliver its service?
4. What countermeasures are feasible?

For example:

A. Risk: The auction house does not meet its functional contract, for example, does not send confirmation e-mail to the right address.
    1. Low likelihood because this is standard functionality
    2. Failure can be serious for high priority e-mails
    3. Estimated cost of detection is low; could be checked when the service sends an e-mail to itself via the external e-mail service
    4. Stop using the service and choose a different service provider
B. Risk: The auction house does not meet its reliability contract.
    1. Fairly high likelihood in case of high load
    2. Failure can be serious
    3. High estimated cost as this requires quantitative testing
    4. Implement checking algorithms

The risks are ranked according to their likelihood of occurrence and their potential impact, taking into account the cost of detection and reaction. Thus, in the example the test of e-mail functionality would be ranked high since its impact is high, and the cost manageable. Also, despite the high cost, the testing of the auction house's reliability is ranked high because of the high impact.

Contract Test Case Definition

Once the goal and relative priority of each risk have been identified, the next step is to define contract test cases (CTCs) to uncover the most highly ranked contract risks. The aim of these CTCs is to uncover at run-time a failure in the service's ability to fulfil the part of the contract that leads to the risk in question.

There are two basic criteria for defining CTCs depending on whether quantitative or qualitative information is required from the execution of run-time tests. Qualitative tests return binary (pass/fail) information depending on whether or not a service fulfils a contract as understood by the client application. This form of run-time test is therefore the most basic and is the most widely applicable. Quantitative tests return a numeric measurement of the level of reliability to which a service implements the contract as understood by client application. This kind of run-time test is therefore only needed if the contract has an associated reliability requirement.

Both forms of testing rely on the ability to determine whether a particular invocation of a service's operation succeeds or fails from the perspective of the client. There are three basic ways in which such an invocation can be judged to have failed:

1. The operation completes, but returns a result that was not the expected one;
2. The operation does not complete and returns some indications to the caller that it was unable to do so (e.g., an error message); and
3. The operation does not complete within a required period of time.

In principle, all three forms can be used in both quantitative as well as qualitative testing. However, since forms (2) and (3) do not require an expected result to be determined, they are particularly suited to quantitative testing. The creation of expected results for the first form of failure has traditionally been one of the biggest stumbling blocks to quantitative testing because it is difficult if not impossible to do automatically.

Qualitative Contract Test Case Definition

The goal of qualitative CTCs is to uncover mismatches between the service provider's understanding (i.e., interpretation) of its contracts and those of the application using it. The CTCs are therefore designed to maximize the chances of uncovering contract understanding mismatches at run-time. Qualitative test cases are similar to the test cases defined in the functional and structural test case design for defect testing. However, since it is assumed that the service has already been tested at development-time to detect coding defects, the focus is on test cases which reveal problems in the service's behaviour due to dependencies on its environment or due to implicit assumptions. In general, the types of "misunderstanding" of a contract that can lead to perceived failure of a service fall into the following two categories, that is, syntactical misunderstandings and semantic misunderstandings.

Syntactical misunderstandings can arise in several parts of a provided interface. In statically typed languages such as Java, the compiler will return an error message when, for example, either a method name does not exist or parameter types of the called method do not match. It is possible to invoke an operation of a Web service without taking the nature of its interface inaccount, but in most cases, invocations are at least checked against, if not created from, the signature information in the WSDL file (such as Figure 12).

Thus, in the AuctionHouse case study, if the AuctionHouse service attempted to invoke the transferMoney() operation of the Bank service with the following type profile

transferMoney(int, int, double)

whereas the operation defined by the Bank service had the following signature

transferMoney(String, String, double).

the Java compiler will return an error. Such a misunderstanding can quite easily occur when using Web services. Since this depends on the programming language used to implement the application or using service we do not further discuss this type of misunderstanding here.

Semantic misunderstandings come from an operation's input parameters. When two or more parameters have the same type the correct order cannot be inferred unambiguously from the WDSL file. This means that the client of a service might assume a different order of input parameters than the called service, probably leading to a nunexpected result. So if, for example, the Bank has a transferMoney() operations with the following intended meaning of its parameters

transferMoney(String fromAccount, String toAccount, double amount)

while the client expects the opposite

transferMoney(String toAccount, String fromAccount, double amount)

the invocation of the operation fails. Even though this kind of semantic misunderstanding can only happen with parameters of the same type, it happens quite often. This is something that can easily be checked via a run-time test. Test cases should be defined for all operations where such parameter swapping is likely. All possible permutations of the parameters need to be checked.

When a third party service is used, it often happens that the client does not know what the valid input values are, and, thus, invokes the operation with *invalid input parameter values*. It is also unknown to the client how the used service will react to the invalid values. Services differ in the way they handle such cases. Some services use default values, others return an error message. This leads to a *different understandings of exception handling*. Therefore, the client should create tests that invoke operations with invalid (boundary) values and check the service's reaction.

If no error occurs during the execution of an operation, the called service will return an output value. The returned output and expected result can differ in various ways. An important distinction in this regard is between functional and extra-functional differences. A functional difference is, for example, the *accuracy of the output*. This kind of difference can occur when the bank uses an additional (third-party) service for converting a certain amount of money between two currencies. The output might be perfectly correct, but whereas the client expected a precision of three decimal places the bank returned a precision of only two. In contrast, extra-functional differences relate to *quality properties* such as response time. When the response time of the AuctionHouse for the bidding operation is too long, it becomes unusable. However, the quality is dependent on the whole system (environment) so that no general conclusions can be drawn from one single test case. Therefore, multiple test cases need to be run, the quality property measured (here the response time), and the average value determined. If this average value lies within a certain range, it will be classified as acceptable.

It can also happen that the service called by the client functions correctly, but still delivers a wrong output. This is the case when the called service depends on other servers in order to fulfil its provided functionality. Unfortunately, such a server usually cannot be detected directly. When the AuctionHouse uses a Bank service to access certain functionality and the bank itself uses a CurrencyConverter service then an error in the interaction between the Bank and the CurrencyConverter cannot be detected by the AuctionHouse. Constructing test cases that invoke a chain of operations is a possibility. The problem is that there might not be enough information available to construct such dependence chains.

Quantitative Contract Test Case Definition

Quantitative contract test cases are used to determine, to a given level of confidence, whether a service delivers its functionality with a level of reliability. A prerequisite for quantitative tests of a service is an extended specification which includes usage profile information of the kind outlined in Section 0. We therefore assume that all provided services have been specified according to the approach.

To attain a reasonable level of confidence in the reliability bound, quantitative tests usually require many more test cases than qualitative tests. The minimum number of test cases that must be executed is a function of the desired reliability threshold and the desired level of confidence. Following Brenner, Atkinson, Malaka, Merdes, Paech, and Suliman (2007) the number of required test cases can be calculated based on the given values for failure rate and confidence. The failure rate f for each operation was already specified earlier in the extra-functional requirements (Section 0). For the bid() operation the failure rate is $f = 0.002$.

In order to calculate the minimum number of test cases, the confidence in the test result is needed. Clearly, only one test case could be run and if no error is detected with this test case, the failure rate is said to be 0 and, thus, better than required. But the confidence in this test result cannot be high. On the other hand, it is obvious that to obtain higher confidence, the more test cases need to be run. In our example we assume a target confidence (c) of 95%.

When the number of test cases, n, is greater than 100 the calculation can be simplified. Then the Poisson distribution can be assumed and the term $\ln(1 - c)$ can be looked up in a table containing the values for the parameter a of the Poisson distribution. For $c = 0.95$, this is approximately $a = 3$, implying that during the test case execution no errors occur. So,

$$n = a / f = 3 / 0.002 = 1500$$

This means that 1500 test cases need to run without an error before we can be 95% sure that the failure rate of the bid() operation is smaller or equal to 0.002. If we accept one error during the test case execution, the minimum number of test cases required to hold the assumptions $f = 0.002$ and $c = 0.95$ raises to 2,400 ($= 4.8 / 0.002$). This provides an estimate for the required numbers of test cases.

RELATED WORK

The idea of testing services at run-time to determine if they are acceptable is related to the notion of quality of service. Several approaches for building Web services focus on QoS, such as availability, security, and throughput (Menasce, 2002). Typically, a global model of the interactions is created which is then evaluated so that adaptation strategies can be defined (Porter & Katz, 2006). However, the creation of such a global model takes a lot of effort and in dynamic contexts, such as Web services, it will change very quickly. Menasce, Ruan, and Gomaa (2004) propose an architecture where the server monitors its own quality and adapts accordingly. Our proposed approach differs from these approaches in that it focuses on functional qualities, that is, on whether the functionality provided by the service fits to the functionality required by the service consumer. This question is often considered as part of service matching. However, as always with software, additional testing is needed to uncover defects.

Numerous component-based development approaches have also developed techniques for enhancing systems testability using metadata provided by the component supplier, such as component behaviour specification, test cases together with coverage data, quality of service information, as well as specific information on code such as dependencies between variables (Orso, Harrold, & Rosenblum, 2000). This information is provided, for example, in the form of testable beans which comprise a testing interface and a traceability interface (Gao, Tsao, & Wu, 2003). The former enables the test to be set up, executed, and evaluated. The latter enables access to the history of test results. The wrapper approach separates the code for the metadata clearly from original code (Edwards, 2001). The notion of built-in tests enhances the testing interface with test cases (Gross, 2005). The test cases can be applied to the provided interface of the component (self-test) (Wang, King, Patel, Patel, & Dorling, 1999), or to the interface of its server components (contract test). This idea has been adapted to Web services where the service provider provides test cases for the service which can be applied by the service consumer to the service (Bruno, Canfora, DiPenta, Esposito, & Mazza, 2005).

Today, the main challenge of testing is still to define a test strategy which minimizes the relationship between test costs and defect costs. Such a strategy comprises a test focus (what should be minimized through the test), the test intensity (how much test effort should be spent on each risk), the test plan (who tests what), the test case definition method, the test case order, the test end criteria (when to stop testing), and the reaction to the test result (Borner, Illes, & Paech, 2007).

In component- and service-oriented systems, the main risk is a misunderstanding between the service and its clients. These risks are integration test risks, and can be classified according to typical defects. Wu, Pan, and Chen (2001) use such defects classification together with a global component interaction model to derive the test cases. Similarly, architecture-based approaches like that of Bertolino, Corradini, Inverardi, and Muccin (2000) and Muccini, Bertolino, and Inverardi (2004) use a global interaction model. As mentioned above, such global models are costly and, thus, it is important to identify typical defects of component interactions from the viewpoint of individual components.

The test cases can either be defined by hand, generated from models, or generated from the test history. Smythe (2006) discusses generation from models at development time. Run-time generation would save space, but requires an execution. In our method we do not give specific support for run-time generation. This is still a question for further research.

Another issue is *when* test cases are executed at run-time. Web service quality assurance approaches so far concentrate on run-time tests triggered and evaluated by humans, for example, after a new service is released. However, this will not be sufficient for a true service-oriented architecture where client-service relationships change very often. Merdes, Malaka, Suliman, Paech, Brenner, and Atkinson (2006) show how tests can be triggered and evaluated by the components themselves. This requires specific testing times and test reactions.

Obviously, the run-time test strategy will always be based on heuristics. Therefore, it is important to monitor and evaluate the test execution. This topic is still in its infancy, even for development-time testing. For run-time tests, evaluation strategies such as mutation test (Delamaro, Maldonado, & Mathur, 2001) and benchmarks (Zhu, Gorton, Liu, & Bui, 2006) need to be adopted. It is necessary to distinguish the quality of individual services as well as of the overall system (where the test strategies of several services interact). So far, our method does not provide specific support for this evaluation.

SUMMARY AND CONCLUSION

We have a presented a method for maximizing the testability of services by systematically ensuring that all information in their model-based specifications are included in their interfaces. As explained, there are numerous other approaches for designing tests of Web services based on their published interfaces, but these all "start" *after* the published interface has been fixed and encoded in a WSDL document or something similar. The novelty of the approach outlined in this chapter is that it addresses the problem of testability *before* the precise interface of the component has been fixed. In fact, it works by extending the basic functional interface beyond what it would normally be in normal methods.

The methodology exploits the fact that complex services are systems which are (or should be) designed using a systematic process of specification, realization, and implementation. More specifically, it exploits the fact that not all the information in the specification of a service (and thus in the contract) takes the form of operations that are accessible at run-time by clients. Semantic information such as externally visible states and attributes are often encapsulated within the body of service implementation, where they are accessible to development-time tests but not third-party client tests at run-time.

Since the main contribution of the approach is how to construct the concrete (i.e., WSDL) interface of a service rather than how to use them, it is compatible with most other approaches to service testing. In fact, we believe it naturally complements them. As part of the MORABIT project (2007), we have developed a prototype infrastructure to directly implement the kind of run-time tests supported in the approach and are currently in the process of building a tool to support the view-based specification of services upon which it is based.

REFERENCES

Atkinson, C., Bayer, J., Bunse, C., Kamsties, E., Laitenberger, O., Laqua, R., et al. (Eds.). (2001). *Service-based product line engineering with UML*. Addison Wesley.

Atkinson, C., Brenner, D. (Eds.), Paech, B., Malaka, M., Borner, L., Merdes, M., et al. (2006). *The MORABIT development method (MORABIT Deliverable M3)*. Mannheim, Germany: University of Mannheim.

Austin, D., Babir, A., Ferris, C., & Garg, S., (2004). Web services architecture requirements. *W3C working group*. Retrieved October 27, 2007, from http://www.w3.org/TR/wsa-reqs/

Bertolino, A., Corradini, F., Inverardi, P., & Muccini, H. (2000). *Deriving test plans from architectural descriptions*. Paper presented at International Conference on Software Engineering, Limerick, Ireland.

Boehm, B. (1984). Verifying and validating software requirements and design specifications. *IEEE Software*, 205-218.

Borner, L., Illes, T., & Paech, B. (2007). *The testing process: A decision based approach*. Paper presented at the Second International Conference on Software Engineering Advances (ICSEA 2007), Cap Esterel, France.

Brenner, D., Atkinson, C., Malaka, R., Merdes, M., Paech, B., & Suliman, D. (2007). Reducing verification effort in component-based software engineering through built-in testing. *Information Systems Frontiers, 9*(2-3), 151-162.

Bruno, M., Canfora, G., DiPenta, M., Esposito, G., & Mazza, V. (2005). *Using test cases as contract to ensure service compliance across releases.* Paper presented at the International Conference on Service Oriented Computing (LNCS 3826).

Delamaro, M. C., Maldonado, J. C., & Mathur, A. P. (2001). Interface mutation: An approach for integration testing. *IEEE Transactions on Software Engineering, 27*(3), 228-247.

Edwards, S. H. (2001). A framework for practical, automated black-box testing of component-based software. *Software Testing, Verification and Reliability, 11*, 97-111.

Gao, J. Z., Tsao, H. S. J., & Wu, Y. (Eds.). (2003). *Testing and quality assurance for component-based software.* Artech House Computing Library.

Gross, H. G. (Ed.). (2005). *Component-based software testing with UML.* Springer.

Juhlin, B. D. (1992). *Implementing operational profiles to measure system reliability.* Paper presented at Third International Symposium on Software Reliability Engineering, Research Triangle Park, NC.

Menasce, D. A. (2002). QoS issues in Web services. *IEEE Internet Computing,* 72-75.

Menasce, D. A., Ruan, H., & Gomaa, H. (2004). *A framework for QoS-aware software components.* Paper presented at Workshop on Software and Performance, San Francisco.

Merdes, M., Malaka, R., Suliman, D., Paech, B., Brenner, D., & Atkinson, C. (2006). *Ubiquitous RATs: How resource-aware run-time tests can improve ubiquitous software systems.* Paper presented at 6th International Workshop on Software Engineering and Middleware, Portland.

Meyer, B. (1992). Applying design by contract. *IEEE Computer, 25*(10), 40-51.

MORABIT project. (2008). Retrieved October 27, 2007, from http://www.morabit.org/

Muccini, H., Bertolino, A., & Inverardi, P. (2004). Using software architecture for code testing. *IEEE Transactions on Software Engineering, 30*(3), 160-171.

Orso, A., Harrold, M. J., & Rosenblum, D. S. (2000). *Component metadata for software engineering tasks.* Paper presented at 2nd International Workshop on Engineering Distributed Objects (EDO), Davis.

Porter, G., & Katz, R.H. (2006). Effective Web service load balancing through statistical monitoring. *Communications of the ACM, 49*(3), 49-54.

Smythe, C. (2006). *Initial investigations into interoperability testing of Web services from their specification using the unified modelling language.* Paper presented at the International Workshop on Web Services Modeling and Testing (WS-MaTe), Palermo, Italy.

Sommerville, I. (Ed.). (2004). *Software engineering.* Addison Wesley.

Suliman, D., Paech, B., Borner, B., Atkinson, C., Brenner, D., Merdes, M., et al. (2006). *The MORABIT approach to run-time component testing.* Paper presented at Second International Workshop on Testing and Quality Assurance for Component-Based Systems (TQACBS 2006), Chicago.

Voas, J. M., & Miller, K. W. (1995). Software testability: The new verification. *IEEE Software*, 17-28.

Wang, Y., King, G., Patel, D., Patel, S., & Dorling, A. (1999). On coping with real-time software dynamic inconsistency by built-in tests. *Annals of Software Engineering, 7*, 283-296.

Wu, Y., Pan, D., & Chen, M.H. (2001). *Techniques for testing component based systems.* Paper presented at 7th IEEE International Conference on Engineering of Complex Computer Systems (ICECCS'01), Skovde, Sweden.

Zhu, L., Gorton, I., Liu, Y., & Bui, N. B. (2006). *Model driven benchmark generation for Web services.* Paper presented at ICSE-Workshop Service-Oriented Software Engineering, Shanghai, China.

Chapter XI
Aspect–Oriented Framework for Web Services (AoF4WS):
Introduction and Two Example Case Studies

Ghita Kouadri Mostefaoui
Oxford University Computing Laboratory, UK

Zakaria Maamar
Zayed University, UAE

Nanjangud C. Narendra
IBM India Research Lab, India

ABSTRACT

This chapter presents our research initiative known as aspect-oriented framework for Web services (AoF4WS). This initiative looks into the role of aspect-oriented programming in enhancing Web services with nonfunctional properties that are orthogonal to the primary functional properties of Web services, without the need for extensive reprogramming. This enhancement achieves a separation between the functional and nonfunctional aspects of Web services, thereby resulting in easier adaptability and maintainability. We have initially chosen to focus on security and self-healing nonfunctional requirements. The AoF4WS initiative is therefore demonstrated using two projects, SC-WS and SH-WS, which respectively stand for security concerns of Web services and self-healing Web services. Our contributions are relevant to the design phase in an aspect-oriented software development lifecycle.

INTRODUCTION AND MOTIVATIONS

Web services are an attractive approach for implementing loosely-coupled business processes, which usually spread over companies' boundaries (Ma, 2005). Over the last few years several efforts have been put into the development of standards related to Web services definition, announcement/discovery, and composition, just to cite a few. The dynamic nature of the business world highlights the continuous pressure on businesses to reduce expenses, increase revenues, generate profits, and remain competitive. This calls for a quick reaction to the market trends, a quick handling of users' needs, a quick adaptation to unforeseen changes, and last but not least, a quick understanding of forthcoming challenges. To boost the acceptance level of Web services by the IT community as the technology of choice when developing flexible processes, Web services need to adapt to changing nonfunctional requirements with minimal reprogramming and minimal maintenance effort, so that they can be kept independent from the core Web services functionality. Security and self-healing are samples of nonfunctional requirements, and we will be highlighting them in this chapter.

Integrating security and self-healing capabilities into Web services calls for a clear separation between "business" and "management" concerns along which a Web service is defined (Figure 1). For this purpose, we adopt an aspect-oriented programming (AOP) approach to specify and implement this separation (Cottenier & Elrad, 2004; El-Manzalawy, 2005). This approach is part of our long-term research initiative known as aspect-oriented framework for Web services (**AoF4WS**). This initiative aims at examining the role of aspects in decoupling various concerns in Web services like security and self-healing. The separation between "business" and "management" sides emphasizes the noninvasive requirement that needs to be taken into consideration during the development cycle of a nonfunctional requirement. The mechanisms related, for instance, to security should be confined into one module and thus, should not scatter over the rest of modules of the Web service. Figure 1 illustrates the way concern separation occurs in a fictive Web service referred to as HotelBooking. The business side focuses on details directly related to hotel booking, like checking room availability, rate verification, and confirming client reservation. The management side of a Web service gathers all modules, such as security, self-healing, and monitoring that back the operations of this Web service. Constituents of the management side to be implemented as aspects need to be factored out of the core logic of the Web service.

In the following, we describe the two projects that we have chosen as part of the Ao4FWS initiative. The SC-WS project stands for security concerns of Web services and the SH-WS project stands for self-healing Web services. In Section 2 we present some basic definitions necessary for understanding the chapter. A motivating scenario is also presented in this section. SC-WS and SH-WS projects are described in Section 3 and Section 4, respectively. The chapter concludes in Section 5.

Figure 1. Concern separation in a Web service

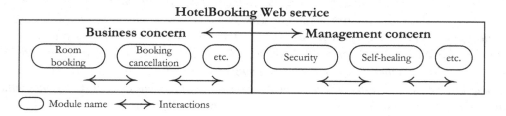

BACKGROUND

Some Definitions

Web Service

For the World Wide Web Consortium (W3C), a Web service is a software application identified by a URI, whose interfaces and binding are capable of being defined, described, and discovered by XML artifacts and supports direct interactions with other software applications using XML-based messages via Internet-based applications. Several standards are associated with Web services like ebXML registry services, Web service description language (WSDL), universal description, discovery, and integration (UDDI), simple object access protocol (SOAP), and WS-security (WSS).

Aspect-Oriented Programming

Ortiz, Hernández, and Clemente (2004a) define aspects as units of encapsulation that are built upon two elements: join points and advices. Join points determine the places or pointcuts where the behavior alteration of an application will happen, and advices identify the new code to be injected in response to this alteration. Aspect-oriented programming has emerged as a programming paradigm that allows gathering of a concern code into one single module. Security, performance, and logging are examples of such concerns that need to be separated from the code of the core application. This approach provides a clean separation between functional and nonfunctional concerns allowing fast update and maintenance of the application code.

Aspect-Oriented Programming for Web Services

Cibrán and Verheecke (2003) promote modularizing Web services management with AOP. That was motivated because of the hard-wiring technique that is nowadays used for integrating Web services into applications. Hard-coding has several deficiencies when it comes to working out how to adapt to changes, what if a service or network fails, and how to deal with issues related to peers, such as checking for availability, switching to other services, and so forth. Charfi and Mezini (2004) apply AOP to workflow languages like business process execution language for Web services (BPEL4WS) in order to achieve modular and dynamic adaptability of Web services composition. This is done using aspect-oriented BPEL (AO4BPEL), which extends BPEL with additional features that permit, for instance, viewing business rules as aspects. In another work, Ortiz Hernández, and Clemente (2004b) adopt an aspect-oriented approach to develop solutions for Web services composition (of type orchestration) and interaction patterns. Their work was motivated by the lack of standards associated with composition. More particularly, Ortiz et al. raised multiple questions related, for instance, to the possibility of reusing interaction patterns previously implemented, and the efforts to put in for modularizing these patterns rather than scattering the code.

Motivating Scenario

In the following, we detail a motivating scenario, trip composite service (T-CS$_1$), that will be used for illustrating the two projects discussed in this chapter. The scenario is about Amin who is visiting Melissa back in her home city, Oslo. They agree to meet in a coffee shop, not far from Melissa's office since she finishes work late on that day. Amin has two options to reach the meeting place, that is, by taxi or by bus. Figure 2 illustrates the specification of Amin scenario using a combination of state chart diagrams and service chart diagrams (Maamar, Benatallah, & Mansoor, 2003).

At his hotel, Amin browses some Web sites about transportation in Oslo. A site has itinerary WS that proposes routes between two specific places, for example, between Amin's hotel and the coffee shop. The proposed routes are subject to weather forecasts: cold weather results in recommending taxis, otherwise public transportations like tramways and buses. Parallel to consulting with weather WS itinerary WS requests details about the origin and destination places using location WS. The use of location WS is highly appreciated by Amin since he is not familiar with the city.

In case weather WS forecasts bad weather, a taxi booking is made by taxi WS upon Amin's approval. In case of pleasant day, Amin uses public transportation. The location of both Amin's hotel and coffee shop are submitted to bus schedule WS, which returns, for example, the bus numbers Amin has to ride. Potential traffic jams force bus schedule WS to regularly interact with traffic WS that monitors the status of the traffic network. This status is fed into bus schedule WS so adjustments to bus numbers and correspondences between buses can occur.

SC-WS PROJECT: DECOUPLING SECURITY CONCERNS IN WEB SERVICES

Related Work

The open and dynamic nature of the environment in which Web services operate poses various challenges and threats to their security. New Web services appear while others disappear without prior notice. Furthermore, messages among component Web services of a composite Web service have to be checked for integrity, confidentiality, and authentication purposes. The need to secure Web services is discussed by Moorthy and Gandhirajan (2005), as the use of Web services continues to increase. This increase is dependent on how much Web services are a serious development alternative to other rival middleware

Figure 2. Specification of Amin scenario

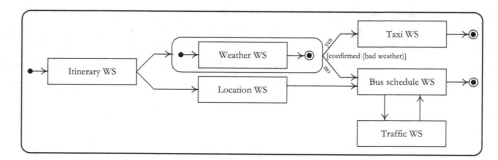

like CORBA and RMI. Indeed, some still consider Web services as distributed objects that react upon request only (Birman, 2004). Enhancing Web services with extra capabilities can happen along three perspectives as reported by Maamar, Benslimane, and Narendra (2006). The first perspective is about deploying Web services that assess the environment before they take part in any composition. The second perspective is about reducing the semantic heterogeneity gap between independent Web services that have all agreed to participate in a composition. Finally, the third perspective is about conciliating contextual information of Web services using ontologies.

WS-security (2002) is a Microsoft and IBM specification dedicated to Web services security. It is an emerging standard for securing messages among Web services engaged in interactions. For this purpose, WS-security defines how security tokens are contained in SOAP messages. WS-security is extensible to other security models, such as secure sockets layer (SSL), kerberos, and public key infrastructure (PKI). Nowadays, the majority of secure communication measures rely on the transport layer security (TLS). TLS secures interactions by using encryption and makes servers and clients collaborate in order to decide on the authentication process to adopt during data transfer. Unfortunately, TLS does not scale well to complex transactions like those involving Web services (Nakamur, Hada, & Neyma, 2002). Traditional security techniques such as virtual private network (VPN) and SSL cannot secure the large number of requests that Web services expect to receive. The W3C's Web services architecture adopts PKI to secure communications over public networks (W3C, 2005). PKI, however, has a complex infrastructure that negatively affects its deployment cost, processing time, and so forth. Moreover, PKI has the reputation of being quite cumbersome. This could prove to overkill the Web services security to be engaged in intense interactions (Sandhu, 2003). The extensible access control markup language (XACML) is an OASIS standard, which describes both a policy language and an access control decision service interface. A policy is extensible and aims at describing general access control requirements. The request/response style for setting access controls allows forming a query to ask whether or not a given action should be allowed; examples of the queries are permit, deny, indeterminate, or not applicable.

Architecture

Taking into account the context in which Web services operate has been proven to be mandatory when developing Web services. Context-aware Web services result in considering the features of the environment in which the Web services are to be executed (Maamar et al., 2006). These features are multiple and can be related to users (e.g., stationary user, mobile user), their level of expertise (e.g., expert, novice), computing resources (e.g., fixed device, mobile device), time of day (e.g., in the afternoon, in the morning), and so forth. Context is relevant to both functional and nonfunctional properties of Web services.

Figure 3 presents the way aspects are handled in the SC-WS project (Kouadri Mostéfaoui, Maamar, Narendra, & Sattanathan, 2006). Three levels of abstraction exist in this figure: composite, component, and resource. The constituents of each level are related to a particular type of context denoted by C-context, W-context, and R-context, respectively. The rationale of each context type is given by Maamar, Kouadri Mostefaoui, & Mahmoud (2005). The connection between composite, component, and resource levels is implemented with "participate in," "oversee," and "operate upon" relationships, respectively. Some key features of the SC-WS project are as follows: multilevel concern separation using aspects, and contextual tracking of the security requirements of Web services.

Figure 3. Overview of the SC-WS architecture

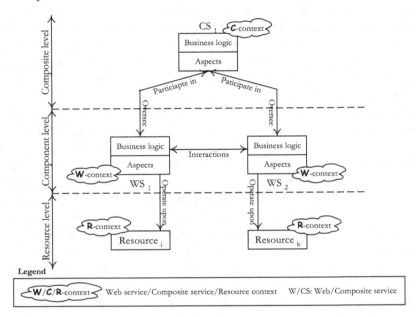

The composite level is about context-aware specifications of composite Web services. Each specification is split into two parts: business logic and aspects. The business-logic part reflects the overall objective that the composite Web service has to reach (e.g., hotel booking) using a set of component Web services. The aspect part reflects the cross-cutting concerns that are included in the operation of the composite Web service, and which are orthogonal to this overall objective. The business logic specifies the process by which user functional requirements are met, whereas aspects model user nonfunctional requirements such as security and reliability.

The component level is about context-aware Web services. Similar considerations apply to Web services, which are split into two parts: business logic and aspects. The business-logic part shows the actions that a component Web service has to individually or collectively carry out in order to enable reaching the composite Web service's overall objective. The aspect part shows the nonfunctional requirements that manifest themselves as cross-cutting concerns affecting the actions and interactions of the Web service.

The resource level is about context-aware resources. Resources represent the computing means on which Web services operate. The scheduling of execution requests of Web services is prioritized when enough resources are not available to satisfy them all at once. Moreover, resource allocation to Web services is subject to the context in which the Web services evolve. For instance, the computing requirements of a Web service need to be checked against the computing capabilities of the resources prior to performing resource allocation.

Configuration of Security Aspects

The development of the SC-WS project happened along two dimensions. The first dimension is the need for an adaptive approach that triggers security services (to be implemented as aspects) upon request. For instance, in a specific situation, only authentication aspect is activated, while an extra-logging aspect is activated in another situation. We refer to this dimension in the SC-WS development as composite configuration. It only targets the composite Web services. The second dimension shows the need for a fine tuning of each security aspect associated with composite configuration. For instance, the authentication aspect can be set to accept a timeout of 10 seconds when requesting clients' credentials. We refer to this dimension in the SC-WS development as component configuration. It only targets Web services.

The identification of a configuration that includes both composite and component levels calls for an additional technology to support aspect-oriented programming in modularizing crosscutting concerns at each level. This technology corresponds to frames. Frames permit achieving this support and are defined as wrappers around code snippets (e.g., source code, HTML code). A frame contains variation points that permit adding, deleting, or adapting functionality in a specific application. This happens using various commands like overriding, extension, substitution, selection, and iteration.

Composite Configuration of Security Aspects

Figure 4 illustrates the operation of the SC-WS project in a configuration of type composite. This operation consists of selecting the security aspects that should be able to protect the whole Web services environment (these aspects are referred to as active in Figure 4). The selection process combines contextual information and policies. Contextual information offer details on the environment that surrounds each element (e.g., Web service, composite Web service, resource), and policies suggest the appropriate security aspects based on these details.

In addition to W/C/R-contexts of Web services, composite Web services, and resources in the SC-WS project, a new type of context that is just dedicated to security is added (Figure 4). S-context is fed with details obtained out of W/C/R-contexts and gets involved in triggering policies for weaving active security aspects. According to Kouadri Mostéfaoui, a security context is a state of the working

Figure 4. Operations in SC-WS

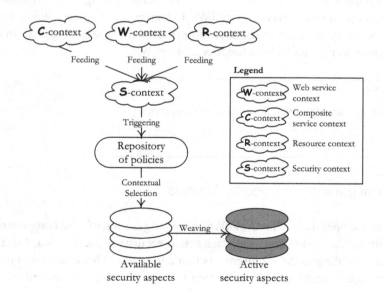

environment that requires taking one or more security actions. A security context is formed by a set of information collected from the user's environment and the application environment and that is relevant to the security infrastructure of both the user and the application (Kouadri Mostéfaoui, 2004). In Figure 4, the feeding process is an event-trigger system that gathers contextual information from appropriate sources like contexts of Web services and contexts of resources. Additional sources could be used for feeding the security context, such as physical sensors in the environment or user inputs (Schmidt, Beigl, & Gellersen, 1999). Based on the content validity of each context, policies are triggered. In the following, and relying on a previous work by Sattanathan, Narendra, and Maamar (2005), we overview some arguments that populate each type of context and illustrate the specification of a policy in Ponder. We have selected Ponder due to its expressiveness and ease of use (Damianou, Dulay, Lupu, & Sloman, (2001).

Some arguments in W-context are: signature (establishes the identity of the Web service so that messages to peers are identified), security mechanism (sets the encryption/decryption mechanism needed for authenticating messages received from peers), security status (indicates the status of authenticating the received message in terms of success or failure), and violation (indicates the type of security violation that a message was subject to). Arguments in C-context are similar to arguments of W-context but are interpreted at the composition level. Some arguments in R-context are: signature (establishes the identity of the Web service that operates on top of the resource), and violation (indicates the type of security violation that the Web service is involved in). Finally some arguments in S-context are as follows: signature per Web service/composite Web service/resource, security mechanism per Web service/composite Web service/resource, security status per Web service/composite Web service/resource, and security violation per Web service/composite Web service/resource. The main role of S-context is to report on which authentication mechanisms (i.e., username/password pairs, binary certificate, etc.), certificate algorithms, and so forth are supported by all components, whether Web service, composite Web service, or resource, and when they are active.

Policies are information which can be used to modify the behavior of a system (Lupu & Sloman, 1999). The use of policies in the SC-WS project permits managing Web services at a higher level where guidelines for conducting composition of Web services are separated from guidelines for securing Web services. The following is a policy in Ponder that authorizes activating a certain security aspect following the invocation request that a Web service (WS_1) receives from a peer (WS_2). This security aspect depends on the types of authentication and encryption mechanisms featuring WS_2. In this policy, details about these mechanisms are available in the S-context of WS_2.

```
inst oblig AuthorizeWS₂{
on ServiceRequest(s,t);
when S-context.authentication(s,"Kerberos",1) and S-context.encryption(s,"DES",1)
subject s = / WS₂;
target t = /WS₁;
action t.activate(aspectᵢ);
```

Component Configuration of Security Aspects

Figure 5 illustrates the operation of the AoF4WS in a configuration of type component. This configuration aims at supporting the customization of each active-security aspect that was identified in composite configuration and according to the requirements that a user sets. This is achieved using frames. Some examples of user requirements are authentication to happen within 10 seconds and AES-128 is the

Figure 5. Framed security aspects generation

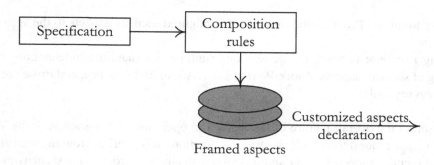

encryption algorithm. In Figure 5, we also present the way a customized aspect is defined, which is adapted from Greenwood and Blair (2004):

- **Specification:** It is about the developer's security specification to be customized. This consists of setting the values of the metavariables and selecting the different options available in the framed aspect. For example, a specification sets the concrete value of a timeout variable that is contained in a framed authentication aspect code.
- **Composition rules:** They control the way aspects are bound together. For example, an aspect's parameter (e.g., timeout) already defined in the specification can be constrained to a specific interval. The weaving process will then occur upon these constraints.
- **Framed aspect:** It is a parameterized version of the original security aspect that was established in the configuration of type composite. In addition to the generalized aspect code that a famed aspect contains, more elements are added, such as conditional compilation and parameterization.

The reader may wonder about the relationship between policies defined earlier and composition rules. Policies are responsible for selecting security aspects to be activated according to the current context of the whole Web services environment. A composition rule defines how the selected security aspects will be woven in order to secure specific Web services. A composition rule is seen as a policy at the micro level of the aspect. The composition rules apply to the set of aspects once these aspects are selected and customized following their respective specifications.

Putting it all Together

In previous contributions (e.g., Greenwood & Blair, 2004; Loughran & Rashid, 2003), weaving of aspects—for generic applications—is based on a simple schema, that is, on the adaptation of the aspects at the composite level (see above for more details on composite configuration of security aspects). The SC-WS—more specific to Web services—adds an extra step that consists of running an adaptation at the component level by integrating a set of relevant contextual information. Compared to Figure 5, Figure 6 illustrates the operation of the SC-WS after combining composite and component configuration. The new elements in the SC-WS are as follows:

- **Web services environment:** Includes the different component Web services of a composite Web service.
- **Security monitor:** Provides the right set of configured security aspects to the Web services environment.
- **Nanning runtime:** Is based on the Nanning runtime tool (nanning.codehaus.org/) for runtime weaving of security aspects. AspectWerkz, JAC, JAsCo, AOPAlliance, and Prose are examples of other weaving tools.

Figure 6 shows the overall picture of the SC-WS in operation. A transaction in the Web services environment (e.g., a request to use a Web service's functionality) requires from the security monitor to set the needed security aspects (i.e., a request is automatically forwarded to the security monitor before being fulfilled). Component and composite configurations of the AoF4WS engage in collaboration to fulfill this transaction. In the first step, that is, composite configuration, a list of security aspects (e.g., authentication, logging) that need to be included in the security framework is produced. The selected security aspects are then framed in the second step, that is, component configuration. The second step is about how each single aspect will be customized in order to properly respond to the context of use (e.g., type of protocol used by the privacy service). The final set of framed aspects is then concretely woven using Nanning runtime and applied in order to secure the transactions in the Web services environment.

Illustration using Amin Scenario

Refer to Figure 2 for a specification of the Amin scenario. The T-CS$_1$ puts together an itinerary for Amin. Two of the most significant component Web services of T-CS$_1$ are taxi booking Web service (TB-WS$_1$) and bus schedule Web service (BS-WS$_2$). In the C-context of T-CS$_1$, Blowfish algorithm is set as part of

Figure 6. Composite and component configuration of security aspects

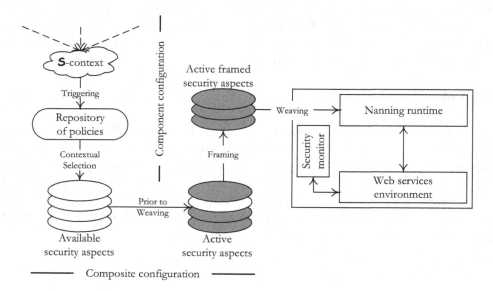

the security mechanism. In the W-contexts of TB-WS$_1$ and BS-WS$_2$, DES and AES algorithms are set, respectively. TB-WS$_1$ uses a resource, which is an online database through which up-to-date information on available taxis are provided. In the R-context of this database, authentication information is presented so TB-WS$_1$ gets to access this database.

Based on the W/C/R-contexts discussed earlier, the S-context arguments of T-CS$_1$ are instantiated. Some of them are: DES algorithm for BS-WS$_2$, Blowfish algorithm for T-CS$_1$, security status for TB-WS$_1$ accessing the database resource ("access granted"), and security violation (if any has occurred; in our case, so far, no). The S-context information is then used to populate the policy repository with the appropriate policies. A sample of policy is to authorize the invocation of TB-WS$_1$ upon request of T-CS$_1$, assuming that the security conditions are met.

```
inst oblig AuthorizeTaxiWebService{
on ServiceRequest(s,t);
when S-context.authentication(s,"Blowfish",1) and S-context.encryption(t,"DES",1)
subject s = /T_CS1;
target t= /TB_WS1;
action s.invoke(t);
```

In other words, when trip Web service authenticates itself to taxi service, this latter is supposed to accept the invocation request from trip service. A similar bus schedule request can also happen, as shown below.

```
inst oblig AuthorizeBusScheduleWebService{
on ServiceRequest(s,t);
when S-context.authentication(s,"Blowfish",1) and S-context.encryption(t,"AES",1)
subject s = /T_CS1;
target t= /BS_WS2;
action s.invoke(t);
```

Based on the policies defined above, the list of appropriate security aspects is generated (i.e., DES aspect, Blowfish aspect, and AES aspect). Since the above policies are needed for Amin, the appropriate authentication code is weaved into the respective Web services (TB-WS$_1$ and BS-WS$_2$) in order to ensure that the necessary security checks are carried out during the composition of these Web services. The actual weaving itself is carried out via frame technology, as follows. Prior to the weaving process, each framed security aspect—identified by the list generated earlier—is customized according to the values set in the specification, as illustrated in Figure 6 (component configuration of security aspects). Afterwards the framed versions of these framed security aspects are woven using the Nanning runtime.

Summary

In the SC-WS project, we argue for an adaptive security strategy in Web services environments using framed aspects, which are the combination of frames and aspect-oriented programming. Frames enhance aspect-oriented programming by separating the specification of a security aspect from the aspect code itself. This approach allows for a fine-grained variation of security aspects according to the context of use.

SH-WS PROJECT: SELF-HEALING WEB SERVICES

The development of self-healing Web services means enhancing them with self-healing properties, such as how to deal with a timeout response from a critical request and how to resume operation after a major crash. One of the recommendations we put forward while designing and coding self-healing functionalities is to keep them separate from the design and code implementing the business logic of a Web service. Concern separation permits avoiding cross-cutting issues and emphasizes the noninvasive requirement that needs to be integrated into the development strategy of self-healing Web services. The inappropriate handling of this requirement leads into a code that is scattered all over the Web service and, thus, becomes difficult to localize and maintain. This maintenance exercise is extensive, expensive, and error-prone. In this chapter we suggest using aspect-oriented programming to design and develop self-healing Web services. The use of self-healing permits develops Web services that are more agile and robust, responsive to (unpredictable) changes in the environment, thereby resulting in reduced downtime, capable of self-diagnosis, and proactively seeking to avoid "unsafe" configurations. Multiple challenges face the development of self-healing Web services, including how to trigger the self-healing process, how to model and track Web services engaged in self-healing operations, how to adjust control and data flow among these Web services, and how to automatically modify this flow with little disruption.

Related Work

Baresi, Ghezzi, and Guinea (2004) select the selection stage of Web services in order to illustrate the importance of self-healing mechanisms. Shutting-down a system because of a Web service failure is no longer acceptable, whether in critical-systems or not. The execution environment should be able to identify new Web services and even to reorganize the process to find a solution that uses what is available, if a perfect match does not exist. Baresi et al.'s proposal revolves around special-purpose probes, that is, monitors, to allow the execution environment to detect anomalous conditions such as a nonresponding Web service. Their proposal is built-upon two techniques: defensive process design and service runtime monitoring. The approach they follow is mainly based on assertions of prepost and invariant conditions; these facilities are inspired from some programming languages such as Eiffel. The resulting proposal suggests the use of such facilities in order to implement recovery actions at the code level.

Ardissono, Console, Goy, Petrone, Picardi, Segnan, et al. (2005) propose a framework for adding diagnostic capabilities to Web services, using a model-based perspective. The objective is to develop self-healing Web services. The framework associates each Web service with a local diagnoser that relates hypotheses about incorrect outputs of this Web service to misbehavior of the Web service itself, or to incorrect inputs from other peers in composition scenarios. Besides the local diagnoser, a global diagnoser is deployed at the composite level. It coordinates the local diagnosers, exchanging messages with them and sometimes computes diagnoses without relying on the feedback of these local diagnosers. Pencole, Cordier, and Grastien (2005) model Web service workflows as discrete-event systems using a model-based reasoning approach. Such a model is the first step towards tracing the evolution of the workflow and diagnosing faults at run-time. The result is a tool for monitoring and diagnosing Web services.

Although the research outcomes in the above projects are promising, two major concerns still remain to be handled: How do we develop self-healing Web services without altering their underlying code? And how do we interleave monitoring, diagnosis, and adaptation as part of the self-healing process

256

without interrupting the execution of the unaffected Web services? Modularizing both concerns using software engineering techniques like object-oriented is hard to achieve. This is where aspect-oriented programming comes into play, as will be described below.

Monitoring Model

As part of the self-healing process, the ability of Web services to self-coordinate is important, that is, being able to monitor the progress of their execution without the overhead of a centralized coordinator. Of course, the composite Web service can always implement a centralized monitoring. However, this turns out to be a bottleneck to the architecture and imposes an unacceptable performance overhead. A decentralized monitoring model that could also permit centralized monitoring, if needed, is deemed appropriate.

Our monitoring model complies with the distributed tuplespace-based approach described by Maamar, Benslimane, Ghedira, & Mahmoud (2005) and depicted with Figure 7. The lifecycle of the monitoring model highlights the following elements: composite Web service issuing invitations of participation to component Web services, component Web services deploying Web service instances upon invitation acceptance, and monitoring being conducted at composite and component levels.

The operation of the monitoring model of Figure 7 assumes that a Web service instance is self-aware. The Web service instance has access to the description of the specification of the composite Web service. This permits to the Web service instance to know and assess the constraints under which it operates in terms of execution time, execution chronology, and acceptable data, just to cite a few. For monitoring purposes at the Web service level, a Web service instance is supposed to post all its activities on the tuplespace that is connected to its Web service. The composite Web service has all access to the tuplespace subject to some access rights verification. It is interesting to note that any failure or delay is automatically reported in the tuplespace, which permits immediate solutions to be deployed. To keep the chapter self-contained, the way a tuplespace operates is excluded. Readers are referred to Maamar, Benslimane, Ghedira, Mahmoud, and Yahyaoui's (2005) work.

Figure 7. Monitoring model for self-healing Web services

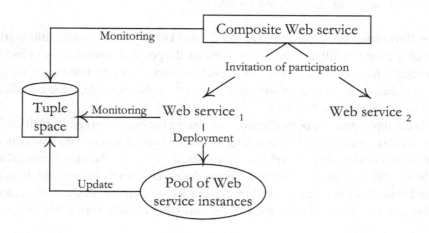

257

Applied in the Amin scenario, the monitoring step is concretized as the following. When a Web service detects an error within its execution, it raises an exception by updating its respective tuplespace. Upon receipt of the exception, the tuplespace reports it to the rest of participating Web services that have expressed interests in this kind of exception. If bus schedule WS detects an error, this information will be recorded and propagated as an exception to traffic WS and weather WS.

Diagnosis Model

As part of the self-healing process, diagnosis continues monitoring. Diagnosis is the process of discovering the cause and nature of a fault (Ardissono et al., 2005). When a Web service instance fails, the cause can either lie within this Web service instance, or within a peer or resource that the Web service instance in question depends on. In the Amin scenario, if the bus schedule WS signals a failure, two options exist: either the bus schedule WS itself is not able to send the schedule due to an internal error, or the bus schedule WS has not received the right input from the location WS so it can send an appropriate bus schedule to Amin.

Two types of dependency exist between any pair of Web service instances $WS\text{-}I_i$ and $WS\text{-}I_j$, where $WS\text{-}I_j$ succeeds $WS\text{-}I_i$ in the composite Web service specification: control flow and data flow. In a data flow dependency, $WS\text{-}I_j$ requires data from $WS\text{-}I_i$ in order to execute successfully. For example, the bus schedule WS requires the location data from the location WS so a bus schedule is provided. $WS\text{-}I_i$ can create, modify, forward, or consume the data.

- **Data creation:** $WS\text{-}I_i$ is the source of the data. $WS\text{-}I_i$ is therefore to be diagnosed as the cause of failure since the data are being erroneous.
- **Data modification:** A different Web service instance is the source of the data. This requires checking whether the modification operation implemented by $WS\text{-}I_i$ produces the expected result. If so, then the data need to be traced back to their source, in order to determine where the error occurred.
- **Data forwarding without modification:** Another Web service instance $WS\text{-}I_k$ before $WS\text{-}I_i$ in the composite Web service specification, is the possible failure cause. Therefore, the data should be traced back to their source until the failure-causing Web service instance is identified.
- **Data consumption:** $WS\text{-}I_i$ is the final destination of the data that will become an input for the creation/modification of another data variable.

In a control flow dependency, the output of $WS\text{-}I_i$ should satisfy certain preconditions that are needed for $WS\text{-}I_j$ to execute successfully. In the Amin scenario, the positive confirmation of bad weather is the precondition needed for taxi WS to execute. The precondition value generated by $WS\text{-}I_i$ is based on the data created/modified by it. In case of any error in this data, for example, wrong confirmation of bad weather, the source would be $WS\text{-}I_i$ itself.

The distributed tuplespace supports diagnosis by tracing the execution results in the reverse direction in which the execution occurred, while checking where the control and/or data flow dependencies have been violated. This will stop once all Web services where the data variables have been created have been covered by the tracing process. As described above, the execution results are stored/maintained in the tuplespace, and hence they can be retrieved from there for verification. In the Amin scenario, a partial list of data flow sequences could be: location WS → bus schedule WS, traffic WS → bus schedule WS, and weather WS → bus schedule WS. The consumption of location, traffic, and weather data results in creating the bus schedule for Amin. Any error in bus schedule WS means that the data flow sequences will be traversed in the reverse direction up to the sources of these data and verified to determine where the error occurred. First, the bus schedule calculation is checked; if that is correct, the location/weather/traffic calculations are checked to determine which of these data variables are erroneous. Since these three data variables are created afresh by their respective Web services, the checking will stop there.

Adaptation Model

Having detailed how the monitoring and diagnosis models operate, we discuss hereafter the adaptation as the last step of the self-healing process. The adaptation occurs using what we call exception trace, exception context, and multiplexing aspects (Figure 8). The exception trace relies on the data flow that is stored in the tuplespace and obtained by a reverse analysis of the content of the tuplespace. The exception context is the state of the Web services when the failure occurred. Multiplexing aspects trigger the adaptation actions based on the exception trace and the context.

Web services failures range from internal errors to some other external factors like network congestion. Handling exceptions is then highly dependant on the source and type of failure. To keep track of a failure source and type, an exception trace is generated out of the tuplespace. An effective adaptation strategy should be supported by an appropriate exception handling at the code level. This is dependant on the features of the programming language. In Java, java.lang.Exception and java.lang.RuntimeException packages are dedicated classes for exception handling.

The adaptation strategy we discuss in this chapter relies on the exception and the current context as well. Recovering from a timeout failure when the requested Web service is overloaded may be handled by a retry process. The same exception due to the Web service constant unavailability requires a dynamic binding to another Web service. As a result, Web services should be continually aware of the

Figure 8. Aspects during adaptation

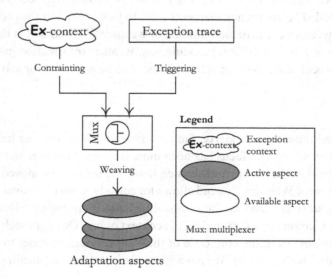

Adaptation aspects

259

current context in order to adopt the right strategy for exception handling. The following suggests some examples of contextual elements constraining the adaptation strategy:

Contextual element	Description
Exception time	When the exception was observed.
Exception location	At which point of the Web services composition the exception occurred.
Previous exceptions	Number of times the exceptions were reported at the same point of the Web services composition.

In Figure 8, the multiplexer supports multiplexing aspects. Multiple aspects mean different strategies to adopt for handling different exceptions. Multiplexing is a well-known technique in the field of electrical engineering (Wikipedia, 2005). This technique supports mixing the inputs from multiple sources into one connection. In the self-healing process, multiplexing is used to simultaneously combine exception traces and current exception context so the right self-healing strategy is derived. In order to implement the concept of multiplexing aspects, we follow a policy-based approach. The primary use of policies is to perform actions according to the occurring events and detected changes. Our main motivation in adopting a policy-based approach is to support the adaptation of self-healing actions by taking advantage of the up-to-date information that context caters over occurred exceptions. We use the well-known Ponder language for representing the policies, due to its expressiveness and ease of use (Damianou et al., 2001). We use obligation policies as a class of Ponder policies, which are event-driven condition-action rules for actions that must be performed on specified objects of the target domain. For weather WS, the policy for activating the aspect relating to weather confirmation could be as follows:

```
inst oblig SelfHealing{
on Exception(t);
when context-elt1 = "4 PM" and context-elt2 = "Weather Confirmation" and context-el3 = "3"
subject t = /WeatherService;
action t.activate(aspecti);}
```

The activation of aspect$_i$ would result in changing weather WS code, so the correct weather information for Amin is recomputed. The contextual elements refer to those listed in the previous table: exception occurred at 4 PM, in weather confirmation module of weather WS, and this is the third time this error occurs. In case the error was in a different module, say, weather information gathered from a satellite imagery, a different aspect other than aspect$_i$ would need to be activated for self-healing purposes.

Summary

As a nonfunctional and must-have property, fault tolerance of Web services has been extensively investigated in the last few years. The focus has been more on error detection and recovery in composite Web services execution flow. In the current chapter, however, we have proposed a reusable framework that achieves self-healing of Web services and allows for consideration of recovery actions as structured units. Implemented as software aspects, the self-healing actions are triggered based on the type of the fault in the composite Web services flow and on the context of use. Our approach aims at separating the fault-tolerance mechanisms from the core code of the Web services in order to allow for a structured and easy maintenance of Web services. We have also positioned our self-healing technique within our previously introduced AoF4WS framework that uses aspects for decoupling various concerns in Web services. Future work will involve developing an implementation to demonstrate our technique.

CONCLUSION

The AoF4WS research initiative is devoted to highlight the added-value of aspect-oriented programming in implementing nonfunctional requirements of Web services. It is also intended to identify the core technologies that realize these requirements. In this chapter, we introduced the AoF4WS initiative that so far encompasses two research projects, namely SC-WS and SH-WS. Both projects use the well-known aspect-oriented programming technique to decouple cross-cutting concerns in Web services. Such a decoupling promotes a clear separation between the operational and nonfunctional aspects of Web service executions, thereby resulting in easier adaptability and maintainability. As a future work, we are looking at extending our framework by tackling other nonfunctional requirements, such as performance. In addition, we will be investigating the issues involved in implementing several aspects simultaneously, which could result in semantic interference between the aspects (Durr, Staijen, Bergmans, & Aksit, 2005).

REFERENCES

Ardissono, L., Console, L., Goy, A., Petrone, G., Picardi, C., Segnan, M., et al. (2005). Towards self-diagnosing Web services. In *Proceedings of the IFIP/IEEE International Workshop on Self-Managed Systems & Services (SelfMan'2005) held in conjunction with The 9th IFIP/IEEE International Symposium on Integrated Network Management (IM'2005),* Nice, France.

Baresi, L., Ghezzi, C., & Guinea, S. (2004). Towards self-healing service compositions. In *Proceedings of the First Conference on the Principles of Software Engineering (PRISE'2004),* Buenos Aires, Argentina.

Birman, K. (2004, December). Like it or not, Web services are distributed objects. *Communications of the ACM, 47*(12).

Charfi, A., & Mezini, M. (2004). Hybrid Web service composition: Business processes meets business rules. In *Proceedings of the 2nd International Conference on Service Oriented Computing (ICSOC'2004),* New York.

Cibrán, M., & Verheecke, B. (2003). Modularizing Web services management with AOP. In *Proceedings of the 1st European Workshop on Object Orientation and Web Services (ECOOP'2003) held in conjunction with The 17th European Conference on Object-Oriented Programming (ECOOP'2003),* Darmstadt, Germany.

Cottenier, T., & Elrad, T. (2004). Validation of aspect-oriented adaptations to components. In *Proceedings of the 9th International Workshop on Component-Oriented Programming (WCOP'2004) held in conjunction with The 18th European Conference on Object-Oriented Programming (ECOOP'2004),* Oslo, Norway.

Damianou, N., Dulay, N., Lupu, E., & Sloman, M. (2001). The ponder specification language. In *Proceedings of the Workshop on Policies for Distributed Systems and Networks (Policy'2001)*, Bristol, UK.

Durr, P., Staijen, T., Bergmans, L., & Aksit, M. (2005). Reasoning about semantic conflicts between aspects. In *Proceedings of the 2ⁿᵈ European Interactive Workshop on Aspects in Software (EIWAS'2005)*, Brussels, Belgium.

EL-Manzalawy, Y. (2005). *Aspect oriented programming*. Retrieved August 2005, from http://www.developer.com/design/article.php/3308941

Greenwood, P., & Blair, L. (2004). *Dynamic framed aspects for policy-driven auto-adaptive systems*. Retrieved August 2004, from http://www.comp.lancs.ac.uk/computing/aose/papers/dynFr_daw04.pdf

Kouadri Mostéfaoui, G. (2004). *Towards a conceptual and software framework for integrating context-based security in pervasive environments*. Unpublished doctoral thesis (No. 1463), University of Fribourg and Paris 6 University.

Kouadri Mostéfaoui, G., Maamar, Z., Narendra, N. C., & Sattanathan, S. (2006). Decoupling security concerns in Web services using aspects. In *Proceedings of the 3ʳᵈ International Conference on Information Technology: New Generations (ITNG'2006)*, Las Vegas.

Loughran, N., & Rashid, A. (2003). Supporting evolution in software using frame technology and aspect orientation. In *Proceedings of the Workshop on Software Variability Management*, Groningen, The Netherlands.

Lupu, E., & Sloman, M. (1999, November/December). Conflicts in policy-based distributed systems management. *IEEE Transactions on Software Engineering, 25*(6).

Ma, K. (2005, March/April). Web services: What's real and what's not? *IT Professional, 7*(2).

Maamar, Z., Benatallah, B., & Mansoor, W. (2003). Service chart diagrams: Description & application. In *Proceedings of the Alternate Tracks of The 12ᵗʰ International World Wide Web Conference (WWW'2003)*, Budapest, Hungary.

Maamar, Z., Benslimane, D., Ghedira, C., Mahmoud, Q. H., & Yahyaoui, H. (2005). Tuple spaces for self-coordination of Web services. In *Proceedings of the 20ᵗʰ ACM Symposium on Applied Computing (SAC'2005)*, Santa Fe, NM.

Maamar, Z., Benslimane, D., & Narendra, N. C. (2006). What can context do for Web services? *Communications of the ACM*.

Maamar, Z., Kouadri Mostéfaoui, S., & Mahmoud, Q. (2005, July-September). On personalizing Web services using context. *International Journal of E-Business Research, Special Issue on E-Services, 1*(3). IGI Global, Inc.

Moorthy, K. R., & Gandhirajan, A. (2005). *The foundations of Web services security*. Retrieved August, from http://www.developer.com/services/article.php/3496326

Nakamur, Y., Hada, S., & Neyma, R. (2002). Towards the integration of Web services security on enterprise environments. In *Proceedings of the Workshop on Web Services Engineering 2002 (WebSE'2002) held in conjunction with The IEEE/IPSJ Symposium on Applications and the Internet (SAINT'2002)*, Nara, Japan

Ortiz, G., Hernández, J., & Clemente, P. J. (2004a). Decoupling non-functional properties in Web services: An aspect-oriented approach. In *Proceedings of the 2ⁿᵈ European Workshop on Web Services and Object Orientation (EOOWS'2004) held in conjunction with the 18ᵗʰ European Conference on Object-Oriented Programming (ECOOP'2004)*, Norway.

Ortiz, G., Hernández, J., & Clemente, P. J. (2004b). Web services orchestration and interaction patterns: An aspect-oriented approach. In *Proceedings of the 2ⁿᵈ International Conference on Service Oriented Computing (ICSOC'2004)*, New York.

Sandhu, R. (2003, January/February). Good-enough security: Toward a pragmatic business-driven discipline. *IEEE Internet Computing, 7*(1).

Sattanathan, S., Narendra, N. C., & Maamar, Z. (2005). Towards context-based tracking of Web services security. In *Proceedings of The 7ᵗʰ International Conference on Information Integration and Web Based Applications & Services (iiWAS'2005)*, Kuala Lumpur, Malaysia.

Schmidt, A., Beigl, M., & Gellersen, H. W. (1999, December). There is more to context than location. *Computers & Graphics Journal, 23*(6).

W3C. (2005). *Working group.* Retrieved June 1, 2008, from http://www.w3.org/

Web services security. (2002). *Version 1.0.* Retrieved August 2005, from http://www.verisign.com/wss/wss.pdf

Wikipedia. (2005). *The free encyclopedia.* Retrieved June 1, 2008, from http://en.wikipedia.org/wiki/Multiplexing/

Yan, Y., Pencole, Y., Cordier, M. O., & Grastien, A. (2005). Monitoring Web service networks in a model-based approach. In *Proceedings of the 3ʳᵈ European Conference on Web Services (ECOWS'05)*, Vaxjo, Sweden.

Chapter XII
Open Security Framework for Unleashing Semantic Web Services

Ty Mey Eap
Simon Fraser University, Canada

Marek Hatala
Simon Fraser University, Canada

Dragan Gašević
Athabasca University, Canada

Nima Kaviani
University of British Columbia, Canada

Ratko Spasojevic
TELUS Security Solutions, Canada

ABSTRACT

The lack of intrinsic and user control in the identity management of today Internet security hampers the research in the area of Semantic Web and service-oriented architectures. Semantic Web research is seeking to develop expert Web services that are a composition of specialized Web services of multi-organizations. To unleash these emergent Web services, we propose an open security framework that is based on the concept of personal identity management. Despite the resistance from today's Internet security dominated by domain-centric identity management, we believe that when all the alternatives are exhausted, the industry will come to the conclusion that the concept of personal identity management is the only approach to provide true user-centric identity management and give users control over the management of their identities.

INTRODUCTION

The service-oriented architecture (SOA) framework features reusability, loose coupling, abstraction, and discoverability. These features are essential for model driven engineering and providing a strong foundation for Semantic Web services; it is a design philology that pushes the boundaries of traditional design to offer highly qualified Web services. Services have the intelligence to trigger a chain of events and to collaborate with other services. In the SOA paradigm, a Web service can be a composition of multiple services located across multiple networks and can have different security settings and authentication requirements. Some services are composed dynamically on the fly, based on the availability and the accessibility of services within the composition framework (Cotroneo, Graziano, & Russo, 2004). Moreover, services can use different authentication systems that require user identities other than the one who invokes the composite service. Consider a company providing a risk assessment service to companies in the transportation business. To assess the risk, this expert service needs to have driving and health records of the employees and vehicle maintenance reports, accident reports, and so forth from a number of outsourcing companies. The risk service needs to collaborate with many services, and the access to these services may require different sets of user credentials. However, current Internet security infrastructure cannot support such context rich Web services. Currently, there is no mechanism for a risk assessment service to access employees' personal information. The employees must retrieve their records from the healthcare and driver license services and make the records available to the risk assessment service. Outsourcing companies must do the same for their accident and maintenance reports. The procedure is costly, and at best, companies can conduct their risk assessment once a year. This short scenario demonstrates the need for a new design of the Internet security framework that is capable of allowing services to collaborate with each other while strengthening the protection of privacy. The risk assessment service is a type of services that the future Internet users expect from the Internet technology and is a typical expert service that can improve the quality of Web services.

Traditional Internet security is designed for standalone systems. Over the recent years, the growing number of online services has changed the requirements of Internet security and forced the industry to develop new security infrastructures to respond to this challenge. In the context of a federation, single sign-on (SSO) was developed to allow users access multiple services using a single login. However, the SSO framework relies on user interaction to perform the authentication and user vigilant to make sure that the Web sites they access and the authenticating sites are legitimated. Unlike Web applications, Web services act on behalf of a user. The SOA must layout the whole security framework and ensure that all services are secured, and security policies must be in place to allow services to collaborate safely with each other. Since access to the services within a composition requires different sets of credentials, a SOA-security must be able to obtain user consent dynamically during the runtime.

The solution to the SOA security lies in the concept of personal identity management (PIdM). Encapsulated in the open security framework (OSF), the PIdM concept takes user-centric identity a step farther to encompass users as the enablers of the service collaboration and as the administrators of the identity management. Each user has a personal identity provider (PIdP), which is an intelligent agent that can act according to user security policy settings to release user consent at runtime. This allows services to collaborate in a multiparties transaction. Local laws, rules, and regulations could take precedent over user rights to privacy, but the policies must be made transparent to the users. PIdPs log all transactions so that users can determine if a violation of their privacy has occurred and take an immediate action to address the problem. The framework is a novel approach designed to meet the requirements of the

SOA security and limit the liability of each party involved in the framework; users see to their security and privacy and a PIdP guarantees the authenticity of user consent claims while relying parties only release user data if user designated PIdPs show proofs of user consents. OSF advocates the rights and freedoms of every user, allowing each user to choose a PIdP that is appropriated to the user's individual needs. The framework is more versatile and user-centric than Windows Live™ ID service. Formerly known as Passport service, Windows Live ID service is designed to manage identity and trust within the Windows Live ecosystem. Web sites using Windows Live ID infrastructure must redirect users to Windows Live ID sign-in page hosted by Microsoft. Once authenticated, Microsoft authentication sends users back to the Web sites, and the Web sites are entitled to request user identity data. In other words, Windows Live ID is an SSO that comes with a designated Microsoft identity provider. Nevertheless, Windows Live ID reflects the necessity of each user having a PIdP, but OSF does not envision a single Microsoft identity provider to service every Internet user. The digital world can and should have several PIdPs offering identity services tailored to the users' needs.

BACKGROUND

In this chapter, we discuss security at the abstract level and assume that the readers have the knowledge of Internet security technologies such as public key infrastructure (PKI) and Web services (WS) security. When speaking of an affiliation claim, we assume that issuing relying parties use PKI technology to sign claims, and target relying parties can use the same technology to validate those claims. This is a typical use of PKI certification mechanism. An affiliation claim is a digital certificate issued by a relying party, and as a certificate, a claim can be validated, and the issuer can revoke or put an expiration date on that claim. Readers should also have some knowledge in logic programming and Semantic Web technologies, in particular the use of ontology or markup languages to represent a knowledgebase. In part, security policies are a knowledgebase implemented using some kinds of logic programming or rule languages. Access rights are determined by applying security policies onto a reasoning engine (i.e., Jess or Jena) or a logic-programming interpreter (i.e., Prolog). Nevertheless, this section does provide some backgrounds and definitions of the technologies discussed in this chapter.

Definitions

- **Identity Provider (IdP):** An IdP is a trusted entity that can verify the authenticity of a user during registration, has the authority to issue sets of credentials, is able to authenticate users, and finally provides identity management (IdM) services to relying parties.
- **Personal Identity Provider (PIdP):** A PIdP is an IdP that answers directly to users. In addition to an IdP functions, a PIdP provides a number of functionalities for users to manage their identity data. It also serves as an intermediary between two relying parties allowing the two parties to establish trust with each other.
- **Relying-party (RP):** An RP is a trusted service provider that relies on a third IdP for its IdM. An RP may or may not have registered users. An RP that has registered users is a home-based RP for those users. All RPs can sign affiliation claims for users, but affiliation claims from a home-based RP are more credible than a nonhome-based RP.

Web Service (WS) Security Technology

The two basic technologies in the SOA-security are PKI and WS security. The public-key cryptography is not only valuable for providing secure communication between two parties, it also provides a certification mechanism, known as third-party trust, for a trusted party to issue signed certificates and vouch the trustworthiness of third parties. Certification authority (CA) is an example of a trusted party. Although we assume that RPs and PIdPs use some kinds of certification mechanism to authenticate each other, the certification authority infrastructure is not in the scope of this chapter. RPs and PIdPs in OSF may use commercial root CAs such as VeriSign, Entrust, and AlphaTrust, but there is no reason that a PIdP cannot act as a CA as long as it can provide adequate security for the third parties.

Public Key Infrastructure (PKI) in WS Security

Simple object access protocol (SOAP) is a standard protocol for Web services, which is mainly an XML-based message embedded in the HTTP protocol. SOAP can be sent over a secure channel using transport layer security or secure sockets layer (TLS/SSL). Currently, PKI is the mainstream technology used in TLS/SSL to establish mutual authentication and provide strong cryptography for secure communications. The connections can be anonymous using self-signed certificates or using CA-signed certificates in the context of certification authentication. Today's secure Web sites, including those that need strong security such as financial Web sites, are using self-signed certificate connections. However, self-signed certificates only guarantee secure connections between clients and target Web servers. Users must supply username and password for their authentication. A CA-signed certificate proves the authenticity of the owner. Known as a certification authentication, a connection using CA-signed certificate can provide stronger security, but the mechanism requires the management of certificates. Before accessing a server, users must get their certificates from CAs and have them installed on their computers. As a result, certification authentication is not common in the public networks.

Web Service Security Standard

Sending SOAP message over TLS/SSL is secure, but there is no supported protocol for WS clients to send security tokens to target service providers. In 2002, the OASIS Technical Committee proposed a WS security specification as a standard for secure exchanges of security tokens between WS clients and WS servers. Shown in *Figure 1*, the WS security standard defines a framework and vocabularies for embedding security tokens in a SOAP message, making it possible for a target service provider to extract the tokens from a SOAP message.

Identity Management

A key component in Internet security is the IdM. Traditional IdMs are mainly domain-centric IdMs; usually, each service provider has its own IdM system. Even in the same organization, a user may be asked to login multiple times because each service provider needs to verify the authenticity of the user. In addition, to eliminate risks of privacy violation, domain-centric IdM systems are designed as well-protected silo systems, so that the sharing of user information, intentionally or unintentionally, is not possible. As the number of online services grows, Internet security researchers had to reconsider

Figure 1. WS security SOAP message example

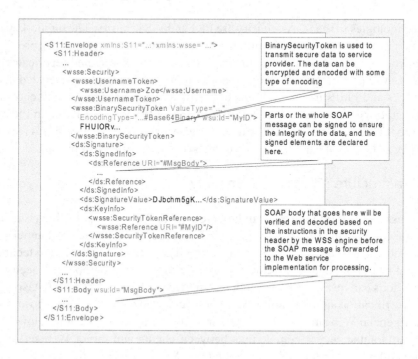

fundamental changes in the IdM (Juels, Winslett, & Goto, 2006) and found that the answer is in the user-centric IdM. This new IdM paradigm shifts the focus towards users and provides stronger user control (Bhargav-Spantzely, Camenisch, Gross, & Sommer, 2006; Clauß, Kesdogan, & Kölsch, 2005; Juels et al., 2006; Recordon & Reed, 2006). Users have greater flexibility in how and where to store their identities, and have the control over sharing and using those identities; this gives users stronger assurance for privacy (Juels et al., 2006). Current IdM research is striving to support this idea. However, since there is no universal set of criteria to measure "user centricity" of a system (Bhargav-Spantzely et al., 2006; Clauß et al., 2005; Juels et al., 2006), each proposed IdM supports different sets of user-centric criteria and none addresses specifically the SOA security issues.

Domain-Centric Identity Management

This section analyzes three well-known domain-centric IdMs: Kerberos (Cervesato, Jaggard, Scedrov, & Walstad, 2005), the central authentication system (CAS) (http://www.ja-sig.org/products/cas/), and Shibboleth (Morgan, Cantor, Carmody, Hoehn, & Klingenstein, 2004). These three IdMs had introduced the concept of federated identities allowing businesses and organizations to share their resources over the Internet. However, as shown in the following discussion, they lack of flexibility and cannot support the requirements of the SOA-security. We intentionally omit Windows Live ID in this discussion because the technology is based on the SSO, the same technology proposed by CAS and Shibboleth. The only exception is that Windows Live ID requires all users to use Microsoft for their IdP.

Kerberos is an authentication system that allows users logged in to their terminals to access resources and services on the network of their respective organizations (Cervesato et al., 2005). When a user logs in to the user's terminal, the Kerberos client authenticates the user to a designated Kerberos server, a trusted third party, known as the key distribution center (KDC). The KDC has two components: an authentication server (AS) and a ticket granting service (TGS). If successful, the AS issues a "ticket granting ticket" and a session key for the Kerberos client. As the name suggests, the ticket allows the Kerberos client to request tickets for the user to access any service on the network. Since the ticket is granted for a specific service, the KDC must be aware of the existence of that service. As a result, Kerberos is used mainly in a private network.

The CAS, designed mainly for Web applications, provides a central authentication service for different RPs. Although the CAS is used mainly within an organization, it can also be a federated IdM. When a user tries to access a member RP, the RP redirects the user to the CAS login page. If the authentication is successful, the CAS sends the user back to the RP with a ticket that the RP must validate before granting access to the user. The CAS is a SSO in the sense that a user can use the same login to access Web applications on different RPs. However, since each new RP needs a new CAS ticket, users must login every time they access a new RP during a session. Nevertheless, CAS does eliminate replications of identity data across a network.

Proclaimed as a "Web SSO" and a federated IdM, Shibboleth makes it possible for users to authenticate at their respective IdPs and access resources on different RPs within a trust federation (Morgan, 2004). When users access a member RP, the RP redirects users to their IdPs, which, of course, must be a trusted IdP. If successfully authenticated, the IdPs send users back to the RP with a SAML token embedded in the HTTP header. A SAML token is an encrypted random number (crypto-handler) associated with a user login session. RPs must validate the token before using it to get user identity data such as affiliation or nickname according to the policy of the federation. As a result, anonymity is possible if the policies limit the release of user attributes.

User-Centric Identity Management

Microsoft believes that InfoCard system would strengthen security and privacy on the Internet (Jones, 2006). InfoCard uses Cameron's seven laws of identity as its design principles (Cameron, 2006). The law states that the IdM

1. Must put users in control and protect users against deception,
2. Should limit the disclosure of identity information for a constraint use,
3. Must only disclose identity information to parties having a necessary and justifiable place in a given identity relationship,
4. Must support both omnidirectional (public) identity to facilitate the discovery and unidirectional (private) identity to prevent unnecessary release of correlation identity information,
5. Should be able to work with multiple IdPs,
6. Must define the human user to be a component of the distributed system integrated through unambiguous human/machine communication mechanisms, and
7. Must provide users with a simple and consistent experience while enabling separation of contexts through multiple operators and technologies.

InfoCard is an interoperable architecture designed to allow Internet users to use context-specific identities from different IdPs in various online interactions (Jones, 2006). When users access an InfoCard compliant site, the site returns a login page that has embedded InfoCard tags. An InfoCard add-on would recognize tags and pop up a visual "Information Card" (law 7) and ask users to select an appropriate identity for the target site (law 1). If the target site is not in the list of visited sites, InfoCard displays a warning with information it has about the site. The user has a choice to decline or trust the site (law 3). InfoCard provides a system for each user to manage their credentials. Users can configure all their credentials into the InfoCard system and use them without having to reenter them. However, it is not true that users can select any set of credentials. The credentials must be the credentials required by the target site. Users must know which sets of credentials they can use for a particular site, and they still have to remember all their credentials to reconfigure the InfoCard system (e.g., switching to another desktop). To help them remember their credentials, users may have to use the old habit of writing down their usernames and passwords on a piece of paper. InfoCard does not propose any change to the existing IdM framework and, hence, cannot offer strong user control.

OpenID (http://openid.net) puts the Yadis protocol on the Internet map. Yadis is a service discovery system that allows a RP to determine, without end-user intervention, the most appropriate protocol to use and to authenticate a user based on a given Yadis ID (Miller, 2006). The ID can be a URL or any other identifier, such as an OASIS extensible resource identifier (XRI), that can resolve to a URL. When a user accesses a Yadis compliant site, the site asks the user to enter the Yadis ID. The site would be able to resolve the user's IdP and use a SSO mechanism to authenticate the user. In 2006, OpenID introduced authentication2.0 to make OpenID compliant to Cameron's fifth law of identity. Authentication2.0 allows a user to use private digital addresses for different RPs (Recordon & Reed, 2006). A digital address is a new ID that users associate to one of their profiles. Also in 2006, Sxip proposed Identity2.0 (Hardt, 2006), a framework that describes the concept of an ID that can be trusted and used anywhere. Identity2.0 strongly supports OpenID. Sxipper is Sxip's Firefox add-on that allows a user to log in using a username or an Identity2.0 authentication mechanism such as OpenID. Sxip envisions the Identity2.0 as a standard identity system that can identify unambiguously who a user is on the Internet. Obviously, OpenID and Sxip are moving towards the concept of personal identity management, but currently, the solutions only address Web applications and do not enforce user consent and user control.

OPEN SECURITY FRAMEWORK FOR SERVICE-ORIENTED ARCHITECTURES

The open security framework (OSF) introduces the concept of PIdP to simplify the design of the IdM that allows users to participate in the management of their personal security. Moreover, the OSF breaks down the responsibility and liability of each party participating in the security framework and makes security and privacy easier to manage. Since users are responsible for watching over their security and privacy, relying parties only have to focus on the security of the resources and the access policies. PIdPs, on the other hand, are striving to provide enhanced security features that help prevent security breaches and give users tools to fight against identity theft. A PIdP should maintain a trust management component that keeps track of all RPs to help users determine the legitimacy of an RP. Similarly, RPs can trust users certified by a PIdP to be authentic, and design a monitoring-based trust management system to hold users accountable for their actions and to reward good users. On request, an RP can vouch for a user's reputation to allow the user to access resources on other RPs. In summary, each party in the OSF is an intelligent entity that can gather knowledge to assess security risks.

As the root for all security stands, trust is the key to the Internet security. Users must trust that systems they access would not violate their privacy and learn to recognize which service providers are legitimated. On the other hand, a service provider must trust that users would use information and services according to the agreements it has with the users and should have a mechanism to verify the authenticity of the users they trust. However, traditional security frameworks do not included users in the trust decision. Institutions make all the decisions regarding trust. To provide a SSO solution across multiple organizations, a trust federation is the common approach (e.g., Shibboleth and Liberty Alliance). However, building trust policies for a federation involves a lengthy negotiation. A federation must have a well-written trust policy agreement among identity and service providers. Due to this complexity, a federated trust is difficult to achieve. Building a trust federation for a similar type of organizations is feasible, but building a trust federation for organizations that need different levels of security is a challenge. Furthermore, in a federation framework, users do not have much freedom, and service providers cannot have the same level of trust for remote users since they are anonymous users. Federations have to hide remote user identities to protect their privacy (Clauβ et al., 2005). Unfortunately, anonymity is a double-edged sword. On one hand, it provides some privacy protection to users, but on the other hand, it increases security risks (Davenport, 2002; Farkas, Ziegler, Meretei, & Lörincz, 2002). It allows malicious users to violate trust and privacy of other users without suffering any consequence. In addition, for an anonymous algorithm to be effective, it must be supported by the use of a proxy or a network protocol that hides users' IP addresses (Kim, Kim, & Kim, 2005).

In the OSF, trust is dynamic and personal. Each party in the OSF must build a knowledgebase for trust management to determine whom it can trust. However, conceptually, an RP can trust each user to be authentic since identity theft is practically impossible in OSF. Users would immediately detect and correct the problem if an identity theft has occurred. Each RP only has to concentrate on the trust management that determines the trust level of each user and RPs that provide references for the user. On the other hand, PIdPs can build a knowledgebase regarding RPs to help users determine the trust level of each RP. This trust model is very close to a real life trust model.

Personal Identity Provider (PIdP)

A PIdP has some similarities to a home-site in terms of Sxip or OpenID. It provides storage for identity data and assists users in the management of their identities. Its functions include:

1. Providing a smart and strong authentication for users with different levels of security (e.g., a user may use a set of credentials that have security level 1 to access the user's blog or a chat room; a second set of credentials with security level 2 to access academic computing services; a third set of credentials with security level 3 to access online financial services; and so on).
2. Allowing users to consent to an RP request for authentication confirmation to make sure that the persons attempting to access the resources are themselves.
3. Managing user profiles and identity data.
4. Allowing users to access their profiles using different sets of credentials with different levels of security.

5. Managing signed affiliation-claims for each user.
6. Logging all transactions and making them transparent to users.
7. Detecting anomalies and alerting users of a possible security risk.
8. Building a knowledgebase for RP reputations to advice users on the security risks.

An Empirical Analysis of the OSF

The following subsections use scenarios to conduct empirical analysis of the OSF. The analysis will show that OSF can strengthen today's Internet security while providing a strong security solution for the SOA. The first scenario describes a registration process to a service provider. This scenario demonstrates the user centricity of the OSF. Instead of designating users to use its authentication system, a service provider relies on users to choose a PIdP for their authentication; the service provider becomes then the RP. Through this process, users verify the security mechanism while the RP verifies user-designated PIdPs. Once registered, the users become members of the RP and can call the RP their home-based RP. The second scenario describes the authentication confirmation process when a user attempts to access resources on a home-based RP. This scenario is also similar to the third scenario where users access resources of an RP using affiliation claims from their home-based RPs. The fourth scenario demonstrates the use of the OSF in a secure electronic payment. The scenario shows that it will be difficult for a thief to use a stolen credit card in the OSF. Finally, we return to the risk assessment scenario, discussed earlier in the introduction section, and discuss how the OSF resolves risk assessment security issues.

Scenario 1: Registration to RP

In *Figure 2*, to register to an RP, John enters his ID into the RP request form (e.g., jdoe@www.pidp.ca). Since the ID is a combination of an identifier and a URL to a PIdP, the RP is able to locate John's PIdP and requests a reference to John's profile from the PIdP. This profile is a custom profile that John wants for that particular RP. Therefore, in the request, the RP specifies what information it needs for the profile.

Figure 2. Register to an RP

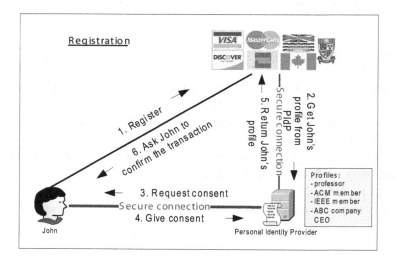

Assuming that John has successfully authenticated with the PIdP, the PIdP prepares a registration form using identity data it has and asks John to modify and/or fill in the missing information. The profile is saved on the PIdP database, and the reference is sent to the RP allowing the RP to retrieve John's updated profile when needed. Once registered, the RP becomes John's home-based RP and can issue its affiliation with John to allow John to access resources on a partner RP. John can create a new ID that matches the security level required by the RP and prevent identity correlation. John can register to as many RPs as he wants. A browser add-on similar to Sxipper or InfoCard (Chappell, 2006) can help John securely login to his PIdP. The add-on can intercept login forms and automatically fill in appropriate John IDs with respect to home-based RPs. In the SOA, the procedure for accessing a service is similar for all scenarios. Before accessing a service, a WS client would retrieve the access policies from the RP to determine the required attributes and ask users to preauthorize the release of the required identity data. To complete the preauthorization transaction, the PIdP issues a consent-claim ticket, which is the WS client embedded in the request to the RP. In turn, the RP uses the ticket to validate user consent and to get user identity data from the PIdP. All SOA processes are regulated by policies. Depending on the level of security, the preauthorization can have a time limit, and when the RP presents the ticket to validate user consent, it may be asked to show a proof of identity or use a secure communication that requires certification authentication.

Scenario 2: Access Resources on a Home-Based RP

In *Figure 3*, when John accesses resources on a home-based RP, the RP requests John's PIdP for a proof of John's consent. The process is as follows. The RP responds to John with a login page that has a special tag in the HTTP header. If John uses an OSF browser add-on, it automatically captures the login page and sends John's ID to the RP. In this case, John does not have to intervene in steps 2 and 3. With the ID, the RP can request the consent from John's PIdP, which in turn asks John to give his consent. This

Figure 3. Access resources on a home-based RP

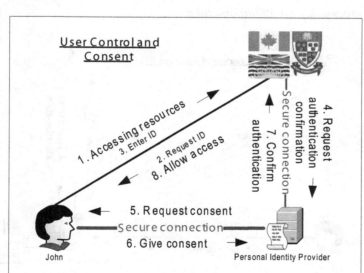

process makes sure that John is the person who is attempting to access the resources on the RP. John can set rules and allow the add-on to release the consent on his behalf. John only has to login once to the add-on and can surf the net securely without worrying about the authentication. Without an add-on, John needs to type in his ID into the login form. The RP will use redirection method to get the proof of John's consent from his PIdP. The process is transparent to John. He knows what he consents to and he can review the consents he has made later. In the SOA, this scenario follows the same process as in Scenario 1. A WS client determines the required attributes, asks the user to preauthorize the PIdP to release consent, and uses the ticket issued by the PIdP to access the resource on the RP, and the RP would use the ticket to validate user consent as in Scenario 1.

Scenario 3: Access Resources using an Affiliation-Claim

The concept of vouching for a user's affiliation, or in a simple term, providing reference for a user, simplifies the design of trust policies and allows each RP to design their own trust policies independently. If one RP has an agreement with another RP, the agreement can be written as a trust policy. For example, if a user presents a signed affiliation-claim from Simon Fraser University (SFU), the user is allowed to access resources based on the user role defined at SFU. Continuing with this example, in *Figure 4*, John is attempting to access resources on UBC the Web site. Since UBC is not John's home-based RP, the PIdP sends a list of John's home-based RPs to the UBC RP. In the trust policies, UBC RP has SFU as a trusted partner. It requests an affiliation-claim from John's PIdP signed by the SFU RP. Once John consents to the affiliation claim request, the PIdP prepares an affiliation claim and has it signed by the SFU RP. Once signed by the SFU RP, the affiliation claim is only valid if and only if John's PIdP presents it to the UBC RP on John's behalf. This scenario is an example of the RP trust management. In the SOA, a WS client would determine what home-based RPs would be appropriate to issue affiliation claims for the request. The client makes the request for the required affiliation claims and attaches the claims with the request to access the target RP service.

Figure 4. Access resources using an affiliation-claim

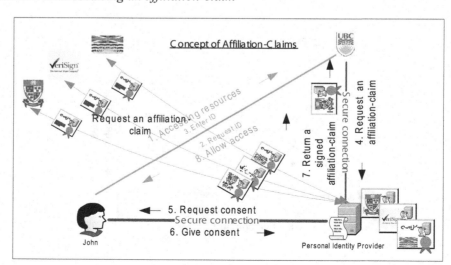

Scenario 4: Secured Electronic Payment

Figure 5 shows a secure credit card payment through the OSF. In this scenario, John is purchasing products on Amazon, Sears, or eBay. During the checkout, the merchant Web site asks John to supply his ID. The merchant payment system resolves the location of John's PIdP and asks the PIdP to release John's profile and credit card number. The PIdP asks John to give his consent and select one of his profiles. The PIdP sends the profile to the merchant. To complete the transaction, the merchant needs a payment approval from John's credit card company, which also must get the consent from John via his PIdP. The consent can also be given through a cell phone. After a cashier had ringed in all the purchased items, John swipes his credit card. The cash register system calls the card company for credit approval. In turn, the card system asks John's PIdP for John's consent. Assuming that John had previously registered his phone number, John would receive a text message from his PIdP. John simply types in the keys to authorize the transaction. John can also set rules and preauthorize purchases to certain stores where he shops regularly. Meanwhile, the PIdP can also determine security risks. For example, if John is connecting to his PIdP from his computer, then John cannot be at another place using his credit card. This payment process is safer than an electronic wallet payment. In this scenario, the process in a SOA needs an extra step. Instead of sending a single consent-claim ticket, a WS client would send two tickets. The first ticket is similar to Scenarios 1 to 3; the ticket is used by the merchant service to retrieve user profiles. The second ticket is forwarded to the credit card service by the merchant service to confirm user consent on the payment. Tickets must be validated and can be used by the designated merchant and credit card services.

These four scenarios show that the proposed OSF enhances security and gives users full control over the release of their identity data. The framework is transparent to users and makes users the participants of the IdM. The ability to get user consent according to user setting policies allows the OSF to deal with special needs for releasing user consent. Due to this ability, service composition that requires credentials of another user is possible. In the risk assessment discussed in the introduction section, employees can

Figure 5. A secured electronic payment

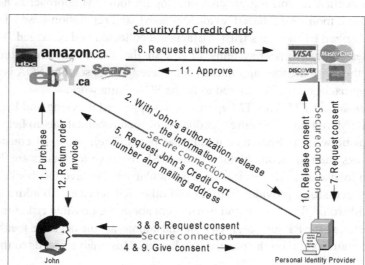

preauthorize the risk assessment service to access their driving health records. This preauthorization can be specific and allows the risk assessment service to access only specific parts of their records. The outsourcing companies can proceed the same way for the maintenance and accident reports. The policies can be part of the hiring agreements and outsourcing contracts. In the OSF, the risk assessment service can go as far as including a risk assessment of employees of the outsourcing companies. This risk assessment service is a typical Semantic Web service, which today's Internet security infrastructures cannot support. The OSF will enable the deployment of such Semantic Web services. Since users consent to the release of their identity data, the OSF does not violate user privacy. Moreover, user consents can be written as policies. Rules, laws, and regulations can be written into the PIdP policies to allow the PIdP to release user consent in case of an emergency or in case a user is incapacitated.

Trust Management (TM)

Some researchers include authentication and authorization in the TM discussion. Although authentication, authorization, and the use of PKI are important security procedures, they are static and could be considered as the basic Internet security, and their usages are standards and are defined and regulated by the IdM. TM must look into the semantics of the data beyond the basic Internet security. Knowing who John is does not mean that John is a trusted person. However, if John were a physician, people would trust John for his medical advices. This section discusses TM in terms of the cognitive trust, which is a trust knowledge acquired over time. Some researchers refer to this type of TMs as soft-policy TM.

Although researchers recognize the importance of TM, there is no consensus in the literature on what constitutes TM. Trust is a composition of many different attributes, such as reliability, dependability, honesty, truthfulness, security, competence, and timeliness, which may have to be considered depending on the environment in which trust is being analyzed (Grandison & Sloman, 2000). Therefore, TM can be seen as an activity of collecting and analyzing evidences relating to competence, honesty, dependability, and reliability with the purpose of assessing trust decisions. The lack of a consensus leads to an adoption of different approaches, and each approach focuses on a specific context of the TM. For a context-specific problem such as TM, each proposed infrastructure must provide ad-hoc solutions for its framework. This section is working towards developing four TM approaches needed in the OSF: recommendation-based, monitoring-based, evidence-based, and reputation-based TM. These four approaches are characterized by the ways trust artifacts are collected and managed. The majority of the proposed TM focuses on peer-to-peer systems. Li and Singhal (2007) have reported a number of TM approaches, among those are the four approaches considered in this section. SOA is not a true peer-to-peer system. The approaches must be tailored to fit the SOA framework.

Recommendation-based TM. This TM approach has appeared in Xiong and Liu's (2004) proposal for their distributed TM system, which uses feedbacks or recommendations to help the establishment of trust relationships between unknown or unfamiliar peers. Their proposal considers both positive and negative feedbacks and interaction history. In the OSF, negative feedbacks are the irregularities or complaints reported by users or RP services on a particular RP. Positive feedbacks are the number of services that a RP successfully provides to users and other RP services. To address complaints from users on a RP, a PIdP would flag the RP and warn users about the possible risk. On the other hand, if other users continue to use the RP service, then it should counteract the negative feedbacks. Prior access history also holds certain weight on the positive feedbacks. This analysis leads to the equation below:

$$T(r,t) = I(r,t) - \left[\sum_{r,u \in F, u \neq r} C(u,r,t) \bullet W(u,t) \div \sum_{r,u \in F, u \neq r} S(r,u,t) \right] \qquad (1)$$

Where

- F is a set of services and users in the OSF
- u denotes a user or a service who requests access to r's service
- r denotes a relying party who provides the service
- t denotes the number of transactions
- $T(r,t)$ is r's trust value evaluated by u
- $I(r,t)$ is a function that computes initial value of r, which eventually converges to 1
- $C(u,r,t)$ is a degree of dissatisfaction that u has with r
- $W(u,t)$ is the weight factor of u
- $S(r,u,t)$ is a value of quality of services r provides to u

The equation gives a new RP an initial value $I(r,t)$, which converges to 1. Therefore, a new RP should have a trust value around the trust threshold. Each complaint $C(u,r,t)$ has certain weights $W(u,t)$ depending on whether the complaint is originated from a user or from a service, and a user holds a status such as an administrator or a repeat user has more weight than a new user in the system. The sum of complaints divides by the sum of satisfied services will adjust the trust level other time dynamically. Each SOA must decide on the trust level threshold, which is somewhere in the neighborhood of initial value. The distrust is when the trust value is below the threshold. This equation penalizes new RPs severely if there are complaints from users, especially from repeated users or users with administrative status.

Monitoring-based TM. Li and Singhal (2007) report a number of the monitoring-based TM models. However, the models are too specific for peer-to-peer and wireless networks. The OSF needs a simple monitoring-based TM model for RPs to monitor users and other RP services and suggests the following equation:

$$T(u,t) = I(u,t) - \sum_{u \in F} B(u,t) \div \sum_{u \in F} S(u,t) \qquad (2)$$

Where

- F is a set of services and users in the OSF
- u denotes a user or a service who request access to r's service
- t denotes the number of transactions
- $T(u,t)$ is r's trust value evaluated by the relying party
- $I(u,t)$ is a function that computes initial value of u, which eventually converges to 1
- $B(u,t)$ is a degree of dissatisfaction that the relying party has with u
- $S(u,t)$ is a value of normal accesses u has over time

Similar to Equation 1, Equation 2 gives an initial value for trust in $I(u,t)$. Therefore, Equation 2 would penalize repeated users less than new users.

Evidence-based TM. Eschenauer, Gligor, and Baras (2002) consider trust as a set of relationships established with the support of evidences that can be anything from a public key to an address, and an entity can generate evidence for itself and for other entities. In the OSF, evidences are claims that vouch for a user from RPs, PIdPs, and other users. The PIdPs can provide a mechanism for a user to issue a claim and vouch for another user. The mechanism certifies the authenticity of the issuer as well as the user. This allows a TM to validate and evaluate the claim.

Reputation-based TM. Reputation is a social evaluation of the public towards a person or an organization and is context dependent. eBay, Amazon Auctions, and OnSale Exchange are good examples of online marketplaces that use reputation-based TM, which are based mainly on ratings of other peers (Sabater & Sierra, 2005). In the OSF, rating information can be included in the claims that vouch for a user. However, the rating should only be visible only to the trust evaluators. The following equation evaluates trust based on reputation ratings and the weight of the individuals who perform the rating.

$$T(u) = \sum_{i=0}^{n} R \ (r,u) \bullet W \ (r,t) \div n \tag{3}$$

Where

- u denotes a user being evaluated
- r denotes an individual who performs the rating
- t denotes the number of ratings r has made
- n denotes the number of ratings
- $Ri(r,u)$ is the rating value r gives for u
- $Wi(r,t)$ is the weight factor of r
- $T(u)$ is u's trust value based on his reputation rating

Security Policies

The term "security policy" is somewhat ambiguous and overused in the literature. Chang, Chen, and Hsu (2003) define security policy as "descriptions of requirements and mechanisms for securing the communication between participating parties" while Hartel, Eck, Etalle, and Wieringa (2005) define it as "a set of rules that constrain the behavior of a system." Meanwhile, Ortalo (1998) defines security policy as "a set of laws, rules, and practices that regulate how sensitive information and other resources are managed, protected and distributed within a specific system." Oxford Dictionary defines policy as a principle or a course of actions used to guide decisions. A policy does not have any value unless actions are taken to implement the policy. For example, a policy of *reducing greenhouse effect* has no value if governments do not take any action to implement this policy. Subsidizing hybrid cars, fining big polluting industries, funding alternative fuel research, and so forth are some of the actions that implement the greenhouse effect policy. In computer systems, actions are written as rules so that software can interpret and perform the actions. Therefore, the so-call policy languages are logic languages used to represent rules that implement a policy (e.g., PeerTrust, Cassandra, Rei, KAoS). As shown by Kaviani, Gasevic, Hatala, Clement, and Wagner (2007), rules written in these so-called policy languages can be mapped or rewritten in rule languages. Therefore, a security policy implies a set of rules, and writing a policy means writing a set of rules that defines the actions for enforcing a policy. Let us consider the following policy description: "To access resources of an RP, users must be a member of that RP or a member of an RP of that RP trusted circle." The description may be clear enough for a human being to enforce the policy, but unlike humans, computers can only execute rules or instructions. Policy designers must expand the policy descriptions into sets of conditions and actions. These are what rule languages are about (i.e., sets of conditions and actions):

1. If user X presents an affiliation claim signed by an RP in the trusted list, and if the signature is authentic, and if a trusted PIdP has certified the claim, and if the trust management has not flagged the user, then grant user X permission to access the resources.
2. If user X satisfies authentication requirement, then grant user X permission to access the resources.
3. When a user accesses protected items, ask the user for ID. If ID is recognized as a member, then ask PIdP to confirm user authentication. If confirmed, grant user access to the resources. Otherwise, provide a list of trusted RPs and ask for a signed affiliation claim. If the user presents an affiliation claim signed by an RP in the trusted list, and if the signature is authentic, and if a trusted PIdP has certified the claim, and if the trust management has not flagged the user, then grant user X permission to access the resources.

The rules above are not yet executable. They are written in plain English. This step is probably necessary for policy designers to evaluate the accuracy of the policy interpretation. The next step is to put these rules into the rule-based languages so that computer software can execute them. Figure 6 shows a version of these rules implemented in the REWERSW rule markup language (R2ML), which in turn, needs to be adapted for the rule engine used by a particular service provider.

The first two steps (i.e., defining a policy and deciding on rules) require human interventions. Only human can interpret a policy and implement rules to enforce a policy. The interpretation of a policy can differ from one designer to another. Designers can choose different alternatives to enforce a policy. In the above rules, the first two rules combined are equivalent to the third rule, but the third rule adds details on how to handle user ID and how to determine a local user from a remote user. The differences continue to expand when designers put these rules into a rule-based language or implement them in a logic programming language. Writing rules in a markup language such as R2ML is a good way for sharing the rules within a community of practice, but the community must use the same vocabularies or provide vocabulary mappings to keep consistency and interoperability.

Rule Language Interoperability and Flexibility

There are many ways that a policy designer can write rules to enforce the same policy. A designer can also use different vocabularies that have similar definitions. Furthermore, designers can choose different rule languages, and each rule language fits better for a specific interpreter or reasoning engine. All these create a challenge for security policy interoperability. Keep in mind that policy interoperability is a requirement in a service composition framework and hence in the SOA. A service composer must understand the policies of a service to determine if a user can access that service before including the service in a composition. Similarly, understanding business rules of a business partner is a crucial step for a business-to-business (B2B) communication. As a result, rule-based language initiatives have been working to provide interoperable rule languages.

Rule markup language (RuleML) is another proposal for rule interchange format (RIF), which aims to provide a framework for an integrated rule markup approach. It tries to enable participants in the rule community at large to collaborate in establishing translations between existing tag sets and to converge

Figure 6. Access control policy in R2ML

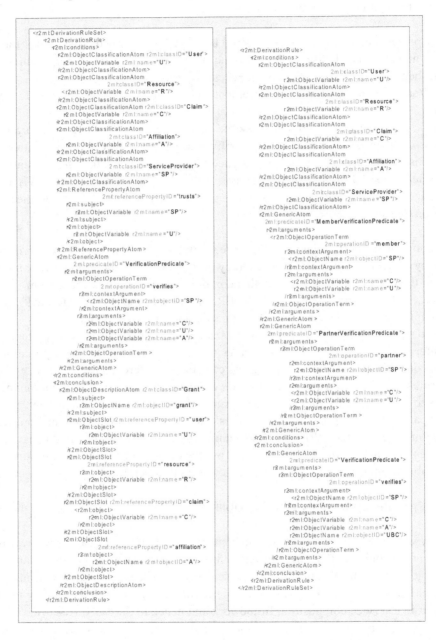

on a shared rule-markup vocabulary (http://www.ruleml.org/). The language is an extensible specification for rule interchange that permits both forward and backward rules. RuleML has generated other rule language derivatives, such as SWRL and SWRL FOL. Semantic Web rule language (SWRL) is a combination of the OWL-DL and OWL-Lite, sublanguages of the OWL Web ontology language, and the unary/binary datalog RuleML sublanguages of the RuleML. It aims to enable Horn-like rules to be combined with an OWL knowledgebase by extending OWL axioms to include Horn-like rules (Horrocks, Patel-Schneider, Boley, Tabet, Grosof, & Dean, 2004). These rule languages are in evolution. Policy designers must be aware of the changes in rule languages and rewrite their policy rules.

W3C launched the RIF Working Group in November 2005 with a goal to bring together business rules and Web architecture to produce a standard for a new rule language that allows rules written for one application to be published, shared, merged and reused in other applications and by other rule engines. The working group has been chartered at least through November 2007 to resolve the rule language interoperability.

R2ML is a general rule interchange language that possesses expressivity for representing four types of rules (i.e., integrity, derivation, reaction, and production) and addresses all RIF requirements. Besides rules, R2ML has its own set of constructs for representing vocabularies and domain ontologies similar to UML or OWL. The R2ML current version is 0.4 (Wagner, Giurca, & Lukichev, 2006), and its abstract syntax is defined with a metamodel by using OMG's metaobject facility (MOF). This means that the whole language definition is represented by using UML diagrams, as MOF uses UML's graphical notation. There are transformations between R2ML and SWRL, OWL, OCL, Jess, Jena, and JBoss rules already implemented. Also there has been efforts (Kaviani et al., 2007) in exploiting the use of R2ML to define policies that can be later exchanged to other policy languages, such as KAoS, Rei, PeerTrust, and so forth. A full description of R2ML in the form of UML class diagrams is given in R2ML Spec (2006), while more details about the language are discussed by Wagner et al. (2006).

OSF Approach for Security Policies

Normally, security policies are shared within a community of practice. The community must agree on the choice of vocabularies and rule engines and on the mapping of vocabularies and rule languages. Code sharing practice of open source community is a good model for sharing security policies. Consider a policy as a block of code or software to be shared. Designers do not have to reveal every detailed implementation. The designers only have to provide an abstract description of the policy, which could be written in rule or logic language shorthand. For example, the following rules (grant(user, affiliation) ← trust(affiliation) v member(user); trust (a) ← a = AU v a = UVic) can represent an access control policy. The rules simply say that if a user is its member or a member of a trusted RP, the RP should grant access to the user. Then, it provides a list of trusted RPs. The policy description contains enough instructions to allow a service composer agent (SCA) to determine if a user meets preliminary requirements to access a service and preselect a list of services that can be used in a service composition. Then, the SCA can enquire the services directly if the user has the access rights and build a knowledgebase for matching users with services to help in the preselection process. Therefore, applying security policies does require a Semantic Web expert. Developers can use a policy (i.e., a set of rules) as long as they know the function of that policy and trust its source, which is similar to using a software component.

The SCA must build a knowledgebase regarding the reliability of each service as well as the success rate for each user to access a particular service. One may look at this knowledgebase as TM since it fits into the category of collecting evidences for determining the dependability of services in relation to a user. Similarly, in addition to affiliation claims, relying parties must monitor access behaviors of every user and use them as evidences to determine the trust level they should put on a user. Bad users are anomalies; their access methods usually do not fit access patterns of regular users in the same category. RPs use TM to protect resources and services from bad users while SCAs use it to find reliable services

Figure 7. Service composition framework

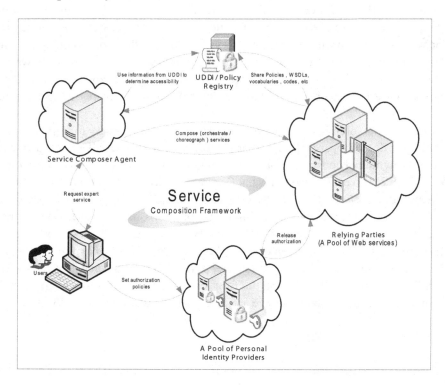

for users. However, SCAs may concern strictly on the technical aspect, which is mostly evidence-based TM. Another TM that helps protect users from malicious RPs is the recommendation-based TM implemented on PIdPs. Although users have the last words whether or not to access a service, OSF must help users making this decisions. One way to provide this help is keeping a knowledgebase for all RPs. Users and SCAs can report bad RPs, and a PIdP can use the information to alert other users and SCAs. Although each component would use a mixed of different types of TMs, SCAs lean toward evidence-based TM while RPs lean toward monitoring-based and reputation-based TM, and PIdPs lean more on recommendation-based TM.

FUTURE TRENDS

The challenge in Internet security over the next few years is to tear down the garden walls that public and private sectors have built over the years to protect sensitive data and allow them to share data securely with each other while strengthening the protection of privacy. Despite of the industry intention to move toward open and intelligent security systems, the legacy of the existing systems drastically hampers this effort. A solution to help ease the transition from domain-centric to user-centric IdM is to adapt user-centric IdM for today's domain-centric IdM. New security solutions such as the OSF must prove beyond doubt that they can support current security requirements. We have conducted an imperial study and have shown that the OSF can support today's most critical security requirements. However, security is context-specific and dependent on the best practices of the users. Replacing a security infrastructure is not a simple task. Users must learn new ways to handle security and work with new security systems. Future Internet security would rely heavily on expert systems to make trust decisions. Hence, it must be supported with strong security policies. The garden walls will eventually be replaced with security policies, and security administrators will need some time to digest these changes in the security practices. Therefore, the study of security in the next few years will be in the area of trust management and security policy modeling and best practices for the security policy design.

CONCLUSION

We have shown that the OSF can support today's most critical security requirements while having the flexibility to provide security for the SOA environment. Having one agent, a personal identity provider, to manage the identity data, makes it easy for users to monitor their personal security and prevent identity theft. As users adhere to different relying parties, they build their reputation and are able to make strong arguments when joining new relying parties. OSF can provide numerous functionalities to strengthen the Internet security and help users make the right decisions. Each critical component keeps a knowledgebase and is able to make trust decisions based on the most current available trust information. Negotiating shared resource policies between institutions becomes easier when the negotiation is one-to-one. Trust federation is formed dynamically as institutions begin to share resources with each other. Therefore, trust management in the OSF is individual-based and based on a real life trust model. It is highly dynamic and flexible. Moreover, OSF makes it possible for complex expert services that require multiple sets of credentials to operate. The framework allows users to set policies to preauthorize their consents for the release of their personal data and allow services to collaborate with each other. Changes toward user-centric and open security are imminent, and the transition is expected to be rather difficult. One way to ease this transition is to build personal identity providers that can share user identity data and give a choice to users to select a personal identity provider to manage all their identity data from a single point of entry. Undoubtedly, OSF provides a security framework for ongoing research in the area of Semantic Web services to move forward and offer better quality of Web services.

REFERENCES

Bhargav-Spantzely, A., Camenisch, J., Gross, T., & Sommer, D. (2006). User centricity: A taxonomy and open issues. In *Proceedings of the Second ACM Workshop on Digital Identity Management, DIM '06* (pp. 1-10). Alexandria: ACM Press.

Camenisch, J., Gross, T., & Sommer, D. (2006). Enhancing privacy of federated identity management protocols: Anonymous credentials in WS-security. In *Proceedings of the 5th ACM Workshop on Privacy in Electronic Society, WPES '06* (pp. 67-72). Alexandria: ACM Press.

Cameron, K. (2005). *The laws of identity Microsoft Corporation.* Retrieved June 10, 2007, from http://msdn2.microsoft.com/en-us/library/ms996456.aspx

Cervesato, I., Jaggard, A. D., Scedrov, A., & Walstad, C. (2005). Specifying Kerberos 5 cross-realm authentication. In *Proceedings of the 2005 Workshop on Issues in the Theory of Security, WITS '05* (pp. 12-26). Long Beach: ACM Press.

Chang, S., Chen, Q., & Hsu, M. (2003). Managing security policy in a large distributed Web services environment. In *Proceedings of the 27th Annual International Conference on Computer Software and Applications, COMPSAC 2003* (pp. 610-62). Pleasanton: IEEE Press.

Chappell, D. (2006). *Introducing windows CardSpaceMicrosoft Corporation.* Retrieved June 10, 2007, from http://msdn.microsoft.com/library/default.asp?url=/library/en-us/dnlong/html/introinfocard.asp

Clauβ, S., Kesdogan, D., & Kölsch, T. (2005). Privacy enhancing identity management: Protection against re-identification and profiling. In *Proceedings of the 2005 Workshop on Digital Identity Management, DIM '05* (pp. 84-93). Fairfax: ACM Press.

Clauβ, S., & Schiffner, S. (2006). Structuring anonymity metrics. In *Proceedings of the Second ACM Workshop on Digital Identity Management, DIM '06* (pp. 55-62). Alexandria: ACM Press.

Cotroneo, D., Graziano, A., & Russo, S. (2004). Security requirements in service oriented architectures for ubiquitous computing. In *Proceedings of the 2nd Workshop on Middleware for Pervasive and Ad-Hoc Computing, MPAC '04* (pp 172-177). Toronto: ACM Press.

Davenport, D. (2002). Anonymity on the Internet: Why the price may be too high. *Communications of the ACM, 45*(4), 33-35.

Eschenauer, L., Gligor, V. D., & Baras, J. (2002). On trust establishment in mobile ad-hoc networks. *Lecture Notes in Computer Science, 1*(2845/2003), 47-66.

Farkas, C., Ziegler, G., Meretei, A., & Lörincz, A. (2002). Anonymity and accountability in self-organizing electronic communities. In *Proceedings of the 2002 ACM Workshop on Privacy in the Electronic Society, WPES '02* (pp. 81-90). Washington: ACM Press.

Grandison, T., & Sloman, M. (2000). A survey of trust in Internet applications. *IEEE Communications Surveys and Tutorials, 1*(3), 2-16.

Hardt, D. (2006). *ETech 2006: Who is the dick on my site? Sxip.* Retrieved June 10, 2007, from http://identity20.com/media/ETECH_2006/

Hartel, P., Eck, P., Etalle, S., & Wieringa, R. (2005). Modelling mobility aspects of security policies. *Lecture Notes in Computer Science, 1*(3362/2005), 172-19.

Horrocks, I., Patel-Schneider, P. F., Boley, H., Tabet,S., Grosof, B., & Dean, M. (2005). *SWRL: A Semantic Web rule language combining OWL and RuleML.* Retrieved June 15, 2007, form http://www.w3.org/Submission/SWRL/

Jones, M. B. (2006). *The identity metasystem: A user-centric, inclusive Web authentication solution.* Retrieved June 10, 2007, from http://research.microsoft.com/~mbj/papers/InfoCard_W3C_Web_Authentication.pdf

Juels, A., Winslett, M., & Goto, G. (2006). Abstract. In *Proceedings of the Second ACM Workshop on Digital Identity Management, DIM '06.*

Kaviani, N., Gasevic, D., Hatala, M., Clement, D., & Wagner, G. (2007). Integration of rules and policies for Semantic Web services. *International Journal of Advanced Media and Communication (IJAMC)*.

Kim, B. R., Kim, K. C., & Kim, Y. S. (2005). Securing anonymity in P2P network. In *Proceedings of the 2005 Joint Conference on Smart Objects and Ambient Intelligence, SOc-EUSAI '05* (pp. 231-234). Grenoble: ACM Press.

Li, H., & Singhal, M. (2007). Trust management in distributed systems. *Computer, 1*(40), 45-53.

Miller, J. (2006). *Yadis specification 1.0.* Retrieved June 10, 2007, from http://yadis.org/papers/yadis-v1.0.pdf

Morgan, R. L., Cantor, S., Carmody, S., Hoehn, W., & Klingenstein, K. (2004). Federated security: The shibboleth approach. *EDUCAUSE Quarterly, 24*, 8-22. Retrieved June 10, 2007, from http://www.educause.edu/apps/eq/eqm04/eqm0442.asp

Ortalo, R. (1998). A flexible method for information system security policy specification. *Lecture Notes in Computer Science, 1*(1485/1998), 67-84.

Recordon, D., & Reed, D. (2006). OpenID 2.0: A platform for user-centric identity management. In *Proceedings of the Second ACM Workshop on Digital Identity Management, DIM '06* (pp. 11-16). Alexandria: ACM Press.

Sabater, J., & Sierra, C. (2005). Review on computational trust and reputation models. *Artificial Intelligence Review, 1*(24), 33-60.

Wagner, G., Giurca, A., & Lukichev, S. (2006). A usable interchange format for rich syntax rules integrating OCL, RuleML and SWRL. In *Proceeding of 15ᵗʰ International World Wide Web Conferences*. Edinburgh: ACM Press.

Xiong, L., & Liu, L. (2004). PeerTrust: Supporting reputation-based trust for peer-to-peer electronic communities. *Knowledge and Data Engineering, IEEE Transactions, 1*(16), 843-857.

Chapter XIII
Providing Web Services Security
SLA Guarantees:
Issues and Approaches

Vishal Dwivedi
Infosys Technologies Limited, India

Srinivas Padmanabhuni
Infosys Technologies Limited, India

ABSTRACT

This chapter underlines the importance of security service level agreements (SLAs) for Web services. As Web services are increasingly incorporated in the mainstream enterprises, the need for security has led to various standards. However unlike nonfunctional requirements such as performance, scalability and so forth, which are quantitative and are enforced through SLAs, security is represented only through policies. There exist quite a few frameworks for security at different levels of enactment; however, what is clearly missing is an approach to represent security SLAs and enacting them for a Web service environment. In this chapter, we primarily focus on two aspects. We first focus on the security requirements for Web services and the currently available stack of security mechanisms and frameworks for achieving security at various levels of Web service implementation. The second focus is on how these could be utilized to build security SLAs, which could be enforced on Web services. Later in the chapter we suggest a conceptual model to represent these SLA clauses and present an approach to enact them.

INTRODUCTION

The increased adoption of service-oriented architecture (SOA) in enterprise context has drawn attention to nonfunctional aspects as security and privacy. Web services, being the building blocks of SOA, require service level agreement (SLA) guarantees not only for performance attributes such as reliability and availability but also for other nonfunctional attributes such as security and privacy. The raison d'être for Web services is that they could be used to compose new services. In that sense the conventional notions of "trusted party paradigms" for composition also apply to the Web services. Not only does a secure service composition have to be ascertained but it has to be also ensured that the provider of the Web services could give security SLA guarantees.

In this work we capture some of the security requirements for composition and execution of Web services. We address some of the issues related to security and privacy in the Web services domain, and we discuss some of the current approaches followed to address them. Right from network level security protocols like secure socket layer (SSL), transport layer security (TLS), and so forth, to the SOAP level, and until the federation level security standards, we look at the existing security stacks for Web services. We explore how SLAs are enacted in terms of other nonfunctional requirements like performance and availability and present a mechanism to represent security SLAs. Towards the end we present a conceptual model to represent the security SLAs and an approach to enact them.

BACKGROUND

SLAs have been commonly used to specify nonfunctional requirements which ascertain the criteria for the correct operation of the system. Typical nonfunctional requirements which are covered through SLAs today include reliability, scalability, cost and so forth, most of which are measurable attributes. The need for a Web service security SLA arises from the fact that Web services are designed to be composed from candidate services, the credentials of each required to be verified for an enterprise level service orchestration. A security SLA would typically comprise of the following quality of service (QoS) attributes:

- **Access Control:** Provision of only need-to-know information/privileges.
- **Authorization and Authentication:** The prevention of data/information access by invalid users.
- **Availability:** The prevention of degradation or interruption as a consequence of failures.
- **Confidentiality:** The prevention of unauthorized disclosure of data.
- **Integrity:** The prevention of unauthorized modification of data.

There exist quite a few approaches, standards, and frameworks which address the above issues for implementing security for Web services. Security assertion markup language (SAML) is an XML standard designed by OASIS for exchanging authentication and authorization data between service and identity providers. Not only does it provided support for transport-level security (through SSL 3.0 and TLS 1.0), but it also ensured message-level security (using **XML signature** and **XML encryption**). Later, Liberty alliance extended SAML for identity management. Although SAML was used as a de-facto industry standard for exchanging authorization information, it was limited by its declarative limitations and was followed by extensible access control markup language (XACML), which provided support for a more declarative-access control-policy definition. Later in 2006, W3C defined WS-policy as a XML-based standard for definition and specification of Web services policies (on security and QoS, etc.)

In spite of all these frameworks and standards, security SLAs were never enacted in real life. In this work we discuss the need for security SLAs, some of the current work towards providing security SLA guarantees, and towards the end we suggest our approach for enactment of security SLAs.

SECURITY REQUIREMENTS FOR WEB SERVICES

Security SLAs would work with typical security attributes that represent the overall set of security QoS requirements of the concerned system. In case of Web services, while the core security requirements of online systems apply, they need to be aware of the specific requirements of Web services. In this section, we shall cover the basic requirements of Web services security.

Any implementation of SOA has three fundamental roles, that is, 1) service provider, 2) service requestor, and 3) service registry, and three fundamental operations, that of 1) publish, 2) find, and 3) bind (as shown in Figure 1). The service provider *publishes* details pertaining to service invocation with a services registry. The service requestor *finds* the details of a service from the service registry. The service requestor then invokes (*binds*) the service on the service provider.

Figure 2 highlights the mapping of **security requirements** to the stakeholders in any Web services system. The crucial requirements in Web services security are highlighted below.

- **Access control and authorization:** The core need to provide for only need-to-know information/access is applied in Web services at multiple levels. Such mechanisms in Web services need to provide for service level access control; additionally, they also need to accommodate individual operation (method) level access control. The standards primarily used in Web services access control and authorization include XACML and WS-policy.
- **Authentication:** The phenomenon of providing access to services to only genuine users is of prime concern in Web services. In Web services, the crucial issue in authentication is that at the message level, the fact of having being authenticated is carried across by clients in standards-based format in Web services messages/headers to allow for interoperability between different authenticating systems.
- **Single sign-on:** Diverse provider systems communicate with each other via Web services, and it becomes impractical to maintain mutual access control information and authentication databases. A useful solution in this context is the provision of **single sign-on**, wherein the diverse systems map

Figure 1. Service oriented architecture

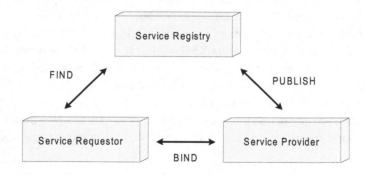

Figure 2. Security requirements in service oriented architecture

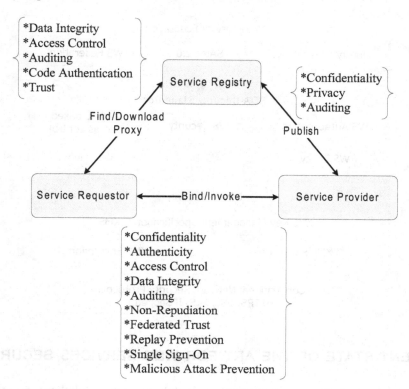

credentials to each other; an authentication at one source is accepted at other providers within the time-to-live period of the credential. A useful standard for single sign-on in Web services systems in SAML. A useful use case of single sign-on in Web services is that of federated identity, wherein users can federate their identities across heterogeneous Web sites and services.

- **Availability:** The prevention of degradation or interruption in a Web service is crucial in business context. It is hence imperative that appropriate measures be put in place for avoiding denial-of-service attacks on Web services, and likewise avoiding malicious content attacks like viruses, Trojan horses, XML buffer overflow attacks, and so forth. An appropriate mechanism deployed in Web services is the usage of **XML firewalls**, which unlike packet filtering firewalls can accommodate for content introspection at the gateway and operate at higher levels of TCP/IP stack.
- **Confidentiality and privacy:** In the context of Web services, it if often necessary that not only a provision be made for prevention of disclosure of the whole service message, but additionally quite often there is a need to prevent disclosure of only part of a message while leaving the whole message intact. Standards like XML encryption allow for such partial message level encryption.
- **Data integrity:** The requirement of prevention of tampering of a piece of data is applicable in the case of Web services to parts of a message, in addition to the conventional need for preserving integrity of a whole piece of data. This is due to the fact that in a Web services scenario, while parts of a message should not be altered, some parts need to be modified while passing through intermediaries like proxies, a service bus, and so forth. Such requirements are met by the **XML signature** standard, which allows for partial signing of XML documents.

Figure 3. Web services security standards stack

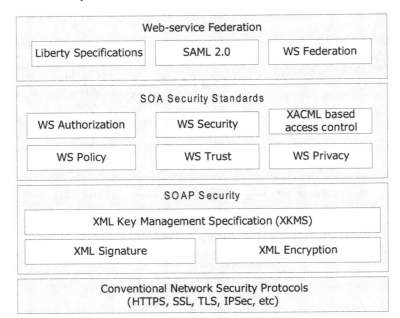

THE CURRENT STATE OF THE ART FOR WEB SERVICES SECURITY

In view of the special requirements of the security needs of Web services, a plethora of standards are being worked at W3C, OASIS, IETF, and other standards bodies to enable faster adoption of Web services.

The standards for security in Web services extend standard mechanisms like encryption, digital signature, and public-key infrastructure to handle XML and Web services specific nuances and problems. Some of the protocols are work-in-progress and some have been standardized already. Hence the adoption of some of these protocols is not complete, and in fact there are proprietary protocols implemented by some vendors already. A top-level hierarchy of Web services standards is presented in Figure 3.

The W3C defines a Web service as a software system designed to support interoperable machine-to-machine interaction over a network. Quite often Web services are implemented as Web APIs that can be accessed over a network, such as the Internet, and executed on a remote system hosting the requested services. These Web services are thus accessed by sending SOAP messages to service endpoints, which perform certain operations and respond with SOAP responses for corresponding results or faults. Thus the Web service security not only comprises of securing these messages over the network but also provides the correct level of access control. At the base layer of Figure 3 we represent the conventional network security protocols such as HTTPS, SSL, TLS, and so forth. These ensure secure point-to-point messaging.

Thus at the bottom layer of Web services security standards, these standards are attempts to remap the existing concepts in Web-based security to XML message level security. In that sense these protocols stress on message-level security in contrast to session level protocols in the Web-based world. All the protocols at this level specify how to carry security data as part of XML documents. The ability to encrypt/sign only parts of XML documents is a critical part of security requirements for Web services as mentioned in the previous section.

At a higher level we represent the currently practiced approaches of encrypting the SOAP messages to ensure integrity and authenticity during transfer. The multihop data transfer scenarios in Web services require partial signing of SOAP requests which could be achieved through a XML signature. As specified by Padmanabhuni and Adarkar (2003), such XML signatures could be:

- **Detached**, wherein the XML signature is separated from the content it signs.
- **Enveloped**, wherein the XML signature is over the XML content it signs.
- **Enveloping**, wherein the XML signature is over the content found within an object element of the signature, which could be provided as a reference to a URI.

The structure of such a signed XML document can be seen in Figure 4.

XML encryption ("XML encryption spec," 2002) and XML key management specification (XKMS) ("XKMS spec," 2001) are some other approaches used to secure a SOAP message and ensure its integrity. While XML encryption allows selective encryption of the XML data, XKMS allows effective registration and management of public keys.

On a further higher level we place the SOA security standards stacks which utilize the functionality below. Today there exist quite a few Web service security standards right from SOAP level security to authentication and authorization management. The prominent amongst them are the following:

WS-security describes how to attach **signature** and encryption headers to SOAP messages. In addition, it describes how to attach security tokens—including binary security tokens such as X.509 certificates and Kerberos tickets—to messages. ("WS-security spec," 2002)

WS-policy represents a set of specifications that describe the capabilities and constraints of the security (and other business) policies on intermediaries and endpoints (e.g., required security tokens, supported encryption algorithms, and privacy rules) and how to associate policies with services and endpoints. ("WS-Policy Spec," 2002)

WS-trust describes a framework for trust models that enables Web services to securely interoperate by requesting, issuing, and exchanging security tokens. ("WS-Trust Spec," 2007)

WS-privacy describes a model for how Web services and requestors state privacy preferences and organizational privacy practice statements. (WS-privacy)

Figure 4. Structure of XML signature document

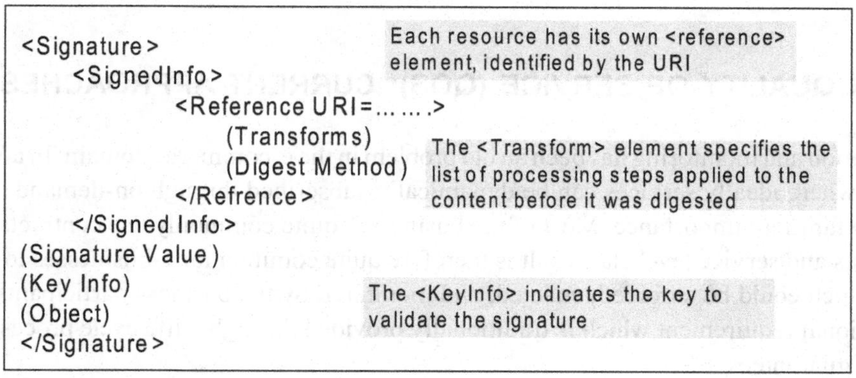

```
<Signature>                          Each resource has its own <reference>
    <SignedInfo>                     element, identified by the URI
        <Reference URI=.........>
            (Transforms)             The <Transform> element specifies the
            (Digest Method)          list of processing steps applied to the
        </Refrence>                  content before it was digested
    </Signed Info>
(Signature Value)
(Key Info)
(Object)                             The <KeyInfo> indicates the key to
</Signature>                         validate the signature
```

WS-secure conversation describes how to manage and authenticate message exchanges between parties, including security context exchanges and establishing and deriving session keys. ("WS-secure conversation spec," 2005)

WS-authorization describes how to manage authorization data and authorization policies. ("WS authorization spec," 2003)

XACML stands for extensible access control markup language ("XACML spec," 2003). It is a declarative access control policy language implemented in XML and a processing model describing how to interpret the policies.

One standard way to handle security requirements is to annotate WSDL with nonfunctional requirement descriptors. WS-security tokens can then be associated with either i) the binding associated with the operations or ii) the operations themselves. The examples for both can be found below:

```
<wsdl: binding name
="DOCSTYLESummationOPENSAMLUSESoapBinding"
type ="impl:DocService">
<wsdlsoap:binding style="document"
transport="http://scemas.xmlsoap.org/soap/http"/>
 -<wsdl:operation name ="calculateAddition">
   <wsdlsoap: operation soapAction=""/>
  -<wsdl:input name ="calculateAdditionRequest">
     <wsdlsoap:body use="literal"/>
  -<wsdl:output name ="calculateAdditionResponse">
     <wsdlsoap:body use="literal"/>
   </wsdl:output>
 </wsdl:operation>
</wsdl:binding>
```

```
<wsdl:operation name="calculateAddition">
  <wsdlsoap: operation soapAction=""/>
 -<wsdl:input name="calculateAdditionRequest">
     <wsdlsoap:body encodingStyle"http://schemas.xmlsoap.org/
     soap /encoding/" namespace="http://RPCServices"
     use ="encoded"/>
   <wsdlsoap:header message="wsse:SecurityHeader"
     namespace ="http://docs.oasis-open.org/wss/2004/01/oasis-
     200401 -wss-wsssecurity-secext-1.0.xsd" part="userToken"
     use ="literal" />
 </wsdl:input>
 <wsdl:output name="calculateAdditionResponse">
   <wsdlsoap:body encodingStyle"http://schemas.xmlsoap.org/
     soap /encoding/"       ------
 </wsdl:operation>
</wsdl:binding>
```

WSS security tags associated with the binding   *WSS security tags associated with operations*

On a further higher level we place the layer of Web service federation which ensures that user identities across various locations can be securely recognized through a single sign-on infrastructure. The whole approach of federated identity management is based on leveraging the trust relationships across the organizations. The security standards which we defined above ensure that in spite of the existence of multiple heterogeneous protocols which manage the identities, the users are allowed means like single sign-on across disparate applications. Liberty specifications ("Liberty specifications," 2007) and WS-federation ("WS-federation spec," 2003) are two specifications which have become quite popular today for federated identity management.

SLAS FOR QUALITY OF SERVICE (QOS): CURRENT APPROACHES

SLA specification and monitoring has been an old problem in the e-commerce domain. In a Web services environment where ideally services can be dynamically subscribed through on-demand mechanisms, SLAs assume far more importance. Most of the businesses quite commonly use contracts as means to lay down trusts and service level clauses. It is therefore quite common for e-businesses to rely on SLA guarantees which could be enforced, enacted, and monitored by the business participants. Security is one nonfunctional requirement which is traditionally provided through a life cycle process rather than through SLA guarantees.

Some of the current approaches for SLA provisioning include provisioning through e-contracts, that is, providing support through business process monitoring based on rules and alerts. IBM's Web service level agreements (WSLA) project provides a framework for specifying and monitoring SLAs for Web services. The WSLA project essentially provides an XML language for SLA specification and a run-time comprising of several SLA monitoring services. SweetRules (supporting Situated Courteous Logic Programs in RuleML) and SweetDeal (supporting e-contracting) were proposed by Grosof and Poon (2003) as systems for specification of business rules which could be enacted and monitored. There exist other approaches, too, for SLA provisioning and monitoring, with the principal idea of using rules for QoS monitoring.

IBM's WSLA Approach for Web-Service SLA Management

A contract defines the relationship between two of more parties by defining the clauses to be followed and hence the SLAs to be adhered too. In terms of Web services, a service contract defines the actors (e.g., the service provider, service consumer, integrators, the infrastructure providers, etc.), the obligations, the permissions, prohibitions, and the SLAs. Thus, overall, it captures the obligations of one party to the other and the SLAs which one agrees to adhere to. IBM's WSLA provides a framework for SLAs for Web services. WSLA is thus one standard for monitoring and managing services. It is therefore designed to have a flexible SLA definition language and a run-time architecture which could help in SLA monitoring.

WSLA along with SLA management ensures workload management, resource provisioning and measurement, and management of monitoring of Web services through a distributed monitoring framework. The SLAs are represented in XML as an SLA template which are translated into configuration information for various WSLA components.

As shown in Figure 5 WSLA uses metrics for SLA monitoring and enactment. Typical metrics comprise of the following:

- **Resource Metrics:** retrieved directly from the resource residing in the service provider tier.
- **Composition Metrics:** Composed out of resource or other composed metrics according to a specific algorithm.
- **Business Metrics:** Relate SLAs parameters to financial terms specific to a service customer.
- **SLA Parameters:** Put the metrics available from a service provider in the context of a specific customer/

And the typical SLA monitoring services comprise of the following:

- **Establishment and Deployment Service:** Negotiation and authoring.
- **Measurement Service:** Measures resource metrics and aggregates them in SLA parameters.
- **Condition Evaluation Service:** Notifies the parties about the violation of SLA.
- **Management Service:** Takes action to correct problems that occurred due to the violation of SLA.

The WSLA framework ensures that SLAs could be created by the customers, deployed in a distributed manner,. and could be enacted and monitored by services. By allowing a formal specification of

Figure 5. WSLA approach for differentiation based on SLAs

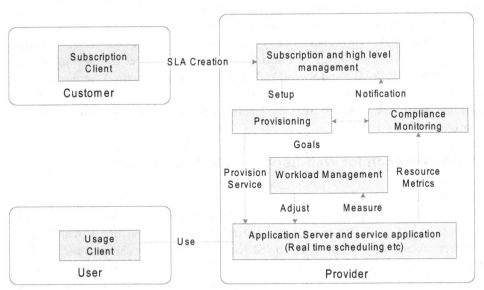

Figure 6. The WSLA SLA monitoring model

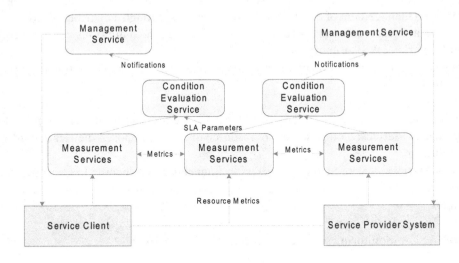

SLAs (in a language as shown in Figure 7), which are captured through metrics that could be aggregated to satisfy the service contract clauses, it ensures that service obligations of parties are met and are monitored continuously.

Issues with Current Approaches

Web service-based architectures which focus intensively on XML messaging have brought about a big change in the manner in which security mechanisms are dealt with. They have moved the focus from

Figure 7. The WSLA XML language

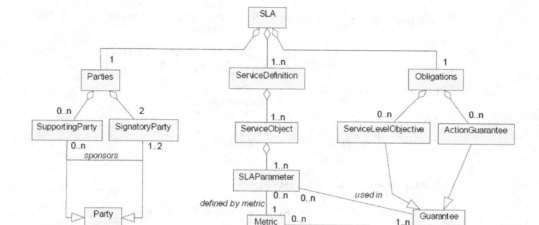

traditional channel-level security management to message-level security management. Even the availability of the Web services has ensured a high level of lose coupling of system security wherein single sign-on approaches ensure distributed identity management. However, in spite of all these approaches, the problem which still lurks around is that how an organization can ensure security and provide definite SLA guarantees. Security in itself is unbounded, and hence, there is often a requirement to draw a line between service and operating margins. Unless there are SLAs defined, this is a difficult task.

Currently there exist a gamut of security specifications and their implementations by different vendors. But what is lacking is a standard way to provide them as SLA guarantees, like the aspects related to performance and availability. Frameworks like WSLA ("WSLA-spec," 2003), which provide support for service guarantees based on performance measures using composite metrics, do not support security metrics. The biggest issue has been in regard to the qualitative nature of the security attributes, which necessitate a process-based approach.

THE NEED FOR SECURITY SLAS

Most of the current works in the SLA provisioning domain have focused mainly on nonfunctional parameters like availability, reliability, performance, and so forth. Although there has been a huge amount of work in the domain of Web service security, provisioning of SLAs based on security attributes has not been worked upon much. In an e-business scenario comprising of Web services, trust is a major factor which could be guided by SLA guarantees. Although random dynamic service composition over the Web seems like an ideal scenario, business pragmatism demands a level of understanding before

Figure 8. The role of business level agreements in SLA formation

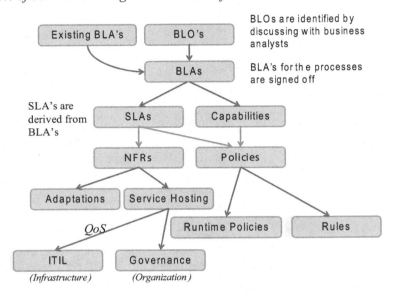

services are composed from candidate services. Such trust can only be achieved if the parties ensure a SLA guarantee for their services, which would encompass authorization, authentication, confidentiality, and integrity.

While frameworks like WSLA are good for monitorable, operational nonfunctional requirements, security is mostly considered aspectual and hence considered quite difficult to monitor. The typical enactment of security is often similar to functional requirements where it is enacted more as a process rather than as an SLA. It should be taken into consideration that the rationale behind any SLA monitoring is to ascertain that business level objectives (BLOs) are met. These BLOs translate into business level agreements (BLAs), which in turn form the basis of SLAs.

HANDLING SECURITY REQUIREMENTS: CURRENT APPROACH

Web services security is normally captured as nonfunctional aspects during service identification (requirements phase). These are then converted into security policies which are then aggregated to form enterprise-wide security policy descriptions. Some of these policies, when they become a part of business level objectives, could form the SLAs between any two parties. These security SLAs are mostly nonquantifiable, but, nevertheless, they are an integral part of BLOs and must be adhered too.

As shown in Figure 10, a security requirement necessitating the secure credential transfer across domains is broken down into policies, which are mapped to the enterprise security policy. Although these policies could be enacted using the enterprise applications, governance proves to be a major issue. One of the major concerns for the service environments thus proves to be formulating the requirements into SLAs and then implementing them and monitoring them for their proper enactment. Thus the key step here is to map the security requirements to the activities and clauses and to the corresponding security mechanisms provided by the different implementations. Traditionally this problem has been

Figure 9. Handling security during service identification and requirements analysis

Influencing Factors			Technical Requirements for security							
Information Sensitivity Level (Confidential, Secret, Operational or Public)	Trust Boundaries Involved		Authentication	Authorization	Message Encryption	Message Integrity	Audit	Flow of Security Context	Non Repudiation	Security Policy
	From	To								
Confidential/Major	Trusted	Trusted	O	O			O		O	
	Trusted	Semi-trusted								
	Trusted	Un-Trusted								
	Semi-trusted	Trusted	O	O			O			O
	Semi-trusted	Semi-trusted								
	Semi-trusted	Un-Trusted								
	Un-Trusted	Trusted								
	Un-Trusted	Semi-trusted								
Operational/Minor	Trusted	Trusted								
	Trusted	Semi-trusted	O							
	Trusted	Un-Trusted								
	Semi-trusted	Trusted								
	Semi-trusted	Semi-trusted								
	Semi-trusted	Un-Trusted								
	Un-Trusted	Trusted	O				O			O
	Un-Trusted	Semi-trusted								

handled through rules as by Grosof and Poon (2003), and exceptions (as in Chiu, Li, & Karlapalem, 1999), which are checked during the task execution. A security contract (as shown in Figure 11) which specifies the security clauses, tasks, and their participants could be a good starting point for the above policy specification. This contract could then be enacted to ensure that the security SLAs are met.

Figure 11 gives a conceptual model for a Web service contract specifying clauses to be satisfied by a service-based infrastructure. The principal components of the above include contract clauses which are derived from the SLAs to be met, the tasks required to fulfill the clauses, the respective security mechanisms they require, and the exceptions which a task throws up. The above conceptual model is derived from the **EC^{FS}** model (Tiwari, Dwivedi, & Karlapalem, 2007) which we use for process security.

ENUMERATING SECURITY SLA COMPONENTS FOR A SERVICES SECURITY CONTRACT

As per the definition of SLAs, that is, "a formally negotiated agreement between two parties which allows for monitoring of the agreement by specifying the levels of availability, serviceability, performance, operation or other attributes of the service which must be adhered too by the parties," it is imperative

Figure 10. Translating security requirements into policies

Security Requirement Statement	#	Security Policy
The services need authentication supporting multiple ways of passing on the credentials allowing both consumers from within and outside the domain to be able to use the service.	P1	All connections made out side the domain will have to be through secured channel (https).
	P2	128 bit keys should be used to encrypt passwords and other confidential data. The service has to support TDES, RSA and AES symmetric key algorithms, MD5 and SHA1 hashing functions.
	P3	The username should be supported with either password or Kerberos tickets for authentication. A PKI infrastructure should be associated with the transfer of the credentials in case of connections made outside domain.

Map to existing Enterprise security policy / Add new policies

#	Enterprise security policy descriptions
GP1	All connections to the Internet must go through a properly secured connection point to ensure the network is protected when the data is classified confidential.
GP2	Access to the network and servers and systems should be achieved by individual and unique logins, and should require authentication. Authentication includes the use of passwords, smart cards, biometrics, or other recognized forms of authentication.
GP3	Monitoring must be implemented on all systems including recording logon attempts and failures, successful logons and date and time of logon and logoff.

that security, although a qualitative measure, could be specified and enacted through SLA attributes.

Some of the security SLA criteria could be built using one or many amongst the following attributes:

- Authentication mechanism/level
- Authorization mechanism/level
- Message encryption mechanism
- Message integrity mechanism
- Possibility of audit
- Nonrepudiation
- Security policy
- Information sensitivity level: public, operational, secret, confidential
- Interaction level: (semi/un/totally) trusted to (semi/un/totally) trusted
- Level of federation
- Type of WSDL annotator used for service descriptions annotated with security NFRs
- Translating security requirement into policies
- Introducing security policies as aspects into services
- And many more such aspects

These SLA parameters along with the desired mechanism or level as agreed to by the parties are then encapsulated to form a security contract containing clauses, the contract activities, and the parties concerned. These security contract clauses are then enacted through discrete tasks. Thus policies, as defined in Figure 10, would form the input for clauses which are enacted through a set of tasks and rules which could be either manual or automated.

Figure 11. A conceptual model for a services security contract

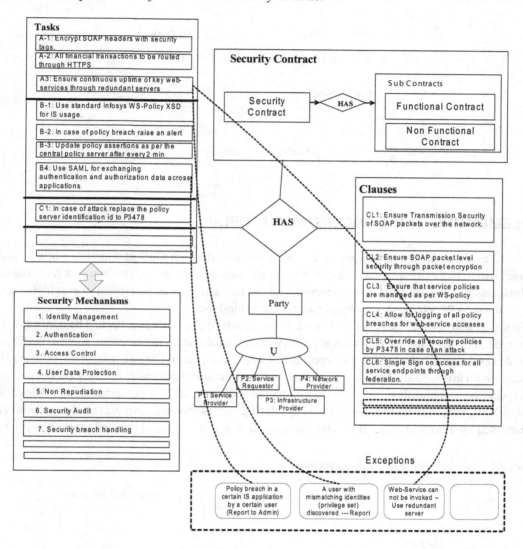

Specifications like WS-policy ("WS-policy spec," 2002) and WS-security ("WS security spec," 2002) help to specify some of the above properties as assertions, which could be simple or declarative with conditions attached. Although the WS-policy specification does not specify how it is to be used, there has been some work where it has been integrated along with the service WSDL. Where certain security requirements necessitate a process rather than a simple conditional assertion, the **EC**[FS] security framework (as described in the next section) can be utilized for the same. Some of our work (e.g., Tiwari et al., 2006) mentions how EC[FS] is utilized to provide SLAs for security using metaworkflows.

Figure 12. A conceptual model for a services security contract

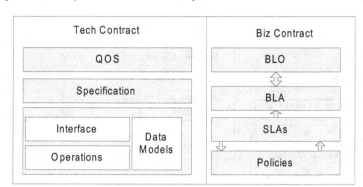

IMPLEMENTING THE CONCEPTUAL MODEL

Figure 12 explains how a tech contract could be handled through QoS parameters while a business contract which has more qualitative aspects is based more on aspects such as business level objectives and business level agreements. The conceptual model in Figure 11 can be broken in executable activity party clauses (**APC clauses**), which are enacted as a rule-base.

Figure 13 above describes the security SLA conformance checking approach. The major issue with security SLAs is that they involve checking policy conformance rather than measurement of performance attributes as defined in the WSLA-like approach. These policies could be either business policies or tech policies which are most of the times aspectual and are monitored manually or using processes.

Aspects such as multilevel security definition and security criteria representation could be captured within a XML language (as in Figure 14), encapsulating parties, clauses, activities, and exception criteria as discussed by Tiwari et al. (2007), who describes how processes could be used to enact security.

Figure 13. Checking security SLA conformance

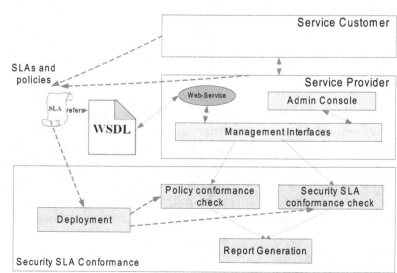

The set of clauses ensures that processes follow the defined security mechanisms which could be audited by any party. An e-contract thus lays down a set of deterministic tasks and rules which need to be followed during process execution.

Implementing security e-contract at systems level needs significant caution and effort as we need to guarantee that

1. All security conditions specified in clauses are correctly implemented.
2. No other operation can be performed (or information is extracted) than what has been specified to be done on a task by a specific role (or user).

Certain SLAs which are totally process-oriented can be enacted using our extended e-contract framework for security (EC^{FS} framework) which allows the modeling, design, and deployment of security e-contracts and their monitoring through security metaworkflows, which could ensure both intrusive and nonintrusive monitoring (in the latter case for auditing purposes).

The EC^{FS} framework is mainly utilized in scenarios which involve process-based security. Although the work (i.e., Tiwari et al., 2007) focuses mainly on RBAC and TBAC coupling over processes for granting need to know privileges, similar could be extended to implement metaworkflows for ensuring processes security. The APC constructs as defined in Figure 14 along with the event condition action (ECA) rules are utilized to implement these metaworkflows which ensure security. The usage of the framework is particularly in scenarios involving policy enactment through workflows, which is typical for a security environment.

The EC^{FS} has the following four main layers:

1. **Document layer:** This layer comprises of XML-based e-contract specifications, the examples of which could be any of the following: RuleML, ECML, tpaML, ebXML, and so forth.
2. **Conceptual layer:** This layer comprises of the metamodel of the security e-contract, the UML structure for which is given in Figure 11. It is mainly used for representing the activities, clauses,

Figure 14. A collection of activity party clauses (APC) which form the rule base for service contract

Party	`<Party`
	 `    <PNO> ...... <>`
	 `    <Activity 1> <Activity 2> ....`
	 `</Party>`

Activity	`<Acknowledgement No =" ">`
	 `< ..........>`
	 `<Operation name =" " type =" ">`
	 `<Clause > <Exp>`

Clause	`<Clauses>`
	 `<ClauseNo ...... >`
	
	 `</Clauses>`

the actors, their interrelationships, and the security mechanisms which should guide the activities under specific contract clauses.

3. **Logical layer:** This layer comprises of the data model, event condition action (**ECA**) rules, APC constructs, and is mainly used to map the e-contract to underlying business processes.

4. **Implementation layer:** This layer provides for the workflow management and execution infrastructure along with the service infrastructure (Web services) for business activity monitoring (BAM) and in this case monitoring the execution of processes which were defined through an e-contract.

Figure 15 (which is based on the work of Tiwari et al., [2007]) represents the four layers of the EC^{FS} framework. In Figure 11 we represent a sample Web services security contract. The contract defined above lays down clauses which define rules. Exceptions from the clauses are provided as rules which can be triggered or may trigger certain tasks. A set of tasks need to be executed to fulfill a particular clause by ensuring a particular security mechanism. The given e-contract is then represented in XML (similar to Fig 11) consisting of a set of ordered pairs of clauses, activities, and actors. Our security metamodel is similar to ER^{EC} metaschema template but differs in being domain-specific and using security mechanisms for realization of the clauses through tasks. We further use the notion of metaworkflows as defined by Chiu et al. (1999), which provides support for handling exceptions, business rules, and workflow instances. These metaworkflows in practice help us to achieve a level of abstraction over workflow instances and are designed to enable monitoring support in our EC^{FS} framework. In the security perspective, not only do they help in auditing but they can also be used as a vigilant entity, observing the accesses of workflow instances in the implementation layer. A snapshot of these metaworkflows

Figure 15. EC^{FS} security framework for e-contracts

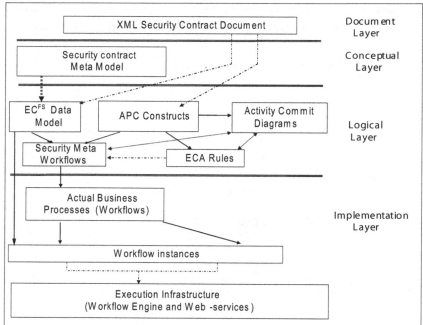

could be exposed to the outside world as process dashboards or they could be designed to provide data to underlying Web services to provide static data about executing workflow instances and their level of abeyance of the security clauses. Any breach of a laid down clause could raise an exception, which could be logged and captured by the all the parties.

CONCLUSION AND FUTURE DIRECTIONS

This chapter focuses on SLAs for Web services security. Security has been a key nonfunctional requirement for Web services, however, there has been very minimal work done on security SLA representation and enactment. Part of it is due to the fact that unlike typical nonfunctional requirements that deal with quantifiable parameters like workload, scheduling, and so forth, security requirements are most of the times nonquantifiable. This necessitates a policy- or process-based approach. We focus on covering some typical Web service security requirements and modeling them into security SLAs. We present a conceptual model to represent security SLAs in terms of a contract framework. In doing so, we review the existing approaches for representing SLAs for Web services and we enhance them by a contract-based approach. In order to enrich the model, we enlist typical attributes for a security SLAs. We conclude by providing an implementation approach for the contract-based framework for modeling Web service security.

One of the future works in this direction could be to translate our current contract-based approach to existing specifications for Web service monitoring (i.e., WSLA etc.). It could then be possible to model some of the security requirements as security SLAs in an enterprise environment and enact them through the contract framework.

REFERENCES

Chiu, D., Li, Q., & Karlapalem, K. (1999). A meta modeling approach to workflow management systems supporting exception handling. *Information Systems Journal, 24*(2), 159-184

Erradi, A., Padmanabhuni, S., & Varadharajan, N. (2006). *Differential QoS support in Web services Management.* Paper presented at the IEEE International Conference of Web Services (pp. 781-788).

Extensible access control markup language 3 (XACML) version 2.0. Retrieved August 10, 2007, from http://docs.oasis-open.org/xacml/2.0/access_control-xacml-2.0-core-spec-os.pdf

Grosof, B., & Poon, T. (2003) *SweetDeal: Representing agent contracts with exceptions using XML rules, ontologies, and process descriptions.* Paper presented at the 12th International Conference on the World Wide Web (pp. 340-349).

IBM Web services tool kit. Retrieved August 10, 2007, from http://www.alphaworks.ibm.com/tech/Web-servicestoolkit

Keller, A., & Ludwig, H. (2003). The WSLA framework: Specifying and monitoring service level agreements for Web services. *Journal of Network and Systems Management, Special Issue on E-Business management, 11*(1). Plenum Publishing Corporation.

Kulkarni, N., & Padmanabhuni, S. (2007). *An architectural framework for non functional requirements in enterprise SOA adoption.* Paper presented at WICSA 2007 (p. 36).

Liberty specifications for identity management. Retrieved August 10, 2007, from http://www.project-liberty.org/resource_center/specifications

Ludwig, H., Keller, A., Dan, A., & King, R. (2002). *A service level agreement language for dynamic electronic services.* Paper presented at the Fourth IEEE International Workshop on Advanced Issues of E-Commerce and Web-Based Information Systems (pp. 25-32).

OASIS Web services security (WSS). Retrieved August 10, 2007, from http://www.oasis-open.org/committees/wss

Padmanabhuni, P., & Adarkar, H. (2003). Security in service- oriented architecture: Issues, standards, and implementations. *Service-oriented software system engineering: Challenges and practices* (Chapter XIV). IGI Publications.

Project Liberty specification. (2003, January 15). Retrieved August 10, 2007, from http://www.project-liberty.org/specs/archive/v1_1/liberty-architecture-overview-v1.1.pdf

Tiwari, R., Dwivedi, V., & Karlapalem, K. (2007). *SLA driven process security through monitored e-contracts.* Paper presented at the IEEE International Conference of Service Computing (SCC'07) (pp. 28-35).

TrustBridge project details of Microsoft. Retrieved August 10, 2007, from http://msdn.microsoft.com/library/default.asp?url=/library/en-us/dnWebsrv/html/wsfederate.asp?frame=true

Web services trust language (2005, February). *WS-trust specification.* Retrieved August 10, 2007, from http://schemas.xmlsoap.org/ws/2005/02/trust/

WS-authorization specification (2003, July). Retrieved August 10, 2007, from http://www.w3c.or.kr/~hollobit/roadmap/ws-specs/WS-Authorization.html

WS-federation specification. (2003, July 18). Retrieved August 10, 2007, from http://www-106.ibm.com/developerworks/Webservices/library/ws-fed/

WSLA-spec (2003, January 28). *Web service level agreement (WSLA) language specification.* Retrieved August 10, 2007, from http://www.research.ibm.com/wsla/WSLASpecV1-20030128.pdf

WS-policy specification. (2002, December 18). Retrieved August 10, 2007, from http://msdn.microsoft.com/library/default.asp?url=/library/en-us/dnglobspec/html/wspolicyspecindex.asp

WS-privacy. Retrieved August 10, 2007, from http://www.serviceoriented.org/ws-privacy.html

WS-secure conversation spec. (2005, February). *Web services secure conversation language.* Retrieved August 10, 2007, from http://specs.xmlsoap.org/ws/2005/02/sc/WS-SecureConversation.pdf

WS-security specifications. (2002, April 5). Retrieved August 10, 2007, from http://msdn2.microsoft.com/en-us/library/ms951257.aspx

WS-trust specifications. (2007, March). Retrieved August 10, 2007, from http://docs.oasis-open.org/ws-sx/ws-trust/200512

XACML spec. (2003, February 18). *Extensible access control markup language (XACML)*. Retrieved August 10, 2007, from http://www.oasis-open.org/committees/download.php/2406/oasis-xacml-1.0.pdf

XKMS spec. (2001, March). *XML key management specification (XKMS)*. Retrieved August 10, 2007, from http://www.w3.org/TR/xkms

XML encryption spec. (2002, December 10). *XML encryption syntax and processing*. Retrieved August 10, 2007, from http://www.w3.org/TR/xmlenc-core/

Section IV
Maintainability and Management

Chapter XIV
Adoption of Web Services in Digital Libraries:
An Exploratory Study

Fatih Oguz
Valdosta State University, USA

ABSTRACT

This chapter describes a research study with an objective to explore and describe decision factors related to technology adoption. The study utilized theories of diffusion of innovations and communities of practice as frameworks and a case study of Web services (WS) technology in the digital library (DL) environment to develop an understanding of the decision-making process. A qualitative case study approach was used to investigate the research problems and data was collected through semistructured interviews, documentary evidence (e.g., meeting minutes), and a comprehensive member check. Face-to-face and phone interviews were conducted with respondents from five different DL programs in the U.S., selected based on distinctive characteristics (e.g., size of the DL program). Findings of the research suggest that the decision-making process is a complex procedure in which a number of factors are considered when making WS adoption decisions. These factors are categorized as organizational, individual, and technology-specific factors.

INTRODUCTION

With the advent of the Internet and specifically the World Wide Web (WWW) application, means of accessing data and information have changed forever. The Internet brought great opportunities for libraries as well as dilemmas and problems, such as technology choice and readiness.

Digital libraries (DL) were envisioned as network-accessible repositories in the 1990s. Now, DLs extend the classical brick-and-mortar library concept, bring value to society, and transform information landscape by improving and changing the means of knowledge access, creation, use, and discovery across disciplines, regardless of temporal and geographical barriers (Larsen & Watctlar, 2003; Reddy & Wladawsky-Berger, 2001).

The speed of technological advances in information technologies (IT) in the last 10 years has enabled DLs to provide innovative resources and services to people. The information landscape is changing as a result of the revolutionary developments in IT, incompleteness of content on Internet, ever increasing digital content along with the evolution of networked technologies and applications, lack of standards, ineffective information retrieval mechanisms, and minimal cataloging. These factors present challenges to the future of DL development efforts (Borgman, 1999; Reddy & Wladawsky-Berger, 2001).

The concept of Web services (WS) has emerged as the next generation of Web-based technology for exchanging information. This effort began with the submission of the SOAP 1.1 to the World Wide Web Consortium (W3C) (Barefoot, 2002). WS are self-contained applications that can be described, published, invoked, and located over the Internet (or any network). Once a Web service is deployed, other applications can discover and invoke the service. WS provide a programmable interface for other applications without requiring custom programming and proprietary solutions regardless of the operating systems and programming languages to share information as opposed to providing users with a graphical user interface (Boss, 2004).

According to the W3C, a Web service is defined as a software system designed to support interoperable machine-to-machine interaction over a network by using XML for sending and receiving messages (Booth, Haas, McCabe, Newcomer, Champion, Ferris, et al., 2004). Simplicity and flexibility of XML made it a definitive standard for data transmission and storage. XML is an open standard and can be accessed and processed by any tool capable of reading and writing American standard code for information interchange (ASCII) text. By definition, the only requirement for a Web service is to use XML.

The basic WS platform is composed of XML and a transport protocol. HTTP is the commonly used transport protocol on the Internet (Hickey, 2003). XML, simple object access protocol (SOAP), and Web services description language (WSDL) are tools to create WS. A Web service provides the framework for creating the next generation of distributed systems by which organizations can encapsulate existing business processes, publish them as services, search for and subscribe to other services, and exchange information throughout and beyond the enterprise (Adams, Gisolfi, Snell, & Varadan, 2002). Besides recognizing heterogeneity of networked resources and applications as a fundamental ingredient, WS are independent of platform and the development environment can be packaged and published on the Internet. Also, WS enable just-in-time integration and interoperability with legacy applications (Oguz & Moen, 2006).

The development and widespread deployment of more intelligent knowledge environments that not only support scholarly inquiry and communication but also that are open, accessible to all, and transparent in their operation remains as a fundamental challenge for DL practitioners and researchers.

DL applications need to have some room to accommodate future technological innovations regardless how they are built, using off-the-shelf software vs. custom-built, and thus decision makers who include managers, coordinators, designers, and developers need to make important decisions at some point in time to adopt or reject an innovation, including a specific technology, application, framework or idea related with DLs. Decision makers who need information about an innovation may seek this information through both informal and formal communication channels while making such critical decisions.

In the context of DLs, roles and influence of informal communication channels on the decision-making process to adopt or reject WS technology has not been investigated before. The adoption of a new technology, WS, which is its early stages of adoption in the DL environment, may provide a significant opportunity to investigate decision factors. The goal of this study is to shed a light on the decision-making process to adopt or reject a new technology, WS, in the context of DLs.

As technologies rapidly change and the information landscape is transformed, DLs find themselves dealing with the issues of technology adoption decisions to exploit this dynamically changing technology environment to meet their users' needs and expectations. Therefore, understanding the decision-making process regarding adoption of WS technologies in the context of DLs is important.

BACKGROUND

This study used the diffusion of innovations (DOI) and communities of practice (CoPs) as theoretical frameworks and a case study of WS technologies in the DL environment to develop an understanding of the decision-making process.

Diffusion of Innovations and Communities of Practice as Theoretical Frameworks

The DOI research methodology provides required instruments, both quantitative and qualitative, to assess the rate and pattern of diffusion of an innovation and identifies various factors that facilitate or hinder its adoption and implementation (Fichman, 1992). These major factors include properties of the innovation, characteristics of adopters, and the means leading to adoption.

An innovation can be an idea, behavior, practice, or object perceived as new by the adopter (e.g., organization, individual). The concept of newness may be determined by the human reaction to it as well as the time passed since its discovery or first use. If the idea seems new to an individual or organization, it is considered an innovation (Daft, 1978; Rogers, 1995).

DOI researchers study the characteristics of the innovation to explain the rate of adoption of an innovation. Rogers (1995) classifies characteristics of innovations into five general categories: relative advantage, compatibility, triability, observability, and complexity. Innovations with greater relative advantage, compatibility, triability, observability, and less complexity are more likely to be adopted faster than others that lack these characteristics (Rogers, 1995). However, there are structural factors (e.g., formalization and centralization) as well as other innovation characteristics (e.g., cost, profitability, social approval) influencing adoption of an innovation, and therefore Rogers' DOI theory needs to be extended to accommodate such factors, specifically in organizational settings (Daft, 1978; Damanpour, 1991). In addition, Tornatzky and Klein (1982) found that relative advantage, compatibility, and complexity have the most consistent relationships with the adoption of innovations across a wide range of industries.

Rogers (1995, p. 23) defines a social system as "a set of interrelated units that are engaged in joint problem-solving to accomplish a common goal" and the members or units of a social system may be composed of individuals, organizations, and informal groups. Patterned social relationships (e.g., hierarchical positions) among the members of a social system define the social structure of a system which, in return, can facilitate or delay the diffusion of an innovation and lays out a framework for making predictions about the human behavior in a system since such structure provides regularity and stability to human behavior (Rogers, 1995).

Established behavior patterns called norms are the ruling principles of a social system, which may also influence diffusion (Rogers, 1995). In other words, norms serve as a guide or a standard for the members against which they can assess their own behavior. Norms may slow the diffusion process when an innovation does not comply with the norms of a social system even if the adoption of an innovation offers important benefits for the system (Raghavan & Chand, 1989).

The innovation-decision can be made by an individual member of a system as well as by the entire system. The decision can be made collectively by reaching a consensus among the members of a social system or by a relatively few individuals who possess status, power, or technical expertise (Rogers, 1995). A decision made by an individual to adopt or reject a new idea independently from other members of a system is called an optional-innovation decision (Rogers, 1995). An adoption decision may be influenced by the norms of the system and informal communication channels. In this case, the decision is made by an individual member of the system rather than the entire social system, and the individual member is fully responsible for the consequences of the decision. Collective-innovation decisions are made by members of a system through a consensus to adopt or reject a new idea. All the units within the social system are expected to comply with the decision. However, reaching a collective decision may be a time-consuming process because it is made by a consensus among the members. Authority-innovation decisions are made by a select set of members of a social system who have authority and higher status in the organizational chart; in this decision-making process an individual member has little or no influence on the decision. In organizational settings, collective and authority-innovation decisions are more common than the optional-innovation decisions, and authority-innovation decisions result in higher rate of adoption than others (Rogers, 1995).

Diffusion of an innovation is a social process that is influenced by various factors such as characteristics of the innovation (e.g., relative advantage) and the decision-making unit (e.g., individual characteristics), depending on the level of adoption (individual vs. organizational). The information about the innovation is communicated through formal (e.g., mass media) and informal in the course of the innovation-decision process. Rogers (1995) suggests that having some exposure to mass media and informal communication channels such as interpersonal networks increases a potential adopter's chance of knowing about an innovation earlier than others. This chapter specifically focuses on CoPs which serve as an informal communication channel.

CoPs are composed of people who share a concern, common problems, or a passion about the domain, and who want to gain more knowledge and expertise pertaining to the domain by interacting regularly (Wenger, McDermott, & Snyder, 2002). CoPs provide a learning environment through social participation, where participation refers to being active participants in the practice and building a sense of identity associated with the CoP to which they belong.

CoPs embody individuals with diverse backgrounds and social structures (e.g., other CoPs, organizations), which in turn, reduce the learning curve and rework, and promote innovation by enabling them to share and disseminate both tacit and explicit knowledge (Lesser & Storck, 2001). Sharing tacit knowledge requires personal interaction and CoPs provide such an informal learning platform through conversation and apprenticeship, for example. Members of the community become aware of their peers' expertise, knowledge, and skills through creating a venue for them to interact with each other. Thus, they are able to compare, verify, and benchmark their professionally developed expertise in the field against their colleagues' knowledge. When these benefits of CoPs are considered, their contribution to DL development efforts is vital in making informed technology, specifically WS, adoption decisions. The literature (e.g., Borgman, 1999; Marchionini, 1998) and nature of DL development efforts (e.g., open source) suggest the existence of informal structures such as CoPs.

As the organizations, specifically commercial ones, expand in size, geographical coverage, and complexity, knowledge has become the key to improving organizational performance and the formation of informal social groups like CoPs become a natural part of organizational life (Lesser & Storck, 2001; Wenger et al., 2002). CoPs make knowledge an integral part of their ongoing activities and interactions. Interpersonal interactions play an important role, especially in sharing tacit knowledge; the learning tools utilized by CoPs such as storytelling, conversation, and apprenticeship increase the efficient use of knowledge. CoPs act as a "living repository" for collective knowledge through creating a value for both the members and the organizations supporting and sponsoring these social structures (Wenger et al., 2002).

The DL conferences, funding agencies, workshops, and professional societies (e.g., Association for Computing Machinery) play important roles both in building and cultivating the CoPs in the DL field, and such meetings serve as a breeding ground for future collaboration in DL development efforts (Borgman, 1999). In addition, the experts in the field reached a consensus that "efforts associated with development of digital libraries are primarily collaborative" in a Delphi study conducted by Kochtanek and Hein (1999, p. 253).

Web Services in Digital Libraries

In general, DLs enable far broader range of users than traditional physical and organizational arrangements (e.g., libraries) to access information. Gathering, organizing, sharing, and maintaining such information resources require a flexible, scalable, and interoperable infrastructure (Larsen & Watctlar, 2003). Interoperability is an important issue where various system architectures, operating systems, and programming languages are required to communicate with each other. In addition, DL development efforts are closely related with the progress in general purpose technologies such as high-speed networking, security, and interoperability (Marchionini, 1998). However, the size, heterogeneity, and complexity of the today's information resources become critical factors when building DL systems because such factors may create immense challenges for interoperability, or the ability to ensure seamless information exchange across multiple DLs and information resources (Akscyn & Witten, 1998; Gonçalves et al., 2002; Marchionini, 1998). Marchionini (1998) addresses interoperability in two levels. The first level is the efforts to create standards for data storage and transmission, for query representation, and for vocabulary control; DLs adopt such standards and modify their content and services at the local level. However, standards development is a complex social process and requires consensus among stakeholders (Moen, 1997). The second level encourages individual DLs to create standards-based services that can be easily accessible and used by other DLs.

A vision set forth for the DLs by the President's Information Technology Advisory Committee (PITAC) Panel on Digital Libraries is that of providing the means of searching and accessing all human knowledge anytime and anywhere via Internet for all citizens (Reddy & Wladawsky-Berger, 2001). One of the key issues in accomplishing this vision is improving the ability to store and retrieve digital content across disparate and independent systems and collections by improving interoperability among diverse DL implementations (Reddy & Wladawsky-Berger, 2001). Thus, interoperability is an important factor to consider in the DL environment when making decisions to adopt WS technologies.

Important decisions have been made in the past as to adopt or reject a new technology for various reasons including the pursuit of this vision, delivering content in more efficient and advanced manner, and social status (e.g., being a pioneer in offering new DL services) (Pasquinelli, 2002). Some of the key technologies and standards related with interoperability that have been adopted in the past in DL environments such as the ANSI/NISO Z39.50 protocol, open archives initiative protocol for metadata harvesting (OAI-PMH), and open URL.

Hickey (2003) lists various ways of using WS technology in DLs from registering different types of objects and search services to navigating hierarchies and decomposing objects into simpler objects. The search/retrieve Web service (SRW) is a standardized Web service built on the 20 years of experience of the Z39.50 information retrieval protocol. SRW provides an easy way to implement the protocol with the power of older and more complex Z39.50 (Sanderson, 2004). Even some libraries are replacing Z39.50 with WS technologies as the protocol of choice between library portals and online electronic resources (Boss, 2004). WS facilitate access to electronic databases, and digital libraries providing access to such resources benefit from this technology (Boss, 2004).

The flexible and extensible digital object and repository architecture (Fedora) system, designed by the Cornell University Information Science and The University of Virginia Library's Digital Library Research and Development Group (DLR&D), is a promising open source digital library software initiative. Fedora was originally implemented based on CORBA architecture; however, the next release (Fedora 2.0) has adopted a service-oriented approach (SOA) based on WS ("Tutorial 1: Introduction," 2005). DSpace is another open source system, developed by Hewlett-Packard and MIT Libraries, to store the digital research and educational material produced by an organization or institution as a repository. Greenstone is yet another open source digital library software from New Zealand Digital Library Project at the University of Waikato that has a focus on publishing (Don, Buchanan, & Witten, 2005). The DELOS network pays close attention and contributes to the use of WS technologies in digital libraries. EBSCO publishing, a provider of a broad range of full-text and bibliographic databases, has introduced its WS interface to EBSCOhost, an electronic journal service for academic and corporate subscribers, forming a basis of real-time communications among library systems, portals, and all other systems in the future (Boss, 2004).

The major strength of WS is its reliance on XML. Given the characteristics of WS technologies and current use in DLs and e-commerce, WS are poised to play an important role as a technology providing interoperable standards-based access to DLs.

MAIN THRUST OF THE CHAPTER

This chapter attempts to explore and describe factors, activities, processes, and forces involved in the decision-making process related to adoption of WS technologies in DLs.

Research Problems and Methodology

The research strategy consisted of two components: a qualitative methodology and a case study. This strategy provided a framework of methods and data that would yield answers to the two research questions: (1) What are the key decision factors that lead decision makers to adopt or reject WS in the DL environment? and (2) What are the activities and entities that influence the decision regarding adoption of WS technologies in the DL environment?

The exploratory and descriptive nature of the study justified the use of a qualitative research approach that allows discovery and description of the social processes involved in decision making. Although quantitative methods have been predominant in information technology (IT) adoption research (Choudrie & Dwivedi, 2005), this chapter aims to develop a better understanding of decision factors influencing adoption of WS technologies in the context of DLs.

In-depth information about this complex social process involving decision makers was acquired through semistructured interviews and documentary evidence (e.g., meeting minutes and reports). The interview respondents and academic libraries that they are associated with were selected based on characteristics of DL programs identified by Greenstein and Thorin (2002). These characteristics included age of the program, staff size, and organization and orientation of the program. Seven respondents with different responsibilities (administrative vs. technical) were interviewed from five different DL programs in the US. These DL programs included big (i.e., staff size) programs such as California Digital Library and University of Texas at Austin and relatively smaller ones such as University of North Texas and University of Texas at Dallas.

Following Patton's (2002) guidelines, purposeful sampling, specifically maximum variation sampling, was employed when selecting the respondents who had the best knowledge, expertise, and overview about the topic of the research. The maximum variation sampling aimed at "capturing and describing the central themes that cut cross great deal of variation" (Patton, 2002, p. 234).

The respondents were from DL programs at the California Digital Library, University of North Texas, University of Texas at Dallas, University of Texas at Austin, and a university in the American Southeast. Some of the participating libraries are members of various influential professional societies and organizations in the DL field, including Digital Library Federation (DLF), Association of Research Libraries (ARL), and Coalition for Networked Information (CNI). Seven interviews were conducted with administrators and technical personnel who were involved in the decision-making process at these five academic libraries' DL programs.

Patton (2002) sets no rules for the sample size in qualitative inquiry by arguing that "the validity, meaningfulness, and the insights generated from qualitative inquiry have more to do with the information richness of the cases selected and the observational/analytical capabilities of the researcher than with sample size" (p. 245). The researcher stopped conducting interviews when data saturation was reached to meet the research goal, that is, to understand and describe decision factors related to WS adoption. Data saturation is defined as the point in a data collection process where new information becomes redundant (Bogdan & Biklen, 1992). Romney, Batchelder, and Weller (1986) conclude that samples as small as four participants could be enough to meet research objectives where purposeful sampling is carefully carried out to include information-rich respondents.

Documentary evidence provided additional and clarifying information supplemental to the data collected through interviews. Further, a comprehensive member check was conducted which allowed to obtain additional information from respondents and to have study findings reviewed by them. This final verification process allowed respondents to evaluate the researcher's interpretation of findings and analysis of data from their perspectives (Lincoln & Guba, 1985; Patton, 2002).

Results and Findings

Data revealed a number of factors that influenced and informed the decision-making process in WS adoption. These factors are categorized at organizational, individual, and technical levels.

Characteristics of DL programs that appeared to influence the decision-making process and categorized as organizational level factors included: organizational culture, program's relationships with surrounding academic units and external partners, management style and work structure, focus and direction of a program, formalization (e.g., flexibility in hierarchal order), functional differentiation in a program, size and age of a program, administrative attitude toward change, financial resources, technology readiness (e.g., expertise, technology infrastructure), and program's expectations (e.g., user needs). These organizational level factors appeared to play a critical role, especially in influencing members' information-seeking and communication behaviors. Individual level factors included members' connectedness with their colleagues, skill-set (e.g., competence), participation in CoPs, perception of organizational culture and goals, and openness to new ideas. Technical level factors included: interoperability, modularity, scalability, flexibility, addressability, rapid deployment of services, subscription service, and open-standards base of WS.

Some of the organizational level factors include management style, focus and direction of the program, size and age of the program, and organizational culture. Organizational level factors were closely associated with the organization itself and indirectly impacted by a DL program's staff, for example. Administrative personnel had an influence on some of organizational level factors (e.g., management style). Other factors could be regarded as more individual characteristics of DL staff members in terms of their information-seeking and communication behavior. Impact of individual level factors on decision-making vary from one technology to another depending on role of the technology (i.e., mission critical vs. non-mission critical) in the DL program.

Respondents identified financial concerns as a critical factor in guiding technology adoption decisions, and these concerns included: initial cost, ongoing cost, payoff, budgetary restrictions, and funding requirements. However, the extent of influence of these factors on WS adoption decisions appeared to vary from one DL program to another depending on the DL program's expectations from the technology and needs, focus, and direction of the program. These expectations and needs were closely related with size and age of the program. Data suggested that as programs grew in size over time, so did their collections, responsibilities, and user expectations. For example, although respondents formed positive opinions regarding open source software, they were aware that the lack of necessary skills in the program would be an important factor when getting a project initiated and providing technical support if they chose to use open source software. In addition, acquiring necessary technology skills through hiring new staff members and additional training were also factors impacting cost. Lack of technical expertise as a decision factor appeared to reflect the importance of Davis' (1989) "ease of use," Tornatzky and Klein's (1982) "ease of operation," and Rogers' (1995) "complexity" as innovation characteristics since adopters' technical background and skills were closely associated with perception of these characteristics.

Technology readiness of the DL program was another organizational factor that appeared to have an influence in the decision-making process. Technology readiness had two aspects: a human aspect (e.g., expertise, staffing), and the technological compatibility of WS technologies with existing technical infrastructure (i.e., hardware, software, and standards). In addition, technology readiness was also closely associated with availability of financial resources in case a hardware or software upgrade was needed. Respondents noted that compatibility of WS technologies with their existing technological infrastructure was an important factor that informed the decision-making. Tornatzky and Klein (1982) found compatibility as one of the most addressed innovation attributes. Compatibility also refers to consistency of an innovation with existing values and norms of the DL program. Furthermore, technology readiness was also an important factor for triability purposes. Small scale experiments were generally conducted in DL programs prior to making an adoption decision.

Individual level adoption decisions could be made especially for the use of WS technologies in nonmission critical applications. A personal positive experience with WS, existing skill-set, potential benefits for the work (i.e., Davis' [1985] perceived usefulness), and having easy access to experienced-based knowledge through CoPs appeared to influence an individual's perception and lowered the individual's learning curve. Technology and specific factors such as interoperability, modularity, flexibility, and WS subscription service were also decision factors in this case. In DL programs where WS had already been adopted, adoption decisions were made collectively and WS technologies were used for major and mission-critical applications. Both organizational and technology-specific factors were taken into consideration.

Another important decision factor was technology-specific benefits offered by WS, including interoperability, modularity, and open standards. WS provides an interoperable platform and is built on open standards (e.g., XML) where programs written in different programming languages and running on different operating systems are able to communicate with each other based on open standards and protocols. Data suggested that interoperability was an important factor since WS would not require major changes in existing technical infrastructure. In addition to interoperability, respondents identified additional technology-specific factors. For example:

- **Modularity and flexibility:** Ability to act as building blocks to create distributed applications through reuse of existing applications that can be published and accessed over the internet or intranets.
- **Rapid deployment of Services:** Development time for new applications or services is greatly reduced through use of standard interfaces (e.g., WSDL) and open standards.
- Scalability: Ability to handle a growing amount of usage loads (e.g., Web caching, load balancing).
- **WS subscription service (UDDI):** A registry services for WS and allows other WS applications to automatically discover services and use them.

Small DL programs often looked to older and bigger DL programs when it came to adopting new technologies and standards. Their limited financial resources, staff size, and skill set were important barriers preventing them from taking initiatives that might be considered risky. These initiatives included technologies or standards that have not been tried or are in early stages of adoption in other DL programs. They often chose to rely on experiences of other DL programs so that they would be less likely to fail and run into unexpected problems. As for bigger programs, it appeared that they sometimes wanted to be the first or early adopters of some technologies in the DL environment to set an example for other programs. Though setting an example for other DL programs or wanting to be an early adopter was not a key decision factor, it was one of the factors occasionally taken into consideration in the decision-making processes.

Data suggested that availability of financial resources, focus and direction, size and age, collection size, users' and programs' expectations, and technology readiness were important factors influencing decision makers. Especially when making an optional-innovation decision, a potential adopter's existing technical skill-set and connectedness with the adopter's colleagues were key factors. At the technical level, interoperability, modularity, scalability, flexibility, addressability, rapid deployment of services, subscription services, and the open standards base of WS were key decision factors leading decision makers to adopt or reject WS in the DL environment.

Figure 1 presents a conceptual framework for the study informed by the theoretical frameworks in light of results and findings discussed earlier. Organizational and technical (i.e., technology specific) level factors have an influence both on adopters' information seeking behaviors and on the adoption decision itself depending on the type of innovation decision (i.e., optional, collective, and authority) made. Individual level factors (i.e., individual characteristics) guide adopters' information seeking activities (e.g., participation in CoPs) and influence their perception of organizational values which in turn inform adopters' contribution to the decision-making process. As shown in Figure 1, potential adopters may acquire information about an innovation through formal (e.g., mass media) and informal (e.g., interpersonal) communication channels. The information acquired through these channels includes perceived characteristics of an innovation that may play a key role as decision factors in the decision-making process. Data suggested that use of information collected through these channels in the decision-making process vary due to adopters' degree of participation in CoPs, characteristics of knowledge (explicit vs. tacit) acquired, and factors at organizational, technical, and individual levels.

On the other hand, there were number of activities that members of DL programs participated in, entities that provided them with guidance, processes that helped them develop an understanding of WS, motivations that encouraged or discouraged them towards WS technologies, and forces that informed and guided their information seeking and communication behaviors. These activities, entities, processes, and forces were in play when making a decision regarding adoption of WS technologies in the DL environment.

Figure 1. Conceptual framework

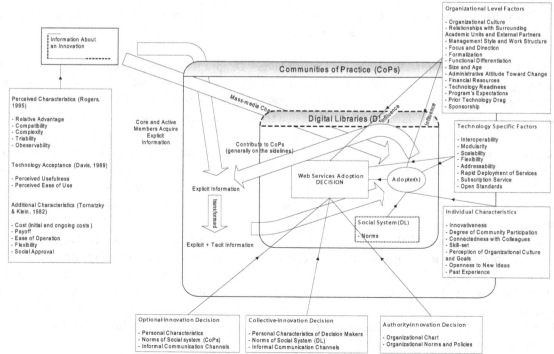

DL programs had good ties with surrounding academic departments and information services, including other library departments, IT department, library and information school, and faculty. DL programs benefited from such connections not only by accessing their expertise but also by acquiring their content and collections.

DL staff members' interactions with others appeared to be maintained informally and the organizational structure of DL programs encouraged informal communication. Informality in communicating with others is one of the key characteristics of CoPs. Respondents interacted with their colleagues who were part of their own DL programs, as well as people from libraries, other university units, or external institutions and organizations to advance and share their knowledge and contribute to the field. Informal communication was also cited as an important part of the technology assessment process.

Some of the participating academic libraries were members of various professional associations and organizations which have an influence on DL-related issues, including use of DL technologies, digital preservation, standards, and DL development activities. Participation in these organizations (e.g., DLF, CNI, ARL) provided venues for DL programs to share their work and connect with other DL programs. The DLF promotes work on DL structures, standards, preservation, and use, CNI is interested in various areas critical to present and future of DLs, and ARL is one of the sponsor organizations of CNI and its member institutions are very active in the field. Further, these organizations engage in collaborative activities with each other in pursuit of their missions and goals. Collegial activities that were made possible through these relationships with these external entities appeared to play a central role in formation and continuation of informal communities that can be characterized as CoPs. Entities in the DL environment generally included CoPs, surrounding academic units and external partners, funding agencies, and the program itself.

In addition, attending national and international conferences were the most commonly used venues to obtain new information and served as a breeding ground for building personal contacts with colleagues. These collegial activities were regarded as communal activities. Preexisting personal contacts and the connections established in various venues with other institutions, organizations, and DL initiatives appeared to be very important for information access and sharing purposes.

CoPs attracted individuals with diverse backgrounds and skills from all around the world regardless of their geographical locations and provided an informal learning platform for their members. These CoPs were generally built and maintained in an online environment and occasionally supported with face-to-face interactions. In addition to distributed virtual CoPs, there were other CoPs, which may be subgroups of a broader CoP, that were locally networked and physically located. Participation of members in discussions in CoPs enabled online communities to cultivate and nurture knowledge acquired thorough experience, print, or other online resources and, in turn, these discussions enhanced and improved members' understanding of the technology. In other words, this mediating process gave rise to cross-fertilization of ideas and appeared to improve credibility of the knowledge generated and housed in CoPs. CoPs provided a living repository for the knowledge generated within the community while they were also perceived as places where up-to-date and quality information could be acquired. CoPs were also used to verify information acquired from different sources.

The conceptual framework (see Figure 1) helped to structure the data-found analysis in a format which may help the reader see this very complex landscape and understand this complex social process. Further, this chapter provided evidence that Rogers' DOI model needs to be complemented with organizational level factors identified by other researchers such as Daft (1978), Davis (1989), and Tornatzky and Klein (1992) to understand and describe diffusion of innovations in organizational settings.

CONCLUSION

This research was an exploratory and descriptive study to shed a light on the decision-making process to adopt or reject a new technology, WS, in the context of DLs and the unit of analysis was the decision to adopt or reject a new technology. The information landscape is transformed as technologies rapidly change and DLs often find themselves in a critical position to make a decision whether to adopt or reject emerging technologies such as WS.

Since the study employed a qualitative case study approach that supported the exploratory and descriptive nature of the research, results and findings of the study are not intended to be statistically generalizable to other technology adoption cases. However, detailed description in the narrative may assist the reader of this case study research to determine applicability of these findings to other technology adoption decisions in the reader's own setting.

This chapter provides evidence that CoPs as informal communication channels practice play an important role in enabling staff members of a DL program to access up-to-date and experienced-based knowledge, providing a distributed problem-solving and learning platform, facilitating informal communication and collaborative activities among DL programs, and informing the decision-making process. Technical characteristics (e.g., interoperability, open standards), compatibility with existing technical infrastructure, applicability to existing DL projects, total cost of ownership (e.g., licensing, maintenance cost), technical expertise in the DL program (e.g., staffing, training, learning curve), and success of a pilot project are cited as key decision factors influencing adoption Web services technologies in the DL environment. This chapter provides an adequate foundation for further research on the impact of organizational, individual, and technology-specific factors on decision-making processes in the DL environment.

The complexity of the decision-making process and the variety of factors that informed and influenced this process are reflected. A review of the relevant literature suggests that this is a complex process, and the findings inform and provide details about the complexity, as presented in Figure 1. The theoretical frameworks selected for this chapter proved useful to achieve the goal of the study. The chapter attempts to provide a complete account of decision factors related with adoption of WS technologies in the DL environment. An outcome of this study suggests that an exploratory and descriptive study such as this is an important step towards understanding the decision-making process as technologies rapidly change in the DL environment.

ACKNOWLEDGMENT

The author thanks Corrie Marsh for her valuable feedback in writing of this chapter and to Dr. William Moen for his guidance and support for this research.

REFERENCES

Adams, H., Gisolfi, D., Snell, J., & Varadan, R. (2002). Best practices for Web services: Part 1 - formation of a semantic framework. *IBM developerWorks*. Retrieved March 5, 2004, from http://www-106. ibm.com/developerworks/Webservices/library/ws-best1/

Akscyn, R. M., & Witten, I. H. (1998). *Report of First Summit on international cooperation on digital libraries.* Retrieved May 3, 2005, from http://Web.archive.org/Web/20010529104724/ks.com/idla-wp-oct98/

Barefoot, D. (2002). *Web services primer.* CapeScience.

Bogdan, R. C., & Biklen, S. R. (1992). *Qualitative research for education: An introduction to theory and methods* (2nd ed.). Boston: Allyn and Bacon.

Booth, D., Haas, H., McCabe, F., Newcomer, E., Champion, M., Ferris, C., et al. (2004, February). *Web services architecture* (W3C Working Group Note 11). The World Wide Web Consortium (W3C).

Borgman, C. L. (1999). What are digital libraries? Competing visions. *Information Processing & Management, 35*(3), 227-243.

Boss, R. W. (2004). *Web services.* Retrieved November 1, 2005, from http://www.ala.org/ala/pla/pla-pubs/technotes/Webservices.htm

Choudrie, J., & Dwivedi, Y. K. (2005). Investigating the research approaches for examining technology adoption issues. *Journal of Research Practice, 1*(1).

Daft, R. L. (1978). A dual-core model of organizational innovation. *Academy of Management Journal, 21*(2), 193.

Damanpour, F. (1991). Organizational inertia and momentum: A dynamic model of strategic change. *Academy of Management Journal, 34*(3), 555-591.

Davis, F. D. (1989). Perceived usefulness, perceived ease of use, and user acceptance of information technology. *MIS Quarterly, 13*(3), 318.

Don, K., Buchanan, G., & Witten, I. H. (2005). *Greenstone 3: A modular digital library.* Retrieved November 1, 2005, from http://www.sadl.uleth.ca/greenstone3/manual.pdf

Fichman, R. G. (1992, December). *Information technology diffusion: A review of empirical research.* Paper presented at the Thirteenth International Conference on Information Systems (ICIS), Dallas.

Gonçalves, M. A., Fox, E. A., Watsom, L. T., & Kipp., N. A. (2002). Streams, structures, spaces, scenarios, societies (5s): A formal model for digital libraries. *ACM Transactions in Informations Systems (TOIS), 22*(2), 270-312.

Greenstein, D., & Thorin, S. E. (2002). *The digital library: A biography.* Digital Library Federation.

Hickey, T. B. (2003). *Web services for digital libraries.* Paper presented at the Cross Language Applications and The Web 27th Library Systems Seminar, Bern, Switzerland.

Kochtanek, T. R., & Hein, K. K. (1999). Delphi study of digital libraries. *Information Processing & Management, 35*(3), 245-254.

Larsen, R. L., & Watctlar, H. D. (2003). *Knowledge lost in information.* Report of the NSF Workshop on Research Directions for Digital Libraries.

Lesser, E. L., & Storck, J. (2001). Communities of practice and organizational performance. *IBM Systems Journal, 40*(4), 831-931.

Lincoln, Y. S., & Guba, E. G. (1985). *Naturalistic inquiry.* Beverly Hills, CA: Sage Publications, Inc.

Marchionini, G. (1998). Research and development in digital libraries. In A. Kent (Ed.), *Encyclopedia of library and information science* (Vol. 63, pp. 259-279). New York: Marcel Dekker.

Moen, W. E. (1997). *The Development of ANSI/NISO Z39.50: A Case Study in Standards Evolution.* Unpublished Dissertation, Syracuse University.

Oguz, F., & Moen, W. E. (2006). *Texas library directory Web services application: The potential for Web services to enhance information access to legacy data.* Paper presented at the International Conference on Next Generation Web Services Practices (NWeSP'06), Korea.

Pasquinelli, A. (2002). *Digital library technology trends.* Retrieved December, 9, 2005, from http://www.sun.com/products-n-solutions/edu/whitepapers/pdf/digital_library_trends.pdf

Patton, M. Q. (2002). *Qualitative research and evaluation methods* (3rd ed.). Thousand Oaks, CA: Sage Publications, Inc.

Raghavan, S. A., & Chand, D. R. (1989). Diffusing Software-Engineering Methods. *IEEE Software, 6*(4), 81-90.

Reddy, R., & Wladawsky-Berger, I. (2001). *Digital libraries: Universal access to human knowledge: A report to the President.* President's Information Technology Advisory Committee (PITAC), Panel on Digital Libraries.

Rogers, E. M. (1995). *Diffusion of Innovations* (4th ed.). New York: The Free Press.

Romney, A., Batchelder, W., & Weller, S. (1986). Culture as consensus: A theory of culture and informant accuracy. *American Anthropologist, 88*, 313-338.

Sanderson, R. (2004). *SRW: Search/retrieve Webservice version 1.1.* Retrieved February 2, 2005, from http://srw.cheshire3.org/SRW-1.1.pdf

Tornatzky, L. G., & Klein, K. J. (1982). Innovation characteristics and innovation adoption-implementation: A meta-analysis of findings. *IEEE Transactions on Engineering Management, 29*(1), 28-45.

Tutorial 1: Introduction. (2005). Retrieved August 15, 2005, from http://www.fedora.info/download/2.0/userdocs/tutorials/tutorial1.pdf

Wenger, E., McDermott, R., & Snyder, W. M. (2002). *A guide to managing knowledge: Cultivating communities of practice.* Boston: Harvard Business School Press.

Chapter XV
Service Evolution and Maintainability

Bijoy Majumdar
Infosys Technologies Limited, India

Krishnendu Kunti
Infosys Technologies Limited, India

Mohit Chawla
Infosys Technologies Limited, India

Terance Bernard Dias
Infosys Technologies Limited, India

Lipika Sahoo
Infosys Technologies Limited, India

ABSTRACT

Change is the only constant, and this concept holds good for services too. Service maintenance is the most tedious and longest phase of service lifecycle. The more complex the service, the more difficult it is to maintain it. Service maintenance and service evolution mandate a series of best practices and selective models to apply for better execution and administration. In this chapter we detail the challenges faced in service evolution management and the key activities involved, and their role in service-oriented architecture (SOA) quality.

INTRODUCTION

Organizations develop service components with rigor supporting different standards and sufficing the interoperability requirements to collaborate with all the stakeholders in the business transaction. But in the face of business competition and changing requirements, the challenge is not only in developing these assets but also maintaining their quality as they evolve with the changing business requirements. Like other objects in the IT environment, services too are subject to aging and may fail to keep up with the ever changing requirements. But services quality and flexibility mandate strict vigilance and maintainability of software services. Thus, to realize the benefits of *service-oriented architecture* (SOA) completely, service evolution and service maintainability become key underlying components of service quality practice.

Service evolution can be defined as the process of change that the service might undergo to meet direct or indirect change in business requirements. Service evolution starts after the development, at the deployment stage of the service, and ends at the service decommission stage. During this period, the service might be changed to include enhancements, bug fixes, and so forth. Managing this change in service is called service maintainability. In a broad perspective, service maintainability encapsulates versioning, monitoring, change management, and reporting. Services, being self-contained, independent components, need slightly different approaches in each of these activities, as explained in the following sections.

CHALLENGES IN SERVICE EVOLUTION

It is important that during the service development lifecycle, the phases of service evolution are also considered so that stakeholders are involved in acts beyond the focus of just developing some business functionality to adapt quickly to the unexpected change in requirement. To effectively address the challenges that one faces during service evolution, one needs to focus on the explicit support around the services and their environment for a sustainable quality in the future. The challenges faced in different aspects of service evolution are explained below. Also the approaches to address these different challenges are different.

Service Model and Support

The service model helps to set the uniform mindset across all stakeholders in the design (Zimmermann, Krogdahl, & Gee, 2004), development, and maintenance phase of service lifecycle. The modeling approach does help to create a framework to work with in boundaries and enhances the system. Each existing model caters to a specific problem in service development. Some examples of models are:

- Model driven architecture (MDA) streamlines the process of integration
- Web services resource framework (WSRF) defines a generic and open framework for modeling and accessing stateful resources using Web services
- Business process execution language (BPEL) defines the orchestration of services across domains
- Domain-specific languages fill the gap between general purpose languages and particular application domains by providing a language with notation and concepts geared to the domain
- Information technology infrastructure library (ITIL) is a set of concepts, techniques, and frameworks to manage software infrastructure and its operations

All models might not be justifiable for all architectures. Appropriate decisions to judiciously select models need to be made in the initial phase of service development. The model designed can be incremental and would need to coexist with other models in the system. Model factor helps the system to work within the scope of the specifications but provides a better traceability for any changes/enhancements. The model helps to build a blueprint for the smooth execution of service evolution.

Modeling caters to the reoccurring aspects of a service requirement or deals with the environment for service performance and monitoring. Therefore, service models need to interact with the service component and the underlying development environment. Evolution is related to the entire systems involved. The modeling approach does help to create a framework to work within boundaries and enhance the system with help of these models. For example, domain-specific languages fill the gap between general purpose languages and particular application domains by providing a language with notation and concepts geared to the domain. But model engineering brings in lock-in to the concepts and abstractions adopted during the process. Service models for a system are to be selected and engineered for a sustainable service evolution where changes in different artifacts can be reflected easily.

Supporting Coevolution

Different artifacts, documents service components, and stakeholders exist in different units or regions of an organization. Modification of one in one unit may not be communicated properly to or understandable to other unit. The problem occurs when there is a need of integration or need of realignment. The design models, service models, and service components at different levels of infrastructure, information, operation, and organization would require being consistent and coevolve for the service evolution.

Integration of Heterogeneous Services

Integration of various services is another challenge that keeps erupting in a service lifecycle. Services are independent pieces of business functionality on different systems, platforms, and wrapping heterogeneous data sources. These services need to integrate from time to time, not only to meet business requirements but also for better and reliable management at the organization level. The traceability propagates from finer grained service, data informational services, to integration and organizational service.

For standard-based service integration, service definition standards like Web services description language (WSDL) fits the bill as it explains the service interface; but a more flexible model encompassing a service will provide the needed help in defining the custom integration protocol in the multisiloed business environment.

Change Management and Versioning

Iterative and incremental development brings in another challenge in service evolution. Modification of a service component not only brings in the concept of build change management but also a service versioning mechanism, catering to notifying the internal and external stakeholders of the service. Appropriate tools are available for the software components change management but a strategy is required for explicit change management across silos and business entities.

Awareness and Transition of Stakeholders

Strategically at the organization level, there needs to be understanding of the implications of service evolution and the imperatives of service maintainability at every level of the organizational hierarchy. Transition of best practices and guidelines is to be propagated to different managers and users or consumers of the service. This will entertain a greater involvement of the stakeholders in the evolution and collaborate with each other to ease out the challenges in the lifecycle. SOA or services have brought in the alignment between business and IT as well as cross-silo business development, which mandates a more stringent awareness and transition.

Sustaining Service Quality: Monitoring and Management

The phenomenon of software aging, coined by Dave Parnas (1994), and the laws of software evolution postulated by Lehman, Ramil, Wernick, Perry, and Turski (1997) agree that, without active counter-measures, the quality of a software system gradually degrades as the system evolves. Service quality can be sustained by monitoring the aspects of performance, availability, and reliability of runtime service and managing the service by feedback/reports. Differential quality of service (QoS) languages like Web service level agreement (WSLA) and Web services offerings language (WSOL) help define contracts to specify agreed-upon, nonfunctional characteristics of Web services (in the form of service level objectives [SLOs]), as well as a model for measuring, evaluating, and managing the compliance with these characteristics. Having a platform that does monitoring and management across services distributed over geographically and technically different locations is a challenge.

IN A NUTSHELL: ENCOMPASSING MODELS AND STRATEGIES

Service design, development, and its management need to dwell into strategies and follow standards to productize a better future for the service evolution. These strategies and service model redefines the roadmap. Along the path during creation or development of services, one needs to design the policies and environment in and around the service component that helps in the longevity and easier manageable services.

Service maintainability has crossed software boundaries in terms of managing and monitoring the IT assets of an industry. Through the service wrappers (Java wrappers for mainframe programs), or be it OS services, it can be reused, managed, and monitored while still retaining the security, robustness, and reliability characterized by legacy systems. Cross-silo monitoring over heterogeneous systems get people of processes and environments in sync, and most of the time this happens from a single point of control.

During design and development of services, the following phases of service evolution also need to be considered and should be planned for accordingly:

1.   Service publishing and deployment
2.   Service access management
3.   Service monitoring
4.   Service model and registry

5. Service versioning
6. Service decommission

Service monitoring, service model, and service versioning are critical to service lifecycle. There have been various methodologies under each of them to sustain the service quality. An organization can choose among the methodologies or specifications to suite their specific SOA environment/strategy and each of these methodologies helps to address the challenges for service evolution in their own way. The following sections will explain in detail the methodologies in service monitoring, service model, and service versioning. For continuity, the other aspects are also explained in brief.

Service Publishing and Deployment

Once a service is created, it needs to be deployed and the stakeholders need to be made aware of the service. This is known as "publishing the service." In service publishing, one needs to define contracts in services that are exposed to the partners in a standard manner. An example of such a contract is the WSDL. The WSDL represents messages exchanged, interface, bindings, endpoints, and so forth of the service which needs to be made available to the service users. Something like XML registries (universal description, discovery, and integration [UDDI] or ebXML registry) can be used to publish the service information.

Service Access Management

Service access management basically addresses challenges and helps to assist the QoS system in maintaining the access to these services throughout the lifecycle. It deals with managing the authentication, authorization, and so forth required to access the service as opposed to message security, which deals with securing the messages being passed between the service provider and consumer (Shin, 2003).

Standards have special relevance to SOA security implementations, especially Web services, since Web services are based on a set of standards and their real value can be realized only when standards are followed. In view of the special requirements of the access security needs of Web services and grid, a plethora of standards are being worked on at W3C, OASIS, IETF, GGF, and other standards bodies to enable faster adoption of Web services and grid technologies.

Since services are diverse and exposed to various consumer, policy management needs to be in place. Services are not only diverse but geographically distributed, which at times are seamlessly integrated; a sense of federated security comes into play for such maintainability and cohesiveness of services across administrative domains. Let us take a look at a few SOA security solutions that can assist in a multidevelopment environment and run in heterogeneous administrative domains.

SOA Policy Enforcement

Consider a typical SOA environment involving several service consumers and various services, each with various security measures associated with them (e.g., authorization, authentication, encryption, digital signatures, etc.) and each service having been traditionally developed on a per-application basis, and very often by service developers that, in addition to having to worry about complexity of security, are also concerned with rolling out their applications and service logic. There are a lot of security complexities that developers need to worry about, if they do not have the notion of runtime governance. But by bringing runtime governance into the SOA picture, the complications of security can be offloaded in a centralized manner. The user access policies framework is to be designed to sustain changes in access control and varying user data

Federated Security with Open Standards

In a standard distributed system, users frequently need to access multiple resources to complete a single business transaction. With the advent of single sign-on (SSO), users can log on to the system once and can remain authenticated for all the systems throughout a complete business transaction (Svoboda, 2002).

Although the single sign-on concept is appealing, employing it is not at all easy because enterprise systems often have anecdotal security requirements and a large range of fundamental technologies on which they are deployed. Single sign-on can be developed for applications that are deployed either locally or over a network. In the case of a network, after the user signs on—using Java authentication and authorization service (JAAS)—to the primary domain, a security assertion and markup language (SAML) assertion can be sent over the wire to different applications (Majumdar et al., 2006). In local networks, user credential data are exchanged directly between applications. Proprietary solutions for managing Web access and SSO are used by many organizations. These solutions manage sign-in sessions within a particular security domain, but where users need their sessions to flow across domains a standard mechanism is required. One of the functions that SAML defines is this standard mechanism for SSO. SAML also defines a protocol that allows organizations to exchange attributes about a user independent of SSO. Figure 1 depicts the blend between the JAAS and SAML.

Figure 1. JAAS and SAML blend

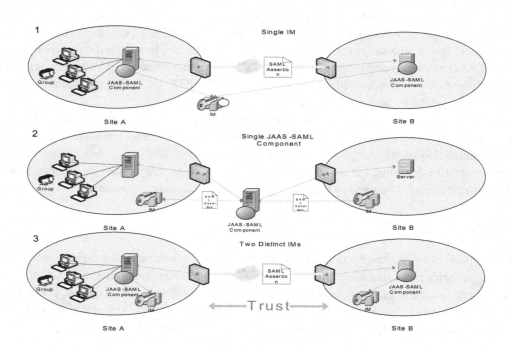

Service Monitoring and Management

While it is true that most of the times services evolve because of changes in business requirements, the data gathered from monitoring service are often the most valuable sources for information on what part of the service needs to be improved. Therefore, it is one of the main factors that drive service evolution.

In the erstwhile software applications, monitoring was limited in scope and purview. For example, in a mainframe application, monitoring was restricted to the jobs running within the mainframe and upon completion; all job failures were reported, leaving little or no scope for real-time transparency. This not only impaired performance but also led to the generation of similar reports for all kinds of users. Say an application is accessed by two kinds of entities, that is, the application owner and the application user. While the application owner would be interested in the overall performance of the application, the user might be keener on individual jobs, the reason for their failure, and possible fixes. In such cases, a generic report would be of little use to the user as an elaborate report will be to the owner. However, things changed when services entered the playfield.

Given the heterogeneous and highly distributed nature of SOA applications, service management becomes critical to manage and monitor the overall infrastructure of an SOA-based application. Thus in a service-based ecosystem, monitoring interoperable services and bringing in real time visibility and control to services deployed across multiple machines, service lifecycle, and quality management, and service level agreements and service usage monitoring are some of the key features desirable in any Web services management framework (Tosic, 2004). In this section we shall discuss the purpose of service monitoring and the upcoming standards and approaches regarding the same.

Monitoring Aspects

While the decentralized nature of SOA applications, which can otherwise be thought as a dynamic network of independent/interdependent services, makes service monitoring a challenging task, the loose coupling and openness inherent in Web services make the request/response cycle readily intercepted, thus enabling easy monitoring and management. At an abstract level, service monitoring should achieve the following features:

1. Automated performance management
2. Hawk-view of service dependencies across disparate systems
3. Metering service usage
4. Understanding the system behavior and detect problems
5. Notification

At a more granular level, service monitoring can be understood to be composed of various core functionalities like the following:

- **Usage monitoring:** This includes metering and reporting the usage of a particular service or a set of services. It may be required to monitor the service usage depending on the total number of hits, or selective usage monitoring depending on the total number of hits by a particular consumer. This could be useful in assessing the number of times a particular client has accessed a service.

- **Performance monitoring:** This includes assessing essential features relating to service performance such as response time, service load checking, fault tolerance, service performance in clustered environments, and so forth. This enables one to determine whether a service is efficiently handling a certain number of requests in an expected time. Performance monitoring helps analyze the impact of performance issues resulting due to a particular service, on the whole system, which further allows for an estimation of the overhead that will be incurred due to these.

- **Fault monitoring:** This includes identifying failed service invocations, faulty request processing, and either generating the error logs or notifying the appropriate application component for fault handling.

- **Service availability monitoring:** This includes monitoring the availability of a service, checking the active time for a service, and identifying the downtime period and duration. Requests may be simulated at regular intervals to hit a particular service and check the responsiveness. This only checks if a service is listening at a particular port or not. To check if it is running at peak efficiency, performance monitoring needs to be done once availability has been verified.

- **Service level agreements (SLA) checks:** SLA is a collection of service level objectives which serve as a contract of sorts between the service provider and the service consumer. The various parameters are either stated as requirements by the provider or are arrived at upon negotiation with the consumer. Typical SLO contents might state performance requirements, priority specifications, security or QoS agreements, and so forth. Service monitoring includes performing SLA checks and notify the violations thereon.

- **Others:** Some miscellaneous monitoring activities might include tasks like incoming data validation, schema checks, and notification. Also multistep transactions which involve multiple requests processing across multiple systems should be managed and monitored. To monitor the integrity of such transactions, the context metadata may be used by the monitoring tools to coordinate the steps involved in the transactions. Another important feature of service monitoring involves providing dashboard reports to higher management in terms of the USP of the services-feedback to access management and infrastructure management group. An infrastructure team can prescribe for an increase in the number of instances for the services and have a clustered version of the same service for better performance and client satisfaction.

Using preconfigured dashboards, monitoring operations, and reporting tools, not only can real-time errors be isolated but also the results thus obtained can be used for effective trend and impact analysis. Decision makers have a wide range of monitoring tools to choose from, most of which provide a rich set of capabilities for efficient SOA management, which very well includes service monitoring.

Service monitoring is not only checking the health of the services but also a feedback mechanism to solutions providing differential QoS features. It also helps in redefining the architecture model to suit the ever changing world. A challenge to sustain software quality can be fulfilled by service monitoring and in turn providing reports/statistics to stakeholders of the services.

Differential QoS

Standard for Web Service Management: OASIS Web service distributed management (WSDM) is an important standard for Web services management. It allows for exposing management functionality in a reusable way through two specifications: one for management using Web services (MUWS) and the other for management of Web services (MOWS). Service monitoring reports can be used to process differential service requirements rather than merely processing the requests in the order of arrival. Both generic and customizable service level checks can be supported. For instance, the runtime conditions may be monitored and dynamic negotiation of service levels can be done depending on the request submitted and the provider's capabilities. A QoS monitoring engine can be put in place to monitor the load and to gather QoS metrics, thereby enabling the provider to ensure that the performance expectation is being met and prioritization and SLA compliances are preserved.

Standards for SLA Checks. XML-based grammar like WSLA and Web service offerings language (WSOL) enable the definition of agreed upon contracts including NFRs of Web services specified as SLOs and also the ideal management and checking of such compliances. While WSLA mostly adheres to custom made SLAs and management infrastructure for establishing SLA enforcement and services monitoring, WSOL enables the specification, monitoring, and management of classes of service for Web services. Web service offering infrastructure (WSOI) enables the monitoring of Web services described in WSOL and implements the dynamic adaptation of algorithms and protocols.

These standards put together with service monitoring practices allow us to ensure business agility through guaranteed transaction performance, middleware and infrastructure health, resource monitoring, and CPU utilization checks. Thus, service monitoring plays a key role in providing a comprehensive insight to performance and efficiency of services deployed across enterprises and businesses. Both active and passive monitoring is essential to make management, infrastructure, and development decisions. By bringing a dynamic Web of services under a single lens, monitoring not only allows easy development of SOA-based applications but also facilitates more manageable application components and IT assets.

Typical architecture for services management with differential QoS support. The current practice regarding QoS differentiation in terms of performance and throughput is to use hardware-based techniques to either allocate dedicated resources for different QoS levels (i.e., physical partitioning) or by the over-provisioning of resources to absorb traffic fluctuations. The major drawbacks of these mechanisms are added complexity, higher cost, and inefficient resource utilization.

Supporting differential QoS for services should apply differentiation techniques at the message layer rather than at lower protocol layers, such as HTTP or TCP. This allows content-based request classification while leveraging the metadata carried in the message requests (mostly headers). Furthermore, differential QoS support should be transparent without requiring any changes to the application server, OS, the service client, or the service implementation. Hence, unmodified commodity services platforms can be used without costly changes while avoiding specific hardware or OS prerequisites.

This section discusses a typical architecture that involves differential QoS support added to SM platforms (see Figure 2). The following subsections describe key components of such architecture as discussed by Chatterjee, Chaudhuri, Das, Dias, and Erradi (2005) and Erradi, Varadharajan, and Padmanabhuni (2005).

Request classifier is a key requirement for supporting differentiated QoS and has the ability to classify the incoming requests according to a classification criterion or a set of criteria. For example, a classifier component can use the requester attributes metadata, which are generated by the authentication handler, to map the request to a service class. SAML could play a key role in service classification because of its wide acceptance as a standard in identity management to encode the user's access rights, authentication information, and other user attributes such as the user's role and service level (e.g., gold, silver, etc.).

Admission control is used to control throughput and to prevent the system from being overwhelmed in the presence of overload by keeping the maximum amount of load within the system capacity. Admis-

Figure 2. Architecture for SM diff QoS support

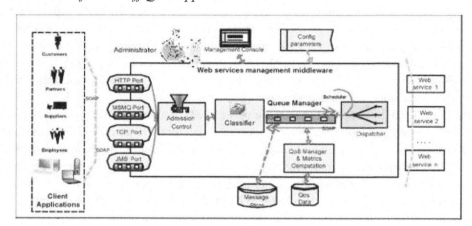

sion control requires three prerequisites: determining the load that a particular service call will generate on a system, knowing the current load on the system, and the capacity of the service implementation. Admission control is also responsible for identifying appropriate scheduling algorithms to enable differentiation in service, such as weighted round-robin scheduling, and at the same time honoring all the SLAs. In terms of implementation, this is probably the most difficult component of the architecture.

There are various ways to implement the request dispatcher, particularly the queue manager component:

- The *look-ahead parameter approach* uses a single queue where requests are queued according to their arrival order. The scheduling algorithm can use a look-ahead parameter (k) that specifies the number of positions that will be searched from the head of the queue looking for requests of a given priority. If no request of the desired priority is found, the algorithm is repeated for the next lower level and so on. The higher the value of k, the better is the service given to higher priority requests. If k = 1, requests will be serviced according to their arrival order.
- *Multiqueue dispatcher with a queue manager* implements a set of logical first-in-first-out (FIFO) queues, one for each service class. The scheduler then dispatches the pending requests according to the configured scheduling scheme.
- *Multidimension-queue with look-ahead parameter dispatcher* can be used to implement more complex service request classification schemes, where you can have a dimension for each parameter. The look-ahead parameter can be configured for each dimension. This method has the disadvantage of increased complexity in case of complex request classification rules.

Service Model and Registry

The model defines the environment for the service to act and react. The more robust and open the model the more longevity and robust is the service. A model will encompass mechanism to coexist with other environments and help the other systems to locate and access the service. A model also helps to manage the service within the boundaries of organization constraints and rules. Let us look at the various models and methodologies to build an environment around the service for better manageability and scalability.

The service model is a model (language, diagrammatic depiction, etc.) used to describe or represent the services (or collection of services) within an enterprise. In an enterprise, services may exist at different layers of the IT environment. These layers are outlined in Figure 3.

In an SOA environment, how IT (business or technical) requirements are translated into services is very important. The common functionalities/infrastructure in the different existing or future requirements need to be identified and exposed as services so that the same service can be used across different requirements. Also there is a possibility that some functionality/infrastructure that already exists needs to be exposed as a service for some new requirement to use. In order to see all the promises of SOA manifest, it is important that the enterprise follows some service model; it becomes easier to define the relationship between requirements and services and hence identify dependency and overlapping functionalities/infrastructure.

The model (or combination of models) used by the enterprise should be able to cover all layers in an IT environment and the interaction between them (Deursen, Visser, & Warmer, 2007). The model should also cover dimensions of the services. Some of the models used in enterprises and that cover different dimensions of the service are the following.

Design Time Models

Design time models are services models used at the time of design of services. IBM's service-oriented modeling and architecture (SOMA) (Arsanjani, 2004) is one such example. SOMA helps user through the process of identifying, specifying, and realizing service. It helps align the business and IT goals by using service modeling that connects business models to IT models. The user can also validate business goal to service realization. The model maps business goals to processes and gives a componentized view of the main activities, the events that trigger those, inputs, outputs, faults, and so forth.

In the identification stage, the SOMA approach identifies the needed services and also helps determine which already exist and which need to be created. Then the services are specified by defining their

Figure 3. Service layers

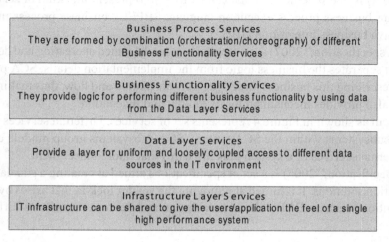

331

multiple aspects, or service model, including dependencies, composition, and messages to be exchanged. SOMA also provides a framework for deciding which services should be exposed to partners based on business needs and also a container in which the services will be deployed. In the realization stage, the framework helps you take decisions that specify how it is anticipated that the service will serve the purpose it was built for. SOMA can be used for design time modeling of the services.

Runtime Models

Runtime service models are used to represent the runtime state of the services. Web services resource framework (WSRF) ("WSRF specification," 2004) is an example of a runtime service model. WSRF is an OASIS standard that provides a standard way to model and manage the state of different resources that are being used in a Web service interaction. It is a set of six Web services standards. One of these six specifications is the WS-ResourceProperties. The WS-ResourceProperties specification standardizes the definition of properties for a particular resource and operation and XML needed to access and manipulate these properties. It also standardizes the association of a WS-resource to a Web service interface.

A WS-resource can be any resource that is being used in a Web service interaction. Therefore, it can also be something like the server on which hosts the Web service. A set of properties can be associated with this resource which specifies the service level agreement or performance parameters for the service. These performance parameters can be constantly monitored based on the defined values and updated to reflect current capabilities of the resource being used by the service.

The WSRF model can used to represent the runtime capabilities of the service or some other metadata information about the service.

Aggregation Models

Aggregation models are used to represent how services are linked together to provide a business functionality. In an enterprise there might high level services that are formed by different kinds of aggregation (e.g., orchestration or choreography) of lower level services. It is important to have a model that represents this kind of interaction between heterogeneous services (Hanson, 2003). Service component architecture (SCA) is one specification that can be used to represent this kind of services. Some of the other models are business process execution language (BPEL), business process modeling language (BPML), and Java business integration (JBI).

SCA ("SCA specification," 2007) is an architecture model aimed at creating and deploying standardized services. It separates the business logic from the implementation details. SCA provides consistent interfaces for describing this business logic code's encapsulation and flow, thus making them accessible as a service. It also provides mechanism for its lookup and invocation.

A SCA system as shown in Figure 4 represents set of services. Different services are represented as different SCA subsystems within the SCA system. SCA subsystems group module components, entry points, and external services of a system plus the wires that interconnect them.

JBI ("JBI specification," 2005) is a set of specifications aimed at creating a standard-based architecture for integration solutions. It is aimed at removing the vendor lock-in that arises by using proprietary integration solutions such as EAI tools. It provides an architecture that allows different applications

Figure 4. SCA module

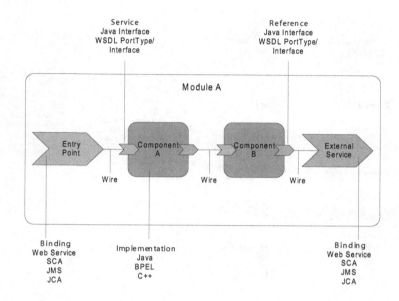

to integrate with each other using XML messages and WSDL interfaces. Figure 5 depicts the basic components of JBI architecture.

Business process management (BPM) follows the model-driven architecture concept. The process definition from the model is captured with a process definition language like BPEL or BPML, a modeling language for business processes from the Business Process Management Initiative (www.bpmi.org). Unlike ebXML, which is geared to public interfaces, BPML is designed to model private processes.

BPEL is an extensible XML language that enables the definition of composite applications. The base activities describing a BPEL process as well as the communication interfaces of the resulting processes are Web services. BPEL is the result of the merging of two Web service composition languages, namely XLANG from Microsoft and WSFL from IBM.

Service Sharing Model

A service sharing model is a representation of the service in such a way that it facilitates easy search and usage of the service. UDDI ("UDDI v3.0.2 specification," 2005) is a sharing model that allows sharing of services in a standard way. UDDI is an XML-based registry and provides a standard-based method for publishing and finding service descriptions. It provides support for defining both business and service information.

The UDDI specification enables businesses to quickly, easily, and dynamically find and transact with one another. UDDI enables a business to:

1. Describe its business and its services;
2. Discover other businesses that offer desired services; and
3. Integrate with these other businesses.

Figure 5. JBI architecture

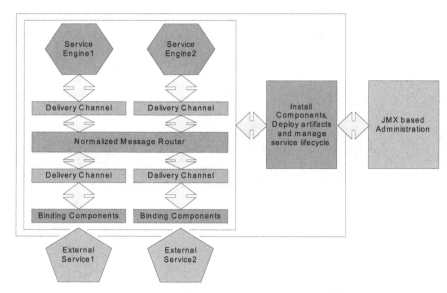

To develop componentized Web-based services, UDDI provides a standardized and simple way of categorizing and identifying businesses, services, and their technical specifications. Shown below is the data structures used in a UDDI registry. Figure 6 shows UDDI data structures.

1. *BusinessEntity* – It allows the description of the business.
2. *BusinessService* – It is the set of services offered by the business.
3. *BindingTemplate* – Every service can have a set of binding templates which have details of how the service can be invoked. It refers to a *TModel*.
4. *TModels* - A *TModel* represents each distinct specification, transport, protocol, or namespace. *TModels* can be reused by multiple *BindingTemplates* and this promotes interoperability. *TModels* are also used for the following purposes within UDDI:
   1. Transport and protocol definitions such as HTTP and SMTP
   2. Value sets including identifier systems, categorization systems, and namespaces
   3. Structured categorizations using multiple value sets called "categorization groups"
   4. Postal address formats
   5. Find qualifiers used to modify the behavior of the UDDI *find_object* APIs
   6. Use type attributes that specify the kind of resource being referred to by a URI reference

One or more *BusinessService* elements can come under a *BusinessEntity*; *BusinessService* contains *BusinessTemplates*, which in turn contains *TModels*. Each of them contains identifier and *CategoryBag* elements. *IdentifierBags* are to identify specific services or businesses and *CategoryBags* organize UDDI registry entries in a structured way. A mapping between *BindingTemplates* and *TModels* can be placed by harnessing the *IdentifierBag* and/or *CategoryBag*. *CategoryBag* can also be used to add categorization information.

Figure 6. UDDI data structures

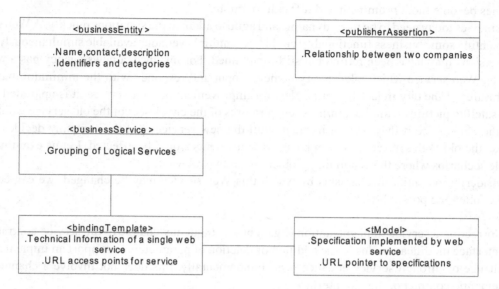

A SOA environment also requires some kind of model that can help services coevolutionize apart from heterogeneous service interaction. UDDI is a model that helps in representing the static information about services, that is, information required to use the service. UDDI acts as a central registry to find services and information about them. An enterprise level registry helps to find the latest service information and thus evolve parallel.

Taxonomy

Taxonomy is a very important part of a registry. Taxonomy is nothing but classification of objects into finite number of groups. Using registries, it becomes possible to define taxonomies and these taxonomies can be associated with businesses, services, and technical details which make it easier to categorize, identify, and search them. So having a proper enterprise level and interenterprise level taxonomy is important since objects will be searched based on this taxonomy. For example, if a "discount calculation" service is already available which calculates the discount to be given to a customer based on some complex rules, this service is available only in systems used in stores. Say the discount service is categorized under a "billing" category. Now if the user is also given the option of buying goods online and the same service needs to be used to calculate the discount, the team developing the online system needs to know the taxonomy followed by the other teams so that they can find the appropriate service from the registry. This can be done by following a uniform/standard enterprise level registry taxonomy.

Service Versioning

SOA and Web services have gained industry wide acceptance. Standardization of various aspects such as security, communication protocol, discovery and registration, and so forth has added to its pace of adoption. However, aspects of service management become important as a business grows and versioning issues become more prominent and difficult to ignore.

Businesses today need to be more dynamic and agile to adapt to the situations quickly. A Web service implementing some business functionality could have multiple versions available simultaneously, while older versions may have been retired but still maintained. For instance, a news agency has a weather reporting Web service which takes a city name as input and responds with the minimum/maximum temperatures of the city in last 24 hours. Now for improvement of their service, it is upgraded to also return satellite pictures with the min/max temperatures of the city. Users of the old service would keep using the old service if they are not intimate with the new service or if the company decides to discontinue the old Web service, in which business with clients would be affected. Let us examine some possible scenarios where the versioning problem would be relevant.

Considering potential mechanisms by which this Web service may be changed, we can come up with the following possibilities:

- Correcting a service implementation (e.g., a bug without any change to the service contract).
- Interface modification due to the addition or deletion of parameters to support an implementation change or through service enhancement. Fundamentally, this does not involve a change to the semantic contract of the old interface.
- Service implementation change (with no change to the service interface) due to change in the business rules.

Real-life businesses are bound to change due to issues varying from business rule changes to service-level improvement. And if a service has a large number of clients, handling the change is even harder, as either all the clients' needs to be intimate with the change or the change should be small enough so that it does not affect business, otherwise it would mean violation of the SLA. In the following, various options ranging from design to implementation level techniques have been proposed to manage issues related to service versioning. A number of techniques including usage of UDDI (Majumdar et al., 2006), configuration management solution (Brown & Ellis, 2004; Kenyon, 2003), XML namespaces, and WS-addressing standard (Anand, Kunti, Chawla, & Marwah, 2005) have been explored to address the issue.

UDDI-Based Option for Version Management

According to the UDDI ("UDDI v3.0.2 specification," 2005) v3 specification, "Subscription provides clients, known as subscribers, with the ability to register their interest in receiving information concerning changes made in a UDDI registry. These changes can be scoped based on preferences provided with the request." UDDI supports updating user information but does not show version information. A UDDI data model is rich enough to enhance the current model to include service versioning.

We can add versioning information in the *CategoryBag* by using the key name "Version" and key value as the version number. Although *BindingTemplate* and *BusinessService* are already linked, with UDDI v3, having *CategoryBags* in *BindingTemplates*, we can explicitly map *BindingTemplates* and *BusinessServices* by putting the service name in the *BindingTemplate's CategoryBag*.

Now as *TModel* is linked to *BindingTemplate*, the service consumer requires mentioning which service version the consumer wants to use. *TModels* can then be searched based on version numbers.

At runtime, the service consumers can retrieve *TModels* associated with a particular *BindingTemplate* and then search for a particular version number in their *CategoryBags*.

Version Management using XML Namespaces

XML namespaces may be used to provide a different mechanism for handling interface change. XML schema's "*targetNamespace*" attribute is used to provide a scoping mechanism; therefore, this attribute may be used to identify changed interfaces. A naming convention used for namespaces may be predefined and communicated to consumers through the service documentation. One simple approach may be to add a version number to the original namespace URL. Alternatively, a timestamp may be used to augment the URL. Consider a change to a WSDL, similar to the aforementioned change to add an additional parameter to an operation. In this case, we may indicate the modification by changing the namespace attribute to something as follows:

targetNamespace=http://www.mydomain.com/Webservices/weather/Service_v1.1.wsdl
or
targetNamespace=http://www.mydomain.com/Webservices/2005/01/05/ weather /Service.wsdl

In the second example, the versioning is accomplished by placing the WSDL scoped by the time-stamp of the change.

Requests which are associated with the previous version, that is, those that are associated with the older namespace, may be handled by a couple of different options. One option is to generate an error on the server and provide data to the user on the new implementation. This approach would result in service consumers having at least one guaranteed failure per service change during service invocation. Therefore, if a service undergoes multiple modifications within a short time frame, this can lead to poor quality of service delivered to the consumer.

A more graceful approach is to provide an intermediate Web service that can accept requests and then make a decision to forward the requests to the correct implementation based on the timestamp/version rules. This would not add a significant amount of overhead to the existing implementation and it may be the preferred option given the expected frequency of service changes.

WS-Addressing for Version Management

The WS-addressing specification can be used to provide an efficient solution for tackling issues related to versioning in Web services. WS-addressing enhances the WS-versioning standard to address versioning mechanism. As mentioned in the problem definition section, three broad scenarios have been identified in relation to version management of services, namely implementation change, implementation correction, and interface change. WS-addressing can also be used to address scenarios in which the endpoint URL of a Web service changes.

Implementation Correction or Change: There can be a scenario where implementation of a service changes or is being rectified. In such a case the client will continue using the service without any knowledge that the service has changed. WS-addressing can be used to solve the issue by adding a custom tag to indicate any change in implementation; for instance, a tag named <implementation> has been included in a response message to indicate the change in the implementation logic.

```
</wsa:ReferenceProperties>
    <Implementation>
        The Implementation has been changed.
        The new interest calculation method is P*T*9/100 instead of P*T*8.2/100
    </Implementation>
</wsa:ReferenceProperties>
```

Whenever the implementation changes, the information pertaining to the specific change is included in this tag for a certain period of time. When there has been no change performed to the implementation of the service, an empty implementation tag is provided. Similarly, the client can include an implementation tag that indicates the last-accessed implementation version, so if the implementation has changed since the last client request the service can send the required information. However, usage of custom tags to convey versioning information must be done only after an agreement between the client and the service.

Interface Change: In this scenario, the number of parameters, or the type of parameters associated with the interface, changes. In this case an error message needs to be communicated to the client that should also contain information communicating the details of the change. In case a client request does not match the required interface definition, WS-addressing can be used to tackle the change by including some custom header tags that indicate interface change. For instance, a custom tag called <*interface*> is used to communicate the information related to the change to the client.

```
</wsa:ReferenceProperties>
    <Interface>
        The interface has been changed.
        For future usage, please refer to new WSDL file
    </Interface >
</wsa:ReferenceProperties>
```

Endpoint Change: In this scenario the endpoint of a service is changed and the responsibility of forwarding the request to the new endpoint is delegated to some dummy service for a period of time. In such a scenario the requirement is to communicate the new URL to the existing users. Figures 2 and 3 show such a scenario. In a traditional approach the dummy service takes the responsibility of invoking the new service and sending the response back to the client. There is no way the new service can send the response directly to the client. Moreover, custom headers need to be added in order to communicate the changed location to the client. Use of WS-addressing headers can solve the aforementioned issues, and the "<*from*>" tag in the response effectively communicates the new URL to the client. Furthermore, the service can send the response directly to the client based on the "<*ReplyTo*>" tag of the request message.

Service Decommission

To retire an older version of a service we may intimate the users for a particular duration of time, informing the expiry date of the older version and the availability of the newer version of the service. This can be implemented by the approach suggested earlier of adding a custom tag to indicate any change;

for instance, a tag named <serviceExpiry> can be included in a response message to notify users of a version's expiration. As illustrated above, WS-addressing can be used to implement the approach suggested.

A decommission of service is as important as the deployment or publishing of it over time with a different version evolving. Decommissioning is not just a matter of deactivating the service but a process of letting the consumers know in advance of the deactivation, do not accept request for such services, or reroute the request to new service, acknowledging the incorrect client users, probably suspend the service for a stipulated period, run the deactivated service for a period with acknowledging the state.

FUTURE TRENDS

The current trend in defining a model for the services is to bring in the concept of domain specific language (DSL) to bridge the gap of business vertical domains. Added to this flavor, there needs to be some level of semantic interoperability between models or information for better understanding and execution of a service architecture model. Service versioning can take a leap by maintaining and exchanging metadata information of services. Ontology can be used to maintain metadata about services or as simple as exchanging service policies complying with WS-policy standards.

CONCLUSION

As mentioned in this chapter, service maintainability and evolution need to be regarded as integral parts of the design and development phase. The chapter has explained a few key encompassing models and standards that service architecture needs to detail out in the initial design phase. The disciplines prescribed by a SOA practitioner needs to fall in place in defining service versioning, defining parameters for service monitoring, and mapping the same to quality of services provided to their end customers. A service model not only develops a framework but also the bridge that helps to collaborate with other systems and businesses. A service can sustain business agility and acquisitions by following the disciplines and strategies imbided in the service models and models to ensure service quality.

REFERENCES

Anand, S., Kunti, K., Chawla, M., & Marwah, K. (2005). Best practices and solutions for managing versioning of SOA Web services. *SOA World Magazine*. Retrieved July 24, 2007, from http://soa.syscon.com/read/143883.htm

Arsanjani, A. (2004). Service oriented modeling and architecture. *IBM developerworks*. Retrieved July 10, 2007, from http://www.ibm.com/developerworks/library/ws-soa-design1/

Brown, K., & Ellis, M. (2004). Best practices for Web services versioning. *IBM developerworks*. Retrieved on July 16, 2007, from http://www.ibm.com/developerworks/Webservices/library/ws-version/

Chatterjee, A., Chaudhuri, A., Das, A. S., Dias, T., & Erradi, A. (2005). Differential QoS support in Web services management. *SOA World Magazine*. Retrieved July 20, 2007, from http://Webservices. sys-con.com/read/121946.htm

Deursen, A. V., Visser, E., & Warmer, J., (2007). *Model-driven software evolution: A research agenda*. Retrieved July 15, 2007, from http://swerl.tudelft.nl/twiki/pub/EelcoVisser/ModelDrivenSoftwareEvolutionAResearchAgenda/DVW07.pdf

Erradi, A., Varadharajan, N., & Padmanabhuni, S., Dr. (2005). *WS-DiffServ: A middleware for differentiated service delivery*. Paper presented at the International Conference on Service-Oriented Computing (pp. 781-788). IEEE Computer Society Press.

Hanson, J. (2003). Coarse-grained interfaces enable service composition in SOA. *TechRepublic*. Retrieved July 20, 2007, from http://articles.techrepublic.com.com/5100-22-5064520.html#Listing%20C

Java business integration (JBI) specification. (2005). *Java community process*. Retrieved July 11, 2007, from http://www.jcp.org/en/jsr/detail?id=208

Kenyon, J. (2003). Web service versioning and deprecation. *Web Services Journal*. SYS-CON Publications, Inc. Retrieved on July 17, 2007, from http://Webservices.sys-con.com/read/39678.htm

Lehman, M., Ramil, J. F., Wernick, P., Perry, D. E., & Turski, W. M. (1997). *Metrics and laws of software evolution - the nineties view*. Paper presented at the International Symposium of Software Metrics (pp. 20-32). IEEE Computer Society Press.

Majumdar, B., Chaudhuri, A. P., & Sitaram. V., (2006). SOA requires enterprise application security integration architecture. *Search software quality*. Retrieved July 27, 2007, from http://searchsoftwarequality.techtarget.com/tip/0,289483,sid92_gci1168738,00.html

Majumdar, B., Verma, A., & Mysore, U. (2006). Enhance UDDI to manage Web services. *IBM developerworks*. Retrieved July 27, 2007, from http://www.ibm.com/developerworks/Webservices/library/ws-uddisecure/

Parnas, D. (1994). *Software aging*. Paper presented at the International Conference of Software Engineering (pp. 279-287). IEEE Computer Society Press.

Service component architecture (SCA) specification. (2007). *Open service oriented architecture*. Retrieved July 10, 2007 from http://www.osoa.org/display/Main/Service+Component+Architecture+Home

Shin, S. (2003). Secure Web services. *JavaWorld*. Retrieved on July 17, 2007, from http://www.javaworld.com/javaworld/jw-03-2003/jw-0321-wssecurity.html?page=1

Svoboda, Z. (2002). Securing Web services with single sign-on. *TheServerSide*. Retrieved on July 18, 2007, from http://www.theserverside.com/tt/articles/article.tss?l=Systinet-Web-services-part-6

Tosic, V. (2004). *Service offerings for XML Web services and their management applications*. Unpublished doctoral dissertation, Carleton University, Ottawa, Canada.

Universal description, discovery and integration (UDDI) specification. (2005). *OASIS*. Retrieved on July 21, 2007 from http://uddi.xml.org/

WS-resource framework (WSRF) specification. (2004). *Globus alliance*. Retrieved on July 22, 2007, from http://www.globus.org/wsrf/

Zimmermann, O., Krogdahl, P., & Gee, C. (2004). Elements of service-oriented analysis and design. *IBM developerworks*. Retrieved on July 19, 2007, from http://www.ibm.com/developerworks/Webservices/library/ws-soad1/

Chapter XVI
The Role of Web Services:
A Balance Scorecard Perspective

Pauline Ratnasingam
University of Central Missouri, USA

ABSTRACT

This chapter aims to examine the extent of Web services usage and quality, applying the balanced score-card methodology in a small business firm as an exploratory case study. This chapter contributes to guidelines and lessons learned that will inform, educate, and promote small businesses on the importance of maintaining the quality of Web services.

INTRODUCTION

The Internet, a rapidly expanding global computer and communication infrastructure, has facilitated the emergence of digitization and globalization that in turn has permitted businesses to extensively engage in foreign investments. Forrester Research suggests that e-commerce in the U.S. will grow 19%, reaching $230 billion by 2008. Today, firms are attempting to attain their value chain goals by offering to sell products and services. Web services have become a significant part of small business, as they are used to facilitate the seamless flow of business transactions and are known to offer many benefits.

However, studies also show that the lack of effective use, quality, and security in Web service applications is one of the main reasons why firms fail to realize the full potential of their IT investments (Benko & McFarlan, 2003). It is imperative that small businesses focus on the quality of Web services and their operations given the extent to which Web service applications are used in business processes in this fast changing market conditions. Enforcing and maintaining the quality of Web services does not only involve a set of security analyses and audit procedures that most firms conduct periodically, but rather it is a continual process that needs to align a rigorous methodology. Such methodology is the balanced scorecard, which is a set of quantifiable measures that aim to monitor and manage a firm's strategic performance. This chapter aims to examine the extent of Web services usage and quality by applying the balance scorecard methodology in a small business firm.

The balanced scorecard is needed to align, monitor, and adjust the factors that impact the quality of Web services. Previous studies applying the balanced scorecard in the context of Web services and quality is limited. Only 10% of the organizations executed their implementation strategy to apply the balanced scorecard methodology because they experienced barriers in formulating a vision, allocating resources (i.e., human resources), and managing change (Niven, 2003). This chapter aims to examine the extent of Web services usage and quality, applying the balanced scorecard methodology in a small business firm as an exploratory case study. The next section discusses the theory of balanced scorecard and Web services followed by the development of a framework which integrates the critical success factors. Then we discuss the research method and provide a description of the background information of the firm. We then test the framework via an exploratory case study and report the findings. The findings contribute to guidelines and lessons learned that will inform, educate, and promote small businesses on the importance of maintaining the quality of Web services. Finally, we conclude the chapter with contributions and directions for future research.

BACKGROUND INFORMATION: THE BALANCED SCOREBOARD

The balanced scorecard deployed to measure the effective use and quality of Web services among small businesses focuses on a system that enforces measurement and feedback, thereby imposing quality, continuous improvement, employee empowerment, and strategic performance that aim to sustain the competitive and strategic objectives. The balanced scorecard measures the performance of Web services in a small business firm from four perspectives, namely, learning and growth, internal business processes, customer, and financial perspectives, which are discussed below. Each of these four perspectives is further categorized by their objectives (as in what are their outcomes?) measures (as in how to achieve their outcomes?) targets, that is, accountability (as in how do we know that we have achieved it?), and initiatives (as in what actions to take?). Further, the balanced scorecard is based on three time dimensional timelines, namely, yesterday, today, and tomorrow. The next section presents a discussion of the four perspectives.

1. The *learning and growth perspective* aims to measure the human, information, and organizational capital. Human capital includes the skills, knowledge, expertise, the extent of training given to employees, and the business cultural attitudes. Do small business employees have the skills/competencies to operate the Web service application and align it with their internal business processes effectively in order to meet their customers' objectives of using Web services? Information capital aims to measure effective communication and information sharing. Do small business employees possess the information required to achieve objectives? Organizational capital aims to monitor the soft areas of the employees, such as, learning and growth, culture, leadership, knowledge sharing, and teamwork. Do small businesses have the ability to sustain growth and change that in turn enhances the quality of Web services?

2. The *internal business process perspective* aims to measure performance that permits small businesses to be aware of the quality of their products and services. Web services, considered as system quality, are defined as "the conformance to explicitly stated functional and performance

requirements, explicitly stated development standards, and implicit characteristics that are expected of all professionally developed software" (Solano, De Ovalles, Rojas, Padua, & Morales, 2003, p. 67). Similarly, Ortega, Perez, and Rojas (2000) suggest that product effectiveness should include characteristics such as timeliness, functionality, reliability, usability, efficiency, maintainability, and probability. Small businesses need to be aware of the following questions when assessing the quality of their Web services performance. Does our internal business processes applying Web services conform to the mission of small businesses? Does the internal business processes meet our customer requirements? There are two types of processes under strategic management. First, the mission oriented-process focuses on the strategic goals of small businesses, and second, the support processes are more repetitive and are used in the daily operations that in turn enforce benchmarking. The balanced scorecard provides a diagnostic feedback into the various internal processes, thereby guiding and improving the business processes involved in the use of Web services on a continuous basis. What must small businesses do well internally in order to achieve the objectives they set forth to achieve quality in Web services? Where does the Web services "process" start, and where does it end?

3. The ***customer perspective*** focuses on meeting the needs of the customers, retaining existing customers, and gaining customer satisfaction. What do customers expect or demand from the use of Web services? Dimensions of customers experience include time, quality, price or cost, accessibility, reputation, and relationship. Who do we define as our customers? How do our customers see us? How do Web services create value for our customers?

4. The *financial perspective* aims to provide timely and accurate financial information. By implementing a centralized database, it is hoped that processing can be standardized and automated. Further, both risk assessment and cost benefit analysis can be easily conducted in order to ensure that the bottom line of small businesses is achieved. What accountability do small businesses that use Web services have to financial stakeholders? In many respects, the financial perspective represents "end in mind" of the small business strategic vision. Small business managers are able

Figure 1. The balanced scorecard perspectives

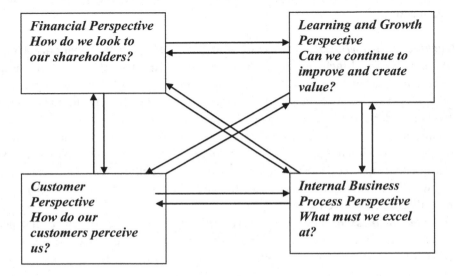

to examine the outcomes of their business performance that provide strategic financial feedback and show the trends of their business performance using Web services overtime. Figure 1 presents the perspectives of the balanced scorecard.

WEB SERVICES

Web services are creating a service-oriented architecture that provides technical solutions and e-collaborations among value chain partners (Chan, Kellen, & Nair, 2004; Yen, 2004). Web services refer to a new breed of Web applications as self-contained, self-describing modular applications that can be published, located, and invoked across the Web. Businesses use existing software components specified as services to perform business operations in a "service-oriented architecture." Similarly, Web services refer to a set of software applications or components developed using a specific set of application programming interface (API) standards and Internet-based communication protocols. The objective is to enable these applications or components to invoke function calls and exchange data among themselves over the standard Internet infrastructure. We define Web services as "modular Internet-based business functions that perform specific business tasks to facilitate business interactions within and beyond the organization." Further, Web services generate sustainable competitive advantage for firms supporting their core competencies and adding value to the execution of the corporate strategy. The technology's fullest potential will not be realized if it is used only for improving the operational efficiency of existing business processes. Therefore, we focus on the quality of Web services usage by applying a rigorous methodology called the balanced scorecard methodology as it measures the effective use and quality of Web services from four perspectives, namely, learning and growth, internal business processes, customer, and financial perspectives, thereby providing a holistic view.

The Web Services Architecture

The Web services architecture is made up of three layers of technology. At the foundation (the bottom layer) is the software standards and communication protocols that provide a common language for Web services and enable applications to be connected. Standards and protocols are often cited as the strategic value that Web services bring (Hagel, 2002; Hagel & Brown, 2001). The service grid (the middle layer) provides a set of shared utilities from security to third-party auditing, to billing and payment so that critical business functions and transactions over the Internet can be conducted. This layer publishes the services that serve as entry points for queries to find service descriptions. In short, the service grid plays two roles. First, it helps the Web service requestors and providers to find and connect with one another; secondly, it creates a trusted environment essential for carrying out mission-critical business activities, thereby contributing to technology trust. Finally, the top layer consists of a diverse array of application services. It is in this top layer where the day-to-day operations will be most visible to employees, customers, and trading partners. The top layer performs the service binding and invocation. Similarly, three are layers of Web services, namely, basic services, composite services, and managed services. While basic services manage the publication, discovery, selection, and binding, composite services facilitate the coordination, conformance, monitoring, and quality of service. Finally, managed services provide the market certification rating and operations support.

Table 1 presents the three layers of the Web services architecture adapted from Hagel and Brown (2001).

FRAMEWORK OF THE BALANCED SCORECARD FOR WEB SERVICES

The framework of balanced scorecard for Web services was developed by integrating the theory of balanced scorecard and Web services. The framework consists of critical success factors or indicators that make up the objectives, measures, targets, and initiatives. The goal of these critical success factors is to evaluate the effective use and quality of Web service applications. Table 2 below illustrates the framework of the balanced scorecard in Web services, which serves as a measurement tool, thereby ensuring the quality of Web services.

RESEARCH METHOD

Case studies were chosen as an appropriate method to evaluate the effective use and quality of Web services among small businesses as it elicited subtle and rich data needed, thereby increasing our understanding in the use and quality of Web services applying the balanced scorecard methodology (Yin, 1994).

We attempted to identify the critical success factors in the effective use and quality of Web services by deploying the balanced scorecard framework for small businesses based on the objectives (what are the outcomes?) measures (how to achieve the outcomes?), targets, that is, accountability and initiatives (how do we know that we have achieved it?), and initiatives (what actions to take?) for all the four perspectives (i.e., learning and growth, internal business processes, customer, and financial perspectives).

In this study we interviewed the managers of the firm in the agricultural industry. Initial entry into the case site was obtained by making telephone calls to key representatives in the organization. A brief description and purpose of the study was discussed before requesting them to participate. The telephone conversation was followed by an e-mail to the respondents with an attachment of the file describing the

Table 1. The Web services architecture

Top Layer – Application Service Web services runs on any application platform as long as it has a Web server connected to the Internet.
Middle Layer – Service Grid The service grid layer provides four types of utilities: (1) Service management utilities (i.e., provisioning, monitoring, ensuring quality of service, synchronization, conflict resolution) (2) Resource knowledge management utilities (i.e., directories, brokers, registries, repositories, data transformation) (3) Transport management utilities (i.e., message queuing, filtering, metering, monitoring, routing, resource orchestration) (4) Shared utilities (i.e., security, auditing, and assessment of third party performance, billing and payment)
Bottom Layer – Software Standards and Communication Protocols Software standards include: (1) Web service description language (WSDL) to describe the Web service (2) Universal, description, discovery and integration (UDDI) to advertise, syndicate as a central organization for registering, finding, and using Web services) (3) Web services flow language (WSFL) to define work flows (4) XML (format for data exchange and description) (5) Communication protocols including simple object access protocol (SOAP) to communicate that are for calling Web services, HTTP, and TCP/IP)

Table 2. Framework of the balanced scorecard in Web services

Balanced Scorecard Perspectives	Relationship to Effective use and Quality of Web Services via the Critical Success Factors (or Indicators)
(1) **(1) Learning and growth perspective** *How can we continue to improve and create value in the use of Web services?*	**Objectives:** employees must be well trained and are expected to perform their day-to-day business operations applying Web services **Measures:** provide online training, user manuals, standard operating procedures, help desk, and reward employees with high productivity **Targets:** fewer customers and stakeholder complaints **Initiatives:** ongoing monitoring of employees performance, focus on the culture, climate, and commitment of the organization.
(2) **Internal business process perspective** *What processes do we need to excel further when using Web services?*	**Objectives:** to achieve high quality and productivity of the services provided via Web services **Measures:** apply best business practices, reliable, accurate, and timely information. Focus on the usability, interoperability of the system **Targets:** increased profit and fewer customers and stakeholders complaints **Initiatives:** ongoing audit and applying the quality assurance plan on a regular basis
(3) **Customer perspective** *How can we enhance our business reputation with our customers via Web services?*	**Objectives:** satisfaction of customers and stakeholders, reputation of the firm and the quality of their products and services **Measures:** open, frequent communications, providing excellent quality services, provide value for money and reliable operations **Targets:** increase in profit and sales **Initiatives:** training employees, ongoing weekly meetings with employees; regular review and reflection of the goals and mission of the company
(4) **Financial perspective** *How are we perceived by our shareholders and other stakeholders invested in our firm?*	**Objectives:** increase in profits, rate of return **Measures:** increased productivity, increase quality of services provided, apply the return on capital employed, economic value added and free cash flow **Targets:** profit figures, increased shareholders value **Initiatives:** advertising their company products, attending trade shows, business conferences and seminars, word of mouth, control operating costs, maximize potential use of Web services

purpose of the study. Once confirmation of their willingness to participate in the study was received, appointment dates for interview sessions were arranged with the managers in the firm. Evidence for the exploratory case study data came from the hand written notes taken during the two (90 minutes) face-to-face interviews and the tape recorded data. In addition, analysis of existing documents relating to Web service applications, day-to-day interactions, operating procedures, Web sites, and internal security policies were analyzed. The tape recorded data was transcribed to identify concepts via pattern matching to the balanced scorecard framework.

FINDINGS: BACKGROUND INFORMATION OF FIRM A

Firm A is a small business seed manufacturer and seller of wild flower and bird seeds located in Kingsville. It is a family owned business with 10 employees and the owner has been in this business for 23 years. They sell a variety of wild flowers seeds including the annual mix, shade, and suns. They also supply bird seeds to regular stores, residential customers, and fulfill large bids from the government for beautifying the land, such as for the city of Blue Springs and the Tiffany Springs highway. Their main form of Web service application is their business-to-consumer (B2C) Web site implemented in 2003, which has embedded IT solutions, e-mail, and fax. Table 3 presents the background information of Firm A.

In this section we report the findings of the exploratory case study from the hand written notes taken during the face-to-face interview with the manager of Firm A.

Web Services Quality in the Learning and Growth Perspective

Firm A found that the learning capability in applying best business practices was important for their business performance. Although only six employees were assigned to operate their computer systems, they had to abide to best business practices that included changing their passwords every 10 days and not disclosing pricing information to any other employees other than the manager and two other employees in the accounts department. Each employee was given limited access rights and was unable to see the detail information of the transaction.

The manager noted, *"We continually improve our employee skills by providing training to our employees in order to increase the potential use of Web services."*

Web services were deployed to facilitate information sharing and collaboration among employees and business units.

Web Services Quality in Improving Internal Business Processes

The internal business process perspective focused on the quality and use of Web services in activities such as supply chain management, customer relationship management, and research and development. The balanced scorecard provided a systemic quality approach to assess Web services as it allowed the software processes to be efficiently and effectively balanced. The manager noted, *"We applied the quality assurance plan which included the following critical success factors: timeliness of obtaining information or processing the transaction, accuracy as in achieving integrity in the content of the mes-*

Table 3. Background information of firm A

Background Characteristics	Firm A
Type of industry	Agricultural industry
Size of Firm	Small business
Type of ownership	Family owned
Number of employees	10
Type of Web service application	B2C Web site & embedded IT solutions
Type and number of customers/business partners	Regular store customers, government bid contracts, Web customers
Annual revenue in US$	$1.5 million
How long have they being in business?	23 years
Mode of attracting customers	Advertise in the local newspaper, Web page

sage, confidentiality, access rights, non-repudiation, reusability, portability, reliability, security and efficiency of the Web service applications were considered in this perspective."

The manager indicated that, *"Further, with industry-accepted standards and protocols, Web services provided a standard interface allowing integration among heterogeneous platforms, thus facilitating efficient and effective collaboration between departments that use different IT systems. Finally, Web services' service-oriented architecture allows firms to build a flexible IT infrastructure that enables faster decision-making and response to market changes."*

Hence, through the orchestration of modular, loosely coupled software components, Web services enable an "assemble line approach" to software development, resulting in a responsive IT infrastructure for designing and building faster application development and enterprise applications.

We argue that Web services technology, with its industry-accepted standards and protocols, can enhance internal business operations by enabling process automation, increasing interoperability and reducing integration complexity, and improving process design.

Web Services Quality in Improving Customer Retention and Relationships

The customer perspective is the core of the business strategy. The manger noted, *"Our Web services and IT solutions offered us with unique business processes and customer value propositions that determined the correct business processes thereby creating better customer relationships."*

The manager also noted, *"We have key attributes of Web services that create customer value propositions such as; enhanced customer intimacy via open communications, improved customer retention, and better customer value. Beyond the quality and specifications of its products and services we try to satisfy our customers by meeting their needs and offering quality goods and services."*

These attributes that serve as critical success factors were derived from the balanced scorecard methodology which comprises of objectives, measures, targets, and initiatives.

The manager indicated, *"Web services made our firm's IT infrastructure more flexible and adaptable, affording the organizational agility to meet the ongoing customers' changing requirements."*

Web Services Quality in Improving Financial Position

The use of the balanced scorecard methodology allowed for improved capability of learning and innovation, better internal business processes, and the enhanced customer value that in turn served as performance drivers for increased financial returns.

The manager noted, *"Web services has directly influenced our shareholder value as it influenced our firm's financial strategy, productivity and revenue growth."*

Further, he added, *"For example, in the financial perspective we aimed to create value for the shareholders and there is a balance between growth and productivity. Further, return on capital employed and economic value indicators are added."*

LESSONS LEARNED

The findings suggests a cyclic process that was created with the use of the balanced scorecard approach to evaluate the quality of Web services applications and in order to integrate quality, provide a strategic map, and indicate how information will be disseminated so that the potential use of Web services can be attained. The processes adapted from Kaplan and Norton (2000) included:

- **Analysis of the sector, its development and role of company:** Refers to the identifications of the key goals in the use of Web services and establishing the characteristics and requirements for the industry.
- **Establishing or confirming the company's strategic plan:** Refers to the establishment or confirmation of a strategic plan, intensifying the internal and external analysis of the earlier processes, and ensuring that agreements are arrived towards the quality of Web services.
- **Translating the strategy into operational terms:** Refers to the actual actions taken to ensure that best business practices, standards, and quality procedures that were followed in the use of Web services. For example, in the financial perspective they aim to create value for the shareholders and there is a balance between growth and productivity. Return on capital employed and economic value indicators are added. Likewise, in the customer's perspective, the growth in terms of volume generated from customers was examined. Further, segments that value quality and innovation were emphasized. In the internal business process perspective they try to differentiate between basic operating processes and operating excellence in the support services via the use of Web services. The product and service quality were measured through the product quality index indicator using the market share in order to gain profit from the investment in the financial perspective. Finally, in the learning and growth perspective, three strategic objectives were identified, namely, basic competencies and skills (referring to the skills expected of the employees), technology (referring to the Web services applications used in the value chain), and climate for action (referring to organization commitments that must be implemented by the human resources department).
- **Aligning the organization with the strategy:** Refers to the alignment of business unit goals with the organization's goal in the use of Web services.
- **Making the strategy everyone's daily job:** Refers to the linking of the employees with the business unit and the organization's strategy.
- **Making the strategy an ongoing process:** Refers to proposing a process for managing the strategy by integrating the tactical management and the strategic management in the use of Web services.
- **Promoting change through management leadership:** Refers to the involvement of the management team in the change process.

CONCLUSION

In this chapter we discussed the role of Web services usage and quality, applying the balanced scorecard methodology. We developed a framework that presented the balanced scorecard's four business perspectives (i.e., learning and growth, internal business processes, customer, and financial perspectives) and tested it via an exploratory case study of a small business firm within the agricultural industry. Then we reported the findings based on the impact of Web services quality on the four perspectives. The findings suggest that the lessons learned evolve over a set of processes that are aimed at integrating quality into the potential use of Web services.

The contribution of this study was attributed to the framework, which provided guidelines for measuring Web services usage and quality, applying the key Web services features that gave rise to business values that were matched with strategic initiatives that small businesses can have in each of the business perspectives. Web services further drive the quality of IT strategy as it is fully aligned with overall business strategy, thereby focusing on the key organizational capabilities and sustainable competitive advantage.

This study contributes to the theory as it extends the current literature of Web services to include the balanced scorecard framework of measure to its usage and quality. Further, the study contributes to practice as small businesses using Web services will benefit from the balanced scorecard as they will have a system which provides them with timely, cost-effective, scalable, manageable and reliable feedback on their strategic performance. The business issues including effective organizational performance and successful strategy implementation will be greatly enhanced. Further, the balanced scorecard gives a holistic view of the small business by simultaneously examining its performance from four perspectives. It is able to translate an organization's vision and strategy into specific objectives, monitored through a coherent set of performance indicators. Future research should aim to apply the balanced scorecard framework for Web services via a survey or multiple case studies with firms across different sections in the industry so that the findings can contribute to a generic framework.

REFERENCES

Benko, C., & McFarlan, F.W. (2003). *Connecting the dots: Aligning projects with objectives in unpredictable times*. Boston: Harvard Business School Press.

Chan, S. S., Kellen, V., & Nair, C. (2004). *Adopting Web services for B2B e-collaboration: Research directions*. Paper presented at the International Resources Management Association Conference, Innovations through Information Technology (pp. 1191-1193).

Hagel, J. (2002). Edging into Web services. *The McKinsey Quarterly, 4*.

Hagel, J., III, & Brown, J. S. (2001). Your next IT strategy. *Harvard Business Review, 79*(9), 105-115.

Kaplan, R., & Norton, D. (2000). *The strategy focused organization*. Harvard Business School Press.

Niven, P. R. (2003). *Balanced scorecard. Step-by-step for government and non-profit agencies*. John Wiley & Sons.

Ortega, M., Perez, M., & Rojas, T. (2000). *A model for software product quality with a system focus*. Paper presented at the 4th World Multi Conference on Systematic Cybernatics.

Solano, J., De Ovalles, M. P., Rojas, T., Padua, A. G., & Morales, L. M. (2003, Winter). Integration of systemic quality and the balanced scorecard, privacy and security in e-business. *Information Systems Management*, 66-81.

Yen, V. C. (2004). *Applications development with Web services*. Paper presented at the International Resources Management Association Conference, Innovations through Information Technology (pp. 875-876).

Yin, R. K. (1994). *Case study research: Design and methods* (2nd ed.). Thousand Oaks, CA: Sage Publications.

APPENDIX: CASE STUDY QUESTIONNAIRE

A) Demographic Section

1. Name of your organization?

2. Your job title?

3. How long have you worked in your present organization?
A. Less than a year
B. Between 1-5 years
C. Between 6-10 years
D. Between 11-20 years
E. Over 20 years

4. How long have you had your present position?
A. Less than a year
B. Between 1-2 years
C. Between 3-5 years
D. Between over 5 years

5. What is your organization's reach?
A. Local
B. Regional
C. National
D. Global

6. What is your organization's size?
A. Large > 500 employees
B. Small-Medium-Enterprise 1-499 employees

7. Please name the type of industry your organization is or provide the NAICS code?

8. Please indicate which of the following terms best describes your organization's main business activity
A. Retail/wholesale trade
B. Manufacturing/distribution
C. Computers/communications
D. Financial services
E. Education
F. Health
G. Government services
H. Other services
I. Other --

9. What is the main role of your organization?

A. Buyer
B. Seller
C. Manufacturer
D. Supplier

10. Please indicate which of the following types of business transactions are actively supported by the IT systems in your organization?

A. Purchase orders
B. Invoices
C. Advance shipping notices
D. Product information
E. Payment transactions

11. Please indicate the type of business applications and tools your organization implemented, or will be implementing?

A. EDI – Value-Added-Network
B. Internet-based EDI
C. Extranets
D. Intranets
E. E-mail
F. B2C or B2B shopping cart
G. Other types of Web service applications
H. Other --

12. Please indicate the number of business partners your organization has? (business partners refer to those who are contracted legally to do business with the firm)

A. 1-20
B. 21-50
C. 51-100
D. 101-499
E. Over 500

13. Approximately what is your annual revenue, in millions? (please estimate)

A. 0-1m
B. 1-10m
C. 10-100m
D. 100-500,
E. 500-1,000m
F. Over 1,000m

14. Approximately how much does your organization spend annually on information technology? (please estimate)

A. 0-100,000
B. 100,000-500,000
C. 500,000-1m
D. 1-5m
E. Over 5m

15. Please indicate how your organization chose your business partners?

A. Advertising on your Web page
B. Screening of business partners
C. Based on past reputations
D. Other --

16. When did your organization start implementing a balanced scorecard system? Please indicate the year.

17. Please indicate the importance of implementing a balanced scorecard system in your organization's current business strategy

A. No importance/not considered
B. Small consideration
C. Nominally part of strategy
D. Substantially part of strategy
E. Crucial to strategy

18. On average how often does your organization meet face-to-face with your business partners?

A. At least once per week
B. At least once per month
C. More than once a month
D. Other ---

19. Please indicate how your organization maintains your business partners

A. Verbal agreements
B. Legal business partner agreements (written)
C. Screening of business partners (based on a performance assessment)
D. Other --

Questions on your Firm's Application of the Balanced Scorecard on Web Services

How did your firm implement a balanced scorecard methodology?

What is the vision of your organization towards the use of Web services?

Do your employees have a solid understanding of your firm's use of Web services?

Why was the balanced scorecard important in measuring your business performance?

What benefits did your firm experienced from the quality of Web service applications?

What risks/challenges did your firm experienced from using Web services?

Learning and Growth Perspective

Do small business employees have the skills/competencies to operate the Web service application and align it with their internal business processes effectively in order to meet their customers' objectives of using Web services?

Do small business employees possess the information required to achieve objectives?

Do small businesses have the ability to sustain growth and change that in turn enhances the quality of Web services?

How does the balanced scorecard impact the quality of Web services in the learning and growth perspective?

How was the data gathered, analyzed, evaluated for feedback so that appropriate actions can be taken to improve the learning and growth perspective?

What skills do your employees possess regarding performance management and more specifically, developing performance measures in the balanced scorecard framework?

(This question relates to what qualification requirements do the senior employees who undertake the role of a balanced scorecard auditor or quality control manager has? The purpose is to ensure that they have the adequate skills to completely measure the firm's performance).

Do your employees have the right skills/competencies to operate the Web service applications?

Do your employees have the tools and information they require to make effective decisions that impact customer outcomes?

Do your employees possess the information required to achieve objectives?

Does your organization have the ability to sustain growth and change?

Do your employees face difficulties when accessing critical information needed to serve customers?

Internal Business Process Perspective

Does the internal business processes applying Web services conform to the mission of small businesses?

Does the internal business processes meet their customer requirements?

What must small businesses do well internally in order to achieve the objectives they set forth to achieve quality in Web services?

Where does the Web services "process" start, and where does it end?

How does the balanced scorecard impact the quality of Web services in the internal business processes? How were the data gathered, analyzed, evaluated for feedback so that appropriate actions can be taken to improve the internal business process perspective?

Do your employees know how their day to day actions contribute to the organization's success? (how and why)

What must your firm do well internally in order to achieve the objectives set forth in the customer perspective?

Customer Perspective

What do customers expect or demand from the use of Web services? Dimensions of customers experience include; time, quality, price or cost, accessibility, reputation, and relationship.

Who do we define as our customers?

How do our customers see us? How does Web services create value for our customers?

How does the balanced scorecard impact the quality of Web services and its relationship with customers' perspectives? What factors are evaluated in the customers' perspective?

How the data was gathered, analyzed, evaluated for feedback so that appropriate actions can be taken to improve the customer perspective?

Who does your firm define as your customers?

What do your customers expect or demand from your firm? (factors pertaining to time, quality, price or cost, accessibility, reputation, relationship and image).

Do you require anything from your customers? (in order to meet your customers demands – is there anything you need from them?)

You have a unique value proposition for customers (for example cost, technical superiority, customer intimacy).

What factors does your firm excel in as in evidence of past successes thereby providing accountability to your stakeholders that you are satisfying customer expectations?

(This question relates to what factors do the firm excel in as in evidence of past successes thereby providing accountability)

Financial Perspective

What accountability do small businesses that use Web services have to financial stakeholders?

How does the balanced scorecard impact the quality of Web services performance from a financial perspective? What factors are evaluated in the financial perspective?

How are the data gathered, analyzed, evaluated for feedback so that appropriate actions can be taken to improve the financial perspective?

What reporting mechanisms are deployed in your firm in order to enforce accountability?

Does your firm create significant value from intangible assets such as employee knowledge and innovation, customer relationships, and a strong culture. (how and why)

Does your senior management team spend time together discussing variances from plan and other financial issues? (How often?)

Does your organization clearly define the performance targets for both financial and non-financial indicators? (how and why)

Compilation of References

3GPP. (2003). *Open service architecture workgroup.* Retrieved May 21, 2008, from http://www.3gpp.org/TB/CN/CN5/CN5.htm

3GPP. Retrieved May 23, 2008, from http://www.3gpp.org/

Aalst, W. v. D., et al. (2003). Workflow mining: A survey of issues and approaches. *Data Knowledge Egineering, 47*(2), 237-267.

Abbott, M. (2005), *Business transaction protocol.*

Abramowicz, W., Filipowska, A., Kaczmarek, M., Kaczmarek, T., Kowalkiewicz, M., Rutkowski, W., et al. (2006). *Service interdependencies: Insights into use cases for service compositions.* Paper presented at the IFIP 2006.

Abramowicz, W., Haniewicz, K., Kaczmarek, M., & Zyskowski, D. (2006). *Automatic Web services interactions - requirements, challenges and limits from the F-WebS system perspective.* Paper presented at the International Conference on Next Generation Web Services Practices, Seoul, Korea.

Abramowicz, W., Haniewicz, K., Kaczmarek, M., & Zyskowski, D. (2006). *Filtering of Semantic Web services with F-WebS system.* Paper presented at the The Semantic Web: ASWC 2006 Workshop.

Abramowicz, W., Kaczmarek, M., & Zyskowski, D. (2006). *Duality in Web services reliability.* Paper presented at the International Conference on Internet and Web Applications and Services (ICIW'06). Guadeloupe, French Caribbean.

Abramowicz, W., Kaczmarek, M., Kowalkiewicz, M., & Zyskowski, D. (2005). *A survey of QoS computation for Web services profiling.* Paper presented at the 18th International Conference on Computer Applications in Industry and Engineering (ISCA), Honolulu.

Abramowicz, W., Kaczmarek, M., Kowalkiewicz, M., & Zyskowski, D. (2006). *Architecture for service profiling.*

Paper presented at the Modelling, Design and Analysis for Service-Oriented Architecture Workshop in conjunction with the 2006 IEEE International Conferences on Services Computing (SCC 2006) and Web Services (ICWS 2006), Chicago.

Adams, H., Gisolfi, D., Snell, J., & Varadan, R. (2002). Best practices for Web services: Part 1 - formation of a semantic framework. *IBM developerWorks.* Retrieved March 5, 2004, from http://www-106.ibm.com/developerworks/Webservices/library/ws-best1/

Agarwal, V., Dasgupta, K., Karnik, N., Kumar, A., Kundu, A., Mittal, S., et al. (2005, May 10-14). A service creation environment based on end to end composition of Web services. In *Proceedings of the WWW Conference,* Chiba, Japan (pp. 128-137).

Akamai. Retrieved May 23, 2008, from http://www.akamai.com/

Akscyn, R. M., & Witten, I. H. (1998). *Report of First Summit on international cooperation on digital libraries.* Retrieved May 3, 2005, from http://Web.archive.org/Web/20010529104724/ks.com/idla-wp-oct98/

Ali, A. S., Rana, O. F., Al-Ali, R., & Walker, D. W. (2003, January) UDDIe: An extended registry for Web services. In *Proceedings of the 2003 Symposium on Applications and the Internet Workshops (SAINT'03 Workshops),* Orlando, FL (p. 85). IEEE Press.

Alonso, G., Agrawal, D., Abbadi, A. E., Kamath, M., Gnthr, R., & Mohan, C. (1996). Advanced transaction models in workflow contexts. In *Proceedings of the 12th International Conference on Data Engineering,* New Orleans (pp. 574-581).

Ambler, S. W. (2002). *Agile modelling: Effective practices for extreme programming and the unified process.* John Wiley & Sons.

Ambler, S. W. (2005). *Managing agile projects.* Lightning Source UK Ltd.

Amendolia, S. R., Brady, J. M., McClatchey, R., Mulet-Parada, M., Odeh, M., & Solomonides, T. (2003). MammoGrid: Large-scale distributed mammogram analysis. In *Proceedings of the 18th Medical Informatics Europe Conference (MIE '03)* (pp. 194-199).

Anand, S., Kunti, K., Chawla, M., & Marwah, K. (2005). Best practices and solutions for managing versioning of SOA Web services. *SOA World Magazine*. Retrieved July 24, 2007, from http://soa.sys-con.com/read/143883.htm

Anbazhagan, M., & Nagarajan, A. (2002, January). *Understanding quality of service for Web services.* IBM Developerworks Website.

Anderson, R. (1996). Patient confidentiality: At risk from NHS-wide networking. In B. Richards & H. de Glanville (Eds.), *Current perspectives in healthcare computing* (pp. 687-692). BJHC Books.

Anderson, R. (1999). Information technology in medical practice: Safety and privacy lessons from the United Kingdom. *Medical Journal of Australia, 170,* 181-185.

Andorf, C., Dobbs, D., & Honavar, V. (2007). Exploring inconsistencies in genome-wide protein function annotations. *BMC Bioinformatics.*

Andrews, T., Curbera, F., Dholakia, H., Goland, Y., Klein, J., Leymann, F., et al. (2003). *BPEL4WS version 1.1 specification.* Retrieved May 21, 2008, from ftp://www6.software.ibm.com/software/developer/library/ws-bpel.pdf

Ankolekar, A., Burstein, M., Hobbs, J. R., Lassila, O., Martin, D., McDermott, D., et al. (2002). DAML-S: Web service description for the Semantic Web. In S. Verlag (Ed.), *First International Web Conference* (pp. 348-363). Sardinia, Italy: Springer Verlag.

Answar, S., Baral, C., & Tari, L. (2005). *A language for modular ASP: Application to ACC tournament scheduling.* Paper presented at the ASP Workshops.

Apple QuickTime. Retrieved May 23, 2008, from http://www.apple.com/quicktime/

Ardissono, L., Console, L., Goy, A., Petrone, G., Picardi, C., Segnan, M., et al. (2005). Towards self-diagnosing Web services. In *Proceedings of the IFIP/IEEE International Workshop on Self-Managed Systems & Services (SelfMan'2005) held in conjunction with The 9th IFIP/IEEE International Symposium on Integrated Network Management (IM'2005),* Nice, France.

Arkin, A., Askary, S., Fordin, S., Jekeli, W., Kawaguchi, K., Orchard, D., et al. (2002). *Web service choreography interface (WSCI).* Retrieved May 21, 2008, from http://www.w3.org/TR/wsci/

Arsanjani, A. (2004). Service oriented modeling and architecture. *IBM developerworks.* Retrieved July 10, 2007, from http://www.ibm.com/developerworks/library/ws-soa-design1/

Atkinson, C., Bayer, J., Bunse, C., Kamsties, E., Laitenberger, O., Laqua, R., et al. (Eds.). (2001). *Service-based product line engineering with UML.* Addison Wesley.

Atkinson, C., Brenner, D. (Eds.), Paech, B., Malaka, M., Borner, L., Merdes, M., et al. (2006). *The MORABIT development method (MORABIT Deliverable M3).* Mannheim, Germany: University of Mannheim.

Au, T. C., Kuter, U., & Nau, D. (2005). *Web service composition with volatile information.* Paper presented at the International Semantic Web Conference (ISWC).

Austin, D., Babir, A., Ferris, C., & Garg, S., (2004). Web services architecture requirements. *W3C working group.* Retrieved October 27, 2007, from http://www.w3.org/TR/wsa-reqs/

Avizienis, A., Laprie, J.-C., & Randell, B. (2001). Fundamental concepts of dependability. In *Proceedings of the 3rd IEEE Information Survivability Workshop (ISW-2000),* Boston (pp. 7-12). IEEE Press.

Baida, Z., Gordijn, J., Omelayenko, B., & Akkermans, H. (2004). *A shared service terminology for online service provisioning.* Paper presented at the Sixth International Conference on Electronic Commerce (ICEC04), Delft, The Netherlands.

Balduccini, M., Gelfond, M., & Nogueira, M. (2006). Answer set based design of knowledge systems. *Annals of Mathematics and Artificial Intelligence.*

Balke, W.-T., & Wagner, M. (2003). Cooperative discovery for user-centered Web service provisioning. In L.-J. Zhang (Ed.), *Proceedings of the International Conference on Web Services (ICWS)* (pp. 191-197). LasVegas: CSREA Press.

Banerji, A., Bartolini, C., Beringer, D., Chopella, V., Govindarajan, K., Karp, A., et al. (2002). *WSCL: The Web services conversation language.* Retrieved May 21, 2008, from http://www.w3.org/TR/wscl10/

Baral, C., Dzifcak, J., & Takahashi, H. (2006). *Macros, macro calls, and use of ensembles in modular answer set programming.* Paper presented at the International Conference on Logic Programming.

Barbedo, J. G. A., & Lopez, A. (2004). A new strategy for objective estimation of the quality of audio signals. *IEEE Latin America Transactions (Revista IEEE America Latina), 2*(3).

Barefoot, D. (2002). *Web services primer*. Cape-Science.

Baresi, L., Ghezzi, C., & Guinea, S. (2004). Towards self-healing service compositions. In *Proceedings of the First Conference on the Principles of Software Engineering (PRISE'2004)*, Buenos Aires, Argentina.

Baresi, L., Guinea, S., & Plebani, P. (2005, September). *WS-policy for service monitoring*. Paper presented at the 6th VLDB Workshop on Technologies for E-Services *(TES'05)* (Vol. LNCS 3811). Springer Press.

Barry, D. (2003). *Web services and service-oriented srchitectures: The savvy manage's guide*. Morgan Kauffman.

Basin, D., Doser, J., & Lodderstedt, T. (2003). Model driven security for process-oriented systems. In *Proceedings of the Eighth ACM Symposium on Access Control Models and Technologies SACMAT '03* (pp. 100-109). New York: ACM Press.

Bassiliades, N., Antoniou, G., & Vlahavas, I. (2006). DR-DEVICE, a defeasible logic reasoner for the Semantic Web. *International Journal on Semantic Web and Information Systems, 2*(1), 1-41.

BEA Systems. (2006, May). *Introducing BEA tuxedo ATMI*. Retrieved July 30, 2007, from http://edocs.bea.com/tuxedo/tux91/

BEA. (2004). *WebLogic plateform*. Retrieved May 21, 2008, from http://www.bea.com

Becker, M. (2005). *CASSANNDRA: Flexible trust management and its application to electronic health records*. Unpublished doctoral thesis, University of Cambridge Computer Laboratory.

Benatallah, B., Sheng, Q. Z., Ngu, A. H. H., & Dumas, M. (2002). Declarative composition and peer-to-peer provisioning of dynamic Web services. In *ICDE* (pp. 297-308). San Jose, CA: IEEE Computer Society.

Benharref, A., Dssouli, R., Glitho, R., & Serhani, M. A. (2006). *Towards the testing of composed Web services in 3rd generation networks*. Paper presented at the IFIP International Conference on Testing of Communicating Systems (TestCom) (Vol. 3964, pp. 118-133). New York: Springer Verlag.

Benharref, A., Glitho, R., & Dssouli, R. (2005). *Mobile agents for testing Web services in next generation networks*. Paper presented at MATA 2005 (Vol. 3744, pp. 182-191). Montreal, Canada: Springer Verlag.

Benko, C., & McFarlan, F.W. (2003). *Connecting the dots: Aligning projects with objectives in unpredictable times*. Boston: Harvard Business School Press.

Berners-Lee, T., & Fischetti, M. (1999). *Weaving the Web: The original design and ultimate destiny of the World Wide Web by its inventor*. Harper.

Berners-Lee, T., Hendler, J., & Lassila, O. (2001). The Semantic Web. *Scientific American, 284*(5), 34-43.

Bertolino, A., Corradini, F., Inverardi, P., & Muccini, H. (2000). *Deriving test plans from architectural descriptions*. Paper presented at International Conference on Software Engineering, Limerick, Ireland.

Bézivin, J., Hammoudi, S., Lopes, D., & Jouault, F. (2004, September). Applying MDA approach for Web service platform. In *Proceedings of the Eighth IEEE International Enterprise Distributed Object Computing Conference (EDOC'04)*, Monterey, CA (pp. 58-70). IEEE Press.

Bhargav-Spantzely, A., Camenisch, J., Gross, T., & Sommer, D. (2006). User centricity: A taxonomy and open issues. In *Proceedings of the Second ACM Workshop on Digital Identity Management, DIM '06* (pp. 1-10). Alexandria: ACM Press.

Bhiri, S., Perrin, O., & Godart, C. (2005, May 10-14). Ensuring required failure atomicity of composite Web services. In *Proceedings of the WWW Conference*, Chiba, Japan (pp. 138-147).

Birman, K. (2004, December). Like it or not, Web services are distributed objects. *Communications of the ACM, 47*(12).

Birolini, A. (1991). *Qualität und Zuverlässigkeit technischer Systeme. Theorie, Praxis, Management*. Springer Press.

Birolini, A. (1997). *Zuverlässigkeit von Geräten und Systemen* (4th ed.). Springer Press.

Bistarelli, S., Montanari, U., & Rossi, F. (1997). Semiring-based constraint satisfaction and optimization. *J. ACM, 44*(2), 201-236.

BitTorrent. Retrieved May 23, 2008, from www.bittorrent.com

Boehm, B. (1984). Verifying and validating software requirements and design specifications. *IEEE Software*, 205-218.

Boehm, B., & Turner, R. (2004). *Balancing agility and discipline: A guide for the perplexed.* Addison-Wesley.

Bogdan, R. C., & Biklen, S. R. (1992). *Qualitative research for education: An introduction to theory and methods* (2nd ed.). Boston: Allyn and Bacon.

Boley, H., Grosof, B., Sintek, M., Tabe, S., & Wagner, G. (2002). *RuleML design, version 0.8.* Retrieved May 30, 2008, from www.ruleml.org/indesign.html

Booth, D., & Liu, C. K. (2005). *Web service description language primer.*

Booth, D., Haas, H., McCabe, F., Newcomer, E., Champion, M., & Ferris, C. (2004, February). *Web services architecture.* Retrieved October 31, 2007, from http://www.w3c.org/TR/ws-arch/

Booth, D., Haas, H., McCabe, F., Newcomer, E., Champion, M., Ferris, C., et al. (2004, February). *Web services architecture* (W3C Working Group Note 11). The World Wide Web Consortium (W3C).

Borgman, C. L. (1999). What are digital libraries? Competing visions. *Information Processing & Management, 35*(3), 227-243.

Borner, L., Illes, T., & Paech, B. (2007). *The testing process: A decision based approach.* Paper presented at the Second International Conference on Software Engineering Advances (ICSEA 2007), Cap Esterel, France.

Boss, R. W. (2004). *Web services.* Retrieved November 1, 2005, from http://www.ala.org/ala/pla/plapubs/technotes/Webservices.htm

Brady, J. M., Gavaghan, D. J., Simpson, A. C., Mulet-Parada, M., & Highnam, R. P. (2003). eDiaMoND: A grid-enabled federated database of annotated mammograms. In F. Berman, G. C. Fox, & A. J. G. Hey (Eds.), *Grid computing: Making the global infrastructure a reality* (pp. 923-943). Wiley.

Brenner, D., Atkinson, C., Malaka, R., Merdes, M., Paech, B., & Suliman, D. (2007). Reducing verification effort in component-based software engineering through built-in testing. *Information Systems Frontiers, 9*(2-3), 151-162.

Broens, T. H. F., Pokraev, S., Sinderen, M. J. van, Koolwaaij, J., & Costa, P. D. (2004). *Context-aware, ontology-based, service discovery.* Paper presented at the European Symposium on Ambient Intelligence (EUSAI), Eindhoven, The *Netherlands* (Vol. 3295, pp. 72-83). Berlin/Heidelberg: Springer. Retrieved June 5, 2008, from http://eprints.eemcs.utwente.nl/7420/

Brose, G. (2003). Securing Web services with SOAP security proxies. In *Proceedings of the International Conference on Web Services* (pp. 231-234).

Brown, K., & Ellis, M. (2004). Best practices for Web services versioning. *IBM developerworks.* Retrieved on July 16, 2007, from http://www.ibm.com/developerworks/Webservices/library/ws-version/

Bruno, M., Canfora, G., DiPenta, M., Esposito, G., & Mazza, V. (2005). *Using test cases as contract to ensure service compliance across releases.* Paper presented at the International Conference on Service Oriented Computing (LNCS 3826).

Bueno, F., Cabeza, D., Carro, M., Hermenegildo, M., López-García, P., & Puebla, G. (1997). *The Ciao Prolog system.* Unpublished manuscript.

Cai, L., Tu, R., Zhao, J., & Mao, Y. (2007). Speech quality evaluation: A new application of digital watermarking. *IEEE Transactions on Instrumentation and Measurement, 56*(1), 45-55.

Calimeri, F., & Ianni, G. (2005). *External sources of computation for answer set solvers.* Paper presented at the Logic Programming and Non-Monotonic Reasoning.

Calinescu, R., Harris, S., Gibbons, J., Davies, J. W., Toujilov, I., & Nagl, S. (2007). Model-driven architecture for cancer research. In *Proceedings of the 5th IEEE International Conference on Software Engineering and Formal Methods.* IEEE Computer Society Press.

Calyam, P., & Lee, C.-G. (2005). *Characterizing voice and video traffic behavior over the Internet.* Paper presented at the 20th International Symposium on Computer and Information Sciences (ISCIS 2005), Istanbul, Turkey.

Camenisch, J., Gross, T., & Sommer, D. (2006). Enhancing privacy of federated identity management protocols: Anonymous credentials in WS-security. In *Proceedings of the 5th ACM Workshop on Privacy in Electronic Society, WPES '06* (pp. 67-72). Alexandria: ACM Press.

Cameron, K. (2005). *The laws of identity Microsoft Corporation.* Retrieved June 10, 2007, from http://msdn2.microsoft.com/en-us/library/ms996456.aspx

Canfora, G. (2005). User-side testing of Web services. In *Proceedings of the 9th European Conference on Software Maintenance and Reengineering.* IEEE Computer Society Press.

Canfora, G., & Di Penta, M. (2006). Testing services and service-centric systems: challenges and opportunities. *IT Professional, 8*(2), 10-17.

Cao, P., & Irani, S. (1997). Cost-aware WWW proxy caching algorithms. In *Proceedings of the 1997 Usenix Symposium on Internet Technologies and Systems (USITS-97)*.

Cao, P., & Liu, C. (1997). Maintaining strong cache consistency in the World-Wide Web. In *Proceedings of the 7th International Conference on Distributed Computing Systems*.

Caprotti, O., Dewar, M., & Turi, D. (2004). Mathematical service matching using description logic and owl. In A. Asperti, G. Bancerek, & A. Trybulec (Eds.), *Mathematical knowledge management (mkm)* (Vol. 3119, pp. 73-87). Bialowieza, Poland: Springer.

Cardoso, J., Sheth, A. P., Miller, J. A., Arnold, J., & Kochut, K. (2004). Quality of service for workflows and Web service processes. *Journal of Web Semantics, 1*(3), 281-308.

Casati, F., Castellanos, M., Dayal, U., & Shan, M. C. (2004, November 2004). *Probabilistic, context-sensitive and goal-oriented service selection.* Paper presented at the ICSOC'04, New York.

Casati, F., Shan, E., Dayal, U., & Shan, M.-C. (2003). Business-oriented management of Web Services. *Communications of the ACM, 46*(10), 55-60.

Case, J., Fedor, M., Schoffstall, M., & Davin, J. (1990). *Simple network management protocol (SNMP)* (RFC 1157).

Castro, L., Swift, T., & Warren, D. (2002). *XASP: Answer set programming with XSB and smodels.* Retrieved May 30, 2008, from xsb.sourceforge.net/manual2/node149.html

Cavano, J., & McCall, J. (1978, November). A framework for the measurement of software quality. In *Proceedings of the ACM Software Quality Assurance Workshop* (pp. 133-139). ACM Press.

CenterSpan. Retrieved May 23, 2008, from http://www.centerspan.com/

Cervesato, I., Jaggard, A. D., Scedrov, A., & Walstad, C. (2005). Specifying Kerberos 5 cross-realm authentication. In *Proceedings of the 2005 Workshop on Issues in the Theory of Security, WITS '05* (pp. 12-26). Long Beach: ACM Press.

Chan, H., & Grosof, B. (1999). *CommonRules.* Retrieved May 30, 2008, from www.alphaworks.ibm.com/tech/commonrules

Chan, S. S., Kellen, V., & Nair, C. (2004). *Adopting Web services for B2B e-collaboration: Research directions.* Paper presented at the International Resources Management Association Conference, Innovations through Information Technology (pp. 1191-1193).

Chang, S., Chen, Q, & Hsu, M. (2003). Managing security policy in a large distributed Web services environment. In *Proceedings of the 27th Annual International Conference on Computer Software and Applications, COMPSAC 2003* (pp. 610-62). Pleasanton: IEEE Press.

Chang, Y.-C., Carney, T., Klein, S. A., Messerschmitt, D., & Zakhor, A. (1998). Effects of temporal jitter on video quality: Assessment using psychophysical methods. In *Proceedings of the SPIE: Human Vision and Image Processing*.

ChangSup, K., Sungwon, K., In-Young, K., Jongmoon, B., & Young-Il, C. (2006). *Generating test cases for Web services using extended finite state machine.* Paper presented at the IFIP International Conference on Testing of Communicating Systems (TestCom) (pp. 103-117). New York: Springer Verlag.

Chankhunthod, A., Danzig, P., Neerdaels, C., Schwartz, M., & Worrell, K. (1996). A hierarchical Internet object cache. In *Proceedings of the 1996 USENIX* (pp. 153-163).

Chappell, D. (2006). *Introducing windows CardSpace-Microsoft Corporation.* Retrieved June 10, 2007, from http://msdn.microsoft.com/library/default.asp?url=/library/en-us/dnlong/html/introinfocard.asp

Charfi, A., & Mezini, M. (2004). Hybrid Web service composition: Business processes meets business rules. In *Proceedings of the 2nd International Conference on Service Oriented Computing (ICSOC'2004)*, New York.

Chatterjee, A., Chaudhuri, A., Das, A. S., Dias, T., & Erradi, A. (2005). Differential QoS support in Web services management. *SOA World Magazine.* Retrieved July 20, 2007, from http://Webservices.sys-con.com/read/121946.htm

Chinnici, R., Moreau, J.-J., Ryman, A., & Weerawarana, S. (2007). *Web service description language, version 2.0.*

Chiu, D., Li, Q., & Karlapalem, K. (1999). A meta modeling approach to workflow management systems supporting exception handling. *Information Systems Journal, 24*(2), 159-184

Choudrie, J., & Dwivedi, Y. K. (2005). Investigating the research approaches for examining technology adoption issues. *Journal of Research Practice, 1*(1).

Christensen, E., Curbera, F., Meredith, G., & Weerawarana, S. (2001). *Web services description language (wsdl) 1.1* (W3C note). Retrieved June 5, 2008, from http://www.w3.org/TR/wsdl

Cibrán, M., & Verheecke, B. (2003). Modularizing Web services management with AOP. In *Proceedings of the 1st European Workshop on Object Orientation and Web Services (ECOOP'2003) held in conjunction with The 17th European Conference on Object-Oriented Programming (ECOOP'2003)*, Darmstadt, Germany.

Clark, A. (2006). *Clarifying video quality metrics.* Retrieved May 23, 2008, from http://www.tmcnet.com/news/2006/04/11/1561303.htm

Clark, A., & Pendleton, A. (2006). *RTCP XR - IP video metrics report blocks.* Retrieved May 23, 2008, from http://www.telchemy.com/reference/draft-clark-avt-rt-cpxr-video-01.pdf

Clark, D. D., Shenker, S., & Zhang, L. (1992). Supporting real-time applications in an integrated services packet network: Architecture and mechanism. *SIGCOMM Comput. Commun. Rev., 22*(4), 14-26.

Clauß, S., & Schiffner, S. (2006). Structuring anonymity metrics. In *Proceedings of the Second ACM Workshop on Digital Identity Management, DIM '06* (pp. 55-62). Alexandria: ACM Press.

Clauß, S., Kesdogan, D., & Kölsch, T. (2005). Privacy enhancing identity management: Protection against re-identification and profiling. In *Proceedings of the 2005 Workshop on Digital Identity Management, DIM '05* (pp. 84-93). Fairfax: ACM Press.

Claypool, M., & Tanner, J. (1999). The effects of jitter on the perceptual quality of video. In *Proceedings of the ACM Multimedia*, Orlando.

Cohen, R., Katzir, L., & Raz, D. (2002). Scheduling algorithms for a cache pre-filling content distribution network. In *Proceedings of the IEEE InfoCom'02.*

Conti, M., Kumar, M., Das, S. K., & Shirazi, B. (2002). Quality of service issues in Internet Web services. *IEEE Transactions on Computers , 6*(51), 593-594.

Cornwall, A. (2002). Electronic health records: An international perspective. *Health Issues, 73*.

Cotroneo, D., Graziano, A., & Russo, S. (2004). Security requirements in service oriented architectures for ubiquitous computing. In *Proceedings of the 2nd Workshop on Middleware for Pervasive and Ad-Hoc Computing, MPAC '04* (pp 172-177). Toronto: ACM Press.

Cottenier, T., & Elrad, T. (2004). Validation of aspect-oriented adaptations to components. In *Proceedings of the 9th International Workshop on Component-Oriented Programming (WCOP'2004) held in conjunction with The 18th European Conference on Object-Oriented Programming (ECOOP'2004)*, Oslo, Norway.

CPXe. (2005). *I3A standards - initiatives - CPXe.* Retrieved May 21, 2008, from http://www.i3a.org/i_cpxe.html

Cruz, R. L. (1995). Quality of service guarantees in virtual circuit switched networks. *IEEE Journal on Selected Areas in Communications, 13*(6), 1048-1056.

Curbera, F., Khalaf, R., Mukhi, N., Tai, S., & Weerawarana, S. (2003). The next step in Web services, *Communications of the ACM, 46*(10), 29-34.

Daft, R. L. (1978). A dual-core model of organizational innovation. *Academy of Management Journal, 21*(2), 193.

Damanpour, F. (1991). Organizational inertia and momentum: A dynamic model of strategic change. *Academy of Management Journal, 34*(3), 555-591.

Damianou, N., Dulay, N., Lupu, E., & Sloman, M. (2001). The ponder specification language. In *Proceedings of the Workshop on Policies for Distributed Systems and Networks (Policy'2001)*, Bristol, UK.

Dan, A., Ludwig, H., & Pacifici, G. (2003). *IBM.* Retrieved May 25, 2008, from http://www-106.ibm.com/developerworks/library/ws-slafram

Davenport, D. (2002). Anonymity on the Internet: Why the price may be too high. *Communications of the ACM, 45*(4), 33-35.

Davis, F. D. (1989). Perceived usefulness, perceived ease of use, and user acceptance of information technology. *MIS Quarterly, 13*(3), 318.

Dean, M. (2001). *RuleML experiments with GEDCOM.* Retrieved May 30, 2008, from www.daml.org/2001/02/gedcom-ruleml

Deering, S., & Hinden, R. (1998). *Internet protocol, version 6 (IPv6) specification* (RFC No. 2460). The Internet Society.

Delamaro, M. C., Maldonado, J. C., & Mathur, A. P. (2001). Interface mutation: An approach for integration testing. *IEEE Transactions on Software Engineering, 27*(3), 228-247.

Deora, V., Shao, J., Gray, W. A., & Fiddian, N. J. (2003). A quality of service management framework based on user expectations. In M. E. Orlowska, S. Weerawarana, M. P. Papazoglou, & J. Yang (Eds.), *ICSOC*(Vol. 2910, pp. 104-114). Trento, Italy: Springer.

Deursen, A. V., Visser, E., & Warmer, J., (2007). *Model-driven software evolution: A research agenda*. Retrieved July 15, 2007, from http://swerl.tudelft.nl/twiki/pub/EelcoVisser/ModelDrivenSoftwareEvolutionAResearchAgenda/DVW07.pdf

Di Marzo Serugendo, G., & Fitzgerald, J. (May 2006). *Dependable self-organising software architectures - an approach for self-managing systems* (Tech. Rep. BBKCS-06-05). Birkbeck College, London, UK.

Don, K., Buchanan, G., & Witten, I. H. (2005). *Greenstone 3: A modular digital library*. Retrieved November 1, 2005, from http://www.sadl.uleth.ca/greenstone3/manual.pdf

Dorai, C., & Kienzle, M. (2004). Challenges of business media. *IEEE Multimedia, 11*(4).

Dssouli, R., Saleh, K., Aboulhamid, E., En-Nouaary, A., & Bourhfir, C. (1999). Test development for communication protocols: Towards automation. *Computer Networks, 31*(17), 1835-1872.

Durr, P., Staijen, T., Bergmans, L., & Aksit, M. (2005). Reasoning about semantic conflicts between aspects. In *Proceedings of the 2nd European Interactive Workshop on Aspects in Software (EIWAS'2005)*, Brussels, Belgium.

Ebrahimi, T., & Pereira, F. (2002). *The MPEG-4 book*. Prentice Hall.

Edwards, S. H. (2001). A framework for practical, automated black-box testing of component-based software. *Software Testing, Verification and Reliability, 11*, 97-111.

Eenoo, C. V., Hylooz, O., & Khan, K. M. (2005). *Addressing non-functional properties in software architecture using ADL*. Paper presented at the 6th Australian Workshop on Software and Systems Architectures - AWSA'05, Brisbane, Australia.

Eger, K., & Killat, U. (2006). *Bandwidth trading in unstructured P2P content distribution networks*. Paper presented at the Sixth IEEE International Conference on Peer-to-Peer Computing (P2P'06) (pp. 39-48).

Eiter, T., Ianni, G., Schindlauer, R., & Tompits, H. (2006). *Effective integration of declarative rules with external evaluations for Semantic-Web reasoning*. Paper presented at the European Semantic Web Conference.

Eiter, T., Leone, N., Mateis, C., Pfeifer, G., & Scarcello, F. (1998). *The KR system dlv: Progress report, comparisons, and benchmarks*. Paper presented at the International Conference on Principles of Knowledge Representation and Reasoning (pp. 406-417).

Eiter, T., Lukasiewicz, T., Schindlauer, R., & Tompits, H. (2004). *Combining ASP with description logics for the Semantic Web*. Paper presented at the Principles of Knowledge Representation and Reasoning,.

Elkhatib, O., Pontelli, E., & Son, T. C. (2006). *A tool for knowledge base integration and querying*. Paper presented at the AAAI Spring Symposium.

Elmagarmid, A. K. (1992). *Database transaction models for advanced applications*. Morgan Kaufmann.

EL-Manzalawy, Y. (2005). *Aspect oriented programming*. Retrieved August 2005, from http://www.developer.com/design/article.php/3308941

Erl, T. (2005). *Service-oriented architecture: concepts, technology, and design*. Prentice-Hall.

Erradi, A., Padmanabhuni, S., & Varadharajan, N. (2006). *Differential QoS support in Web services Management*. Paper presented at the IEEE International Conference of Web Services (pp. 781-788).

Erradi, A., Varadharajan, N., & Padmanabhuni, S., Dr. (2005). *WS-DiffServ: A middleware for differentiated service delivery*. Paper presented at the International Conference on Service-Oriented Computing (pp. 781-788). IEEE Computer Society Press.

Eschenauer, L., Gligor, V. D., & Baras, J. (2002). On trust establishment in mobile ad-hoc networks. *Lecture Notes in Computer Science, 1*(2845/2003), 47-66.

Extensible access control markup language 3 (XACML) version 2.0. Retrieved August 10, 2007, from http://docs.oasis-open.org/xacml/2.0/access_control-xacml-2.0-core-spec-os.pdf

Eysenbach, G. (2001). What is e-health? *Journal of Medical Internet Research, 3*(2), e20.

Facciorusso, C., Field, S., Hauser, R., Hoffner, Y., Humbel, R., Pawlitzek, R., et al. (2003). A Web services matchmaking engine for Web services. In K. Bauknecht, A. M. Tjoa, & G. Quirchmayr (Eds.), *EC-Web* (Vol. 2738, p. 37-49). Prague, Czech Republic: Springer.

Farkas, C., Ziegler, G., Meretei, A., & Lörincz, A. (2002). Anonymity and accountability in self-organizing electronic communities. In *Proceedings of the 2002 ACM Workshop on Privacy in the Electronic Society, WPES '02* (pp. 81-90). Washington: ACM Press.

Farrel, J., & Lausen, H. (2006). *Semantic Annotations for WSDL*. DERI Innsbruck.

Farrell, J. A., & Kreger, H. (2002). Web services management approaches. *IBM Systems Journal, 41*(2), 212-227.

Fenton, N. E., & Pfleeger, S. L. (1997). *Software metrics: A rigorous and practical approach* (2nd ed.). Boston: PWS Pub.

Fernández, J., Pazos, J. J., & Fernández, A. (2004). High availability wit clusters of Web services. In *Proceedings of the 6th APWeb* (pp. 644-653).

Fernández, J., Pazos, J., & Fernández, A. (2004). An architecture for building Web services with quality-of-service features. In *Proceedings of the 5th WAIM.*

Fernández, J., Pazos, J., & Fernández, A. (2005). Optimizing Web services performance using caching. In *Proceedings of the 2005 NWeSP* (pp. 6-16).

Fichman, R. G. (1992, December). *Information technology diffusion: A review of empirical research.* Paper presented at the Thirteenth International Conference on Information Systems (ICIS), Dallas.

Foster, I. (2002). What is the grid? A three point checklist. *GRID Today, 1*(6). Retrieved May 20, 2008, from www.gridtoday.com/02/0722/100136.html

Fowler, M. (2000). *Refactoring: Improving the design of existing code.* Addison-Wesley.

Frantzen, L., Tretmans, J., & de Vries, R. (2006). Towards model-based testing of Web services. In A. Bertolino & A. Polini (Eds.), *Proceedings of the International Workshop on Web Services Modeling and Testing (WS-MaTe 2006)* (pp. 67-82).

Freenet. Retrieved May 23, 2008, http://freenet.sourceforge.net/

Frølund, S., & Koistinen, J. (1998). Quality of services specification in distributed object systems design. In *Proceedings of the 4th Conference on USENIX Conference on Object-Oriented Technologies and Systems (COOTS '98)* (Vol. 5, No. 4, pp. 179-202).

Frølund, S., & Koistinen, J. (1998, December). Quality of service specification in distributed object systems design. *Distributed Systems Engineering Journal, 5*(4).

Fu, X., Bultan, T., & Su, J. (2004). Analysis of interacting BPEL Web services. In *Proceedings of the 13th International Conference on World Wide Web* (pp. 621-630).

Fuchs, H., & Färber, N. (2005). ISMA interoperability and conformance. *IEEE Multimedia, 12*(2), 96-102.

Fu-Zheng, Y., Xin-Dai, W., Yi-Lin, C., & Shuai, W. (2003). *A no-reference video quality assessment method based on digital watermark.* Paper presented at the 14th IEEE Proceedings on Personal, Indoor and Mobile Radio Communications, 2003. PIMRC 2003, 3(7), 2707 - 2710.

Gao, J. Z., Tsao, H. S. J., & Wu, Y. (Eds.). (2003). *Testing and quality assurance for component-based software.* Artech House Computing Library.

Ge, Z., Ji, P., & Shenoy, P. (2002). *A demand adaptive and locality aware (DALA) streaming media server cluster architecture.* Paper presented at the ACM Conference on Networking and Operating System Support for Audio and Video (NOSSDAV'02), Miami.

Geddes, J., Lloyd, S., Simpson, A. C., Rossor, M., Fox, N., Hill, D., et al. (2005). NeuroGrid: Using grid technology to advance neuroscience. In *Proceedings of the 18th IEEE Symposium on Computer-Based Medical Systems (CBMS)*. IEEE Computer Society Press.

Gelfond, M., & Lifschitz, V. (1988). *The stable model semantics for logic programming.* Paper presented at the Logic Programming: Proceedings of the Fifth International Confl and Symp. (pp. 1070-1080).

Gene Ontology Consortium. (2007). *The gene ontology.* Retrieved May 30, 2008, from www.geneontology.org

Gene Ontology, Edit 1.101. (2007). Retrieved May 30, 2008, from http://www.geneontology.org/ontology/gene_ontology_edit.obo

Georgiadis, L., Guérin, R., Peris, V., & Sivarajan, K. N. (1996). Efficient network QoS provisioning based on per node traffic shaping. *IEEE/ACM Trans. Netw., 4*(4), 482-501.

Ginsberg, A., Hirtle, D., McCabe, F., & Patranjan, P.-L. (2006). *RIF use cases and requirements.* W3C.

Gnutella. Retrieved May 23, 2008, from http://www.gnutella.wego.com/

Golbreich, C. (2004). *Combining rule and ontology reasoners for the Semantic Web.* Paper presented at the RuleML.

Goodman, B. D. (2002). Accelerate your Web services with caching. *developerWorks Journal.*

Grandison, T., & Sloman, M. (2000). A survey of trust in Internet applications. *IEEE Communications Surveys and Tutorials, 1*(3), 2-16.

Gray, A. R., & MacDonell, S. G. (1997). Comparison of techniques for developing predictive models of software metrics. *Information and Software Technology, 39*(6), 425-437.

Greenfield, P., Fekete, A., Jang, J., & Kuo, D. (2003, September). Compensation is not enough. In *Proceedings of the 7th International Enterprise Distributed Object Computing Conference (EDOC'03)*, Brisbane, Australia (Vol. 232, pp. 16-19).

Greenstein, D., & Thorin, S. E. (2002). *The digital library: A biography.* Digital Library Federation.

Greenwood, P., & Blair, L. (2004). *Dynamic framed aspects for policy-driven auto-adaptive systems.* Retrieved August 2004, from http://www.comp.lancs.ac.uk/computing/aose/papers/dynFr_daw04.pdf

Grønmo, R., & Jaeger, M. C. (May 2005). Model-driven methodology for building QoS-optimised Web service compositions. In *Proceedings of the 5th IFIP International Conference on Distributed Applications and Interoperable Systems (DAIS'05)*, Athens, Greece (pp. 68-82). Springer Press.

Grønmo, R., Skogan, D., Solheim, I., & Oldevik, J. (2004, March). Model-driven Web services development. In *Proceedings of 2004 IEEE International Conference on e-Technology, e-Commerce and e-Service (EEE'04)*, Taipei, Taiwan (pp. 42-45). IEEE Press.

Grosof, B. (1999). *A courteous compiler from generalized courteous logic programs to ordinary logic programs.* IBM T.J. Watson Research Center.

Grosof, B., & Poon, T. (2003) *SweetDeal: Representing agent contracts with exceptions using XML rules, ontologies, and process descriptions.* Paper presented at the 12th International Conference on the World Wide Web (pp. 340-349).

Gross, H. G. (Ed.). (2005). *Component-based software testing with UML.* Springer.

Gudgin, M. (2004, June 15-17). Secure, reliable, transacted; Innovation in Web services architecture. In *Proceedings of the ACM International Conference on Management of Data*, Paris (pp. 879-880).

Hagel, J. (2002). Edging into Web services. *The McKinsey Quarterly, 4.*

Hagel, J., III, & Brown, J. S. (2001). Your next IT strategy. *Harvard Business Review, 79*(9), 105-115.

Hamilton, G. (1997). JavaBeans™ API specification 1.01. *Sun Microsystems.* Retrieved October 31, 2007, from http://www.es.embnet.org/Doc/Computing/java/beans/beans.101.pdf

Hanson, J. (2003). Coarse-grained interfaces enable service composition in SOA. *TechRepublic.* Retrieved July 20, 2007, from http://articles.techrepublic.com.com/5100-22-5064520.html#Listing%20C

Hardt, D. (2006). *ETech 2006: Who is the dick on my site? Sxip.* Retrieved June 10, 2007, from http://identity20.com/media/ETECH_2006/

Hartel, P., Eck, P., Etalle, S., & Wieringa, R. (2005). Modelling mobility aspects of security policies. *Lecture Notes in Computer Science, 1*(3362/2005), 172-19.

Heckel, R., & Mariani, L. (2005). Automatic conformance testing of Web services. In *Proceedings of the FASE 2005* (Springer Verlag LNC S3442, pp. 34-48).

Heflin, J., & Hendler, J. (2000). Searching the Web with SHOE. Paper presented at the *Artificial Intelligence for Web Search, Papers from the AAAI Workshop. WS-00-01* (pp. 35-40). Menlo Park, CA: AAAI Press.

Hendriks, R. C., Heusdens, R., & Jensen, J. (2007). An MMSE estimator for speech enhancement under a combined stochastic–deterministic speech model. *IEEE Transactions on Audio, Speech and Language Processing, 15*(2), 406-415.

Hickey, T. B. (2003). *Web services for digital libraries.* Paper presented at the Cross Language Applications and The Web 27th Library Systems Seminar, Bern, Switzerland.

Hirtle, D., & Boley, H. (2005). *The modularization of RuleML.* Retrieved May 30, 2008, from www.ruleml.org/modularization

Ho, S., Loucks, W. M., & Singh, A. (1998). Monitoring the performance of a Web service. In *IEEE Canadian Conference on Electrical and Computer Engineering* (Vol. 1, pp. 109-112). Waterloo, Ontario, Canada: IEEE Press.

Hoffmann, J., & Nebel, B. (2001). The FF planning system: Fast plan generation through heuristic search. *Journal of Artificial Intelligence Research, 14*, 253-302.

Horrocks, I., Patel-Schneider, P. F., Boley, H., Tabet, S., Grosof, B., & Dean, M. (2005). *SWRL: A Semantic Web rule language combining OWL and RuleML.* Retrieved June 15, 2007, form http://www.w3.org/Submission/SWRL/

Horrocks, I., Patel-Schneider, P., Boley, H., Tabet, S., Grosof, B., & Dean, M. (2004). *SWRL: A Semantic*

Web rule language combining OWL and RuleML (No. SUBM-SWRL-20040521). W3C.

HP. (2007). *Open view.* Retrieved May 21, 2008, from http://www.managementsoftware.hp.com

Hu, X., He, G., & Zhou, X. (2006). *PEAQ-based psychoacoustic model for perceptual audio coder.* Paper presented at the 8th International Conference on Advanced Communication Technology, 2006, ICACT 2006, Phoenix Park, Korea.

IBM Corporation Software Group. (2007, March). Providing a messaging backbone for SOA connectivity. *IBM service oriented architecture solutions white paper.* Retrieved October 31, 2007, from ftp://ftp.software.ibm.com/software/integration/wmq/WS_MQ_Messaging_Backbone_for_SOA.pdf

IBM Corporation. (2006, June). *An architectural blueprint for autonomic computing* (4th ed.) (IBM Tech. Rep.). Retrieved October 31, 2007, from http://www-03.ibm.com/autonomic/pdfs/ACwpFinal.pdf

IBM Web services tool kit. Retrieved August 10, 2007, from http://www.alphaworks.ibm.com/tech/Webservicestoolkit

IEC. (1997). *Dependability and quality of service* (IEC 60050:191) International Electrotechnical Commission.

ISMA. (2004). Retrieved May 23, 2008, from http://www.isma.tv/

ISO. (1997). *ISO/ITU-T recommendation X.641 — ISO/IEC 13236: Information technology - quality of service - framework.* Author.

ISO. (n.d.). *Open system interconnection-distributed transaction processing (OSI-TP) model* (ISO IS 100261). Author.

ISO/IEC. (1989). *7498, information processing systems -- open systems interconnection – basic reference model.* Author.

ISO/IEC. (1998). *9596, information technology -- open systems interconnection -- common management information protocol.* Author.

ITU-T Recommendation H.263. (1996). *Video coding for low bit rate communication.* Author.

ITU-T Recommendation J.144-2004. (2004). *Objective perceptual video quality measurement techniques for digital cable television in the presence of a full reference.* Author.

Jade. (2007). *Java agent development framework.* Retrieved May 21, 2008, from http://jade.tilab.com

Java business integration (JBI) specification. (2005). *Java community process.* Retrieved July 11, 2007, from http://www.jcp.org/en/jsr/detail?id=208

Jeffay, K., & Stone, D. (1995). An empirical study of delay jitter management policies. *Proceedings of ACM Multimedia Systems, 2*(6), 267-79.

Jiang, Y., Xin, G.-M., Shan, J.-H., Zhang, L., Xie, B., & Yang, F.-Q. (2005). A method of automated test data generation for Web services. *Chinese Journal of Computers, 28*(4), 568-577.

Jin, L., Machiraju, V., & Sahai, A. (2002, June). *Analysis on service level agreement of Web services* (Tech. Rep. No. HPL-2002-180). USA: Software Technology Laboratories, HP Laboratories.

Jones, M. B. (2006). *The identity metasystem: A user-centric, inclusive Web authentication solution.* Retrieved June 10, 2007, from http://research.microsoft.com/~mbj/papers/InfoCard_W3C_Web_Authentication.pdf

Juels, A., Winslett, M., & Goto, G. (2006). Abstract. In *Proceedings of the Second ACM Workshop on Digital Identity Management, DIM '06.*

Juhlin, B. D. (1992). *Implementing operational profiles to measure system reliability.* Paper presented at Third International Symposium on Software Reliability Engineering, Research Triangle Park, NC.

Jürjens, J. (2002, September). *UMLsec: Extending UML for secure systems development.* Paper presented at the Uml 2002 - The Unified Modeling Language: 5th International Conference, Dresden, Germany (Vol. 2460/2002, pp. 1-9). Springer Press.

Kabir, M., Manning, E., & Shoja, G. (2002). Request-routing trends and techniques in content distribution network. In *Proceedings of the International Conference on Computer and Information Technology,* Dhaka, Bangladesh.

Kalepu, S., Krishnaswamy, S., & Loke, S. W. (2004). Verity: A QoS metric for selecting Web services and providers. In *Fourth International Conference on Web Information Systems Engineering Workshops* (pp. 131-139). Rome, Italy: IEEE Computer Society.

Kangasharju, J., Roberts, J., & Ross, K.W. (2002). Object replication strategies in content distribution networks. *Computers and Communications, 24*(4), 367-383.

Kant, K., Tewari, V., & Iyer, R. (2001). *Peer to peer computing: The hype, the hard problems, and quest for solutions.* Paper presented at the IEEE International Conference on Network Protocols 2001.

Kaplan, R., & Norton, D. (2000). *The strategy focused organization.* Harvard Business School Press.

Kath, O., Blazarenas, A., Born, M., Eckert, K.-P., Funabashi, M., & Hirai, C. (2004, September). Towards executable models: Transforming EDOC behavior models to CORBA and BPEL. In *Proceedings of the 8th International Enterprise Distributed Object Computing Conference (EDOC'04),* Monterey, CA (pp. 267–274). IEEE Press.

Kautz, H., & Selman, B. (1996). Pushing the envelope: Planning, propositional logic, and stochastic search. In *Proceedings of the 13th National Conference on Artificial Intelligence (AAAI-96)* (pp. 1194-1199).

Kaviani, N., Gasevic, D., Hatala, M., Clement, D., & Wagner, G. (2007). Integration of rules and policies for Semantic Web services. *International Journal of Advanced Media and Communication (IJAMC).*

Keller, A., & Ludwig, H. (2003). The WSLA framework: Specifying and monitoring service level agreements for Web services. *Journal of Network and Systems Management, 11*(1), 57-81.

Kent, S., & Atkinson, R. (1998). *Security architecture for the Internet protocol* (RFC No. 2401). The Internet Society.

Kenyon, J. (2003). Web service versioning and deprecation. *Web Services Journal.* SYS-CON Publications, Inc. Retrieved on July 17, 2007, from http://Webservices.sys-con.com/read/39678.htm

Kifer, M., de Bruijn, J., Boley, H., & Fensel, D. (2005). *A realistic architecture for the Semantic Web.* Paper presented at the RuleML.

Kikuchi, Y., Nomura, T., Fukunaga, S., Matsui, Y., & Kimata, H. (2000). *RTP payload format for MPEG-4 audio/visual streams* (RFC 3016).

Kim, B. R., Kim, K. C., & Kim, Y. S. (2005). Securing anonymity in P2P network. In *Proceedings of the 2005 Joint Conference on Smart Objects and Ambient Intelligence, SOc-EUSAI '05* (pp. 231-234). Grenoble: ACM Press.

Kochtanek, T. R., & Hein, K. K. (1999). Delphi study of digital libraries. *Information Processing & Management, 35*(3), 245-254.

Koenen, R. (2002). *MPEG-4 overview* (MPEG Output document, N4668). Jeju, Korea.

Kouadri Mostéfaoui, G. (2004). *Towards a conceptual and software framework for integrating context-based security in pervasive environments.* Unpublished doctoral thesis (No. 1463), University of Fribourg and Paris 6 University.

Kouadri Mostéfaoui, G., Maamar, Z., Narendra, N. C., & Sattanathan, S. (2006). Decoupling security concerns in Web services using aspects. In *Proceedings of the 3rd International Conference on Information Technology: New Generations (ITNG'2006),* Las Vegas.

Kowalkiewicz, M., Ludwig, A., Kaczmarek, M., & Zyskowski, D. (2005). *Documented mechanisms for dynamic service prpofiling and agreement life-cycle management* (ASG internal deliverable, FP6-IST-004617).

Krause, H. (2005). *Next generation service delivery: Adaptive services grid, European project, 2007.*

Kreger, H. (2001). *Web services conceptual architectures (WSCA 1.0)* (white paper). IBM Software Group.

Kritikos, K., & Plexousakis, D. (2006). Semantic QoS metric matching. In *Proceedings of the European Conference on Web Services, Ecows '06* (pp. 265-274). Washington, D.C.: IEEE Computer Society.

Kritikos, K., & Plexousakis, D. (2007). Requirements for QoS-based Web service description and discovery. *Compsac, 02,* 467-472.

Kulkarni, N., & Padmanabhuni, S. (2007). *An architectural framework for non functional requirements in enterprise SOA adoption.* Paper presented at WICSA 2007 (p. 36).

Kumar, S., Xu, L., Mandal, M. K., & Panchanathan, S. (2006). Error resiliency schemes in H.264/AVC standard. *Elsevier Journal of Visual Communication and Image Representation (Special issue on Emerging H.264/AVC Video Coding Standard), 17*(2).

Kuropka, D., & Weske, M. (2006, January). *Die adaptive services grid platform: Motivation, potential, funktionsweise und anwendungsszenarien.* Paper presented at the EMISA Forum.

Kuster, U., Koenig-Ries, B., Stern, M., & Klein, M. (2007, May 8-12). *DIANE: An integrated approach to automated service discovery, matchmaking and composition.* Paper presented at the WWW 2007, Banff, Alberta, Canada.

Kuter, U., Sirin, E., Nau, D., Parsia, B., & Hendler, J. (2005). Information gathering during planning for Web service composition. *Journal of Web Semantics (JWS) 3*(2-3), 183-205.

Laera, L., Tamma, V., Bench-Capon, T., & Semeraro, G. (2004). *SweetProlog: A system to integrate ontologies and rules*. Paper presented at the RuleML.

Langworthy, D. (2005). *WS-atomictransaction*.

Langworthy, D. (2005). *WS-business activity*.

Langworthy, D. (2005). *WS-coordination*.

Laprie, J. (1992). *Dependability: Basic concepts and terminology*. Wien, Austria. Springer Press.

Laprie, J. (1995). *Dependable computing: Concepts, limits and challenges*. Paper presented at the 25th International Symposium on Fault-Tolerant Computing, Pasadena (pp. 42-54).

Lara, R., & Olmedilla, D. (2005, June). *Discovery and contracting of Semantic Web services*. Paper presented at the Position Paper for the Workshop on Frameworks for Semantics in Web Services, Innsbruck, Austria.

Larsen, R. L., & Watctlar, H. D. (2003). *Knowledge lost in information*. Report of the NSF Workshop on Research Directions for Digital Libraries.

Le Callet, P., Viard-Gaudin, C., Pechard, S., & Caillault, É. (2006). No reference and reduced reference video quality metrics for end to end QoS monitoring. *IEICE Transactions on Communications, 2006 E89-B*(2), 289-296.

Lee (2003, October). Matching algorithms for composing business process solutions with Web services. In *Proceedings of the 4th International Conference on E-Commerce and Web Technologies (ECWEB'03)*, Prague, Czechoslovakia (pp. 393-402). Springer Press.

Lee, D., Netravali, A. N., Sabnani, K. K., Sugla, B., & John, A. (1997). *Passive testing and applications to network management*. Paper presented at the International Conference on Network Protocols (pp. 113-122). Atlanta: IEEE Computer Society.

Lee, K., Jeon, J., Lee, W., Jeong, S.-H., & Park, S.-W. (2003, November). *Qos for Web services: Requirements and possible approaches*. World Wide Web Consortium (W3C).

Lee, Y. W., Strong, D. M., Kahn, B. K., & Wang, R. Y. (2002). Aimq: A methodology for information quality assessment. *Information Management, 40*(2), 133-146.

Lehman, M., Ramil, J. F., Wernick, P., Perry, D. E., & Turski, W. M. (1997). *Metrics and laws of software evolution - the nineties view*. Paper presented at the International Symposium of Software Metrics (pp. 20-32). IEEE Computer Society Press.

Lesser, E. L., & Storck, J. (2001). Communities of practice and organizational performance. *IBM Systems Journal, 40*(4), 831-931.

Levesque, H., Reiter, R., Lesperance, Y., Lin, F., & Scherl, R. (1997). GOLOG: A logic programming language for dynamic domains. *Journal of Logic Programming 31*(1-3), 59-84.

Leymann, F. (2001). *Web service flow language (WSFL) 1.0*. Retrieved May 21, 2008, from http://www-4.ibm.com/software/solutions/Webservices/pdf/WSFL.pdf

Li, B., Xu, D., & Nahrstedt, K. (2001, October). Towards integrated runtime solutions in QoS-aware middleware. In *Proceedings of the ACM Multimedia Middleware Workshop (M3W 2001)*, Ottawa, Canada (pp. 11-14). ACM Press.

Li, H., & Singhal, M. (2007). Trust management in distributed systems. *Computer, 1*(40), 45-53.

Li, W. (2001). Overview of fine granularity scalability in MPEG-4 video standard. *IEEE Transactions on Circuits and Systems for Video Technology, 11*(3), 301-317.

Liberty specifications for identity management. Retrieved August 10, 2007, from http://www.projectliberty.org/resource_center/specifications

Liebesman, S. (1994, July). ISO 9000: An introduction. *Using ISO 9000 to improve business processes* (Chapter 1). AT&T Corporate Quality Office.

Lifschitz, V. (1999). *Answer set planning*. Paper presented at the International Conference on Logic Programming (pp. 23-37).

Lifschitz, V. (2002). Answer set programming and plan generation. *Artificial Intelligence, 138*(1-2), 39-54.

Lincoln, Y. S., & Guba, E. G. (1985). *Naturalistic inquiry*. Beverly Hills, CA: Sage Publications, Inc.

Little, M. (2003), Transactions and Web services, *Communications of the ACM, 46*(10), 49-54.

Liu, C., Peng, Y., & Chen, J. (2006). *Web services description ontology-based service discovery model*. Paper presented at the International Conference on Web Intelligence (WI 2006).

Liu, F., Chou, W., Li, L., & Li, J. (2004). WSIP - Web service SIP endpoint for converged multimedia/multimodal communication over IP. In *Proceedings of the IEEE International Conference on Web Services (ICWS'04)*, San Diego.

Liu, Y., Ngu, A. H. H., & Zeng, L. (2004). QoS computation and policing in dynamic Web service selection. In S. I. Feldman, M. Uretsky, M. Najork, & C. E. Wills (Eds.), *WWW (alternate track papers & posters)* (pp. 66-73). New York: ACM.

Liu, Y., Ngu, A. H. H., & Zeng, L. (2004, May). *QoS computation and policing in dynamic Web service selection.* Paper presented at the 13th International Conference on World Wide Web (WWW), New York.

Lodderstedt, T., Basin, D. A., & Doser, J. (2002, September). SecureUML: A UML-based modeling language for model-driven security. In *Proceedings of the 5th International Conference on the Unified Modeling Language,* Dresden, Germany (Vol. 2460, pp. 426-441). Springer Press.

Loughran, N., & Rashid, A. (2003). Supporting evolution in software using frame technology and aspect orientation. In *Proceedings of the Workshop on Software Variability Management*, Groningen, The Netherlands.

Ludwig, H., Keller, A., Dan, A., & King, R. (2002). *A service level agreement language for dynamic electronic services.* Paper presented at the Fourth IEEE International Workshop on Advanced Issues of E-Commerce and Web-Based Information Systems (pp. 25-32).

Ludwig, H., Keller, A., Dan, A., King, R. P., & Franck, R. (2003). Retrieved May 25, 2008, from http://www.research.ibm.com/wsla

Ludwig, H., Keller, A., Dan, A., King, R. P., & Franck, R. (2003, January). *Web service level agreement (WSLA) language specification* (IBM Tech. Rep.). Retrieved July 30, 2007, from http://www.research.ibm.com/wsla/WSLASpecV1-20030128.pdf

Lupu, E., & Sloman, M. (1999, November/December). Conflicts in policy-based distributed systems management. *IEEE Transactions on Software Engineering, 25*(6).

Ma, K. (2005, March/April). Web services: What's real and what's not? *IT Professional, 7*(2).

Maamar, Z., Benatallah, B., & Mansoor, W. (2003). Service chart diagrams: Description & application. In *Proceedings of the Alternate Tracks of The 12th International World Wide Web Conference (WWW'2003)*, Budapest, Hungary.

Maamar, Z., Benslimane, D., & Narendra, N. C. (2006). What can context do for Web services? *Communications of the ACM.*

Maamar, Z., Benslimane, D., Ghedira, C., Mahmoud, Q. H., & Yahyaoui, H. (2005). Tuple spaces for self-coordination of Web services. In *Proceedings of the 20th ACM Symposium on Applied Computing (SAC'2005)*, Santa Fe, NM.

Maamar, Z., Kouadri Mostéfaoui, S., & Mahmoud, Q. (2005, July-September). On personalizing Web services using context. *International Journal of E-Business Research, Special Issue on E-Services, 1*(3). IGI Global, Inc.

Majumdar, B., Chaudhuri, A. P., & Sitaram. V., (2006). SOA requires enterprise application security integration architecture. *Search software quality.* Retrieved July 27, 2007, from http://searchsoftwarequality.techtarget.com/tip/0,289483,sid92_gci1168738,00.html

Majumdar, B., Verma, A., & Mysore, U. (2006). Enhance UDDI to manage Web services. *IBM developerworks.* Retrieved July 27, 2007, from http://www.ibm.com/developerworks/Webservices/library/ws-uddisecure/

Marchionini, G. (1998). Research and development in digital libraries. In A. Kent (Ed.), *Encyclopedia of library and information science* (Vol. 63, pp. 259-279). New York: Marcel Dekker.

Marek, V., & Truszczynski, M. (1999). Stable models and an alternative logic programming paradigm. *The logic programming paradigm: A 25-year perspective* (pp. 375-398).

Marick, B. (1998). When should a test be automated? In *Proceedings of the International Quality Week, 1998.*

Martín-Díaz, O., Cortés, A. R., Benavides, D., Durán, A., & Toro, M. (2003). A quality-aware approach to Web services procurement. In B. Benatallah & M.-C. Shan (Eds.), *Technologies for e-services (TES)* (Vol. 2819, pp. 42-53). Berlin: Springer.

Martinez, J. (2002). MPEG-7: Overview of MPEG-7 description tools, part 2. *IEEE Multimedia, 9*(3), 83-93.

Masry, M., & Hemami, S. (2004). A metric for continuous quality evaluation of compressed video with severe distortion. *Signal Processing: Image Communication, 19*(2).

Matena, V., & Stearns, B. (2000). *Applying Enterprise JavaBeans™: Component-based development for the J2EE™platform.* Addison Wesley.

Maximilien, E. M., & Singh, M. P. (2002). Conceptual model of Web service reputation. *SIGMOD Rec., 31*(4), 36-41.

Maximilien, E. M., & Singh, M. P. (2002a). Reputation and endorsement for Web services. *ACM SIGecom Exchanges, 3*(1), 24-31.

Maximilien, E. M., & Singh, M. P. (2002b). *Conceptual model of Web services reputation.* SIGMOD Record.

Maximilien, E. M., & Singh, M. P. (2004, November, 2004). *Towards autonomic Web services trust and selection.* Paper presented at the ICSOC'04, New York.

Maximilien, E. M., & Singh, M. P. (2004, September). A framework and ontology for dynamic Web services selection. *IEEE Internet Computing,* 84-93. IEEE Press.

May, W., Alferes, J., & Amador, R. (2005). *Active rules in the Semantic Web: Dealing with language heterogeneity.* Paper presented at the RuleML.

McBreen, P. (2003). *Questioning extreme programming.* Addison-Wesley.

McCarthy, J. (1959). Programs with common sense. In *Proceedings of the Teddington Conference on the Mechanization of Thought Processes* (pp. 75-91).

McDermott, D., Dou, D., & Qi, P. (2002). *PDDAML: An automatic translator between PDDL and DAML.*

McIlraith, S., & Son, T. C. (2002). Adapting GOLOG for composition of Semantic Web services. In *Proceedings of the Eighth International Conference on Principles of Knowledge Representation and Reasoning (KR'2002)* (pp. 482-493).

Mehrotra, S., Rastogi, R., Silberschatz, A., & Korth, H. (1992, June 9-12). A transaction model for multidatabase systems. In *Proceedings of the 12th IEEE International Conference on Distributed Computing Systems (ICDCS92)*, Yokohama, Japan (pp. 56-63).

Melzer, I., & Sauter, P. (2005). A comparison of WS-business-activity and BPEL4WS long-running transaction. *Kommunikation in Verteilten Systemen, Informatik aktuell.* Springer.

Menasce, D. A. (2002). QoS Issues in Web services. *IEEE Internet Computing, 6*(6), 72-75.

Menasce, D. A. (2002). QoS issues in Web services. *IEEE Internet Computing, 6*(6), 72-75.

Menasce, D. A. (2002). QoS issues in Web services. *IEEE Internet Computing,* 72-75.

Menasce, D. A., Ruan, H., & Gomaa, H. (2004). *A framework for QoS-aware software components.* Paper presented at Workshop on Software and Performance, San Francisco.

Menasce, D. A. (January 2003). Automatic QoS control. *IEEE Internet Computing, 7*(1), 92-95.

Merdes, M., Malaka, R., Suliman, D., Paech, B., Brenner, D., & Atkinson, C. (2006). *Ubiquitous RATs: How resource-aware run-time tests can improve ubiquitous software systems.* Paper presented at 6th International Workshop on Software Engineering and Middleware, Portland.

Meyer, B. (1992). Applying design by contract. *IEEE Computer, 25*(10), 40-51.

Microsoft Windows Media. Retrieved May 23, 2008, from http://www.microsoft.com/windows/windowsmedia/default.mspx

Microsoft. (2003, February). *Enterprise UDDI services: An introduction to evaluating, planning, deploying, and operating UDDI services.* Retrieved October 31, 2007, from http://www.microsoft.com/windowsserver2003/technologies/idm/uddi/default.mspx

Miller, J. (2006). *Yadis specification 1.0.* Retrieved June 10, 2007, from http://yadis.org/papers/yadis-v1.0.pdf

Montagut, F., & Molva R. (2006, September 18-22). *Augmenting Web services composition with transactional requirements.* Paper presented at the ICWS 2006, IEEE International Conference on Web Services, Chicago (pp. 91-98).

Moorthy, K. R., & Gandhirajan, A. (2005). *The foundations of Web services security.* Retrieved August, from http://www.developer.com/services/article.php/3496326

MORABIT project. (2008). Retrieved October 27, 2007, from http://www.morabit.org/

Morgan, R. L., Cantor, S., Carmody, S., Hoehn, W., & Klingenstein, K. (2004). Federated security: The shibboleth approach. *EDUCAUSE Quarterly, 24,* 8-22. Retrieved June 10, 2007, from http://www.educause.edu/apps/eq/eqm04/eqm0442.asp

MPEG 4: ISO/IEC International Standard, 14 496-2. (1998). *Information technology—coding of audio-visual objects: Visual.* Author.

MPEG-2: ISO/IEC International Standard 13 818-2. (1994). *Generic coding of moving pictures and associated audio information: Visual.* Author.

MPEG4IP. Retrieved May 23, 2008, from http://mpeg4ip.sourceforge.net/

Muccini, H., Bertolino, A., & Inverardi, P. (2004). Using software architecture for code testing. *IEEE Transactions on Software Engineering, 30*(3), 160-171.

Nakamur, Y., Hada, S., & Neyma, R. (2002). Towards the integration of Web services security on enterprise environments. In *Proceedings of the Workshop on Web Services Engineering 2002 (WebSE'2002) held in conjunction with The IEEE/IPSJ Symposium on Applications and the Internet (SAINT'2002)*, Nara, Japan

Napster. Retrieved May 23, 2008, from http://www.napster.com/

Nau, D., Cao, Y., Lotem, A., & Muñoz-Avila, H. (1999). SHOP: Simple hierarchical ordered planner. In *Proceedings of the 16th International Conference on Artificial Intelligence* (pp. 968-973).

Nick, J., Chung, J. Y., & Bowen, N. S. (1996). Overview of IBM system/390 parallel sysplex. In *Proceedings of 10th International Parallel Processing Symposium (IPPS)* (pp. 488-495). IEEE Computer Society.

Niemelä, I. (1999). Logic programming with stable model semantics as a constraint programming paradigm. *Annals of Mathematics and Artificial Intelligence, 25*(3,4), 241-273.

Niemelä, I., & Simons, P. (1997). Smodels: An implementation of the stable model and well-founded semantics for normal logic programs. In *Proceedings ICLP & LPNMR* (pp. 420-429).

Niven, P. R. (2003). *Balanced scorecard. Step-by-step for government and non-profit agencies.* John Wiley & Sons.

Noia, T. D., Sciascio, E. D., Donini, F. M., & Mongiello, M. (2003). A system for principled matchmaking in an electronic marketplace. In *Proceedings of the 12th International Conference on World Wide Web, WWW '03* (pp. 321-330). New York: ACM Press.

Noll, J. (2004). *ASG based scenarios in telecommunications, telematics and enhanced enterprise IT.* Retrieved May 26, 2008, from http://asg-platform.org

O'Sullivan, J., Edmond, D., & Hofstede, A. T. (2002). What's in a service? Towards an accurate description of non-functional properties of Web services. *Distributed and Parallel Databases,* (12), 117-133.

OASIS Web services security (WSS). Retrieved August 10, 2007, from http://www.oasis-open.org/committees/wss

OASIS. (2004, November). OASIS Web services reliable messaging TC. *WS-Reliability 1*(1). Retrieved July 30, 2007, from http://docs.oasis-open.org/wsrm/ws-reliability/v1.1/wsrm-ws_reliability-1.1-spec-os.pdf

OASIS. (2005). *Universal description, discovery, and integration.* Retrieved May 21, 2008, from http://www.uddi.org/

OBO download matrix. (2007). Retrieved May 30, 2008, from http://www.berkeleybop.org/ontologies/

Offutt, J., & Xu, W. (2006). Generating test cases for Web services using data perturbation. *SIGSOFT Software Engineering Notes, 29*(5), 1-10.

OGF. (2007). Web services agreement specification (WS-Agreement) (Open Grid Forum Recommendation Documents [REC]). *OGF Grid Resource Allocation and Agreement Protocol Working Group.* Retrieved October 31st, 2007, from http://www.ogf.org/documents/GFD.107.pdf

Oguz, F., & Moen, W. E. (2006). *Texas library directory Web services application: The potential for Web services to enhance information access to legacy data.* Paper presented at the International Conference on Next Generation Web Services Practices (NWeSP'06), Korea.

Oldham, N., Verma, K., Sheth, A., & Hakimpour, F. (2006). Semantic WS-agreement partner selection. In *Proceedings of the 15th International Conference on World Wide Web, WWW '06* (pp. 697-706). New York: ACM Press.

OMG. (1995). *The common object request broker: Architecture and specification.* Framingham, MA: Object Management Group, Inc.

OMG. (2001). *Model driven architecture* (ormsc/2001-07-01). Needham, MA. Object Management Group, Inc.

OMG. (2001). *Unified modeling language specification version 1.4* (OMG formal document/01-09-67). Needham, MA. Object Management Group, Inc.

OMG. (2004). *UML profile for modelling quality of service and fault tolerance characteristics and mechanisms* (ptc/2004-06-01). Needham, MA. Object Management Group, Inc.

Orso, A., Harrold, M. J., & Rosenblum, D. S. (2000). *Component metadata for software engineering tasks.* Paper presented at 2nd International Workshop on Engineering Distributed Objects (EDO), Davis.

Ortalo, R. (1998). A flexible method for information system security policy specification. *Lecture Notes in Computer Science, 1*(1485/1998), 67-84.

Ortega, M., Perez, M., & Rojas, T. (2000). *A model for software product quality with a system focus.* Paper presented at the 4th World Multi Conference on Systematic Cybernatics.

Ortiz, G., Hernández, J., & Clemente, P. J. (2004). Decoupling non-functional properties in Web services: An aspect-oriented approach. In *Proceedings of the 2nd European Workshop on Web Services and Object Orientation (EOOWS'2004) held in conjunction with the 18th European Conference on Object-Oriented Programming (ECOOP'2004)*, Norway.

Ortiz, G., Hernández, J., & Clemente, P. J. (2004). Web services orchestration and interaction patterns: An aspect-oriented approach. In *Proceedings of the 2nd International Conference on Service Oriented Computing (ICSOC'2004)*, New York.

OWL Services Coalition. (2003). *OWL-S: Semantic markup for Web services.*

Padmanabhan, V. N, Wang, H. J., Chou, P. A., & Sripanidkulchai, K. (2002). *Distributing streaming media content using cooperative networking.* Paper presented at the ACM Conference on Networking and Operating System Support for Audio and Video (NOSSDAV) 2002, Miami.

Padmanabhuni, P., & Adarkar, H. (2003). Security in service- oriented architecture: Issues, standards, and implementations. *Service-oriented software system engineering: Challenges and practices* (Chapter XIV). IGI Publications.

Pai, V., Aron, M., Banga, G., Svendsen, M., Druschel, P., Zaenepoel, W., et al. (1998). *Locality-aware request distribution in cluster-based network services.* Paper presented at the 8th International Conference on Architectural Support for Programming Languages and Operating Systems (ASPLOS-VIII), San Jose, CA.

Pan, Y., Tu, P. H., Pontelli, E., & Son, T. C. (2004). *Construction of an agent-based framework for evolutionary biology: A progress report.* Paper presented at the Declarative Agent Languages and Technologies (DALT).

Papazoglou, M. P. (2003). Service-oriented computing: Concepts, characteristics and directions. In *Proceedings of the 4th International Conference on Web Information Systems Engineering, WISE '03* (pp. 3-12). Rome: IEEE Computer Society.

Parasoft. (2006). *SOATest.* Retrieved May 21, 2008, from http://www.parasoft.com/jsp/products/home.jsp?product=SOAP

Parastatidis, S., Webber, J., Watson, P., & Rischbeck, T. (2005). WS-GAF: A framework for building grid applications using Web services. *Concurrency and Computation: Practice and Experience, 17*(2-4), 391-417.

Parhami, B. (1988). From defects to failures: A view of dependable computing. *SIGARCH Comput. Archit. News, 16*(4), 157-168.

Park J-T., Baek, J-W., & Won-Ki Hong, J. (2001, May). Management of service level agreements for multimedia Internet service using a utility model. *IEEE Communication Magazine.*

Parnas, D. (1994). *Software aging.* Paper presented at the International Conference of Software Engineering (pp. 279-287). IEEE Computer Society Press.

Pasquinelli, A. (2002). *Digital library technology trends.* Retrieved December, 9, 2005, from http://www.sun.com/products-n-solutions/edu/whitepapers/pdf/digital_library_trends.pdf

Patton, M. Q. (2002). *Qualitative research and evaluation methods* (3rd ed.). Thousand Oaks, CA: Sage Publications, Inc.

PDDL Technical Committee. (1998). *Planning domain definition language.* Author.

Perform output caching with Web services in visual C#.NET. (2003). Microsoft Support.

Perkins, D., & McGinnis, E. (1997). *Understanding SNMP MIBs.* Upper Saddle River, N.J.: Prentice Hall PTR.

Pettichord, B. (1996). Success with test automation. In *Proceedings of the Quality Week, 1996.*

Pitt-Francis, J., Chen, D., Slaymaker, M. A., Simpson, A. C., Brady, J. M., van Leeuwen, I., et al. (2006). Multimodal imaging techniques for the extraction of detailed geometrical and physiological information for use in multi-scale models of colorectal cancer and treatment of individual patients. *Computational Mathematical Methods in Medicine, 7*(2/3), 177-188.

Pontelli, E., Son, T. C., & Baral, C. (2006). *A framework for composition and inter-operation of rules in the Semantic Web.* Paper presented at the RuleML.

Porter, G., & Katz, R.H. (2006). Effective Web service load balancing through statistical monitoring. *Communications of the ACM, 49*(3), 49-54.

Powell, J., & Buchan, I. (2005). Electronic health records should support clinical research. *Journal of Medical Internet Research, 7*(1), e4.

Power, D. J., Politou, E. A., Slaymaker, M. A., & Simpson, A. C. (2005). Towards secure grid-enabled healthcare. *Software: Practice and Experience, 35*(9), 857-871.

Preist, C. (2004, November). *A conceptual architecture for Semantic Web services.* Paper presented at the International Semantic Web Conference 2004 (ISWC 2004).

Project Liberty specification. (2003, January 15). Retrieved August 10, 2007, from http://www.projectliberty. org/specs/archive/v1_1/liberty-architecture-overview-v1.1.pdf

Psytechnics video. Retrieved May 23, 2008, from IP metric http://www.psytechnics.com

Radha, H., van der Schaar, M., & Chen, Y. (2001). The MPEG-4 fine-grained scalable video coding method for multimedia streaming over IP. *IEEE Transactions on Multimedia, 3*(1).

Rainer, W. (2005). *Web service composition using answer set programming.* Paper presented at the Workshop on Planning, Scheduling, and Configuration.

Rajahalme, J., Conta, A., Carpenter, B., & Deering, S. (2004). *IPv6 flow label specification* (RFC No. 3697). The Internet Society.

Ran, S. (2003). A Framework for Discovering Web Services with Desired Quality of Services Attributes. In *International Conference on Web Services* (pp. 208-213). Las Vegas, Nevada: CSREA Press.

Ran, S. (2003). A model for Web services discovery with QoS. *ACM SIGecom Exchanges, 4*(1), 1-10.

Rao, J., & Su, X. (2004). *A survey of automated Web service composition methods.* Paper presented at the SWSWPC.

Ratakonda, K., Turaga D. S., & Lai, J. (2006). *QoS support for streaming media using a multimedia server cluster.* Paper presented at the IEEE Globecom 2006.

Real Networks. Retrieved May 23, 2008, from http://www. realnetworks.com/products/media_delivery.html

Recordon, D., & Reed, D. (2006). OpenID 2.0: A platform for user-centric identity management. In *Proceedings of the Second ACM Workshop on Digital Identity Management, DIM '06* (pp. 11-16). Alexandria: ACM Press.

Reddy, R., & Wladawsky-Berger, I. (2001). *Digital libraries: Universal access to human knowledge: A report to the President.* President's Information Technology Advisory Committee (PITAC), Panel on Digital Libraries.

Ricca, F. (2003). *The DLV Java wrapper.* Paper presented at the Italian Congress on Computational Logic (CILC).

Rix, A. W., Beerends, J. G., Hollier, M. P., & Hekstra, A. P. (2001). Perceptual evaluation of speech quality (PESQ): A new method for speech quality assessment of telephone networks and codecs. In *Proceedings of the IEEE Acoustics, Speech, and Signal Processing, Conference (ICASSP '01)*, Salt Lake City, Utah.

Roczniak, A., Janmohamed, S., Roch, C., El Saddik, A., & Lévy, P. (2006, May 17-19). SOA-based collaborative multimedia authoring. In *Proceedings of the 2nd Montréal Conference on e-Technologies (MCeTECH '06)*, Montréal, Canada.

Rogers, E. M. (1995). *Diffusion of Innovations* (4th ed.). New York: The Free Press.

Rohani, B., & Zepernick, H.-J. (2005). An efficient method for perceptual evaluation of speech quality in UMTS. In *Proceedings of Systems Communications, 2005.*

Roman, D., et al. (2006). *WWW: WSMO, WSML and WSMX in a nutshell.* Paper presented at the First Asian Semantic Web Conference (ASWC 2006).

Romney, A., Batchelder, W., & Weller, S. (1986). Culture as consensus: A theory of culture and informant accuracy. *American Anthropologist, 88*, 313-338.

Rosa, N. S., Cunha, P. R., Freire, L., & Justo, G. R. (2002, March 29, 2005). *Process NFL: A language for describing non-functional properties.* Paper presented at the 35th Annual Hawaii International Conference (HICSS), Hawaii.

Rosenberg, J., & Schulzrinne, H. (2002). *SIP: Session initiation protocol* (RFC 3261). IETF Network Working Group.

RTSP. Retrieved May 23, 2008, from http://www.ietf. org/rfc/rfc2326.txt

Rusinkiewicz, M., & Sheth, A. (1995). Specification and execution of transactional workflows. *Modern database systems: The object model, interoperability, and beyond* (pp. 592-620).

Sabata, B., Chatterjee, S., Davis, M., Sydir, J. J., & Lawrence, T. F. (1997). Taxomomy of QoS specifications. In *Proceedings of the 3rd Workshop on bject-Oriented Real-Time Dependable Systems (WORDS '97)* (pp. 100-107). Washington, D.C.: IEEE Computer Society.

Sabater, J., & Sierra, C. (2005). Review on computational trust and reputation models. *Artificial Intelligence Review, 1*(24), 33-60.

Sahai, A., Durante, A., & Machiraju, V. (2002). *Towards automated SLA management for Web services* (Tech. Rep. No. HPL-2001-310). Palo Alto, CA: Software Technology Laboratory, HP Laboratories.

Sahai, A., Machiraju, V., Sayal, M., & Casati, F. (2002, October). *Automated SLA monitoring for Web services.* Paper presented the Management Technologies for E-Commerce and E-Business Applications: 13th IFIP/IEEE International Workshop on Distributed Systems: Operations and Management, Montreal, Canada (Vol. 2506, pp. 28-41). Springer Press.

Sahai, A., Machiraju, V., Sayal, M., Jin, L. J., & Casati, F. (2002). *Automated SLA monitoring for Web services.* Paper presented at the 13th IFIP/IEEE International Wokshop on Distributed Systems (DSOM) (pp. 28-41).

Salamatian, K., & Fdida, S. (2001). Measurement based modeling of quality of service in the Internet: A methodological approach. In *Proceedings of the Thyrrhenian International Workshop on Digital Communications IWDC'01* (pp. 158-174). London: Springer-Verlag.

Salamon, W. J., & Wallace, D. R. (1994). *Quality characteristics and metrics for reusable software.* National Institute of Standards and Technology.

Sanderson, R. (2004). *SRW: Search/retrieve Webservice version 1.1.* Retrieved February 2, 2005, from http://srw.cheshire3.org/SRW-1.1.pdf

Sandhu, R. (2003, January/February). Good-enough security: Toward a pragmatic business-driven discipline. *IEEE Internet Computing, 7*(1).

Sattanathan, S., Narendra, N. C., & Maamar, Z. (2005). Towards context-based tracking of Web services security. In *Proceedings of The 7th International Conference on Information Integration and Web Based Applications & Services (iiWAS'2005)*, Kuala Lumpur, Malaysia.

Schmidt, A., Beigl, M., & Gellersen, H. W. (1999, December). There is more to context than location. *Computers & Graphics Journal, 23*(6).

Schmidt, D. C. (1999, January). Why software reuse has failed and how to make it work for you. *C++ Report.*

Schmietendorf, A., Dumke, R., & Reitz, D. (2004). SLA management - Challenges in the context of Web-service-based infrastructures. In *IEEE International Conference on Web Services (ICWS)* (pp. 606-613). San Diego, CA: IEEE Computer Society.

Schuldt, H., Alonso, G., & Schek, H. (1999, May 31-June 2). Concurrency control and recovery in transactional process management. In *Proceedings of the Conference on Principles of Database Systems*, Philadelphia (pp. 316-326).

Schulzrinne, H. (1996). *RTP profile for audio and video conferences with minimal control* (Standards Document RFC 1890).

SDP. Retrieved May 23, 2008, from http://www.ietf.org/rfc/rfc2327.txt

Serhani, M. A., Dssouli, R., Hafid, A., & Sahraoui, H. (2005). A QoS broker based architecture for efficient Web services selection. In *International Conference on Web Services (ICWS)* (Vol. 2005, pp. 113-120). Orlando, FL: IEEE Computer Society.

Serhani, M. A., Dssouli, R., Sahraoui, H., Benharref, A., & Badidi, M. E. (2005, September). QoS integration in value added Web services. In *Proceedings of the Second International Conference on Innovations in Informal Technology (IIT'05)*.

Service component architecture (SCA) specification. (2007). *Open service oriented architecture.* Retrieved July 10, 2007 from http://www.osoa.org/display/Main/Service+Component+Architecture+Home

ShaikhAli, A., Rana, O. F., Al-Ali, R., & Walker, D. W. (2003). UDDIe: An extended registry for Web services. In (pp. 85-89). Orlando, FL, USA: IEEE Computer Society.

Sheth, A., Cordoso, J., Miller, J., & Kochut, K. (2002, July). *QoS for service-oriented middleware.* Paper presented at the 6rh World Multiconference on Systemics Cybernetics and Informatics (SCI02).

Shin, S. (2003). Secure Web services. *JavaWorld.* Retrieved on July 17, 2007, from http://www.javaworld.com/javaworld/jw-03-2003/jw-0321-wssecurity.html?page=1

Simons, P., Niemelä, N., & Soininen, T. (2002). Extending and implementing the stable model semantics. *Artificial Intelligence, 138*(1-2), 181-234.

Simpson, A. C., Power, D. J., Slaymaker, M. A., & Politou, E. A. (2005). GIMI: Generic infrastructure for medical informatics. In *Proceedings of the 18th IEEE Symposium on Computer-Based Medical Systems (CBMS).* IEEE Computer Society Press.

Simpson, A. C., Power, D. J., Slaymaker, M. A., Russell, D., & Katzarova, M. (2007). On the development of secure service-oriented architectures to support medical research. *The International Journal of Healthcare Information Systems and Informatics 2*(2), 75-89.

Sivashanmugam, K., Sheth, A. P., Miller, J. A., Verma, K., Aggarwal, R., & Rajasekaran, P. (2003). Metadata and semantics for Web services and processes. In W. Benn, P. Dadam, S. Kirn, & R. Unland (Eds.), *Datenbanken und informationssysteme: Festschrift zum 60. geburtstag von gunter schlageter* (pp. 245-271). Hagen: FernUniversitÄat in Hagen, Fachbereich Informatik.

Skogan, D., Grønmo, R., & Solheim, I. (2004, September). Web service composition in UML. In *Proceedings of the 8th IEEE International Enterprise Distributed Object Computing Conf (EDOC'04),* Monterey, CA (pp. 47-57). IEEE Press.

Slaymaker, M. A., Simpson, A. C., Brady, J. M., Gavaghan, D. J., Reddington, F. & Quirke, P. (2006). A prototype infrastructure for the secure aggregation of imaging and pathology data for colorectal cancer care. In *Proceedings of the 19th IEEE Symposium on Computer-Based Medical Systems (CBMS).* IEEE Computer Society Press.

Smythe, C. (2006). *Initial investigations into interoperability testing of Web services from their specification using the unified modelling language.* Paper presented at the International Workshop on Web Services Modeling and Testing (WS-MaTe), Palermo, Italy.

Solano, J., De Ovalles, M. P., Rojas, T., Padua, A. G., & Morales, L. M. (2003, Winter). Integration of systemic quality and the balanced scorecard, privacy and security in e-business. *Information Systems Management,* 66-81.

Sommerville, I. (Ed.). (2004). *Software engineering.* Addison Wesley.

Son, T. C., & Pontelli, E. (2006). Planning with preferences using logic programming. *Theory and Practice of Logic Programming, 6,* 559-607.

Son, T. C., Baral, C., Tran, N., & McIlraith, S. (2006). Domain-dependent knowledge in answer set planning. *ACM Transactions on Computational Logic, 7*(4).

Son, T. C., Baral, C., Tran, N., & McIlraith, S. (2006). Domain-dependent knowledge in answer set planning. *ACM Transactions on Computer Logic, 7*(4), 613-657.

Son, T. C., Tu, P. H., Gelfond, M., & Morales, R. (2005). Conformant planning for domains with constraints: A new approach. In *Proceedings of the the Twentieth National Conference on Artificial Intelligence* (pp. 1211-1216).

Son, T., & Pontelli, E. (2007). *Planning for biochemical pathways: A case study of answer set planning in large planning problem instances.* Paper presented at the Software Engineering for Answer Set Programming.

Spencer, B. (2002). *The design of j-DREW, a deductive reasoning engine for the Semantic Web.* Uni. Pol. Madrid.

Sripanidkulchai, K. (2001). *The popularity of Gnutella queries and its implications on scalability.* O'Reilly's. Retrieved May 23, 2008, from www.openp2p.com

Stoica, I., Morris, R., Karger, D., Kaashoek, M., & Balakrishnan, H. (2001). *Chord: A scalable peer-to-peer lookup service for Internet applications.* Paper presented at the ACM Special Interest Group on Communications Conference (SIGCOMM 2001), San Diego.

Subrahmanian, V. S., & Zaniolo, C. (1995). Relating stable models and AI planning domains. In *Proceedings of the International Conference on Logic Programming* (pp. 233-247).

Suliman, D., Paech, B., Borner, B., Atkinson, C., Brenner, D., Merdes, M., et al. (2006). *The MORABIT approach to run-time component testing.* Paper presented at Second International Workshop on Testing and Quality Assurance for Component-Based Systems (TQACBS 2006), Chicago.

Sumra, R., & Arulazi, D. (2003, March). *Quality of service for Web services: Demystification, limitations, and best practices.* Developer.com Website.

Svoboda, Z. (2002). Securing Web services with single sign-on. *TheServerSide.* Retrieved on July 18, 2007, from http://www.theserverside.com/tt/articles/article.tss?l=Systinet-Web-services-part-6

Sycara, K., Burstein, M., Hobbs, J., Lassila, O., Mc Dermott, D., McIlraith, S., et al. (2003). *Owl-s 1.0 release.* Retrieved June 5, 2008, from http://www.daml.org/services/owl-s/1.0/

Syrjanen, T. (1998). *Lparse 1.0: User's manual.* Helsinki University of Technology.

Szyperski, C. (1997). *Component oriented programming.* Addison-Wesley.

Takishima, Y., Wada, M., & Murakami, H. (1995). Reversible variable length codes. *IEEE Transactions on Communications, 43,* 158-162.

Tang, S., Liebetruth, C., & Jaeger, M. C. (2003). *The OWL-S matcher software.* Retrieved May 29, 2008, from http://flp.cs.tu-berlin.de/

Thatte, S. (2003). *Business process execution language for Web services version 1.1 (BPEL).*

The Policy RuleML Technical Group. (2004). *RuleML-powered policy specification and interchange.* Author.

Tian, M., Gramm, A., Nabulsi, M., Ritter, H., Schiller, J., & Voigt, T. (2003, October). *QoS integration in Web services*. Gesellschaft fur Informatik DWS 2003, Doktorandenworkshop Technologien und Anwendungen von XML.

Tiwari, R., Dwivedi, V., & Karlapalem, K. (2007). *SLA driven process security through monitored e-contracts*. Paper presented at the IEEE International Conference of Service Computing (SCC'07) (pp. 28-35).

Toma, I. (2006). *Non-functional properties in Web services*. DERI.

Tornatzky, L. G., & Klein, K. J. (1982). Innovation characteristics and innovation adoption-implementation: A meta-analysis of findings. *IEEE Transactions on Engineering Management, 29*(1), 28-45.

Tosic, V. (2004). *Service offerings for XML Web services and their management applications*. Unpublished doctoral dissertation, Carleton University, Ottawa, Canada.

Tosic, V., Esfandiari, B., Pagurek, B., & Patel, K. (2002). *On requirements for ontologies in management of Web services*. Revised Papers presented at the International Workshop on Web Services, E-Business, and the Semantic Web CAISE '02/WES '02 (pp. 237-247). London: Springer-Verlag.

Tosic, V., Ma, W., Pagurek, B., & Esfandiari, B. (2003). *On the dynamic manipulation of classes of service for xml Web services* (Research Rep. No. SCE-03-15). Ottawa, Canada: Department of Systems and Computer Engineering, Carleton University.

Tosic, V., Ma, W., Pagurek, B., & Esfandiari, B. (2004, April). Web service offerings infrastructure (WSOI): A management infrastructure for XML Web services. In *Proceedings of the IEE/IFIP Network Operations and Management Symposium (NOMS'04),* Seoul, South Korea (p. 817-830). IEEE Press.

Tosic, V., Pagurek, B., & Patel, K. (2003). WSOL: A language for the formal specification of classes of service for Web services. In L.-J. Zhang (Ed.), *Proceedings of the International Conference on Web Services (ICWS)* (pp. 375-381). Las Vegas: CSREA Press.

Tosic, V., Patel, K., & Pagurek, B. (2002, May). WSOL: Web service offerings language. In *Proceedings of the Workshop on Web Services, e-Business, and the Semantic Web - WES (at CAiSE'02),* Toronto, Canada (Vol. 2512, pp. 57-67). Springer Press.

Tran, D., Hua, K., & Do, T. (2002). Scalable media streaming in large P2P networks. In *Proceedings of the ACM Multimedia Conference (SIGMM 2002),* Juan Les Pins, France (pp. 247-256).

Tran, D., Hua, K., & Do, T. (2004). A peer-to-peer architecture for media streaming. *IEEE Journal on Selected Areas in Communications, Special Issue on Recent Advances in Service Overlay Networks, 22*, 121-133.

TrustBridge project details of Microsoft. Retrieved August 10, 2007, from http://msdn.microsoft.com/library/default.asp?url=/library/en-us/dnWebsrv/html/wsfederate.asp?frame=true

Tsai, W. T., Paul, R., Cao, Z., Yu, L., & Saimi, A. (2003). Verification of Web services using an enhanced UDDI server. In *Eighth IEEE International Workshop on Object-Oriented Real-Time Dependable Systems* (pp. 131-138). Guadalajara, Mexico: IEEE.

Tsai, W. T., Zhang, D., Chen, Y., Huang, H., Paul, R. A., & Liao, N. (2004, November). A software reliability model for Web services. In *Proceedings of the IASTED Conference on Software Engineering and Applications,* Cambridge, MA (pp. 144-149). IASTED/ACTA Press.

Tu, P. H., Son, T. C., & Baral, C. (2006). Reasoning and planning with sensing actions, incomplete information, and static causal laws using logic programming. *Theory and Practice of Logic Programming, 7*, 1-74.

Turaga, D. S., & van der Schaar, M. (2007). Cross-layer packetization and retransmission strategies for delay-sensitive wireless multimedia transmission. *IEEE Transactions on Multimedia, 9*(1), 185-97.

Turaga, D. S., Chen, Y., & Caviedes, J. (2002). *PSNR estimation for compressed pictures*. Paper presented at the IEEE International Conference on Image Processing (ICIP), Rochester, NY.

Turaga, D. S., el Al, A. A., Venkatramani, C., & Verscheure, O. (2005, July). *Adaptive live streaming over enterprise networks*. Paper presented at the ICME.

Turaga, D. S., Ratakonda, K., & van der Schaar, M. (2001). *Enterprise multimedia streaming: Issues, background and new developments*. Paper presented at the IEEE International Conference on Multimedia and Exposition, Amsterdam, Holland.

Tutorial 1: Introduction. (2005). Retrieved August 15, 2005, from http://www.fedora.info/download/2.0/user-docs/tutorials/tutorial1.pdf

UDDI Spec Technical Committee. (2003). *UDDI version 3.0.1*. Retrieved June 9, 2008, from http://www.oasis-open.org/committees/uddi-spec/doc/tcspecs.htm

UDDI. (2004). *UDDI Version 3.0.2*. UDDI Spec Technical Committee.

Universal description, discovery and integration (UDDI) specification. (2005). *OASIS*. Retrieved on July 21, 2007 from http://uddi.xml.org/

Uyar, A., & Fox, G. (2005, May). Investigating the performance of audio/video service architecture I: Single broker. In *Proceedings of the 2005 International Symposium on Collaborative Systems*.

Uyar, A., & Fox, G. (2005, May). Investigating the performance of audio/video service architecture II: Broker network. In *Proceedings of the 2005 International Symposium on Collaborative Systems*.

Valente, S., Dufour, C., Groliere, F., & Snook, D. (2001). An efficient error concealment implementation for MPEG-4 video streams. *IEEE Transactions on Consumer Electronics, 47*(3), 568-578.

van den Lambrecht, C. J. (1996). *Color moving pictures quality metric*. Unpublished doctoral thesis, EPFL.

van der Meer, J., Mackie, D., Swaminathan, V., Singer, D., & Gentric, P. (2003). *RTP payload format for transport of MPEG-4 elementary streams* (RFC 3640).

van der Schaar, M., & Chou, P. (2007). *Multimedia over IP and wireless networks: Compression, networking, and systems*. Elsevier Press.

van der Schaar, M., Turaga, D. S., & Sood, R. (in press). Stochastic optimization for content sharing in P2P systems. *IEEE Transactions on Multimedia*.

van der Schaar, M., Turaga, D. S., & Stockhammer, T. (2005). *MPEG-4 beyond video compression: Object coding, scalability and error resilience*. Digital Library of Computer Science and Engineering, Morgan Claypool.

van Emden, M., & Kowalski, R. (1976). The semantics of predicate logic as a programming language. *Journal of the ACM., 23*(4), 733-742.

Van Gelder, A., Ross, K., & Schlipf, J. (1991). The well-founded semantics for general logic programs. *Journal of ACM, 38*(3), 620-650.

Van Hentenryck, P., & Saraswat, V. (1996). Strategic directions in constraint programming. *ACM Computing Surveys, 28*(4), 701-726.

van Schewick, B. (2007). Towards an economic framework for network neutrality regulation. *Journal on Telecommunications and High Technology Law, 5*.

Venkatapathy, S., & Holdsworth, C. (2002). *An introduction to Web services gateway*. Retrieved May 25, 2008, from http://www-106.ibm.com/developerworks/Webservices/library/ws-gateway/

Video Quality Experts Group (VQEG). Retrieved May 23, 2008, from http://www.its.bldrdoc.gov/vqeg/

Vijayananda, K., & Raja, P. (1994). *Models of communication protocols for fault diagnosis*. Swiss Federal Institute of Technology.

Vinosky, C. (2002). Web services interaction models. Current practice. *IEEE Internet Computing, 3*(6), 89-91.

Voas, J. M., & Miller, K. W. (1995). Software testability: The new verification. *IEEE Software*, 17-28.

Voran, S., & Wolf, S. (2000). *Objective estimation of video and speech quality to support network QoS efforts*. Paper presented at the 2nd Internet2/DoE Quality of Service Workshop, Houston.

VQEG 2000. *Final report from the video quality experts group on the validation of objective models of video quality assessment*.

VQmon. Retrieved May 23, 2008, from http://www.telchemy.com/vqmonsavm.html

W3. (2004). *Web services endpoint management architecture requirements*. Retrieved May 22, 2008, from http://dev.w3.org/cvsWeb/2002/ws/arch/management/ws-arch-management-requirements.html?rev=1.7

W3C. (1999). *HTTP*. Retrieved May 22, 2008, from http://www.w3.org/Protocols/

W3C. (2001). *Web services description language*. Retrieved May 22, 2008, from http://www.w3c.org/TR/wsdl

W3C. (2002). *Web services management concern* (white paper). W3C Consortium.

W3C. (2003, November). *QoS for Web services: Requirements and possible approaches*. Author.

W3C. (2004). *Owl-s: Semantic markup for Web services*. Retrieved May 26, 2008, from http://www.w3.org/Submission/OWL-S/

W3C. (2004). *Simple object access protocol*. Retrieved May 22, 2008, from http://www.w3c.org/TR/soap

W3C. (2005). *Working group*. Retrieved June 1, 2008, from http://www.w3.org/

W3C. (2006). *eXtensible markup language*. Retrieved May 22, 2008, from http://www.w3c.org/XML

W3C. (2007). *WSDL 2.0*. Retrieved May 26, 2008, from http://www.w3.org/TR/wsdl20

Wagner, G., Giurca, A., & Lukichev, S. (2006). A usable interchange format for rich syntax rules integrating OCL, RuleML and SWRL. In *Proceeding of 15th International World Wide Web Conferences*. Edinburgh: ACM Press.

Wahli, U. (2002). *Self-study guide: WebSphere studio application developer and Web* services (1st ed.). Retrieved May 22, 2008, from http://www.books24x7.com/marc.asp?isbn=0738424196

Wang, G., Chen, A., Wang, C., Fung, C., & Uczekaj, S. (2004, September). Integrated quality of service (QoS) management in service-oriented enterprise architectures. In *Proceedings of the 8th International Enterprise Distributed Object Computing Conference (EDOC'04)*, Monterey, CA (pp. 21-32). IEEE Press.

Wang, Y., & Zhu, Q.-F. (1998). Error control and concealment for video communication: A review. *Proceedings of the IEEE, 8*(5), 974-997.

Wang, Y., King, G., Patel, D., Patel, S., & Dorling, A. (1999). On coping with real-time software dynamic inconsistency by built-in tests. *Annals of Software Engineering, 7*, 283-296.

Wang, Y., Riebman, A. R., & Lin, S. (2005). Multiple description coding for video delivery. *Proceedings of the IEEE, 93*(1), 57-70.

Warrier, U., Besaw, L., LaBarre, L., & Handspicker, B. (1990). *The common management information services and protocols for the Internet (CMOT and CMIP)* (RFC 1189).

Web services invocation framework. (2007). Retrieved May 25, 2008, from http://ws.apache.org/wsif

Web services security. (2002). *Version 1.0*. Retrieved August 2005, from http://www.verisign.com/wss/wss.pdf

Web services trust language (2005, February). *WS-trust specification*. Retrieved August 10, 2007, from http://schemas.xmlsoap.org/ws/2005/02/trust/

Weller, S. (2002). *Web services qualification*. Retrieved May 25, 2008, from http://www-106.ibm.com/developerworks/library/ws-qual

Wenger, E., McDermott, R., & Snyder, W. M. (2002). *A guide to managing knowledge: Cultivating communities of practice*. Boston: Harvard Business School Press.

Whitehead, J. (1998). Collaborative authoring on the Web: Introducing WebDAV. *Bulletin of the American Society for Information Science, 25*(1), 25-29.

Wiegand, T., Sullivan, G. J., Bjontegaard, G., & Luthra, A. (2003). Overview of the H.264/AVC video coding standard. *IEEE Transactions on Circuits and Systems for Video Technology, 13*(7), 560-76.

Wikipedia. (2005). *The free encyclopedia*. Retrieved June 1, 2008, from http://en.wikipedia.org/wiki/Multiplexing/

Wikipedia. Retrieved May 23, 2008, from http://en.wikipedia.org/wiki/Voice_over_IP

Winkler, S. (2005). *Digital video quality*. Wiley Interscience.

Wolf, S., & Pinson, M. (1999). Spatial-temporal distortion metrics for in-service quality monitoring of any digital video system. In *Proceedings of the SPRI Multimedia Systems*.

Woods, J. (2006). *Multidimensional signal, image, and video processing and coding*. Elsevier.

Worrell, K. (1994). *Invalidation in large scale network object caches*. Unpublished master's thesis, University of Colorado.

WS-authorization specification (2003, July). Retrieved August 10, 2007, from http://www.w3c.or.kr/~hollobit/roadmap/ws-specs/WS-Authorization.html

WSDL. (2001). *Web services description language*. Retrieved May 22, 2008, from http://www.w3c.org/TR/wsdl

WS-federation specification. (2003, July 18). Retrieved August 10, 2007, from http://www-106.ibm.com/developerworks/Webservices/library/ws-fed/

WSLA-spec (2003, January 28). *Web service level agreement (WSLA) language specification*. Retrieved August 10, 2007, from http://www.research.ibm.com/wsla/WSLASpecV1-20030128.pdf

WS-policy specification. (2002, December 18). Retrieved August 10, 2007, from http://msdn.microsoft.com/library/default.asp?url=/library/en-us/dnglobspec/html/wspolicyspecindex.asp

WS-privacy. Retrieved August 10, 2007, from http://www.serviceoriented.org/ws-privacy.html

WS-resource framework (WSRF) specification. (2004). *Globus alliance*. Retrieved on July 22, 2007, from http://www.globus.org/wsrf/

WS-secure conversation spec. (2005, February). *Web services secure conversation language.* Retrieved August 10, 2007, from http://specs.xmlsoap.org/ws/2005/02/sc/WS-SecureConversation.pdf

WS-security specifications. (2002, April 5). Retrieved August 10, 2007, from http://msdn2.microsoft.com/en-us/library/ms951257.aspx

WS-trust specifications. (2007, March). Retrieved August 10, 2007, from http://docs.oasis-open.org/ws-sx/ws-trust/200512

Wu, D., Parsia, B., Sirin, E., Hendler, J., & Nau, D. (2003). *Automating DAML-S Web services composition using SHOP2.* Paper presented at the The SemanticWeb – ISWC.

Wu, W., Fox, G., Bulut, H., Uyar, A., & Huang T. (2006, May). Service oriented architecture for VoIP conferencing: Research articles. *International Journal of Communication Systems Archive, 19*(4).

Wu, Y., Pan, D., & Chen, M.H. (2001). *Techniques for testing component based systems.* Paper presented at 7th IEEE International Conference on Engineering of Complex Computer Systems (ICECCS'01), Skovde, Sweden.

XACML spec. (2003, February 18). *Extensible access control markup language (XACML).* Retrieved August 10, 2007, from http://www.oasis-open.org/committees/download.php/2406/oasis-xacml-1.0.pdf

Xiang, Z., Zhang, Q., Zhu, W., & Zhong, Y. (2001). *Cost-based replacement policy for multimedia proxy across wireless Internet.* Paper presented at the IEEE GlobeCom'01, San Antonio.

Xiang, Z., Zhang, Q., Zhu, W., Zhang, Z., & Zhang, Y.-Q. (2004). Peer-to-peer based multimedia distribution service. *IEEE Transactions on Circuits and Systems for Video Technology, 6*(2), 343-55.

Xiaoying, B., Wenli, D., Wei-Tek, T., & Yinong, C. (2005). WSDL-based automatic test case generation for Web services testing. In *International Workshop on Service-Oriented System Engineering* (pp. 207-212). Beijing, China: IEEE Computer Society.

Xiong, L., & Liu, L. (2004). PeerTrust: Supporting reputation-based trust for peer-to-peer electronic communities. *Knowledge and Data Engineering, IEEE Transactions, 1*(16), 843-857.

XKMS spec. (2001, March). *XML key management specification (XKMS).* Retrieved August 10, 2007, from http://www.w3.org/TR/xkms

XML encryption spec. (2002, December 10). *XML encryption syntax and processing.* Retrieved August 10, 2007, from http://www.w3.org/TR/xmlenc-core/

Xu, D., Hefeeda, M., Hambrusch, S., & Bhargava, B. (2002). On peer-to-peer media streaming. In *Proceedings of the IEEE International Conference on Distributed Computing Systems (ICDCS 2002),* Wien, Austria.

Xu, W., Offutt, J., & Luo, J. (2005). Testing Web services by XML perturbation. In *Proceedings of the 16th IEEE International Symposium on Software Reliability Engineering* (pp. 257-266).

Yan, B., & Ng, K. W. (2003). A novel selective motion vector matching algorithm for error concealment in MPEG-4 video transmission over error-prone channels. *IEEE Transactions on Consumer Electronics, 49*(4), 1416-1423.

Yan, Y., Pencole, Y., Cordier, M. O., & Grastien, A. (2005). Monitoring Web service networks in a model-based approach. In *Proceedings of the 3rd European Conference on Web Services (ECOWS'05),* Vaxjo, Sweden.

Yen, V. C. (2004). *Applications development with Web services.* Paper presented at the International Resources Management Association Conference, Innovations through Information Technology (pp. 875-876).

Yin, R. K. (1994). *Case study research: Design and methods* (2nd ed.). Thousand Oaks, CA: Sage Publications.

Yiu, W.-P. K., Jin, X., & Chan, S.-H. G. (2007). Challenges and approaches in large-scale P2P media streaming. *IEEE Multimedia, 14*(2), 50-59.

Yu, T., & Lin, K.-J. (2005). Service selection algorithms for composing complex services with multiple QoS constraints. In B. Benatallah, F. Casati, & P. Traverso (Eds.), *ICSOC* (Vol. 3826, pp. 130-143). Amsterdam, The Netherlands: Springer.

Yu, T., & Lin, K.-J. (2005, March). A broker-based framework for QoS-aware Web service composition. In *Proceedings of the 2005 IEEE International Conference on e-Technology, e-Commerce, and e-Services (EEE'05),* Hong Kong, China (pp. 22-29). IEEE Press.

Yuming, J., Chen-Khong, T., & Chi-Chung, K. (2000). Challenges and approaches in providing QoS monitoring. *International Journal of Network Management, 10*(6), 323-334.

Zeng, L., Benatallah, B., Dumas, M., Kalagnanam, J., & Sheng, Q. Z. (2003, May). *Quality driven Web services composition.* Paper presented at the 12th International Conference on World Wide Web (WWW), Budapest, Hungary.

Zeng, L., Benatallah, B., Dumas, M., Kalagnanam, J., & Sheng, Q. Z. (2003). Quality driven Web services composition. In *Proceedings of the 12th International Conference on World Wide Web, WWW '03* (pp. 411-421). New York: ACM Press.

Zeng, W., & Liu, B. (1999). Geometric structured based error concealment with novel applications in block based low-bit-rate coding. *IEEE Transactions on Circuits and Systems for Video Technology, 9*(4), 648-665.

Zhang, F. P., Yang, O. W., & Cheng, B. (2001). *Performance evaluation of jitter management algorithms.* Paper presented at the Canadian Conference on Electrical and Computer Engineering, 2001, Toronto, Canada.

Zhang, Q., Xiong, Y., & Zhu, W. (2001). *Testing scheme QoS probing tool—uProbe* (Microsoft internal report). Microsoft.

Zhang, Q., Yang, F., & Zhu, W. (2005). Cross-layer QoS support for multimedia delivery over wireless Internet. *EURASIP Journal on Applied Signal Processing 2005, 2*, 207-219.

Zhang, Z.-L., Wang, Y., Du, D. H. C., & Su, D. (2000). Video staging: A proxy-server-based approach to end-to-end video delivery over wide-area networks. *IEEE/ACM Transactions on Networking, 8*, 429-442.

Zhou, C., Chia, L.-T., & Lee, B.-S. (2004). DAML-QoS ontology for Web services. In *Proceedings of the IEEE International Conference on Web services (ICWS '04)* (pp. 472-479). Washington, D.C.: IEEE Computer Society.

Zhou, C., Chia, L.-T., & Lee, B.-S. (2004, July). DAML-QoS ontology for Web services. In *Proceedings of the IEEE International Conference on Web Services (ICWS'04),* San Diego (pp. 472-479). IEEE Press.

Zhu, L., Gorton, I., Liu, Y., & Bui, N. B. (2006). *Model driven benchmark generation for Web services.* Paper presented at ICSE-Workshop Service-Oriented Software Engineering, Shanghai, China.

Zhu, Q. F., & Kerofsky, L. (1999). Joint source coding, transport processing, and error concealment for H.323-based packet video. In *Proceedings of the SPIE Visual Communications and Image Processing* (Vol. 3653, pp. 52-62).

Zimmermann, O., Krogdahl, P., & Gee, C. (2004). Elements of service-oriented analysis and design. *IBM developerworks.* Retrieved on July 19, 2007, from http://www.ibm.com/developerworks/Webservices/library/ws-soad1/

About the Contributors

Khaled M. Khan has recently joined the Department of Computer Science and Engineering at Qatar University. He also holds an honorary adjunct fellow position in the School of Computing and Mathematics at the University of Western Sydney, Australia. Prior to these, Dr. Khan served at University of Western Sydney for 7 years as an academic in computing. He was the head of programs for the postgraduate studies at the University of Western Sydney. He taught computing for the last 18 years at various universities in Asia, Europe, Africa, and Australia. His research interests include software security, software component, software architecture, Web services, and service-oriented software. He received his PhD in computing from Monash University and a BS and an MS in computer science and informatics from the University of Trondheim, Norway. He also holds another bachelors degree from the University of Dhaka, Bangladesh. Dr. Khan has published more than 50 refereed papers. He contributed to the IEEE-ACM Computing Curricula 2001.

* * *

Witold Abramowicz (http://www.kie.ae.poznan.pl/members/wabramowicz/) is the chair of Department of Information Systems at Poznan University of Economics, Poland. His particular areas of interest are information retrieval and filtering, and knowledge management in MIS. He received his MSc from The Technical University of Poznan, Poland, PhD from The Wroclaw Technical University, Poland, and habilitation from The Humboldt University Berlin, Germany. He worked for three universities in the Switzerland and Germany for 12 years. He is an editor or coauthor of 21 books and over 140 articles in various journals and conference proceedings. He chaired 15 scientific international conferences and was a member of the program committees of 180 other conferences. He is member of the editorial boards of some international journals, including *Wirtschaftsinformatik (A list), Comparative Technology Transfer, International Journal of Web Services Practices, International Journal of Web-based Learning,* and *Teaching Technology*. Currently Professor Abramowicz is involved in seven research projects in the 6th Framework Program EU. Professor Abramowicz is vice president of the Polish Association of Management Information Systems.

Jose J. Pazos Arias received a master's degree in telecommunications engineering from the Polytechnic University of Madrid (Spain-UPM) in 1995. He received a PhD degree in computer science from the Department of Telematics Engineering, the Polytechnic University of Madrid (Spain-UPM) in 1995. He is the current director of the Networking and Software Engineering Group in the University of Vigo, and has been since 1998. He is currently working on middleware and applications for Interactive Digital TV.

Colin Atkinson has been the leader of the Software Engineering Group at the University of Mannheim since April 2003. Before that he was as a professor at the University of Kaiserslautern and project leader at the affiliated Fraunhofer Institute for Experimental Software Engineering. His research interests are focused on the use of model-driven and service-based software engineering approaches in the development of dependable computing systems. He received a PhD and MSc in computer science from Imperial College, London in 1990 and 1985, respectively, and received his BSc in mathematical physics from the University of Nottingham in 1983.

Chitta Baral is a professor at the Arizona State University. He obtained his B.Tech (Hons) from IIT, Kharagpur (1987) and his MS (1990) and PhD (1991) from the University of Maryland. He works in the areas of knowledge representation, logic programming, and reasoning about actions and change. His research has been supported over the years by NSF, NASA, and ARDA/DTO/IARPA. He received the NSF CAREER award in 1995. He authored the book *Knowledge Representation, Reasoning, and Declarative Problem Solving* about answer set prolog in 2003. For more about him and his research please see http://www.public.asu.edu/~cbaral/

Abdelghani Benharref received a PhD in computer engineering from Concordia University (Canada) in 2007, a master's in network and telecommnication from Ecole Nationale Superieure d'Informatique et d'Analyse des Systemes (Morocco) in 2000, and a bachelor's in computer science from Cadi Ayyad University (Morocco) in 1998. His interest domains include but not limited to Web services, Web services composition, management of Web service, QoS of Web services, software testing, protocol design, and validation.

Daniel Brenner received a degree in business information systems from the University of Mannheim, Germany in 2004. He then joined Prof. Dr. Colin Atkinson's Software Engineering Group at the University of Mannheim where he is currently conducting research in the field of component and service testing.

Mohit Chawla is a technical specialist with the SOA and Web Services Center of Excellence at Infosys Technologies, Hyderabad. His primary area of interest is SOA, with a specific focus on Web services implementations on various platforms. He is also interested in developing applications using emerging WS-* standards. He is currently focused on SOA-based enablement of legacy systems. He can be reached at Mohit_chawla@infosys.com

Terance Dias works as part of the SOA and Web Services COE (Center of Excellence) for Infosys Technologies, a global IT consulting firm, and has substantial experience in publishing papers, presenting papers at conferences, and defining standards for SOA and Web services. The SOA and Web Services COE specializes in SOA, Web services, and other related technologies. His main areas of interests include virtualization, grid computing, and SOA technologies. He can be reached at terance_dias@infosys.com

Rachida Dssouli has been a full professor in the Department of Electrical and Computer Engineering since 2001. She received her master's (1978), DEA (1979), Doctorat de 3eme Cycle in networking (1981) from l'Université Paul Sabatier (Toulouse, France) and her PhD in computer science from Université de Montréal. She published more than 150 papers in journals, and referred conferences in her area of research. She has published in *IEEE Transaction on Software Engineering, IEEE Networks, International Journal of Web Information Systems, Information and Software Technology, Journal of Computer Networks, Computer Networks,* and *ISDN Systems.* Her research interests are in communication software engineering, testing based on formal methods, requirements engineering, systems engineering, and telecommunication service engineering. Dr. Dssouli was nominated Director of Concordia Institute for Information and Systems Engineering in June 2002. Her mandate was the creation of an interdisciplinary research and learning institute dedicated for graduate studies.

Vishal Dwivedi is a junior research associate at SOA/Web-services Centre of Excellence at SET-Labs, the R&D arm of Infosys Technologies Ltd, and holds a MS degree from IIIT Hyderabad, India. He specializes in business process management and service-oriented architectures. He has published award winning conference papers in this area. He is currently pursuing research on service identification approaches and service level guarantees for SOA adoption.

Ty Mey Eap is a PhD candidate at Simon Fraser University. He received his BSc and MSc from the Simon Fraser University. His primary interests lie in areas of Internet security, Web service security, service oriented architecture, e-learning management, artificial intelligence, and Semantic Web. He has authored/coauthored more than 20 research papers and has been involved in divert projects funded by NSERC, SSHRC, Canarie, and A.W.Mellon Foundation (USA).

Dragan Gašević is an assistant professor at the School of Computing and Information Systems at Athabasca University. Dr. Gašević received his Dipl. Ing., MSc, and PhD degrees in computer science from the Department of Computer Science, University of Belgrade, Serbia, in 2000, 2002, and 2004, respectively. His primary interests lie in areas of service-oriented architectures, Semantic Web, model-driven engineering, technology enhanced learning, and Petri nets. Dr. Gašević has authored/co-authored more than 150 research papers and authored *Model Driven Architecture and Ontology Development,* a book published by Springer in 2006.

Silvan Tecumseh Golega is a master student at the Hasso-Platner-Institut of the Universität Potsdam, Germany. Silvan received a BSc from the Hasso-Platner-Institut in 2006 after pending one year at the Universidad Rey Juan Carlos in Madrid, Spain. Silvan performed the practical work of his master's thesis under the supervision of Frederic Montagut at SAP Research, France on the topic "Composition and Coordination of Transactional Business Processes." He contributed to the work presented in this chapter during his stay at SAP Research.

Marek Hatala is an associate professor at Simon Fraser University - School of Interactive Arts and Technology and the director of the Laboratory for Ontological Research. Dr. Hatala received his MSc in computer science and PhD in cybernetics and artificial intelligence from the Technical University of Kosice. His primary area of expertise is information and knowledge management, security in SOAs, policies, interoperability in SOA, and distributed systems. Dr. Hatala is currently a theme leader in the NSERC Research Network LORNET, which includes collaboration with industrial partners (Theme budget is $1.3M/5Y).

Michael C. Jaeger has received a German diploma in computer engineering and a PhD degree from the Berlin University of Technology. His doctorate thesis covers the problem of optimising e-service compositions considering multiple quality-of-service criteria. This involved also the application of the thesis findings using Web service technologies. His research interests are distributed systems, modelling, and SOA. Before his track on SOA, he worked also in projects covering knowledge management, Semantic Web, and Semantic Web services. During his time as doctorate student, he served as a graduate research assistant and participated in externally funded projects.

Monika Kaczmarek is a research assistant and a PhD student at the Department of Information Systems at Poznan University of Economics, Poland. She was involved in the Adaptive Services Grid Project FP6-2003-IST-2-004617 working on the dynamic service profiling mechanism. Currently, she works in the Semantics Utilised for Process management within and between Enterprises project (FP6-IST-026850), aiming at bridging the gap between business and the IT world by enabling at least semiautomation of the BPM lifecycle. Her major areas of interest are Web service and Semantic Web service technology, knowledge representation techniques, information filtering and retrieval, as well as business process management.

Nima Kaviani is a PhD student in the department of Electrical and Computer Engineering in the University of British Columbia, Canada. His research interests mainly form around authentication and authorization in mobile networks, identity 2.0, trust, and policy management. He has also an extensive background on robotic, multiagent reasoning, and multiagent planning.

Ghita Kouadri Mostefaoui is currently a research officer at Oxford University computing laboratory. She is involved in the GIMI project, which is a large scale middleware collaborative research project that is concerned with the development of a secure IT infrastructure to support medical research. Before joining Oxford University, she worked as a postdoctoral fellow at the University of Montreal, Canada, and as a research and teaching assistant at the University of Fribourg (Switzerland). Her research interests include software engineering, context-based security, and Web services. She received an MS degree (predoctoral school) in computer science from Ecole Polytechnique Fédérale de Lausanne, Switzerland, in 1999, and a PhD in computer science from both the University of Fribourg and Université Pierre et Marie Curie (Paris 6) in 2004.

Kyriakos Kritikos is a PhD student in the Department of Computer Science, University of Crete and a researcher at the Information Systems Laboratory of the Institute of Computer Science, FORTH in Greece. He received his BSc and MSc degrees in computer science from the University of Crete. His research interests concern the following areas: Semantic Web service description and discovery, QoS modeling, constraint solving and optimization, and distributed systems. He has been a PC member at the NWESP 2005-2007, SOAS 2006-2007, ICABS 2007 international conferences, and at the NFPSLA-SOC 2007 international workshop.

Krishnendu Kunti is working as a technical architect with SETLBAS SOA Center of Excellence, Infosys Technologies LTD. Krishnendu has been extensively published in leading journals, conferences, and books; he has also been involved in a number of real life SOA-based projects. He has lead the development of the Infosys SOA testing framework "ACCORD SOA Solution," and has been involved in the formulation of go to market strategy. His areas of interest include SOA testing, data services, and application architecture in general. He can be reached at krishnendu_kunti@infosys.com

Xiaoqi Ma graduated from Nanjing University of Science and Technology, China, with a distinct BEng degree in 1997. He received his master's degree from the Institute of Software, Chinese Academy of Sciences in 2003. He got his PhD degree from the University of Reading in 2007. He is currently a research officer of Oxford University Computing Laboratory. His research interests include computer security, software engineering, operating systems, and real-time

Zakaria Maamar is an associate professor in the College of Information Technology at Zayed University, Dubai, United Arab Emirates. His research interests include Web services, software agents, and context-aware computing. Maamar has published several papers in various journals, such as *ACM Transactions on Internet Technology* and *IEEE Transactions on Knowledge and Data Engineering*, and conference proceedings. Maamar has a PhD in computer sciences from Laval University.

Bijoy Majumdar is a member of the SOA and Web Services COE (Center of Excellence) for Infosys Technologies, a global IT consulting firm, and has substantial experience in publishing papers, presenting papers at conferences, and defining solutions for SOA and Web services. Bijoy works as a technical architect in designing enterprise solutions with leading-edge technologies. At present, he is heading the homegrown BPM platform development and handles the collaboration strategy with different lines of business. He can be reached at bijoy_majumdar@infosys.com

Rainer Malaka is Professor and Chair for Digital Media in the Computer Science Department of the Universität Bremen, and a member of the "TZI — Center for Computing Technologies." Until recently he headed the research department of the European Media Laboratory (EML). Rainer Malaka's research group works on projects dealing with mobile assistance systems, language understanding, geographical information systems, and computer vision. The focus of Dr. Malaka's work is on intelligent mobile systems.

Matthias Merdes earned degrees in physics from the Universities of Illinois (UIUC) and Heidelberg, Germany. After working as a software developer in the areas of medical informatics and geoinformatics, he spent several years in scientific research in the field of software engineering. He is now a senior software developer in a start-up company.

Refik Molva is a full professor and the head of the Computer Communications Department at Eurecom Institute in Sophia Antipolis, France. His current research interests are in security protocols for self-organizing systems and privacy. He has been responsible for research projects on multicast and mobile network security, anonymity, and intrusion detection. Beside security, he worked on distributed multimedia applications over high-speed networks and on network interconnection. Prior to joining Eurecom, he worked as a research staff member in the Zurich Research Laboratory of IBM where he was one of the key designers of the KryptoKnight security system. He also worked as a network security consultant in the IBM Consulting Group in 1997. Refik Molva has a PhD in computer science from the Paul Sabatier University in Toulouse (1986) and a BSc in computer science (1981) from Joseph Fourier University, Grenoble, France.

Frederic Montagut is a PhD candidate at SAP Research in Sophia Antipolis, France. Frederic obtained his engineering diploma from Telecom INT, France, and the Diploma of Advanced Studies (MSc) in network and distributed systems from Nice – Sophia Antipolis University, France in 2004. He joined SAP Research in October 2004 working under the supervision of Pr. Refik MOLVA, Eurecom Institute. Frederic is involved in different research projects in the field of pervasive computing and e-government. His current research interests ranges from decentralized workflow management systems, transactional coordination of workflows, to workflow security.

Nanjangud C Narendra is a research staff member at IBM India Research Lab in Bangalore, India. His research interests are in software engineering, Web services, and SOA. He has 15 years R&D experience in IBM, Hewlett Packard India, and Motorola India. He is the author or coauthor of over 70 publications in international conferences and journals. He is also a program committee member of several well-known international conferences such as ACM Symposium on Applied Computing and AAMAS.

Fatih Oguz is an assistant professor in the Master of Library and Information Science Program at Valdosta State University. He received his PhD from University of North Texas. His research interests include the Web services, Web-based database applications, information architecture, and open source software solutions. He is coauthor of "Texas Library Directory Web Services Application: The Potential for Web Services to Enhance Information Access to Legacy Data" presented at the International Conference on Next Generation Web Services Practices (NWeSP), Korea in 2006. Additional information about Oguz and a selection of his writings can be found at http://www.valdosta.edu/mlis/faculty/oguz.shtml

Srinivas Padmanabhuni is a principal researcher with the Web Services Centre of Excellence in SETLabs, the R&D arm of Infosys Technologies, and specializes in Web services, service-oriented architecture, and grid technologies alongside pursuing interests in Semantic Web, intelligent agents, and enterprise architecture. He has been selected for Who's Who in Asia first edition. He serves on editorial board of journals and program committees for international conferences. Dr Padmanabhuni has authored several conference papers, book chapters, and journal articles alongside speaking at strategic forums. He holds a PhD degree in computing science from University of Alberta, Edmonton, Canada.

Barbara Paech holds the chair in Software Engineering at the University of Heidelberg. Until October 2003, she was department head at the Fraunhofer Institute Experimental Software Engineering. Her teaching and research focuses on methods and processes to ensure quality of software with adequate effort. She has headed several industrial, national, and international research and transfer projects. She is spokeswoman of the special interest group "Requirements Engineering" and the section "Software Engineering" in the German computer science society. She holds a PhD in computer science from the Ludwig-Maximilans-Universität München (1990) and a habilitation in computer science from the Technical Universität München (1998)

Dimitrios Plexousakis is a professor and chair of the Department of Computer Science, University of Crete, and a researcher at the Information Systems Laboratory of the Institute of Computer Science, FORTH in Greece. He received his BSc degree in computer science from the University of Crete and MSc and PhD degrees in computer science from the University of Toronto. His research interests span the following areas: knowledge representation and knowledge base design; formal knowledge representation models and query languages for the Semantic Web; formal reasoning systems with focus on dynamic action theories and belief revision; business process; and e-service modeling, discovery, and composition.

Enrico Pontelli is a professor of computer science at New Mexico State University. He received his PhD in 1997 and a MS in computer science from the University of Houston in 1992. His main areas of interest are knowledge representation and reasoning, logic and constraint programming, parallel processing, bioinformatics, and assistive technologies. He has published over 140 peer-refereed publications. He is the director of the knowledge representation, logic, and advanced programming laboratory and the associate director of the NMSU Center for Bioinformatics. His research has received support from various agencies, including a NSF Career Award.

David Power received a BEng in mechanical and materials engineering from Loughborough University in 1993. He studied for an MSc in computation at the University of Oxford for which he received a distinction. He then moved to the University of Bath where he was awarded a PhD in computing. He has since returned to the University of Oxford where he currently works as a researcher on a number of high profile projects in the field of distributed medical systems. His current research interests are in the formal modeling of data access and the design of access control systems.

Krishna Ratakonda received MS and PhD degrees in electrical and computer engineering from University of Illinois at Urbana Champaign in 1997 and 1999. He joined IBM Research as a research scientist in 1999, where he currently manages the Process Automation group. Prior to that, he managed the Content Servers group in Research that contributed core components of IBM DB2 Content Manager. At Illinois, he received awards for outstanding graduate research from both the School of Engineering and Department of Electrical Engineering. He has authored over 40 papers, six patents, and served as session chair in multiple academic and industry conferences.

Pauline Ratnasingam is an associate professor of MIS, Department of Computer Information Systems, Harmon School of Business Administration, University of Central Missouri (UCM). Before joining UCM, she was an assistant professor at the School of Business Administration, University of Vermont, Burlington, Vermont. She received her PhD from Erasmus University, Rotterdam School of Management, The Netherlands in 2001. She lectured on topics such as project management, management of information systems, and electronic commerce in Australia, New Zealand, Europe, and America. She is an associate member of the Association of Information Systems, and is a member of the Information Resources Management Association and Academy of Management. Her research interests include business risk management, Internet-based B2B e-commerce, organizational behavior, and trust. She is a recipient of a National Science Foundation Grant and has published several articles related to this area in national and international conferences, refereed journals, and chapters in books. Her biography is also published in the 58th Edition of Marquis Who's Who – Who's Who in America.

Douglas Russell graduated from the University of Reading in 2004 with a MEng in computer science and cybernetics. He then took up a post in the Oxford University Computing Laboratory as a Research Officer in the Secure Distributed Data Access Group. His research interests include distributed systems and security.

Lipika Sahoo currently works with the SOA and Web Services Centre of Excellence in SETLabs, the technology research division at Infosys Technologies, India. Her core area of work involves dynamic adaptability and management of Web services. She is currently involved in various research activities within the group relating to MDA and AOSD. She can be reached at Lipika_Sahoo@infosys.com

Mohamed Salem joined the college of information technology at the University of Wollongong in Dubai in February 2004. He worked previously as a software engineer for several years, collaborated in research with IBM Center of advanced studies (Toronto) and HP Protocol Test Center (Montreal), and worked for some time as a product analyst for a start-up software company in Canada. His areas of interests and expertise are in both technical and nontechnical aspects of computing, including, but not limited to, software engineering, performance analysis and scalability, innovation, and ethics in information technologies. He was appointed in 2005 as faculty fellow with the IBM Toronto Laboratory Centre for Advanced Studies and is a member of the steering committee of the North African and Middle East ACM Programming contest. Dr. Mohamed Salem received a Master of Science and Philosophiae Doctor in computer science from the University of Montreal (Canada). While a postgraduate student, he received the IBM Centre for Advanced Studies PhD fellowship for three consecutive years and the "Bourse d'excellence de la Francophonie" from the Canadian International Development Agency.

Mohamed Adel Serhani received his master's in computer science (specialization software engineering) from University of Montreal, Canada in 2002. He received the PhD degree in electrical and computer engineering in 2006, from Concordia University, Montreal, Canada. He is currently an assistant professor in the College of Information Technology, U.A.E University, Al Ain, U.A.E. His research area is on Web services engineering that includes service selection and discovery, service lifecycle, QoS integration in SOA, end-to-end QoS management for Web services, QoS, and Web services composition. He also worked on the application of artificial intelligence techniques, mainly fuzzy logic to software engineering, object-oriented metrics, and software quality.

Andrew Simpson gained a first class honours degree in computer science from the University of Wales, Swansea and an MSc and a DPhil from the University of Oxford. Andrew is currently a university lecturer in software engineering at the University of Oxford, where he is Director of Studies for Oxford's Software Engineering Programme. Previously he was a principal lecturer in computing at Oxford Brookes University. Andrew's current research interests are associated with the analysis, design, and development of large-scale distributed systems. Andrew is a Chartered Engineer and a Charted IT Professional.

Mark Slaymaker received his BSc from City University before joining CHIME at UCL to work on medical informatics. Subsequent to this he worked on image processing of X-ray images and gained a PGDCCI from the Open University. He is currently working at the Oxford University Computing Laboratory on the GIMI project as well the Imaging and Pathology Demonstrator, and prior to these the eDiaMoND project. He has a particular interest in security for medical informatics and in parallel to his project commitments is working towards a DPhil in software engineering.

Tran Cao Son is an associate professor of computer science at New Mexico State University. He earned his MS in mathematics from the Technical University of Dresden (1986), and MS and PhD in computer science from the Asian Institute of Technology (1992) and University of Texas at El Paso

(2000), respectively. He is interested in knowledge representation and reasoning, logic programming, planning, commonsense reasoning, and intelligent agents, and is the associate director of the KLAP. He has published over 65 peer-referred publications, and most can be downloaded from http://www.cs.nmsu.edu/~tson. His research has been supported by NSF, NASA, NIH, and NMSU.

Ratko Spasojevic is a senior security consultant for TELUS, with more than 14 years of security, application, and data networking experience. Mr. Spasojevic is a specialist in secure Internet communications and online (user-centered) identity management, and actively participates in BC CIO's Identity Management Forum. He has been participating in the SIAN project and is currently working on the Information Sharing Framework (ISF) project for broader public sector in collaboration with the BC government, which tries to leverage user-centered identity management principles for developing secure and privacy protection service-oriented architectures.

Deepak S. Turaga received the B Tech degree in electrical engineering from IIT, Bombay in 1997 and the MS and PhD degrees in electrical and computer engineering from Carnegie Mellon University, Pittsburgh in 1999 and 2001, respectively. He is currently a research staff member at the IBM T. J. Watson Research Center, Hawthorne. His research interests lie primarily in statistical signal processing, multimedia coding and streaming, machine learning, and data mining applications. He is an associate editor of the *IEEE Transactions on Multimedia, IEEE Transactions on Circuits and Systems for Video Technology,* and *Journal for the Advances in Multimedia.*

Ana Fernández Vilas received a master's degree in telecommunications engineering from the University of Vigo (Spain-UVigo) in 1996. She received a PhD degree in computer science from the University of Vigo in 2002. She is currently working in the Interactive Digital TV laboratory, and has been since 2002. She is at present an associate professor in the Department of Telematics Engineering at the University of Vigo. She is currently working on Web services technologies and ubiquitous computing environments.

Julio A. Fernández Vilas received a master's degree in computer science from the University of A Coruna (Spain-UDC) in 1992. He has been working as a mainframe system administrator from 1990 to 2004. He has been the director of "Mainframe System" department since 2004 at a Spanish savings bank (Caixa Galicia). He has been working on a PhD on Web services since 2002, and he is currently working on a universal integration framework based on Web services.

Matthias Werner has studied electrical engineering, control theory, and computer engineering, and received his PhD from the Humboldt University of Berlin. He worked at the University of Texas at Austin, the University of Technology at Berlin, with Microsoft Research Lab at Cambridge, and Daimler Research. His research interests are in the area of nonfunctional system properties, especially real-time and dependability, as well as in architectural and composability aspects. Currently, he is head of the operation systems group of the Computer Science Department at the University at Chemnitz.

Graeme Wilson completed his undergraduate studies in computing science at the University of Ulster in 2004, prior to postgraduate study in neuroscience at Oxford University in 2005. He is currently a research officer at the Oxford University Computing Laboratory, working on the Generic Infrastructure for Medical Informatics (GIMI) project.

Dominik Zyskowski is a PhD student and research assistant at the Department of Information Systems, Poznan University of Economics. He was involved in the ASG FP6-2003-IST-2-004617 where he was leading the team working on the dynamic service profiling component. Currently he is with SUPER FP6-IST-026850 and Knowledge Web FP6-507482 projects. He is an author and co-author of several international publications on Semantic Web services, quality of service, and BPM. His research interests also include management information systems, e-marketplaces of Semantic Web services, service-oriented architectures, semantic description of Web services, and knowledge management.

Index